INDEX
TO
THE LOUISIANA
HISTORICAL QUARTERLY

The INDEX TO THE LOUISIANA HISTORI-
CAL QUARTERLY is printed in a limited
edition of 500 copies, of which 50 de luxe
copies (numbered 1 to 50) are signed by the
compiler. The de luxe edition also includes an
extra set of the drawings.

This is copy No. ....

INDEX TO THE LOUISIANA HISTORICAL QUARTERLY

COMPILED AND DECORATED BY

BOYD CRUISE

WITH AN INTRODUCTION BY

CHARLES "PIE" DUFOUR

A FIREBIRD PRESS BOOK

PELICAN PUBLISHING COMPANY
Gretna 1998

Copyright 1956
L. Kemper Williams

Index Louisiana Historical Quarterly
January 1917 thru October 1950
Volumes I thru XXXIII

Manufactured in the United States of America
Published by Pelican Publishing Company, Inc.
1000 Burmaster Street, Gretna, Louisiana 70053

America
Orleans

For Brig.-General and
Mrs. L. Kemper Williams

PREFACE

For many years I have been vitally interested in many phases of the rich historical background of Louisiana. When Brig-Gen. L. Kemper Williams suggested that I prepare an Index to the Louisiana Historical Quarterly for his personal use, I accepted the task with eagerness and pleasure. Being primarily a painter I soon realized that my knowledge of the gentle arts of compiling, indexing, typing, and finally of binding and publishing was being "weighed and found wanting." Therefore I beg indulgence for the mistakes which I have, undoubtedly, made in this work.

My sincere thanks go to Gen. and Mrs. L. Kemper Williams for the opportunity to do this volume and to Charles L. Dufour, Harold Schilke and Harold and Bonnie Kate Leisure for their valuable assistance. For other important and varied aid I am greatly indebted to the following: Robert and Annette Andrews, Aime Pierre Claudet, Weeks Hall, Bessie Mae Jones, Rai Murray and the New Orleans Public Library, David and June Nixon, Elizabeth Norsworthy, Rose Oliver and the Library of the Louisiana State Museum, Leonard Oppenheim and the Tulane University Law Library, Paul Schaeffer, Jeanne Marie Schrewe, and the Presbytere of the Louisiana State Museum.

Boyd Cruise

New Orleans, Louisiana
February 1, 1956

FOREWORD

Anyone who has ever worked in the field of Louisiana history realizes what a rich mine of material the Louisiana Historical Quarterly is.

It is a mother lode of fascinating facts about the colorful story of Louisiana, but like most rich deposits it yielded its greatest rewards only to the greatest diggers.

The historical gold in the Louisiana Quarterly was, like the real article, where you found it. But finding it called for not only the instincts of a researcher but for the manual labor of a prospector. And, too, for a great waste of time.

Let us assume that you wanted to find out something about Mardi Gras Bayou, near the mouth of the Mississippi, where Iberville spent his first night in Louisiana on Mardi Gras, 1699.

What did you have to do? If you lived in New Orleans, you probably went to the Public Library, where a card index on the Louisiana Quarterly, by no means complete, may be found. If you owned the complete file of the Louisiana Quarterly yourself, or lived beyond reach of the New Orleans Public Library, you did your researching the hard way. You went to the stacks and pulled from the shelves, one at a time, 33 different volumes and looked up Mardi Gras Bayou in 33 different indexes. The first 25 volumes you investigated proved fruitless, but Volume 26 yielded a citation to Mardi Gras Creek, the same stream you were interested in. You then continued through the rest of the 33 volumes for other possible references.

Unless you have been indulging in secret practice, the process of taking down 33 volumes, looking through the index of each and returning the books to the shelves can hardly be done in less than an hour. I know because I have tried it.

If you have ever had such an experience in running down information in the Louisiana Historical Quarterly, you have doubtless asked, along with thousands of scholars and students: "Why doesn't someone make an index to the entire Louisiana Quarterly?"

This book makes that question superfluous. Compiled and edited by Boyd Cruise, distinguished New Orleans artist and himself a keen student of Louisiana history, it is what scholars and students and historical-minded laymen have needed for years.

We are all familiar with the patter used to sell us deodorants, motor oil, toothpaste, razor blades, TV sets, etc. We are told they are 16 percent more effective; 22 percent more heat-resistant; 37 percent more acid-preventive; 43 percent sharper by micro-test; 51 percent clearer image and so on, ad bunkum. What we are seldom, if ever, told is that these things are "more than." They're just "more."

Boyd Cruise's Index to the Louisiana Historical Quarterly is 33 times more efficient; 33 times more easy; and I may go so far as to say, 33 times more "heat" resistant than the 33 separate indexes to the existing volumes of the Louisiana Quarterly.

Mr. Cruise, with the same infinite patience and meticulous craftmanship that he brings to his drawing board and canvases, has reversed the "do-it-yourself" trend in research in the Louisiana Quarterly. He has, with this book, done it for you. He has, to coin a cliche, "packaged" the various indexes for you.

It may be asked, how did a sensitive artist like Boyd Cruise get mixed up in so prosaic an undertaking as preparing a cumulative index to an historical quarterly.

The answer, of course, is simple. Boyd Cruise is not only a sensitive artist, but he is a sound student of Louisiana history, made so not only by the exigencies of his profession but by the curiosity of a fine and versatile intellect as well.

Proof of this is ample, in this very book. For each letter of the alphabet in the Index, Mr. Cruise has created magnificent headings, headings which touch upon almost every facet of Louisiana—history, natural history, customs, folklore, products, industry, literature, architecture, etc. For each of these headings, admirable examples of the work of a great artist, Mr. Cruise did extensive research before he put pencil to paper, and, as Weeks Hall, himself a perceptive artist and brilliant critic, once wrote of Boyd's work, he executed them, "never allowing skill to become facility."

Boyd Cruise has painted in many mediums and in many manners, as Weeks Hall points out, but "invariably with thoroughness and achievement." It is with "thoroughness and achievement" that Mr. Cruise lent his hand and time—he has worked, off and on, for two years and intensively for the past six months—to this Index.

Let me quote Weeks Hall again: "Living in one of the finest old houses in New Orleans, he has recorded, with an unequalled eye and a sympathetic understanding, the very beautiful old buildings of his quarter. In some instances, he has not only painted these buildings as they are today, but, after the most painstaking research, he has also painted them, with the utmost fidelity, as they were at the height of their period. In this phase, these pictures, extraordinary as they were in themselves, have great added historical value."

Such are Boyd Cruise's credentials as an historian. His credentials as an artist, for those few who are unfamiliar with his work, will be found throughout this book. You will notice, in two of the headings, only illustrations. "No one in Louisiana," said Mr. Cruise, "has to be told that magnolias stand for 'M' and pelicans for 'P'."

In compiling the Index, Mr. Cruise first correlated the indexes of each of the 31 volumes of the Louisiana Historical Quarterly, a staggering undertaking in itself. In addition, he himself indexed the volumes, Nos. 32 and 33, to which no index is available. Then he integrated his work into the 31 indexes, now edited into one compilation.

Mr. Cruise did not stop with merely straight indexing; everything is cross-indexed. For instance, in your search for data on Mardi Gras Bayou, you would have found it under "bayou" as well as under "Mardi Gras."

The result of Boyd Cruise's scholarship is a book that librarians, scholars, students and mere amateurs in Louisiana history will welcome with enthusiasm. He has cut numberless hours off everybody's future research projects in Louisiana history. That this book, because of Boyd Cruise's art work as well as for its utility, will soon be a collectors' item, I have no doubt.

In closing, I would like to express agreement with Weeks Hall: "Boyd Cruise knows what he is doing ... His contribution is as distinct as it is valuable. This will be instantly recognizable to those who know."

CHARLES L. DUFOUR

New Orleans
19 March 1956

ABBADIE, D' AND W. FLA., v.22, p.20, 21, 27, 29.

Abbey, Kathryn T., "Land Ventures of General Lafayette in the Territory of Orleans and the State of Louisiana," v.16, p.359.

Abbott, Maj. H. L., member of levee board, v.31, p.542.

Abbot map referred to, v.31, p.605.

Abbot, M., topographical survey of Crowley, v.27, p.1135.

Abbot Brothers, noted, v.23, p.568.

Abbott, David, originated system of upland irrigation making possible rice industry of Crowley, v.27, p.1157-58, 1159.

Abell, Judge E., fights convention, v.31, p.1080; removed, v.31, p.1089.

Abolitionists, noted, v.25, p.349, 350, 689, 690, 1002, 1003, 1071, 1116.

Aborn, Joseph, sketch, v.28, p.822n.; noted, v.28, p.823, 845n.; letters of, v.28 p.899, 905-06, 910.

Abram, Maurice, noted, v.22, p.180.

Absenteeism, in British West Florida, v.19, p.196-98.

"Abstracts by William Price of State Papers Preserved in the Louisiana Historical Society with notes," by Grace King, v.1, sec.1, p.10.

Abstracts of French and Spanish Documents Concerning Early History of Louisiana, v.1, sec.1, p.103; sec.3, p.224.

Academies of Louisiana, historical sketch of, v.30, p.738-757; list of by Parishes, v.30, p.738-972; bibl., v.30, p.973-978.

"Academy Movement in Louisiana," by James William Mobley, v.30, p.738-978.

Academy of Music, N.O., v.26, p.391.

Acadia College, historical sketch of, v.30, p.757-759.

"Acadia," Hebert plantation, v.31,, p.493.

Acadia Literary and Commercial College, v.27, p.1176.

Acadian education, in La., v.18, p.397-406.

"Acadian-Signal," v.2, p.1188.

Acadians, in Iberville Parish, v.24, p.163, 937; folklore in La., v.24, p.752-55; arrival in New Orleans, v.23, p.558; French Charities to, 1755-1799, v.21, p.656-68.

Acadia Parish Board of Health, fight against yellow fever, v.27, p.1136.

Acadia Parish School Board, v.27, p.173, 1175, 1177, 1179.

Acadia Parish, v.27, p.380; early history and formation of by division of St. Landry, v.27, p.1119-21; contest for parish seat of, v.27, p.1122-23, 1124; Crowley selected parish seat, v.27, p.1125-26; erection of court house, v.27, p.1126-27; officials of 1888, v.27, p.1127; new court house, 1903, v.27, p.1132-1133; discovery of oil, v.27, p.1134; repair of court house and erection of Agri. Building, v.27, p.1140-41, 1155; growth of rice in, v.27, p.1157, 1159, 1160; cotton crop, v.27, p.1162; cattle industry, v.27, p.1163; other crops, v.27, p.1163; agencies aiding farmers, v.27, p.1163; growth of rice mills in, v.27, p.1165-68; cotton gins, v.27, p.1168; oil developments, v.27, p.1169-70, 1172, 1173; developments of education, v.27, p.1175-84; newspapers, v.27, p.1184-89, 1199; public welfare organizations, v.27, p.1205-1207, 1208; resolution of thanks to those helping in food disaster, v.27, p.1220; German colony in, v.23, p.513; location of, v.23, p.558; Populist Legis. from, v.26, p.1109.

Acadia Rice Mill, first mill est. in Acadia, v.27, p.1164.

"According to the Code," by J. S. Kendall, v.23, p.141-61.

"Account of the Credit and Debit of the Funds of the City of New Orleans for the Year 1789," ed. by Henry P. Dart, by Laura L. Porteous, v.19, p.584-94.

Acme, La., noted, v.25, p.397.

Acosta, Joaquin, noted, v.24, p.674, 678.

Acosta, Lt. Thomas de, Sp. Commandant of Manchac, v.25, p.936.

Act of Sale, La., 1769, v.21, p.674-76.

"Adah Isaacs Menken," by Leo Shpall, v.26, p.162-68.

"Adaias, The Spanish Post of the," Phanor Breazeale, v.7, p.304.

Adai Indians in Grant Parish, v.23, p.1109; description, v.23, p.1120.

Adair, John, and Burr Conspiracy, v.23, p.160.

Adais, Sp. fort established at, v.26, p.687-88, 698.

Adam, Adolphe, manuscript of opera in L.S.U. Music School Library, v.24, p.347.

Adamoli, Guilio (New Orleans, 1867), v.6, p.271.

Adams, Capt. ———, privateersman, v.22, p.1080-1081.

Adams, Capt. Thomas Scott, and bagging factory, v.26, p.1066; Farmers' Alliance leader, v.26, p.1070; declined nomination for gov., v.26, p.1079; anti-lotteryite cand. for Sec. of State, v.26, p.1081; advocated Populist Dem. Alliance, v.26, p.1084-1085.

Adams, Henry, noted, v.23, p.1000.

Adams, John, noted, v.24, p.701, 711; death of, v.24, p.1013, 1014; ancestry, v.23, p.1000.

Adams, John, II, attacked by Jarvis, v.24, p.1106.

Adams, John Quincy, election to presidency, v.24, p.936, 957; noted, v.24, p.711, 934, 1065, 1091, 1137; appraisal by James Brown, v.24, p.944, 1137; European reaction to 1825 message, v.24, p.982, 983; political opposition to, v.24, p.997; questions of reelection, v.24, p.1001-02, 1004, 1042, 1096-97, 1123-24; and 1826 election, v.24, p.1027; status of administration, 1827, v.24, p.1044; supporters of, v.24, p.1115; commentary on Jefferson letter, v.24, p.1140; antimasons, v.24, p.1159; and Unitarian Church, v.24, p.1165; Senator from Mass., v.31, p.281, 363-4; opinion of Sumter, v.31, p.295; governorship of Claiborne, v.31, p.365, 366; quoted, v.31, p.367; noted, v.25, p.44, 86, 133; and tariff, v.25, p.48, 49, 50, 81, 82, 83, 117, 1016, 1044.

Adams, Mrs. John Quincy, praised as a hostess, v.24, p.944, 963; noted, v.24, p.1091.

Adams, R. McC. B., "New Orleans and the War of 1812," I, II, III, v.16, p.221, 479, 681; IV, V, VI, v.17, p.169, 349, 502.

Adams, Samuel, noted, v.24, p.701.

Adams, Thos. A., Chairman of Com. of 100 of the Fusion Party, v.27, p.568.

Adams, Thomas E., noted, v.23, p.1176n.

Adams, T. S., Rep. of State Farmers' Union at anti-lottery conv., v.27, p.1057; suggested as nominee for gov. by combine of anti-lottery and Farmers' Union, v.27, p.1086, 1088; declined nomination, v.27, p.1090; cand. sec. of state, v.27, p.1090; noted, v.31, p.836, 837; cand. for gov., v.28, p.1152; opposition to as cand. for gov., v.28, p.1154-55, 1156; withdrawal, v.28, p.1157; nom. sec. of state, v.28, p.1158; noted, v.28, p.1162, 1171.

Adams, William R., and "N.O. Crescent," v.30, p.271; "Daily Delta," v.30, p.303.

Adams, Wirt, noted, v.23, p.244.

Addison, Britton, noted, v.23, p.422.

Addison, Geo., began "Rayne Signal," v.27, p.1184.

Address by Honorable Frank M. Dixon, v.32, p.231.

Address, by House of Representatives of Louisiana to the People of France, (1831), v.3, p.399.

Adelle vs. Beauregard, v.24, p.303.

Administrative Papers, 1493-1865, in Middle American Research Institute, v.24, p.332.

"Admiralty, A case in, in Louisiana, 1741," Henry P. Dart, and Heloise H. Cruzat, v.7, p.5.

Admiralty Court, at Galveston, v.22, p.764-1065.

"Admission of Louisiana into the Union," by Lillie Richardson, v.1, p.333.

"Adventures of Denis Braud, First printer of Louisiana," by Henry P. Dart, translation by Laura L. Porteous, v.14, p.349.

Affleck, Thomas, papers in L.S.U. Archives, v.24, p.340-41.

Africa and Voodooism, noted, v.25, p.366.

"Aftermath of Reconstruction in Louisiana, The," by Margaret T. Leach, v.32, p.631.

Agosti, Antonio, arrest mix-up, v.31, p.746.

Agramonte, Dr. Aristides, papers in Agramonte Memorial Library, L.S.U., New Orleans, v.24, p.320, 321.

Agrarian Movement, beginnings of in La., v.26, p.1062-74; People's Party, v.26, p.1074-1124.

"Agreement Between Louis Cezard LeBreton and Jean Baptist Goudeau, as Overseer on His Plantation, 1744," translated by Heloise H. Cruzat, v.9, p.590.

Agricultural Colony in La., Jewish, v.20, p.821-31.

"Agricultural Review," acquires property of "De Bow's Review," v.29, p.393.

Agricultural Society of Baton Rouge, v.24, p.58.

Agriculture, early, in La., v.18, p.285-86; change in La., 1860-1880, v.16, p.407-29; Guano deposits on Galapagos Island, v.23, p. 162-69; history of rice production in La., v.23, p.554-88; in early La., v.23, p.88; after Civil War in South, v.23, p.1237-1238; St. Charles Parish, v.21, p.1114-15.

Ahrens, Dr. J. B., pastor of German Methodist Church, v.24, p.146.

Ahrens, Henry, newspaperman, "Old Days on the N.O. Picayune," v.33, p.337.

Ailenroc, M. R., See Cornelia Randolph Murrell, v.25, p.150.

Aime, Valcour, noted, v.21, p.1120-21.

Aird, James, noted, v.23, p.59, 391.

Aird, John, noted, v.23, p.391.

Aird, William, and W. Fla. Assembly, v.22, p.312, 317, 943; v.23, p.23ff; noted, v.23, p.391.

Aiton, Arthur S., A Letter in Answer to Dr. Stenbergs Article, v.19, p.1075-77.

Aix, health resort, v.24, p.944, 956, 1037.

Akkerman, Treaty of, v.24, p.1070.

Alabami Indians, description, v.23, p.1121.

Alause, Henri, noted, v.24, p.671.

"Albatross," federal boat, v.29, p.1108, 1109.

Albemarle Bend, old Mississippi River Channel, v.31, p.600.

Albrecht, Andrew C., author, "Ethical Precepts Among the Natchez Indians," v.31, p.569-97; "The Origin and Early Settlement of Baton Rouge, La.," v.28, p.5-68.

Alcorn, James L., Miss. Senator, investigation of La. Politics, 1873, v.27, p.579.

Alderman, E. A., noted, v.25, p.806.

"Alerta," slaver, v.23, p.438.

Alexander I, death of, v.24, p.980.

Alexander, Dr. W. W., noted, v.25, p.781.

Alexander, Eliza, noted, v.24, p.1156.

Alexander, George D., organizer of Thatcher Institute, v.30, p.798.

Alexander, James, noted, v.22, p.433, 435.

Alexander, J. E., noted, v.23, p.885; v.31, p.397; author on Louisiana, v.31, p.406, 408, 412.

Alexander, Mark, and sugar tariff, v.25, p.70.

Alexander, Mr. and Mrs. James Caroline Desgranges lived with, v.27, p.171.

Alexandre, Captain, v.24, p.628.

Alexandria and Cheneyville Railroad, sketch of, v.30, p.1127-1128.

Alexandria Female Academy, v.30, p.895.

Alexandria Institute, v.30, p.897.

Alexandria, La., burning of, by Federals, v.18, p.22-34; in 1860, v.21, p.1151ff.; in the 1820's, v.23, p.1007; distributing point for slaves, v.24, p.23; headquarters for Richard Taylor, v.24, p.68; Civil War engagements described, v.24, p.73-75, 84-88, 94-101; noted, v.25, p.50, 324, 397, 398, 399; noted, v.26, p.973, 1024; fall of, to Federals, v.26, p.1044; noted, v.26 p.1045, 1048; v.27, p.483; population 1860, v.27, p. 488; Dick Taylor organized military dept. in, v.27, p.521, 541, 633; N.O. trade with, v.27, p.952; Farmers' Union meeting, v.27, p.1087, 1198, 1201, 1218, 1227; dam built in river, v.32, p.130; departure of Federal Army, v.32, p.131; cotton in, v.32, p.134.

Algiers, French expedition against, v.24, p.1041, 1047, 1056.

Algiers, La., noted, v.24, p.144.

Alien and Sedition laws of 1798, noted, v.24, p.719, 727.

Allain, T. T., instrumental in establishment of S. Univ., v.25, p.769; senator, v.27, p.990; favored lottery bill of 1890, v.27, p.1033.

Allard, ———, noted, v.23, p.141-42.

Allbritton, Richard, member St. Helena Police Jury, v.23, p.407ff.

Allegiance to the Union, oaths under Butler in N.O., v.24, p.499-501.

Allen, C. H., noted, v. 23, p.556.

Allen, Gen. Henry Watkins, succeeded Moore as gov. of La., v.26, p.1043; refugee from U. S. with Moore, v.26, p.1046.

Allen, Henry Watkins, noted, v.21, p.1131, 1212; cotton contracts with merchants, v.23, p.1229-31; noted, v.24, p.84; injured in Battle of B. Rouge, v.27, p.522; official report relative to Fed. troops in W. La., v.27, p.1226-28; management of 4th La. Reg't falls in his hands, v.29, p.1048, 1049, 1051; headquarters in Bay St. Louis, v.29, p.1053; directs completion of fort at Ship Island, v.29, p.1053; succeeds Col. Barrow as commander of reg't, v.29, p.1056; events in Corinth, v.29, p.1057; gives commands to Tennessee companies for Gov. of Tenn., v.29, p.1063; at battle of Shiloh, v.29, p.1063-1064; wounded at Shiloh, v.29, p.1064-1065; encourages men at Ten Mile Creek, v.29, p. 1071; gives commands to men at Ten Mile Creek and Corinth, v.29, p.1072, 1073; noted, v.29, p.1074, 1075; encounter with Chaplain over tent, v.29, p.1080; receives disabling wound, v.29, p.1086-1088; noted, v.29, p.1090; promoted to Brig. Gen'l, v.29, p.1147; Confederate Governor, v.31, p.1033, 1078; candidate for governor, v.31, p.1058, 1060-1061; funeral, v.31, p.1085; noted, v.31, p.64.

Allen, Samuel C., and 1824 tariff bill, v.25, p.40.

Alligator Bayou (Creek), v.28, p.779, 780.

Alliquot, Jeanne, noted, v.25, p.363.

"Allotment of Building Sites in New Orleans, 1722," Heloise H. Cruzat, v.7, p.564.

Allston, (Hugh) & Co., noted, v.23, p.557.

"Almirante," schooner belonging to Laffites, v.23, p.783.

Almonester, Madame (Madame Castillon), struggle for control of hospital, v.31, p.30-6; renounces title to hospital, v.31, p.38-9.

Almonester y Roxas, Don Andres, Will of, v.6, p.21; noted, v.19, p.123-127; and Catholic Church in New Orleans, v.21, p.1070n.; noted, v.22, p.388, 628, 681, 684; sketch of, v.31, p.20-1, 28; rebuilds New Orleans Charity Hospital, v.31, p.21-5; struggle for control of hospital, v.31, p.25-8; death, v.31, p.29; rebuilds church, v.31, p.902; noted, v.31, p.949.

Alspaugh, Granville L., sketch of, v.29, p.1229-1230; letters to mother written during Civil War, v.29, p.1230-1240.

Alspaugh, Jermiah B., brief sketch, v.29, p.1229.

Alston, Capt. Solomon, noted, v.21, p.83-84.

Alston, Theodosia Burr, noted, v.22, p.1083-1084.

"Altamira Case," by Stanley Faye, v.25, p.5-23.

Altamira, Juan Bautista de, in N. O., 1806, v.25, p.6; real name of Picornell, v.25, p.8; plot in N. O., v.25, p.9-10; captured, v.25, p.15-18; in prison, v.25, p.19-23.

Alter, Charles E., noted, v.23, p.240.

Alvarez, ———, noted, v.24, p.649.

Alvord, J. W., Inspector of Schools and Finances, v.25, p.742-43.

Alwes, Berthold C., "The History of the La. State Lottery Co.," v.27, p.964-1118.

Amacker, O. P., opposed lottery, v.27, p.1043.

Ambrister, R. C., and Andrew Jackson, v.24, p.938.

Amelia Island, Aury driven out, v.23, p.774, 780; taken possession by U. S., v.23, p.791-794; noted, v.24, p.644; surrender to the U. S., v.24, p.646.

Amelung, Ferdinand Louis, and Andrew Jackson, v.21, p.392n, 397n.

America, See A. L. Boimare.

American Baptist Home Mission Society, v.25, p.768, 782, 783, 787.

American Colonization Society, v.25, p.344, 345, 350, 351, 387; benefited by McDonogh's legacy, v.26, p.158.

American Co., under Caldwell, v.28, p.91, 95, 103, 105, 106ff., 114ff.; under Russell & Rowe, v.28, p. 186ff.

American Historical Association, Annual Report of, for 1914, Notes on by William Beer, v.1, sec.1, p.117.

American Legion Memorial Hospital, v.27, p.1199.

"American Libre," privateer vessel, v.24, p.645, 646, 647, 653, 671, 676.

American Lumberman, survey work in Bogalusa, v.29, p.101-104.

American Old Catholic Church, New Orleans, v.24, p.323.

"American Party in Louisiana, History of," by W. Darrell Overdyke, Chapt. I, v.15, p.486; Chapts. II, III, IV, V, v.16, p.84, 256, 409, 608; affiliation of Richard Taylor with, v.24, p.54-55; noted, v.25, p.679, 680-682, 691, 692, 704. See also Know Nothing Party.

American Protective Tariff League denounced Caffery, v.27, p.811.

American Revolution, in W. Fla., v.22, p.43.

American Rice Milling Co., v.27, p.1172, 1175.

"American Siddons, The," by John Smith Kendall, v.28, p.922-40.

American Sugar Refining Co., sugar trust, Caffery's opposition to, v.27, p.819.

American System, v.25, p.29, 32, 48, 49, 63, 65, 70, 79, 83, 104.

American Theatre, in N. O., noted, v.26, p.375, 377, 384, 390, 391, 392; fire of, v.26, p.393-94; closed, v.26, p.1153; St. Philip St., v.28, p.105-10; Orleans St., v.28, p.110-13, 114-120; Camp St., description, v.28, p.121-22, 144-45; 1824-1833; v.28, p.121-86; repairs to, v.28, p.154; Caldwell ends management of Camp St. Theatre, Russell and Rowe take over, v.28, p.186; seasons 1833-36, v.28, p.186-204; 1836-37, v.28, p.212-18; 1837-38, v.28, p.224-25; Barrett assumes direction, v.28, p.235; season 1838-39, v.28, p.235-40; 1839-40, v.28, p.245-47; 251-52; on Magazine St., v.28, p.252; Poydras St., 1840-41, v.28, p.247-63; description, v.28, p.257-58; season 1841-42, v.28, p.269-74; destroyed by fire 1842, v.28, p.274; Mrs. Duff appeared in, v.28, p.927-33.

American Theatrical Commonwealth Co., in N. O., v.28, p.96ff.

"American Vessels in New Orleans, Procedure for Sale of, 1803," by Laura L. Porteous, v.10, p.185.

Americans vs. Creoles, See Creoles vs. Americans.

Amiant, Bernarde, noted, v.21, p.1011.

Amigoni, Julius Caesar, noted, v.22, p.734, 1036.

Amistad, case of the, v.22, p.1048-49.

Amite Collegiate Institute, v.30, p.917-919.

Amite River, grants on, v.22, p.35; land grants on, v.23, p.382, 383; noted, v.25, p.935, 939, 941.

Amlet, ———, noted, v.22, p.387.

Amoss, ———, and W. Fla., v.22, p.46.

Amusement tax, on billiard tables, v.23, p.412.

Amusements, in Carrollton, v.21, p.266-67; in Donaldsonville, 1860, v.21, p.1123; horse racing at Natchitoches, v.21, p.1168.

"An Architectural History of the Royal Hospital and the Ursuline Convent of New Orleans," by Samuel Wilson, Jr., v.29, p.559-659.

Anaya, Juan Pablo y, Mexican Agent, v.22, p.739, 1031; activities in New Orleans, v.21, p.206; agent of Mexican Patriots, v.25, p.300, 663.

"Ancestry of Edward Livingston of La.: The Livingston Family," by James A. Padgett, v.19, p.900-37.

Anciaux's Wharf, Savannah, noted, v.24, p.613.

Ancient Congo Queens, noted, v.25, p.367.

Anderson, Annie Davis, second wife of Wickliffe, v.25, p.719.

Anderson, Charles D., noted, v.23, p.1179.

Anderson, Harrod C., Collection in L.S.U. Archives, v.24, p.341.

Anderson, John, noted, v.23, p.77; and 1828 tariff, v.25, p.45.

Anderson, Thomas C., as a member of La. Returning Board, trial of, v.25, p.713; Senator, 1872, v.27, p.557; and Election of 1872, v.28, p.1134; noted, v.31, p.775; member Returning Board, v.31, p.1093; indicted, v.31, p.1108, 1111-2.

"Andes," frigate of Cochrane's fleet, v.24, p.674, 675.

Andreassen, John Christian Ludwig, "Mississippi River Ice at New Orleans," v.21, p.349-53; noted, v.24, p.308; inventory of manuscript collection, v.24, p.345, 349; "Check list of Historical Records Survey & Survey of Fed'l Archives Publications for La.", v.27, p.613-23; "Internal Improvements in Louisiana, 1824-1837," v.30, p.5-119.

Andrews, John W., noted, v.24, p.491.

Andrews, Penelope Lynch Adams, wife of P. O. Hebert, v.31, p.528.

Andrus, Martin J., Tax collector, Acadia, v.27, p.1131.

Andry, Michael, noted v.22 p.815.

Anduze, Father Aristide, authorized by Moni, v.31, p.907; activities, v.31, p.908; struggle with Blanc, v.31, p.909-59; services withdrawn, v.31, p.914; to Blanc, v.31, p.941, 953; in Paris, v.31, p.961.

Anegada Channel noted, v.24, p.648.

"An Evening with Gayarre," by Rudolph Matas, v.33, p.269-293.

"An Interesting Medico-Historical Exhibit," by Jane Grey Rogers, v.6, p.588.

Annals of Dominican Sisters in Dominican College Library, v.24, p.326.

"Anna Maria," ship, v.24, p.375, 376.

Ann(e), daughter of Henry Clay, v.24, p.1119, 1153.

Annexation of Texas, La. and, v.19, p.89-118; political issue, v.25, p.127, 1002-1005.

Annual Chronological Records of the English Theatre at N. O., 1806-1842, v.28, p.361-490.

Anse la Butte, oil field near Breaux Bridge, v.27, p.1095.

"Ante-Bellum Career of Leonidas Polk, The," by Vera Lea Dugas, v.32, p.245.

Anti-Lottery League of La., initial meeting, v.27, p.1054; organization and election of officers, v.27, p.1054-55, 1056; first public meeting, v.27, p.1055; later meetings, v.27, p.1055-56; reception for legislators, v.27, p.1056; state conv. in B. R., v.27, p.1057, 1086; merged with Farmers' Union, v.27, p.1058; Dem. Anti-Lottery State Ex. Com. organized, v.27, p.1058-61; Campaign highlights, 1890, v.27, p.1063-66; sentiment favoring Anti-Lottery mail bill aroused by, v.27, p.1075, 1086, agreement with Farmers' Union, v.27, p.1086-87; Const. of, v.27, p.1103-1104; list of leaders of, v.27, p.1104-1109; formation of, v.28, p.1150-51; combined with Farmers' Alliance, v28, p.1152ff.; organized, v.32, p.499.

Anti-Lottery Postal Law, upheld by Supreme Court, v.27, p.789; effects of early laws on, v.27, p.1073; history of, v.27, p.1074-75; passage in Cong., v.27, p.1076; provisions, v.27, p.1076; debate, v.27, p.1076; effects of, v.27, p.1077; attitude of the press, v.27, p.1078-79; law enforced, v.27, p.1079-81; U. S. Sup. Court rules constitutional, v.27, p.1081-82, 1111, 1112.

Antimasons, noted, v.24, p.11533; and John Quincy Adams, v.24, p.1159; and Richard Rush, v.24, p.1159; issue in 1832 politics, v.24, p.1167.

Antinullification Proclamation, prepared by Edward Livingston, v.24, p.700; public reaction to, v.24, p.722.

Antioquia, noted, v.24, p.673.

"Antiquities of the Ouachita Valley," by Clarence B. Moore, noted, v.25, p.627.

Antoine, Arthur, introduced bill to create "N. O. Lottery Co.," v.27, p.980.

Antoine, Arthur, Negro rep. from St. Mary, v.28, p.1136.

Antoine, C. C., Negro partner of Pinchback in factorage concern in N. O., v.27, p.538-39; Pinchback said to have cheated, v.27, p.544; claimant for lt.-gov., 1782, v.27, p.560, 576; and election of 1872, v.28, p.1134; cand. for lt.-gov., 1876, v.28, p.1138; negro cand. for lt.-gov. on Kellogg ticket, v.29, p.402, 403, 404, 406, 414; noted, v.29, p.429; acting gov. in Kellogg's absence, v.29, p.426, 440, 449, 460, 484; opinion on Federal troops in La., v.29, p.432; cand. for lt.-gov., v.31, p.536; takes oath of office, v.32, p.399-400.

Antoines restaurant, N. O., noted, v.26, p.774.

"Antoinette," schooner, v.24, p.369, 371.

"Antonio Bonafacio," schooner of Laffites v.23, p.776.

"Antonio de Sedella, Fray," compiled by Clarance Wyatt Bispham, v.2, p.369, p.24, noted, v.31, p.901, 902; and Father Walsh, v.31, p.904; and Dubourg, v.31, p.905; death, v.31, p.906.

Apodaca, Juan, Ruiz de, viceroy of New Spain, v.22, p.744; sketch of, v.23, p.759-60; noted, v.23, p.777; expedition against champ d'Asile settlement, v.23, p.792ff.; opposes Laffite's plan, v.23, p.809; noted, v.23, p.853.

Apostolicals, in France, v.24, p.1026-27.

Appalachi Indians, in Grant Parish, v.23, p.1109; noted, v.23, p.1122.

Appleton, John James, representative at Naples, v.24, p.976-77, 998, 1006, 1020, 1031, 1136; and 1833 tariff, v.25, p.99-100.

Appointments, Edward Livingston's views on, v.24, p.712.

"Appreciation, An, of Fray Antonio de Sedella," by Clarence Wyatt Bispham, v.2, p.24.

Aragon y Villegas, Padro de, teacher in Spanish school, v.22, p.683.

"Aram, Marie, Emancipation of the Slave, 1744," by Henry P. Dart, v.3, p.551.

Aranda, Conde de (Pedro Pablo Abraca de Bolea), sketch, v.21, p.21n; letter from Carondelet noted, v.21, p.24n.

"A Rare Confed. La. State Document and Its History," by Jas. A. McMillen, v.27, p.1226-28.

Arathusa, pen name of Cable, v.24, p.171.
Arbuckle, Mathew, and Andrew Jackson, v.21, p.383.
Arbuthnot, Alexander, and Andrew Jackson, v.24, p.938.
Arcade Theatre, v.28, p.251.
Arcadia, in 1860, v.21, p.1188.
Arcadia Male and Female College, v.30, p.791.
Archer, Henry, Confed. Soldier, v.26, p.949.
Archer, John, Confed. Soldier, v.26, p.949.
Archer, Wm. S., noted, v.23, p.1010.
Archibald, Gunner, noted, v.23, p.388.
Archinard, John Joseph, Chief surgeon second La. Vol. reg't, v.26, p.795; head of mess, v.26, p.805; his fight against poor health conditions at post near Miami, v.26, p.818-22; appointed brigade surgeon by Gordon, v.26, p.822; inspection of camp at Jacksonville, v.26, p.823; appointed brigade surgeon and ordered to Santiago by McKinley, v.26, p.824; in Cuba, v.26, p.833; promoted, v.26, p.835.
Archinard, Paul E., N. O. physician, v.26, p.818.
Architecture of New Orleans, v.22, p.700-701.
Archives of Louisiana, See Louisiana.
"Archives of Paris, History of Calendar of Documents in, Relating to Mississippi Valley," Mrs. N. M. Miller Surrey, v.7, p.551.
Archives, See Index to the Records of the Superior Council of Louisiana and the Spanish Judicial Records of Louisiana; also Editor's Chair.
Arditi, Salvatore and Mafia incident, v.22, p.501.
Argentina, flag of, v.24, p.680.
"Argentina," pirate vessel, v.24, p.362.
"Argo," sinking of yacht, v.33, p.326.
Argote, Antonio, merchant and Spanish agent, v.22, p.75, 796-98, 814.
Argote, Pedro Marin, Spanish Consular agent in New Orleans, v.21, p.681.
Arismendi, Juan Baptista, noted, v.24, p.665, 666.
Ariza, Angel Benito de, consular secretary, v.21, p.678; v.22, p.797; v.23, p.739, 766, 770.
Arizona Academy, v.30, p.817-818.
Arkansas, plan for colonization, v.21, p.61.
"Arkansas Post of La.: Spanish Domination," by Stanley Faye, v.27, p.629-716.
"Arkansas Post of La.: French Domination," by Stanley Faye, v.26, p.633-721.

Arkansas Post of La., description of 1687, v.26, p.633-35; Tonti in charge of, v.26, p.636-45; Iberville plans to command, v.26, p.646; search for gold in, v.26, p.647-61; John Law & Co. and settlers of, v.26, p.661-70; armed forces withdrawn, v.26, p.670-72; fight against Chickasaw, v.26, p.672-86; and illicit Sp. trade, v.26, p.687-707; strength of 1748, v.26, p.708; new commander, reconstruction and reinforcements of, v.26, p.708-13, 715; description of 1757, v.26, p.716-18; flood, v.26, p.718-19; rehabilitation, v.26, p.719-20; La. ceded to Spain, v.26, p.720-21; brief history of, v.26, p.731-32; noted, v.26, p.736; fortification maintained by O'Reilly, v.26, p.740; noted, v.26, p.745; v.27, p.629, 630, 631; naming of, v.27, p.632; lack of law and order, v.27, p.632; de Clovet in charge, v.27, p.632; salary to officials of, v.27, p.634; of peace to, v.27, p.636; strength of, v.27, p.637-38; lack of religious guidance, v.27, p.638-39; population of, v.27, p.639-40; site of, v.27, p.640-41; Labuxiere interpreter arrested as traitor, v.27, p.641-42; dealings with Indians, v.27, p.642-43, 644; De Villiers in charge of, v.27, p.645-46; peace with Osage, v.27, p.646; friendship with Kaskaskia, v.27, p.648; trade arrangements with Blommart, v.27, p.649-50, 651-52; trouble with Osage, v.27, p.650-51, 652; and contraband traders, v.27, p.653-654; Willing visits, v.27, p.655-56; Blommart sends spy to, v.27, p.658; agitation for movement of to higher ground, v.27, p.659; crops ruined by drought, v.27, p.661, 662, 663, 664; Ger. soldiers at, v.27, p.670; attempt to conquer for Eng. by rebels, v.27, p.671; DeVilliers replaced by Jacob Durbeuil Saint-Cyr as commander, v.27, p.672, 674, 675, 676; Colberts antipathy toward, v.27, p.676; his reported plot to attack, v.27, p.677; DeVilliers in command, v.27, p.677, 678, 679; letter of commander in re; peace with Chicksaw, v.27, p.680; Durbeuil takes command, v.27, p.682; reinforcements to, v.27, p.682, 683; conditions of, v.27, p.682-83; Gov. wished to abandon, v.27, p.683; attacked by Colbert, v.27, p.683-85; location, conditions and inhabitants of, v.27, p.688-90; need of new fort, v.27, p.699-700; repair by inhabitants, v.27, p.700-701; destruction by floods, v.27, p.701-702; construction of new fort delayed, v.27, p.702-703; new fort built, v.27, p.703-704; outpost established, later abandoned, v.27, p.707-708; poor conditions of 1793, v.27, p.709-710; new comdt., v.27, p.712; council of Sp. decides to repair, v.27, p.712; Villemont in command, v.27, p.713; various spellings of the name, v.27, p.713; St. Stephens established, v.27, p.714; transfer of, v.27, p.715; name remains, v.27, p.716; noted, v.28, p.688, 690, 691.

Arlee, Stephen, petition of, v.23, p.374.

Armand, Dr. ———, outfits privateer, v.22, p.1033.

Armand, Franz, noted, v.24, p.392.

Armant, Louis, noted, v.22, p.74.

Armas, Octave de, and St. Louis Cathedral, v.31, p.918, 920.

Armesto, Manuel Andres Lopez de, noted, v.22, p.106, 123, 683.

Armistead, Samuel, cand. for secy. of state, v.31, p.535.

Armory Hall, noted, v.26, p.375.

Armstrong College, See Lampton Literary and Industrial College, v.25, p.789.

Armstrong, Duval, newspaperman, "Old Days on the N. O. Picayune," v.33, p.323-24.

Armstrong, Guy, newspaperman, "Old Days on the N. O. Picayune," v.33, p.323.

Armstrong, Henry S., columnist, "N. O. Times," v.30, p.285.

Armstrong, Solomon, and W. Fla. Rev., v.21, p.112; complaint against, v.21, p.123-124.

Army of Northern Virginia, business papers of in La. Hist. Assn. depository, v.24, p.315.

Army of Tennessee, papers of in La. Hist. Assn. depository, v.24, p.315.

Army of Virginia, materials of in La. Hist. Assn. depository, v.24, p.315.

Army Posts, Four Forgotten, I, II, III, IV, by J. Fair Hardin v.16, p.5, 279, 441, 670.

Arndt, Karl J. R., "The Genesis of Germantown, Louisiana: or The Mysterious Past of Louisiana's Mystic, Count de Leon," v.24, p.378-433; ed. "A Bavarian's Journey to New Orleans and Nacogdoches in 1853-54," v.23, p.485-500.

Arnold, Thomas D., and 1833 tariff, v.25, p.100.

Arnould, Louis, introduced bill which became act #44 of 1879, v.27, p.994; bill against lottery, v.31, p.751.

"Arpents de face," noted, v.25, p.164.

Arpin, Madame, La. educator, v.30, p.858.

Arredondo, Antonio, defeats Toledo's expedition, v.22, p.728.

Arredondo, Joaquin de and J. Lafitte, v.23, p.814; and Toledo, v.23, p.827, 1001-02.

Arriola, Andres de, noted, v.22, p.941.

Arroyo, Hondo, noted, v.25, p.292; v.26, p.688, 690; and the disputed neutral ground between Texas and La., v.28, p.1023-1103 passim.

Arroyo, Oscar, as't. sec. of state senate, 1857, v.26, p.981; member Returning Board, v.31, p.1094.

Arthur, Chester A., succeeds to presidency of U. S. on death of Garfield, v.29, p.745; noted, v.29, p.753.

Arthur, Stanley Clisby, "The Emblematic Bird of Louisiana," v.2, p.248; noted, v.24, p.317; works cited, v.24, p.320, 349.

Artigas, Jose, noted, v.22, p.1092; v.23, p.127.

Art, in La. v.18, p.382-96.

Art, James Robb, a patron of, v.23, p.246.

Ascantia, See Bayou Manchac, v.25, p.933.

Ascension Parish, in 1860, v.21, p.1122-25.

"Ascension Parish, Story of," by Sidney A. Marchand, Review by Edith Dart Price, v.14, p.569.

Ascension Red Cypress Co., v.30, p.1034-1036.

Asensio, Father Felipe, noted, v.31, p.917, 948.

Ashe, Thomas, author, v.31, p.395, 398, 413.

Ashland, Home of Henry Clay, v.24, p.1147, 1153.

Assumption Parish, La., v.25, p.162, 216; sugar area, v.25, p.187.

Assumption Parish Papers in L.S.U. Archives, v.24, p.341.

Astor, John Jacob, business relations with James Brown, v.24, p.1146; noted, v.24, p.1042, 1150, 1159.

Aswell, James B., noted, v.25, p.806, 807; pres. Normal Ind. cand. for Gov., v.28, p.1222-23; accusations against, v.28, p.1227-28.

"Atalanta," privateer vessel, v.24, p.368.

Atchafalaya Bay, v.28, p.797, 800, 810.

"Atchafalaya Lottery," river improvement lottery, v.31, p.717.

Atchafalaya plantation area, v.25, p.55.

Atchafalaya Railroad and Banking Company, v.30, p.71.

Atchafalaya River, description of, v.24, p.42; noted, v.25, p.398, 932, 938; La Salle discovers, v.25, p.927-28; noted, v.26, p.983; v.28, p.297, 739, 754, 758, 761, 781, 785, 793, 796, 799, 808, 829, 838ff., 888, 1129.

Athenaeum Theatre temporarily used by Caldwell, 1824, v.28, p.274.

Athens, Ala., captured, v.24, p.103.

Atherton, Lewis E., "John McDonogh and the Miss. River Trade," v.26, p.37-43.

Atlanta Male and Female Institute, v.30, p.935.

Atlantic and Ohio Company, to back telegraph construction, v.31, p.437.

"Atrevido," vessel, v.24, p.653, 654, 656, 660, 675; captured by Haitian gunboat, v.24, p.676.

Attakapas College, v.30, p.912.

Attakapas, plan for colonization, v.21, p.61. Cotton area of La., v.25, p.27; plantations of, v.25, p.54, 204, 371; Description of country 1838, v.24, p.39-42; papers in L.S.U. archives, v.24, p.341.

Attakapas, Post of, deBlanc as commander, v.22, p.77; noted, v.22, p.811, 814, 815, 816; region claimed by Spain, v.26, p.690, 745.

"Attakapas Steam Co.," v. 28, p.823n.

"Attempted Escape of John and Josiah Hayward, English Prisoners, from the jail in New Orleans in 1744," Henry P. Dart, text translated by Heloise H. Cruzat, v.9, p.361.

Atwood, W. P., noted, v.23, p.216.

Aubaredo, Guillermo de, noted, v.22, p.1040.

Aubert, F. C., duel of, v.23, p.452.

Aubry, Capt. Philippe, Fr. official in command in N. O., v. 26, p.312, 739.

Aubry, Charles, noted, v.22, p.30.

Aubry, Charles Philipe de, letters from, v.23, p.392-395, 402.

Aucoin, Sidney Joseph, "The Political Career of Isaac Johnson, Gov. of La., 1846-1850," v.28, p.941-989.

Auctions, slave, v.22, p.147-151.

Aude, Madame Eugenie, La. educator, v.30, p.960-965.

Audibert, Charles M., letter to Skipwith, v.21, p.87-88, 139-141, 145-147, 150-152; naval agent for W. Fla., v.21, p.137n., 761n.; and the Beaudin Claim, v.25, p.949-950.

Audubon College, v.30, p.880.

Audubon, John James, v.18, p.389-390; books by, v.25, p.198, 206.

Audubon, Mrs. John James, school of, v.25, p.157, 206, 158.

Aufrere, Antoine, suit against, v.21, p.1010-1012.

"Auguste Davezac's Mission to the Kingdom of the Two Sicilies, 1833-1834," by Howard R. Marraro, v.32, p.791.

Augustin, D., candidate for St. Louis Cathedral Warden, v.31, p.913; noted, v.31, p.922.

Augustin, James M., newspaperman, "Old Days on the N. O. Picayune," v.33, p.336.

Augustin, Major John, quoted, v.24, p.765, 766-767.

Augustin, ———, duels of, v.23, p.149-150.

"Aurore," early slaver, v.23, p.866.

Aury, Adrien, death of, v.24, p.685.

Aury, Louis Michel, South American naval officer, v.21, p.208; and the Laffites, v.21, p.219; and privateers, v.21, p.-1087ff.; captures brig, Indefatigable, v.21, p.1090ff.; expedition of, v.22, p.736ff.; pirate settlement at Galveston, v.22, p.764, 1065; noted, v.22, p.1033, 1044, 1045, 1053, 1059, 1060, 1063, 1091; boats of, v.23, p.118ff.; filibustering expedition of, v.23, p.758, 761; leaves Galveston for Matagorda Bay, v.23, p.768, 770, 773, 774; noted, v.23, p.784; at Santo Domingo, v.23, p.851; noted, v.24, p.16, 21; sketch of early life, v.24, p.611-612; commissioned by New Granada, 1813, v.24, p.614; at Cartagena, 1813, v.24, p.615-620; new commission, v.24, p.619; at Aux Cayes, v.24, p.620-629; description of and contrast with Brion, v.24, p.623-624; and New Orleans associates, v.24, p.627-631ff.; at Galveston Bay, v.24, p.631-643; search for new prospects, v.24, p.644-648; negotiations for adding vessels to Venezuelan fleet, v.24, p.651; action at Fourcher and Saba, v.24, p.652-653; at Mona Passage, v.24, p.653-654; commission from Madariaga, v.24, p.656; at old Providence, v.24, p.654-660; up the River Dulce, v.24, p.661-665; offer from Spain for reconciliation, v.24, p.670; back to old Providence, v.24, p.670; complaints against Brion, v.24, p.672-673; proposition from Cancino, v.24, p.675; treatment of Captain Ferrero, v.24, p.676-677; invitation from El Choco, v.24, p.678-680; expedition to Central America, v.24, p.680-685; homecoming, v.24, p.690-693; quarrel with Brion, v.24, p.691-697; death, v.24, p.697.

Aury, Victorie, noted, v.24, p.611, 685.

Austin, Black, noted, v.23, p.146.
Austin, Dr. C. E., backer of N.O. "Democrat," v.31, p.739.
Austin, J. E., on de Feriet Returning Board, v.28, p.1135.
Austin, Moses, arrival at Bexar, v.31, p.640-641; aided by Bastrop, v.31, p.641; compared with Bastrop, v.31, p.642; leaves Texas, v.31, p.642; death, v.31, p.643.
"Austin, Stephen F., Founder of Texas, 1793-1836," by James E. Winston, v.9, p.398.
Austin, Stephen F., and de Bastrop in Texas, v. 20, p.418-424; activities in New Orleans, v.22, p.750; letters as source, v.31, p.608; at Natchitoches, v.31, p.643; at Bexar, v.31, p.644; goes to Mexico, v.31, p.645; obtains Mexican sanction, v.31, p.646; efforts to influence government, v.31, p.652-653; plans, v.31, p.654-655; on slavery, v.31, p.669-670; will, v.31, p.676.
Austin, Willis, Confed. soldier, v.26, p.974.
Australian ballot system, adopted in La., v.26, p.1112; proved successful, v.26, p.1116-117.
Austria, negotiations against Russian campaign, v. 24, p.1141.

"Autobiography of George Mason Graham," ed. by Dr. G. M. Stafford, v.20, p.43-57.
"Autobiography of Charles Gayarre," Introduction by Henry P. Dart, v.12, p.5;
Aux Cayes, noted, v.24, p.620, 653, 655, 658.
Avery, Daniel D., cand. for secy. of state, v.31, p.501.
Avery, Dr. Dudley, and W. Fla. Rev., v.21, p.131; identified, v.21, p.733n.
Avery, Gen. Dudley, noted, v.25, p.786.
Avery Island, noted, v.24, p.70.
Avoca Drainage District, drainage project, v.30, p.676, fig.3, p.699.
Avoyel Indians, in Grant Parish, v.23, p.1109, 1119; noted, v.25, p.398.
Avoyelles Academy, sketch of, v. 30, p.761.
Avoyelles, cotton area of La., v.25, p.27; Parish of, v.25, p.120, 324, 337, 353, 362, 398; hills, v.25, p.397.
Avoyelles Cypress Co. v.30, p.1034-1036.
Avoyelles Parish, in 1860, v.21, p.1145-1153; revolutionary agitators in, v.22, p.67.
Ayures, ———, noted v.22, p.815.
Aznosola y Voani, Jose, noted, v.24, p.367.

BABIN, ARISTIDES, SEC. OF STATE SEN., 1857, v.2, p.981.
Babington, Bill, 1st ruler of Bogalusa baby coronation, v.29, p.119.
Babled, Charles L., Hospital steward, v.26, p.795-796; supervised Fr. Doctors Mess, v.26, p.805.
Bachelor Bend, old Mississippi River channel, v.31, p.600.
Bach, Father Ferdinand, investigates cemetery incident, v.31, p.942; death, v.31, p.943.
Bach, reproductions of, in Howard-Tilton Memorial Library, v.24, p.330.
Bacon, A. B., minority report on Lottery, v.31, p.722.
Badger, A. S., noted, v.22, p.508.
Badins, Louis, revolutionary agitator, v.22, p.67.
Bael, Francisco, trader sent to Indians, v.28, p.1099.
Baermann, H., unpublished music of, in L.S.U. Music School Library, v.24, p.347.
Bagging trust, denounced by farmers, v.26, p.1064-1065.
Baggs, W. B., introduced bill prohibiting sale of lottery tickers, v.27, p.1096.
Bahia, noted, v.24, p.641.
Bailey, B. W., Populist candidate for Cong., 4th district, 1894, v.26, p.1093-1094, 1095, 1097; La. rep. to Nat'l populist convention, v.26, p.1119.

Bailey, J. W., Populist House leader, v.28, p.1183.
Bailey's Dam in Red River Campaign, v.18, p.18-21, 857-858.
Bailey, Theodorus, noted, v.24, p.467.
Bailly, Pierre, deposition of, v.23, p.706, 708-709.
Baily, Cap't Theodorus, v.29, p.341.
Bain, Alexander, Scottish telegraph inventor, v.31, p.466; gains patent, v.31, p.466; used by O'Reilly, v.31, p.467; instrument ruled legal, v.31, p.470.
Baird, Gen., assistant commissioner Freedman's Bureau, v.32, p.181, 196, 197, 216.
Baird, Joseph B., W. Florida, Convention printer, v.21, p.711n.
Baird, Major General Absalom, noted, v.25, p.741.
Baird, Samuel T., Dem. rep., v.26, p.1116, 1123.
Baispinel, de, engineer of early 18th century, v.29, p.559.
Baker, Joshua, authorized to clean out Bayou Pigeon and Grand River, v.28, p763n.; noted, v.28, p.818n.
Baker, Marion, newspaperman, v.33, p. 421-422; ed. N.O. "Picayune," sketch of, v.30, p.263.
Baker, Page, v.30, p.294; newspaperman, v.31, p.740; edits "Democrat," v.31, p.785; noted, v.33, p.423.

Baldwin, Joshua, noted, v.22, p.1133; noted, v.23, p.204, 219, 220; Whig rep., v.25, p.1095, 1096, 1097, 1098.

Baldwin, Samuel, naval agent for State of Fla., 1810, v.21, p.136, 137n., 138; and W. Fla. Rev., v.21, p.740.

Baldwin, Lt. Charles C., resigned, v.26, p.835.

Balize, privateersmen at, v.22, p.1076-1077; noted, v.24, p.370; v.24, p.629; noted, v.26, p.8, 9; post on Southern pass of Miss., first called "Toulouse," v.26, p.73; maintained by O'Reilly, v.26, p.740; noted, v.26, p.750; Laussats impressions of, 1803, v.26, p.752; noted, v.28, p.684, 686, 747, 748, 768, 883ff.

Ballinger, John, sketch, v.21, p.93n.; orders of W. Fla. Conventions Comm., v.21, p.93-95, 108; letter from Skipwith, v.21, p.145; agent of state of Fla. to Cong., v.21, p.189; and W. Fla. Rev., v.21, p.719n.; noted, v.29, p.76.

Ballot Reform League, v.26, p.1108.

Ballowe, Hewitt L., "The Lawd Sayin' the Same," reviewed, v.31, p.154-56.

Ball, William P., newspaperman, v.33, p.327.

Balmer, Ch., collection in L.S.U. Music School Library, v.24, p.347.

Baltimore, and privateering, v.23, p.799-800.

Balzer, Helen, noted, v.24, p.381.

Bancroft, George, letter to from Charles Gayarre, v.33, p.252-254; noted, v.33, p.231n., 236, 255, 268.

Bancroft, Hubert Howe, quoted on Bastrop's identity, v.31, p.607.

"Banett's report, Louisiana in 1724," Translated by Heloise H. Cruzat, v.12, p.121.

Bangs, Lt.-Col. J. S., Jr., recommended Pinchback for commissioner, v.27, p.531.

Bank Bill in La., 1842, v.25, p.114, 115, 129.

Banker, Ed. H., N.O. minstrel, sketch of, v.30, p.141-142.

Banking in N.O., and J. Robb, v.23, p.173ff.; in La., v.23, p.243-244; after the Civil War, v.23, p.255, 1209.

Bank of Commerce and Trust Co. of Crowley, v.27, p.1171-1172.

Bank of Louisiana, noted, v.24, p.481; in N.O., v.25, p.164, 172, 195.

Bank of Orleans, v.25, p.987.

Bank of Rapides, noted, v.24, p.742-743.

Bank Question, Ed. Livingston's position on, v.24, p.703; Clay and, v.24, p.1166; in politics, v.24, p.1169.

"Banks Expedition of 1862, The," by Geo. Winston Smith, v.26, p.341-60.

"Bank's, General, Red River Campaign," by Richard Hobson Williams, v.32, p.103.

Banks, Nathaniel Prentiss, raids up Red River, v.18, p.5-15, 855-858; sets up local government in New Orleans, v.18, p.562ff.; noted, v.23, p.1197ff.; letter from G. S. Denison, v.23, p.1198-1199; letter from Lincoln, v.23, p.1212; and Christ Church, v.23, p.1245; noted, v.24, p.82, 84, 87, 93, 97, 99; successor of Butler in N.O. v.24, p.525-526, 530-531; and Negro education, 1863, v.25, p.738, 742, 744, 748, 753, 787; organized Southern expedition, 1862, v.26, p.351-355; landed in N.O. and replaced Butler, v.26, p.355-357; and Red River Campaign, v.26, p.974n.; noted, v.26, p.1043; La. under, v.26, p.1058; conscription in N.O. under, v.27, p.519-520; replaces Butler in N.O., v.27, p.525; interview with Pinchback, v. 27, p.530; refused Pinchback's commission, v.27, p.531; noted, v.29, p.1241; v.30, p.524-529; noted, v.30, p.534; and Charity Hospital, v.31, p.63-64; birth and early life, v.31, p.558; orator and journalist, v.31, p.558-559; elected to Congress, v.31, p.559; and Mass. constitution, v.31, p.559; Governor of Mass., v.31, p.559; in army, v.31, p.560; at New Orleans, v.31, p.561; Port Hudson, v. 31, p.560-561; Congressman, v.31, p. 561-562; U.S. Marshal, v.31, p.562; retirement and death, v.31, p.562-563; Louisiana Governor, v.31, p.1011; fight with Wells, v.31, p.1028, 1030-1032; removed, v.31, p.1034; correspondence with Gen. Halleck, v.32, p.104, 105, 106; headquarters of the army, v.32, p.106; message from Gen. Steele, v.32, p.107; Messages from Gen. Grant, v.32, p.116, 127; message to Gen. Sherman, v.32, p.126; from Gen. Sherman, v.32, p.116; Message from Gen. Smith, v.32, p.127; noted, v.32, p.111, 113, 114, 115, 116, 118, 120, 121, 123, 124, 125, 126, 128, 130, 131, 132, 135, 137, 138, 139, 140; Red River Campaign, v.19, p.150-195.

Bankston, Peter, v.29, p.83.

Bankston, W. P., appointed to Bogalusa police force, v.29, p.113.

"Banner of Liberty," populist newspaper, v.26, p.1118.

Bannister, Rinaldo, noted, v.23, p.482.

Baonavia y Zapata, Don Bernando, Comdt. of armies, Sp. Council held to discuss Indian trade, v.28, p.1088.

Baptists, in New Orleans, v.21, p.828-829; in Calcasieu Parish, v.32, p.622; in St. Mary Parish, v.32, p.76.

Baptist, William, inventor of pullboat system for cypress, v.30, p.1002.

Baracoa, privateers plan to attack, v.23, p.443.

Bar Association of N.O., invitation to Clay, v.27, p.740; honors Clay, v.27, p.762; memorial exercise for Webster, v.27, p.763.

Barataria Bay, activities at, v.21, p.202n., 204-205.

Baratarians, noted, v.25, p.300; pirates and part played in Battle of N.O., v.28, p.730-731.

Bartaria, pirates of, v.22, p.803-804; used in shipping specie, v.22, p.1013, 1015-1017; privateersman at, v.22, p.1018, 1024; auction, v.22, p.1027; privateers establishments at, v.23, p.428-444; description of, v.23, p.438-439; description of, v.24, p.12-13; base for privateers, v.24, p.14-15; and Battle of N.O., v.24, p.26; noted, v.24, p.367, 369, 362; noted, v.25, p.934.

Barba, noted, v.24, p.46.

Barbat, Alphonse, official of Confed. navy, v.27, p.480, 481.

Barbe, Dr., Charter member Medical Society of La., v.26, p.59.

Barbe-en-fume, Gianni, noted, v.24, p.628.

Barbe, Marbois, book on La. Treaty, v.24, p.1137.

Barbin, Aristide, reasons for voting for Lottery Bill of 1890, v.27, p.1037-1039.

Barbin, Nicolas Godefroy, attorney for the Vacant Estates, v.21, p.1010.

Barbour, James, minister to London, v.24, p.1111, 1129, 1136, 1138, 1143, 1159.

Bard, Samuel F., candidate for supt. of ed., 1855, v.25, p.680.

Bares, Basile J., N.O. musician, v.31, p.135.

Barker, Jacob, noted, v.24, p.533; v.30, p.273.

Barker, William, and W. Fla. Rev., v.21, p.83.

Barlow, Rev. ———, pastor in New Orleans, v.22, p.454.

Barlow, S. L. M., noted, v.24, p.52, 119.

Barnes, Captain, noted, v.24, p.362.

Barnes, Caroline, v.27, p.8; birth of paternity questioned, v.27, p.25, 27-40, 61; marriage to John Barnes, v.27, p.29; legatee in will of Clark, v.27, p.66, 67; noted, v.27, p.75-76, 80, 81, 83, 97, 99, 101, 102, 131-133, 134, 137-142, 145, 146, 147, 149, 150, 152, 155, 156, 157, 159, 160, 161, 162, 165, 168, 170, 174; made defendant in Gaines bill of equity, v.27, p.190; legal opinion in re birth, v.27, p.191, 193, 194, 195, 215, 216, 217, 218, 219, 220, 221, 222, 223, 224, 228-235, 237, 253, 267-269, 271, 278, 282, 284, 308.

Barnes, Edward F., inventor v.31, p.437; defends Columbian Telegraph, v.31, p.468; arrested, v.31, p.462.

Barnes, John, marriage to Caroline Desgrange, v.27, p.29, 36, 138, 161, 163, 171; named defendant in Gaines bill in equity, v.27, p.190, 219, 233.

Barnett, Charles, noted, v.24, p.992, 1059.

Barnett, Maurice, real estate auctioneers, v.26, p.145.

Barnett, substitute for Sheldon, v.24, p.948, 987, 1068, 1091, 1096, 1097-1098, 1102, 1125, 1134.

Barnwell, R. G., agent for "De Bow's Review", v.29, p.360-362; editor of "Review" after De Bow's death, v.29, p.391-392.

Baron, Pierre, appointed by Louis XV to study in La., v.29, p.577; appointed engineer-in-chief of convent building, v.29, p.577; dismissed as engineer, v.29, p.578.

Barr, Agnes Gibson, claim vs. Davenport for Barr property, v.28, p.1090-1092, 1095.

Barrancas, Amargo, noted, v.22, p.810; v.23, p.429.

Barrancas, de Margot, importance of post, v.21, p.54-55.

Barr and Davenport, House of Sp. Trading firm, v.28, p.1074, 1087; partners and organization of, v.28, p.1089-1096; activities of, v.28, p.1096-1097; merchandise handled by, v.28, p.1097-1098; setbacks of, v.28, p.1098-1100; return to prosperity, v.28, p.1100-1101; Sp. attitude toward, v.28, p.1101-1103.

Barran, Peter Dulcide, deposition of, v.23, p.727-728.

Barranquilla, noted, v.24, p.688, 690.

Barrecco, John, and the Mafia, v.22, p.832ff.

Barrecco, Paul, and the Mafia, v.22, p.832ff.

Barrett, Charles, "Address on Celebration of the Founding of New Orleans," Translated from French by Miss Grace King, v.2, p.259.

Barrett, George H., assumes direction of American Theatre, 1838, v.28, p.235; season 1838-1839, v.28, p.235-240.

Barrett, J. T., pres. Acadia Lit. & Com. College, v.27, p.1176; head of Acadia College, v.30, p.758-759.

Barrett, T. C., Lt. Gov. of La., v.29, p.109.

Barriere, Michael Bernard, noted, v.22, p.814.

Barringer, Daniel L., and sugar tariff, v.25, p.67.

Barroto, ———, noted, v.22, p.939.

Barrow, Alexander, opposes annexation of Texas, v.19, p.99-101, 118; and 1842 tariff, v.25, p.116, 117, 119, 139, 141; and annexation of Texas, v.25, p.127, 1004; and 1844 tariff, v.25, p.131, 1044; his death, v.25, p.1058; body taken to La., v.25, p.1073; Rep. from W. Fel. with Johnson, v.28, p.950, 951; death of, v.28, p.970; noted, v.28, p.982.

Barrow, Bennett H., diary, in L.S.U. Archives, v.24, p.341.

"Barrow, Civil War Diary of Willie Micajah Barrow," I, II, by W. H. Stephenson and E. A. Davis (edited by), v.17, p.436, 712.

Barrow, Crowley, noted, v.22, p.985.

Barrow, Robert I., made Col. of 4th La. Reg't, v.29, p.1049.

Barrow, William, and W. Fla. Rev., v.21, p.76, 687n.; and W. Fla. Assembly, v.22, p.956; noted, v.23, p.45.

Barr, William, organized trading firm, v.28, p.1089; mother claims property, v.28, p.1090-1091, 1095; sketch, v.28, p.1091-1092; activities of House of Barr and Davenport, v.28, p.1096ff.; Sp. attitude toward, v.28, p.1101-1102; death, v.28, p.1103.

Barry, J. E., Judge, public offices in Crowley, v.27, p.1131.

Barry, Richard, noted, v.23, p.391.

"Bar, The Louisiana," by T. C. W. Ellis, v.4, p.81.

Bartlett, Cosam J., Major 1st La. Inf., v.26, p.798, 799.

Bartlett, Napier, early N.O. newspaperman, v.29, p.776-777.

Barton, Dr. Edward H., son-in-law of Fulwar Skipwith, v.31, p.309; noted, v.22, p.466, 490; Dean of Medical College after Luzenberg, v.26, p.57; on Charity Hospital Board, 1836, v.26, p.58; on Medical Board of Censors, v.26, p.60; noted, v.26, p.76.

Barton, John, N.O. actor, v.31, p.978.

Barton, Thomas P., application for diplomatic post, v.24, p.1101.

Baru, noted, v.24, p.617.

Basil, Florence, noted, v.22, p.815.

Basket, Thomas, petition of, v.23, p.404.

Bass and Benckenstien, oil well in Jennings, La. pool, v.29, p.500, 501, 503.

Bass, Charles C., article cited, v.24, p.334, 349.

Basso, Hamilton, noted, v.24, p.354.

Bastard, Count, noted, v.24, p.1036.

Bastrop Claim Case, v.25, p.1085.

Bastrop, Felipe Enrique Neri, Baron de, role in American settlement of Texas, v.31, p.606-679; name discussed, v.31, p.607; identity, v.31, p.607-608; petitions, v.31, p.613-614, 616, 624, 626; contract for colony, v.31, p.614, 615, 624; Ouachita settlement, v.31, p.616-628; goes to Texas, v.31, p.631-632; petitions to settle at Bexar, v.31, p.632-633; seeks trading privileges, v.31, p.635; opinions of, v.31, p.639-640; aids Austin, v.31, p.641-643; compared with Austin, v.31, p.642; serves as intermediary, v.31, p.645; commissioner of Austin Colony, v.31, p.647-648; elected deputy, v.31, p.648; continued interest in colony, v.31, p.649-650; election to legislature, v.31, p.651-652; work in interest of colonization, v.31, p.656-658, 659-660; efforts at Mexican concession, v.31, p.662-668; and slavery question, v.31, p.670; death and burial, v.31, p.672-673; will, v.31, p.673-676; Edward's accusations, v.31, p.677-678; evaluation of, v.31, p.679.

Bastrop Land Grant, v.20, p.289-462.

Bastrop, La., noted, v.25, p.931; in 1860, v.21, p.1198.

Bastrop Masonic Female Institute, v.30, p.842-843.

Batchelder, G. F. C., noted, v.23, p.1198.

Batchelor, A. A., pressure on to vote for lottery, v.27, p.1047.

Bateman, F. B., school board member of 1st Bogalusa school, v.29, p.100.

Bateman, Fred, Lt. in Troop "F" of La. Inf., v.29, p.82.

Bates, Ephraim, noted, v.23, p.420.

Bates, Hannah, wife of Elnathan Smith, sketch of, v.29, p.287.

Bates, Thomas C., pres. N.O., Baton Rouge and Vicksburg Railroad, v.30, p.1216, 1223-1224.

Bates, W. D., Farmers' Alliance leader, v.26, p.1070.

Baton Rouge Academy, sketch of, v.30, p.766.

Baton Rouge Bayou, v.28, p. 5, 35, 40.

Baton Rouge College, sketch of, v.30, p.770-772.

Baton Rouge Collegiate Institute, sketch of, v.30, p.777-778.

Baton Rouge, Daily Capitolian Advocate, obituary of Randolph, v.25, p.215.

Baton Rouge Female Seminary, sketch of, v.30, p.779-780.

Baton Rouge, Grosse Tete and Opelousas Railroad, v.25, p.697-698; history of, v.30, p.1209-1217.

Baton Rouge, Grosse Tete and Opelousas Plank Road Company, created, v.31, p.512.

Baton Rouge Incorporated Academy, sketch of, v.30, p.769-770.

"Baton Rouge, Lafayette's Visit to, April 1825," translated by R. W. Colomb, v.14, p.178.

Baton Rouge, Louisiana, "The Historic Capital of La.," by J. St. Clair Favrot, v.12, p.611; West Florida— The Capture of Baton Rouge by Galvez, Sept. 21, 1779, From reports of the English officers, v.12, p.255; West Florida — Documents Covering a Royal Land Grant on the Mississippi and Amite Rivers, transcribed from the originals in the Cabildo, v.12, p.630; and W. Fla. Convention, v.21, p.702ff.; Catholic Church of, v.22, p.99; early land grants near, v.23, p.382; Agric. Soc. of, v.23, p.874; attacked by Breckenridge, v.23, p.1192; captured by Banks, v.23, p.1198; Spanish post, v.25, p.13; noted, v.25, p.49, 63, 120, 126, 127, 140, 186, 204, 324; agricultural society of, v.25, p.58; and tariff, v.25, p.79; and nullification, v.25, p.91; made capital, v.25, p.1044; captured by Galvez, v.26, p.311, 742-743; noted, v.26, p.663; defense plan of, v.26, p.745; State Dem. Conv. in 1859, v.26, p.984, 986, 987, 989; question of removing capital from, v.26, p.993; special legis. sess. in 1860, v.26, p.995; secession conv. in, v.26, p.998-1001; agricultural experiment station, v.26, p.1064; occupied by Galvez, v.27, p.338; population 1860, v.27, p.488, 490; fall of, v.27, p.520; attempt of Brecken- ridge to recapture, v.27, p.521-522; evacuated by Federals, v.27, p.522; Repub. Conv. in 1872, v.27, p.552; surrender to Galvez, v.27, p.661, 662, 663, 698; Taylor pres. from, v.27, p.725; Clay visits, v.27, p.741; encounter of Clay and Taylor in, v.27, p.757, 758; provisions for moving capital to, v.27, p.989, 1032, 1046; state conv. of Anti-Lottery League in Aug., 1890, v.27, p.1057, 1086; State Farmers' Union Conv., v.27, p.1057, 1077; Dem. State Nominating Conv. in, v.27, p.1088, 1089, 1096, 1199; origin of name, v.28, p.5-8, 44-47; physiographic characteristics of region of, v.28, p.9-15; map of area, v.28, p.11; subdivisions of, v.28, p.14; levees of, v.28, p.14-15; traffic outlets, v.28, p.15; capital in, v.28, p.15; climate and weather, v.28, p.16-18; soils of area, v.28, p.18-19; trees in area and other vegetation, v.28, p.19-22; animal life of, v.28, p.22-24; Indian mounds and middens give evidence of prehistoric Indians in, v.28, p.24-30; earliest explorations, v.28, p.30-34; location of Red Pole, v.28, p.35-44; early maps showing, v.28, p.39-40; Indian origin and settlement, v.28, p.48-57; Fr. settle, v.28, p.58-65; D'Artaguette family founders of, v.28, p.60-63, 67; land office discontinued, 1861, v.28, p.300; made capital, v.28, p.967; election of 1896, v.28, p.1181; supports telegraph, v.31, p.439; telegraph reaches, v.31, p.448.

Baton Rouge Reach, straight course of Miss. R. at B.R., v.28, p.10, 15, 35; map of, v.28, p.36; noted, v.28, p.38, 40, 63, 67.

Baton Rouge, Regulations to be observed by the Syndics and Alcalds of the Jurisdiction of, v.9, p.405.

Batson Prairie, oil field, v.27, p.1169.

Battigne, Bellegarde, noted, v.24, p.628.

Battigne, Captain Marcellin, privateer, v.23, p.434, 436, 437.

Battigne, Joseph, noted, v.22, p.1047.

Battle of Missionary Ridge, v.29, p.705-706.

Battle of New Orleans, Battle of N.O. Number (Editor's Chair), v.9, p.111; "Contemporary Account of the Battle of N.O. by a Soldier in the Ranks," v.9, p. 11; "General Court-Martial of or Trial of Brevet Lieutenant Colonel Mullins," v.9, p.33; "General David M. Morgan's Defense of the Conduct of the La. Militia in the Battle on the left side of the

River," v.9, p.16; "Letter of the Duke of Wellington (May 22, 1815) on the Battle of New Orleans," v.9, p.5; "Massachusetts Volunteer in the Battle of N.O., A," v.9, p.30; "Ogden's Troop of Horse in the," v.10, p.381; Nathan and Reuben Kemper in, v.21, p.86; noted, v.23, p.1018; report in La. Hist. Assn. depository, v.24, p.314-315; noted, v.25, p.304; noted, v.26, p.960, 976; noted, v.27, p.495, 734; Commemoration of 1844, v.27, p.748, 764; Favrot's description of Aftermath of, v.28, p.725-28; "A Letter from the, from John A. Fort," with Introductory note by E. A. Parsons, v.32, p.225; noted, v.33, p.168-169.

Battle of Pleasant Hill, v.32, p.119-125.

Battle of Sabine Crossroads, v.32, p.119-125.

"Battle of September 14, 1874, in New Orleans," by Col. F. L. Richardson, v.3, p.498; noted, v.32, p.231.

"Battle of St. Paul's, The," quoted, v.24, p.503-505.

Batture Controversy, Livingston's, v.19, p.357-374; documents relating to controversy, v.23, p.679-732; Controversy, v.23, p.1064-1071; case concerning, v.23, p.1029-1031.

Batz, de, architect, v.29, p.573, 577, 608.

Baudier, Roger, work on Catholic Church cited, v.24, p.312, 349; Catholic historian, v.31, p.898.

Baudoin, ———, noted, v.23, p.146.

Baudouin, Father, Jesuit priest, v.31, p.900.

Baume, Jose de la, noted, v.31, p.628; sold out to Bastrop, v.31, p.631; settles in Texas, v.31, p.631; Bastrop will, v.31, p.676.

Baume, Victoriana de, Bastrop heiress, v.31, p.675.

Bautte, Hippolyette Prudent de (Prudent d'Artlys), v.31, p.992.

"Bavarian Organist Comes to New Orleans," by Robert T. Clark, Jr., v.29, p.14-42.

"Bavarians Journey to N.O. and Nacogdoches in 1853-1854," ed. by K. J. R. Arndt, v.23, p.485-500.

Bayard, James A., noted, v.24, p.116.

Bayard, Thomas F., noted, v.24, p.58.

Bayley, Dr. Robert A., son of G. W. R. Bayley, v.30, p.1080, 1095.

Bayley, George Willard Reed, as assistant state engineer, v.30, p.1067; Chief. Engr. and Land Agent, N.O., Opelousas and Great Western Railroad, v.30, p.1069, 1072-1078; City Surveyor of N.O., v.30, p.1071; Division Engr., N.O., Mobile and Chattanooga Railroad, v.30, p.1078; Chief Engr., Louisiana Levee Company, v.20, p.1082; member Levee Commission of Engineers, v.30, p.1082; member State Board of Health, v.30, p.1080; on Education Committee, N.O. Mechanics Society, v.30, p.1083-1089; member, N.O. Chamber of Commerce, v.30, p.1084-1085; member La. Legislature, v.30, p.1087-1097; Resident Engr., Eads Jetty Company, v.30, p.1097-1100; and New Orleans Pacific Railroad, v.30, p.1100-1105; sketch of, v.30, p.1105-1115; "History of the Railroads of Louisiana," v.30, p.1116-1325.

Bayou Bartholomew, noted, v.25, p.628, 629, 930.

Bayou Boeuf, Cathcart's survey of, v.28, p.765, 787ff.; noted, v.24, p.84, 97.

"Bayou Boeuf Lottery," river improvement lottery, v.31, p.717.

Bayou Bourbeau, noted, v.24, p.79.

Bayou Caillou, noted, v.25, p.54.

Bayou de la Digue, noted, v.25, p.324.

Bayou de Large (Buffalo Bayou), v.28, p.802n., 803.

Bayou des Allemands, noted, v.24, p.70, 83.

Bayou Fountain, v.28, p.12, 24, 25.

Bayou Garrison, figures in location of Red Pole site, v.28, p.35, 37, 38.

"Bayou Goula Guards," noted, v.25, p.212.

Bayou Goula Indians, description of, v.23, p.1123; noted, v.25, p.163; v.28, p.34, 51, 56, 57, 83.

Bayou Goula, La., noted, v.25, p.150, 161, 170, 172, 174, 187, 189, 202; sugar area, v.25, p.163-164; v.28, p.32.

Bayou Goula Plantation, noted, v.25, p.174; sale of, v.25, p.213, 214.

Bayou la Butt, noted, v.25, p.163.

Bayou Lafourche, noted, v.24, p.71; center of Acadian culture, v.24, p.753; noted, v.25, p.934, 938-939; v.28, p.51, 739, 754.

Bayou Long, v.28, p.786ff.

Bayou L'Outre, noted, v.25, p.627.

Bayou Manchac, noted, v.25, p.13, 14; found by Iberville, v.25, p.933; suggested site for city, v.25, p.934; inter colonial boundary, v.25, p.935; British interest in, v.25, p.935; Sp. interest in, v.25, p.935-937, 939; international boundary, v.25, p.939; effort made to clear, v.25, p.940, 941-942; Sp. forbidden use of, v.25, p.940-944; lost importance, v.25, p.942; noted, v.26, p.665; noted, v.28, p.24; Iberville's party camps near, v.28, p.32, 33, 34; believed site of Red Pole by some historians, v.28, p.35; figures in location of Red Pole site, v.28, p.37, 38, 40, 44; noted, v.28, p.694.

Bayou Mardi Gras, noted, v.26, p.754.

Bayou Milkomme (Mellam), v.28, p.787ff.

Bayou Monte Sano, v.28, p.12, 13, 25, 36; southern boundary of Pousset Grant, determines site of Indian Village, v.28, p.42.

Bayou Natchez, noted, v.25, p.361.

Bayou Natchitoches, noted, v.25, p.398.

Bayou Petite Sorel, v.28, p.779, 780.

Bayou Pierre, noted, v.24, p.93; v.25, p.400; trading post established at, v.28, p.1088, 1089, 1099, 1101.

Bayou Pigeon, clearing of authorized, v.28, p.298; noted, v. 28, p.837.

Bayou Plaquemine, noted, v.25, p.163, 164; found by Iberville, v.25, p.933; navigable, v.25, p.934-935; Sp. attempt to build palisade, v.25, p.937-938; noted, v.28, p.739, 752n., 754, 758, 759, 760, 762; Cathcart's survey, v.28, p.834ff.; noted, v.28, p.883.

Bayou Rapides, noted, v.24, p.96.

Bayou Reed, Cathcart's survey, v.28, p.766ff.

Bayou Road, noted, v.25, p.14.

Bayou Robert, noted, v.24, p.96, 97; v.26, p.976; v.28, p.828ff.

Bayou Sale, v.28, p.828ff.

Bayou Sara, located, v.21, p.93n.; in 1860, v.21, p.1134-1136; noted, v.25, p.157; scene of conflict between Negroes and Whites, v.25, p.709-710; v.28, p.942, 943.

Bayou Shafer, v.28, p.791, 792, 797.

"Bayous, Louisiana's Dreamy," by Evelyn Soule, v.13, p.253.

Bayou Snipe, noted, v.25, p.361.

"Bayous of Louisiana," by Harnett T. Kane, rev'd by Andre Lafargue, v.28, p.349-351.

Bayous of northeast La., description of, by Filhiol, v. 20, p.477ff.

Bayou Sorel (Sorrel), v.28, p.786, 888, 889, 834ff.

"Bayou St. John, and New Orleans in 1766," by William Beer, v.6, p.19; in Sp. period, v.22, p. 642; noted, v. 22, p.816; Houmas settled, v.28, p.57; noted, v.25, p.14; v.26, p.665, 741, 747, 748, 806-807; and Orleans Navigation Co. Case, v.28, p.979.

Bayou Teche, noted, v.24, p.71, 85; center of Acadian Culture, v.24, p.753; Cathcart's survey of, v.28, p.738, 739, 752; water routes to from the Miss., v.28, p.754n.; noted, v.28, p.760, 761, 762n., 763, 766ff., 786, 793, 808ff., 835ff., 883, 888, 1129 ;noted, v.32, p.17-18; plan to clear for navigation, v.32, p.22.

Bay Roundel Bayou, noted, v.25, p.398.

Beaird, S. J., Confed. soldier, v.26, p.952, 968.

Beale, Robert G., noted, v.25, p.681.

"Beales Rifles," noted, v.25, p.384.

Beall, A. K., tells of development of Bogalusa, v.29, p.96-97, 98, 101.

Beall, Brig. Gen'l W. R. N., placed in command of Port Hudson, v.29, p.1094, 1096, 1122.

Bean, Ellis P., sketch, v.22, p.730-731.

Bean, Jacob, Opelousas planter demanded return of slaves, v.28, p.1071.

Bean, Peter, noted, v.22, p.1031n.

Beard, Cornelius, noted, v.23, p.534.

Beard, James A., noted, v.23, p.180, 200.

Beard, Joseph A., slave dealer, v.22, p.152.

Beasley, Consul in charge of Brown Wills, v.24, p.1150.

"Beast Butler," noted, v.24, p.531.

Beatly, Dr. F., noted, v.26, p.76.

Beattie, Taylor, rep. cand. for Gov. 1879, v.28, p. 1140.

Beaubois, Father Nicolas Ignatius de, Jesuit priest of N.O., v.25, p.730; comes to N.O. to help procure Jesuit Mission from France, v.29, p.563; letter concerning delayed arrival of Nuns, v.29, p.564; impatiently awaits arrival of Nuns, v.29, p.565; serves as chaplain of convent, v.29, p.569; claims to be superior of Nuns, v.29, p.570; recalled as result of dispute, v.29, p.571-572; noted, v.29, p.591.

Beaudin, Alex., West Fla. claims against U.S., v. 25, p.948-950.

Beaumont, Chantreau de, settlers for concession, v.21, p.966.

Beauregard Centennial, May 28, 1918: Address by Col. H. J. de la Vergne, "General Beauregard before the Civil War," v.1, p.297; Address by Milo B. Williams, "General Beauregard and General Blanchard in the Mexican War," v.1, p.299.

Beauregard, Henri Toutant, noted, v.24, p.356.

Beauregard, P. G. T., "A Sketch of General," by his son, R. T. Beauregard, v.2, p.276; noted, v.23, p.1183, 1187; noted, v.24, p.354; noted, v.24, p.61, 78, 104, 106, 107; orders in Jackson Barracks Library, v.24, p.313; manuscripts in Howard-Tilton Memorial Library, v.24, p.328; reinforcements from N.O., v.24, p.445; reaction to Butler's Order #28, v.24, p.495; independent candidate in N.O. 1858, v.25, p.692-693; ordered firing on Sumter, v.27, p.776; commissioner of La. Lottery, v.27, p.979; in defense of Lottery Co., v.27, p.987; semi-annual drawing, 1879, v.27, p.1002-1003, 1015; as commissioner, v.27, p.1016-1020, 1099; and Carrollton Railroad, v.30, p.1126-1127; pres. N.O., Jackson and Great Northern Railroad, v. 30, p.580-481, 1140-1144; and lottery company, v.31, p.742; as inventor, v.21, p.243; noted, v.24, p.359.

Beauregard, R. T., "A Sketch of General G. T. Beauregard," v.2, p.276.

Beauregard, Santiago, noted, v.22, p.664.

Beauvais, Arnaud, and sugar tariff, v.25, p.58, 60.

Beaver River, noted, v.24, p.426.

Beck, Charles, Confed. naval officer, v.27, p.484.

Beckwith, Admiral, noted, v.23, p.434.

Bedford Springs, resort, v.24, p.1100, 1166.

Bedsole, Vergil L., noted, v.24, p.308.

"Beechwoods," school of Mrs. J. J. Audubon, v.25, p.157.

"Bee," v.27, p.518; suppressed by Butler, v.27, p.500-501; friendly to Clay, v.27, p.733; noted, v.33, p.406-407.

Bee, General H. P., noted, v.32, p.123, 128.

Bee, Hamilton P., noted, v.24, p.89, 90, 91, 92, 94, 95.

Beer factory, establishment in La., 1788, v.21, p.13.

Beer, H., lottery offer, v.27, p.1035, 1049.

Beer, William, Louisiana Data Recently Acquired by U.S. Congressional Library, v.1, sec. 1, p.116; Notes on Annual Report of American Historical Association, for 1914, v.1, sec. 1, p.117; Contemporary English View of Trade at Close of French Dominion, v.6, p.221; List of Writings of Grace King, v.6, p.378; New Orleans and Bayou St. John in 1766, v.6, p.19; Visit of Illinois Indians to France in 1725, v.6, p.189; In Memoriam, by Henry P. Dart, v.10, p.249; "William Beer, 1849-1927," by Edward Laroque Tinker, v.11, p.59; "Introduction to Early Census Tables of La.," Translated by J. K. Ditchey, v.13, p.205; Collection of in Howard-Tilton Memorial Library, v.24, p.328.

Beethoven, reproductions of in Howard-Tilton Mem. Library, v.24, p.330.

Begue, Hippolyte, head cook of Fr. doctor's mess, v.26, p.805.

Behan, Wm. J., and White League, v.23, p.528; on the lottery question, v.27, p.1042.

Bel, Dr. George S., first Director of New Charity Hospital, v.31, p.95.

"Beleaguered City: Richmond, (1861-1865)," by Alfred Hoyt Bill, rev'd by Walter Prichard, v.30, p.352-353.

Bell, ————, noted, v. 23, p.420.

"Bell and Everett Union Club," of Amite, La., v.29, p.685.

Bellechasse, Joseph D.D., noted, v.27, p.7; Clark conveys property to in interest of Myra, v.27, p.45, 47-48; letter of, v.27, p.47; Myra visits, v.27, p.48; noted, v.27, p.56, 59; testimony of, v.27, p.60; executor of will, v.27, p.66, 67, 69; testimony of, v.27, p.72-76; noted, v.27, p.85, 86, 90; testimony of, v.27, p.103; evidence against, v.27, p.115; testimony of, v.27, p.119, 125, 133, 134, 137, 153, 154, 155, 159, 160, 161, 164, 165, 172; in re Clark's will of 1813, v.27, p.173, 174, 190; deposition of, v.27, p.206, 208, 214, 224, 236, 237, 262, 267, 269, 280, 310; noted, v.22, p.808; sketch, v.22, p.810.

Bell, Edwin, work on "De Bow's Review," v.29, p.363, 379, 391, 392..

Bellegarde, Capt., ————, noted, v.22, p.1047-1049.

"Belle Grove" Plantation, near White Castle, v.25, p.207.

Belle Isle, noted, v.24, p.40; v.28, p.765, 808ff.; minerals on, v.28, p.830; noted, v.28, p.832; Cathcart found excellent live oaks on, v.28, p.886-887, 891.

"Belles Demoiselles Plantation," work of Cable, v.24, p.168.

Bellestre, Francisco de, Commander of Barrancas, 1816, v.21, p.809.

Bellevue, in 1860, v.21, p.1179-1180.

Bellevue Seminary, v.30, p.793.

Bellewood Academy, v.30, p.900-902.

Bellew, Page, Cathcart's pilot, v.28, p.771; sketch, v.28, p.771n.; noted, v.28, p.829.

Bell, Isaac, merchant, v.24, p.1014, 1047, 1048, 1127.

"Bellisle, Installation as Town Major," Introduction by Henry P. Dart, Translated by Heloise H. Cruzat, v.14, p.235.

Bellisle, ———, noted, v.22, p. 661n.

Bell, John M., Dem. candidate for sheriff in N.O., 1855, v.25, p.690-691; candidate for state senator, 1846, v.25, p.1036, 1038; and the senatorial election of 1848, v.25, p.1094-1096.

Bell, Joseph M., acting recorder of N.O., v.27, p.512; sentenced Pinchback to 2 yrs. in jail, v.27, p.529.

"Bells, The," comment on by Cable, v.24, p.174.

Bell, T. F., pres. anti-lottery conv., 1890, v.27, p.1057-1058; v.28, p.1150-1151; nom. Adams, v.28, p.1157.

Bell, William, noted, v.24, p.40.

Belly, Pierre, v.28, p.842n.

Belmont Crevasse, v.26, p.1072.

Belmonti, Louis, and case of Sally Miller, v.22, p.160.

"Belona," a vessel, v.24, p.629, 632, 633, 634, 643, 653, 656, 672, 679, 681, 682, 684, 687.

Beluche, Commodore, letter of, v.24, p. 367; noted, v.24, p.662.

Beluche, Rene, noted, v.22, p.1025, 1040, 1044, 1075, 1076, 1081, 1082; noted, v.23, p.429; and expedition of P. Lafitte, v.23, p.771-772; privateer, v.23, p.810.

Benavides, Father, noted, v.22, p.939.

Bengston, Rev. W. H., cited, v.24, p.147.

Benguerel, Madame, ———, gives evidence that Degrange was bigamist, v.27, p.53-54, 103-104, 137, 151, 153, 154, 155, 159, 160; testimony, v. 27, p.208, 215, 224-225, 238, 262, 265, 266, 288.

Benjamin, Judah Philip, forced to flee the Confederacy, v.19, p.964-968; early life and family, v.19, p.970-975; leader of N.O. Bar, v.19, p.978; and La. constitutional convention, 1844-1845, v.19, p.980-981; a progressive sugar planter, v. 19, p.985-986; attitude toward slavery and internal improvements, v.19, p.986ff.; and McDonogh Case, v.19, p.989-992; and La. Constitutional Convention of 1852, v.19, p.992; and Know Nothings, v.19, p.993-996; in U.S. Senate, v.19, p.997-1014; and "Creole" case, v.19, p.1023-1026; att'y Gen. of Confederacy, v.19, p.1031-1033; Secretary of War, v.19, p.1033-1038; and King Cotton, v.19, p.1040-1045; flight to England, v.19, p.1049; Queen's Counsel, v.19, p.1051; retirement, v.19, p.1054; Letters of, to Ambrose D. Mann, v.20, p.738-793; noted, v.22, p.1136; mission to Ecuador, v.23, p.162-169; and election of 1851, v.23, p.180, 187; supported by Robb, v.23, p.192; and railroad convention, v.23, p.199; noted, v.23, p.244, 483, 1095; tribute to by Marti, v.23, p.259-264; Democratic candidate for La. Senate, 1858, v.24, p.55, 56; noted, v.24, p.441, 442, 444; noted, v.25, p.142, 979, 980, 998, 1007; disputed election of, v.25, p.1009, 1079, 1083; senatorial election of 1848, v.25, p.1095, 1108; U.S. Senator, v.26, p.980, 982, 997; noted, v.27, p.740, appears before Bar Assoc. honoring Webster, v.27, p.763; Sec. of State under Jeff Davis, v.29, p.1242; personality sketch, v.29, p.1243-1244; noted, v.29, p.1245, 1246, 1248; arranges peace conference, v.29, p.1252-1253.

"Benjamin, Judah Philip, or Jewish Prophecy Fulfilled," by Joseph M. Pilcher, v.3, p.478.

Benoit, A., Farmers' Alliance leader, v.26, p.1070; Populist cand. for Cong., 1894, v.26, p.1095; noted, v.28, p.1176, 1177.

"Benoit, Juan, Marriage Contract with Elena Montanary," Translated by Laura L. Porteous, v.9, p.385.

Benthuysen, Alfred C. Van, Capt. of the Confed. Marine Corps from La., v.27, p.485.

Benton, Colonel of Lake Providence, v.23, p.1141.

Benton, Thomas H., noted, v.23, p.1046n., 1143; documents of in Bibliotheca Parsoniana, v.24, p.311; and Clay, v.24, p.1001, 1037, 1045; friendship for Jackson, v.24, p.1041, 1135; U.S. Senator and 1833 tariff, v.25, p.102; encounter with Calhoun, v.25, p.1069; suggested as peace commissioner to Mexico, v.25, p.1072; noted, v.25, p.1113.

Berard vs. Berard et al, v.25, p.314.

Bercier, Eusebe, noted, v.23, p.477.

Berkeley, William, and rice cultivation, v.23, p.545.

Berkley, John, noted, v.24, p.922.

Berkley Springs, resort, v.24, p.1100.

Bermudez, Edward, duel of, v.23, p.449-451.

Bermudez, J., on Charity Hospital Board, 1836, v.26, p.58.

Bermudez, Jose Francisco, noted, v.24, p.16, 622.

Bermudez Tea, noted, v.24, p.960, 970, 973, 975.

Bernard, Duke of Saxe-Weimar Eisenach, noted, v.31, p.397, 407, 412, 415.

Bernard, Louisiana educator, v.31, p.851.

Bernardi, Jubilus S., collection in L.S.U. Music School Library, v.24, p.347.

"Bernardo de Galvez's Siege of Pensacola in 1781," (As Related in Robert Farmar's Journal), ed. by James A. Padgett, v.26, p.311-329.

Bernardy, Charles, Witness to marriage of Desgrange and Barbara Orci, v.27, p.87, 91, 94, 98.

Bernardy, Victoria, Witness to marriage of Desgrange and Barbara Orci, v.27, p.87, 91, 94, 98.

Berner riots, noted, v.24, p.201.

Bernhardt, Sarah, her great fame, v.26, p.770, 773; her first visit to N.O., v.26, p. 770-772, 773-775; her birth and early life, v.26, p.772; acquired the title "divine" in "Ruy Blas," v.26, p.772-773; her private life, characteristics and personal appearance, v.26, p.775, 777, 780, 781; later visits to N.O., v.26, p.775-776; last visit to N.O., 1917, v.26, p.776-777; her hunting expeditions, v.26, p.777-778; her best known plays, v.26, p.778-780; her itinerary in the U.S., 1910, v.26, p.781-782; her death, v.26, p.782.

Bernstein, Albert, v.29, p.96.

Bernstein, Isaac, lottery suit, v.31, p.825.

Berrien, John McPherson, noted, v.24, p.1157, 1159.

Bertel, Etienne, noted, v.22, p.406, 417.

Berwick Bay and Texas Railroad Company, v.30, p.1173.

Berwick Bay, during the Civil War, v.23, p.1196; noted, v.24, p.71, 72, 77, 95; Cathcart's survey, v.28, p.765, 785, 791ff., 812.

Berwick Lumber Company, v.30, p.1012.

Berwick, Thomas, petition of, v.23, p.365-366; noted, v.28, p.791n.; sketch, v.28, p.793n.

Bessieres, conspiracy of, v.24, p.950, 958-960.

Bethel Church, 1st Baptist Church in present boundaries of La., v. 29, p.83-84.

Bettersworth, John K., "Protestant Beginnings in N.O.," v.21, p.823-45.

Bettner, Dr. G., noted, v.26, p.76.

Beugnot, Dr. J. F., Charter member Medical Society, v.26, p.59; his "Essay on Yellow Fever," v.26, p.64-65; noted, v.26, p.75, 104.

Beverly, letter of Andrew Jackson, noted, v.24, p.1063, 1064.

"Bibliographic and Analytical Notes on the Principal Works Published on Florida and Ancient Louisiana," Compiled by A. L. Boimare, 1853 (Published from original MS. in the French), v.1, sec. 2, p.9.

"Bibliography of New Orleans Magazines," by Max L. Griffin, v.18, p.493-556.

Bibliotheca Parsoniana, summary of holdings, v.24, p.310-311.

"Bi-Centennial Medallion, The New Orleans," by Andre Lafargue, v.7, p.87.

Bi-Centennial of New Orleans, See New Orleans.

Bickel, David A., noted, v.23, p.478.

Bickham, Abner, identified, v.21, p.715n.

Bickham, James S., trustee of Franklin Academy, 1838, v.29, p.84.

Bickham, John, donates land for Washington Parish Courthouse, v.29, p.79.

Biddle, Nicholas, documents in Bibliotheca Parsoniana, v.24, p.311.

Bienvenu, Mary Anne, noted, v.24, p.355.

"Bienville," A Poem, by Mrs. S. B. Elder, v.2, p.177.

"Bienville, Iberville and, 1699-1712," by Henry Plauche Dart, v.2, p.72.

Bienville, Jean Baptist le Moyne de: Introduction to Bienville Number by the Editor, (Mr. John Dymond), v.1, sec.3, p.5; Illustration of Seal of, v.1, sec. 3, p.4; "New Orleans Under," by Heloise Hulse Cruzat, v.1, sec.3, p.54; "Notes on Life and Services of," by Grace King, v.1, sec.3, p.39; Seal of, v.1, p.374; Sidelights on Louisiana History (See Louisiana), v.1, sec.3, p.87; Will of, Made in 1765, v.1, sec.3, p.52; "Renounces a debt due by Serigny, His Deceased brother, 1738," by Heloise H. Cruzat, v.8, p.216; "A Geneological Sketch," by Andre Lafargue, v.8, p.252; "Claims Against the Company of the Indies for Back Salary, 1737," by Henry P. Dart, with Documents and Translated by Heloise H. Cruzat, v.9, p.210; "Lands in Louisiana, Documents Concerning, 1719,1737," Text and Translation by Heloise H. Cruzat, Introduction by Henry P. Dart, v.10, p.5, 161, 364, 538; "Lands of in La.,

1719-1740, Documents Concerning," Translated from Book of Concessions by Heloise H. Cruzat with Introduction by Henry P. Dart, v.11, p.87, 209, 463; "Documents Covering the Impeachment of," Introduction by Henry P. Dart, Translated by A. G. Sanders, v.14, p.5; and Fort de la Boulaye, v.19, p.847ff.; land holdings in La., v.20, p.897ff.; Land grants, v.21, p. 222-224; and introduction of rice, v.23, p.548, 549; plan to introduce slaves, v.23, p.864; noted, v.25, p.629; explores Miss. River, v.25, p.934; noted, v.26, p.649; to command post on Ohio River, v.26, p.651; Comd't-Gen. of La., v.26, p.654-656; Gov. of La., v.26, p.668, 674-679; succeeded by Boisbriant, v.26, p.669; withdraws troops from Ark., v.26, p.669; and trade in Sp. territory, v.26, p.693; noted, v.26, p.717; succeeded Sauvole, v.26, p.726; sent to erect fort on Mobile River, v.26, p.726; reappointed Gov., v.26, p.729; noted, v.26, p.730, 731, 732, 739, 753; Gov. of La., v.28, p.32, 58; suppressed Natchez, v.28, p.59; noted, v.28, p.65, 72; letter to Maurepas, v.28, p.683; and Favrot, v.28, p.684; founded N.O. in 1718, v.29, p.559; noted, v.29, p.562; succeeded as Gov. of La. colony by Perier, v.29, p.563; noted, v.29, p.569, 591, 596, 599; and N.O. Charity Hospital, v.31, p.7, 9, 12; influences Du Pratz, v.31, p.581.

Bienville Parish, in 1860, v.21, p.1186-1190.

Bierck, Harold A., Jr., "Dr. John Hamilton Robinson," v.25, p.644-669.

Bigney, Mark F., ed. "N.O. Times," v.30, p.283; noted, v.30, p.182, 287.

Bill, Alfred Hoyt, "The Beleaguered City: Richmond, (1861-1865)," rev'd, v.30, p.352-353.

Billings, E. C., counselor in support of Pinchback, v.27, p.592; Judge of U.S. Circuit Court, declares Act #44 unconstitutional, v.27, p.998-999, 1000, 1009, 1010, 1013.

Billings, Josh, comment on by Cable, v.24, p.172-173.

Bill of Abominations, v.25, p.43ff., 92.

"Biloxi Bi-Centennial," by Andre Lafargue, v.4, p.459.

Biloxi Indians, in Grant Parish, v.23, p.1109; description of, v.23, p.1122.

Biloxi, ship lists of passengers leaving France, 1718-1724, v.21, p.965-978.

"Biloxi, The Founding of," Bi-Centennial Address by Andre Lafargue, v.3, p.617.

"Bio-Bibliography of Grace Elizabeth King," by Bess Vaughan, v.17, p.751.

"Bird of Louisiana, The Emblematic," by Stanley Clisby Arthur, v.2, p.248.

"Birds of America," by Audubon, v.25, p.206.

Bird, T. J., Commissioner of Bureau of Agr., v.26, p.1069.

Bisbee, DeWitt F., noted, v.22, p.201, 204.

Bisland, John, and Family, collection in L.S.U. Archives, v.24, p.341.

Bispham, Clarence Wyatt, "Contest for Ecclesiastical Supremacy in the Mississippi Valley, 1763-1803," v.1, sec.3, p.154; "Fray Antonio de Sedella, An Appreciation," v.2, p.24; "Fray Antonio de Sedella," compiled by, v.2, p.369; "New Orleans, A Treasure House for Historians," v.2, p.237.

Bjork, David, "Documents Relating to Alexandro O'Reilly," v.7, p.20.

Black Bayou, noted, v.25, p.54.

"Black Code," in La., 1803, v.21, p.1076; in Sp. La., v.22, p.623, 659; of O'Reilly, v.24, p.310; in La., v.25, p.731, 732; noted, v.32, p.154, 156, 157, 183, 364, 365.

Blackman, Judge W. F., v.28, p.1174.

Blackmar, A. E., N.O. music publisher, v.31, p.145-146.

Black Republicans, noted, v.24, p.435.

Black River, description of, by Filhiol, v.20, p.477; noted, v.25, p.204, 397; course of, v.25, p.929, 931, 932.

Blackstone, William, noted, v.24, p.708.

Blackwell, Jacob, noted, v.23, p.76; member of W. Fla. Council, v.23, p.353ff.

Blackwell, Joseph, petition of, v.23, p.366.

Blaine, James G., noted, v.24, p.116.

Blaird, James, Confed. soldier, v.26, p.952, 954, 959, 962, 964.

Blair, Francis P., noted, v.24, p.1157.

Blairs Landing, noted, v.24, p.92, 93.

Blake, Joachim, noted, v.23, p.835.

Blake, William, sketch, v.28, p.755n.; noted, v.28, p.758, 759, 841n.

Blanc, Antoine, Bishop of N.O., v.23, p.1032-1033; noted, v.25, p.363; noted, v.31, p.898; administers diocese, v.31, p.906; Bishop, v.31, p.906; appoints Rousselon, v.31, p.909; appointment made provisional, v.31, p.912; appoints Maenhaut, v.31, p.914; refuses to officiate, v.31, p.931; attends council, v.31,

Blanc—Boatner

p.941; letter to wardens, v.31, p.944-945, 961-962; withdraws priests, v.31, p.947; suit, v.31, p.950-955; defense of position, v.31, p.957.

Blanc, Evariste, noted, v.23, p.1003; suit over land, v.23, p.1093-1094.

Blanchard, B. P., witness in case to prove Pinchback duly elected to House of Rep., v.27, p.587, 588; State registrar of Voters in Orleans Parish, v.27, p.584.

Blanchard, Charles, noted, v.22, p.989.

"Blanchard, Gov. Newton C.," by Paul Sompayrac, v.6, p.56.

Blanchard, Newton C., noted, v.25, p.806; successful cand. for cong., 1890, v.26 p.1077; defeated Guice, 1892, v.26, p.1091; his speech launching Foster's candidacy for re-election, v.26, p.1099; possible choice for U. S. Senator by Legislature, v.26, p.1111; succeeded White in Senate, v.27, p.808; and the Wilson Gorman Bill, v.27, p. 809, 810; fight for sugar duty, v.27, p.813, 814; fight for bounty due, v.27, p.817; favored Calcasieu River project, v.27, p.842; introduced ordinance on lotteries, 1879, v.27, p.999; appt'd by Foster to U. S. Sen., v.28, p.1167, 1169; noted,, v.28, p.1170; selection of successor in Sen., v.28, p.1184; favored primary system, v.28, p.1196.

Blanchard, Olivia, "The Death Mask of Napoleon at the Cabildo, New Orleans," v.8, p.71.

Blanchet, Peter, noted, v.22, p.982.

Blanc, S. P., La. midshipman, v.27, p.483.

Blanc Tract Case of Myra Clark Gaines, v.20, p.33ff.

Blanding, Oscar C., Candidate for Sec. of State, v.29, p.402.

Bland, Theodoric, noted, v.22, p.763.

Blanque, Jean, noted, v.22, p.808; sketch, v.22, p.811.

"Blanque," privateer of Laffittes, v.23, p.747.

Blardone, George, promoted, v.26, p.835, 837.

Blenk, Archbishop, noted, v.24, p.139.

Blennerhassett, Harman, documents in Bibliotheca Parsoniana, v.24, p.311; island and Burr Conspiracy, v.25, p.12.

Blessington, Lady, letter of in N. O. Public Library, v.24, p.325.

Bliss, Capt. T. R., noted, v.23, p.1177.

Bliss, Elizabeth Taylor, noted, v.24, p.50.

Bliss, William Wallace, noted, v.24, p.50.

Blockade, effects of in N. O., 1862, v.24, p.448.

Blom, Franz, noted, v.24, p.331.

Blommart, John, and W. Fla. Assembly, v.22, p.956; v.23, p.5ff.; noted, v.23, p.391.

Blonin, Louis, noted, v.22, p.628.

"Blood on the Banquette," by J. S. Kendall, v.22, p.819-856.

Bloomer, Robert, incorporator of La. Lottery Co., v.27, p.975.

Blossman, Dick, early N. O. police reporter, v.29, p.53.

"Blossom," noted, v.23, p.436.

Blouier, Luis, noted, v.22, p.624.

Blount, F. S., Mobile attorney, v.29, p.345.

Blunt, Raford, noted, v.25, p.766.

Blythe, James, private instructor of Wickliffe, v.25, p.670.

"Blythewood," Hudson plantation, v.25, p.171, 172; purchased by Randolph, v.25, p.174, 196, 198, 199, 200, 207, 211, 214; sale of, v.25, p.201, 213.

Boardman, Israel, noted, v.23, p.77.

Board of Administrators of Charity Hospital, of New Orleans, v.31, p.46ff.

Board of Currency, noted, v.25, p.702.

Board of Education, 1864, work of, v.25, p.738-740.

Board of Internal Improvements, v.30, p.29-35; created by Legis. to administer Special U. S. reclaiming funds to Territory of Orleans, v.28, p.293-294.

Board of Levee Commissioners, v.28, p.302-305.

Board of Military Affairs, creation of in La., 1860, v.26, p.996.

Board of Public School Directors in City of Jefferson, v.25, p.745, 752.

Board of Public Works, and railroad expansion, v.25, p.695-698; replaces Swamp Land Com., created, v.28, p.293-295; abolished, v.28, p.295; Const. of 1852 provided for reviewing of, v.28, p.295-296; established 1859, composition and function of, v.28, p.296-298; abolished because of Civil War, v.28, p.298-299; creation of, v.30, p.42-44; reports of, v.30, p.44-47; changes in by Gov. White, v.30, p.49-50; noted, v.30, p.52.

Board of Swamp Land, Commissioners, cretion and work of, v.25, p.694-695; v.28, p.287-290; abolished, v.28, p.293.

Boatner, C. J., Dem. cand. for Congress, 1894, v.26, p.1095; supported McEnery

forces, 1892, v.28, p.1161; noted, v.28, p.1172.
Bob Acres, railroad station on Jefferson estate, v.26, p.1157.
Bobe, M., memoire of, concerning convent after transfer of colony to Sp., v.29, p.616-617.
Boca Chita, noted, v.24, p.617, 619.
Boca Grande, noted, v.24, p.617.
Body of Liberties of Massachusetts, noted, v.24, p.701.
Boelitz, Herman, noted, v.24, p.131.
Boeuf River, Course of, v.25, p.929, 930.
Bogaerts, Rev., noted, v.24, p.139.
"Bogalusa American," v.29, p.168.
"Bogalusa Enterprise," v.29, p.129, 135, 136, 163, 168.
Bogalusa, La., settlers of, v.29, p.86; pre-Bogalusa days, v.29, p.86-90; location of, v.29, p.91, 103, 113-114; a saw mill town in the making, v.29, p.91-100; sections of, v.29, p.100-101; "American Lumberman" survey mill, v.29, p.101-107; town named, v.29, p.107; incorporated, v.29, p.108-113; city's tax record, 1919-1938, v.29, p.115; special occasions, v.29, p.116-120; sawmill closed, v.29, p.120-122; industries of, v.29, p.122-132; reforestation program, v.29, p.124-126; becomes paper mill town, v.29, p.127-131; industrial relations, v.29, p.132-136; educational system, v.29, p.136-149; religion of, v.29, p.149-153; civic, social and recreational organizations of, v.29, p.154-169; transportation of, v.29, p.169-172; Pearl River navigation project, v.29, p.172-174; traffic outlets, v.29, p.174-176; communication facilities, v.29, p.176-178; first natural gas in 1930, v.29, p.178; electric power of, v.29, p.178-179; water and sewerage systems, v.29, p.179-180; fire protection, v.29, p.180; list of city officials from 1914-1942, v.29, p.190-193; members of fraternal orders, v.29, p.193-196; bibl., v.29, p.196-200.
"Bogalusa News," v.29, p.168-169, 184.
Bogalusa Paper Company, v.29, p.107, 128-131, 134, 183.
Bogel, A. J., treasurer of insane asylum, named in Wickliffe impeachment, v.31, p.693.
Boggs, W. B., proposed silver resolution, v.26, p.1099.
Bogner, Howard F., "Sir Walter Scott in N. O., 1818-1832," v.21, p.420-517.

Bogue Chitto, v.29, p.83, 87.
Bogue Lusa Creek, v.29, p.80, 89n., 91, 99, 103n., 104, 107, 114.
Boguier, Sebastian, noted, v.24, p. 636, 637, 685.
Boildieu, Francois Adrien, manuscript of operas in L. S. U. Music School Library, v.24, p.347, 348.
Boimare, A. L., "Bibliographic and Analytical Notes on the Principal Works Published on Florida and Ancient Louisiana, 1853," v.1, sec.2, p.9.
Boisbriant, Pierre Duque de, Commander of the Illinois, v.26, p.654, 656; succeeded Bienville as Gov. in N. O., v.26, p.669; in charge of Biloxi colony, v.26, p.726; builds Fort Chartres, v.26, p.728, 736; noted, v.26, p.753.
Boisfontaine, Pierre Baron, v.27, p.7; testimony on Myra Gaines birth, v.27, p.41, 43-56; testimony of, v.27, p.60, 68-71, 67, 75, 85, 88, 90; evidence against, v.27, p.115; testimony of, v.27, p.119, 125, 133, 134, 137, 161, 168-169, 172; deposition of, v.27, p.206, 208, 214, 224, 236, 271, 280, 281, 282, 285.
Boisgervais, Jacques Robert, noted, v.24, p.359.
Boissiere, J. S., noted, v.24, p.372; plan to rescue Napoleon, v.24, p.27, 373-376.
Boissiere-Laresche duel, noted, v.24, p.769.
Boissoneau, A. J., promotion of, v.26, p.835, 836.
Boland, Mother Loretta, noted, v.24, p.334.
Bolivar Bend, old Mississippi River Channel, v.31, p.600.
"Bolivar," schooner of filibusters, v.23, p.850; privateer vessel, v.24, p.366, 367, 369, 370, 371, 372, 376.
Bolivar, Simon, filibuster, v.23, p.837, 1009n., 1078; noted, v.22, p.1039, 1043, 1047, 1050, 1062; fled 1812 to Cartagenia, v.24, p.613, 615; title of "Liberator" by New Granada, v.24, p.615; enmity with del Castillo and Marmion, v.24, p.616; at Aux Cayes, v.24, p.621; enmity of Venezuelan and Cartagenan leaders for, v.24, p.622; preparations at Port-au-Prince for expedition, v.24, p.640; noted, v.24, p.647, 1076; raising of soldiers and supplies in Great Britain, v.24, p.649-650; in New Granada uplands, v.24, p.666; formed republic of Columbia, v.24, p.667; enlarged army, v.24, p.675; drive toward the sea, v.24, p.686; relations with Brion, v.24, p.688-689; up

the Magdalena, v.24, p.693-696; order to Aury, v.24, p.694; plans for government, v.24, p.1027.

Bolton, G. W., thought lotteries morally wrong, v.27, p.1039, 1058.

Bonamy, Alexis Caesar, justice of peace, v.23, p.697-698ff.

Bonaparte, Jerome, auction of gallery of, v.23, p.246.

Bonaparte, Joseph, noted, v.23, p.755, 862; and Fr. settlement in Texas, v.23, p.779; betrayal by Toledo, v.23, p.829, 830.

Bonaparte, Lucien, noted, v.23, p.862.

Bonaparte, Napoleon, noted, v.24, p.5, 373-376; attempted rescue, v.24, p.27, 373-376; papers in Bibliotheca Parsoniana, v.24, p.310, 311.

Bonavia, Bernardo, Mil. Gov. of Texas, v.28, p.1080, 1081.

"Bonded Debt of New Orleans, 1822-1920, inclusive," by H. P. Phillips, v.3, p.596.

Bond, Richard F., Commissioned, v.26, p.836.

Bone, Fanny Z. Lovell, "Louisiana in the Disputed Election of 1876," I, II, v.14, p.408, 549; III, IV (Conclusion), v.15, p.92, 234.

Bonham, Milledge L., Jr., "The Flags of Louisiana," v.2, p.439; "The Rebel Reefer Furls His Last Sail," v.11, p.582; "Morganalia," v.17, p.706.

Bonham, Milledge L., "The Letters of John Muir, British Consul at New Orleans on the Financial and Economic Disturbance in New Orleans on the Eve of Secession," v.13, p.32.

Bonin, Miss Estelle, queen of rice festival, v.27, p.1209.

Bonnaud, Arnaud, director of Duverney Concession, v.21, p.982.

Bonne, Albert, petition of, v.23, p.374.

Bonnet Carre, crevasse near, v.26, p.1072.

Bonnevie, Citizen, arrest of, v.22, p.90.

"Bonnie Blue Flag," noted, v.24, p.498.

Bonquois, Dora J., "The Career of Henry Adams Bullard, La. Jurist, Legislator and Educator," v.23, p.999-1106.

Book Reviews: Flemming's "The Freedmen's Saving Bank," by James E. Winston, v.10, p.562; Read's "More Indian Place Names in La.," by Henry P. Dart, v.11, p.445; Rowland's "Varina Howell, wife of Jefferson Davis," by Grace King, v.11, p.466; Rowland's and Sander's "Mississippi Provincial Archives, 1729-1740, French Dominion," by Henry P. Dart, v.11, p.111; Vogel's "The Capuchins in French La., 1722 - 1766," by Henry P. Dart, v.11, p.620; "Le Chevalier de Pradel," by Edith Dart Price, v.12, p.134; "The Southern Frontier," by Henry P. Dart, v.12, p.136; Carpenter, Dr. Jesse T., "The South as a Conscious Minority," by Henry P. Dart, v.14, p.637; Longino, Dr. Luther, "Thoughts, Visions and Sketches of North Louisiana," by Fair Hardin, v.14, p.239; Marchand, Sidney A., "Story of Ascension Parish," by Edith Dart Price, v.14, p.569; Saxon, Lyle, "Lafitte the Pirate," by J. Fair Hardin, v.14, p.441; Thomas' "Forgotten Frontiers," by Francis P. Burns, v.15, p.712; Ettinger's "The Mission to Spain of Pierre Soule, 1853-1855," by Henry P. Dart, v.15, p.708; Greer's "A Texas Ranger and Frontiersman, The Days of Buck Barry in Texas," by Henry P. Dart, v.15, p.711; Read's "French Louisiana," by Henry P. Dart, v.15, p.710; Rowland's "Varina Howell, Wife of Jeff. Davis," by Henry P. Dart, v.15, p.350; Rowland and Sander's "Provincial Archives, 1704 - 1742, French Dominion," Vol. III, by Henry P. Dart, v.15, p.707; Surveyer's "Bench and Bar of Quebec," by Henry P. Dart, v.15, p.118; Whitaker's "Commercial Policy of Spain in Florida and Louisiana, 1778-1803," by Henry P. Dart, v.15, p.345; Waldo G. Leland, "Guide to Material for American History in the Libraries and Archives of Paris," by Henry P. Dart, v.16, p.168; Grace King's "Memories of a Southern Woman of Letters," by Henry P. Dart, v.16, p.164; Jay K. Ditchy's "Les Acadians Louisianais et Leur Parler," by Henry P. Dart, v.16, p.166; Simone de la Delery and Gladys Anne Renshaw's "France d'Amerique," (Illustrated by Dagmar Renshaw), by Edith Dart Price, v.16, p.168; Simone de la Souchere Delery's "A La Poursuite des Aigles," by Rene J. Le Gardeur, Jr., v.33, p.151-153.

"Books, and Booksellers in New Orleans, 1730-1830," by R. P. McCutcheon, v.20, p.606-618; circulating library in antebellum La., v.23, p.131-140.

Bookstores in Sp. New Orleans, v.22, p.686.

Bookter, Alexander, noted, v.23, p.419, 420, 421.

Booth, A. B., "Confederate Military Records of Louisiana," v.4, p.369; People's Party elector, v.26, p.1087; cand. for Gov. on first Populist ticket, 1896, v.26, p.1101; double crossed party, v.26, 1101-1102; populist divided over, v.26, p.1104; Chairman Populist State Ex. Comm., v.28, p.1175; cand. for Gov., v.28, p.1176; withdrawal from race, v.28, p.1179.

Booth, Edward, introduced bill to repeal acts # 25 of 1868 and #9 of 1874, v.27, p.982, 988, 1056.

Bopp, J. S., noted, v.24, p.432.

Boquilla de Piedras, importance of, v.23, p.849-850; noted, v.24, p.637, 641.

Bordelon, Louis, candidate for governor, v.31, p.501.

Bordier, Jeanne, noted, v.22, p.398, 407; sues Gravier, v.22, p.412-413.

Bore, Jean Etienne de, first mayor of N. O., v.20, p.169; and sugar cane cultivation, v.22, p.668.

Borland, Euclid, opposed lottery, v.27, p.1040; termed a "wide awake Mex. lottery magnate," v.27, p.1047, 1056.

Bosco Field, v.27, p.1170.

Bossie, Francois, noted, v.22, p.68.

Bossier, General, noted, v.24, p.766.

Bossier Parish, La., in 1860, v.21, p.1179-1182; and the Cong. election of 1894, v.26, p.1097.

Bossier, Pierre E., noted, v.25, p.124; and 1844 tariff bill, v.25, p.131.

Bostick, J. Wallace, early N. O. newspaperman, v.29, p.788-789.

Boston Club, noted, v.24, p.117.

Boucher, Cadet, noted, v.23, p.695.

Bouchereau, Louis, noted, v.23, p.554.

Bouchet, Antoine, privateer, v.23, p.433.

Boudousquie, Antoine, royal printer, v.22, p.685n.

Boulaye, see de la Boulaye.

Bouligny, Col. Francois, Sp. Lt.-Gov. of La., v.25, p.939; studies Manchac, v.25, p.939.

Bouligny, Dominique, settled estate of Maison Rouge, v.20, p.336; and 1826 tariff bill, v.25, p.43; and 1828 tariff, v.25, p.46, 47.

Bouligny, Francisco, noted, v.22, p.661n., 795.

Bouligny, Louis, Claimant of Maison Rouge Grant, v.20, p.336ff.

Bouligny, M. Louis, in charge at Balize, 1803, v.26, p.752.

Bouligny, ———, noted, v.23, p.1080.

Boundaries of La. and U. S., 1790, v.21, p.17; of W. Fla., v.21, p.172-73.

"Boundaries of Texas and Louisiana, Report to Mexican Republic Concerning," by Fray Jose Maria Puelles, 1828, v.1, sec.1, p.21.

"Boundary of Louisiana, Western," by Gaspar Cusachs, v.1, sec.1, p.9.

Bouney, B. F., pres. Masonic Institute of Clinton, v.30, p.830.

Bouquay, Jean, noted, v.22, p.685.

Bourdesoulle, Guilleminot, trial of, v.24, p.991.

Bourdin, Bernard, noted, v.22, p.734.

Bourges, Alfred, introduced bill to authorize lottery drawing for charitable institution, v.27, p.971.

Bourg, John G., becomes Battalion Adjutant of 1st Reg't of La. Inf., v.29, p.82.

Bournety, E. F., Genoyer de, (French Consul), Address on Joan of Arc, v.1, p.277.

Bouvee, G. E., on Lynch Returning Board, v.28, p.1135.

Bovee, George, v.30, p.596-598; noted, v.30, p.583; sec. of state removed by Warmoth, v.31, p.700; named in Warmoth impeachment articles, v.31, p.702.

Bowen, Dr. William Shaw, describes La. Lottery drawing, v.27, p.1016-20.

Bowie, James, noted, v.23, p.1147.

Bowker, Thomas, noted, v.23, p.369.

Bowles, Evan, sketch, v.28, p.766n.

Bowles, William Augustus, sketch, v.21, p.22n., 24n.; noted, v.22, p.795.

Bowman, Eliska, Methodist missionary in New Orleans, v.21, p.824-825; noted, v.22, p.429, 430-431.

Bowman, William R., noted, v.22, p.465, 469.

Boyard, Etienne, noted, v.22, p.685.

Boyce, C. W., editor of "Constitutional," v.31, p.1004; noted, v.31, p.1022.

Boyce, Henry, pres. Louisiana Central Steam Railroad Co., v.30, p.1218-1224; elected U. S. Senator, v.31, p.1069.

Boyd Collection, L.S.U. Museum, v.24, p.346.

Boyd, Thomas Duckett, collection in L.S.U. Archives, v.24, p.341; story of by M. M. Wilkerson, v.24, p.321, 348, 353; noted, v.25, p.806.

Boyer, Jean Pierre, noted, v.24, p.998.

Boyers School, v.30, p.851.

Boykins, Capt., noted, v.23, p.420.

Boyland, T. N., noted, v.22, p.508.

Boyle, William D., noted, v.22, p.470; named judge to succeed Johnson, v.28, p.959.

Boys' Grammar School of N. O., v.30, p.869.

Boys' Institute, v.30, p.896.

"Boy's Recollection of the War Between the States," by W. O. Hart, v.11, p.253.

Brackenridge, Henry Marie, author, v.31, p.395.

Bradburn, W. P., sketch, v.21, p.1127.

Braddish, Geo., v.28, p.750n.

Bradford, David, officer of Confed. Marine Corps from La., v.27, p.485.

Bradford, E. A., noted, v.24, p.117.

Bradford, James Morgan, and W. Fla. Rev., v.21, p.709n.; noted, v.22, p.432, 433, 435, 436; noted, v.28, p.948.

Bradford, ———, printer, v.22, p.374.

Bradish, Ebenezer, noted, v.22, p.433.

Bradley, John, noted, v.23, p.357, 368, 404.

Brady, Rev. John, noted, v.22, p.99.

Bragg, Braxton, noted, v.24, p.67, 101, 102; Gen. of the Confed. army, v.26, p.964.

Bragg, Jefferson D., "La. in the Confederacy," rev'd, v.25, p.823-824.

Brahilov, engagement in War between Russia and Turkey, v.24, p.1120.

Brahms, reproduction in Howard-Tilton Memorial Library, v.24, p.330.

Brand, William F., noted, v.22, p.462, 470.

Brashear City, noted, v.24, p.72, 76, 79; noted, v.32, p.52.

Brashear, Dr. Walter, noted, v.24, p.40; noted, v.25, p.1039; on committee for support of schools, v.25, p.1042-1043, 1057, 1058; sketch, v.28, p.813n.; noted, v.28, p.832n.

Brashier, Esther, married Philander Smith, v.29, p.285.

Brassac, Father Hercules, advice to Blanc, v.31, p.943; noted, v.31, p.961.

"Braud, Adventures of Denis, First Printer of Louisiana," by Henry P. Dart, Translation by Laura L. Porteous, v.14, p.349.

Braud, Denis, director first N. O. Charity Hospital, v.31, p.15-16.

Braughn, G. H., named in Kellog impeachment, v.31, p.713; backs Greeley, v.31, p.538.

"Brave Mardi Gras: A New Orleans Novel of the 60's," by W. Adolphe Roberts, rev'd by Andre Lafargue, v.29, p.793-796.

Brazillier, ———, noted, v.23, p.374.

Brazos de Santiago, Mexico, v.24, p.369.

"Breakbone fever," noted, v.24, p.168.

Breau's Bridge, noted, v.24, p.41.

Breaux, John A., headed anti-lottery Repub. ticket, v.27, p.1092; v.28, p.1160.

Breaux, Joseph A., justice, dissenting opinion in Morris vs. Mason, v.27, p.1052; superintendent of education, v.31, p.803.

Breazeale, Phanor, "Uncle Tom's Cabin" and "The Spanish Post of the Adaias," v.7, p.304; "The Diary of a Young Lawyer of Natchitoches of 1836," edited by William S. Toumey, I, II, v.17, p.64, 315; Dem. rep., 1898, v.26, p.1123.

Breckinridge, John C., attack on Baton Rouge, v.23, p.1192; noted, v.24, p.59; Dem. candidate for vice pres., v.25, p. 686; the election of 1860, v.25, p.707, 1105.

Breedin, R. K., trustee of 1st Bogalusa school, v.29, p.100.

Breed, John, member of St. Helena Police Jury, v.23, p.407ff.; noted, v.23, p.419.

Breedlove, James W. (Andrew Jackson's Correspondence with James W. Breedlove), v.6, p.179.

Breland, Earnest, Lt. in Troop "F" of La. Inf., v.29, p.82.

Brent, Daniel, to Mr. Pleasanton, suggestion, limitations of W. Fla. Claims, v.25, p.948.

Brent, James F., and the Const. Con. of 1844 in La., v.25, p.1005ff.

Brent, Joseph L., noted, v.24, p.91, 104; pres. La. State Agr. Society, v.26, 1064.

Brent, Mrs. J. L., Collection in La. State Museum, v.24, p.319.

Brent, William L., and 1824 tariff bill, v.25, p.37, 38, 39, 40, 42, 43; and 1826 tariff bill, v.25, p.43, 49, 50, 60, 61; noted, v.28, p. 767n.

Brewer, C. A., County agent of Acadia, v.27, p.1163.

Brewster, O. H., Chosen speaker of the House, 1872, by Warmoth, v.27, p.549.

Brian, Hardy L., and cong. campaign of 1890, v.26, p.1077; ed. comrade, v.26, p.1077; La. rep. to Cincinnati Conv., v.26, p.1077-1078; noted, v.26, p.1091, 1103; Populist nominee, 1898, v.26, p.1123.

Brian, Rev. B. F., Senator People's Party, v.26, p.1083, 1091.

Brice, Albert G., noted, v.22, p.204; diary in Xavier Univ. Library, v.24, p.337.

Bricklin, in N. O., 1794, v.23, p.683.

Brickmaking on Randolph plantation, v.25, p.187.

Briede, Kathryn C., "A History of the City of Lafayette," v.20, p.895-964.

Briggs, Isaac, and Claiborne candidacy, v.31, p.355-356, 357-358, 375.

Briggs, Joseph, Claiborne's secretary, v.31, p.360.

Bright, George U., noted, v.22, p.1108.

Bright, Jessie D., noted, v.24, p.58.

Brincio, ———, noted, v.22, p.1150.

Bringier, Myrthe, noted, v.24, p.52, 54.

Briniac, Alexander, member of St. Helena Police Jury, v.23, p.406ff.

Brink, Florence Roos, author "Literary Travellers in Louisiana Between 1803 and 1860," v.31, p.394-424.

Brion, Luis, noted, v.22, p.1042, 1043, 1047; and the Lafittes, v.23, p.807; identified, v.24, p.615; commander of the "Dardo," v.24, p.617-619, 621; rivalry with Aury, v.24, p.622-625, 685-686, 691-697; at Aux Cayes, v.24, p.640; posted Joly as pirate, v.24, p.643; Admiral of Venezuela, v.24, p.648; carried supplies for Bolivar, v.24, p.650; "Savior of His Country," v.24, p.652; aid from army accepted, v.24, p.653; at Margarita Island, v.24, p.662, 666; Admiral of Colombia, v.24, p.667; outlawed commissions of St. Bart's, v.24, p.669; at Rio Hacha, v.24, p.679; financial needs, v.24, p.688; insanity and death, v.24, p.697.

British plans to aid South America revolutionists, v.24, p.649-650.

"British Proclamation of 1763, Creating West Florida," Introducttion by Editor, Louisiana Historical Quarterly, v.13, p.610.

"British West Florida, 1763-1783," by Cecil Johnson, rev'd, v.26, p.1181-1185.

Brodhead, Richard, and sugar tariff, v.25, p.137-138.

Broglie, Duke de, noted, v.24, p.1036.

Bromfield, Louis, "Wild Is The River," rev'd, v.29, p.791-793.

Brookman, Capt., ———, privateer, v.22, p.1042.

Brooks, Philip Coolidge, "Diplomacy of the Borderlands," rev'd by Harris G. Warren, v.24, p.205-206.

Brooks, R. J., Negro Rep. representative from St. Mary, v.28, p.1138.

Brooks, Wm., Confed. naval engineer from La., v.27, p.484, 485.

Brouard, Ange-Michel, noted, v.23, p.435-441; noted, v.22, p.1024, 1041.

Broussard, I. B., post adjutant of Acadia Post Am. Legion, v.27, p.1200; sec.-treas. of rice festival, v.27, p.1209.

Broussard, Robert F., congressman, v.26, p.792, 1116, 1123; opposed Sanders as Senator, v.28, p.1223; noted, v.28, p.1229.

Broutin, Francisco, noted, v.22, p.631; petition of, v. 23, p.374.

Broutin, Ignace Francois, writes concerning site of Ursuline Convent, v.29, p.563-564; noted, v.29, p.569, 573; name omittted from cornerstone, v.29, p.577; replaced by Baron as engineer-in-chief, v.29, p.577; assumes position as engineer-in-chief again, v.29, p.578, 580; noted, v.29, p.599, 601, 608.

Browder, Frederick A., and W. Fla. Rev., v.21, p.97, 755.

Brown, Bedford, and sugar tariff, v.25, p.71.

Brown, Clair A., co-ed., "Southern La. and Southern Ala. in 1819," the "Journal of Jas. Leander Cathcart," v.28, p.735-921.

Browne, George, election of, v.23, p.377.

Browne, Lieut.-Gov. of W. Fla., v.21, p.1024; Montfort and W. Fla. Assembly, v.22, p.943, 961, 979.

Brown, Eliphalet, noted, v.22, p.433.

Brownell, Thomas Church, noted, v.22, p.464.

Browne, Monfort, and W. Fla. Assembly, v.23, p.6ff., 24, 26; lieutenant gov. of W. Florida, v.23, p.353ff.; complaint against, v.23, p.370.

Browne, Peter A., noted, v.23, p.1000.

Brown, Everett S., "The Orleans Territory Memorialists to Congress, 1804," v.1, sec.1, p.99.

Brown, George, noted, v.23, p.42.

Brown, Isaac N., Capt. of Confed. Navy, v.27, p.480.

Brown, James, secy. of State of Ky., v.20, p.58; moved to N. O., v.20, p.58; aided in preparation of La. Civil Code, v.20, p.59; member of constitutional convention of 1811-1812, v.20, p.59; senator, v.20, p.59; minister to France, v.20, p.59; death, v.20, p.60; letters from to Presidents of the U. S., v.20, p.61-136; noted, v.22, p.433, 435; papers in L.S.U. Archives, v.24, p.341; letters to Clay in Library of Congress, v.24, p.921; suits in Ky., v.24, p.922, 926-927, 929, 1099; legal success, v.24, p.923-924; views of the importance of La., v.24, p.930-934; opinions on national politics, v.24, p.934-938, 944, 957, 1018, 1037-1038, 1041, 1044, 1064-1065, 1075, 1076, 1078, 1080, 1082, 1088, 1090, 1096-1097, 1099, 1106, 1120, 1123-1124, 1125-1126, 1127, 1129, 1133-1134, 1136, 1137-1138, 1140-1141, 1143, 1146, 1148, 1153-1154, 1155, 1157, 1150-1160, 1163-1164, 1167-1168; diplomatic duties in France, v.24, p.938-942, 985, 990, 1017, 1039-1040, 1043-1044, 1062, 1142; health of, v.24, p.943, 944-945, 947, 949, 956, 969, 975, 985, 989, 995, 1003, 1004, 1007, 1014, 1031, 1032, 1037, 1047, 1093, 1100, 1140, 1147, 1152, 1156, 1161, 1162, 1163, 1166, 1168, 1171ff.; financial status, v.24, p.974-975, 987-988, 994, 1005-1006, 1015, 1019, 1037, 1039, 1089, 1098-1099, 1133, 1144, 1145-1146, 1161-116, 1165, 1171-1172, 1173ff.; plans for private life, v.24, p.1100, 1133, 1135, 1142, 1144-1145, 1146, 1147; in New York, v.24, p.1144; in Phila., v.24, p.1145; plans to visit La., v.24, p.1147, 1150, 1152, 1156, 1159, 1160, 1163, 1164, 1168, grief on the death of his wife, v.24, p.1148ff.; suits with Keene, v.24, p.1150, 1169, 1174; concern over his niece, v.24, p.1148, 1151, 1154-1155, 1156, 1158, 1160; death, v.24, p.1177; and 1819 tariff bill, v.25, p.34; noted, v.27, p.79, 107, 108, 454; in La. history, v.27, p.720; brother-in-law of Clay, letter of, v.27, p.741; suit of heirs of vs. Humphrey heirs, v.27, p.742-745; sketch, v.28, p.843n.; and Orleans, v.31, p.368-369, 371; quoted, v.31, p.376; noted, v.31, p.389.

Brown, J. N., v.28, p.841n.

Brown, John, Brother of James Brown, v.24, p.1060.

Brown, John W., See district executive committee of People's Party, v.26, p.1093.

Brownlow, William Gannaway, noted, v.23, p.1181.

Brown, Mary Louisa, noted, v.24, p.794.

Brown, Mason, noted, v.24, p.1174.

Brown, Mrs. James, enjoyment of social life, v.24, p.1005, 1047, 1142; illness, v.24, p.1057, 1059, 1068, 1073, 1075, 1078, 1079, 1083, 1084-1085, 1086-1088, 1089, 1091, 1093, 1099, 1105-1106, 1112, 1114, 1116, 1117, 1120, 1124, 1125, 1127, 1129, 1133, 1135, 1136, 1139, 1142, 1144, 1145, 1147, 1148; purchases for friends in America, v.24, p.966, 972, 974, 1042, 1047, 1041, 1057, 1060-1061, 1068, 1076, 1117, 1126-1127; death of, v.24, p.1148ff.; willed property to J. B. Humphreys, v.27, p.742, 744.

Brown, Samuel, brother of James Brown, v.24, p.927, 929, 1020, 1060, 1110, 1116, 1127.

Brown, Shepherd, Commandant and alcade in St. Helena, v.21, p.131n., 187n., 707n.; Judge of St. Helena Parish, v.23, p.202, 406ff.; McDonogh's business partner, v.26, p.37-43.

Brown, S. L., ed. "N. O. Republican," v.30, p.307-308.

Brown, William G., supt. of ed., v.25, p.763; noted, v.25, p.764; negro candidate for Sup't of Public Instruction, v.29, p.403; sup't of ed. during Kellogg's regime, v.29, p.437; cand. for sup't of ed., v.31, p.536.

Brown, William, noted, v.22, p.433, 434; v.24, p.774, 779, 781.

Bruce, G. W., Farmers' Alliance leader, v.26, p.1070.

Bruce, James, noted, v.22, p.364, 986.

Bruce, Mrs. William Cabell, noted, v.24, p.736.

Brugman, Pierre, privateer, v.22, p.1041-1043; v.23, p.436.

Bruin, Joseph, slave dealer, v.22, p.152.

Brumbaugh, Martin G., noted, v.25, p.806.

Bruns, Dr. H. D., called Lottery Co. moral evil, v.27, p.1055.

Bruns, Mrs. H. Dickson, vice-pres. Women's Anti-Lottery League, v.27, p.1061.

Brusle, Louise Elizabeth, married Claude Joseph Favrot, v.28, p.684.

Bruton, G. A., opposed lottery question, v.27, p.1039.

"Brutus," formerly "Superior," v.24, p.643, 646, 648.

Bryant, Christie, v.28, p.781n., 792, 829.

Bryant, Luke, v.28, p.791n.

Bry, Henry, opinion against Bastrop, v.31, p.617.

Bryne, Maurice, noted, v.23, p.560.

Buard, Marie Elizabeth, wife of Ed. Murphy, v.28, p.1090.

Buatt, J. Matt, mayor of Crowley, v.27, p.1145, 1151, 1211.

Buchanan, Admiral Franklin, Confed. naval officer, v.27, p.482.

Buchanan, James, election of, v.23, p.1162.

Buchanan, Judge A. M., and case of Sally Miller, v.22, p.61.

Buchanan, R. C., noted, v.30, p.549.

Buck, Charles F., noted, v.23, p.511; Dem. cand. for Cong., 1894, v.26, p.1095; for mayor of N. O., 1896, v.26, p.1107.

Buckholz, Louis, resigned, v.26, p.835.

Buckingham, James S., author on Louisiana, v.31, p.397, 412, 416-417, 418, 421.

Buckner, H. S., noted, v.23, p.204, 211, 214, 226.

Buckner, S. B., noted, v.24, p.101.

Buenos Aires, privateering commissions of, v.23, p.796-797; agents in the U. S., 1810, v.24, p.613; flag of, v.24, p.656, 664.

Buerki, Dr. Robin, investigation of Charity Hospital, v.31, p.96.

Buhler, Edith Smith (see Smith, Edith), eldest daughter of Elnathan Smith, v.29, p.287-288; children of by 1st marriage, v.29, p.288.

Buhler, John Christian, 1st husband of Edna Smith, v.29, p.288.

"Building Sites in New Orleans, 1722, Allottment of," Heloise H. Cruzat, v.7, p.564.

Building trade in Sp. New Orleans, v.22, p.672.

Buisson, Pierre Benjamin, v.33, p.151-152.

Bullard, Charles, noted, v.23, p.1003, 1140.

Bullard, Elizabeth Adams, noted, v.23, p.999.

Bullard, Henry Adams, early life and family in Mass., v.19, p.9; lawyer in Phila., v.19, p.10; recruit in Mexican revolution, v.19, p.10-11; lawyer in Natchitoches, v.19, p.12; district judge in La., v.19, p.13; member of Congress, v.19, p.13; on Supreme Court of La., v.19, p.13; Secretary of State of La., v.19, p.14; professor of law, v.19, p.15; in La. Legislature, v.19, p.15; first president of La. Historical Soc., v.19, p.7-20; Judge, and case of Sally Miller, v.22, p.164; noted, v.22, p.735; ancestry, v.23, p.999-1000; education, v.23, p.100; filibustering activities, v.23, p. 1000-1002; lawyer in Natchitoches, v.23, p.1002-1003; family, v.23, p.1003-1008; in La. House of Rep., v.23, p.1003-1007; in Alexandria, v.23, p.1007; in Cong., v. 23, p.1008-1022; joins Whigs, v.23, p.1008; and tariff of 1832, v.23, p.1012-1017; on La. Sup. Ct., v.23, p.1021-1028, 1029-1037; Sec. of State of La., v.23, p.1028-1029; Law digest, v.23, p.1031-1032; evaluation as jurist, v.23, p.1031-1039; and La. Hist. Soc., v.23, p.1039-1046; address to People's Lyceum, v.23, p.1047; and New England Soc., v.23, p.1047-1048; and La. Colonization Soc., v.23, p.1048-1050; eulogy on A. Porter, v.23, p.1050-1051; on F. Martin, v.23, p.1051-1053; on S. S. Prentiss, v.23, p.1054-1055; dean and prof. in Un. of La. Law School, v.23, p.1055-1063; and Batture controversy, v.23, p.1064-1071; and Lopez expedition, v.23, p.1071-1079; and election of 1850, v.23, p.1079-1089; in Cong., v.23, p.1089; cases before U. S. Sup. Court, v.23, p.1090-1095; death, v.23, p.1095; tribute to, v.23, p.1095-1098; succession of, v.23, p.1098-1100; evaluation of, v.23, p.1100-1101; bibl. on, v.23, p.1101-1106; and tariff, v.25, p.83-84, 85, 86, 87, 103, 296, 303; noted, v.25, p.1083; first pres. of N. Eng. Soc. of N. O., v.27, p.739; Louisiana Supreme Court, Blanc decision, v.31, p.959-60.

Bullard, Henry Bass, noted, v.23, p.1003.

Bullard, Julia Laurence, noted, v.23, p.1003.

Bullard, Marianne, noted, v.23, p.1003.

Bullard, Rev. John, noted, v.23, p.999.

Bullard, Virginia, noted, v.23, p.1003.

Bullitt, Cuthbert, acting collector of customs, N. O., v.23, p.1137, 1200.

Burbank, Major Nat., early N. O. newspaperman, v.29, p.773.

Burch, J. E., Farmers' Alliance Com., v.28, p.1152.

Burch, William, duel, noted, v.24, p.770.

Bureau, Freedmen's, see Freedmen's Bureau.

Bureau of Finance, organized by Shepley in N. O., v.27, p.512.

Bureau of Free Labor, v.32, p.157, 162.

Bureau of Reclamation, v.30, p.655.

Bureau of Refugees, Freedmen and Abandoned Lands, v.25, p.740-741; regulations of, v.25, p.741; Howard cited on, v.25, p.741; noted, v.25, p.751; bill creating, v.32, p.151.

Bureau of Streets and Landings, organized in N. O. by Shepley, v.27, p.512.

Burge, Col. H. W., noted, v.23, p.1185.

Burges, Tristram, and sugar tariff, v.25, p.64-65.

Burial Mounds used by Indians for burial purposes, v.28, p.27-28, 29, 30.

Burkdall, A. R., editor of "Signal," v.27, p.1185-1186.

Burke, E. A., personal encounter with Kellogg, v.29, p.439n.; personal representative of Gov. Nicholls of La. in Wash., v.29, p.731-732, 736; noted, v.29, p.735; political enemy of E. J. Ellis, v.29, p.747; makes friends with Ellis, v.29, p.749; owner and editor "Times Democrat," v.30, p.144; owner of N. O. "Democrat," v.31, p.785; control of "Democrat," v.27, p.1002.

Burke, Glendy, noted, v.23, p.199, 200, 214.

Burke, John, N. O. police chief, v.31, p.1040.

Burke, Walter J. (Gov. Luther E. Hall), v.6, p.46.

Burke, William, noted, v.22, p.430.

Burkhart, George, noted, v.23, p.1142.

Burns, Francis P., "Charles M. Waterman, Mayor of New Orleans," v.7, p.466; "The Spanish Land Laws of La.," v.11, p.557; Book Review, Thomas, "Forgotten Frontiers," v.15, p.712; "West Florida and the Louisiana Purchase," v.15, p.391; "White Supremacy in the South: The Battle for Constitutional Government in New Orleans, July 30, 1866," v.18, p.581-616; "Notes on the Legislature and Litigation Affecting the Title of Saint Louis Cathedral," v.18, p.363-376; "The Graviers and the Faubourg Ste. Marie," v.22, p.385-427; "Henry Clay Visits N. O.," v.27, p.717-782; "Lafayette Visits New Orleans," v.29, p.296-304.

Burnside, John, noted, v.23, p.245, 249.

Burnside, La., v.28, p.843n., 844n.

Burns, John, appointed to Bogalusa police force, v.29, p.113.

Burr, Aaron, and schemes for settlement in Ouachita, v.20, p.407ff.; noted, v.22, p.101, 799; conspiracy material in Bibliotheca Parsoniana, v.24, p.310, 311; letters of Claiborne and Wilkinson on, in La. State Museum, v.24, p.319; noted, v.24, p.699.

Burr Conspiracy, and Marquis de Casa Irujo, v.25, p.8, 11, 292, 293, 645.

Burson, Caroline Maude, "The Stewardship of Don Estevan Miro, 1782-1792," rev'd by Walter Prichard, v.24, p.537-541.

Burthe, Andre, early N. O. police reporter, v.29, p.51-52; elected Recorder of Second District, N. O., v.29, p.52.

Burthe, D. F., Soule's opponent for state senate, 1846, v.25, p.1036, 1038.

Burthe, D. O., and College of Jefferson, v.31, p.853.

Burton, William, pioneer cypress lumberman, v.30, p.1015-1016.

Burwell, William M., acquires property of "De Bow's Review," v.29, p.393; early N. O. newspapermen, v.29, p.773; sketch of life, v.29, p.773-774.

Bush, Louis, noted, v.24, p.83; at reception for anti-lottery legislators, v.27, p.1056; presiding Dem. Anti-Lottery State Com., v.27, p.1091; chairman meeting anti-lottery faction, v.28, p.1158.

Bushnell, David I., Jr., "The Choctaw of St. Tammany Parish," v.1, sec.1, p.11.

Butler, Andrew Jackson, noted, v.24, p.483; activities described, v.24, p.483-484.

Butler, Benjamin F., in New Orleans, v.18, p.558-562; in N. O., v.23, p.1135, 1182ff.; and Christ Church, v.23, p.1241-1257; noted, v.29, p.451; contracts with Richard Taylor, v.24, p.70-71; orders of in Bibliotheca Parsoniana, v.24, p.311; appointed to command in N. O., v.24, p.450; landing with troops in N. O., v.24, p.465; headquarters in St. Charles Hotel, v.24, p.465; negotiations with Mayor Monroe, v.24, p.466-470; press complaints, v.24, p.470-471; money raising devices in N. O., v.24, p.476-477; cleaning of N. O., v.24, p.477-479; financial operations, v.24, p.480-484; decline of social life in N. O., v.24, p.484-485; quotation from diary of, v.24, p.486; harsh discipline, v.24, p.486-488, 490-492; execution of Mumford, v.24, p.489-490; bitterness of women toward, v.24, p.492-498; nickname "Spoon," v.24, p.501-502; censorship of press and clergy, v.24, p.502; steps in reconstruction, v.24, p.506-507; problem of foreigners in N. O., v.24, p.507-516; Negro problem, v.24, p.517-524; departure from N. O., v.24, p.524-530; estimate of, v.24, p.531-532; transactions of, v.24, p.532-536; attorney general, v.24, p.1170; concurred with Stanton in plan for invading Texas, v.26, p.341-343; promised safe transit of cotton, v.26, p.346; letter to from Chase, v.26, p.348; replaced by Banks, v.26, p.354-356; commanding officer at N. O., v.26, p.1036; arrival in N. O., v.27, p.487, 495-496; description of, v.27, p.496-497; reception in N. O., v.27, p.497-499; declared martial law, v.27, p.499-500; attitude toward press, v.27, p.500-501; control of churches, v.27, p.501-502; his "woman order," v.27, p.502-504; refused to commute sentence of Mumford, v.27, p.504-505; restoration of economic processes, v.27, p.506; public works program, v.27, p.508-509; monetary stabilization, v.27, p.509-511; in re slavery, v.27, p.511; reorganized N. O. City Gov't under military control, v.27, p.512-513; "cracks down" on N. O., v.27, p.514-518; July 4 celebration in N. O., 1862, v.27, p.519; disarming order, v.27, p.522; recalled, v.27, p.524-525; order to free men of color to take up arms in Union Army, v.27, p.529; Repub. Rep. from Mass. proposed that Pinchback be seated in Congress, v.27, p.582, 583, 584; inscription on Clay's monument, v.27, p.777, 778, 779; counsel for lottery co., v.27, p.991; sentences traitor to be hanged as example for others, v.29, p.342, 343; interviews wife of doomed man and pledges aid, v.29, p.343-344; his account of scene of execution, v.29, p.344; public sentiment against him, v.29, p.345-346, 347; upheld by few in North, v.29, p.346, 347; fulfills pledge to widow, v.29, p.347-351; widow's son plots revenge against him, v.29, p.352-353; press comments after his death, v.29, p.353; softens in old age, v.29, p.353-354; and Charity Hospital, v.31, p.60-63.

Butler, Charles A., on com. to supervise primary, 1892, v.27, p.1094; v.28, p.1161.

Butler, Judge Thomas, defeated for Congress, v.28, p.949.

Butler, Loudon, Confed. Maj., v.26, p.958.

Butler, Louise, "West Feliciana, a Glimpse of Its History," v.7, p.90; "The Louisiana Planter and His Home," v.10, p.317.

"Butler Regime in La.," by Thos. Ewing Dabney, v.27, p.487-526.

Butler, Thomas Langford, sketch, v.21, p.386.

Butler, Thomas, noted, v.22, p.470; and 1819 tariff bill, v.25, p.34.

Buzzaeott, cooking apparatus, v.26, p.808.

Byerly, Dan, N. O., newspaperman, v.31, p.704, 786.

Byerly, D. C., established "N. O. Bulletin," sketch of, v.30, p.293-295.

Byrne, Thomas, noted, v.24, p.369.

Byron, Lord, noted, v.24, p.422; portrait of, v.24, p.941.

CABALLERO, JERONIMO, SKETCH OF, v.21, p.23n.

Caballero, Jose Antonio, noted, v.22, p.103; letter from Casa Calvo, v.22, p.129.

"Cabarets of New Orleans in the French Colonial Period," by Henry P. Dart, v.17, p.578-583.

Cabell, General W. L., connected with La. Lottery Co., v.27, p.1015, 1098, 1099, 1101; challenge of, v.27, p.1102.

Cabello, Don Domingo, Gov. of Texas, opposed open trade with La., v.28, p1077.

Cabildo Archives, see Louisiana, Superior Council Records.

"Cabildo of Mexico City, 1524-1534, History of the," by Louise K. Dyer, v.6, p.395.

"Cabildo, The Story of the Ancient," by Charles Patton Dimitry, v.3, p.57; The, of New Orleans, (Editor's Chair), v.5, p.279; Spanish Colonial, (Editor's Chair), v.6, p.478.

"Cabin, Uncle Tom's," Phanor Breazeal, v.7, p.304.

"Cable, George W.," Henry P. Dart, v.8, p.647; work on New Orleans Picayune, v.24, p.168-186; views on questions of the day, v.24, p.184-185; quoted, v.24, p.184-185; quoted, v.24, p.452, 455, 457; noted, v. 24, p.454, 455.

Caddo Academy of Greenwood, v.30, p795.

Caddo Academy of Shreveport, v.30, p.797.

Caddo Indians, session of Site of Shreveport, La., v.18, p.775-779; building of Caddo Indian Agency, v.18, p.780-785; Caddo Indian Treaty, v.18, p.792-796; history of tribe, v.18, p.872-946; in Grant Parish, v.23, p.1109; description of, v.23, p.1111ff.; noted, v.25, p.398, 625, 928, 930, 931.

Caddo Lake, noted, v.29, p.59n., 61, 65, 66; bed drilled for oil, v.29, p.59, 68-69.

Caddo Oil and Gas Field, first gas found in 1870, v. 29, p.59; more gas than oil found, v.29, p.60; wildgassers produce much waste, v.29, p.60, 61, 62, 63, 64, 65, 67; waste of gas acted on by Gen'l Assembly of La. in 1906, v.29, p.61; in 1908, v.29, p.63; in 1910, v.29, p.67; action on waste gas by Dept. of Interior, v.29, p.64; Pres. T. Roosevelt signs withdrawal order, v.29, p.64-65; Pres. Taft establishes Petroleum Reserve No. 4, v.29, p.66; disastrous oil fire in 1911, v.29, p.68; drilling in Caddo Lake, v.29 p.68-69; saturated gas contained great quantities of gasoline, v.29, p.69; Supreme Court decisions concerning oil claims, v.29, p.69-71.

Caddo Parish, La., before the white man came, v.18, p. 761-763; exploration and coming of the pioneers, v.18, p.763-765; first American expedition up Red River, v.18, p.765-769; great raft in Red River and its removal, v.18, p.769-775; cession of site of Shreveport by Caddo Indians, v.18, p.775-785; founding of Shreveport, v.18, p.785-791; Caddo Indian Treaty, v.18, p.792-796; establishment of Caddo Parish, v.18, p.805-811; invaded by Texan army v.18, p.819-820; Caddo-Texas treaty, v.18, p. 821; Western boundary and international boundary, v.18, p.833-837; old trails and roads, v.18, p.837-845; century of steam boating on Red River, v.18, p.845-854; coming of railroads, v.18, p.854-855; war period, v.18, p.855-858; post war days and decline of river trade, v.18, p.858-863; in 1860, v.21, p.1174-1179; and the Cong. election of 1894, v.26, p.1097.

Cade, C. Taylor, fusion cand. sec. of state, 1900, v. 28, p.1192.

Cadena, Francisco, agent in Haiti, v.24, p.622, 626, 627, 629, 632, 634; Indian trader, v.28, p.1086.

Cadet, Pierre, noted, v.22, p.1034.

Cadillac, Antoine de la Mothe, commandant of post on Straits of Mackinac, v.26, p.639; reinforced St. Ignace, v.26, p.724; became gov. of Crozat's province, v.26, p.728; sent Bienville to Natchez, v.26, p.729; with Tonti's brother, in control of Detroit post, v.26, p.646; gov. of La., v.26, p.649-651, 653, 656, 687.

Cady, L. W., telegraph contractor, v.31, p.451.

"Cafe des Refugies," New Orleans, v.25, p.304.

Caffery, Bethia Richardson, marriage, v.27, p.785.

Caffery, Central Refining Co., v.27, p.789.

Caffery, Donelson, (Gov. Luther E. Hall), v.6, p.53; "A Louisiana Democrat Out of Line," by E. M. Violette, v.14, p.521; U.S. Senator, bolted and formed Nat'l Dem. party, v.26, p.1115; sugar planter in St. Mary Parish, v.27, p.783; parish judge, v.27, p.783; antecedents, v.27, p.783; birth, early life, education, v.27, p.784; in Civil War, v.27, p.784; practice of laws and sugar planting, v.27, p.784-785; marriage, v.27, p.785; sued by Syper and acquitted, v.27, p.785; during Carpetbag regime, v.27, p.785; cont. conv. of 1879, v.27, p.786-788; member com. to investigate state debt, v.27, p.786-787; anti-lottery campaign, v.27, p.788-790; member Dem. State Nominating Conv., 1891, v.27, p.789; in the Senate, v.27, p.790-791; supports social measures, v.27, p.790-791; anti-trust bill supported by, v.27, p. 791; supports changes in Civil Code of La., v.27, p.791; appointed and elected to U.S. Senate, v.27, p.791-792; maiden speech on the silver question, v.27, p.794-796; reelected to U.S. Senate, 1894, v.27, p.797; sale of U.S. bonds, v.27, p.798; address on nat'l finance, v.27, p.799-800; "La. Dem. out of Line," v.27, p.801; campaign of 1896; v.27, p.801-803; chaiman Nat'l Dem. Party, v.27, p.803; against Teller Resolution, v.27, p.804; his "The New South," address, campaign of 1900, v.27, p.805; views on Tariff, v.27, p.806; champion of sugar planters, v.27, p.806; becomes senior senator from La., v.27, p.806; and the Wilson-Gorman Bill, v.27, p.806, 807-810, 815; denounced, v.27, p.809, 810, 812-813, 821; his stand on bounty question, v.27, p.810-812; fight for sugar duty, v.27, p.813-814; fight to collect bounty due, v.27, p.816-817; opposition to Dingley Tariff act, v.27, p.818-821; opposition to sugar trust, v.27, p.819-820; attitude on Cuban Insurrection, v.27, p.821-822, 823-825; sympathy to Cuban patriots, v.27, p.825; against Morgan Resolution, v.27, p.826; opposed to war with Sp., v.27, p.827-828; in re annexation of Hawaii, v.27, p.829-830; opinion of the result of the Sp. Am. War, v.27, p.831; against acquisition of the Philippines, v.27, p.831-833, 834, 835; against McEnery Resolution, v.27, p.833-834; fought Spooner Amendment to Army Appropriation Bill, v.27, p.835; attitude toward Nicaragua Canal, v.27, p.836-840; support of Rivers and Harbors Bills, v.27, p.841; responsible for appropriation for improvement of Bayou Plaquemine, v.27, p.842-843; efforts to get appropriation for Miss. R. Pass improvements, v.27, p.843-844; objections to Immigration Bill, 1897, v.27, p.844-845; efforts to obtain passage of Quarantine Bill, v.27, p.845-846; presented committee resolutions denying Corbett seat in Senate, v.27, p.846; campaigned for son for gov. of La., v.27, p.847; interest in 4 yr. term only for naval cadets, v.27, p.847; fight against Ship Subsidy Bill, v.27, p.848; retired to private life, v.27, p.849, 850; reestablished friendship with Foster, v.27, p.849-850; became wealthy man, v.27, p.850; death in 1906, v.27, p.850-851;

estimation of, v.27, p.851; bibl., v.27, p.851-853; counsel for Mason, v.27, p.1051; noted, v.28, p.1129, 1130; in partnership with Foster, v.28, p.1132; cand. for Sen. from St. Mary, 1876, v.28, p.1138; chairman anti-lottery faction com., v.28, p.1156-1157; noted, v.28, p.1161; apptd. by Foster to Sen., v.28, p.1167, 1169; noted, v.28, p.1170; his break with the party, v.28, p.1186, 1187; support of fusion ticket, v.28, p.1192.

Caffery, Donelson, Jr., supported for gov. by People's Party, v.26, p.1124; noted, v.27, p.803; cand for gov. on Populist and Repub. fusion ticket, v.27, p.846; Sen. Caffery campaigned for, v.27, p.847; fusion cand. for gov., v.28, p.1192; speech of, v.28, p.1193; defeated, v.28, p.1194; noted, v.29, p.1058.

Caffery, Gertrude, daughter of Sen. Caffery, v.27, p.850.

Caffery, Lucile Roy, "The Political Career of Senator Donelson Caffery," v.27, p.783-853.

Caffery, Lydia Murphy, marriage to Don Caffery, v.27, p.783-784.

Cage, Judge ———, nomination of, v.23, p.1080.

Cage, Thomas A., on the lottery question, v.27, p.1042.

Caillavet, Madame Rose, Zulime gives power of atty. to, v.27, p.26, 29, 31, 34; testimony on birth of Caroline, v.27, p.35; testimony, v. 27, p.41, 44, 45, 76, 78, 82-85, 90, 97, 99, 193; evidence concerning, v.27, p.115; evidence of, v.27, p.125, 133, 134, 137, 138, 143, 146, 147, 148, 149; testimony, v.27, p.152-154, 155, 156, 157, 159, 160, 161, 164-165, 175, 191, 193, 194, 206, 208, 214; ruled unworthy of credit, v.27, p 217-220, 221, 223, 224, 227, 228, 232, 233, 234, 235, 236, 237, 238, 268, 271, 284-285, 288.

Caire, Edward, Confed. naval surgeon, v.27, p.486.

Calcasieu Parish, noted, v. 25, p.120; "Economic and Social Development of," by Grace Ulmer, v.32, p.519; description, v.32, p.519; agricultural developments, v.32, p.527-539; diversified farming, v.32, p.527-530; rice, v.32, p.530-538; farmer's organizations, v.32, p.538; transportation, v.32, p.539-542; railroads, v.32, p.543-544; water transportation, v.32, p.544-546; telegraph and telephone, v.32, p.546-548; lumber industry, v.32, p.548-554; cypress mills, v.32, p.555-556; naval stores, v.32, p.556-558; sulphur, v.32, p.558-561; Jennings oil field, v.32, p.561-565; Welsh Field, v.32, p.565; Vinton Field, v.32, p.565-567; population, v.32, p.567-575; Lake Charles, v.32, p.575-584; Sugartown, v.32, p.584-585; Vinton, v.32, p.585-588; Iowa, v.32, p.588; Welsh, v.32, p.589; Sulphur, v.32, p.590; Jennings, v.32, p.591; West Lake, v.32, p.592; Niblett's Bluff, v.32, p.593; Prien, v.32, p.593; Rose Bluff, v.32, p.593; other small villages, v.32, p.594; social life, v.32, p.596-602; educational developments, v.32, p.602-616; libraries, v.32, p.616; newspapers, v.32, p.617; religious developments, v.32, p.620; Methodists, v.32, p.620; Catholics, v.32, p.621-622; Baptists, v.32, p.622; Presbyterians, v.32, p.623; Episcopalians, v.32, p.624; Lutherans, v.32, p.625; Methodist Episcopal (North), v.32, p.625; minor sects, v.32, p.626; Baptist Orphanage, v.32, p.626; St. Patrick's Sanitarium, v.32, p.627.

Calcasieu River, noted, v.24, p.638; noted, v.28, p.1023, 1024, 1027, 1029, 1034, 1046.

Caldez, Francisco, noted, v.22, p.67n.

Caldwell, B. C., noted, v.25, p.806, 808.

Caldwell, James, and New Orleans Theatre, v.21, p.500; noted, v.22, p.1133; founds N.O. Gas Light and Banking Co., v.23, p.173; noted, v.23, p.244; pioneer of the drama in the South, v.26, p.370; built St. Charles Theatre, v.26, p.370; introduced gas to N.O., v.26, p.371; noted, v.28, p.88; owned Am. theatrical co., v.28, p.103, 104, 106ff.; joins with Phillips, v.28, p.105; sketch, v.28, p.105-106; and Am. Theatre on Orleans St., v.28, p.107-110, 110-113, 114-120; and Camp St. Theatre, v.28, p.121ff.; management of Am. Theatre ends, v.28, p.186; noted, v.28, p.199; opened new St. Charles Theatre, v.28, p.204-205; season 1835-1836, v.28, p.204-212; 1836-1837, v.28, p.218-224; 1837-1838, v.28, p.229-234; agreement bebtween Caldwell and Barrett, v.28, p.235; season 1838-1839, v.28, p.240-245; 1838-1840, v.28, p.247-250; 1840-1841, v. 28, p.253-257; 1841-1842, v.28, p.264-268; withdrawal from theatrical scene in N.O., v.28, p.274; Mary Ann Duff appeared in Am. theatre of, v.28, p.927ff.

Caldwell, Mrs. J. W., treasurer Women's Anti-Lottery League, v.27, p.1061.

Caldwell, Norman W., "The French in the Mississippi Valley, 1740-1750," rev'd. v.25, p.827-828.

Caldwell Parish, in 1860, v.21, p.1200-1203.

Caldwell, Robert, v.24, p.922, 926.

Caleb, Richard, noted, v.23, p.404.

Caleman, Father, of Pensacola, v.21, p.92.

"Calendar of Documents, History of, in Archives of Paris Relating to the Mississippi Valley," Mrs. N. M. Miller Surrey, v.7, p.551.

Calhoun, A. C., Populist cand. for railroad commissioner, v.26, p.1123.

Calhoun, John C., views at variance with Edward Livingston, v.24, p.707, 719; views of the Union, v.24, p.707-708, 710; State Rights leader, v.24, p.716-717; noted, v.24, p.935, 1018, 1148, 1155, 1164; nullification doctrine, v.24, p.1159; and 1816 tariff, v.25, p.32, 105, 123, 1001, 1003, 1060; his view on Mex. War, v.25, p.1061; on the Mo. Comp., v.25, p.1064, 1066, 1067; noted, v.25, p.1069; encounter with Benton, v.25, p.1069-1070, 1072; on slavery and non-intervention, v. 25, p.1111-1115; noted, v.27, p.718; contest with A. Jackson, v.27, p.728; death of, v.27, p.763; N.O. honors jointly with Clay and Webster, v.27, p.763-764, 765-769.

Calhoun, John, noted, v.23, p.203.

Calhoun, Jos. F., Lotteryite cand. for supt. of ed., v.27, p.1090.

Calhoun, J. B., "Regular" cand. for supt. of ed., v.26, p.1081; Dem. cand. for supt. of ed., 1896, v.26, p.1101; cand. supt. of ed., v.28, p.1158, 1173, 1191.

Calhoun, La., Agricultural experiment station, v.26, p.1064; State Agr. Society meeting at, v.26, p.1064, 1066; suggested agr. school at, v.26, p.1065.

Calhoun, Robert Dabney, "A History of Concordia Parish, Louisana," I, II, III, IV, v.15, p.44, 214, 428, 618; V, VI, VII, VIII, v.16, p. 92, 309, 454, 598; IX (Conclusion), v.17, p.96; "Taensa Indians," I, II, v.17, p.411, 642; "The John Perkins Family of Northeast La.," v.17, p.70-88; "The Origin and Early Development of County-Parish Government in La., 1805-1845," v.18, p.56-106; (co-auth.), "The Marquis de Maison Rouge, the Baron de Bastrop and Col. Abraham Morhouse: Three Ouachita Valley Soldiers of Fortune, The Maison Rouge and Bastrop Spanish Land Grants," v.20, p.289-462.

Calkins, Elizabeth, 1st wife of Wm. Henry Sullivan, v.29, p.186.

Callaghan, Charles, Populist cand. for Cong., 1894, v.26, p.1095.

Callao, international expedition against, v.24, p.674.

Callender, Gordon W., (jt. author), "The Miss. Fort Called Fort de la Boulaye, 1700-1715; The First French Settlement in Present-day La.," v.19, p.829-899.

Caller, James, and W. Fla. Rev., v.21, p.117.

Caller, Robert, Jr., letter to J. P. Kennedy, v.21, p.117-118.

Callot, Sieur, well trained architect, v.29, p.577, 578, 579.

Calvo, de Casa, Spanish representative in N.O., v.21, p.677.

Calvo, Santiago de la Puerto y O'Farrill, see Casa Calvo, Marquis de "Calypso," brig, v.24, p.639. 642.

Cambreleng, Churchill C., and sugar tariff, v.25, p.38, 66, 67.

Camden, Arkansas, settlement by Filhiol, v.20, p.465.

Cameron, J. B., People's Party elector, v.26, p.1087.

Cameron Parish, noted, v.23, p.517.

Cameron, Simon, noted, v.24, p.495.

Cameron, William, pioneer in manufacture of cypress shinges, v.30, p.1018-1019.

Cammack, H. C., noted, v.23, p.204.

Camorra, History of, v.22, p.502-504.

"Campaign, Red River, General Banks," by Richard Hobson Williams, v.32, p.103.

Campbell, B. and W. L., slave dealers, v.22, p.152, 153.

Campbell, Capt., began clearing Manchac, v.25, p.935.

Campbell, Dougal, noted, v.22, p.317, 981; and W. Fla. Assembly, v.23, p.23ff., 357, 368.

Campbell, Dr. G. W., on committee to investigate case of Seminole Mary, v.26, p.73-75; noted, v.26, p.76; challenged to duel by Luzenberg, v.26, p.80-83; noted, v.26, p.86, 162.

Campbell, H. J., ousted Sambola as senator, v.27, p.536; withdraws from Pinchback faction, v.27, p.553; Removed by Pinchback from Command of Militia, v.27, p.569; Counsel for Pinchback, v.27, p.587; introduces lottery bill, v.31, p.721; denounced by Sambola, v.31, p.721.

Campbell, Jas. C., Prog. League com., v.27, p.1062.
Campbell, John A., counsel for lottery co., 1879, v.27, p.998; lottery lawyer, v.31, p.764.
Campbell, John, noted, v.33, p.25, 368, 392.
Campbell, Martin Q., Confed. soldier, v.26, p.950.
Campbell, Robert, noted, v.22, p.1112.
Campbell, St. George T., counsel Morse vs. O'Reilly, v.31, p.463.
Campbell Town, and W. Fla. Assembly, v.22, p.39-40, 312, 944, 996; loses representation in W. Fla. Assembly, v.23, p.17; boundaries of, v.23, p.361.
Campbell, William B., noted, v.23, p.217.
Campbell, William S., noted, v..23, p.204, 226, 235.
Camp Chalmette, near N.O., v.26, p.960, 961.
Campeache (Galveston Island) base for privateers, v. 24, p.16; "Snake Island," v.24, p.21; noted, v.24, p.629, 930.
Camp Foster, at N.O. Fair Grounds and named for Gov. Murphy J. Foster, v.26, p.738; Col. Wood's reg't there, v.26, p.797-810; Wood's report of to Gov., v.26, p.811-814.
Campigiano, Ignazio, noted, v.22, p.827.
Campiglio, Paolo, N.O. musician, v.31, p.132-133.
Camp Moore, noted, v.24, p.61; noted, v.26, p.937-957 passim.
Campo de Alange, Conde del (Manuel Jose Antonio Hilario, identified, v.21, p.21n.
Camp of Instruction, at Shreveport, v.24, p.432.
Campomanes, Conde de (Pedro Rodriguez) sketch, v.21, p.21n.
Camp Ouachita, near Vicksburg, v.26, p.967, 969.
Camp Parapet, noted, v.24, p.518.
Camp Pratt, noted, v.24, p.69.
Camp Street Theatre, v.28, p.240; leased for ballroom, v.28, p.247; again opened as Am. Theatre, summer 1840, v.28, p.251-252; became Camp St. Exchange, v.28, p.252.
Canada de la Conde (Juan Acedo y Rico), identified, v. 21, p.23n.
Canadian "Instituteurs," v.25, p.362.
Canal Carondelet, and Orleans Navigation Co. case, v.28, p.979.
Canals, first used in rice irrigation, v.23, p.568-569.

Canas, Hilary, Confed. naval officer, v.27, p.480-481, 483.
Canby, Edward Richard Sprigg, noted, v.23, p.1213, 1219; wounded, v.23, p.1217; and Christ Church in N.O., v.23, p.1244ff.; noted, v.24, p.109, 110, 111; replaces Banks, v.31, p.1034; noted, v.31, p.1064; at odds with Kennedy, v.31, p.1072.
Cancer, Fray Luis, noted, v.22, p.936.
Cancino, Jose Maria, noted, v.24, p.673, 674, 675.
Candia, insurrection at, v.24, p.966.
"Canebrake, Dr. James G. Carson's: A View of an Ante-Bellum Louisiana Plantation," by Dr. Robert C. Reinders, v.33, p.353-363.
"Canebrake" Plantation, located, v.33, p.353-354; food raised, v.33, p.358.
Canellas, Count de, noted, v.24, p.1025.
Cane River, noted, v.21, p.1166; noted, v.25, p.361, 362, 397; noted, v.26, p.731.
Canillas, Father, noted, v.22, p.936.
Cann, Abe A., Confed. soldier, v.26, p.969.
Canning, George, noted, v.24, p.951, 1018, 1021, 1024, 1031, 1036, 1066; effects of his death, v.24, p.1051-1052, 1055; censure of Eastern Policy, v.24, p.1071.
Cannon, Fenelon, noted, v.26, p.1004.
Canon, E. A., candidate for St. Louis Cathedral warden, v.31, p.913; incident, v.31, p.918, 920; noted, v.31, p.942; to Blanc, v.31, p.947-948.
Canonge, B. Z., and S. C. Ord. of Nullification, v.28, p.951.
Canonge, Judge, noted, v.24, p.757.
"Canon of Chile," title of Madariaga, v.24, p.655.
Canovis, noted, v.24, p.968, 1001.
Cantey, Gen'l James, confederate officer, v.29, p.1125, 1168, 1177, 1181-1186.
Cantrel, Michael, noted, v.22, p.815.
Capdeville, Paul, v.28, p.343; address at reburial of Fr. sailors, v.28, p.344.
Cape Horn, noted, v.24, p.647.
Capell, Eli J., collection in L.S.U. Archives, v.24, p.341.
Cap Francois, noted, v.23, p.431.
Capitan de fragata (captain junior grade), noted, v.24, p.615.
Capitan de navio (captain senior grade), noted, v.24, p.619.
Capo, Thomas, noted, v.22, p.827.
Capuchins, and eary education, v.19, p.598-601; in N.O., v.21, p.1069-1070; in N.O., v.22, p.98ff.; order of, noted, v.25,

p.365; in N.O., v.26, p.670; priests in La., 1767, v.27, p.638-639.

"Capuchins in French Louisiana, 1722-1766, The," by Caude L. Vogel, Review by Henry P. Dart, v.11, p.620.

Capuran, Joseph, noted, v.22, p.69, 76.

Carabi, Antonio, noted, v.22, p.813.

Caracas, revolt in, v.23, p.430; agents of in the U.S., 1810, v.24, p.613; fall of, 1812, v.24, p.613.

Cardenas and Lopez expedition, v.22, p.1120-1132.

Cardenas, Louis de Penalver y, La's first bishop, v.27, p.713-714.

Carder, James D., Pastor in N.O., v.22, p.461.

"Career of Dubrevil in French La.," by Henry Plauche Dart, v.18, p.267-331.

"Career of Henry Adams Bullard, La. Jurist, Legislator and Educator," by Dora J. Bonquois, v.23, p.999-1106.

"Career of Paul Octave Herbert, The, Governor of Louisiana," by A. L. Dupont, v.31, p.491-552.

Carey, Dr. V., noted, v.26, p.76.

Carey, Rita Katherine, "Samuel Jarvis Peters," v.30, p.439-480.

Carleton, Eleanor Beatrice, author "The Establishment of the Electric Telegraph in Louisiana and Mississippi," v.31, p.425-490.

Carleton, Henry, noted, v.22, p.418; on La. Sup. Ct., v.23, p.1027, 1028; noted, v.25, p.78.

Carline, Cathcart's pilot, v.28, p.770.

Carlin, Joseph, v.28, p.763n., 766n.

Carman, J. L. & Co., slave auctioneers, v.22, p.154.

Carmelita, schooner of B. Lafon, v.23, p.775.

Carmelites, established convent, v.25, p.731.

Carmon, Mary, noted, v.23, p.391.

Carnatz Institute, v.30, p.865.

Carnival, in France, v.24, p.1140.

"Caroline," naval schooner, v.23, p.442.

Carondelet, Baron de (Francisco Luis Hector de Hoyelles, Seigneur D' Haine St. Pierre), and Ouachita land grants, v.20, p.298ff.; decree issued June 1, 1795, v.20, p.590-605; substance of letters to Florida-blanca, Gayoso de Lemos, Aranda, v.21, p.24n.; treaty with McGillivray noted, v.21, p.25n.; fears of slave revolt, v.21, p.26n.; letter to Alcudia noted, v.21, p.28; letters to de Alange in re invasion of La., v.21, p.33ff.; letters to Godoy, v.21, p.64ff.; and fur trade, v.21, p.71; and French Rev., v.22, p.48ff.; and Batture Controversy, v.23, p.682ff.; noted, v.23, p.1090; papers in Bibliotheca Parsoniana, v.24, p.311; papers in L.S.U. Archives, v.24, p.341; noted, v.26, p.745-751 passim; in re commecre, v.27, p.634; plan for war against Americans, v.27, p.681; succeeded Miro, 1791, v.27, p.708; surveys Miss. R. posts, v.27, p.709; preparation for Clark's expedition, v.27, p.710, 711, 712, 713; and Don Pedro, v.28, p.705ff.; noted, v.28, p.722, 1013, 1014; noted, v.30, p.360, 363, 373n., 376; struggle over control of N.O. Hospital, v.31, p.25-26; reports French influence, v.31, p.610; attempt to minimize American influence, v.31, p.611; and Maison Rouge, v.31, p.612; Bastrop colony, v.31, p.613ff.; seeks approval of Bastrop venture, v.31, p.618-620; replaced, v.31, p.623.

"Carondelet's Levee Ordinance of 1792, Gov.," Text and translation by Laura L. Porteous, v.10, p.513.

Carpenter, Caleb, noted, v.33, p.391.

Carpenter, Dr. Jesse T., "The South as a Conscious Minority," reviewed by Henry P. Dart, v.14, p.637.

Carpenter, Edwin H., Jr., "Latour's Report on Spanish-American Relations in the Southwest," v.30, p.715-737.

Carpenter, James, noted, v.23, p.404.

Carpenter, Matthew, proposed another election in La., 1874, v.27, p.596; investigation of La. Politics, v.27, p.579.

Carpenter, Richard, noted, v.23, p.26, 391; election of, v.23, p.377.

Carpetbaggers, noted, v.25, p.709.

Carraby, Etienne, noted, v.22, p.421, 424.

Carradine, Rev. B., N.O. Methodist Minister protests against acceptance of aid from Lottery Co., v.27, p.1028; Anti-Lottery League Ex. Com., v.27, p.1056; published pamphlet against Lottery Co., v.27, p.1070.

Carrera, Jose Miguel, noted, v.23, p.836.

Carriere, Andre, petition of, v.23, p.374.

Carriere, Zulime, v.27, p.7; sketch, v.27, p.23-24; marriage of to Desgrange, v.27, p.24; children of, v.27, p.24-25; given power of atty. in absence of Desgrange, v.27, p.25-26; birth of Caroline, v.27, p.27-40; alleged marriage to D. Clark, v.27, p.41-43; circumstances of Myra Clark's birth, v.27, p.43-44; married to James Gardette, v.27, p.46, 58, 59, 62; trip to N.Y. to prove bigamy of Desgrange, v.27, p.53-54; marriage to Clark, v.27, p.55-62, 78, 70, 74, 77; in re marriage to Clark, v.27, p.77-82, 83-85; in re-marriage certificate of Desgrange to Barbara Orci, v.27, p.86-91; and Desgrange's trial for bigamy, v.27, p.91-104; record of her petition against Desgrange for alimony, v.27, p.104-107; record of divorce or annulment proceedings, v.27, p.107-114; evidence disproving her marriage to D. Clark, v.27, p.115-133; conflicting evidence, v.27, p.133-178; legal opinion in re facts of her marriages, v.27, p.190-195, 206; decreed legally married to Clark in Patterson Case, v.27, p.207, 210; decision reversed, v.27, p.213-225; dissenting opinion, v.27, p.226-240, 252-255, 259, 261, 262, 265, 267-273, 274, 275, 279-288, 304, 322.

Carrigan, John N., nominee for state supt. of education, v.31, p.501.

Carr, John C., noted, v.25, p.299; civil judge at Natchitoches, v.28, p.1061, 1065; efforts to recover fugitive slaves, v.28, p.1072-73.

Carroll, Joseph W., member of La. Bar Association Committee which prepared memorial to Henry P. Dart, Sr., v.18, p.255-266.

Carroll, Michael B., and privateers, v.23, p.442.

Carroll Parish, in 1860, v.21, p.1211-1214; noted, v.25, p.356.

Carroll's Mill, noted, v.24, p.88.

Carrollton, history of city, v.21, p.220-281; history of, v.22, p.181-215; in 1863, v.23, p.1207; noted, v.24, p.138; collection in Howard-Tilton Memorial Library, v.24, p.330.

Carrollton House, N. O. summer resort, theatrical entertainment in, v.28, p.263-264.

Carrollton Railroad Co., sued by City of N.O., v.22, p.422-423.

Carrollton Star, newspaper, noted, v.32, p.727.

Carrollton Times, newpaper, noted, v.32, p.727.

Carroll, William, General at Battle of New Orleans, v.21, p.229.

Carrying trade, French jealousy of the U.S., v.24, p.1020.

Carson, Catherine, mistress of Canebrake, v.33, p.356.

Carson, Samuel P., noted, v.23, p.1017; and sugar tariff, v.25, p.86.

Cartagena, base for privateers, v.24, p.10; noted, v.24, p.368, 617, 647, 650, 659; agents of in the U.S., v.24, p.613; factions in, v.24, p.615-616; described, v.24, p.617-618.

Carter, Billy, Negro minstrel, sketch of, v.30, p.142.

Carter, Clarence E., (ed.), "Territorial Papers of the U.S., IX, Territory of Orleans," revd., v.25, p.224-226.

Carter, George G., Speaker of House, 1872, opponent of Warmoth, v.27, p.549-550; noted, v.30, p.581; accused by Warmoth, v.30, p.591, 610, 613, 625; attempts to make next in line for governorship, v.30, p.627; events in Legislature, v.30, p.628-632; noted, v.30, p.634.

Carter, G. W., noted, v.23, p.517.

Carter, Hon. Prentiss B., "The History of Washington Parish, Louisiana, as Compiled from the Records and Traditions," v.14, p.36.

Carter, J. W., school board member of 1st Bogalusa school, v.29, p.100.

Carver, Hiram W., councilman of Crowley, v.27, p.1126, 1130, 1171.

Cary, S. L., brings immigrants to S. W. La., v.23, p.559-560; noted, v.23, p.568, 570.

Casa Calvo, Marquis de (Sebastian de la Puerta y O'Farril) causes schism in church, v.22, p.100, 103ff.; report to Caballero, v.22, p.104-111; letters from Sedella, v.22, p.117, 124-125, 130; letters from Walsh, v. 22, p.121-123, 133; letters to Walsh, v.22, p.121, 123-124, 128, 141; letter to Sedella, v.22, p.125; letters from Alderman, v.22, p.125-128, 129; letter to Caballero, v.22, p.129; letters from Vidal, v.22, p.130, 134-138; letter to Vidal, v.22, p.131-132; letter to Gili, v.22, p.132; letter from Gili, v.22, p.138-140; letter to Girod and Lanusse, v.22, p.140; Spanish agent, v.22, p.797-799; noted, v.23, p.429; noted, v.24, p.7; noted, v.28, p.715, 718, 719; Sp. boundary commissioner in N.O., v.28, p.1070-1071; and Bastrop, v.31, p.625, 631, 632, 635.

Casa Irujo, Marquis de, Sp. plenipotentiary, v.25, p.7, 8; and Burr conspiracy, v.25, p.8, 11, 13; visited by Vidal, v.25, p.8; and 1808 incident, v.25, p.14; ordered Vidal to New Orleans, v.25, p.18-19.

Casanave, Gadane, member Returning Board, v.31, p.1093; indicated, v.31, p.1108.

"Case in Admiralty in Louisiana, 1741,"

Henry P Dart and Heloise H. Cruzat, v.7, p.5.

Casey, James F., Collector of the Port, v.27, p.549; appeal to Grant for recognition of Pinchback, v.27, p.565, 568.

Casey, Powell, "Early History of the Washington Artillery," v.23, p.471-484.

Cason, J. B., named in Kellogg impeachment, v.31, p.713.

Caspari, L., view of the Lottery question, v.27, p.1037.

Cassidy, Edward R., designated Chief of Police of Bogalusa, v.29, p.113; mayor of Bogalusa, v.29, p.118, 141, 146, 182, 183.

Cass, Lewis, noted, v.23, p.1046n.

Castanedo, Juan de, letter to Casa Calvo, v.22, p.129; deposition of, v.23, p.711-712.

Castein, Walter, noted, v.24, p,768.

Castellanos, noted, v.24, p.16.

Castillo, Manuel del, noted, v.24, p.616, 618.

Castillon, Jean Batiste Victor, Spanish consular agent in N.O., v.21, p.678; N.O. Consul, v.23, p.739.

Castleton Female Seminary, sketch of, v.30, p.778-779.

Catahoula Academy, v.30, p.808.

Catahoula Institute, v.30, p.810.

Catahoula Lake, noted, v.24, p.83; noted, v.25, p.206.

Catahoula Parish, v.21, p.1203-1207; noted, v.25, p.120; Randolph property in, v.25, p.214-215; and the Granger Movement, v.26, p.1063; Populist Rep. from, v.26, p.1109.

Catalina, noted, v.24, p.654.

"Catalina," Spanish schooner, v.23, p.429.

Catalonia, insurrections in, v.24, p.1066.

Cathcart, James Leander, com. to make survey of timber for naval purposes in La. and Ala., v.28, p 735-736; life of, v.28, p.736-737; salary as navy agent, v.28, p.737, 738; sketch of survey, v.28, p.738ff.; result of survey, v.28, p.740-741; journal, v.28, p.743-883; map of routes in La., v.28, p.748-748; charts of valuable timber found on survey, v.28, p.880ff.; compiled acc't of timber found, v.28, p.883-892; corespondence of concerning survey, v.28, p.892.

Cathedral Square, v.28, p.326, 327, 328; story of the obelisk in, v.28, p.328-348.

Catholic Church, in New Orleans, legislation and litigation of St. Louis Cathedral, v.18, p.363-376; and education in early La., v.19, p.595-634; in N. O., 1855-1858, v.20, p.680-689; affairs of, in La., 1793, v.21, p.26; in N. O., v.21, p.1069-1074; in Iberville Parish, 1860, v.21, p.1128; schism in N. O., v.22, p.98; in Carrollton, v.22, p.209-210; in W. Fla., v.22, p.332, 336, 377; case concerning, v.23, p.1032-1033; in San Antonio, 1854, v.23, p.1150; noted, v.24, p.312, 349; question of in England, v.24, p.1032; question of in the U. S., v.24, p.1122-1123, 1139-1140; and Negro education, v.25, p.360, 361-362, 363, 364, 365, 729-734; in St. Mary Parish, v.32, p.76.

Catholics, in Calcasieu Parish, v.32, p.621.

Catholic Society for the Instruction of Indigent Orphans, noted, v.25, p.364, 733.

Catin vs. D'Orenoy's Heirs, v. 25, p.352.

Catlin, R. H., named in Warmoth impeachment, v.31, p.702.

Caton, Miss, Daniel Clark reported engaged to, v.27, p.57, 58, 59, 79, 121, 122, 167, 168, 216, 286.

Catron, John, justice, v.27, p.126, 205-210; opinion written by in suit of Gaines vs. Relf, Chew and others, v.27, p.213-214, 217-225, 226, 232, 233, 234; dissenting opinion in case of Gaines vs. Hennan, v.27, p.274-276.

Cattle, laws concerning, v.23, p.414-417; in Sabine country, v.24, p.36.

Caucasian Club, organized in Franklin, v.28, p.1133.

Caughey, John, "Willing's Expedition Down the Mississippi, 1778," v.15, p.5; "The Natchez Rebellion of 1781 and Its Aftermath," v.16, p.57; "Bernardo de Galvez in Louisiana, 1776-1783," noted, v.26, p.314, 740.

Caulfield's "The French Literature of Louisiana" (Editor's Chair), v.13, p.484.

"Cause and Results of the Revolution of 1768 in Louisiana, The," by James E. Winston, v.15, p.181.

Cavalier, Z., noted, v.22, p.749.

Cavelier, Jean, noted, v.22, p.5.

Cavellier, ———, noted, v.22, p.815.

"Cazador," schooner, v.24, p.653, 659, 660.

Cazares, E., noted, v.24, p.758.

Cazeres, noted, v.23, p.146.

"Ceard's Case, 1724," by Henry P. Dart, v.5, p.155.

Ceballas, Ciriaco, N. O. leader of filibusters, v.25, p.293.

Cecil, William, noted, v.23, p.1025-1027.

"Celebration of Founding of New Orleans,"

address by Charles Barrett, Trans. from French by Miss Grace King, v.2, p.258.

Celebration of the Twelfth Year of the Louisiana Historical Quarterly, Editor's Chair, v.12, p.620.

Celeron, Jean Baptiste, Madame, see Langloisiere, Suzanne Piot de.

Cemetery, of Germantown settlers, v.24, p.433.

Cenas, ———, noted, v.24, p.776, 777.

Cenas, H. B., chairman Democratic meeting, v.25, p.1037.

Cenas School, v.30, p.873.

Cenotaph, in Lafayette Sq., N. O., honoring Clay, Calhoun and Webster, erection of, v.27, p.765; picture of, v.27, p.766; description of, v.27, p.767, 769.

Censorship, in New Orleans under Butler, v.24, p.502; in France, v.24, p.1024, 1029-1030, 1045, 1069.

Census, of La., 1785, in Bibliotheca Parsoniana, v.24, p.310.

Census, of New Orleans, v.22, p.648-649, 7th by De Bow, v.22, p.479-491.

"Census Tables of Louisiana, Early," Introduction by William Beer, Translation by J. K. Ditchey, v.13, p.205.

Centenary College, bulletin of, v.24, p.339; article about, v.24, p.339, 352; sketch of, v.24, p.338; historical sketch, v.31, p.123-124; Martindale teacher there, v.31, p.124; minutes of board meeting, v.31, p.125-128, 129; history, v.31, p.877-879; noted, v.32, p.777-780.

Centenary of Supreme Court of Louisiana, 1913, v.4, p.5; Invocation, Rev. J. D. Foulkes, S.J., v.4, p.7; Opening Address, Joseph W. Carroll, v.4, p.9; Address of Welcome, Gov. Luther E. Hall, v.4, p.12; The History of the Supreme Court of Louisiana, Henry Plauche Dart, v.4, p.14; The Jurisprudence of the Supreme Court of Louisiana, Charles Payne Fenner, v.4, p.71; The Louisiana Bar, T. C. W. Ellis, v.4, p.81; The Centennial Year, Joseph A. Breaux, v.4, p.106; Prayer, Rt. Rev. Davis Sessums, v.4, p.109; The Justices of the Supreme Court, William Kernan Dart, v.4, p.112.

Centennial-Bi, New Orleans, Medallion, Andre Lafargue, v.7, p.87.

Centennial-Semi, of the 14th Sept. 1874, v.7, p.570.

Centerville, La., noted, v.32, p.51, 71, 83.

"Centinela," ship in Aury expedition, v.24, p.628, 629, 632, 633, 634, 637.

Centralization, nature of, v.24, p.698.

Centreville, description of, v.24, p.41.

Cerre, Gabriel, noted, v.22, p.89.

Cesario's Garage, in Bogalusa, v.29, p.99.

Cession of East and West Florida by Treaty Between U.S. and Spain, v.2, p.154.

Cevallos, Ciriaco, noted, v.22, p.798, 803, 804.

Cevallos, Pedro, noted, v.22, p.804n.; memorial from DeClouet, v.22, p.805-818; noted, v.23, p.833.

Chaille, Dr. S. E., quoted on repeal of pharmacy legislation, v.26, p.340.

Chalaron, Dr. Frank J., assistant surgeon, v.26, p.795; replaced Archinard, v.26, p.824, 835; noted, v.33, p.414.

Chalmet, Delinos, noted, v.22, p.814.

Chalmette, Don Ignacio de, in command at B.R., v.28, p.698.

Chalmette, Favrot's successor at Baton Rouge, v.26, p.743.

Chalmette, obelisk marking site of Battle of N.O., v.28, p.329.

Chalmette, weak condition in 1862, v.24, p.454; silenced by Federal ships, v.24, p.457.

Chamberlain, Deacon Holbrook, philanthropist, v.25, p.783.

Chamberlain, Josephine, wife of E. John Ellis, v.29, p.713.

Chambers, Henry E., "Early Commercial Prestige of New Orleans," v.5, p.451; Review of his "Mississippi Valley Beginnings," v.7, p.672; In Memoriam, Editor's Chair, v.12, p.300.

Chambers, Josiah, on Wells, v.31, p.1005; noted, v.31, p.1017.

Chambers, Noble M., mayor of Crowley, put finances on current basis, v.27, p.1145; chairman Red Cross, v.27, p.1218.

Champagne, John Louis, v.28, p.841n.

Champ d'Aisle, agricultural enterprise, v.22, p.747-749; settlement of French refugees, v.23, p.788; Laffitte's plan to abolish, v.23, p.790-791.

"Champion No. 3," steamer, v.24, p.95.

"Champion No. 5," steamer, v.24, p.95.

Champion vs. Ames, tested constitutionality of law restricting interstate traffic of lottery tickets, v.22, p.1084-1085.

Champlin, Guy R., privateersman, v.22, p.1073-1076; v.23, p.773.

Champomier, P. A., cited on La. sugar, v.25, p.120-121.

Chance, S. W., noted, v.25, p.358.

Chanche, Father John Joseph, Bishop of Natchez, v.31, p.908, 913; noted, v.31, p.931, 938, 939.

"Changes in La. Agriculture, 1860-1880," by G. W. McGinty, v.18, p.407-429.

Chantalon, Augustin, sale of property to Livaudais, fils, v.21, p.674-676; case of, v.21, p.1006ff.

"Chaouachas Plantation, Documents Concerning Sale of," Heloise H. Cruzat, v.8, p.594.

Chapiron, James, petition of, v.23, p.374.

Chapman, Ed., Jr., La. midshipman, v.27, p.483.

Chapman, George, theatrical co. of in N.O., v.28, p.251.

Chapman, Robert, noted, v.23, p.409.

Chappuis, P. J., mayor of Crowley, sketch, v.27, p.1130, 1208.

"Charity Hospital at New Orleans, The: An Administrative and Financial History, 1736-1941," by Stella O'Conner, v.31, p.1-109.

Charity Hospital International Fair, v.31, p.81-82.

Charity Hospital, of La. in New Orleans, First in New Orleans, 1736, v.4, p.359; contract for first in La., v.18, p.280-281; established by Almonester, 1785, v.20, p.583-584; noted, v.22, p.99, 110; donation to, v.22, p.392; in Sp. New Orleans, v.22, p.680-682; register in Rudolph Matas Medical Library, v.24, p.334; noted, v.26, p.918; revenue from gambling house placed at disposal of, v.26, p.924; income from Lottery Co., v.28, p.1141; under the French, v.31, p.7-16; under the Spanish, v.31, p.16ff.; Almonester's hospital, v.31, p.21-35; struggle between city council and Almonester heirs, v.31, p.29-39; becomes state institution, v.31, p.46ff.; measures for revenues, v.31, p.48-50; Sisters of Charity arrive, v.31, p.52-53; new building (1832), v.31, p.54; ante-bellum years, v.31, p.55-59; service during Civil War, v.31, p.60-61; under military government, v.31, p.61-64; during reconstruction, v.31, p.64-68; nursing controversy, v.31, p.70-77; bequests to, v.31, p.80; drives to raise money, v.31, p.81-84; and Goldwater investigation, v.31, p.84-86; under Huey P. Long, v.31, p.86-93; construction of new building, v.31, p.94-95; under Long's henchmen, v.31, p.95-96; reforms of Sam Jones, v.31, p.96-99; bibliography, v.31, p.99-109; under Herbert, v.31, p.520.

Charity Hospital of St. Charles, Almonester's hospital, v.31, p.23-35.

Charivari, described, v.21, p.20.

Charles IV, reestablished Consejo de Estado, v.21, p.8.

Charles X, popularity of, v.24, p.1069, 1071.

"Charles Aloysius Luzenberg, 1805-1848; A History of Medicine in N.O. during the years 1830-1848," by A. E. Fossier, v.26, p.47-137.

"Charles Gayarre, A Biographical Sketch," by Grace King, v.33, p.159.

"Charles Gayarre, Louisiana's Literary Historian," by Wilford B. Yearns, Jr., v.33, p.255.

Charles, John, noted, v.23, p.29.

"Charles," reported captured by pirates, v.24, p.31-32.

Charlevoix, Father, visited B. R., v.28, p.62; attributes change in course of Miss. to human factor, v.28, p.71-72, 84.

"Charlotte Cushman's Apprenticeship in New Orleans," by Nellie Smither, v.31, p.973-980.

"Charlotte, Schooner, Marine Survey of 1777," by Laura L. Porteous, v.13, p.230.

Chase, Rev. Philander, Episcopal rector in N.O., v.21, p.824; v.22, p.436-447, 462-463, 472-473.

Chase, Salmon Portland, appoints collector of customs, N.O., v.23, p.1135; noted, v.23, p.1178, 1181; letter from G. S. Denison, v.23, p.1189; letter of G. S. Denison, v.23, p.1191, 1200; in Mobile, v.23, p.1224; counsel Moore vs. O'Reilly, v.31, p.471.

Chassaignac, Eugene, N.O. musician, v.31, p.132.

Chateaubriand, Francois Rene Auguste de, noted, v.24, p.991.

"Chatsworth," Murphy plantation, v.28, p.1131.

Chauveau, James, identified, v.21, p.785n.

Chauvin brothers, land concessions, v.21, p.224-225.

Chaves, Marquis de, noted, v.24, p.1025.

Chaville, de, engineer of early 18th century, v.29, p.559-560.

Chayton, Captain James, noted, v.24, p.362.

Cheaga, San Juan de, noted, v.22, p.934.

"Check List of Hist'l Records Survey and Survey of Fed'l Archives Publications for La.," by John C. L. Andreassen, v.27, p.613-623.

Chef Menteur, noted, v.26, p.742, 777.

Chelso, Vincent, noted, v.23, p.697.

"Chenal, Petition of Widow Donna Anna, 1773," by Laura L. Porteous, v.11, p.233.

Chenet, H. S., N.O. educator, v.30, p.878-879.

Chenier au Tigre, v.28, p.765, 811, 829, 830, 886.

Cheniere au Caminada, noted, v.24, p.23; v.28, p.884, 885.

Cherbonnier, Pierre, Louisiana educator, v.31, p.855.

Cherbonnier, Victor, comes to Louisiana, v.31, p.851.

Cherokee Indians, mentioned, v.21, p.54.

"Chervin, A Pioneer Epidemiologist," Wm. Colby Rucker, M.S., M.D., v.8, p.434.

Chester, Gov. Peter, complaints against, v.22, p.31-46.

Chestnut, Mary B., quoted, v.24, p.495.

Chetimaches Isles, v.28, p.785, 787.

Chevalier, Capt., ———, noted, v.22, p.1087.

"Chevalier de Pradel, The," by Geo. C. H. Kernion, v.12, p.238.

"Chevallier Bernard de Verges, Reminiscences of," George C. H. Kernion, v.7, p.56.

Chevallier, Jean, noted, v.24, p.612, 613.

Cheves, Langdon, noted, v.24, p.935, 1090.

Chevet, Moses, noted, v.23, p.29.

Chevet, Paul, noted, v.22, p.982; v.23, p.29.

Chevis, W. C., Foster's campaign manager, v.28, p.1224.

Chevis, Will, ed. "Rayne Sentinel," v.27, p.1185-1186.

Chew, Beverly, noted, v.22, p.449, 1080; report on piracy, v.22, p.766; and Wm. Mitchell, v.22, p.1054, 1055; and the Lafittes, v.23, p.771, 784, 788; letter to superior, v.23, p.776, 782; partner of Clark, v.27, p.19; named executor in the will of Clark, 1811, v.27, p.20, 21, 23, 30, 31, 32, 33, 45, 56, 65, 75-76; petition against, v.27, p.126, 127, 128, 141, 173; defendant in Myra Whitney's bill in equity in Circuit Ct. of U.S., v.27, p.180-183; charges against, v.27, p.184-185; filed demurrer, v.27, p.189, 190; Gaines vs., v.27, p.189-204; noted, v.27, p.206, 209, 213, 216, 246, 247, 249, 250, 251, 277, 278, 289, 290, 291; illegal sales of Clark estate, v.27, p.304-307, 310, 315; collector of Customs, N.O., v.28, p.753n.

Chiapas, material on, in Institute of Middle American Research, v.24, p.332.

Chicasaw Indians, in Grant Parish, v.23, p.1109, 1122.

Chicot, Auguste, noted, v.24, p.369, 370, 371.

Chief Justices of 1921-1922, (Editor's Chair), v.6, p.280.

Child, Sargent B., noted, v.24, p.308.

"Children of the Poor, The," quoted, v.24, p.180-181.

Chilton, Thomas, noted, v.24, p.1097.

Chinchuba, legend of, noted, v.24, p.750.

Chinn, Thomas Wither, and nullification, v.25, p.95; noted, v.25, p.1034; Whig Rep. to Cong. from La., sketch, v.28, p.942; and S. C. Ord. of Nullification, v.28, p.951; on West Feliciana Police Jury, v.30, p.54; noted, v.30, p.466.

Chisholm v. Georgia, noted, v.24, p.698, 708.

Chitty, George, noted, v.24, p.367, 371.

C. H. Murray and Company, lottery firm, v.31, p.718, 730.

Choate, Rufus, and 1833 tariff, v.25, p.100.

Choctaw Indians, in W. Fla. Rev., v.21, p.92; trade with French, v.23, p.10; boundary line in W. Fla., v.23, p.371; fight with Creeks, v.23, p.371-372, 375; treaty with, v.23, p.1004; in Grant Parish, v.23, p.1109, 1123, 1124; and the name, B.R., v.28, p.46-47; Houmas a tribe of, v.28, p.48.

"Choctaw of St. Tammany Parish, The," by David I. Bushnell, Jr., v.1, sec.1, p.11.

Choctaw Village, described by Cathcart, v.28, p.850-852.

Chol, Emile, N.O. musician, v.31, p.132.

Cholera, in Philadelphia, v.24, p.1168; fear of in New Orleans, v.24, p.1168-1169.

Chopin, Frederic, plans emmigration, v.31, p.856; advised to stay, v.31, p.857.

Chouteau, Auguste, description of house, v.21, p.340-341.

"Christ Church and General Butler," ed. by J. S. Kendall, v.23, p.1241-1257.

"Christ Church Lottery," noted, v.31, p.717.

Christian Doctrine Society, noted, v.25, p.365.

"Christianstadt," vessel of Swedish registry, v. 24, p.612.

Christie, ———, noted, v.22, p.46.

Christy, Col. William, and naturalization racket, v.31, p.682; prefers charges, v.31, p.683.

Christy, Lt. Arthur H., acting regimental adjutant, v.26, p.831; promoted, v.26, p.835.

Christy's Minstrels, v.30, p.133.
Christy, William, noted, v.22, p.466, 472; petition of, v.23, p.390.
"Chronicles of a Southern Family," by John Smith Kendall, v.29, p.277-295.
Chubbock, Rev. F. E. R., and Christ Church, v.23, p.1241, 1257.
Chun, J. H., Confed. soldier, v.26, p.954; noted, v.26, p.963.
Churches, in Carrollton, v.2, p.272-273; "Christ Church and Gen. Butler," v.23, p.1241-1257.
Church History, "Legislation and Litigation Affecting Title of St. Louis Cathedral," v.18, p.363-376.
Churchill, Thomas J., noted, v.24, p.88, 90, 91, 93.
Church Point, La., v.27, p.1121, 1163; cotton gins in, v.27, p.1168; Farmer's Bank and Trust Co. merged with that of Crowley, v.27, p.1171, 1215.
"Churchwardens, Veterans Versus," by Simone de la Souchere Delery, v.33, p.145-150.
Cienfuegos, Jose, Capt.-Gen. of Cuba, v.23, p.764; letter from P. Laffite, v.23, p.765; letter from L. Noeli, v.23, p.789-792; wary of Lafittes, v.23, p.808; superseded, v.23, p.816; wary of Toledo, v.23, p.829.
"Circulating Library of Ante-Bellum La.," by W. R. Patrick, v.23, p.131-140.
Cirilo, Fray de Barcelona, noted, v.22, p.98.
Citizens Bank Bill, noted, v.25, p.678.
Citizens Bank, noted. v.24, p.513; v.25, p.987, 989, 990, 992.
"City Belle," transport, v.24, p.96.
"Civil Code of Louisiana," law against mixed marriages, v.25, p.309-310, 370.
"Civil Procedure in Louisiana Under the Spanish Regime as Illustrated in Loppinot's Case, 1774," by Henry P. Dart, Translated by Laura L. Porteous, v.12, p.33.
"Civil War Diary of Willie Micajah Barrow, The," I, II, edited by W. H. Stephenson and E. A. Davis, v.17, p.436, 712.
Civil War, the 3rd Regiment La. Infantry at Shreveport, v.18, p.867-870; Shreveport the Confederate capital of La., v.18, p.863-871; Red River Campaign, v.19, p.150-195; Diary of a Federal Soldier in La., 1863, v.19, p.635-667; letters of J. P. Benjamin to A. D. Mann, v.20, p.738-793; New Orleans German Colony in, v.20, p.990-1015; conditions in La. and Texas during, v.23, p.1132ff.; documents in La. Hist. Assn. depository, v.24, p.315; Wickliffe's connection with, v.25, p.707; La.'s contribution to, v.26, p.1005-1043; conditions after, in La. and the South, v.26, p.1055-1062; effect of on trade in N.O., v.27, p.957; the lottery a means of reconstruction in La., v.27, p.969, 973-974; Hy. W. Allen's official report of conduct of Fed'l troops in W. La., v.27, p.1226-1228.
Claiborne Academy, v.30, p.812.
Claiborne, C. C., Jr., and the Const. Con. of 1844, v.25, p.1007ff., 1053.
Claiborne, Charles, noted, v.23, p.193.
Claiborne-Clark duel, noted, v.24, p.773.
Claiborne, Colonel Ferdinand Leigh, letter from Wm. C.C. Claiborne to, v.24, p.730.
"Claiborne, Governor, and the Public School System of the Territorial Government of Louisiana," by Stewart Grayson Noble, v.11, p.535.
Claiborne, Henry Ballatin, Confed. naval officer, v.27, p.481.
Claiborne Parish, in 1860, v.21, p.1183-1186; Populist rep. from, v.26, p.1109.
Claiborne, Richard, identified, v.24, p.729; judge in Rapides Parish, v.24, p.730, 741; desire for Judgeship in Concordia Parish, v.24, p.730-731; law office in New Orleans, v.24, p.732; patent on "duckfoot" paddle, v.24, p.733; work on steam navigation, v.24, p.741-742.
Claiborne, William Charles Cole, and W. Fla. Rev., v.21, p.79, 763-764; letter to from Skipwith, v.21, p.149-50; taking of W. Florida, v.21, p.159, 162-164; criticism of by Skipwith, v.21, p.171; sketch, v.21, p.192n.; letter from Skipwith, v.21, p.201-202; order to militia in N.O., v.21, p.372-374; and Andrew Jackson in N.O., v.21, p.367ff.; Battle of N.O., v.21, p.407n.; letter to Jackson, v.21, p.408n.; and Elisha Bowman, v.22, p.430; and Gutierrez, v.22, p.721-724; and Barataria, v.22, p.756-758, 1032; and New Spain, v.22, p.786-788; election of, v.22, p.808, 809-810; and La. purchase, v.23, p.80; criticism of, v.23, p.152-158; duel with D. Clark, v.23, p.160-161; noted, v.23, p.440, 1082n.; and Barataria pirates, v.23, p.749; reward for Jean Lafitte, v.24, p.18-19; refused Lafitte's aid, v.24, p.20; documents in Bibliotheca Parsoniana, v.24, p.311; letters in La. State Museum, v.24, p.319; collection in L.S.U. Archives, v.24, p.341; noted, v.24, p.729, 734; letter to Secretary of State

Monroe, v.24, p.732; and Jones-Gurley duel, v.24, p.773-781; estimate on La. sugar, v.25, p.26, 153, 295, 300, 303, 328; Gov. of La., v.25, p.660, 662; refused Sp. rights of importation, v.25, p.940-941; claims West Florida, v.25, p.952, 982; on Charity Hospital Board, 1836, v.26, p.58; noted, v.27, p.28; Clark's duel with, v.27, p.57, 65; the transfer of La. to the U.S., v.27, p.329; took over W. Fla. Rep., v.28, p.723; claimed W. Fla. as part of Ter. of Orleans, v.28, p.944; rep. U.S. in transfer of La., v.28, p.1018; and the neutral ground between Tex. and La., v.28, p.1031, 1036, 1037, 1045, 1065; appeal to for protection of slaves escaping into neutral ground, v.28, p.1070; noted, v.28, p.1072, 1073, 1082; appointed commissioner to receive Louisiana, v.31, p.270; instructions concerning Louisiana transfer, v.31, p.273-281; letter to Jefferson, v.31, p.274, 277; provisional governor of Orleans, v.31, p.283; noted, v.31, p.288, 306, 313; and Clark, v.31, p.314, 315, 340; and Dawson, v.31, p.323-324, 334, 342; candidate for Governor of Orleans, v.31, p.353-391; early life, v.31, p.353-354; reputation, v.31, p.355; opposition to administration, v.13, p.357, 359-360, 366-368; appointed governor, v.31, p.361; and N.O. Charity Hospital, v.31, p.31, 33, 39-40; noted, v.33, p.228.

Claims against French government, discussed by Brown, v.24, p.938-939, 942, 943, 945-946, 961, 962, 964, 972, 977, 980-981, 983, 984-985, 988, 990, 1022-1024, 1033-1034, 1042-1043, 1054-1055, 1061-1062, 1081, 1090, 1095-1096, 1106, 1109, 1112, 1116, 1124, 1128, 1130ff., 1139.

Claire, Gabriel Fuselier de la, Sp. Militia Comdt., v.25, p.936.

Clapp, Rev. Theodore, Presbyterian preacher in N.O., v.21, p.823, 824, 826; pastor in N.O., v.22, p.451; noted, v.25, p.1083; v.26, p.76; inauguration of Gov. Isaac Johnson, v.28, p.963; noted, v.33, p.70, 145.

Clare, Aburey, Gottschalk's son, v.31, p.867, 868.

Clare, Ada, and Gottschalk, v.31, p.867-868.

Clark, ———, noted, v.23, p.402.

Clark, Charles, noted, v.24, p.105, 113.

Clark-Claiborne duel, noted, v.24, p.773.

Clark, C. W., on N.O. "Item," v.31, p.785.

Clark, Daniel, U.S. Consul in New Orleans, v.20, p.8; member of Congress, v.20, p.8; duel with Claiborne, v.20, p.8; controversy with Wilkinson, v.20, p.8; wills of, 1811 and 1813, v.20, p.16; and W. Fla. Rev., v.21, p.81-82; owns one fourth of Maison Rouge Grant, v.21, p.166; noted, v.22, p.317, 810; and W. Fla. Assembly, v.22, p.943; treas. W. Fla. Assembly, 1769, v.23, p.74, 76; and Jean Lafitte, v.24, p.15; documents in Bibliotheca Parsoniana, v.24, p.311; noted, v.25, p.15, 18; father of Myra, v.27, p.7, 9; will of, v.27, p.12-13; sketch of, v.27, p.18-23; first delegate from Territory of Orleans to Cong., v.27, p.19, 57; will of May, 1811, v.27, p.20-23; his questioned paternity of Caroline and Myra, v.27, p.25; letter from Desgrange, v.27, p.26-29; and Caroline's birth, v.27, p.28-40; his alleged marriage to Zulime, v.27, p.41-43; circumstances of Myra Clark's birth, v.27, p.43-44; places property in trust for Myra, v.27, p.45-46, 47; last will, v.27, p.48; further evidence regarding marriage to Zulime, v.27, p.53-62, 77-82, 88, 115-133; De la Croix's evidence in re last will, v.27, p.63-64; further evidence in re birth of Myra, v.27, p.64-68, 68-72, 72-76, 91, 97, 99, 100, 103, 104, 105, 106, 107, 111, 112, 114; conflicting evidence, v.27, p.133-178, 191-195, 206; decreed legally married to Zulime in Patterson Case, v.27, p.207, 210, 211; decision reversed, v.27, p.213-215; dissenting opinion, v.27, p.226-240; will of 1813 probated, v.27, p.244-245, 246, 247-248, 249, 250, 251; decision in case of Gaines vs. Hennen regarding validity of marriage, v.27, p.252-253, 255, 259, 261, 262, 267-273, 274, 275, 279-288; estate of, v.27, p.289-293; attempt to revoke probation of will of 1813, v.27, p.293-304; sales of estate of, legal and illegal, v.27, p.304-314, 317, 321, 322, 938; noted, v.28, p.843n.; leads Creole move for statehood, v.31, p.287; early life, v.31, p.310; appointed U.S. Consul, v.31, p.311; impressions of, v.31, p.311-313; opposes Claiborne, v.31, p.313-315; death, v.31, p.316; noted, v.31, p.270, 276, 279, 340, 342, 377, 378-379; duel with Claiborne, v.23, p.384; buys land in Concordia, v.23, p.1091.

Clark, George, noted, v.23, p.204.

Clark, George Rogers, expedition of, v.21, p.34; noted, v.22, p.86, 87, 91.

Clark, John, petition of, v.23, p.383.
Clark, J. S., Pres. S. Univ., 1914, v.25, p.772, 807.
Clark, Mary, mother of Daniel, v.27, p.20, 36, 48, 162-163, 172, 246, 247, 250, 291, 312, 316.
Clark, Robert T., Jr., "The German Liberals in N.O., 1840-1860," v.20, p.137-151; "The New Orleans German Colony in the Civil War," v.20, p.990-1015; "Reconstruction and the N.O. German Colony," v.23, p.501-524.
Clark, Robert T., Sr., "A Bavarian Organist Comes to New Orleans," v.29, p.14-42.
Clark, R. T., clerk of court, Acadia, v.27, p.1127, 1171.
Clark, T. A., noted, v.23, p.1095.
Clark, Waters, noted, v.22, p.433, 435.
Classical and Commercial Institute, v.30, p.878.
"Class Struggle in La.," by R. W. Shugg, rev'd by E. A. Davis, v.23, p.887-888.
Claudel, Calvin A., "Tombs of Historical Interest in the Saint Bernard Cemetery," v.24, p.354-359.
Clausel, Gen., noted, v.23, p.787.
Clay, Clement C., Jr., Confederate secret agent, v.29, p.1247, 1249, 1250.
Clay, Henry, noted, v.23, p.1046n.; guest of New Eng. Soc., v.23, p.1048; noted, v.24, p.736; letters from James Brown, 1804-1835, v.24, p.921-1177; La. supporters, 1822, v.24, p.936; supporter of John Quincy Adams, v.24, p.941; Secretary of State, v.24, p.942ff.; goods bought in Paris by Browns, v.24, p.945, 966, 972, 974, 1042, 1048, 1057, 1060-1061, 1068, 1076, 1117, 1126-1127; personal sorrow, v.24, p.963, 965, 1011; affair with Randolph, v.24, p.999, 1001, 1002; denial of charge made by Jackson, v.24, p.1063; admonitions from Brown on health and temper, v.24, p.944, 963, 965, 979-980, 989, 994, 1001-1002, 1003, 1004, 1007, 1008, 1018, 1020-1021, 1040, 1041, 1042, 1044-1045, 1052, 1053, 1059-1060, 1063, 1064, 1075, 1079, 1088, 1099, 1100, 1106, 1110, 1114-1116, 1133-1134, 1158, 1167; request for loan from Brown, v.24, p.1145, 1146; honored on trip to New Orleans, v.24, p.1147; executor of Mrs. James Brown's will, v.24, p.1150; plans to visit New Orleans, v.24, p.1150, 1153; political fortunes of, v.24, p.1158, 1159-1160; candidate for President, v.24, p.1162; political views of, v.24, p.1166; travel accident, v.24, p.1170; noted, v.25, p.29, 34, 43, 45, 48, 63, 87, 88, 91, 96, 119, 125, 126; and 1816 Tariff, v.25, p.32; and 1824 Tariff Bill, v.25, p.39; in La., 1830, v.25, p.58-59; to J. S. Johnston, v.25, p.58-59, 59-60; supporters of, in La., v.25, p.60; in New Orleans, 1831, v.25, p.74, 114; and 1833 compromise tariff, v.25, p.101-102, 103, 104, 106, 107; plan for 1841, v.25, p.115-116; in 1844 election, v.25, p.126-127, 673, 1003, 1005; statue of in N.O., v.27, p.717; a "Great American," v.27, p.717-718; early life, v.27, p.718-719; study of law, v.27, p.720; marriage, v.27, p.720; children, v.27, p.721; assistance to La. sugar planters, v.27, p.721; his services as Congressman from Ky., v.27, p.721-722; signs Treaty of Ghent, v.27, p.722; Sec. of State, v.27, p.722; cand. for pres., v.27, p.722-723; the Plaquemines Fraud, v.27, p.723-725; final effort made to nominate as pres., v.27, p.725, 726; duels of, v.27, p.727-728; the Compromise Tariff, 1833, v.27, p.728; description of, v.27, p.729-732; reasons for visits to N.O., v.27, p.732-733; attack on Jackson, v.27, p.733-734; enmity to Jackson reflected in treatment in N.O., 1819, v.27, p.734; his speech of May, 1819, in N.O., v.27, p.734; second visit to N.O., 1831, v.27, p.735-736; influence of in senatorial election, v.27, p.735-736; second defeat for pres., v.27, p.736; third return to N.O., 1842, v.27, p.736; N.O.'s reception of, 1842, v.27, p.737-739; guest of honor of N. Eng. Society of N.O., v.27, p.740; appearance in the Sup. Court in N.O., v.27, p.742-745; trips to Mobile, v.27, p.745, 750; Clay Ball, v.27, p.745-747; fourth visit to N.O., 1843, v.27, p.747; social activities, v.27, p.748; trip to Natchez, v.27, p.749; reception of friends, v.27, p.749-750; third defeat for pres., v.27, p.750-751; fifth visit to N.O., v.27, p.751; guest of honor of N. Eng. Soc. of N.O., v.27, p.751-754; address in behalf of Irish, v.27, p.755; final visit to N.O., v.27, p.756; Whigs fail to nominate, v.27, p.757; participates in laying of cornerstone of Customhouse, v.27, p. 760; death of, v.27, p.761-762; N.O. forms Clay monument Assoc., v.27, p.764; Parmele gives reasons for honoring Clay, v.27, p.764-765; joint funeral ceremony, v.27, p.765-769; erection of statue and description, v.27, p.769-775; criticism of statue, v.27, p.775-776; But-

ler's inscription on statue, v.27, p.777, 778; new cornerstone laid, v.27, p.778-779; square and avenue in N.O. named after, v.27, p.779; bibl., v.27, p.780-782; noted, v.32, p.272.

Clay, Henry, Jr., noted, v.24, p.1119, 1136, 1152; marriage of, v.24, p.1167.

Clay, John, noted, v.24, p.924; brother of Henry, a merchant in N.O., v.27, p.733.

Clay, Mrs. Henry, sister of Mrs. James Brown, v.24, p.923, 925, 927, 928, 942, 948, 969, 972, 979, 980, 982, 985, 990, 994, 996, 1000, 1002, 1003, 1007, 1010, 1014, 1020, 1024, 1028, 1030, 1034, 1037, 1038, 1039, 1042, 1047, 1048, 1052, 1057, 1059, 1060, 1061, 1068, 1069, 1075, 1079, 1081, 1083, 1085, 1088, 1091, 1119, 1125, 1126, 1136, 1142, 1145, 1147, 1148, 1153, 1154, 1161, 1162, 1164, 1165, 1166, 1167, 1170, 1174, 1176.

Clayton, —————, noted, v.23, p.422.

Clayton, Joe, Confed. soldier, v.26, p.952; noted, v.26, p.954, 970.

Clayton, Thomas A., Populist campaign manager, v.26, p.1082; leader People's Party in La., v.27, p.1092; Populist, v.28, p.1160.

Clegg, Baxter, pres. Homer College, v.30, p.813-814; noted, v.30, p.816, 966.

Clements, Joseph, noted, v.24, p.367.

Clerical problem, in France, v.24, p.1122.

Cleveland, Grover, noted, v.26, p.1084; carried La., 1892, v.26, p.1090; noted, v.26, p.1094, 1095, 1098; visited Orange Island, v.26, p.1158, 1165.

Clifton, Edward, noted, v.23, p.368.

Clifton, William, noted, v.23, p.74; member of W. Fla. Council, v.23, p.353ff.

Clinton and Port Hudson Railroad, sketch of, v.30, p.1123-1125.

Clinton, Charles, state auditor nominee, v.29, p.402, 403; noted, v.29, p.411, 450; tried for mismanagement of funds and resigns as auditor, v.29, p.448, 456, 457, 470-471; buying of warrants, v.29, p.464-465, 466; candidate for state auditor, v.31, p.536; impeached, v.31, p.703; civil suit instituted, v.31, p.704; named in Kellogg impeachment, v.31, p.713, 714.

Clinton, De Witt, noted, v.24, p.1018; N.Y. support of, v.24, p.1004; coalition with Van Buren, v.24, p.1050.

Clinton Female Academy, historical sketch of, v.30, p.822-824.

Clinton Female Seminary, v.30, p.825.

Clintons, overthrow by Robert R. Livingston in N.Y. ratifying convention, v.24, p.700.

"Clinton, War Times in and Around," by Annie Sanderson Kilbourne, v.13, p.64.

Clird, —————, noted, v.23, p.378.

Cloutierville, La., noted, v.24, p.94, 99; noted, v.25, p.362.

"Clovelly Farms," reclamation project, v.30, p.664, fig.2; description of, v.30, p.696-699; noted, v.30, p.685, 705.

Coates' Bluff, noted, v.25, p.400.

Cobbs, Jacob, noted, v.23, p.420.

Cochran and Rhea, merchants near St. Francisville, v.21, p.76.

Cochrane, Admiral, noted, v.23, p.434.

Cochrane, Lord, noted, v.24, p.647, 649, 658, 674, 956, 1009; at Cagliari, v,24, p.1016.

Cocks, Reginald S., (The Fiction of Grace King), v.6, p.353.

Code, Livingston's Civil and Criminal, of La., v.19, p.342-357.

"Code Noir," of O'Reilly, v.24, p.310; 1724, v.25, p.302; on status of free Negroes, v.25, p.315.

Codrington, Sir Edward, noted, v.24, p.1070.

Coes, George H., N.O. minstrel, v.30, p.137.

Coffee, importation of, v.22, p.669; production of in West Indies, v.24, p.1158.

Cohen, M. M., noted, v.22, p.1143; noted, v.23, p.1095; tried on charge of conspiracy to assassinate Kellogg, v.29, p.422.

Cohen, S., furniture store in Bogalusa, v.29, p.99, 100.

Cohn, Joseph, noted, v.23, p.502.

Cohn, Solomon, noted, v.22, p.200.

Coignard, Louis, noted, v.22, p.94.

Coiron, Jean Joseph, noted, v.23, p.1016n.

"Col. A. P. Kouns," steamer, picture of, v.25, p.432.

Cold Harbor, battle, noted, v.24, p.66.

Cole, Fred, "Annual Meeting of Southern Hist'l Ass'n to be Held in N.O.," v.21, p.959-964.

Cole, H. C., chosen city Health Officer of Bogalusa, v.29, p.114.

Coleman College, history of, v.25, p.787.

Coleman, F. J., engineer of Great Southern Lumber Co., v.29, p.91.

Coleman, H. Dudley, Rep. Lotteryite cand. for Lt.-Gov., v.28, p.1159.

Coleman, Jas. David, Anti-Lottery League Ex. Com., v.27, p.1056-1060.

Coleman, John, N.O. newspaperman, v.33, p.423.

Coleman, O. J., Negro, founded college, v.25, p.787.

Coleman, Rev., ———, noted, v.22, p.1019.

Colfax, La., located, v.23, p.1107; noted, v.25, p.397; race riot, v.29, p.419-420.

"Colfax Riot of April, 1873," by Manie White Johnson, B.A., v.13, p.391.

Colignon, Professor, N.O. musician, v.31, p.138-139.

"Collection of La. Confed. Letters, A," ed. by Frank E. Vandiver, v.26, p.937-974.

College, Centenary, v.32, p.777-780.

College of Immaculate Conception, v.30, p.944.

College of Louisiana, noted, v.25, p.1042; becomes Centenary College of Louisiana, v.31, p.878.

"College of Louisiana Lottery," v.31, p.717.

College of New Orleans, noted, v.25, p.1041.

College of Orleans, Lakanal president, v.31, p.555; brief sketch, v.31, p.556.

College of Rapides, noted, v.24, p.735.

Collegiate Institute, sketch of, v.30, p.774-775.

Colles, James, noted, v.22, p.472.

Collett, Joe, of Bogalusa, v.29, p.92.

Collins, Benjamin, naval agent for W. Fla., v.21, p.138.

Collins, Bridget, noted, v.23, p.391.

Collins, Joseph, and W. Fla. Rev., v.21, p.761n.

Collins, Robert, noted, v.22, p.318, 950, 952, 962.

Collins, T. W., noted, v.23, p.472.

Collins, William, noted, v.23, p.33.

Collom, C. H., Confed. soldier, v.26, p.954.

Collot, General, "Reconnoitering Trip Down Mississippi and His Arrest in New Orleans, 1796," by Heloise Hulse Cruzat, v.1, p.303; "Description of De Bore's Sugar House by," Trans. of, v.1, p.327; "Documents Bearing on the Arrest of," Trans. of, v.1, p.321; description of fortifications of N.O., v.26, p.745-747; description of Fort San Felipe, v.26, p.749-750; noted, v.26, p.752.

Collot, George Victor, arrest of, v.22, p.91, 92.

Collum, E. North, noted, v.31, p.1002; on Wells, v.31, p.1006.

Colombia, Bullard's speech concerning, v.23, p.1008-1010.

Colomb, R. W., "How the Louisiana Purchase was Financed," v.12, p.189; Translated by: "Dufour's Local Sketches, 1847," I, II, III, v.14, p.208, 393, 533; Translated by: "Lafayette's Visit to Baton Rouge, April, 1825," v.14, p.178; Translated by: "Dufour's Local Sketches, 1847," IV, V (Conclusion), v.15, p.78, 268.

"Colonial Forts of La.," by H. Mortimer Favrot, v.26, p.722-754.

"Colonial Louisiana, Education in," by Stuart G. Noble, v.32, p.759.

Colonization, Project of Vilemont, 1795, v.21, p.57-63.

Colson, Gille, noted, v.24, p.6.

Columbia, La., in 1860, v.21, p.1200-1201.

Columbian Telegraph, Zook invention used by O'Reilly, v.31, p.458, 462.

"Columbia," steamer, picture of, v.25, p.433.

Colvin, John J., Sr., "A New York Yankee in New Orleans, September 14, 1874," v.3, p.502.

"Col. Wood's Report to Gov. Foster," general content of, v.26, p.784; copy of, v.26, p.810-841.

Combs, Leslie, letter from, v.24, p.1162.

Comeau, Brother Alfonso, C.S.C., "A Study of the Trustee Problem in the St. Louis Cathedral Church in New Orleans, Louisiana, 1842-1844," v.31, p.897-972.

Comision reservado, great stroke of P. Laffite, v.23, p.766.

Comite River, grants on, v.22, p.35.

"Commerce and Agriculture of Louisiana, 1720-1766, Historical Notes On," by Charles Gayarre, v.2, p.286.

"Commerce of Louisiana During the French Regime, 1699-1763," by N. M. Miller Surrey, Ph.D., Columbia University, Critique by Grace King, v.5, p.19.

Commerce, early in La., v.18, p.287-288; location of Ms. material on Spanish Colonial period, v.21, p.13ff.; Mather and Panton granted trading privileges, v.21, p.13; freedom of trade granted La., v.21, p.20, 26; trade of Fla., v.21, p.27; fur trade on Miss. River, 1795, v.21, p.69ff.; trade with New Spain, v.21, p.362-366; trade in Gulf of Mexico, 1745; v.21, p.631-635; suit in re, v.21, p.1012; instructions given British government of W. Fla., v.21, p.1044ff.; duties in W.

Fla., 1769, v.23, p.61; right of deposit at N.O., v.23, p.79; debts of French in W. Fla. to N.O. merchants, 1769, v.23, p.393; conditions in N.O., 1865, v.23, p.1220; difficulties between France and the U.S., v.24, p.1130ff.

Commercial Exchange, 1851 and railroad movement, v.23, p.200.

Commercial opportunities, for son of Clay, v.24, p.1159.

Commissioner of Public Lands, office established, v.28, p.300; abolished, v.28, p.301.

Commissions by executive, Edward Livingston opposed to, v.24, p.713.

Committee of Enrollment, established first public schools in La., 1863, v.25, p.738.

Committee of One Hundred, group of Fusionists, v.27, p.565, 568.

Committee of Public Safety, v.25, p.212; organized in N.O. for its defense, v.26, p.1018; organized for the defense of the Confederacy west of the Miss., v.26, p.1032; in N.O., 1862, published list of notes thought to be "good" money, v.27, p.509.

Committee of Thirty-Four, raised flag of U.S. over N.O., June 7, 1862, v.27, p.518.

Committee of Two Hundred, Fusionist groups opposing Pinchback, v.27, p.572.

Committee on Banks and Banking, Wickliffe member of, v.25, p.676-677, 678.

Committee on Federal Relations, Wickliffe member of, v.25, p.676.

Committee on Internal Improvements, appointed, v.30, p.28; made joint committee, v.30, p.30; reports of, v.30, p.37; noted, v.30, p.42, 51.

Committee on Public Education, Wickliffe chairman of, v.25, p.675, 676, 677.

"Commodore Aury," by Stanley Faye, v.24, p.611-697.

Common Council of New Orleans, v.25, p.354.

Community property, articles of Custom of Paris, v.21, p.1003-1004.

Compact government, Edward Livingston theory of, v.24, p.704.

Compact theory of union, noted, v.24, p.706.

Compagnie des Indes, and the Miss. Bubble, v.26, p.651-663; bankrupt, v.26, p.663-664; colonies at Ark. post, v.26, p.665-672; gave up charter, v.26, p.672; noted, v.26, p.688, 732.

Company of the Indies, ship lists of passengers leaving France for La., 1718-1724, v.21, p.965-978; papers of in Bibliotheca Parsoniana, v.24, p.310; papers in La. State Museum depository, v.24, p.316; treaty with Ursuline nuns in Ursuline College Museum, v.24, p.335; and N.O. Charity Hospital, v.31, p.8.

"Company of the West, The," 1717-1732, by Henry Plauche Dart, v.2, p.85; storekeeper and cashier of, v.21, p.982.

Compromise of 1850, in La., v.23, p.189; finality of, v.23, p.1089; Soule's opposition to, v.25, p.1116-1117.

"Comrade," People's Party paper, v.26, p.1077; quoted, v.26, p.1080; ownership, v.26, p.1094.

Comstock, John Henry, Confed. naval officer, v.27, p.480, 481-482, 483.

Comstock, William Van, Confed. naval officer, v.27, p.480, 481, 482-483, 484.

"Comte de Maurepas," attacked by pirates, v.24, p.9-10.

Comyn, Valens Stephen, noted, v.22, p.991; and W. Fla. Assembly, v.23, p.5ff.; noted, v.23, p.357, 368; petition of, v.23, p.367, 382; election of, v.23, p.377.

"Concerning the Loyalty of Slaves in North Louisiana in 1863, letters from John H. Ransdell to Governor Thomas O. Moore, dated 1863," Introduction by G. P. Whittington, v.14, p.487.

"Concession of Ste. Catherine at the Natchez," Trans. from French by Heloise H. Cruzat, v.2, p.164.

Concessions, Book of: Documents Concerning Bienville's Lands in Louisiana, v.11, p.89, 209, 463; Jonchere Concession, (The Distribution of Land in Louisiana by the Company of the Indies), v.11, p.553.

Concession at Natchez, Heloise H. Cruzat, v.8, p.389.

Concha, Capt.-Gen. ———, noted, v.22, p.1149.

Concordia Parish, Louisiana, History of, by Robert Dabney Calhoun, I, II, III, IV, v.15, p.44, 214, 428, 618; V, VI, VII, VIII, v.16, p.92, 309, 454, 598; IX (Conclusion), v.17, p.96; in 1860, v.21, p.1207-1211; suit over land by heirs of Gayoso, v.23, p.1090-1093; collection in L.S.U. Archives, v.24, p.341.

Concordia, Spanish post, v.25, p.6, 12, 15; Parish of, v.25, p.120, 397.

Concord Institute, v.30, p.923.

"Concurrent" majority, Calhoun theory of, v.24, p.717.
Confederacy, La. adopts constitution of, v.26, p.1003-1004; La.'s contribution to, v.26, p.1005-1043 passim.
"Confederate Congress, Debates in First" (Editor's Chair), v.6, p.480.
"Confederate Die for the Coinage of Silver Half Dollars, The., by W. O. Hart and Dr. Y. R. LeMonnier, v.5, p.505.
Confederate Memorial Building, erection of, v.27, p.1025-1026.
Confederate Military Records, in La. State Museum, v.24, p.319.
Confederate Organizations Collection, in La. Hist. Assn's depository, v.24, p.315.
Conference at Milan, noted, v.24, p.343.
Confiscation Act, its effect in N. O., v.27, p.514-515, 516.
Confiscation of property, by Butler in New Orleans, v.24, p.501.
Congregation of the Sisters of the Holy Family, v.25, p.363, 731.
"Congreso Mexicano" (formerly "Calypso"), v.24, p.643, 644, 646, 647, 648, 652, 653, 654, 656, 658, 662, 663, 680, 687, 690.
"Congressional Library, Louisiana Data Recently Acquired By," by William Beer, v.1, sec.1, p.116.
Conichi Ranch, Turner's advance to, v.28, p.1032ff., 1036.
Conkling, Roscoe, noted, v.24, p.116.
Connecticut, Fundamental Orders of, v.24, p.701.
Connell, John, noted, v.24, p.975, 1094.
Conrad, Charles M., noted, v.23, p.1079, 1083; noted, v.24, p.441; and nullification, v.25, p.91; and tariff, v.25, p.116, 117, 119; disputed election of, v.25, p.1009; noted, v.25, p.1007, 1011ff.; La. delegate to conv. of seceding states, v.26, p.1002; noted, v.28, p.821n.
Conrad, Frederick, sketch, v.28, p.762n., 821n.
Conrad, N., on Charity Hospital Board, 1836, v.26, p.58.
Conrad, Paul, succeeded Dauphin as pres. La. Lottery Co., 1890, v.27, p.1014; agreed to abide by Postal Law, v.27, p.1083; transfers business of Lottery Co. to Honduras, v.27, p.1098; pres. of La. Lottery, v.31, p.783.
Conrey, Peter, noted, v.23, p.200, 212, 214.
Conscription Act of April 16, 1862, v.24, p.69.

Consejo de Estado, creation of, v.21, p.8.
Conshatta massacre, v.18, p.671-682.
Considine, John, incorporator of La. Lottery, v.27, p.975.
Consolidated Association of Planters of La., collection in L.S.U. Archives, v.24, p.341.
Consolidated government, Edward Livingston theory of, v.24, p.704.
Constantine, Emperor, noted, v.24, p.980, 982, 983, 986.
"Constitucion," noted, v.24, p.620, 625, 626, 642.
Constitutional Convention of La., in 1844-45, v.19, p.980-981; of 1852, v.19, p.992; first, 1812, and the division of N. O., v.25, p.983; noted, v.25, p.1006; of 1844, v.25, p.1005-1036; meeting in Jackson, v.25, p.1006-1010; reassembled in N .O., v.25, p.1010; discussion of term of residence for member of leg., v.25, p.1011-1012; right of suffrage, v.25, p.1012-1015; qualifications for governor, v.25, p.1015, 1016-1021; on apportionment or representation, v.25, p.1021-1027; on amending the const., v.25, p.1027-1028; judiciary reform, v.25, p.1028-1033; education, v.25, p.1033-1034; minor provisions, v.25, p.1034-1035; adjournment, v.25, p.1035; ratification, v.25, p.1035-1036; in 1879, v.32, p.667-684.
Constitutionality, power of a state to decide, v.24, p.720.
"Constitutional" majority, Calhoun theory of. v.24, p.717.
Constitution, controversies over, v.24, p.698-699, 701-702; of 1845 supported by Bullard, v.23, p.1086-1087; of 1864, Lincoln's opinion, v.32, p.1212; of 1864, v.24, p.114; of 1868, on Negro education, v.25, p.753.
Constitution of the Confederate States of America, submitted to La. convention, 1861, v.26, p.1003-1004.
"Constitution of the West Florida Republic," ed. by James A. Padgett, v.20, p.881-894.
"Constitutions of Louisiana With Some Observations on the Constitutional Convention of 1921," by W. O. Hart, v.3, p.570.
Consulado, of Havana, v.24, p.637.
"Consuls, Jurisdiction of the, Tribunals of Criminal Jurisdiction in Ancient Rome," by Charles Gayarre, v.33, p.209-210.
"Contemporary English View of Trade at

Close of French Dominion," by William Beer, v.6, p.221.

"Contest for Ecclesiastical Supremacy in the Mississippi Valley, 1763-1803," by Clarence Wyatt Bispham, v.1, sec.3, p.154.

Contracting estimate of cost of 18th century house in N. O. built by Du Breiul, v.18, p.281-283.

"Contract to Build a Ship in New Orleans, 1769," Translated by Laura L. Porteous, v.9, p.593.

"Controversy on Lafitte's Biography, The," by Gaspar Cusachs, v.3, p.100.

Conturie, Amedie, conflict with Butler, v.24, p.512-514.

Convention, Constitutional, 1879, v.32, p.667-684.

Convention of 1822, noted, v.24, p.964, 1068; controversies over, v.24, p.1130ff.

Conventions, Railroad, Monticello, Miss., 1849, v.23, p.198; Aberdeen, Miss., 1852, v.23, p.228; N. O., 1850, 1851 and 1852, v.23, p.199, 202, 203, 219, 220, 221-223.

Convent of Presentation, v.30, p.938-939.

Convent of St. Michael, noted, v.21, p.1120.

Converse, W. P., noted, v.23, p.226.

Conway, Maggie, first teacher in Crowley, v.27, p.1175.

Conway, Maurice, noted, v.23, p.391.

Conway, Patrick, noted, v.23, p.391.

Conway, Rev. T. W., head of "Bureau of Free Labor," v.32, p.157, 160, 161, 162, 165, 166, 176, 179, 193, 212, 213.

Conway, T. W., noted, v.25, p.741; state supt. of ed., 1869, v.25, p.745, 753-754, 758, 761, 764.

Cook, David T. W., sketch, v.21, p.96n.; and W. Fla. Rev., v.21, p.722n.

Cook, Dr. G. A. M., cand. for Supt. of Ed., first ticket, 1896, v.26, p.1101; on second Populist ticket, v.26, p.1102; cand. for supt. of ed., v.28, p.1176, 1177.

Cook, Jas. V., Confed. naval surgeon, v.27, p.486.

Cook, John F., noted, v.25, p.365, 735.

Cook, Sarah (see Smith, Sarah Cook), wife of Jedediah Smith, v.29, p.285.

Cooley, Dr. E., appeal for protection of slaves, v.28, p.1070.

Cooley, Lt. Charles, noted, v.26, p.836.

Cooley, W. H., opponent of Civil Rights Articles of Const., v.27, p.534.

"Co-operationists," noted, v.24, p.437; proposed cooperation of slave-holding states rather than secession, v.26, p.998.

Cooper, Capt. Geo. A., commander Co. D, under Wood, v.26, p.791.

Cooper, Dick, Confed. soldier, v.26, p.964.

Cooper, Morgan, engineer of Gulf, Mobile and Ohio Railroad, v.29, p.102.

Cooper, William, identified, v.21, p.187n.; and W. Fla. Rev., v.21, p.688n.

Copeland, Edward B., noted, v.23, p.561.

Copeland, Fayette, "Kendall of the Picayune," revd., v.26, p.1168-1170; "The New Orleans Press and the Reconstruction," v.30, p.149-339.

Coppell, ———, British vice consul at N. O., v.23, p.1240.

Coquet, M., proprietor of the St. Philip Theatre, v.28, p.91.

"Coquette," privateer, v.23, p.433.

Corbin, Henry, secretary to Pinchback, v.27, p.555.

Corcoran, Denis, manager "Daily Delta," v.30, p.296-298.

Cordero, Antonio, ordered to comd. Tex., v.28, p.1029; his attempts to enforce claims, v.28, p.1029ff.; neutral ground agreement, v.28, p.1040-1041; boundary, v.28, p.1046; gov. of Tex., conference with Indians, v.28, p.1085; council to discuss problem of Indian trade, v.28, p.1088.

Cordill, C. C., pro-lottery senator, v.28, p.1145.

Cordon bleu balls, noted, v.25, p.310.

Cormier, Louis E., N. O. newspaperman, v.33, p.323.

Cornay, Florian O., Capt. 4th La. Reg't, C.S.A., muster roll of company given, v.30, p.519-522.

Cornelius, Elias, Presbyterian pastor, v.22, p.450-451.

Corn Islands, noted, v.24, p.659.

Corn Laws, of England, v.24, p.1032.

Coronado, Francisco Vasquez, noted, v.22, p.938.

Corona, Jose, injury of by bandits, v.28, p.1064.

Corps, Fabviers, noted, v.24, p.1003.

Corri, H., small theatrical co., v.28, p.274.

Cortes, Manuel, privateersman, v.22, p.1079-1081.

Cortez, Hernando, noted, v.22, p.933.

Cortimigilia, Charley, noted, v.22, p.844ff.

Cortimigilia, Rosie, noted, v.22, p.844ff.

Costa, Tony, noted, v.22, p.828.

Costello, James, Dem. cand. for Rep. from St. Mary, v.28, p.1136.

Costex, Jean, noted, v.23, p.570.

Cottage Grove Seminary, v.30, p.793.

Cotte Blanche Bay, noted, v.24, p.40.

Cotton, export of 1801, v.22, p.668; in military operations in La., v.24, p.81, 86; Cotton, Comparative production of 1832, v.23, p.1013-1015; contracts of merchants with H. W. Allen, v.23, p.1229-1231; in confed. states, v.23, p.1231-1232; Richard Taylor's policies toward, v.24, p.81, 108; burning of in New Orleans, v.24, p.455; noted, v.25, p.25, 27, 53-54; and 1828 tariff issue, v.25, p.49-50; attacked by caterpillar, v.25, p.121; competition with sugar in La., v.25, p.122ff.; staple in Natchez district, v.25, p.153; "Mexican or Petit Gulf," variety, v.25, p.175; production figures, v.25, p.175; plantation system, v.25, p.175ff.; a crop in La., v.27, p.352-353; on Erwin estate, v.27, p.363, 389, 390; in 1860, v.27, p.488; N. O. merchants specialized in, v.27, p.949; factorage system in N. O., v.27, p.951; South's dependence on, v.27, p.957, 958; in Acadia Parish, v.27, p.1162, 1168; influence of, on Red River Campaign, v.32, p.132-137; in La. noted, v.32, p.9; planting of, v.33, p.360; picking, v.33, p.361; amount picked per day, v.33, p.362.

Cotton Bill, intended to relieve cotton planters, vetoed, v.26, p.1015-1017.

Cotton Centennial Exposition, 1884, in N. O., v.27, p.777, 1011.

Cotton gin, early, v.32, p.38.

"Cotton," gunboat, v.24, p.71.

Cotton, Judge John B., supt. of elections in N. O., v.25, p.692.

Cotton, Nathaniel, petition of, v.23, p.367; noted, v.23, p.368.

Cottreaux, Gen. E. P., quartermaster-general of La. Depot, v.26, p.799; unable to obtain supplies, v.26, p.809; in charge of Camp Foster, v.26, p.809.

Cottrell, R. S. (The Natchez Trace), v.6, p.259.

Coutler, E. Merton, "The South During Reconstruction," reviewed, v.31, p.150-154.

Council of State (Supreme), Minutes of Spanish, 1787-1797, v.21, p.5-75.

Council, Superior, of Louisiana, See Superior Council.

County-Parish gov't in La., 1805-1845, v.18, p.56-160.

County Training School movement, v.25, p.808-811.

Coupland, T. V., nominated for Lt.-Gov., v.27, p.547.

Courant, Theodore, N. O., musician, v.31, p.142.

"Courrier," N. O. newspaper, v.25, p.984; quoted on Plaquemines Fraud, v.25, p.1005.

Court of Probates of La., N. O., the Gaines Case, v.27, p.9, 13, 23, 30, 63, 74; proceedings in to probate will of Clark, v.27, p.49, 51, 119, 173, 180, 311, 312.

Courtois, Severe, noted, v.24, p.664, 665, 671.

Court Records of Colonial La., Index to the Spanish Judicial Records, v.18, p.193-233, 456-485, 727-758, 1004-1035; Records of the Superior Council of La., v.18, p.161-192, 430-455, 696-726, 976-1003.

"Courts and Law in Colonial Louisiana," by Henry P. Dart, v.4, p.255.

Courts, Confederate, v.19, p.1032ff.

Courts of Louisiana, and Myra Clark Gaines Case, v.20, p.5-42.

Coushatta Indians, in Grant Parish, v.23, p.1109; noted, v.23, p.1120.

Coushatta, La., riot of, v.29, p.430-431.

Coushatta Male and Female Academy, v.30, p.899-900.

Cousinard, Edward, papers in L.S.U. Archives, v.24, p.342.

Couture, Jean, one of Fr. settlers at Ark. post, v.26, p.633-638passim.; deserted Tonti and joined English, v.26, p.639; led British trading expedition to Ark. post, v.26, p.644; noted, v.26, p.666, 680, 716.

Couvent, Widow Bernard, free woman of color, v.25, p.364, 733.

Couvillier, Alexander, duel of, v.23, p.447-448.

Covington Academy, v.30, p.914.

Covington Female Academy, v.30, p.914.

"Covington," gunboat, v.24, p.96.

Covode, John, on Wells, v.31, p.1037, 1039; investigator, v.31, p.1043.

Cowen, David L., "La. Pioneer in the Regulation of Pharmacy," v.26, p.330-340.

Cowgill, H. J., on committee to incorporate Bogalusa, v.29, p.108, 109, 110; designated Comm. of Public Streets and Parks, v.29, p.113.

Cowpen Island, v.28, p.791, 792, 833.

Coxe, Daniel W., Phila. partner of Daniel Clark, v.20, p.7; claimant of Maison Rouge grant, v.20, p.322ff.; business relations with James Brown, v.24, p.1145-1146; noted, v.27, p.7; business partner of Clark, v.27, p.19, 20; testimony in the Gaines Case, v.27, p.25, 29-40, 56, 57-58, 59, 60, 61, 62, 75-76, 79, 81, 82, 90, 101, 115, 120-122, 129, 131-133, 134, 137, 138-139, 139-142, 144, 145, 147, 148, 149, 155, 157, 158, 159, 160, 161, 162, 163, 164, 165, 166-167, 168, 170, 171-172, 173, 174, 194, 214, 215-216, 217, 218, 219, 221, 222, 228, 229-231, 232, 233, 234, 237, 246, 266, 271, 272, 287.

Coxe, John E., "The N. O. Mafia Incident," v.20, p.1067-1110.

Cox, Isaac Joslin, "Trailways to the Momentous Transfer," v.27, p.329-42.

Cox, Marguerite Victorine, noted, v.24, p.358.

Cox, Nathaniel, Letters of, to Gabriel Lewis, v.2, p.179.

Cox, William, noted, v.22, p.313, 948; noted, v.23, p.24.

Coyteux, Louis, noted, v.22, p.90.

Craig, Elijah, noted, v.24, p.922.

Craighead, John B., administered plantations of Erwin estate, v.27, p.359, 360, 374, 386, 387, 388, 390, 391, 394, 396, 398, 399, 400, 401; agent of heirs of Lavinia Erwin, v.27, p.430, 433, 437, 439, 440, 444, 445, 449, 450, 452, 453, 454, 455, 457, 458, 459, 460, 461, 462, 464, 465, 466.

Craig, John, noted, v.24, p.922.

Craig, Toliver, noted, v.24, p.922.

Craig, William, noted, v.24, p.922.

Crain, Walter O., Confed. naval officer, v.27, p.483, 484.

Crandell, A. W., suggests aid be given by Lottery Co. direct to people, v.27, p.1027; chairman State Dem. Ex. Com., demands for primary, v.27, p.1050, 1092; on com. to supervise primary election, v.27, p.1094; member com. to supervise election, v.28, p.1161.

Crane, B. P., telegraph contractor, v.31, p.451.

Crane, Verner W., The Southern Frontier (Editor's Chair), v.12, p.136.

Crane, William Montgomery, noted, v.24, p.1138.

Crash of 1857, in La., v.25, p.701-702.

Crawford, T. S., opponent of Civil Rights Article of Const., v.27, p.534.

Crawford, William Harris, noted, v.24, p.934, 1137; congressional supporters of, v.24, p.1004.

Creary, James, noted, v.23, p.1198, 1199.

Creek Indians, complaint of, v.23, p.371-372; in Grant Parish, v.23, p.1109, 1120-1121.

"Creole American," newspaper short-lived in Crowley, v.27, p.1186.

"Creole" case, Judah P. Benjamin, v.19, p.1023-1026; case concerning, v.23, p.1033-1034.

"Creole Civilization in Donaldsonville, 1850, According to 'Le Vigilant'" by Lionel C. Durel, v.31, p.981-994.

"Creole Families of New Orleans," Notes on Miss Grace King's Book, v.3, p.612.

"Creole Folk Songs," by Emilie LeJeune, v.2, p.454.

Creole, identified, v.22, p.647-648; described, v.22, p.650-654, 686-688.

"Creole, James Kirke Paulding's, Tale," by Dr. Floyd C. Watkins, v.33, p.364-379.

Creoles, Cable's attitude toward, v.24, p.185; of New Orleans, v.25, p.302, 981; hostilities toward Americans, v.25, p.981-986.

Creole St. Louis, housing in, v.21, p.337-348.

Creoles vs. Americans, v.21, p.167-168.

"Crescent," letters from traveling correspondent, v.21, p.1110-1214.

Crescent Rifles, noted, v.24, p.438.

Crevasse of 1816 in Carrollton, v.21, p.227n.

Criart, W., on Board of Charity Hospital, 1836, v.26, p.58.

Crime, in N. O., v.20, p.952-953, 1067ff.; horse stealing in W. Fla., v.22, p.367; Mafia in N. O., v.22, p.492ff., 818-886; of slaves, v.22, p.623-641; in Sp. N. O., v.22, p.694-700; in St. Mary Parish, v.32, p.84-89.

Criminal Code, of Edward Livingston, v.24, p.724.

"Criminal Jurisdiction, Tribunals of, in Ancient Rome," by Charles Gayarre, v.33, p.205-222.

"Criminal Trial, Before the Superior Council of Louisiana, May, 1747," Introduction by Henry P. Dart, v.13, p.367.

"Criminal Trials in Louisiana, 1720-1766," by Henry P. Dart, v.3, p.279.

"Criolla," ship in Aury expedition, v.24, p.628, 629, 633, 634, 637, 640, 665.

Cripps, Margaret, mother of R. C. Wickliffe, v.25, p.671.

Crittenden, Brigadier-General George, noted, v.24, p.62.

Crittenden, W. L., noted, v.22, p.1149.

Crocker, Raphael, and W. Fla. Rev., v.21, p.738n.

Crocker, Samuel Shaw, and W. Fla. Rev., v.21, p.688n.

Crockett, David, noted, v.23, p.1147.

Crockett, Dr. J. S., noted, v.26, p.76.

Crofton, Edward, noted, v.23, p.357, 368, 378.

Croix, Don Theodore de, Sp. Comdt. gen'l, urged open trade with La., v.28, p.1075-1076.

Croquere, Bastile, noted, v.23, p.146; noted, v.25, p.373.

Cross, J. W., Confed. soldier, v.26, p.952; noted, v.26, p.955.

Cross, K. A., senator, v.27, p.1042; counsel of St. Amant, v.27, p.1048; pro-lottery senator, v.28, p.1145.

Cross Keyes, military engagement at, v.24, p.65.

Crossman, A. D., Mayor of New Orleans and riots, v.22, p.1154, 1155; elected mayor, v.23, p.193; Mayor of N. O., v.25, p.1053; proclaims half-holiday honoring Webster, v.27, p.763.

Crowley Industrial School, for Negroes, v.27, p.1180.

Crowley Industrial Training Institute, v.27, p.1182.

Crowley, Louisiana, description of, v.23, p.562; noted, v.27, p.1120; founders of, v.27, p.1121-1122; stories in re location of, v.27, p.1122; laid out, v.27, p.1123; naming of, v.27, p.1123; plan of, v.27, p.1123; sale of lots, v.27, p.1124-1125; building begun, v.27, p.1124, 1125; victorious in contest for Acadia Parish seat, v.27, p.1125-1126; village organized, v.27, p.1126; new courthouse, v.27, p.1127-1128; growth of business, v.27, p.1128; other growth, v.27, p.1129; incorporated as town, 1898, v.27, p.1129; early leaders, v.27, p.1129-1131; conditions of streets in early 1900's, v.27, p.1131; erection of town hall and market, v.27, p.1131-1132; new parish courthouse, v.27, p.1132-1133; established Board of Health, v.27, p.1133; growth, v.27, p.1133-1134; census of 1903, v.27, p.1134-1135; becomes a city, v.27, p.1135; center of Southwest La. rice industry, v.27, p.1135; extensive street improving program, v.27, p.1135, 1137-1138, 1139-1140; fight against yellow fever, v.27, p.1135-1137; property tax assessed, v.27, p.1137; health program, v.27, p.1138-1139, 1141-1142, 1152; erection of city hall, repairs of courthouse, 1930, v.27, p.1140-1141; businesses of, 1937, v.27, p.1142-1144; finances, v.27, p.1145; history of waterworks and power plant of, v.27, p.1145-1149; fire dept., v.27, p.1149-1151; development of sewerage system, v.27, p.1151-1153; telegraph and telephones, v.27, p.1153-1154; the post office in Crowley, v.27, p.1155-1156; natural gas reaches, v.27, p.1156; "Rice City of Am.," v.27, p.1157; development of rice industry, v.27, p.1157-1162; host to State Cattlemen's Assoc., v.27, p.1163; plans for building paper mill, v.27, p.1168; oil development, v.27, p.1169-1170; financial institutions, v.27, p.1171-1173; railroads in, v.27, p.1173-1174; shipping facilities, v.27, p.1175; development of education, v.27, p.1175-1184; newspapers, v.27, p.1184-1189; churches, v.27, p.1190-1194; lodges, v.27, p.1194-1196; civic organizations, v.27, p.1196-1205; public welfare organizations, v.27, p.1205-1207; health unit, v.27, p.1206; Rice Belt Amateur Fields Trials, v.27, p.1208; Annual Rice Festival, v.27, p.1208-1214; flood disaster of 1940, v.27, p.1214-1221; need for better drainage, v.27, p.1221-22; summary, v.27, p.1222-24; bibl., v.27, p.1224-1225.

Crowley Oil and Mineral Co., v.27, p.1129, 1137, 1169.

Crowley, Pat, section foreman for whom town of Crowley was named, v.27, p.1123.

Crowley Rice Experiment Station, v.27, p.1161.

Crowley University School, v.27, p.1176-1177.

"Crown Colony, 1731-1762," by Henry Plauche Dart, v.2, p.98.

Crown, of de Leon's sacred acts, v.24, p.403.

Crozat, ———, noted, v.24, p.757.

Crozat, Antoine, and slavery in La., v.23, p.865; royal grant to, v.26, p.649-651;

granted 15-year monopoly of trade, v.26, p.728; noted, v.26, p.739.

Crozat (Old Book concerning grant from Louis XIV to Crozat) See Louisiana.

"Crozat's Charter, 1712-1717," by Henry Plauche Dart, v.2, p.74.

"Crozat's Regime in Louisiana, Documents Concerning," Translated by A. G. Sanders, Introduction by Henry P. Dart, First Installment, v.15, p.589; II, v.16, p.293; III, IV, v.17, p.268, 452.

Crozer, John, and W. Fla. Assembly, v.22, p.314, 317, 943.

Crozet, Claudius, Louisiana educator, v.31, p.853.

Crozier, John, and W. Fla. Assembly, v.23, p.5; petition of, v.23, p.363, 378, 390.

Cruzat, Heloise Hulse, "Joan of Arc, the Maid of Orleans," v.1, p.263; "General Collot's Reconnoitering Trip Down the Mississippi and His Arrest in New Orleans, 1796," v.1, p.303; "New Orleans Under Bienville," v.1, sec.3, p.54; "Sidelights on Louisiana History," v.1, sec.3, p.87; "When Knighthood Was in Flower," v.1, p.367; "Concession of Ste. Catherine at the Natchez," Translated from the French, v.2, p.164; "Letters from Pontalba to Miro," Trans., v.2, p.393; "Manon Lescaut, The Real Versus the Ideal," Trans. from the French of Victorian Dejan, v.2, p.313; "The Ursulines of Louisiana," v.2, p.5; "First Charity Hospital for Poor of New Orleans," v.3, p.554 (See Translation, Cabildo Archives, I, II, III, IV), Tr. by: "Nuncupative Will of Philip Haynaud," v.5, p.466 (Original French Text), v.5, p.472; "Suit for Damages for Personal Injuries to a Slave," v.5, p.58; Tr. by: "Early Louisiana Inquest, An," v.6, p.269; Tr. by: "Inauguration of De Vaudreuil," v.6, p.568; Tr. by: "Session of Superior Council of Louisiana in 1744," v.6, p.571; Tr. by: "The Trial of Mary Glass," v.6, p.589; Tr. by: "A Case in Admiralty," v.7, p.5; Tr. by: "Allotment of Building Sites in New Orleans, 1722," v.7, p.564; Tr. by: "Municipal Legislation by the Superior Council of Louisiana," v.7, p.567; Tr. by: "Records of the Superior Council of Louisiana," v.7, p.143, 334, 485, 676; Tr. by: "The Smuggler St. Michel," v.7, p.371; Tr. by: "Bienville Renounces a Debt Due by Serigny, His Deceased Brother, 1738," v.8, p.216; Tr. by: "Concession at Natchez," v.8, p.389; Tr. by: "Documents Concerning Sale of Chaouachas Plantation," v.8, p.594; Tr. by: "First Grand Jury of the Attakapas, The," v.8, p.369; Tr. by: "French Colonial Procedure in Louisiana for the Appointment of Tutors to Minors," v.8, p.218; Tr. by: "Records of Superior Council of Louisiana" (Index), v.8, p.118, 271, 478, 673; Tr. by: "Trial and Sentence of Biron, Runaway Negro Slave, 1728," v.8, p.23; Tr. by: "Wills of the French Colonial Period in Louisiana," v.8, p.411; Tr. by: "Agreement Between Louis Cezard LaBreton and Jean Baptiste Goudeau as Overseer on His Plantation, 1744," v.9, p.590; Tr. by: "Attempted Escape of English Prisoners from the Jail in New Orleans," v.9, p.361; Tr. by: "Bienville's Claims for Back Pay," v.9, p.210; Tr. by: "Inventory of the Estate of Sieur Jean Baptiste Prevost, 1769," v.9, p.411; Tr. by: "Records of the Superior Council of Louisiana," XXIX, XXX, XXXI, XXXII, v.9, p.113, 288, 502, 705; Tr. by: "Documents Concerning Bienville's Lands in Louisiana, 1719-1737," v.10, p.5, 161, 364, 538; Tr. by: "Induction of Laurent MacMahon as Councillor, 1730," v.10, p.529; Tr. by: "Introduction of Jean Francois Pasquier as Councillor-Assessor in The Superior Council of Louisiana, 1737," v.10, p.68; Tr. by: "Records of the Superior Council of Louisiana," XXXIII, XXXIV, XXXV, XXXVI, v.10, p.96, 252, 409; Tr. by: "Distribution of Land in Louisiana by the Company of the Indies, The Jonchere Concession," v.11, p.553; Tr. by: "Documents Concerning Bienville's Lands in Louisiana, 1719-1737," 5th, 6th and 7th Installments, v.11, p.87, 209, 463; Tr. by: "Records of the Superior Council of Louisiana," XXXVII, XXXVIII, XXXIX, XL, v.11, p.119, 288, 470, 624; Tr. by: "Wreck of the La Superbe," v.11, p.179; Tr. by: "Banet's Report, Louisiana in 1724," v.12, p.121; Tr. by: "Records of the Superior Council of Louisiana," v.12, p.134, 304, 467, 647; Tr. by: "Documents Covering the Criminal Trial of Etienne La Rue Before the Superior Council of Louisiana, May, 1747," v.13, p.377; Tr. by: "A Duel in the Dark in

New Orleans, 1747," v.13, p.202; Tr. by: "Records of the Superior Council of Louisiana," v.13, p.119, 307, 488, 660; Tr. by: "Great Storm of 1722 at Fort Louis, Mobile," v.14, p.567; Tr. by: "Installation of De Kerleric as Governor of Louisiana, 1753," v.14, p.235; "In Memoriam," by Henry P. Dart, v.14, p.443; Tr. by: "Records of the Superior Council of Louisiana," LIII, LIV, LV, v.15, p.120, 507; Tr. by: "Savage Law of the French Regime in Louisiana, 1765," v.15, p.482; Tr. by: "Jamaica Pirates and La. Commerce, 1739," v.16, p.209; Tr. by: "Lawsuit Over the Right to Sell the Office of Notary in La. During the French Regime, 1769," v.16, p.587; Tr. by: "Records of the Superior Council of La.," LVI, LVII, LVIII, v.16, p.135, 330, 504; Tr. by: "Marriage Contract Between Pierre Lemoine D'Iberville and Marie Therese Pollet de la Combe," v.17, p.242; Tr. by: "Records of the Superior Council of La.," LIX, LX, LXI, v.17, p.183, 364, 556; LXII, April, 1747, v.18, p.161-192; LXIII, May, 1747, v.18, p.430-455; LXIV, June-Sept., 1747, v.18, p.696-726; LXV, Oct.-Dec., 1747, v.18, p.976-1003; LXVI, Jan. 1748, v.19, p.210-240; LXVII, Feb.-March, 1748, v.19, p.466-509; LXVIII, April-May, 1748, v.19, p.751-777; LXIX, June-July, 1748, v.19, p.1078-1118; LXX, Aug.-Dec., 1748, v.20, p.212-244; LXXI, Jan.-Dec., 1749, v.20, p.486-517; LXXII, Jan.-Dec., 1750, v.20, p.832-839; LXXIII, Jan.-June, 1751, v.20, p.1111-1140; LXXIV, Jan.-May, 1752, v.21, p.282-318; LXXV, June-July, 1752, v.21, p.564-609; LXXVI, Aug.-Sept., 1752, v.21, p.875-908; LXXVII, Oct.-Dec., 1752, v.21, p.1215-1252; LXXXVIII, Jan.-March, 1753, v.22, p.226-258; LXXIX, April-July, 1753, v.22, p.531-574; LXXX, Aug.-Sept., 1753, v.22, p.857-902; LXXXI, Oct.-Dec., 1753, v.22, p.1168-1210; work on Ursulines in La., v.24, p.335, 349.

Cruzat, Joseph, noted, v.23, p.430.
Cryer, Daniel, noted, v.23, p.422.
Cryers, Morgan, noted, v.23, p.422.
Cuba, trade with, v.22, p.779; Lopez expeditions, v.22, p.1095-1167; State Trials, v.22, p.1132-1141; Robb organizes gas company in Havana, v.23, p.174-175; enthusiasm in N. O. over 1873, v.23, p.465; illicit slave trade with, v.23, p.879; Lopez expedition to, v.23, p.1071-1079; agreement of France, England, and the U. S. on Status, v.24, p.983-984; and filibustering, v.25, p.291, 294, 298, 302; proposed annexation of, v.25, p.680; La.'s interest in her struggle for independence, v.26, p.783; revolution in, v.26, p.787-789; noted, v.26, p.803, 817; La. regt. in, v.26, p.827-834.

Cucullu, J. M., noted, v.23, p.204.
Culbertson, John, in the Con. of 1844 in La., v.25, p.1007ff.
Culture of French Colonial La., v.21, p.629-630.
Cuming, Fortesque, member St. Helena Police Jury, v.23, p.411ff., 425.
Cummings, Jesse H., pioneer cypress lumberman, sketch of, v.30, p.1019-1020.
Cummings, William, in duel, v.24, p.997.
Cunningham, Edward, noted, v.24, p.101.
Cunningham, Lieut. E., aide-de-camp to Gen. Smith, letter from, v.32, p.110.
Cunningham, M. J., anti-lotteryite cand. for Atty.-gen., v.26, p.1081; Dem. cand. for Atty.-gen., 1896, v.26, p.1101; Anti-Lottery cand. for Atty.-gen., v.27, p.1090; address to Dem. Anti-Lottery St. Com., v.27, p.1091; suggested cand. Atty.-gen., v.28, p.1158; 1173; noted, v.28, p.1161, 1162.
Cunningham, Thomas S., noted, v.22, p.1037, 1084.
Cunningham, William, and Bowles activities in Fla., v.21, p.22n., 24n.
Cure, Dame Louis, noted, v.24, p.358.
Cure, Martin Randolph, noted, v.24, p.357.
Currency, problems in New Orleans, v.24, p.480-482.
Curry, R. H., opposed lottery, v.27, p.1039.
Curry, Thomas, collaborates with Bullard on Law Digest, v.23, p.1031.
Curtis, Reuben, and W. Fla. Rev., v.21, p.708.
Curto, Gregorio, N. O. voice teacher, v.31, p.862; life, v.31, p.863-864; and Minnie Hauck, v.31, p.862, 864-865; musician, v.31, p.135-36.
Cusachs, Gaspar, "Dario de Galvez," v.1, sec.1, p.9; "Diary of Bernardo de Galvez of Operations Against Pensacola," Trans. from the Spanish, v.1, sec.1, p.44; "Western Boundary of Louisiana," v.1, sec.1, p.9; "Lafitte, the Louisiana Pirate and Patriot," v.2, p.418; "Old Documents, from Collection of," v.2, p.447; "The

Controversy on Lafitte's Biography," v.3, p.100; President Louisiana Historical Society, Death of (Editor's Chair), v.13, p.117; collection in La. State Museum, v.24, p.317, 319.

Cushing, Caleb, noted, v.24, p.58.

Cushing, Courtland, noted, v.23, p.163.

Cushing, D. T., noted, v.29, p.121; work with tung trees, v.29, p.123, 182-183; successor to Wm. H. Sullivan, v.29, p.182.

Cushing, Thomas Humphrey, and W. Fla. Rev., v.21, p.114-115; Col., demanded explanation of Sp. patrols, v.28, p.1035-1036; neutral ground agreement, v.28, p.1039.

Cushman, Charlotte, musical career, v.31, p.973; opinions of, v.31, p.974-975; New Orleans debut, v.31, p.975-976; turns to acting, v.31, p.978.

Custom House Convention, called by Dunn, v.27, p.544-545.

Customhouse—Grant Republican, elections of 1872, v.28, p.1134.

"Custom-House, New Orleans, Historical Sketch on Constitution of," by Charles A. Favrot, v.3, p.467.

Customhouse, officials of Spanish, v.23, p.845.

Custom House Republicans, v.27, p.545, 547, 551; led by Packard, holds state conv., v.27, p.552.

Custom of Paris, articles on Community property, v.21, p.1003-1004.

Cutler, O. N., noted, v.23, p.1230.

Cutler, R. King, elected U. S. senator, v.31, p.1022; president of Const. Convention, v.31, p.1080.

Cuvellier, Col., N. O. educator, v.31, p.852.

Cypress Bayou, v.28, p.771, 773.

Cypress Island, Cathcart's survey, v.28, p.769ff., 783, 836; good live oak, v.28, p.889.

Cypress lumber industry, of Louisiana, description and early history of, v.30, p.979-986; passage and results of Swamp-Land Bill, v.30, p.986-991; surveying and estimation of swamp-land grants, v.30, p.991-994; sale of cypress swamp lands, v.30, p.995-998; development of modern machinery, v.30, p.999-1004; development of shingle mills, v.30, p.1004-1006; pioneers in the industry, v.30, p.1007-1021; in early 20th century, v.30, p.1022-1044; after World War I, v.30, p.1044-1045; charts, v.30, p.1045-1046; future of, v.30, p.1047; bibl., v.30, p.1056.

Cypress Mills, in Calcasieu parish, v.32, p.555-556.

DABNEY, THOMAS E., "THE BUTLER REGIME IN LA.," v.27, p.487-526; "One Hundred Great Years: The Story of the Times-Picayune from Its Founding to 1940," Rev'd, v.27, p.1229-1231.

"Daily Delta," suppressed by Butler, v.27, p.500; Union paper, v.27, p.518.

"Daily Democrat," established, v.31, p.739; fights lottery, v.31, p.743-773; seeks convention, v.31, p.770-773; state printing, v.31, p.773-778; changes hands, v.31, p.779-780.

"Daily Picayune," attitude toward Butler, v.27, p.500; order of suspension not enforced, v.27, p.501; in re conduct of women toward Union men, v.27, p.503, 506, 507, 508, 511; welcomed reorganization of city gov't, v.27, p.513, 518, 519; friendly to Clay, v.27, p.733, 736, 737, 741; established, v.31, p.719; quoted, v.31, p.721, 727, 735, 736, 737, 817, 827; early history, v.31, p.740-741; backs lottery, v.31, p.791, 794-798.

"Daily Signal," of Crowley, v.27, p.1180; "Signal" becomes daily, v.27, p.1186-1187; celebration of fiftieth anniversary, v.27, p.1188-1189; issues for which it has fought, v.27, p.1189.

"Daily States," established, v.31, p.786; quoted, v.31, p.787-789, 791, 792, 796, 799, 808, 809-810, 815, 822.

"Daily True Delta," attitude toward Butler, v.27, p.497, 499; cautioned by Butler, v.27, p.500, 505, 507, 508, 509, 510; denounces abolitionism, v.27, p.511; welcomed reorganization of city gov't, v.27, p.513, 514, 518.

Dakin, James H., diary in L.S.U. Archives, v.24, p.341-342.

"Dakotah," Lottery Co., boats aid in flood relief, v.27, p.1029.

Dalberg, house of, v.24, p.383; noted, v.24, p.418.

Dallas, George M., noted, v.24, p.1164.

Dalrymple, Robert, petition of, v.23, p.390.

Daly, ———, noted, v.22, p.1143.

Damas, Baron Anne-Hyacinthe-Maxence de, French negotiator with James Brown, v.24, p.942, 946, 949, 950, 964, 965, 1008, 1022, 1041, 1042, 1061, 1063, 1067, 1068, 1072, 1078, 1081.

Dana, Charles A., early N. O. newspaperman, v.29, p.784.

Dandridge, Philip P., noted, v.24, p.50.

Daniel, Lucia Elizabeth, "The La. People's Party," v.26, p.1055-1149.

Daniels, Captain, noted, v.24, p.361.

d'Anville, Jean Baptiste Bourguignon, map maker, noted, v.31, p.605.

DaPonta, Henry, suit against Lottery Co., v.27, p.983-984.

Da Ponte, Deny, lottery suit, v.31, p.742.

Daponte, Durand, on Returning Board, v.27, p.557-558; appt'd by Warmoth to Returning Board, v.28, p.1134; member Warmoth Returning Board, v.31, p.700.

Daquin, Major, noted, v.25, p.327.

d'Aquin's school, Columbian Institute, v.30, p.863-864.

Darby, W. A., Confed. soldier, v.26, p.960n.

Darby, William, "A Geographical Description of the State of La.," noted, v.18, p.124; reported on La., 1816, v.25, p.27; map of La., 1816-1817, v.25, p.628, 641; description of neutral ground, v.28, p.1048; noted, v.29, p.78; author on Louisiana, v.31, p.394, 395, 400.

Darcantel, Paul, justice of peace, v.23, p.696ff.

D'Arc, Jeanne, See Joan of Arc.

D'Arcy, John N. (co-author), "Paul de Rastel de Rocheblave," v.18, p.336-343.

"Dardo," vessel, v.24, p.616, 618-619, 625, 649.

D'Arges, Spanish agent in Ky., 1788, v.21, p.14.

Daron, Charles J., candidate for St. Louis Cathedral Warden, v.31, p.913.

D'Artaguette, Bernard Diron, v.28, p.60, 62; one of the family founding B. R., v.28, p.60, 67.

D'Artaguette concession, map showing, v.28, p.39; called B. R. by Broutin, v.28, p.40; early B. R. concession, v.28, p.60, 63.

Dart, Albert Laplace, Translation of "Ship Lists of Passengers Leaving France for Louisiana, 1718-1724," I, v.14, p.516; II, III, v.15, p.68, 453; IV, v.21, p.965-978; v.24, p.317, 349.

Dart, Henry Plauche, "The Archives of Louisiana," v.2, p.349; "Legal Institutions of Louisiana," v.2, p.72; "Criminal Trials in Louisiana, 1720-1766," v.3, p.279; "First Succession Opened in Louisiana, 1717," v.3, p.322; "Superior Council of Louisiana," v.3, p.71 (See also Cabildo Archives, Superior Council Records); "Courts and Law in Colonial Louisiana," v.4, p.255; "History of Supreme Court of Louisiana," v.4, p.14; "Indian Titles to Land in French and Spanish Periods," v.4, p.134; "Mazureau's Oration on Mathews," v.4, p.149; "Servinien's Case," 1752, v.4, p.290; "A Gentleman of Pointe Coupee," v.5, p.462; "Edward Douglas White,", v.5, p.145; "George H. Theard," v.5, p.333; Grace King's "Madame Girard," rev'd. v.5, p.51; "New Orleans in 1758 (The Experiences of William Perry)," v.5, p.53; "Politics in Louisiana in 1724," v.5, p.298; "Remy's Lost History of Louisiana," v.5, p.5; "Suit for Damages for Personal Injuries to a Slave," v.5, p.58 (See Editor's Chair); "Almonaster's Will" (Introduction), v.6, p.21; "Conventional Mortgage of Spanish Colonial Period," v.6, p.255; "Episodes of Life in Colonial Louisiana," v.6, p.35; "De-Vaudreuil, Inauguration of," v.6, p.568; "Miss Grace King's Historical Works," v.6. p.347; "The Lesueur Collection," v.6, p.585; "Original Autograph of Henry De Tonty," v.6, p.576; "Session of the Superior Council of Louisiana" (Introduction to Index), v.6, p.145; "Trial of Mary Glass, The," v.6, p.589; "The Devron Introduction," v.6, p.543; "Chief Justices of 1921-1922," v.6, p.280; "Colonial Archives of Louisiana," v.6, p.111; "Confederate Congress, Debates in First," v.6, p.480; "The Centenary of Francis Parkman," v.6, p.655; "This Number (Jan. 1923) of the Quarterly," v.6, p.112; "Rewards of Public Service, A Digression on the," v.6, p.281; "Spanish Colonial Cabildo," v.6, p.478; "A Case in Admiralty in Louisiana, 1741," v.7, p.5; "Calendar of Documents and the History of Louisiana," v.7, p.674; "Destrehan's Slave Roll" (Introduction), v.7, p.302; "Major William Grant," 1838-1919, v.7, p.658; "Historical Research in Louisiana, 1923," v.7, p.141; "September 14th, 1874" (Introduction), v.7, p.570; "Slavery in Louisiana," v.7, p.332; "The Smuggler St. Michel," v.7, p.371; "Spain and France at Biloxi, 1699," v.7, p.480 (See also Editor's Chair); "American Historian's Raw Materials," v.8, p.268; "George W. Cable," v.8, p.647; "Concession at Natchez" (Introduction), v.8, p.389; "The Eighteenth Century in Louisiana," v.8, p.474; "A Great Louisiana Plantation of the French Colonial Period," v.8, p.589; "Imprisonment for Debt in French Louisiana," v.8, p.549; "Judicial Auction Sale in Louisiana, 1739, A," v.8, p.382; "Something for the Members of the Louisiana Historical Society to Think About," v.8, p.115; "Attempted Escape of English Prisoners from the Jail in

New Orleans in 1744," v.9, p.361; "A Battle of New Orleans Number" (Editor's Chair), v.9, p.111; "Bienville's Claims Against the Company of the Indies for Back Salary, 1737," v.9, p.210; "Editing the Quarterly" (Editor's Chair), v.9, p.703; "Instinct of the Private Collector of Archive Material" (Editor's Chair), v.9, p.499; "Jackson and the Louisiana Legislature, 1814-1815," v.9, p.221; "Louisiana Indigo Plantation (De Vaugine) on Bayou Teche, 1773," v.9, p.565; "Prevost Inventory of the Estate of Sieur Jean Baptiste," (Introduction), v.9, p.411; "Slave Depot of the Company of the Indies at New Orleans" (Editor's Chair), v.9, p.286; "Index to the French and Spanish Archives" (Editor's Chair), v.10, p.407; "William Beer, In Memoriam" (Editor's Chair), v.10, p.249; "Documents Concerning Bienville's Lands in Louisiana, 1719-1737" (Introduction), v.10, p.5, 161, 364, 538; "Edict of December 15, 1721" (Introduction), v.10, p.533; "MacMahon, Laurent, 1st Councillor in the Superior Council of Louisiana, Director of the Company of the Indies at New Orleans, 1730-1731," v.10, p.529; "William R. Irby, In Memoriam," (Editor's Chair), v.10, p.95; "The Tenth Year of the Quarterly" (Editor's Chair), v.10, p.94; Surrey's "Calendar of Manuscripts in Paris Relating to the History of the Mississippi Valley Under the French Domination" (Editor's Chair), v.10, p.564; "Distribution of Land in Louisiana by the Company of the Indies, The Jonchere Concession" (Introduction), v.11, p.533; "Documents Concerning Bienville's Lands in Louisiana, 1719-1737" (Introduction), v.11, p.87, 209, 463; "Public Education in New Orleans in 1800" (Introduction to Lefort Petition), v.11, p.244; Read's "Louisiana Place Names of Indian Origin," v.11, p.286; Rowland and Sanders "Mississippi Provincial Archives, 1729-1740, French Dominion" (Editor's Chair), v.11, p.111; Vogel's "The Capuchins in French Louisiana, 1722-1766" (Editor's Chair), v.11, p.620; "Which Way History?" (Editor's Chair), v.11, p.468; "Wreck of La Superbe in the Gulf of Mexico, 1745" (Introduction), v.11, p.179; "Autobiography of Charles Gayarre" (Introduction), v.12, p.5; "Celebration of the Twelfth Year of the Louisiana Historical Quarterly" (Editor's Chair), v.12, p.630; "Civil Procedure in Louisiana Under the Spanish Regime as Illustrated in Loppinot's Case, 1774," v.12, p.33; Crane's "The Southern Frontier" (Editor's Chair), p.12, p.136; "In Memoriam, Henry E. Chambers" (Editor's Chair), v.12, p.300; "Splendid Work of Rowland and Sanders on the French Archives of Louisiana" (Editor's Chair), v.12, p.464; Caulfield's "The French Literature of Louisiana" (Editor's Chair), v.13, p.484; "Criminal Trial Before the Superior Council of Louisiana, May, 1747," v.13, p.367; "Death of Mr. Cusachs and Mr. Hart" (Editor's Chair), v.13, p.117; "Duel in the Dark in New Orleans, 1747," v.13, p.199; Fisher's "The Intendant System in Spanish America" (Editor's Chair), v.13, p.304; "Governor Warmoth, His Book" (Editor's Chair), v.13, p.655; "Adventures of Denis Braud, First Printer of Louisiana," v.14, p.349; "Documents Covering Impeachment of Bienville" (Introduction), v.14, p.5; "First Cargo of African Slaves for Louisiana, 1718" (Introduction), v.14, p.163; "First Law Regulating Land Grants in French Colonial Louisiana, The," v.14, p.346; "In Memory of Heloise H. Cruzat," (Editor's Chair), v.14, p.443; "Installation of De Kerleric as Governor of Louisiana, 1753" (Introduction), v.14, p.235; "Revolution of 1876 in Louisiana, The," (Editor's Chair), v.14, p.242; "South as a Conscious Minority, The," by Dr. Jesse T. Carpenter, Book Review, v.14, p.637; "Spanish Procedure in Louisiana in 1800 for Licensing Doctors and Surgeons" (Introduction), v.14, p.204; "Work of the Quarterly in 1930," (Editor's Chair), v.14, p.86; "Documents Concerning the Crozat Regime in Louisiana, 1712-1717," (Introduction), v.15, p.589; Ettinger's "The Mission to Spain of Pierre Soule," (Review), v.15, p.708; Greer's "A Texas Ranger and Frontiersman. The Days of Buck Barry in Texas," (Review), v.15, p.711; "Ideals of Grace King," (Editor's Chair), v.15, p.339; "Office of Councillor-Assessor in the Superior Council of Louisiana in the French Regime" (Editor's Chair), v.15, p.117; Read's "Louisiana-French" (Review), v.15, p.710; Rowland's "Varina Howell, Wife of Jefferson Davis" (Review), v.15, p.350; Rowland and Sanders "Mississippi Provincial Archives, 1704-1743, French Dominion," Vol. 3 (Review), v.15, p.707; "Sanitary Conditions in New Orleans Under the Spanish Regime, 1799-1800," (Introduction), v.15, p.610; "Savage Law of the French Regime in Louisiana, 1765," (Introduction), v.15, p.482; "Spain's Report of the War with the British in Louisiana," by Jac Nachbin, (Introduction), v.15, p.468; Surveyer's "Bench and Bar of Quebec," (Review), v.15, p.118; Whitaker's "Commercial Policy of Spain in Florida and Louisiana, 1778-1803," (Review), v.15, p.345; "Whittington, George Purnell, In Memoriam," v.15, p.655; Ditchey's "Les Acadiens Louisianais et Leur Parler," v.16, p.166; King's "Memories of a Southern Woman of Letters" (Review), v.16, p.164; Leland's "Guide to Material for American History in the Libraries and Archives of Paris," v.16, p.168; "Documents Concerning Crozat Regime in La., 1712-1717" by Albert G. Sanders (Introduction), v.16, p.293; "Marriage Contracts of French Colonial Louisiana," v.17, p.229; "Commemorative exercises of the Louisiana Historical Society in Memory of," v.18, p.239-253; Memorial of the La. Bar Assoc., v.18, p.255-266; "The Career of Dubreuil in French Louisiana," v.18, p.267-331; ed. "Account of the Credit and Debit of the Funds of the City of N.O. for the Year 1789," v.19, p.584-594; "Cabarets of N.O. in the French Colonial Period," v.19, p.578-583; ed. "Appointment of Members of the Superior Council of La. in 1762," v.21, p.669-670; "Sale of Real Property in La. in 1769," v.21, p.674-676; "Decision Day in the Superior Council of La., March 5, 1746," v.21, p.998-1020; "Records of Superior Council of La." (Cont.), v.21, p.282-318, 564-609, 875, 908, 1215-1252; ed. "A Murder Case Tried in N.O. in 1773," v.22, p.623-641; noted, v.23, p.1023.

d'Artlys, Prudent, noted, v.31, p.984, 991, 992-994.

Dart, Sally, (Trans. by), "French Incertitude in 1718 as to a Site for New Orleans," I, II, v.15, p.37, 417; (Trans. by), "Jamaica Pirates and Louisiana Commerce, 1739," v.16, p.209; (Trans. by), "Lawsuit over the Right to Sell the Office of Notary in Louisiana During the French Regime" (1769), v.16, p.587; (co-author), "La Dame de Ste. Hermine," v.21, p.671-673.

Dart, William Kernan, "Early Episodes in Louisiana History," v.1, sec.3, p.190; "The Justices of the Supreme Court of La." v.4, p.113; Translations by the late: "Edict of December 15, 1721 providing for Appointment of Dual Tutors to Minors in France and in her colonies" (Introductory note by Henry P. Dart), v.10, p.533; "Ordinance of 1717 Governing Notaries in Louisiana During the French Colonial Period," v.10, p.82.

"Daspit, Francisco, Marriage contract with Maria Barba Zeringue," Translated by Laura L. Porteous, v.9, p.394.

Datcheret, ———, complaint against, v.23, p.393.

Daughters of American Revolution, genealogical records in Howard-Tilton Memorial Library, v.24, p.328.

Daughters of the Cross, noted, v.25, p.362, 733.

Daunoy, Bartholome, noted, v.22, p.814.

"Daunoy, Carlos Felipe Favre, Marriage Contract with Maria Elizabetha Destrehan," Translated by Laura P. Porteous, v.9, p.388.

Daunoy, Carols Gui Favre, noted, v.22, p.632.

Daunoy, Carlos Lejonchere, noted, v.22, p.624, 628.

Daunoy, Charles F., Dem. candidate for State Sen., 1864, v.25, p.1036, 1038.

D'Aunoy, Jeanne Emma, married E. Johns, v.31, p.859.

D'Aunoy, Marie Rose Celeste, married E. Johns, v.31, p.859.

Daunoy, Nicolas, noted, v.22, p.624, 626, 632, 814.

Dauphin, ———, noted, v.23, p.146.

Dauphin, M. A., Pres. Lottery Co., defense of Co., v.27, p.995-996, 1007; use of mails attacked, v.27, p.1007-1008, 1008-1009; libel suit against McClure, v.27, p.1010-1011; sketch, v.27, p.1014; offer of money for flood control, v.27, p.1021, 1028; other charities, v.27, p.1029; message in re lottery Co. in N. Dakota, v.27, p.1074, 1079; pres. Louisiana Lottery, v.31, p.783; noted, v.31, p.784.

Dauphin vs. Key Case, v.27, p.1074.

Dauphine Theatre, Bernhardt at, v.26, p.776.

Dauseville, Raimond Amiant, suit of succession of, v.21, p.1010-1012.

D'Auterive, ———, noted, v.22, p.1024.

Davenport, John, and W. Fla. Rev., v.21, p.804n.

Davenport, Josiah, early Mer Rouge settler, v.20, p.414.

Davenport, Samuel, noted, v.22, p.725; v.25, p.294, 299; sketch, v.28, p.845n.; noted, v.28, p.886; report of, v.28, p.890, 892; noted, v.28, p.1046; land claims in neutral ground, v.28, p.1052; interpreter for joint Am.-Sp. expedition against bandits, v.28, p.1062; noted, v.28, p.1068; organized trading firm, v.28, p.1089; claim against for Barr property, v.28, p.1090-1092; sketch, v.28, p.1092-1093; leader filibusters, v.28, p.1094-1095, 1103, experiments with Sugar Cane, v.28, 1095; Will, v.28, p.1091, 1095-1096; activities of House of Barr and Davenport, v.28, p.1096ff.; Sp. attitude toward, v.28, p.1101-1103.

Davey, Robert C., Dem. Congressman, v.26, p.1116, 1123.

Davezac, Dr. A., Charter member Medical Society, v.26, p.59; noted, v.26, p.76.

Davezac, Dr., brother of Mrs. Livingston, v.24, p.1135.

"Davezac's, Auguste, Mission to the Kingdom of the Two Sicilies, 1833-1834," by Howard R. Marraro, v.32, p.791.

David, Joseph, noted, v.23, p.555.

Davidson, Dr. J. F., possible originator of "no light" theory of small pox treatment, v.26, p.67-70.

Davidson, Thomas Green, nominated for cong., 1860, v.25, p.704; testifies on Myles absence, v.25, p.1103.

Davidson, Thomas J., member of St. Helena Police Jury, v.23, p.407ff.; appointed assessor, v.23, p.407; noted, v.23, p.418, 421.

Davis and Lacaze, Laffite's New Orleans Lawyers, v.23, p.816, 817.

Davis, Benjamin, Baptist minister, sketch, v.28, p.755n.

Davis, Col. Samuel B., v.27, p.8; testimony of, v.27, p.41; brief sketch, v.27, p.43; Myra Clark placed in care of, v.27, p.43-47, 59, 62; testimony about, v.27, p.64-65, 67, 69, 71, 81, 84, 88; testimony of, v.27, p.126-128, 131-133, 134, 137, 165, 168-169, 170, 172, 173; in re Clark's will of 1813, v.27, p.173-174, 190; legal opinion in re to, v.27, p.191, 244, 259, 280, 293.

Davis, David, justice, rendered majority opinion in favor of Mrs. Gaines in case vs. City of N.O., v.27, p.278-293; opinion in case of Gaines vs. de la Croix, v.27, p.308-311.

Davis, Edwin Adams, "Civil War Diary of Willie Micajah Barrow," I, II, v.17, p.435, 712; "Plantation Life in the Fla. Parishes of La., 1836-1846, as reflected in the Diary of Bennet H. Barrow," rev'd, v.20, p.1173-1179; revs, "Origin of Class Struggle in La.," by R. W. Shugg, v.23, p.887-888; noted, v.24, p.308, 340.

Davis, Eliza, her suit against Mrs. Gaines, v.27, p.311-314.

Davis, Henry Winter, noted, v.24, p.113.

Davis, Horatio, noted, v.22, p.1161; St. Louis Cathedral Warden, v.31, p.922.

Davis, I. I., reasons for voting for Lottery Bill of 1890, v.27, p.1042-1043.

Davis, Jackson Beauregard, "The Life of Richard Taylor," v.24, p.49-126.

Davis, Jefferson, noted, v.24, p.50, 62, 67, 88, 97, 104, 107, 110, 113, 441, 442, 530, 532; papers in La. Hist. Assn. depository, v.24, p.15; pres. of the Confed., v.26, p.1008, 1012; documents to from La. asking for more defense, v.26, p.1018-1019; request from Moore for a general, v.26, p.1021-1022; noted, v.26, p.953, 969; communication from meeting of governors, v.26, p.1023-1024; urged to complete railroad and supply Red River defense, v.26, p.1025; more men requested from, v.26, p.1026; noted, v.29, p.285n., 345; destiny of Confederacy depended on him, v.29, p.1242; personality sketch, v.29, p.1243; burdens of administration, v.29, p.1245-1248; peace interview at Richmond and result, v.29, p.1253-1258.

Davis, John, erected Orleans Theatre, v.28, p.90.

Davis, R. M., noted, v.23, p.202.

Davis, Sarah Knox Taylor, noted, v.24, p.50.

Davis, Thomas E., early N.O. newspaperman, v.29, p.790.

"Davis, Varina Howell, Wife of Jefferson Davis," by Eron Rowland, Reviewed by Grace King, v.11, p.463.

Davis, Warren R., noted, v.23, p.1008.

Dawney, Barnet, noted, v.23, p.77.

Dawson, Anna Ruffin, married Chas. G. Johnson, v.28, p.942.

Dawson, Annie R., became wife of R. C. Wickliffe, v.25, p.673.

Dawson, J. B., campaign against E. D. White, v.25, p.104-107, 112, 115, 124, 134; and 1842 tariff, v.25, p.116, 117; and 1844 tariff bill, v.25, p.131, 673; death of, v.25, p.674.

Dawson, John B., v.28, p.942n.; sketch, v.28, p.949n.; W. Fel. Parish judge, v.28, p.954; noted, v.28, p.962.

Dawson, John, sketch, v.31, p.320; carrier of La. Purchase treaty, v.31, p.321; and Lafayette bill, v.31, p.321-322; candidate for governor of Orleans, v.31, p.322.

Dawson, Warrington, "History of the Foundation of New Orleans," Translated from the French of Baron Marc de Villiers, v.3, p.157.

Day, Ben, Confed. soldier, v.26, p.954.

Day, David, noted, v.23, p.45.

Day, David T., of U.S. Geological Survey, v.29, p.61, 63.

Day, Robert S., pres. Prog. League, v.27, p.1062.

Day, Roland, N.O. newspaperman, v.33, p.331.

Day, Thomas, noted, v.23, p.420.

Deal, Ephraim, noted, v.23, p.420, 421.

Dearborn, Henry, documents in Bibliotheca Parsoniana, v.24, p.311.

De Armas, Cristoval, noted, v.22, p.399, 408.

"Deathmask of Napoleon at the Cabildo, New Orleans," Olivia Blanchard, v.8, p.71.

"Death," redoubt of "Impregnable" fort, v.24, p.657.

De Bastrop, Baron (Felipe Enrique Neri), petition and contract with Carondelet, v.20, p.371-378; settlers brought into Ouachita, v.20, p.379-384; career in Tex., v.20, p.402ff.; death and will, v.20, p.430-440.

De Baulne, and Superior Council, v.21, p.1000.

De Benac, and Superior Council, v.21, p.1000.

de Blainville, Jacques, mentioned, v.21, p.1007.

DeBlanc, Armand, Confed. naval engineer from La., v.27, p.485.

DeBlanc, Judge Alcibiade, organized Caucasian Club, v.28, p.1133.

DeBlanc, Louis, and French Rev., v.22, p.65-79; noted, v.22, p.796, 808; sketch, v.22, p.811-812.

de Bore, Etienne, and La. sugar industry, v.25, p.24-25, 186; noted, v.33, p.161-164; appointed Mayor, v.33, p.166.

de Bore, Madame, noted, v.33, p.164.

"De Bow and the Seventh Census," by O. C. Skipper, v.22, p.479-490.

De Bow, B. Frank, brother of J. B. D. De Bow and business mgr. of "Review," v.29, p.355, 358, 359, 362, 363, 364, 367, 368, 369, 379, 391.

De Bow, J. B. D., and the 7th Census, v.22, p.479-491; noted, v.22, p.11-39n.; and railroad convention, v.23, p.199, 200; cited on La., wealth, v.25, p.121; announces re-establishment of "Review," v.29, p.355; work as editor of "Review," v.29, p.356-391; death of, v.29, p.391; on telegraph, v.31, p.482; defends Wells, v.31, p.1040.

De Bow, Mrs. J. B. D., v.29, p.391.

"De Bow's Review," re-establishment announced, v.29, p.355; work begun for re-establishment, v.29, p.355-357; offices set up, v.29, p.358; subscription secured, v.29, p.359-367; cost of "Review," v.29, p.369; press comments on the "Review," v.29, p.371, 388-391; features of the "Review," v.29, p.372-388; public opinion of, v.29, p.391; fate of after De Bow's death, v.29, p.391-393.

"De Bow's Review After the Civil War," by Ottis C. Skipper, v.29, p.355-393.

de Breard, Augustus, agent of de Maison Rouge, v.20, p.318-319.

De Breuil, ———, noted, v.23, p.868.

De Brissot, Julius, and J. P. Benjamin, v.23, p.164.

Debuys, Gaspard, identified, v.21, p.402.

Debuys, John, duel of, v.24, p.768.

DeBuys, William, noted, v.25, p.128, 129, 130; Whig candidate for Gov., 1846, v.25, p.1038; v.28, p.959.

"Decemvirate, The, Tribunals of Criminal Jurisdiction in Ancient Rome," by Charles Gayarre, v.33, p.211-213.

Decentralization, theory of, v.24, p.698.

de Chanfret, Claude Trenaunnay, director of Duverney Concession, v.21, p.982.

"Decision Day in the Superior Council of

La., March 5, 1746," edited by Henry P. Dart, v.21, p.998-1020.

Declaration of Independence, noted, v.24, p.701.

deClouet, Alexander, delegate to convention of seceding states, v.26, p.1002.

deClouet, Alexandre, noted, v.22, p.795; commandant of Ark. Post, v.23, p.386; Post, 1768, v.27, p.632; peace with Osage Indians, v.27, p.636, 646.

deClouet, Alexandre, Jr., noted, v.22, p.815.

deClouet, Balthasar, noted, v.22, p.815.

deClouet, Louis Bronier, memorial to Sp. gov't, v.22, p.795-818.

deClouet, Louis, noted, v.23, p.437n., 847n.

deClouet, Louise Favrot, sister of Don Pedro, v.28, p.688; description of, v.28, p.691.

De Coppens, Gaston, duel of, v.23, p.151-154.

"Decree for La. issued by the Baron of Carondelet, June 1, 1795," ed. by James H. Padgett, v.20, p.590-605.

Dede, Edmond, noted, v.25, p.359.

"Deep Delta Country," by Harnett T. Kane, rev'd, v.28, p.990-992.

Deer Island, v.28, p.765, 798, 800, 810, 886.

Defarges, Jean, privateersman, v.22, p.1083-1084.

DeFeriet Board, Returning Board created by Warmoth, v.27, p.558; v.28, p.1135, 1136; noted, v.29, p.410; appointed, v.31, p.701; certifies Fusion ticket, v.31, p.701; noted, v.31, p.702.

DeFeriet, G., and Returning Board, v.28, p.1105.

De Ferriet, J., noted, v.23, p.203.

De Forest, David Cortes, and privateering, v.23, p.796, 800, 807.

DeForest, J. W., officer under Butler, wrote "Miss Ravenel's Conversion," v.27, p.516.

De Glapion, Christophe, deposition of, v.23, p.726-727.

de Grand Pre, appointed lieut.-gov. of Ouachita, v.20, p.316-317.

De Grange, Joseph H., "Historical Data of Spanish Fort," v.2, p.268.

DeGrange, Zulime, marriage to Daniel Clark, v.20, p.9; implication in Myra Clark Gaines Case, v.20, p.14ff.

Degruis, Jean-Baptiste, improvements in Bayou Plaquemine, v.25, p.938-939.

de Grummond, Jewell Lynn, "A Social History of St. Mary Parish, 1845-1860," v.32, p.16.

Deiler, J. Hanno, "The System of Redemption in Louisiana," translated by Rev. Louis Voss, v.12, p.426; noted, v.24, p.128, 378; cited, v.24, p.129, 130, 131, 132-133, 151-152, 153.

Dejan, Victorin, "Manon Lescaut, The Real Versus the Ideal," Trans. from the French by Heloise H. Cruzat, v.2, p.313.

deLaage, Jules, Chancellor of Fr. Consulate, N.O., v.28, p.340, 342, 343.

de la Baume, Don Gillaume, Commandant of Fort Miro, v.20, p.466.

Delabigarre, Peter, buys land of Gravier, v.22, p.412, 413.

De la Boulaye, first French settlement in present day La., v.19, p.829-99.

de la Buissoniere, Alphonse, noted, v.21, p.1008, 1009.

De la Chaise, ———, procurer, syndic of Cabildo and Batture controversy, v.23, p.683.

Delachaise, Alexandria, and Jesuit land grant, v.22, p.388-390.

Delachaise, Auguste, sketch, v.21, p.37n.; v.22, p.53n.; noted, v.22, p.81, 87, 93.

De la Chaise, Intendant of La. colony, v.29, p.562, 563, 570, 571, 573, 575.

Delachaise, Jacques, George C. H. Kernion, v.7, p.447; "Orders Placing Him in Charge of Louisiana," Translation and Introduction by Edith Dart Price, v.15, p.376.

de la Colina y Escudero Francisco, teacher in Sp. school, v.22, p.683.

de la Croix, F. D., executor named in Clark's will, v.27, p.12, 21-22; petition against probation of will of 1811, v.27, p.22-23, 48; testimony of, v.27, p.63-64, 134, 137, 190, 208, 214; executor of will, v.27, p.65-66, 67, 68, 69, 72, 73, 75, 76, 90, 119, 173; Gaine's suit against for property purchased in bad faith, v.27, p.307-311, 313, 314.

de la Croix, secretary of Aury, v.24, p.685.

De la Francia, largest West Florida claim, v.25, p.944-945.

de la Freniere, Nicholas Chauvin, land grants, v.21, p.224; app't of to Superior Council of La., 1762, v.21, p.669; and Superior Council, v.21, p.1000.

de la Garde, Daurien, partner in Duverney Concession, v.21, p.984.

de la Gautrais, Sieur, petition to Superior Council, v.21, p.1013.

Delagoublaye, Sieur, and lease of Pailloux plantation, v.21, p.996-997.

de la Louere, Flacourt Louis Auguste, judge in Ill., 1844, v.21, p.1015, 1016.

Delanaux, Aristide, noted, v.24, p.731.

Delanglez, S.J., Rev. John, "The Natchez Massacre and Governor Perier," v.17, p.631.

De Lara, Jose Bernardo Gutierrez, noted, v.25, p.294.

De la Rosa, Don Francisco, victim of "no trade" policy of Sp. with La., v.28, p.1080.

De la Salle, Robert, early exploration in La., v.19, p.26-28.

De las Bayares, Guido, noted, v.22, p.936.

Delassize, Nicolas, comdt. at Pointe Coupee, detains Madame de Villiers, v.27, p.674.

Delassus, Adelaide Leonard, wife of Charles de Hault Delassus, v.30, p.368.

Delassus, Carlos Dehault, Governor of West Florida, refuses to appoint Skipwith, v.31, p.304.

De Lassus, Charles Augustus de Hault, commander at New Madrid, v.21, p.37n.; and W. Fla. Rev., v.21, p.79ff.; sketch, v.21, p.95-96; and Skipwith, v.21, p.170; and W. Fla. Rev., v.21, p.693n.

De Lassus, Charles de Hault, friend of Carondelet, v.22, p.87, 93; early career in Sp. army, v.30, p.362; follows family to America, v.30, p.363; with Sp. army in La., v.30, p.363-367; court-martial of, v.30, p.367-368; marriage and later life, v.30, p.368-369; in St. Louis, v.30, p.370, 371; diary of, v.30, p.371-438.

Delassus, Domitilde Joseph Dumont, mother of Charles de Hault, v.30, p.359.

Delassus, Jean Felicite Odille, Madame Pierre Derbigny, sister of Charles de Hault de Lassus, v.30, p.360, 372n., 402-403, 416.

Delassus, Pierre Charles de Hault, father of Charles de Hault, sketch of, v.30, p.359-362.

De Lassus, Pierre de Luziere, friend of Carondelet, v.22, p.87.

Delaunay, Colonel, and Osage Indians, v.24, p.1056-1057, 1076-1077.

Delaunay, Piot, app't to Superior Council of La., 1762, v.21, p.669.

de Laussat, Pierre Clement, Colonial Prefect and High Commissioner of France in La., proclamation issued on arrival in La., v.20, p.161-168; appointed 1st mayor and municipal council of N.O., v.20, p.168-172.

De la Vasselais, Charles, newspaper artist, v.33, p.328.

de la Vergne, Col. H. J., "Address on Col. Chas. D. Dreaux," v.5, p.502; "In Memoriam," v.7, p.121.

De la Villantray, M. de Sauvole, Governor of La., 1699-1702, and Fort de la Boulaye, v.19, p.851-852.

de Lemos, Manuel Gayoso, documents in Bibliotheca Parsoniana, v.24, p.311; gov. of Fort Panmure, refused to carry out Cardonlet's orders, v.27, p.681, 706; warned of Am. attack, v.27, p.708; established Fort San Fernando de las Barrancas, v.27, p.711.

De Leon, Alonzo, noted, v.22, p.939, 940.

de Leon, Count, noted, v.24, p.378, 379; accounts of birth of, v.24, p.381, 383; see Bernhard Muller.

De Leon, Ponce, noted, v.22, p.933.

Delepuch, A., see Med. Board of Censors, v.26, p.60; apothecary, v.26, p.334.

Delery, Chauvin, land grants of, v.21, p.224.

Delery, C., pres. Board of Health of La., repaired monument to Fr. sailors, v.28, p.335.

Delery, Simone de la Souchere, "France d'Amerique," (Book Review by Edith Dart Price), v.16, p.168; author "Some French Soldiers who Became Louisiana Educators," v.31, p.849-876; "A La Poursuite des Aigles," reviewed by Rene J. La Gardeur, Jr., v.33, p.151-153; "Veterans Versus Churchwardens," v.33, p.145-150.

Delgado, Isaac, donates Memorial Building to Charity Hospital, v.31, p.80.

Delgado, Marcos, noted, v.22, p.940.

de Livaudais, Francois Esnould, owner of land grant later known as Faubourg Livaudais, v.20, p.913-916.

Deloach's Bluff, noted, v.24, p.95.

Delondes, Jorge, noted, v.22, p.392.

Delondes, Juan Bautista, noted, v.22, p.391.

Delondes, Santiago, noted, v.22, p.392.

De Los Adaes Mission, noted, v.25, p.399.

del Real, Jose Maria, noted, v.24, p.649, 659.

Delta Farms, drainage project, v.30, p.644, fig.2, p.696-697.

Delta Rifles, nucleus of 4th La. Reg't, v.29, p.1048; noted, v.29, p.1050, 1052, 1062,

1122; nucleus 4th La. Reg't, v.30, p.481.

Delvaux, Jean, sketch, v.22, p.67-78.

De Magny, Catherine, suit of, v.21, p.1009.

de Maison Rouge, Marquis, contract for settlement of Ouachita land "grant," v.20, p.303-304; formal grant of Carondelet to, v.20, p.307; character of, v.20, p.331-332; death and will of, v.20, p.335.

de Maret, Zadie, married Levi Foster, v.28, p.1130.

Demas, Henry, on the lottery question, v.27, p.990, 1042.

Democratic Anti-Lottery State Com., meeting in N.O., v.27, p.1090-1091, 1092.

Democratic Anti-Lottery St. Ex. Com., organization, committees, and work of, v.27, p.1058-1060.

Democratic Party, defeat of in La., 1867, v.27, p.533; 1868, v.27, p.535, 536, 537, 538; union with Warmothites, v.27, p.542, 545, 548, 552; endorsed Greeley, v.27, p.553, 571, 604, 751; split in La., 1891, v.27, p.789; and the silver issue, v.27, p.796-797; La. for free silver, v.27, p.801; Caffery a gold bug, "A La. Dem. out of Line," v.27, p.801-802; and the tariff question, v.27, p.805-821 passim.; members of bolt into Repub. Party, v.27, p.816; Caffery alienates himself from by stand on currency, v.27, p.849; lottery amendment issue in La. gubernatorial race, 1892, v.27, p.1085, 1086; meeting of St. Central Com., v.27, p.1087-1088; St. Nominating Conv., v.27, p.1088; factions hold caucus, v.27, p.1089; split in, v.27, p.1089-1092; efforts to unite, v.27, p.1093-1094; unity achieved, v.27, p.1096.

Democratic Republicans, v.25, p.48, 49, 51, 60, 77; in La., v.25, p.75, 78, 79, 89.

Democratic State Central Committee, v.27, p.790; meeting in N.O., v.27, p.1087-1088; anti-lottery "Foster" faction reorganizes, v.27, p.1090-1091; meeting of McEnery faction Ex. Com., v.27, p.1093; declares against lottery amendment in view of Morris' withdrawal, v.27, p.1093; meeting of factions, v.27, p.1093; efforts to unite, v.27, p.1093-1094; harmony effected, v.27, p.1096.

Democratic State Nominating Conv., 1891, v.27, p.789, 1088, 1089.

Democrats, and suffrage reform in La., v.19, p.392-406; and Judah P. Benjamin, v.19, p.1004ff.; in 1851, v.23, p.186; in La., v.25, p.121, 122, 123, 124, 125, 126, 128, 129, 133, 134, 136, 137, 140, 141, 142, 143, 675, 676, 679, 680-682, 683, 685, 686, 687, 689, 691, 704, 705, 706, 709, 710, 711, 712, 714, 715, 716, 719, 764, 998, 999, 1001, 1003, 1005, 1006, 1007, 1008, 1013-1014, 1035; Dem. Conv., 1845, v.25, p.1036; election, v.25, p.1037-1038; caucus, v.25, p.1038-1039; election of senator, 1847, v.25, p.1058-1059; on the Three Million Bill, v.25, p.1072; sen. election, 1848, v.25, p.1039-1104; pres. campaign, 1848, v.25, p.1105-1110; noted, v.25, p.1053, 1071, 1087, 1116.

De Mortier, Madame, noted, v.25, p.787.

de Nava, Don Pedro, Sp. comdt. prohibited exportation of livestock to La., v.28, p.1096.

Denegre, W. D., noted, v.22, p.520; possible choice for U.S. senator by leg., v.26, p.1111; cand. U.S. sen., v.28, p.1184.

Denham, Reuben, noted, v.23, p.418.

Denison, Alice, noted, v.23, p.1164.

Denison, Dudley C., letters from G. S. Denison, v.23, p.1169ff.

Denison, Eliza, see Jameson, Mrs. John Alexander.

Denison, George Stanton, early life and education, v.23, p.1132; teacher in San Antonio, v.23, p.1132, 1145-1161; practices law, v.23, p.1133, 1166; trip to Mex., v.23, p.1134; trip to north to enlist in Union army, v.23, p.1135, 1176; special agent, Treas. Dept., New Orleans, v.23, p.1135, 1179-1199, 1209-1220; acting surveyor and collector of internal rev., v.23, p.1137, 1200-1208; special agent, Treas. Dept. in Tex., v.23, p.1137, 1228-1233; sugar planter, v.23, p.1137, 1224, 1237-1238; death of, v.23, p.1138, 1239-1240; trip from Vt. to Tex., v.23, p.1138-1145; marriage, v.23, p.1163; letters of, v.23, p.1139-1240; noted, v.24, p.476, 487; worked with Chase on movement into Texas, v.26, p.344; received Hamilton in N.O., v.26, p.349; reported to Chase on corruption in N.O., v.26, p.355.

Denison, James, letters from G. S. Denison, v.23, p.1138ff.

Denison, Joseph Adam, noted, v.23, p.1132.

Denison, Mrs. E. S., letters from G. S. Denison, v.23, p.1139ff.; letter from Mr. Coppell, v.23, p.1239-1240.

Denison, Rachel, letters from G. S. Denison, v.23, p.1181-1182, 1208.

Denmark, claims against France, v.24, p.965.

Dennett, Daniel, early N.O. newspaperman, v.29, p.778.

De Palacios, Joseph, jailed for debt, v.23, p.55.

Department of Archives, L.S.U., v.24, p.308, 340.

Department of Interior, established, v.24, p.989.

Department of Public Works, Est., 1942, v.28, p.299.

De Pauw, Charles, sketch, v.21, p.37; v.22, p.52n., 81, 87.

"Depositories of Manuscript Collections in Louisiana," table of contents, v.24, p.309.

Depot de Fortifications des Colonies, memoirs in La. State Museum depository, v.24, p.317.

De Raoul's daughter married John Rhea, v.21, p.76.

Derbanne, Louis, search for fugitive slaves in neutral ground, v.28, p.1072.

Derbigny, Charles, noted, v.25, p.130; candidate for gov., 1855, v.25, p.681; 1846, v.25, p.1038.

Derbigny, Madame Pierre (Jean Felicite Odille Delassus), v.30, p.360, 372n., 402-403, 416.

Derbigny, Peter, La. gov. noted, v.25, p.48, 60.

Derbigny, Pierre Auguste Charles Bourisgay, noted, v.24, p.1057.

Derbigny, Pierre, N.O. lawyer, v.19, p.331-332; witness in Ouachita land grant case, v.20, p.363; noted, v.22, p.412, 418, 808; sketch, v.22, p.812-813; noted, v.23, p.730; noted, v.30, p.360.

Derbin, Skipworth, noted, v.23, p.422.

"Der Brauer von Preston," manuscript in L.S.U. Music School Library, v.24, p.347.

Derniere Isle (Last Isle), v.28, p.803ff.

de Rojas, Laura A., "The Great Fire of 1788 in N.O.," v.20, p.578-584; "A Consequence of the La. Purchase," v.21, p.362-366.

Deron, Madame, N.O. educator, v.30, p.858-859.

De Russy, Col. engineer in charge of Red River fortifications, v.26, p.1025.

De Russy, Lewis G., engr. in reclamation of marshlands, v.30, p.667; noted, v.30, p.668, 669.

De Russy, noted, v.24, p.78.

"Der Wildschutz," manuscript in L.S.U. Music School Library, v.24, p.347.

de Sanson, Edouard, surgeon on Duvernay Concession, v.21, p.982.

De Saulles, L., noted, v.23, p.204.

Descoudreaux, Charles, in charge at Balize and Manchac, v.27, p.630, 631.

Desfarges, associated with Laffite, v.24, p.363, 365, 366.

Desgrange, Jerome, sketch of, v.27, p.27; marriage to Zulime Carriere, v.27, p.24; children, v.27, p.24-25; trip to France, v.27, p.25-26; letter to Clark, v.27, p.26-29, 41; charged with bigamy, v.27, p.53-55, 57, 61, 62, 70, 78, 80, 81, 82, 83; Latin marriage certificate, v.27, p.86-91; early trial for bigamy in ecclesiastical court, v.27, p.91-104; petitioned by Zulime for alimony, v.27, p.104-107; record of divorce or annulment suit, v.27, p.107-114, 129, 130, 135-136, 138, 142, 143, 146, 147, 148, 149, 150, 151, 152, 153, 154, 156, 157, 158, 159, 160, 161, 163, 164, 166, 167, 169; alimony suit, v.27, p.155; legal opinion in re facts of marriage to Zulime, v.27, p.190-195, 206, 252, 253, 254, 255; declared not a bigamist, v.27, p.213-225; dissenting opinion, v.27, p.226-240; in re ecclesiastical trial of, v.27, p.257-258, 261, 262, 264, 265, 267-273, 275, 283, 284, 286-288.

Deshon, Capt. ———, noted, v.22, p.1021, 1022, 1023, 1024.

Deshotels, O. H., fusion cand. for auditor, 1900, v.28, p.1192.

Deslondes, ———, noted, v.23, p.1064.

Deslondes, Maria Josefa, land granted to, v.22, p.390; will of, v.22, p.391-393.

Deslondes, P. G., negro candidate for Sec. of State, v.29, p.403; v.31, p.536.

De Soto, Hernando, early wanderings in La., v. 20, p.291; noted, v.25, p.399; the Ouachita Valley expedition of 1539-1542, v.25, p.611-643; embarkation and landing, v.25, p.612-613; futile search for gold in Florida, v.25, p.613; trouble with Indians, v.25, p.614-616, 619; discovery and crossing of Miss. R., v.25, p.616-618; in Arkansas, v.25, p.618-626; the Casqui and the Pacaha Indians, v.25, p.618-622; in La., v.25, p.626-640; the disputed route to Ayas, v.25, p.633-636; with the Guachoya and Quigaltam Indians, v.25, p.635-637; in Miss. R. flood, v.25, p.636-638; death of, v.25, p.638; de Moscoco in command, v.25, p.639-

641; in the Miss. Valley, v.25, p.922.

De Soto Parish, La., in 1860, v.21, p.1120; active Farmers' Alliance Group, v.26, p.1067-1068; noted, v.26, p.1077; and the cong. election of 1894, v.26, p.1097.

Despatches of Spanish governors in Howard-Tilton Memorial Library, v.24, p.328.

Despau, Madam Sophie, v.27, p.7, 24, 34; testimony of, v.27, p.35, 39-40, 41, 54, 55, 56, 76-82, 97, 99, 103, 136-137, 138, 142-149, 151-152, 154, 155, 156, 157, 158, 159, 160, 161-162, 164, 165-166, 167, 168, 172, 175, 191, 193, 194, 206, 213, 214, 221, 222, 223, 224, 227-228, 229, 230, 231-232, 233, 234, 235, 236, 237, 238, 262, 268, 270-271, 283-284, 285, 287, 288; noted, v.27, p.37, 38, 57, 58, 60, 68, 85, 90; evidence concerning, v.27, p.115, 122, 125, 133, 141, 150, 153, 163; ruled unworthy of credit, v.27, p.217-220.

Desrayaux, Madame, N.O. educator, v.30, p.848-849; noted, v.30, p.967.

Desrayaux School, v.30, p.848-849.

Dessalines, noted, v.24, p.620.

Destrehan, ———, noted, v.22, p.749.

Destrehan, Jean Baptiste, court case involving, in Loyola University Library, v.24, p.323.

Destrehan, Jean Noel, sketch, v.282, p.844n.

"Destrehan, Marie Elizabetha, Marriage Contract with Carlos Felipe Favre Daunoy," Translated by Laura L. Porteous, v.9, p.388.

Destrehan's Slave Roll, v.7, p.302.

"Destruction and Reconstruction," Manuscript of General Richard Taylor's Book, by Andre Lafargue, v.13, p.46; comments, v.24, p.118-119.

"De Tonty, an Original Autograph of" (Translated from the original by Miss Annie R. King), by Henry P. Dart, v.6, p.576.

de Tourneuille, Chevalier, settlers for concession, v.21, p.965.

De Trepy, Pierre Marie Cabaret, deposition of, v.23, p.722-724.

"Deutcher Courier," N.O. newspaper begun 1842, v.26, p.1097.

Deutsche Gesellschaft, noted, v.24, p.129, 154; history of, v.24, p.159-160.

Deutscher Schulverein, noted, v.24, p.155.

Deutsches Haus, noted, v.24, p.160.

Deutsches National Theatre, noted, v.26, p.375, 388.

"Deutsches Theatre," defined, v.24, p.156; noted, v.26, p.375, 379.

Deva, Bernardo de, noted, v.22, p.814.

De Valetti, Dr. C., Charter member Medical Society, v.26, p.59; noted, v.26, p.75; delivered eulogy at Luzenberg's funeral, v.26, p.103.

Devall, David, brief sketch of life in Confederate Army, v.29, p.1051; Lt. in Nat'l Guards, v.29, p.1074; punishes men for refusing to answer roll call, v.29, p.1074-1075; noted, v.29, p.1147; at Battle of Ezra Church, v.29, p.1178, 1179; no favorite at reg't, v.29, p.1194; becomes Cap't of Nat'l Guard on promotion of Pruyn, v.29, p.1195; encounter with Col. Hunter, v.29, p.1195-1196; at Battle of Jonesboro, v.29, p.1198-1199; noted, v.29, p.1201, 1203, 1208.

Devall, Edith Smith Buhler (see Smith, Edna), second marriage of Edna Smith and children of, v.29, p.289.

Devall, Richard, identified, v.21, p.712n.; second husband of Edna Smith, v.29, p.289.

"DeVaudreuil, Inauguration of," Translated from the original by Mrs. Heloise H. Cruzat, by Henry P. Dart, v.6, p.568.

De Vaugine, Etienne, comdt. at Natchitoches, attempts to monopolize Caddo trade, v.27, p.633, 636.

"De Vaugine's Plantation in the Attakapas on Bayou Teche, Inventory of," Translated by Laura Porteous, with introduction by Henry P. Dart, v.9, p.565.

"Development of Education in La., prior to Statehood," by Martin L. Riley, v.19, p.595-634.

"Development of N.O. as a Wholesale Center," by Harry A. Mitchell, v.27, p.933-963.

De Verbois, N., noted, v.25, p.163.

Deverges, Sieur Bernard, commandant at Balize, gives aid to nuns, v.29, p.565-566; visits France, v.29, p.578, 579.

Devers, Jean, noted, v.22, p.1043.

de Verteuil, Pierre Louis, partner of Paris Duverney Concession, v.21, p.981.

Devesge, Capt. ———, pivateeersman, v.22, p.1044ff.

DeVilliers, Balthazar R., came to La., 1749, v.27, p.629, 630; at Pointe Coupee, v.27, p.630; repair of Fort Carlos III, v.27, p.644; sent to Ark., v.27, p.645-646; dealings with Indians, v.27, p.646, 647-648, 649, 650-651; trading arrangements with Blommart, v.27, p.649-650,

651, 655-656, 657, 658; agitation for movement of Ark. Post, v.27, p.659, 661; claims left bank of Miss. for Sp., v.27, p.662, 663, 668, 670-671; financial straits, v.27, p.672; relieved of command, v.27, p.672, 688; problem of sale of rum to Indians, v.27, p.691-692, 674, 675; Colbert's ill will toward, v.27, p.676, 677; death, v.27, p.677, 683, 702.

DeVilliers, Madam B. R., v.27, p.663-664, 672, 673; detained at Pointe Coupee as an absconding debtor, v.27, p.674, 677.

Devil's Swamp, v.28, p.5, 23, 40.

"Devorador," merchant brig, v.23, p.766.

Devries, Rose, singer, v.31, p.871.

Devron, Dr. Gustave, "A Chapter of Colonial History, 1717-1751," v.6, p.543.

DeWater, Charles, noted, v.24, p.637, 665, 671, 681, 684, 694.

Dhu, Rhoderick, pen-name of Cable, v.24, p.171.

Dialect, use of by Cable, v.24, p.183.

"Diana," Federal gunboat, v.24, p.72, 73; schooner, v.24, p.676.

"Diary of a Young Lawyer of Natchitoches of 1863, The," William S. Toumey, I, II, edited by J. Fair Hardin and Phanor Breazeale, v.17, p.64, 315.

"Diary of Bernardo de Galvez, of Operations against Pensacola," Trans. from the Spanish by Gaspar Cusachs, v.1, sec.1, p.44.

"Diary of Charles Dehault Delassus From New Orleans to St. Louis, 1836," by John Francis McDermott, v.30, p.359-438.

"Diary of Surgeon J. M. Craig, 4th La. Regt., C.S.A., 1864-1865," by John S. Kendall, v.8, p.53.

Dibble, H. C., judge, ruled in favor of Repub. Returning Board, v.27, p.558; counselor in support of Pinchback, v.27, p.592; Republican nominee to Congress, v.29, p.718; judge 8th Dist. Court, v.30, p.602-603; noted, v.30, p.607, 619; and injunction against Lynch Board, v.30, p.641-643; noted, v.30, p.557, 577, 580, 591.

Dibert, Mrs. John, donates tuberculosis hospital, residence for sisters to New Orleans Charity Hospital, v.31, p.80.

D'Iberville, Pierre le Moyne, Sieur, and Fort de la Boulaye, v.19, p.842ff.; report in Bibliotheca Parsoniana, v.24, p.310.

Dickey, Dallas C., "Seargent S. Prentiss, Whig Orator of the South," rev'd, v.29, p.202-203.

Dickinson, Charles H., son-in-law of Joseph Erwin, v.27, p.346; duel with A. Jackson, v.27, p.347-348, 397, 401, 404, 413, 435, 454, 455, 472.

Dickinson, John, noted, v.24, p.701; state printer when Shreveport was Capital of La., v.27, p.1226, 1228.

Dick, John, and Andrew Jackson in La., v.21, p.370ff.

Dickson, Alexander, in W. Fla., v.22, p.38; and the Pensacola siege, v.26, p.316; surrenders Fort Richmond to Galvez, v.26, p.743; articles of Capitulation of B. R., v.28, p.696.

Dickson, Miss Bell, Recording Sec. of Women's Anti-Lottery League, v.27, p.1061.

Dickson, Miss, vice-pres. Women's Anti-Lottery League, v.27, p.1061.

Di Cristina, Paul, and Mafia, v.22, p.835-836.

"Dictator, Jurisdiction of The, Tribunals of Criminal Jurisdiction in Ancient Rome," by Charles Gayarre, v.33, p.211.

"Die for the Coinage of Silver Half Dollars, The Confederate," by W. O. Hart and Dr. Y. R. LeMonnier, v.5, p.505.

Dieppe, health resort, v.24, p.952, 997, 998, 1014, 1120, 1124, 1125, 1129.

Dietrich, M., noted, v.23, p.521.

Diettel, Howard L., noted, v.25, p.207, 208.

"Die Weise Deine von Avenel," manuscript in L.S.U. Music School Library, v.24, p.347.

Diggs' Academy, v.30, p.896.

"Diligent," French privateer, v.24, p.614.

Dillard, James Hardy, noted, v.25, p.781, 793, 808.

Dillard Uiversity, History of, v.25, p.780-782, 811, 814.

Di Martini, Eduardo, and Mafia, v.22, p.835-837.

Dimbinsky, L., La. educator, v.30, p.829; noted, v.30, p.967.

Dimbinsky's School, v.30, p.829.

Dimick, Howard T., "Visits of Josiah Gregg to La., 1841-1847," v.29, p.5-13; "Peace Overtures of July, 1864," v.29, p.1241-1258.

"Diminishing Influences of German Culture in New Orleans Life since 1865," by William Robinson Konrad, v.24, p.126-167.

Dimitry, Alexander, supt. of Ed., noted, v.25, p.1043; v.28, p.971; La.'s first St. Supt. of Ed., v.30, p.872, 968; v.31, p.984-985.

Dimitry, Charles Patton, "The Story of the Ancient Cabildo," v.3, p.57; "The Old 'Mobile Landing' Head of the Basin, in New Orleans," v.3, p.131.

Dimitry's School, v.30, p.865.

Dimitry, Theodore J., manuscripts in Howard-Tilton Memorial Library, v.24, p.328-329.

Dingley Tariff Act, boosted sugar duties, v.27, p.818; rates, v.27, p.819; Caffery's view of, v.27, p.820; passage of, v.27, p.821.

Dinkelspiel, Edward, quartermaster sergeant, v.26, p.795, 800.

Dinkins, Lynn H., pres. Interstate Trust and Banking Co., v.28, p.1225.

Dinnies, J. C., early N.O. newspaperman, v.29, p.775, 776.

Diocese of Natchitoches, noted, v.25, p.362.

"Diplomacy of the Borderlands. The Adams—Onis Treaty of 1819," by Philip Coolidge Brooks, rev'd by Harris G. Warren, v.24, p.205-206.

"Diplomatic Career of Pierre Soule," by J. A. Reinecke, Jr., v. 15, p.283.

Diplomats, expenses and duties of, v.24, p.941, 985, 990, 1005, 1007-1008, 1019, 1039-1040, 1047, 1073-1074, 1084, 1088, 1093, 1097-1098, 1102, 1108-1109, 1119, 1129, 1135.

Dirombourg, early name for B. R., v.28, p.62.

Diron, Dominique, privateersman, v.22, p.1020-1021, 1038; noted, v.24, p.612, 613.

Dirrhammer, Charles, noted, v.23, p.518.

Discriminatory duties, protests against by Brown, v.24, p.1067.

"Discussion in the Continental Congress Relative to Surrendering the Right to Navigate the Miss. River," v.26, p.12-36.

Disease, putrid fever, 1769, at Ill., v.23, p.388.

"Disfranchisement in Louisiana, 1862-1870," by William A Russ, Jr., v.18, p.557-580.

d'Istraia, Count Capo, noted, v.24, p.1104.

"Distribution of Land in British West Florida, The," by Cecil Johnson, v.16, p.539.

"Distribution of Land in Louisiana by the Company of the Indies, The Jonchere Concession," Translated from the Book of Concessions by Mrs. Heloise H. Cruzat with Introduction by Henry P. Dart, v.11, p.553.

"District of Iberville," v.25, p.162.

Ditchy, J. K., "Early Census Tables of Louisiana," v.13, p.205; "Les Acadiens Louisianais et Leur Parler," Book review by Henry P. Dart, v.16, p.166.

Di Trapani, Joseph, noted, v.22, p.855.

Divet, Ecequiel and Clark's expedition, v.21, p.34ff.

Divided sovereignty, theory of, v.24, p.710.

Dix, Dorothy, "Talks on Grace King," v.6, p.359.

Dixon, Frank M., Address by Honorable, v.32, p.231.

Dixon, George Washington, N.O. minstrel, sketch of, v.30, p.128-130.

Dixon, W. H., principal of "Prof. Dixon's Academy," 1840, v.29, p.84.

"D. L. Tally," steamer, picture of, v.25, p.441.

Doane, Col. Charles, chief agent of O'Reilly, v.31, p.439, 440; contractor, v.31, p.441.

Dobbs, A. N., supervised parade on Bogalusa inaugural day, v.29, p.110.

"Doctor John Hamilton Robinson," by Harold A. Bierch, Jr., v.25, p.644-69.

"Documents, Calendar of," Mrs. N. M. Miller Surrey, v.7, p.551.

"Documents Concerning Bienville's Lands in Louisiana, 1719-1737," Text and translation by Heloise H. Cruzat, Introduction by Henry P. Dart, v.10, p.5, 161, 364, 538; from 1719 to 1740—Translated from Book of Concessions, 5th, 6th and 7th Installments, v.11, p.87, 207, 463.

"Documents Concerning Sale of Chaouachas Plantation," Heloise H. Cruzat, v.8, p.594.

"Documents Concerning the Crozat Regime in Louisiana, 1712-1717," by Albert G. Sanders (Introduction by Henry P. Dart), v.16, p.239; I, Memoir from Duclos to Pontchartrain, July 15, 1713, II, Letter from Duclos to Ponchartrain, October 25, 1713; III, IV, v.17, p.268, 452; v.15, p.589, (1) Memoir (Instructions) of the King to Duclos, December 18, 1712, (2) Memoir (Instructions) of the King to Cadillac, December 18, 1712 (3) Memoir (Instructions) of the King to Duclos Carrying His Credentials as First Councillor of the Superior Council, December 24, 1712, (4) Memoir (Instructions) of the King to Duclos Regarding His Management of His Office.

"Documents Concerning the History of the

Indians of the Eastern Region of Louisiana," by Baron Marc de Villiers, George C. H. Kernion, v.8, p.28.

"Documents Concerning West Florida Revolution, 1810," I, II, III, by John J. Kendall, v.17, p.80, 306, 474.

"Documents Covering a Royal Land Grant on the Mississippi and Amite Rivers," Transcribed from the Originals in the Cabildo, v.12, p.630.

"Documents Covering the Beginning of African Slave Trade in Louisiana, 1718," translated by A. G. Sanders, v.14, p.163.

"Documents Covering the Criminal Trial of Etienne Larue, before the Superior Council of Louisiana, May, 1747," Translation by Heloise H. Cruzat, v.13, p.377.

"Documents Covering the Impeachment of Bienville under Direction of Louis XIV Before Diron D'Artaguette, Special Commissioner, at Fort Louis, Mobile, February 24-27, 1708," Trans. by A. G. Sanders, v.14, p.5.

"Documents Covering the Prosecution of Denis Braud, Regidor of the Cabildo, for the Crime of Running Away from Louisiana," translated by Laura L. Porteous, v.14, p.361.

"Documents Covering the Renunciation of Daniel Fagot of the Office of Regidor of Fines in Favor of deGlapion and the Proceedings Resulting Therefrom," Translated by Laura L. Porteous, v.14, p.373.

"Documents Covering the Sale at Auction to Daniel Fagot of the Vacant Office of Regidor of Fines Abandoned by Denis Braud," Translated by Laura L. Porteous, v.14, p.366.

Documents, Historical, "A Letter from the Battle of New Orleans from John A. Fort," with Introductory Note by E. A. Parsons, v.32, p.225.

"Documents in Loppinot Case, 1774," Translated by Laura L. Porteous, v.12, p.38.

"Documents Relating to Alexandro O'Reilly," David K. Bjork, v.7, p.20.

"Documents Relating to the Batture Controversy in New Orleans," ed. by J. A. Padgett, v.23, p.679-732.

"Documents Showing That the U. S. Ultimately Financed the W. Fla. Revolution of 1810," ed. by James A. Padgett, v.25, p.943-970.

Dodge, G. W., pres. La. Red Cypess Co., v.30, p.1037.

Dolliver, Benjamin, privateer, v.24, p.30.

"Domestic Animals and Plants of French Louisiana as Mentioned in the Literature with Reference to Sources, Varieties and Uses, The," by Lauren C. Post, v.16, p.554.

Dominguez, noted, v.24, p.10.

Donaldsonville, La., in 1860, v.21, p.1120-1124; noted, v.22, p.435, 820, 821; Whig Convention, 1850, v.23, p.1083; during the Civil War, v.23, p.1196; distributing point for slaves, v.24, p.23; noted, v.24, p.54, 71, 76, 77, 80; convention of sugar planters, 1842, v.25, p.111-112; noted, v.28, p.38, 739, 754, 755, 757, 842; Creole Civilization in, 1850, according to "Le Vigilant," v. 31, p.981-994.

Donaldson, William, noted, v.22, p.433, 434.

Don Andres Almonester y Roxas, generous N.O. benefactor of 1786, v.29, p.617.

Donation by State of Louisiana to the Family of Thomas Jefferson, 1827, v.8, p.52.

Donato, Martin, noted, v.25, p.319, 371, 732.

Donelson, Mary, married John Caffery, v.27, p.783.

Donelson, Rachel, became Mrs. Andrew Jackson, v.27, p.783.

Don Juan, comment about Rapp in, v.24, p.422.

"Don Juan Filhiol and the Founding of Fort Miro, The Modern Monroe," La., by J. Fair Hardin, v.20, p.463-485.

Donnally, Capt. J. B., rep. cand. sec. of state, v.28, p.1175.

Donnaud, Charles, early N.O. police reporter, v.29, p.53-54.

Donnellan, Dr. J. L., mayor of Carrollton, v.21, p.251; noted, v.22, p.203.

Donnels, William, organizer of United Brotherhood of Carpenters and Joiners of America, v.29, p.133.

"Don Pedro Favrot, A Creole Pepys," by Helen Parkhurst, v.28, p.679-734.

Do Porto Gonzalo, noted, v.22, p.934.

"Dorada," early name of the Firebrand, v.21, p.205; privateer of Laffites, v.23, p.745.

Dorcheat Bayou, noted, v.24, p.432.

Dorch, John, and W. Fla. Rev., v.21, p.722n.

Dorfeuille, G., noted, v.25, p.735.

Dorothee vs. Conquillon et al., v.25, p.313-314.

Dorr, J. W., description of trip over La.,

v.21, p.1110-1214; sketch of, v.21, p.1111.
Dorsey collection, of Caddo Indians, v.24, p.749.
Dorsey, Florence L., "Master of the Mississippi," rev'd, v.25, p.824-27.
D'Ortolant, Bernardo, noted, v.22, p.68.
Doss, W. L., opposed lotteries, v.27, p.1040.
Dostie, Dr. A. P., noted, v.31, p.1011, 1044, 1081; auditor, v.31, p.1044; Wells, v.31, p.1031, 1034; killed, v.31, p.1083.
Douglas, Henry T., noted, v.24, p.98.
Douglas, Stephen A., noted, v.24, p.58.
D'Outremer, Carlier, noted, v.22, p.815.
Dow, Dr. Robert, noted, v.22, p.449.
Dowler, Dr., Charter member Medical Society, v.26, p.59.
Dow, Lorenzo, in Orleans Territory, v.22, p.429.
Dow, Neal, noted, v.23, p.1198-1199.
Downman, Lt., noted, v.23, p.388.
Downman, R. H., "Lumber King of the Southwest," v.30, p.1026, 1028; mills belonging to, v.30, p.1030; noted, v.30, p.1036, 1037.
Downs, Robert B., work on southern libraries, v.24, p.315, 317, 330, 333, 345, 349.
"Downs, Solomon Weathersbee, General, 1801-1854," by Mrs. Minnie Markette Ruffin and Miss Lilla McLure, v.17, p.5; and Maison Rouge Will, v.20, p.339; and election of 1851, v.23, p.186; noted, v.23, p.189; noted, v.25, p.142, 675; and the Const. Con. of 1844, v.25, p.1007ff.; named U.S. Senator, v.25, p.1044, 1053; U.S. Sen. supporting bill for reclaiming swamp lands, v.28, p.279; noted, v.28, p.948; ap't to rep. La. at Memphis R.R. Conv., v.28, p.974.
Doyle, Dr. Henry A., noted, v.25, p.161, 164, 182, 202.
"Drainage Reclamation in the Coastal Marshlands of the Mississippi River Delta," by Robert W. Harrison and Walter W. Kollmorgen, v.30, p.654-709.
Drake, Mrs. Alexander, and N.O. Theatre, v.21, p.497.
Drama, German on the N.O. stage, v.26, p.361-627; brief history of in Am., v.26, p.363-364; of N.O., v.26, p.364-366; development of interest in drama in N.O., v.26, p.369-371; Ger. Theatre, v.26, p.371-376; classical Ger. dramatists, v.26, p.376-400; second rate dramatist, v.26, p.400-433; other dramatists, v.26, p.433-448; conclusion, v.26, p.448-449; bibl., v.26, p.449-453; appendix, I chronological list of theatrical performances in N.O., 1839-1890, v.26, p.454-600; appendix, II alphabetical list of authors of plays on N.O. stage, v.26, p.600-627.
"Dramatische Gesellschaft," noted, v.24, p.157.
Draughon, Amelia (Permelia), mother of G. L. Alspaugh, v.29, p.1229.
"Dr. Beatty," confederate boat, v.29, p.1099-1100; used in capture of "Indianola," v.29, p.1102-1107.
"Dress and Brains," essay by Cable, v.24, p.170.
Dreux, Colonel Charles D., (Dedication of Monument To), Address on, by Col. H. J. de la Vergne, v.5, p.502; first La. officer killed in Civil War, v.29, p.1047.
Drexel, Mothel Katherine, noted, v.25, p.785.
Dreyfous, Felix F., against lottery bill of 1890, v.27, p.1034; reasons for opposition, v.27, p.1040-1041; termed "political traitor," v.27, p.1047, 1056; addressed Anti-Lottery League Conv., v.27, p.1057.
"Dr. James G. Carson's Canebrake: A View of an Ante-Bellum Louisiana Plantation," by Dr. Robert C. Reinders, v.33, p.353-363.
Dronville, ———, noted, v.23, p.397.
"Drop Shot" column, of Cable, v.24, p.168-169, 171, 177, 181, 186.
"Dr. Otto Lerch, 1855-1948," by Dr. A. E. Fossier, v.33, p.343-348.
Duane, William John, noted, v.24, p.936.
Dubois, Capt. ———, privateersman, v.22, p.1081-1083.
Dubois, William, candidate for St. Louis Church Warden, v.31, p.913.
Dubourg, Bishop, noted, v.25, p.365.
Dubreuil, Claude Joseph, arrival in La., v.18, p.267; located at "The Chapitoulas," v.18, p.268; first to make levees and drainage canals, v.18, p.270; contractor of public works for the King, v.18, p.270; active in slave trade, v.18, p.272-273; first sugar planter after the Jesuits, v.18, p.275-276; contract for first Charity Hospital, v.18, p.280-281; contract showing cost of 18th century house in New Orleans, v.18, p.281-283; work as a canal builder, v.18, p.283-284; agricultural activities and commerce in the colony, v.18, p.285-288; memorial of

Madame Dubreuil to the French government, v.18, p.289-291; succession sale of Dubreuil's estate, v.18, p.291-331; canal of, v.23, p.438; and La. sugar industry, v.25, p.24.

Dubreuil, Jean, deposition of, v.23, p.709-710.

Dubreuil, Sieur, general contractor for the second convent, v.29, p.608, 609.

Dubuc, Antoine, secretary of St. Louis Church Wardens, v.31, p.918.

Dubuclet, Antoine, candidate for state treasurer, v.31, p.536.

Dubuclet, Dauterive, sketch, v.28, p.813; claim on Belle Isle, v.28, p.915.

Dubuisson, Etienne, mentioned, v.21, p.984.

Du Buisson, Francois de Montfort, manager of Paris Duverney Concession, v.21, p.981.

"Duc de Montebello," privateer, v.23, p.435.

Duchesne, Mother Philippine, arrives at N. O. from Fr., v.29, p.623-624; leader of Order of Sacred Heart, v.30, p.958-959, 960-961.

Duclot, Louis, printer, v.22, p.685n.

Ducoing, Francois, noted, v.22, p.1066.

Ducoing, Judge John, noted, v.22, p.737, 764, 1066.

Du Colombier, ———, early slave trader, v.23, p.866.

Ducros, Joseph, noted, v.22, p.625; v.23, p.697.

Ducros, P. A., Jr., senator, attempt to bribe, v.27, p.996.

Ducros, R. J., noted, v.22, p.749.

Dudley, W. S., Prog. League Com., v.27, p.1062.

"Duel Between Diplomats, A," by H. G. Morgan, Jr., v.14, p.385.

Dueling, code, v.23, p.141-161; in New Orleans, v.23, p.445-470; code of J. Quintero, v.23, p.453-460; in La., v.24, p.756-782; in N.O., v.25, p.310; prohibited by law, v.25, p.1034; in N.O., v.26, p.78-88.

"Duel in the Dark in New Orleans, 1747," by Henry P. Dart, v.13, p.199.

Du Fernex, Rev. ———, pastor in N.O., v.22, p.456.

Duffel, Dr., noted, v.23, p.1080.

Duff, John R., husband of Mary Ann Duff, v.28, p.924ff.; death of, v.28, p.933.

Duff, Mary Ann, gave up brilliant career as actress to become homemaker in N.O., v.28, p.922-923; life and family of, v.28, p.923-924; marriage to John Duff, v.28, p.924; theatrical career in Am., v.28, p.925-926; appearance in N.O., v.28, p.926, 927-933; death of husband, remarriage, v.28, p.933; retirement to private life, v.28, p.935; separated from husband, left N.O. for life of obscurity, v.28, p.936-937; death, v.28, p.937-938; children of, v.28, p.938-940.

Duff, Mary, daughter of Mary Ann, also actress, v.28, p.938-939.

Duff, William, pioneer in the Eng. Theatre in N.O., v.28, p.90, 91, 92.

Duffy, Sgt. Miles R., promoted, v.26, p.836.

Dufilho, L. J., one of the first registered pharmacists, v.26, p.336, 337.

du Fossat, Guy Soniat, history of La., in Shreve Memorial Library, v.24, p.339.

Dufour, Cyprien, noted, v.23, p.180; v.24, p.757; quoted on Soule, v.25, p.998; reasons for Soule's success, v.25, p.1079; his tribute to Soule, v.25, p.1082.

"Dufour's Local Sketches, 1847," translated under supervision of R. W. Colomb, I, II, III, v.14, p.208, 393, 533; IV, V (Conclusion), v.15, p.78, 268.

Dufour, W. C., commanded 7th Bat'l La., N.G., v.26, p.792; noted, v.26, p.743; made Lt.-Col. 2nd La. Regt., v.26, p.793; acting regimental commander, v.26, p.831.

Dufrocq, John R., noted, v.23, p.203, 204.

Dugas, Vera Lea, "The Ante-Bellum Career of Leonidas Polk," v.32, p.245.

Duggan, J. H., opposed lottery, v.27, p.1043, 1056.

Dujay, Margaret, see Maison Rouge, Margaret.

"Duke de Noailles," ship list of passengers bound from France to La., 1719, v.21, p.974-978.

Dula, John, colored parish judge, forced to resign, v.25, p.709.

Dumas, Henry, instrumental in establishment of S. University, v.25, p.769.

Dumas, Major F. E., v.30, p.548.

Dumoinisseau, Jean-Baptiste, noted, v.22, p.1066.

Dumont de Montigny, quoted, v.31, p.580; source discussed, v.31, p.580-581; noted, v.31, p.601.

Dunbar and Hunter, expedition of, v.25, p.625, 628, 630, 631; concerning Nilco, v.25, p.632, 641.

Dunbar, George T., officer Soc. of Nat'l Hist. and the Sciences, v.26, p.61; noted, v.26, p.79.

Dunbar, William, exploration trip up Ouachita River, v.20, p.393-395; and election of 1851, v.23, p.186.

Duncan, Abner L., legal advisor of James Wilkinson, v.21, p.101, 106n.; and W. Fla. Rev., v.21 p.113, 738n.; supplies for W. Fla. Rev., v.21, p.115; letter to John H. Johnson, v.21, p.115-116, 120, 122; agent of W. Fla., v.21, p.151; and Firebrand affair, v.21, p.205, 206, 208, 210; and Andrew Jackson, v.21, p.368ff., 385n.; and Spanish filibusters, v.21, p.813; and Mexican insurgents, v.21, p.1086; noted, v.22, p.1059; and Spanish insurgents, v.23, p.737; and filibusters, v.23, p.757; and New Orleans Assoc., v.23, p. 763; privateering of, v.23, p.771; member of New Orleans Assn., v.24, p.631; noted, v.25, p.300.

Duncan, G. B., noted, v.23, p.180; v.25, p.1086; v.26, p.88; Luzenberg's attorney, v.26, p.96-97.

Duncan, J. K., noted, v.24, p.453, 463.

Duncan, Lucius C., noted, v.22, p.457, 470, 472.

Duncan, Stephen, collection in L.S.U. Archives, v.24, p.342.

Duncan, William, noted, v.22, p.965.

Dunlap, John, manuscripts in Howard-Tilton Memorial Library, v.24, p.329.

Dunn, A. M., in the Const. Con. of 1844, v.25, p.1010ff.

Dunn, Milton, "History of Natchitoches, Louisiana," v.3, p.26.

Dunn, Oscar J., opponent of Pinchback as delegate to Const. Conv., 1867-1868, v.27, p.533; pres. of Repub. Conv., 1871, v.27, p.541; Pinchback selected for U.S. Senate over, v.27, p.542; acting gov. calls Customhouse meeting of Repub. faction, v.27, p.544-545; death of, v.27, p.546, 562; Negro Lt. Gov., v.30, p.548, 550; in Repub. St. convention, v.30, p.604-605; leads anti-Warmoth men, v.30, p.609-611; as acting gov., v.30, p.612-615; letter of to Greeley, v.30, p.622-623; death, v.30, p.624; noted, v.30, p.198, 620; noted, v.31, p.64, 1042.

Duon, Augustin, noted, v.22, p.420.

Dupaquier, Dr. E. M., Translation of Surgeons' Report in "Suit for Damages for Personal Injuries to a Slave," v.5, p.58.

Dupart, Pierre Delisle, suit against, v.21, p.1010-1012.

Dupas, Dr., Charter member Medical Society, v.26, p.59.

Duplantier, Guy, appointment decision, v.31, p.1031.

Duplanty, Bruce, noted, v.23, p.374.

Duplessis, ———, noted, v.24, p.778-779.

Duplessis, Elias, arrest of, v.22, p.779.

Duplessis, Martin, letter in New Orleans Public Library, v.24, p.325.

Duplessis, P. L. B., and Andrew Jackson, v.21, p.371ff.; member of New Orleans Assn., v.24, p.631.

Duplessis, P. L. B., Jr., survey for light house at mouth of Miss., v.28, p.748n.

Duplessis, W. F., on Charity Hospital Board, 1836, v.26, p.58.

Dupont, Alfred Leonce, author, "The Career of Paul Octave Hebert, Governor of Louisiana," v.3, p.491-552.

Du Pratz, Antoine S. Le Page, author on Natchez culture and Dumont, v.31, p.581; influenced by Bienville, v.31, p.581; quoted concerning Natchez, v.31, p.582-584, 593-594; credibility, v.31, p.585; noted, v.31, p.602; explanation of origin of name, B.R., v.282, p.45, 46; location of B.R., v.28, p.63; attributes change in course of Miss. to human interference, v.282, p.70-71; believed cutoff of Pointe Coupee occurred in 1713, v.28, p.76, 84; his "carte de la Louisiane," v.28, p.40.

Dupree, Stirling, and W. Fla. Rev., v.21, p.109; letter to Kemper, v.21, p.109; complaint against, v.21, p.123-124; at Pascagoula, v.21, p.155; and W. Fla. Rev., v.21, p.799n.

Dupre, George W., state printer, accused of overcharging, v.27, p.987; testified to bribery by Lottery Co., v.27, p.989-991; Lottery gets control of "Democrat," v.27, p.1001-1002; case of involving violation of Anti-Lottery Postal Bill, v.27, p.1081-1083; backs "Democrat," v.31, p.739, 740; attack by Green, v.31, p.774, 775; "Daily States," v.31, p.786; noted, v.31, p.792, 828.

Dupre, Gilbert L., "Imperial St. Landry," v.8, p.420; favored lottery bill of 1890; v.27, p.1033, 1047; Judge, v.28, p.1174.

Dupre, Gov. Jacques, and tariff, v.25, p.59, 75-76.

Dupre, Jacques, v.30, p.81.

Dupre, Raoul, noted, v.23, p.556, 557.

Duprez, Charles H., manager minstrel shows, sketch of, v.30, p.147.

Dupuis, Francois, agent of Aury, v.23,

p.761; member of New Orleans Assn., v.24, p.631.

Dupuis, V. E., People's Party elector, v.26, p.1087.

du Quesnay, Rev. Marie Arthur Guillaume le Mercier, rector of St. Louis Cathedral, v.20, p.680-689.

Duralde, J. V., noted, v.25, p.681.

Duralde, Martin, Jr., v.24, p.1146, 1173, 1175.

Duralde, Martin, noted, v.22, p.814; married daughter of Henry Clay, v.27, p.721, 733, 736.

Durand, Andre, noted, v.22, p.768.

Durand, Jean, noted, v.22, p.685; privateer, v.23, p.431.

Durant, Thomas J., noted, v.24, p.506; and tariff, v.25, p.136-137; Dem. candidate for State Senate, 1846, v.25, p.1036-1037, 1038, 1046; N. O. unionist, v.31, p.1011, 1042; appointed governor, v.31, p.1091.

Durcy, ———, buys part of Jesuit plantation, v.23, p.681.

Durel, Batiste, letter to Casa Calvo, v.22, p.129.

Durel, E., noted, v.24, p.758.

Durel Institute, v.30, p.881.

Durel, Lionel C., "Creole Civilization in Donaldsonville, 1850," According to "Le Vigilant," v.31, p.981-994.

Durell, E. H., noted, v.23, p.521, 522, 1224n.; judge ruled in favor of Repub. Returning Board, v.27, p.558; promulgated order for seizure of state house, v.27, p.559; noted, v.28, p.1135; noted, v.30, p.528, 537; orders Packard to State House, v.30, p.643-645; noted, v.30, p.220-222, 253; restrains Warmoth returning board, v.31, p.700; "midnight order," v.31, p.701; acknowledges Lynch Board, v.31, p.701; noted, v.31, p.1079.

Durnford, Elias, member of W. Fla. Council, v.23, p.23, 354ff.

Durst, John, v.28, p.1068, 1093, 1095.

Duson, C. C., noted, v.23, p.567; sheriff of St. Landry, v.27, p.1121; sketch, v.27, p.1122; co-founder of Crowley, v.27, p.1123; crier at auction of lots, v.27, p.1124; aid to Crowley, v.27, p.1129-30; founder of Eunice, La., v.27, p.1130; memorial ceremony, v.27, p.1208.

Duson, Will, manages "Signal," v.27, p.1187, 1189.

Duson, W. W., noted, v.23, p.567; sketch, v.27, p.1122; co-founder of Crowley, v.27, p.1123; the "guiding spirit" of Crowley, v.27, p.1129, 1171; donated land for school in Crowley, v.27, p.1176, 1178, 1181; owns and edits "Signal," v.27, p.1184-1187; donated land to churches, v.27, p.1190, 1196; memorial ceremony, v.27, p.1208.

"Dutch Gazette," newspaper, noted, v.33, p.406-407.

"Dutch Settlement," or Pattersonville, v.24, p.40.

du Terrage, Baron Marc de Villiers, in Memoriam, v.19, p.1069-1074; works on La., v.24, p.755.

Duties, in controversy between the U. S. and France, v.24, p.1063ff.

Dutillet, Francis, justice of peace, v.23, p.732.

Dutise, Louis, noted, v.25, p.162.

Dutrien, ———, noted, v.22, p.1067.

Dutton, John, Iberville Parish judge, v.27, p.369, 400, 411, 432, 459.

Duvallon, Berquin, noted, v.23, p.871.

Duval, ———, painter, v.22, p.687n.

Duverney, Joseph Paris, inventory of Concession, v.21, p.979-994.

Duvezin, Olivier, surveyor of Jesuit plantation, v.23, p.681.

Duyckinck, Evert A., letters to from Charles Gayarre, v.33, p.223, 224, 225, 227, 228, 231, 232, 234, 236, 237, 239, 241, 242, 244, 246, 247, 249, 250.

Dyer, Brainerd, "Zachary Taylor," rev'd, v.30, p.349-350.

Dyer, Dr. Isadore, noted, v.22, p.679n.

Dyer, Louise K., "History of the Cabildo of Mexico City, 1524-1534," v.6, p.395.

"Dying March," poem by Cable, v.24, p.179-180.

Dykers Institute, v.30, p.870.

Dymond, John, Editor, Louisiana Historical Quarterly, Memorial Presented to the Louisiana Historical Society, March 28, 1922, v.5, p.188; Illustration (Portrait), v.5, p.187; The Quarterly Under Mr. Dymond, by Editor, v.5, p.277; noted, v.22, p.218.

EADS, JAMES B., PROPOSED JETTIES, v.31, p.543-545; noted, v.31, p.738, 784.

Eagar, ———, noted, v.23, p.1211.

Eakin, Paul, noted, v.24, p.307.

Ealer, Joseph E., noted, v.23, p.478.

"Early Career of Pierre Soule," by Arthur Freeman, v.25, p.971-1127.

"Early Census Tables of Louisiana," by William Beer, Translation by J. K. Ditchy, v.13, p.205.

"Early Commercial Prestige of New Orleans," by H. E. Chambers, v.5, p.451.

"Early Economic Life in La., 1804-1824 (An Historical Dialogue)," by Pierre de la Vergne, v.26, p.915-936.

"Early Episodes in Louisiana History," by William Kernan Dart; Foreword, v.1, sec.3, p.190; Trip from France, The, v.1, sec.3, p.191; Life in New Orleans: An Indian Treaty, v.1, sec. 3, p.193; Natchez Tribe, and Their Massacre of the French, v.1, sec.3, p.197.

Early, Gen'l Jubal, commissioner of La. Lottery drawings, v.27, p.979; in defense of Lottery Co., v.27, p.987; semi-annual lottery drawing, 1879, v.27, p.1002-1003, 1015; as commissioner, v.27, p.1016-1020, 1099; and lottery company, v.31, p.742.

Early History of Louisiana, French and Spanish Documents concerning, v.1, sec.3, p.103, 224.

"Early History of the Episcopal Church in N. O., 1805-1840," by G. F. Taylor, v.22, p.428-478.

"Early History of the Flag of the United States," by George A. Simpson, v.8, p.258.

"Early History of the Louisiana State University, The," by J. Fair Hardin, v.11, p.5.

"Early New Orleans Newpapers," by John S. Kendall, v.10, p.383.

E. A. Seminary, sketch of, v.30, p.790-791.

East Baton Rouge Parish, La., elections of 1812, v.21, p.193-198; Parish Juries, v.21, p.200-201; in 1860, v.21, p.1133; noted, v.25, p.156, 162, 321, 322, 324, 337, 348, 388, 389; noted, v.26, p.1101, 1102; Populist legislator from, v.26, p.1109.

East Feliciana Parish, La., Germans in, v.23, p.514; formation, v.28, p.946; Johnson in, v.28, p.948; noted, v.28, 952, 958.

Easton, Dr. R. B., charter member medical society, v.26, p.59; noted, v.26, p.75, 82; signed testimonial justifying Luzenberg, v.26, p.88-89.

Easton, Warren, N. O. Supt. of Schools, v.26, p.142-143.

"Eastport," Federal gunboat, v.24, p.94, 95.
Eaton, S. M., noted, v.23, p.1256.
Ecclesiastical Court, authority questioned, v27, p.11; trial of Desgrange for bigamy, v.27, p.91-104, 149-150, 152, 153-160, 193, 217, 218, 220, 223-224, 227; records of trial called inadmissable as evidence, v.27, p.238-240, 255-258, 264.
"Ecclesiastical Supremacy in the Mississippi Valley, Contest for, 1763-1803," by Clarence Wyatt Bispham: Introduction, v.1, sec.3, p.154; Bibliography (1677-1776), v.1, sec.3, p.158; Documents of Spanish Archives relating to History of U. S. in American Libraries, v.1, sec.3, p.159; Episode of Father Beaubois S. J. and Father Raphael de Luxemburg, Vicar-Generals of Louisiana, v.1, sec.3, p.163; Interesting Fragments, v.1, sec.3, p.186; Triple Struggle for the Vicar-Generalship, 1772-1773, v.1, sec.3, p.181; Vicar-Generalship, The Question of, v.1, sec.3, p.159; "Voyage Du Nord," Record of, concerning "Les Compagnie Des Indes," v.1, sec.3, p.174; War of the Jesuits and Capuchins, 1755-1772, v.1, sec.3, p.176.
Echergaray, Martin de, noted, v.22, p.939.
Echo, La., noted, v.25, p.397.
Eckert, J. W. H., N. O. musician, v.31, p.139.
"Eclair," schooner, v.24, p.648, 653.
"Ecole Des Orphelins Indigents," New Orleans, v.25, p.364, 733.
"Economic and Social Development of Calcasieu Parish, Louisiana," by Grace Ulmer, v.32, p.519.
Economic conditions in Sp. N. O., v.22, p.662-675.
Economy, Pa., noted, v.24, p.422, 424, 429.
Ecore a Fabri, first site of Camden, Ark., v.20, p.465.
Ecores a Margot, noted, v.22, p.50, 63n.
Ecuador, mission of J. P. Benjamin to, v.23, p.162-169.
Ecuyer, Emile, pres. Fr. Union, v.28, p.348.
Edenborn Brake, of cypress, v.30, p.982-984, 1020; noted, v.30, p.1034-1035.
Edenborn, William, v.30, p.983; sketch of, v.30, p.1020-1021.
Eder, Joseph, trip from Germany to New Orleans and Nacogdoches, v.23, p.485-500.
Eder, Rosina, noted, v.23, p.500.
Edgar, H. T., noted, v.24, p.86.
"Edict of December 15, 1721, Providing for Appointment of Dual Tutors to Minors in France and in Her Colonies," Translated by the late William K. Dart, with introductory note by Henry P. Dart, v.10, p.533.
"Edict of October 12, 1716," translated by Henry P. Dart, v.14, p.346.
Editorial Change, Walter Prichard, new editor of the La. Historical Quarterly to replace Henry Plauche Dart, deceased, v.18, p.160a-d.
Editor's Chair, The, see Dart, Henry P.; (John Dymond), v.2, p.122, 229, 343, 486; v.3, p.151, 253, 449, 627; by Henry P. Dart: About Ourselves and You, v.5, p.605; A New History of Louisiana, v.5, p.427; Cabildo of New Orleans, The, v.5, p.279; Delay in Publishing the Quarterly, The, v.5, p.118; Quarterly Under Mr. Dymond, The, v.5, p.277; The, v.7, p.141, 332, 480, 674; by Henry P. Dart, American Historian's Raw Materials, The, v.8, p.268; Eighteenth Century in Louisiana, The, v.8, p.474; Something for the Members of the Louisiana Historical Society to Think About, v.8, p.115; The Quarterly in 1925, v.8, p.671; by Henry P. Dart: Battle of New Orleans, A, v.9, p.111; Editing the Quarterly, v.9, p.703; Instinct of the Private Collector of Archive Material, v.9, p.499; Slave Depot of the Company of the Indies at New Orleans, v.9, p.286; by Henry P. Dart: Archives, Index to the French and Spanish, v.10, p.407; Beer, William, In Memoriam, v.10, p.249; Irby, William R., In Memoriam, v.10, p.95; Quarterly, The Tenth Year of the, v.10, p.94; Surrey's Calendar of Manuscripts in Paris Relating to the History of the Mississippi Valley Under the French Domination, v.10, p.564; by Henry P. Dart: Read's "Louisiana Place Names of Indian Origin," v.11, p.286; Rowland and Sanders' "Mississippi Provincial Archives, 1729-1740, French Dominion," v.11, p.111; Vogel's "The Capuchins in French Louisiana, 1722-1766," v.11, p.620; Which Way History? v.11, p.463; by Henry P. Dart: Celebration of the Twelfth Year of the Louisiana Historical Quarterly, v.12, p.645; Crane's "The Southern Frontier," v.12, p.136; In Memoriam, Henry E. Chambers, v.12, p.300; Splendid Work of Rowland and Sanders on the French Archives of

Louisiana, v.12, p.464; By Henry P. Dart: Caulfield's "The French Literature of Louisiana," v.13, p.484; Death of Mr. Cusachs and Mr. Hart, v.13, p.117; Fischer's "The Intendant System in Spanish America," v.13, p.304; Governor Warmoth's Book, v.13, p.655; by Henry P. Dart: A New Light on the Attitude of Spain in the Louisiana Cession of 1762, v.14, p.636; In Memory of Heloise H. Cruzat, v.14, p.443; Revolution of 1876 in Louisiana, v.14, p.242; Work of the Quarterly in 1930, v.14, p.86; "South as a Conscious Minority, The," by Dr. Jesse T. Carpenter (Book Review), v.14, p.637; by Henry P. Dart: Ideals of Grace King, v.15, p.339; Office of Councillor-Assessor in the Superior Council of Louisiana in the French Regime, v.15, p.117.

Edmonds, James, N. O. newspaperman, v.33, p.422-423.

"Education, in Louisiana in the closing Decades of the Nineteenth Century," by Edwin L. Stephens, v.16, p.38; Acadian, v.18, p.394-406; in La. prior to statehood, v.19, p.595-631; bibliography, v.19, p.631-634; State Seminary of Learning established, v.20, p.53ff, 572-77; in N. O., v.20, p.935-945; founding of Tulane U., v.20, p.1016-1066; in Carrollton, v.21, p.257-265; state aid to, v.21, p.264; of free negroes, v.21, p.1081-1082; in St. James Parish, 1860, v.21, p.1120-1121; in Pointe Coupee Parish, v.21, p.1139; in Plaquemines Parish, 1860, v.21, p.1128, 1129; in De Soto, v.21, p.1172, 1173; in Minden, v.21, p.1184; in Monroe, v.21, p.1195; popular, in E. Fla., v.22, p.101; in N. O., v.22, p.197-198, 443-444, 452, 456, 682-687; private schools, v.22, p.684-685; apprentice system, v.22, p.685; German schools in New Orleans, v.23, p.511; public lands granted for, v.23, p.1004-1006; Bullard's interest in, v.23, p.1044; Univ. of La. established, v.23, p.1056; of Randolph children, v.25, p.202ff.; of free Negroes in La., v.25, p.357, 358-366; of all Negroes, v.25, p.728-821; and the La. Const. Con. of 1844, v.25, p.1033-1034; the conditions prior to 1846, v.25, p.1040-1042; legislation of 1846-1847, v.25, p.1042-1043; in Colonial Louisiana, by Stuart G. Noble, v.32, p.759; in St. Mary Parish, v.32, p.77-81; in Calcasieu Parish, v.32, p.602-616; in La., noted, v.32, p.7.

"Edward Douglas White, Sr., Gov. of La., 1835-1839," by Diedrich Ramke, v.19, p.273-327.

"Edward Livingston: Jeffersonian Republican and Jacksonian Democrat," by William B. Hatcher, revd. by William O. Lynch, v.24, p.542-543.

"Edward Livingston's Place in La. Law," by Ira Flory, Jr., v.19, p.328-389.

"Edward Livingston's View of the Nature of the Union," by William B. Hatcher, v.24, p.698-728.

Edwards, Boliver, noted, v.29, p.682, 683, 707.

Edwards, Daniel, identified, v.21, p.766n.; noted, v.29, p.79.

Edwards, Haden, accusations of Bastrop, v.31, p.677-678.

Egan, Barthes, letter from, v.24, p.100-101.

Egan, Michael, officiated at marriage of Zulime and Gardette, v.27, p.58.

Egan, Thomas, and W. Fla. Rev., v.21, p.706n.

Eggleston's School, v.30, p.845.

Eguia, Jacinto, assumed name of Vidal, v.25, p.13, 15, 16.

"Egypt," plantation of Alexander Sterling, v.21, p.76.

Egypt, troops of in Greek-Turkish War, v.24, p.967; modernization in, v.24, p.1011.

Ehren, Fritz, noted, v.24, p.132.

Elam, James M., noted, v.25, p.124.

"El Bravo," pirate vessel, v.24, p.363, 366.

El Choco, located, v.24, p.673.

Elder and Dreyfus, noted, v.23, p.1230.

Elder, Mrs. S. B., "Bienville" (a poem), v.2, p.177.

"Election Frauds in Plaquemines Parish, Louisiana, 1844," "The Nation" (N. Y.), 1879, v.10, p.402.

"Elections, The Municipal, of 1858," by John S. Kendall, v.5, p.357; "The, of 1860 in Louisiana," by Mary Lilla McLure, v.9, p.601; of 1844 in N. O., v.19, p.109-114; qualifications of candidates in W. Fla., 1769, v.23, p.359; of 1872, v.23, p.521; of 1850, v.23, p.1079-1089; French law of, v.24, p.1113; in 1828, v.24, p.1125-1126; of 1860, in La., v.24, p.434; of 1828, in La., v.25, p.51-53; of 1830, in La., v.25, p.60-61; in N. O. during Wickliffe's governorship, v.25, p.690-93; returns of 1892, 1896, 1912, tables of, v.28, p.1232-1237; of

1878, in La., Results of, v.32, p.649-667; in 1879, results of, v.32, p.667-684; in 1880, v.32, p.684-715.

Elgee, J. K., chairman of committee to design flag for republic of La., v.26, p.1003.

Eliot, John, gov. of W. Fla., v.23, p.24ff., 353; death of, v.23, p.369-370.

Eliot, Margaret Sherburne, noted, v.24, p.307.

Elkins, Lewis, La. educator, v.30, p.916.

Ellery, Abraham R., noted, v.22, p.433, 439.

Ellery, A. R., curator of Desgrange, v.27, p.107, 108, 109.

Ellet, Alfred Washington, noted, v.23, p.1207.

Ellet, Charles, Jr., noted, v.23, p.1207n.

Elliott, Gov. ————, noted, v.22, p.981.

Elliott, Clay, opposition to election law, v.28, p.1186.

Elliott, Judge B. C., impeachment of, v.31, p.682-687; reasons for impeachment, v.31, p.682-683; articles of impeachment, v.31, p.685; trial of, v.31, p.686.

Ellis, Caswell P., family correspondence in L.S.U. Archives, v.24, p.342.

Ellis, Dr. E. M., pres. Crowley Board of Health, fight against yellow fever, v.27, p.1135, 1136.

Ellis, E. John and C. W., and family, collection in L.S.U. Archives, v.24, p.342.

Ellis, E. John, ancestry, birth, early life and education, v.29, p.679-685; interest in politics, v.29, p.685-686; serves in Confederate army, v.29, p.687-705; captured in Battle of Missionary Ridge, v.29, p.705-706; prison life on Johnson's Island, v.29, p.706-712; return to civilian life and marriage, v.29, p.712-713; begins law practice, v.29, p.713; makes name for self in N. O. politics, v.29, p.714-718; nominated for Congress, v.29, p.718-719; elected to Congress, v.29, p.725; ten years in Congress, v.29, p.727-739, 741-752; opens law office in Washington, v.29, p.753; death, v.29, p.754; speeches made, v.29, p.754-757, 759-767; bibl., v.29, p.767-770.

Ellis, Ezekiel Parke, family collection in L.S.U. Archives, v.24, p.342; brief sketch, v.29, p.679-680, 683; death noted, v.29, p.752.

Ellis, Hazel and Nellie and family, collection in L.S.U. Archives, v.24, p.342.

Ellis, John, noted, v.29, p.679.

Ellis, Mrs. E. John, vice-pres., Women's Anti-Lottery League, v.27, p.1061.

Ellis, Sarah, noted, v.29, p.679.

Ellis, Stephen, v.29, p.690, 691, 700, 702.

Ellis, T.C.W., The Louisiana Bar, v.4, p.81; on Anti-Lottery League Ex. Com., v.27, p.1056; birth noted, v.29, p.679; education, v.29, p.680; noted, v.29, p.681, 682, 683, 685, 701-702; member of state Senate, v.29, p.713; noted, v.29, p.726; quarrel with brother, v.29 p.740-741; backer of N. O. "Democrat," v.31, p.739.

Ellis, Wm. C., cashier Crowley State Bank, v.27, p.1171.

Ellsworth, Annie G., sends first telegraph message, v.31, p.426.

Elmore, Minor, early N. O. newspaperman, v.29, p.782.

Elmore, W. A., placed in charge of Eighth District Court by Warmoth, v.27, p.558; judge, not recognized by Pinchback as "somebody in authority," v.27, p.563; the court abolished, v.27, p.567.

"Elmridge," plantation of Judge Peter Randolph, v.25, p.158.

"Elmsby," plantation of Moses Liddell, v.25, p.160.

Ely, Richard T., collection in L.S.U. Archives, p.24, p.342.

Elzey, Brigadier-General Arnold, noted, v.24, p.62.

Emancipation, and national politics, 1822, v.24, p.936.

Emancipation Proclamation, noted, v.32, p.147.

Embargo Act, effect on smuggling, v.23, p.440; enforced in neutral ground, v.28, p.1099-1100; repealed, v.28, p.1100.

Embargo of 1808, and Folch, v.25, p.20-21.

"Emblematic Bird of Louisiana, The," by Stanley Clisby Arthur, v.2, p.248.

"Emfield," Mrs. Moore's plantation, v.26, p.977; wrecked by war, v.26, p.1043-1044, 1045; rented, v.26, p.1047; Moore's death at, v.26, p.1049.

Emigres of France, problems of, v.24, p.943.

"Emma," transport, v.24, p.96.

Emmett, Daniel, Composer of "Dixie," v.31, p.146-147.

Emory, W. H., Gen'l in command of Dept. of Gulf, ordered to uphold Pinchback gov't, v.27, p.570, 573; troops used to uphold Kellogg gov't, v.29, p.410, 422, 434, 443; noted, v.29, p.722, 723, 724, 727.

England, difficulties in manufacturing class, v.24, p.998-999; lowered rank in European opinion, v.24, p.1118-1119; inactivity in European tension, v.24, p.1121.

Engle, Don Pedro, trader sent to Indians, v.28, p.1099.

Englesman, John Cornelius, "The Freedmen's Bureau of Louisiana," v.32, p.145.

English, immigration opposed, v.22, p.695.

English Opera House, v.28, p.103.

English Theatre, hist. of in N. O., v.28, p.84-276, 361-572; bibl. of, v.28, p.275-276; annual chronological records, v.28, p.361-490; list of plays, v.28, p.490-541; list of players, v.28, p.542-563; list of playwrights, v.28, p.563-572.

English Turn, noted, v.22, p.116; preparation to build Fort Miss. at v.26, p.644; noted, v.26, p.665, 742; Iberville erects fort at, v.26, p.726; noted, v.28, p.684, 695, 715n.

Enon School, established, 1887, v.29, p.85.

Ensign, Mary, wife of Samuel Smith, v.29, p.282.

Entail, question of in France, v.24, p.991.

Epidemic, cholera, in Philadelphia, 1832, v.24, p.1166.

"Epidemic, The New Orleans Yellow Fever, of 1853," by Donald E. Everett, v.33, p.380-405.

"Epine," privateer, v.23, p.434, 436; forfeit to U. S., v.23, p.438; noted, v.23, p.437-438.

Episcopal Church, history of, in N. O., v.22, p.428-478; Christ Church, v.22, p.432-454; French Church, v.22, p.455-461; St. Paul's Parish, v.22, p.461-463; Diocese of La., v.22, p.464-471; in New Orleans during the Civil War, v.23, p.1241-1257.

Episcopalians, in Calcasieu Parish, v.32, p.624; in St. Mary Parish, v.32, p.74-75; congregation of Christ's Church Cathedral incorporated, noted, v.33, p.69.

"Era No. 2," steamer, picture of, v.25, p.447.

Erlanger, Abraham, in partnership with Klaw and Charles Jefferson in management of St. Charles, v.26, p.1155.

Erving, George W., noted, v.23, p.831.

Ervin, Joseph, messenger of early Bap't Church in Washington Parish, v.29, p.83.

Erwine, Jas., of N. O., married to daughter of H. Clay, v.27, p.721, 733.

Erwin, Isaac, and W. Fla. Rev., v.21, p. 746n.; son of Joseph Erwin, v.27, p.346, 357, 358, 360; buys land from father, v.27, p.376, 377, 398, 400, 447, 471.

Erwin, James, noted, v.24, p.1146; relations with James Brown, v.24, p.1160, 1161, 1162, 1163, 1164, 1165, 1169, 1172, 1173, 1174, 1175, 1176, 1177.

Erwin, Jane(also Jane Craighead), v.27, p.346, 357, 359.

Erwin, John, v.27, p.357, 359.

Erwin, Joseph, Jr., v.27, p.346, 357, 358, 360.

Erwin, Joseph, noted, v.25, p.207; background and family history, v.27, p.344-345, 346-348; came to La., v.27, p.348, 353; plantations of, v.27, p.354-355; financial difficulties, v.27, p.355-356; estate and will of, v.27, p.356-359; creation and dispersal of estate, v.27, p.361-377; slave transactions, v.27, p.377-385; summary, v.27, p.396-398; will of, v.27, p.399-400; inventory of succession, v.27, p.400-412; sale of slaves belonging to succession of, v.27, p.412-414; bibl., v.27, p.476-478; noted, v.28, p.842n.

Erwin, Lavinia Thompson, wife of Joseph Erwin, v.27, p.348; heir of husband's estate, v.27, p.356, 357; repurchased plantations, v.27, p.359; administered estate, v.27, p.360; death, v.27, p.360, 374, 377; administration of estate, 1831-1836, v.27, p.386-396, 397; estate of, v.27, p.398-399, 412-414; inventory of property of succession of, v.27, p.415-430; acc't of receipts and disbursements, v.27, p.430-465, 470-475; statement of crops, v.27, p.466-470.

Erwin, Leodicia, daughter of Erwin, v.27, p.346, 357.

Erwin, Mrs. James, noted, v.24, p.1011, 1169; inherited diamonds from Brown, v.24, p.1176.

Erwin, Nancy Ann, v.27, p.346, 357, 358.

"Erwin, Spraggins & Wright—Real Estate & Slave Dealers," business firm, v.27, p.353-354, 397.

Esnault, Louis, in duel with Philogene Favrot, v.28, p.732.

Espada y Landa, Juan Joseph Diaz de, noted, v.22, p.101.

Espagnol, Raymond, noted, v.22, p.1066.

Espagnol, Richard, noted, v.22, p.737; noted, v.23, p.766.

Espana, Carlos, trial of, v.22, p.1107-1114.

Espare, ———, and Mafia, v.22, p.824.
Esposito, Giuseppe, and Mafia, v.22, p.494ff.
"Essex," federal gunboat, v.29, p.1093.
"Establishment of the Electric Telegraph in Louisiana and Mississippi, The," by Eleanor B. Carleton, v.31, p.426-490.
Este, Count Maximilian de, noted, v.24, p.423.
Este, house of, v.24, p.381.
Esterhazy, Prince, noted, v.24, p.941.
Estero, noted, v.24, p.617.
Estopinal, Adam, cited, v.24, p.354.
Estopinal, Albert, on Lottery Bill, v.27, p.1042; pres. pro tempore of Sen., v.28, p.1185; cand. Lt.-gov., 1900, v.28, p.1191.
"Ethical Precepts Among the Natchez Indians," by Andrew C. Albrecht, v.31, p.569-597.
Ethridge, Adele Nash, "Indians of Grant Parish," v.23, p.1107-1131.
"Etiology of Cholera," by Dr. Michael Halphen, noted, v.26, p.62.
Ettinger, Amos Aschback, "The Mission to Spain of Pierre Soule" (review) v.15, p.708.
Eubanks, William, and W. Fla. Rev., v.21, p.799.
Eustis, George, noted, v.23, p.1028, 1029, 1061; and the Const. Con. of 1844, v.25, p.1006ff.; made Justice of La. Supreme Ct., v.25, p.1050, 1078, 1083; noted, v.27, p.740; chief-justice of Sup. Ct. in La., v.27, p.762; oration on Clay, v.27, p.769.
Eustis, J. B., Dem. claim of to vacancy in U. S. Senate, Jan., 1876, v.27, p.600-601; Democratic nominee for Congress, v.29, p.718, 719; noted, v.29, p.751.
Evangeline Oil Field, v.27, p.1169, 1170, 1197.

Evans, Harry Howard, "James Robb, Banker and Pioneer Railroad Builder," v.23, p.170-258.
Evans, Henry Clay, explanation of daily lottery drawings, v.27, p.1022-1024; methods of Lottery Co. in advertising through mail, v.27, p.1024-1025.
Evans, John, named in Warmoth impeachment, v.31, p.702.
Evans, Luther H., quoted, v.24, p.305; noted, v.24, p.308.
Everett, Alexander Hill, noted, v.24, p.960, 971, 975, 990, 1006, 1031, 1034, 1055, 1136.
Everett, Donald E., "The New Orleans Yellow Fever Epidemic of 1853," v.33, p.380.
Everett Institute, v.30, p.924-925.
Everett, J. P., La. educator, v.30, p.923.
Evergreen Home Institute, sketch of, v.30, p. 764-766.
Evergreen, noted, v.24, p.85.
Evia, Jose de, noted, v.22, p.795.
Ewell, Major-General Richard S., noted, v.24, p.63.
Ewing, Cortez A. M., "Five Early Louisiana Impeachments," v.31, p.682-715.
Ewing, Robert, Jr., address in memory of Henry Plauche Dart, v.18, p.245-246.
"Exalted Enterprise (The Miss. Question: The La. Answer)," by W. C. Holmes, v.23, p.78-106.
Exchange, rate of, between France and the U. S., v.24, p.974-975, 985, 1006, 1014.
"Expense Account of a Grande Dame of French Colonial La.," by Edith Dart Price, v.21, p.629-630.
"Experiences of a Federal Soldier in La. in 1863," ed. by Walter Prichard, v.19, p.635-667.
Exploration, of lower Miss. R. Valley, v.22, p.933-942.

FABACHER, JOSEPH, AND GERMAN COLONY, v.23, p.513-514; introduced Ger. colony in Acadia, v.27, p.1119.

Fabiani, Gianni, noted, v.24, p.672.

Fabry, Andry de la Bruyere, N. O. notary sent on expedition into New Mexico, v.26, p.693-694; noted, v.26, p.695.

"Fabulous N. O.," noted, v.25, p.637.

Fagot, Charles, noted, v.22, p.815.

Faiquere, Jean-Baptiste, noted, v.22, p.1067.

Fairchild, Henry, noted, v.23, p.357, 368, 383, 386.

"Faithful Picture of the Political Situation in New Orleans at the Close of the Last and Beginning of the Present Year, 1807," Reprinted from Pamphlet with Introduction and Editorial Notes by James E. Winston, v.11, p.359.

Falconer, John, noted, v.23, p.26, 42, 377, 391.

Faliet, Louis de, noted, v.22, p.815.

Falouche, description of, v.23, p.122.

False River Cutoff, formerly Channel of Miss., v.28, p.69; cause of, v.28, p.69-75; possible date of, v.28, p.75-77; human interference not necessary and ineffective, v.28, p.77-81; length of time for change, v.28, p.81-84.

False River, in 1860, v.21, p.1137-1139; origin, v.31, p.598-599; origin of name, v.31, p.598-600.

"Families, History of Louisiana and Some of Its Leading," v.1, sec.1, p.95.

Family Compact and the La. Cession, v.19, p.204-209.

"Family Meetings in French Period, Louisiana," by Henry P. Dart, v.3, p.543, 547.

"Famous Case of Myra Clark Gaines, The," by Nolan B. Harmon, Jr., rev'd by Walter Prichard, v.30, p.338-342.

"Famous Event in the French Colonial History of Louisiana, The Orders of December 8th, 19th, 30th, 1722, Putting Sr. de Sauvoy and Sr. Jacques de la Chaise in Charge of the Colony," Translation and Introduction by Edith Dart Price, v.15, p.376.

Fanchaux, Francois, noted, v.22, p.685.

Fannie, Edythe, 1st ruler of Bogalusa baby coronation, v.29, p.119.

Faquetaique, German settlement of, v.23, p.513.

Fargo, ———, noted, v.23, p.393.

Farias, Gomez, resident in New Orleans, v.18, p.54-55.

Farmar, Major, and W. Fla., v.21, p.1022; and W. Fla. Assembly, v.23, p.23ff.; noted, v.23, p.357, 368; petition of, v.23, p.366-367; election of, v.23, p.377.

Farmer, Robert, and W. Fla., v.22, p.18ff.
Farmers' Alliance, became People's Party, v.26, p.1061; appearance of 1880, v.26, p.1063; platforms and principles of, v.26, p.1067-1069; and the La. Lottery, v.26, p.1070; noted, v.26, p.1074, 1082; and the Congressional Campaign of 1890, v.26, p.1077; meeting at Lafayette, v.26, p.1079; meeting in Monroe, v.26, p.1084; noted, v.26, p.1109; noted, v.27, p.1087-1088; combine with Anti-Lottery League, v.28, p.1152ff.
Farmers' Cooperative Rice Milling Co., formed to erect a mill in Crowley to protect farmers, v.27, p.1164.
Farmers' Union Cooperative Store of W. Monroe, v.26, p.1065.
Farmers' Union, early farmers organization, v.26, p.1061; and bagging trust, v.26, p.1065; purpose of, v.26, p.1066-1067; noted, v.26, p.1074.
Farmerville Institute, v.30, p.922-923.
Farmer, W. W. Capt. Confed. army, v.26, p.972; candidate for Lt. Gov., v.31, p.501.
Farming, in Calcasieu Parish, v.32, p.527-530; in La., noted, v.32, p.10.
"Farragut, Admiral, The Father of," by Charles O. Paullin, v.13, p.37.
Farragut, David G., noted, v.23, p.1184; at Mobile, v.23, p.1214; expedition against New Orleans, v.24, p.449-451, 457, 460-461; N. O. surrendered to, 1862, v.26, p.1020; noted, v.27, p.480, 481, 487, 493, 494, 505; his conquests along the Miss. River, v.27, p.520, 523; noted, v.29, p.341, 342.
Farrar, Edgar H., and Mafia, v.20, p.513, 519.
Farrar, E. H., resolutions asking for cooperation of State Farmers' Union, v.27, p.1057; addressed Anti-Lottery League Conv., v.27, p.1057.
Farrar, Preston W., noted, v.25, p.1075; speaker of La. House, v.25, p.1095, 1103.
Farrell, M. J., noted, v.22, p.509.
"Fashion Plantation," home of Richard Taylor, v.24, p.52-53, 70, 116.
Fatio, Felipe, Spanish consul at New Orleans, v.21, p.214n.; Spanish vice-consul at N. O., v.21, p.682ff.; privateering in Gulf, v.21, p.1088ff.; report on Lafitte's plan to capture privateers, v.21, p.1097-1102; Sp. agent, v.22, p.744; consul at New Orleans, v.23, p.760, 766, 767, 770; and P. Lafitte, v.23, p.775, 776, 806; letter to Cienfuegos, v.23, p.789-792; letter to Onis, v.23, p.793-794; death of, v.23, p.821.
Fatio, Francisco Jose, noted, v.23, p.767.
"Faubourgs Forming the Upper Section of N. O.," by Melconcy C. Soniat, v.20, p.192-211.
Faubourgs, of Nuns, Lafayette, and Livaudais, establishment of above N. O., v.20, p.904-916; Ste. Marie, history, v.22, p.385-427; St. Mary and Batture, v.23, p.680ff.
Fauchet, Jean Antoine Joseph, sketch, v.21, p.41n.
Faulkner, A. W., voted to submit lottery question to people, v.27, p.1037; favored submitting lottery question to people, v.28, p.1144.
Faurvinsky, Theodore, noted, v.24, p.367.
Faust, Millard, Cap't of 1st Reg't of La. Inf., v.29, p.82.
"Favorita," ship in Aury expedition, v.24, p.628, 629, 633, 636.
Favrot, Charles A., "An Historical Sketch on the Construction of the Custom-House, New Orleans," v.3, p.467.
Favrot, Claude Joseph, father of Don Pedro, in La., 1728, v.28, p.683; mil. service, v.28, p.683ff.; commendation of, v.28, p.687; in Fr., v.28, p.687, 688; death, v.28, p.689.
Favrot, Don Pedro, at Sp. Council of War, v.26, p.741; in command at Baton Rouge, v.26, p.743; education and travel, v.26, p.752; at Fort San Felipe, v.26, p.752, 754; documents of, v.28, p.679-682; ancestors, mil. background, v.28, p.682-687; birth and early years, v.28, p.684-685; service at Ark. post, v.28, p.688; visits Fr., v.28, p.688-689; service in Fr., v.28, p.689; termination of service to Fr., v.28, p.689-690; social life in Fr., v.28, p.690, 691; transfer to service of Sp., v.28, p.690, 691-694; relations with Galvez in La., v.28, p.694; plans for defense of N. O., v.28, p.694-695; in comd. at B. R., v.28, p.695-698; at Mobile, v.28, p.699-702; marriage of, v.28, p.699; at Natchez, v.28, p.702-704, 705; letter to Carondelet criticising his policies, v.28, p.706-707; letter to Genet, v.28, p.707-708; given comd. at Plaquemines, v.28, p.708-715; ed. of children, v.28, p.711-713; at B. R., v.28, p.715-716; purchased plantation near B. R., v.28, p.716; reassigned to Plaquemine, v.28, p.716;

coming of Laussat, v.28, p.716-718; transfer of San Felipe to Fr., v.28, p.719-720; retired, v.28, p.720-722; tribute to Louis Grand Pre, v.28, p.722-723; member state legis., 1814, plan for defense of N. O. and La., v.28, p.724-725; letter to his wife in re aftermath of Battle of N. O., v.28, p.725-728; letter from his son describing regard for Napoleon, v.28, p.729-730; sons of, v.28, p.731; death of Philogene, v.28, p.732; death of, v.28, p.732-733; burial plot of, v.28, p.732-34; Society of Children of Am. Rev. bears name of, v.28, p.735.

Favrot, Henry L., adjutant 2nd La. Reg't., v.26, p.795; acting adjutant of brigade, v.26, p.831; change in rank, v.26, p.837.

Favrot, Henry Mortimer, collection in Howard-Tilton Memorial Library, v.24, p.330; "Colonial Forts of La.," v.26, p.722-754.

Favrot, Henry Richmond, collection in Howard-Tildon Memorial Library, v.24, p.330.

Favrot, H. M., of Delta Rifles, v.29, p.1052, 1066; Capt. Co. C, 4th La. Reg't., muster roll of, v.30, p.491-493.

Favrot, Josephine, and Louise de Grand Pre, v.21, p.188n.; letter to friend describing life at Plaquemines, v.28, p.713-715.

Favrot, J. St. Clair, "Baton Rouge, the Historic Capitol of Louisiana," v.12, p.611.

Favrot, Leo M., agent for Negro education in La., v.25, p.794, 797, 798, 802, 807, 809.

Favrot, Maria Francesca, Grave of, v.28, p.733.

Favrot Papers, transcription of, v.24, p.306; in Howard-Tildon Memorial Library, v.24, p.330.

Favrot, Philogene, son of Don Pedro, v.28, p.680; letters of to father, v.28, p.729-730; Judge of W.B.R., v.28, p.731; killed in duel, v.28, p.732.

Favrot, St. Clair, collection in Howard-Tildon Memorial Library, v.24, p.330.

Fay, Edwin Whitfield, history of La. education, cited, v.24, p.335, 349.

Faye, Stanley, "Consuls of Spain in N. O., 1804-1821," v.21, p.677-684; (ed.), "The Garden of Fray Antonio de Sedella," v.21, p.1069-1074; (ed), "The Schism of 1805 in N. O.," v.22, p.98-141; (ed.), "Louis Declouet's Memorial to the Sp. Gov't., Dec. 7, 1814," v.22, p.795-818; (ed.), "Privateersmen of the Gulf and Their Prizes," v.22, p.1012-1094; "Types of Privateer Vessels, Their Armament and Flags, in the Gulf of Mexico," v.23, p.118-130; "Privateers of Guadeloupe and Their Establishment in Barataria," v.23, p.428-444; "The Great Stroke of Pierre Lafitte," v.23, p.733-826; "Commodore Aury," v.24, p.611-687; "The Altamira Case," v.25, p.5-23; "The Forked River," v.25, p.921-942; "The Arkansas Post of La.," v.26, p.59, 60; "Ark. Post of La.: Sp. Domination," v.27, p.629-716.

Fay, R. S., Jr., noted, v.24, p.535, 536.

Fayssoux Collection, inventory of, v.24, p.332, 333, 350.

Fead, George, noted, v.23, p.35.

"Fealing Slave Plantation," home of Judge Peter Randolph, v.25, p.158.

Fearon, H. B., author, v.31, p.395, 415, 416.

Featherstonehaugh, George William, noted, v.23, p.878; author on Louisiana, v.31, p.397, 410; discussion of quadroons, v.31, p.414.

Federalists, noted, v.24, p.717.

Federal Troops, raids on Randolph property, v.25, p.197.

Federative Government, Edward Livingston's definition of, v.24, p.704.

Feliciana bills, and Treaty of 1795, v.25, p.6.

Feliciana Female Collegiate Institute, v.30, p.826-827.

Feliciana High School, v.30, p.828-829.

Feliciana, rebellion in, v.28, p.944; becomes prosperous, v.28, p.945-946; divided into E. and W., v.28, p.946.

"Felix," ship, v.24, p.629, 633.

Fellenberg's Institute, v.30, p.915-916.

Fellowes, Cornelius, noted, v.23, p.244.

Fellows, John Quincy Adams, noted, v.23, p.1144, 1239; noted, v.31, p.1011, 1035; candidate for governor, v.31, p.1015.

Felsing, Wilhelm, noted, v.24, p.147.

Felter, C. W., began "Rayne Signal," v.27, p.1184.

Fencing, schools of, v.23, p.146.

Fenner, Charles E., noted, v.23, p.531.

Fenner, Charles Payne, "Jurisprudence of Supreme Court, Louisiana," v.4, p.71.

Fenner, Dr. E. D., Charter member of Medical Society, v.26, p.59, 60.

Fenner, E. C., address to Prog. League, v.27, p.1063.

Fenner, E., request for aid for Sanitary Assoc. of N. O., v.27, p.1029.
Ferguson, James, noted, v.23, p.358.
Fernandez, Andrew, deposition of, v.23, p.697.
Fernandez, Bernardo, noted, v.22, p.73.
Fernandina, noted, v.24, p.644, 645, 652.
Feron, Madame, and N. O. Theatre, v.21, p.497.
Ferrell's School, v.30, p.878.
Ferrero, Bernardo (Captain Lacaze), noted, v.24, p.645, 653, 671, 689.
Ferret, Philippe, skipper of Precieuse, tests Embargo, v.25, p.941.
Ferrise, Lutande, noted, v.23, p.714.
Ferronnays, Count de la, negotiations with James Brown, v.24, p.1086, 1113, 1117, 1128, 1130ff., 1135, 1143-1144.
Ferrusola, Juan Barno y, noted, v.22, p.81.
Ferry, rates at Colyell Bayou, v.23, p.419; at Nitalbany River, v.23, p.422; laws concerning, v.23, p.422-423.
Ferth, Archibald S., noted, v.22, p.200, 203.
"Fete of Joan of Arc, The, May 16," v.1, p.295.
Fetherstone, William, noted, v.23, p.404.
Ficklen, John Rose, and Reconstruction in La., v.23, p.525-526.
Field, A. P., att'y-gen'l recognized by Pinchback, 1872, v.27, p.567; candidate for Attorney Gen'l, v.29, p.402, 403; cand. for att'y gen'l, v.31, p.536; leader Nat'l Conservation Union Party, v.31, p.1054; accuses Democrats, v.31, p.1059; noted, v.31, p.1081.
Field, Colonel ————, noted, v.22, p.1160.
Field, Flo, "Andres Molinary," v.7, p.455.
Field, Stephen J., justice, majority opinion in Gaines vs. Fuentes written by, v.27, p.300-302.
Fierro, Francisco Garcia del, noted, v.22, p.776-777.
Fifth District Court of Orleans, injunction against Ala. Lottery Co., v.27, p.977.
"Fighting Politician: Major General N. P. Banks," by Fred Harvey Harrington, review by Walter Prichard, v.31, p.559-563.
Filhiol, Don Juan, and Spanish land grants, v.20, p.297ff.; birth and early life in France, v.20, p.463; years in Santo Domingo, Phila., N. O., v.20, p.464; built Fort Miro in 1782, v.20, p.464; instructions to from Gov. Miro, v.20, p.473-475; description of the Ouachita by, v.20, p.476-485; established Ouachita post, v.31, p.613; noted, v.31, p.715, 617, 626.
Filibustering, Lopez expeditions to Cuba, v.22, p.1095-1167; defined, v.25, p.291.
Filibusters, in Pensacola, 1816-1817, v.21, p.806-822; Toledo's reconciliation with Spain, v.23, p.827-863; southern in War of 1812, v.25, p.291-300.
Fillmore Academy, sketch of, v.30, p.793-794.
Fillmore, Millard, and Cuban question, v.22, p.1140; noted, v.23, p.1079.
"Financial and Economic Disturbance in New Orleans on the Eve of Secession," by Milledge L. Bonham, v.13, p.32.
Financial crisis of 1837, v.25, p.112.
Finegan, Joseph, noted, v.29, p.1241.
Finn, Henry James, and N. O. Theatre, v.21, p.501.
"Firebrand Affair: A Forgotten Incident of the Mexican Rev.," by Harris Gaylord Warren, v.21, p.203-212; noted, v.22, p.783, 784.
"Firebrand," privateer of the Lafittes, v.23, p.752; noted, v.24, p.737.
Fire Companies and Fires in New Orleans, in 1788, v.21, p.13; in 1794, v.21, p.53; in Carrollton, v.21, p.244, 269-271; in Sp. New Orleans, v.22, p.646, 696; department of Carrollton, v.22, p.206, 207; Company records in Howard-Tilton Memorial Library, v.24, p.329.
"First Cargo of African Slaves for Louisiana, 1718," Introduction by Henry P. Dart, documents tran. by A. G. Sanders, v.14, p.163.
"First Grand Jury of Attakapas, The," Heloise H. Cruzat, v.8, p.369.
"First Great River Captain, The, Henry Miller Shreve," by J. Fair Hardin, v.10, p.25.
"First Law Regulating Land Grants in French Colonial Louisiana, The," translated by Henry P. Dart, v.14, p.346.
"First Meeting of the Louisiana Historical Society in the Sala Capitular at the Cabildo," by H. Gibbs Morgan, v.14, p.60.
"First Official Flag of the City of New Orleans," address by W. J. Waguespack, v.1, sec.3, p.210.
First State Bank of Bogalusa, organized, v.29, p.98.
"First Succession Opened in Louisiana, The," by Henry P. Dart, v.3, p.322.
"Fiscal System for Louisiana, A New,"

by L. E. Thomas, v.2, p.129.

Fisher, Charles, Jr., Sub-ed. "True American" letter to Luzenberg, v.26, p.91-92.

Fisher, Charles L., Wickliffe's law partner, his attempted assassination, v.25, p.711.

Fisher, Frederick, noted, v.22, p.201.

Fisher, Henry, Negro who gave Bogalusa sections names, v.29, p.101.

Fisher, William, noted, v.25, p.295.

Fisk Free Public Library, noted, v.24, p.324, 349.

Fisk, Harold Norman, noted, v.25, p.398.

Fitzenreiter, Charles, noted, v.23, p.520.

Fitzgerald, William C., Confed. army, v.26, p.969.

Fitzhugh, George, noted, v.29, p.363, 365, 371, 372; work on "De Bow's Review," v.29, p.374-376.

Fitzpatrick, John, mayor of N. O., v.27, p.779; attempt to repeal Lottery Co. charter, v.27, p.991; on Com. to supervise primary, v.27, p.1094; member com. to supervise election, v.28, p.1161.

Fitzpatrick, William H., "Government by Treaty," v.33, p.299, 316.

"Five Early Louisiana Impeachments," by Cortez A. M. Ewing, v.31, p.682-715.

Five Islands Channel, noted, v.24, p.648, 652, 653, 669.

"Flag at Jackson Square, New Orleans, Jan. 8, 1918, Raising the American," Address by Andre Lafargue, v.1, sec.3, p.213.

Flag, incident of in New Orleans, 1862, v.24, p.460-461.

"Flag Legislation in Louisiana," by W. O. Hart, v.7, p.499.

"Flag of the City of New Orleans, First Official," Address by W. J. Waguespack, v.1, sec.3, p.210.

"Flags of Louisiana, The," by Milledge L. Bonham, Jr., v.2, p.439.

Flags, of privateers, v.23, p.126-130; over La., v.24, p. 744-745.

Flanders, Benjamin F., special agent Treas. Dept., v.23, p.1209, 1222n., 1232; noted, v.24, p.506; elected to Cong. in First District of La., 1862, v.27, p.524; La. Representative to Washington, v.30, p.523; agent of Freedmen's Bureau, v.30, p.527; replaces Wells, v.30, p.546; noted, v.30, p.525, 536, 545n., 549; elected to Congress, v.31, p.1010; noted, v.31, p.1011, 1012, 1063; cand. for governor, v.31, p.1013; appointed governor, v.31, p.1091.

Flash, Theo., noted, v.23, p.570.

Fleming, Raymond H., noted, v.24, p.313.

Fleming's "Freedmen's Savings Bank," review, v.10, p.562.

Fleming, Walter L., work on historical activities in Southwest, v.24, p.315, 317, 320, 349.

Fletcher, John, in Concordia, v.2, p.1208-1209.

Fleuriau, Carlos, noted, v.22, p.641.

Fleuriau, Francois, and Superior Council, v.21, p.1000.

Flint, John D., noted, v.25, p.779.

Flint Medical College, in N. O., v.25, p.779.

Flint, Timothy, description of Sabine country, v.24, p.36; noted, v.24, p.38; description of Southwest La., v.24, p.39; minister, writer, educator, v.30, p.746-748; principal College of Rapides, v.30, p.893; noted, v.30, p.914, 964; author, v.31, p.395, 416; quoted, v.31, p.599.

"Flood Control Act," Cong. act of 1928 giving federal aid in the control of Miss., v.28, p.324-325.

Floridablanca, Conde de (Jose Monino y Redondo), created Junta de Estado, v.21, p.8ff.; sketch, v.21, p.21n.; letter from Carondelet noted, v.21, p.24n.

Florida, Concerning works published on, See Boimare, A. L.

"Florida, East and West, Cession of, to U. S. by Treaty Between U. S. and Spain, February 22, 1821," v.2, p.154.

"Florida Episodes, Some ——— of War of 1812," v.1, p.330.

Florida-Louisiana Red Cypress Company, v.30, p.1045.

Florida Parishes, possession taken of, v.18, p.99-104; apportionment of representatives, v.21, p.191-192.

Floridas, report to Napoleon on, v.24, p.310; U. S. designs upon, v.24, p.629; ambitions of New Orleans Association, v.24, p.631-632; British advice of Spanish cession to the U. S., v.24, p.669-670.

Florida, West: "Baton Rouge, the Historic Capital of Louisiana," by J. St. Clair Favrot, v.21, p.611; "West Florida—The Capture of Baton Rouge by Galvez, September 21, 1779, From Reports of the English Officers," v.12, p.255; "West Florida—Documents Covering a Royal Land Grant on the Mississipi and Amite Rivers," transcribed from the originals in the Cabildo, v.12, p.630; Republic of West Florida, v.20, p.881-894.

Floridian Academy, v.30, p.906-907.

Flory, Ira, Jr., Edward Livingston's place

in La. law, v.19, p.328-389.

Flour, importation of, v.22, p.664-665, 669; export of, v.22, p.773-775; concerning sale of, in W. Fla., 1769, v.23, p.55.

Flower, Walter C., and Mafia, v.22, p.513; cand. for mayor of N. O., 1896, v.26, p.1107.

Flower, William, noted, v.23, p.176.

Floyd, John, noted, v.24, p.1045.

Floyd, in 1860, v.21, p.1212.

Flugel, Felix, "Pages From a Journal of a Voyage Down the Mississippi to New Orleans in 1817," v.7, p.414.

"Flush Productions: The Epic of Oil in the Gulf-Southwest," by Gerald Forbes, rev'd, v.26, p.1185-1186.

Foelkel, Valentine, identified, v.21, p.722, 801n.

Folch, Vincente, Gov. of Fla., v.21, p.92n.; and W. Fla. Rev., v.21, p.121, 718n.; noted, v.22, p.798, 806; Gov. of W. Fla., v.25, p.13-14, 15, 17, 19, 20; and Sp. rights of importation, v.25, p.940-941; letter to C. O. of Fort Stoddart, v.25, p.945; Miro's nephew, built Fort San Esteban, v.27, p.704; in command Fort San Fernando de las Barrancas, v.27, p.712; noted, v.28, p.702; comdt. W. Fla., v.28, p.720; noted, v.29, p.75-76.

Folklore, of La. Indian, v.24, p.749-750; Negro, v.24, p.750-752; Acadian, v.24, p.752-755.

"Folk Songs, Creole," by Emile LeJeune, v.2, p.454.

"Folktales, Specimens of the, From Some Ante-Bellum Newspapers of La.," by Arthur K. Moore, v.32, p.723.

Follett, Prescott H. F. (jt. auth.), "The Miss. Fort Called Fort de la Boulaye, 1700-1715, The First French Settlement in Present Day La.," v.19, p.829-899.

"Following the Spanish Trail Across the Neutral Territory in Louisiana," by Leon Sugar, v.10, p.86.

Fonte, ———, noted, v.24, p.649.

Fontenot, Gus, notary of Crowley, sketch, v.27, p.1130.

Fontenot, T. S., Farmers' Alliance leader, v.26, p.1070; chairman, Anti-Lottery League conv., v.27, p.1057.

Food Administration in La., 1917-1918, v.21, p.869-874.

Food, bad condition of, in New Orleans, v.24, p.472-473, 475-476.

Foot Resolution, noted, v.24, p.703, 704, 708, 711, 727.

Forbes and Co. of Mobile, v.21, p.92n.; and W. Fla. Rev., v.21, p.115; and Mobile Society, v.21, p.153n.

Forbes, Gerald, "A History of Caddo Oil and Gas Fields," v.29, p.59-72; "Jennings, First Louisiana Salt Dome Pool," v.29, p.496-509.

"Force Bill," noted, v.23, p.1021.

Ford, J. Franklin, La. educator, supervisor Shreveport Female High School, v.30, p.796; Minden Female College, v.30, p.931; noted, v.30, p.966.

Ford, S. B., Confed. soldier, v.26, p.964.

Fordyce, Col. John R., engineer, on route of DeSoto, v.25, p.611, 614, 616, 618, 622, 625, 627, 637.

Forehand, Anthony, noted, v.22, p.1003.

Foreigners, in New Orleans under Butler, v.24, p.507-516.

"Foreign Languauge Press of New Orleans, The," by John S. Kendall, v.12, p.363.

Foreign Legion, noted. v.24, p.456.

Foreign relations, Mafia incident and Italy, v.22, p.492; N. O. and Latin Am., v.22, p.710-794; Cuban question, v.22, p.1095-1167; duties of executives and Legislative branches toward, v.24, p.713-714.

Forest, David C., identified, v.21, p.218n.

"Forest Home," Randolph plantation, v.25, p.162, 164, 166, 167, 181, 182, 184, 190, 192, 196, 197, 198, 199, 202, 205, 214; sale of, v.25, p.201, 213, 215.

"Forgotten Louisiana Engineer, A: G. W. R. Baley and his 'History of the Railroads of Louisiana,'" ed. by Walter Prichard, v.30, p.1065-1325.

"Forgotten Service" (A Reminiscence of Capt. Henry Miller Shreve), v.3, p.137.

"Forked River, The," by Stanley Faye, v.25, p.921-942.

Forman, B. R., apologia for Lottery Co., v.27, p.1013.

Fornaris, Joseph M., enlisted as private, v.26, p.796; made 1st Lt., v.26, p810.

Forneret, Louis, interpreter, v.22, p.25.

Forno, Henry, noted, v.23, p.477.

Forrest, Nathan Bedford, noted, v.24, p.103, 106, 110; noted, v.29, p.1241.

Forshey, C. G., canal project, v.31, p.544-545.

Forstall, Edmond J., noted, v.23, p.1046; noted, v.24, p.512; and 1842 tariff, v.25, p.118, 120, 1062.

Forstall, Eugene J., noted, v.23, p.528.

Forster, Georg, noted, v.23, p.502, 518.

Forsyth, John, noted, v.22, p.364.

Forsyth, Mrs. Cordelia M., noted, v.23, p.1133.

Fort Adams, and dueling, v.23, p.452.

Fort Aury, located, v.24, p.697.

Fort Beauregard, noted, v.26, p.974n.

Fort Bisland, noted, v.24, p.70, 72.

Fort Boulaye, built at Eng. turn, sometimes called Fort Miss., v.26, p. 726; condition of, v.26, p.752; v.19, p.829-899.

Fort Bourbon, construction of, v.26, p.748; Carondelet's instructions concerning, v.26, p.750-751; noted, v.26, p.753.

Fort Bourgoyne, of N. O., v.26, p.746.

Fort Burgundy, noted, v.22, p.645.

Fort Bute, construction of, v.21, p.1023; at head of Manchac, v.25, p.935; deserted and rebuilt, v.25, p.936; out of existence, v.25, p.939; at Manchac, captured by Galvez, v.26, p.311; noted, v.26, p.742; construction began in 1766, v.27, p.630; British post, v.27, p.642, 656, 658; surrender to Galvez, v.27, p.661, 663, 669, 670.

Fort Butler, noted, v.24, p.77.

Fort Charlotte, noted, v.22, p.20; noted, v.23, p.389.

Fort Chartres, noted, v.22, p.27.

Fort Darby, v.28, p.883, 884.

Fort de la Boulaye, first French settlement in present day La., v.19, p.829-899.

Fort de Russy, noted, v.24, p.85, 98.

Fort Donelson, noted, v.24, p.444.

Fort Hatteras, noted, v.24, p.440.

Fort Henry, noted, v.24, p.444.

Fortier, Alcee, works on La., v.24, p.325, 339, 349, 755; address to Women's Anti-Lottery League, v.27, p.1061; noted, v.30, p.866, 874.

Fortier, Honore, expedition of, v.22, p.1014-1015; noted, v.23, p.441.

Fortier, James J. A., Dedication of Lafayette Public School in New Orleans, Address by, v.9, p.204; noted, v.24, p.744.

Fortier, Jean Michel, noted, v.22, p.799.

Fortier, Ludgere, plantation of, v.22, p.188.

Fortier, Michael, noted, v.22, p.815; noted, v.25, p.327.

Fortin, Louis, promotion of, v.26, p.836.

Fort Jackson, noted, v.24, p.443, 444, 497; bombardment of, v.24, p.450-451; fall of, v.24, p.463; ordered surrendered to La., v.26, p.997.

"Fort Jesup, Fort Selden, Camp Sabine, Camp Salubrity," I, II, III, IV, by J. Fair Hardin, v.16, p.5, 279, 441, 670.

Fort Jesup, established by Gaines, v.20, p.183.

Fort Jesup Masonic Institute, v.30, p.902-903.

"Fort, John A., A Letter From the Battle of New Orleans From," With Introductory Note by E. A. Parsons, v.32, p.225.

Fort Lafayette, noted, v.24, p.505.

Fort Livingston, noted, v.24, p.443.

Fort Macomb, ordered surrendered, v.26, p.1005.

Fort McComb, noted, v.24, p.443.

Fort Miro, founding of by Don Juan Filhiol, v.20, p.296, 463-485; noted, v.25, p.628, 641; site of Monroe, v.26, p.745.

Fort of Arkansas, 1794, mentioned, v.21, p.36.

Fort of Baton Rouge, seized in W. Fla. Rev., v.21, p.93n.; surrendered to Claiborne, v.21, p.178-179; list of stores, 1810, v.21, p.800.

Fort Panmure, noted, v.23, p.386; at Natchez, captured by Galvez, v.26, p.311; surrendered by Dickson, v.26, p.743.

Fort Pickens, noted, v.23, p.1198.

Fort Pike, noted, v.24, p.443.

Fort Pillow, noted, v.24, p.446.

Fort Real Catolica, at Balize, abandoned, v.26, p.740.

Fortress Monroe, noted, v.24, p.113.

Fort Richmond, at Baton Rouge, Galvez's description of, v.26, p.742; surrender to Galvez, v.26, p.742-743; changed by Great Britain to, v.28, p.63, 65, 67.

Fort Rosalie, map of, v.19, p.548, 560, 569.

Fort Royal, capture of, v.24, p.63-64.

Fort Saint Charles, noted, v.22, p.645; in N. O., v.26, p.746.

Fort Saint Ferdinand, of N. O., v.26, p.746.

Fort Saint Jean Baptiste, at Natchitoches, v.26, p.731.

Fort Saint John, noted, v.22, p.645, 764.

Fort Saint Lewis, in N. O., v.26, p.746.

Fort Saint Louis de Carlorette, noted, v.25, p.939.

Fort Saint Louis, noted, v.22, p.645.

Fort Saint Philip, noted, v.22, p.764, 817; noted, v.24, p.443, 444; bombardment of, v.24, p.450-451; noted, v.28, p.750, 751; ordered surrendered to La., v.26, p.997.

Fort San Carlos, see Fort of Baton Rouge.

Fort San Felipe, of Plaquemines, construction of, v.26, p.748; description of by Collot, v.26, p.749-750; noted, v.26, p.751; conditions of, v.26, p.752; Laussat's reception at, v.26, p.752-753.

Fort San Luis de Naches, noted, v.25, p.6; to be built by Piernas, v.26, p.721; abandoned, v.26, p.740.

Fort Santa Teresa, noted, v.24, p.656, 657.
Fort Stoddert and Mobile Society, v.21, p.100n.; location, v.21, p.153n.
Fort Toulouse, noted, v.22, p.20.
"Fortuneo," privateer vessel, v.23, p.432.
"Forward Bogalusa" movement, aims summarized, v.29, p.159n.
Fossier, A. E., "The Funeral Ceremony of Napoleon in New Orleans," v.13, p.246; "Charles Aloysius Luzenberg, 1805-1848," v.26, p.49-137; "Dr. Otto Lerch, 1855-1948," v.33, p.343-348.
Foster, Capt. J. P., noted, v.25, p.707.
Foster, D. N., physician and supt. of ed. of St. Mary, v.28, p.1131.
Foster, James, leased theatre on Camp St. for ball room, v.28, p.247; unsuccessful, v.28, p.251.
Foster, James M., worked for fusion of Democrats and Populists, v.26, p.1114.
Foster, J. H., U. S. reforestation expert, v.30, p.1051; report of, v.30, p.1051-1052; frames Revenue Bill, v.30, p.1052-1053.
Foster, Levi, v.28, p.767n.; sketch, v.28, p.1130.
Foster, Lillian, author on Louisiana, v.31, p.420.
Foster, Murphy J., and N. O. Strike, 1892, v.21, p.556, 557; headed ticket of Anti-Lottery group, 1892, v.25, p.716; noted, v.26, p.783; promised Hood command of La. Regt., v.26, p.792, 794; noted, v.26, p.796; anti-lotteryite cand. for gov., v.26, p.1078, 1079, 1081; the evils of the lottery, v.26, p.1078-1079; campaign of 1896, v.26, p.1099, 1100-1101, 1109-1111; ballot reform, v.26, p.1117-1118; cand. for gov. supported by Caffery, v.27, p.788, 789, 790, 791; resentment against, v.27, p.846-847; supported Heard for gov., 1900, v.27, p.847; elected to succeed Caffery as senator, v.27, p.849; strained relation with Caffery eased, v.27, p.849-850; senator, offered amendments to Lottery Bill of 1890, v.27, p.1041, 1042; opposed lottery bill, v.27, p.1043, 1050, 1056; address at Anti-Lottery League conv., v.27, p.1057; vice-pres. conv., presiding, v.27, p.1058; vice-chairman Dem. Anti-Lottery St. Ex. Com., v.27, p.1059; address to Anti-Lottery St. Com., v.27, p.1091; cand. for gov. of Anti-Lotteryites, v.27, p.1090, 1093, 1094; campaign, v.27, p.1094; election disputed, v.27, p.1094-1095; inauguration, v.27, p.1096, 1097; resolutions to from Women's Anti-Lottery League, v.27, p.1113; noted, v.28, p.767n.; ancestors, birth, early life and ed., v.28, p.1130-1132; cand. for leg., 1872, v.28, p.1136-1137; his work with White League, v.28, p.1137-1138; support of Nicholls, v.28, p.1138; election to Sen. 1879, v.28, p.1139-1140; his work as Sen., v.28, p.1140; efforts in behalf of state schools, v.28, p.1140-1141; his fight against the lottery, v.28, p.1140-1141, 1141-1151; pres. pro tempore of Sen., v.28, p.1141; the 1892 campaign for gov., v.28, p.1152-1162; inaugural address, v.28, p.1164; efforts to heal factional difference, v.28, p.1164-1165; and the N. O. strike of 1892, v.28, p.1165-1166; political appointments, v.28, p.1166-1167; support of Cleveland, v.28, p.1167; message to legis., 1894, v.28, p.1167-1168; provisions for election of police jurors, v.28, p.1168; fight for election laws, v.28, p.1168, 1185, 1186; other bills, v.28, p.1168-1169; and Dem. split over tariff, v.28, p.1169-1170; election of 1896, v.28, p.1170-1183; inaugural address, v.28, p.1183; divided legis., v.28, p.1183-1184; appointment of Sen., v.28, p.1184; const. conv., v.28, p.1185-1186, 1188; support of Bryan split in party, v.28, p.1186-1187; election of delegates to const. conv., v.28, p.1187-1188; special session of legis. to authorize cities to issue bonds, v.28, p.1189-1190; his good neighbor policy, v.28, p.1190; election of 1900, v.28, p.1190-1194; named U. S. Sen., v.28, p.1194; membership in committes, v.28, p.1195; his colleagues, v.28, p.1195; election of, v.28, p.1195-1198; the sugar tariff issue, v.28, p.1195-1212, 1224; railroad legis., v.28, p.1212-1216; action in re House Postal Approp. Bill, v.28, p.1216-1217; interest in flood control, v.28, p.1218-1219; efforts to eradicate boll weevil, v.28, p.1220; B. R. made port, v.28, p.1220; other work in Sen., v.28, p.1220-1221; trip to Japan and Philippines, v.28, p.1221; secured appointment of White as Chief Justice, v28, p.1221; the 1912 campaign, v.28, p.1222-1229; defeat of, v.28, p.1228-1229; app't Collector of Customs, N. O., v.28, p. 1229-1230; private life and death, v.28, p.1230; analysis of, v.28, p.1230-1231; tables of election returns of 1892, 1896, 1912, v.28, p.1232-1237;

bibl., v.28, p.1234-1243; bribery, v.31, p.794; noted, v.31, p.836; nominated for gov., v.31, p.837.

Foster, Rushton, N. O., newspaperman, v.33, p.322.

Foster, T. D., Judge of district, v.28, p.1131.

Foster, Thomas Jefferson, sketch, v.28, p.1130-1131; member of White Camellia, v.28, p.1130, 1134; on police jury, v.28, p.1136.

Foster, Thomas, slave dealer, v.22, p.152.

Foucault, describes hospital in 1766, v.29, p.602, 614-615; noted, v.29, p.625, 626.

Foucher, Pierre, location of plantation, v.21, p.225, 227; v.22, p.190, 813; noted, v.33, p.163.

"Foundation of New Orleans, History of," by Baron Marc de Villiers, v.3, p.157.

"Founding of New Orleans, Celebration of the," Address by Charles Barrett, Trans. from French by Miss Grace King, v.2, p.258.

"Founding of New Orleans, The," by Delaville H. Theard, v.3, p.68.

Fourcher Island, noted, v.24, p.648, 650, 653.

Fournet, Alexander V., cand. for treasurer, 1896, v.28, p.1173.

Fournet, G. A., Dem.-Populist elector, v.26, p.1116.

Fournet, J. A., Dem. cand. for treasurer, 1896, v.26, p.1101.

Fournier, Cesar, privateersman, v.22, p.768, 1079-1081.

Fourniez and St. Pe, noted, v.23, p.393, 395-397.

Fourth La. Regiment, chronology of, v.29, p.1043; organized, v.29, p.1048, 1049; officers of, v.29, p.1049-1050; 1st complete reg't to march through N. O., v.29, p.1051; from Camp Walker to Camp Moore to Ship Island, v.29, p.1051; at Ocean Springs, v.29, p.1051-1052; at Brashear City, v.29, p.1053-1054; ordered to Tenn., v.29, p.1055; at Corinth, v.29, p.1056-1057; part taken in Battle of Shiloh, v.29, p.1059-1070; back to Corinth, v.29, p.1070-1073; ordered to Edward's Station, Miss., to re-organize, v.29, p.1073-1075; events during stay in Vicksburg, v.29, p.1075-1080; from Vicksburg to Camp Moore to Greenwell Springs, v.29, p.1081-1082; from Greenwell Springs to Baton Rouge, v.29, p.1083; battle of Baton Rouge, v.29, p.1083-1090; leaves Baton Rouge for Port Hudson, v.29, p.1090-1091; events at Port Hudson, v.29, p.1091-1095; expedition against and capture of "Indianola," v.29, p.1097-1107; one company participates in siege of Port Hudson, v.29, p.1107-1133; rest of regiment sent to Miss. to intercept Grierson's Raiders, v.29, p.1143-1144; ordered to Jackson, Miss., v.29, p.1144-1145; siege of Jackson, v.29, p.1145-1146; ordered to Mobile, Ala., v.29, p.1146; from Mobile to Dalton, Ga., and back to Mobile, v.29, p.1149-1150; arrival at Marietta, Ga., and Battle of New Hope Church, v.29, p.1151-1152; on Pine Mt., v.29, p.1153-1158; on Kennesaw Mt., v.29, p.1158-1167; Battle of Kennesaw Mt., v.29, p.1167-1168; camped at Chattahooche River, v.29, p.1173-1174; Battle of Ezra Church or Battle of Poor House, v.29, p.1177-1181; brigaded with forces under General Quarles, v.29, p.1181; battle of Peach Tree Creek, v.29, p.1192; move to position before Atlanta, v.29, p.1192-1193; retreat from Atlanta begun, v.29, p.1197; battle of Jonesboro and retreat from battlefield, v.29, p. 1198-1201; occupy Florence, Ala., v.29, p.1202; battle of Franklin, v.29, p.1205-1206; arrival near Nashville, v.29, p.1207; battle of Nashville, v.29, p.1207-1211; most of reg't taken by enemy at Hollow Tree Gap, v.29, p.1212; remainder absorbed into 16th La. and identity lost, v.29, p.1212; reorganized and finally captured at Spanish Fort, v.29, p.1212; of Volunteers, muster rolls of, v.30, p.481-522.

Fourth Mississippi Cavalry, affiliation of Cable with, v.24, p.168.

Fourth Ward Repub. Club, organized by Pinchback in N. O., v.27, p.532.

Fox, James A., pastor in N. O., v.22, p.454, 465, 469, 470.

Foy, Maximilien Sebastien, funeral of, v.24, p.977; noted, v.24, p.991.

Foy, Prosper, papers in Howard-Tilton Memorial Library, v.24, p.329; noted, v.33, p.149.

Franc, Capt. ———, privateersman, v.22, p.1076-1079.

France, Address to People of, by House of Representatives of Louisiana, 1831, v.3, p.399.

France, friendship with the U. S., v.24, p.964-965, 1139; financial condition of, v.24, p.992; theological controversy in,

Franchise—Freeman

v.24, p.1010; naval preparations, v.24, p.1041, 1113; ministry in 1828, v.24, p.1113; rivalry with England, v.24, p.1118-1119; neutral in Russian campaign, v.24, p.1141; education of free colored in, v.25, p.307, 308, 359, 371, 372.

"Franchise," French vessel, v.24, p.612.

Francis, R. W., named in Wickliffe impeachment, v.31, p.693, 695.

"Francis Tillou Nicholls and the End of Reconstruction," by Hilda Mulvey McDaniel, v.32, p.357.

Francis, William, noted, v.22, p.725-726.

Francois, W. T., N. O. musician, v.31, p.141-142.

"Francois Xavier Martin: Second President of the La. Hist. Soc.," ed. by Walter Prichard, v.19, p.43-69.

Franco-Louisiana Alliance, noted, v.24, p.747.

Frankel, Jacob, councilman of Crowley, v.27, p.1126, 1128; sketch of, v.27, p.1130; first postmaster of Crowley, v.27, p.1155, 1171, 1172.

Franklin, Benjamin, noted, v.30, p.739.

Franklin, Gen. W. B., noted, v.32, p.115, 116, 125.

Franklin Infirmary, Hospital built at Luzenberg's proposal, v.26, p.54; fees of, v.26, p.55; noted, v.26, p.66.

Franklin, J. M., La. educator, v.30, p.902.

Franklin, La., ante-bellum library of, v.23, p.131-140; noted, v.24, p.39, 73; description of, v.24, p.40-41; noted, v.28, p.738, 752, 757, 760, 762, 763, 764; Cathcart's survey, v.28, p.766ff., 790, 792, 814; noted, v.28, p.818ff.; founding and naming of, v.28, p.1130; noted, v.28, p.1131, 1132; Caucasian Club in, v.28, p.1133; mass meeting in 1872, v.28, p.1136-1137; noted, v.32, p.17, 23, 47, 50, 52-55, 72, 74, 76, 86, 107, 113.

Franklin, State of, dependent on Spain, v.21, p.17.

Franklin Succession Case, v.25, p.1079.

Franklinton Academy, v.30, p.926-928.

Franklinton, "Central Institute" established, 1890, v.29, p.85.

Franklinton, La., parish seat of Washington Parish, v.29, p.79; noted, v.29, p.81, 82; schools of, v.29, p.84, 85; noted, v.29, p.118.

Franko, Nathan, musician, v.31, p.874-875; background, v.31, p.875-876.

Franko, Sam, noted, v.31, p.874; career, v.31, p.876; background, v.31, p.875-876.

Fransoni, Cardinal, Prefect of Propaganda, v.31, p.946.

Franz, Kaiser, noted, v.24, p.381.

Fraser, Major, —————, noted, v.22, p.1161.

Frayee, W. S., cand. auditor 1900, v.28, p.1191.

Frazer, Alexander, noted, v.23, p.35.

Frazier, Bob, killed in Civil War, v.29, p.1157-1158.

Frederick, Daniel, noted, v.22, p.458.

Frederics, Capt. Karl, on a six-day march, v.26, p.831-832.

Freedman's Aid Society of Methodist Episcopal Church, v.25, p.768, 778, 788.

Freedmen's Bureau, and Negro education, v.25, p.737-747; establishment of, v.25, p.740; regulations of, v.25, p.741; educational policy of, v.25, p.742; records of attendance, v.25, p.742; support of, v.25, p.742-743; made permanent, v.25, p.744; noted, v.30, p.150, 169, 188-189, 527; noted, v.32, p.157, 164; local agents of, v.32, p.162, 163; relief division, v.32, p.164-170; transportation, v.32, p.170; hospitalization, v.32, p.171-175; labor, v.32, p.176-177; Black Codes, v.32, p.183; contract management, v.32, p.189-190; bureau education, v.32, p.191-204; land, v.32, p.204-208; share cropping, v.32, p.209; home colonies, v.32, p.211; homesteading, v.32, p.210-211; justice, v.32, p.213; noted, v.32, p.364.

"Freedmen's Bureau of Louisiana, The," by John Cornelius Englesman, v.32, p.145.

"Freedmen's Saving Bank," by Fleming, reviewed by J. E. Winston, v.10, p.562.

Free Labor, on Randolph plantation, v.25, p.192, 193-194.

Freeland, T. B., and C. J., v.27, p.1167; control of First Nat'l Bank of Crowley, v.27, p.1171; sketch of, v.27, p.1172, 1179, 1187.

Freeman, A. A., Assistant Att'y-Gen'l, v.27, p.1008.

Freeman, Arthur, "The Early Career of Pierre Soule," v.25, p.971-1127.

Freeman, Col. Constantine, Comd. U. S. troops at Natchitoches, v.28, p.1061.

Freeman, Miles J., Confed. naval engineer from La., v.27, p.485.

Freeman, Thomas, surveyor gen'l of southern U. S., v.28, p.894.

Free Market, of New Orleans, v.24, p.456, 474.

"Free Negro in Ante-Bellum Louisiana," by Annie Lee West Stahl, v.25, p.301-396.

"Free Negro in N. O., 1803-1860," by James E. Winston, v.21, p.1075-1085.

Free persons of color, in La., labor done by, v.25, p.179; laws regarding, v.25, p.303, 304, 312-336; religion of, v.25, p.357-358, 360, 361-362, 363, 366-368; education of, v.25, p.357, 358-366, 371-372, 732-733; occupations of, v.25, p.368-374; summary, v.25, p.374-377; glossary, v.25, p.377-380; appendices, v.25, p.381-392; bibliography, v.25, p.392-396.

Free Trade Convention, 1831, v.25, p.71, 79.

"French and Spanish Documents Concerning Early History of Louisiana," v.1, sec.1, p.103; v.1, sec.3, p.224.

French Colonial La., life in, v.21, p.629-630; list of settlers of, v.21, p.965-978.

"French Colonial Procedure in Louisiana for the Appointment of Tutors to Minors," Heloise H. Cruzat, v.8, p.218.

French, culture of in La., v.24, p.745-749, 750-751, 752-755; exploration of in lower Miss. Valley, founding of B. R., v.28, p.31; and settling of B. R. area, v.28, p.58-65.

French, Dr. C. R., identified, v.21, p.733n.

French Government charities to the Acadians, 1755-1799, v.21, p.656-68.

"French Incertitude in 1718 as to a Site for New Orleans," I, II, translated by Sally Dart, v.15, p.37, 417.

French Indian policy, toward the Caddoes, v.18, p.888-891.

"French in the Miss. Valley, 1740-1759," by Norman W. Caldwell, v.25, p.827-828.

French, John, noted, v.23, p.420.

French, Jonas H., acting chief of police in N. O., v.27, p.512; reorganized police force, v.27, p.513.

"French Literature of Louisiana," Caulfield's, by H. P. Dart (Editor's Chair), v.13, p.484.

French Market, distributing point for slaves, v.24, p.23.

"French Opera House, The New Orleans," by Andre Lafargue, v.3, p.368.

"French Press of La.," by Douglas C. McMurtrie, v.18, p.947-965.

French Revolution, propaganda in N. O., v.22, p.697; books censored, v.22, p.796; effect in La., v.23, p.112-113.

French, Samuel G., noted, v.24, p.107.

French Settlement (La.), roads at, v.23, p.418.

French Theatre, New Orleans, v.25, p.309; v.28, p.89.

French Union, noted, v.24, p.747.

French, William Henry, noted, v.23, p.1171.

Freret, Carrie, noted, v.24, p.316.

Freret, James P., noted, v.23, p.176, 187.

Freret, William, removal from office, v.22, p.1165, 1166.

Frey, Frederick, noted, v.22, p.458.

Frey, Thomas, noted, v.23, p.391.

Friars, Joseph, noted, v.23, p.421.

"Friend of Chopin, and Some Other New Orleans Musical Celebrities, The," by John Smith Kendall, v.31, p.856-877.

"Friends of Freedom of the State of Louisiana," New Orleans union society, v.31, p.1011.

"Friends of Mexican Emancipation," v.25, p.299.

"Friends of the Union," in N. O., v.25, p.91-92.

Frissell, Hollis B., noted, v.25, p.795.

Fromanpexima, Richard, noted, v.23, p.404.

Fromentin, Eligius, and 1818 tariff bill, v.25, p.34.

Fromentin, Nicolas, noted, v.22, p.626.

Frost, ———, noted, v.24, p.768.

Fuentes, Joseph, vs. Gaines, and Gaines vs. Fuentes, to revoke will of 1813, v.27, p.293-304.

Fuller, Frank J., La. senator, v.26, p.961.

Fullerton, G. W., sale of "Fashion Plantation" to Richard Taylor, v.24, p.52-53.

Fulton, Alexander, bought mercantile interests of William Miller, v.24, p.735.

Fulton and Miller, traders at Alexandria, v.23, p.1122, 1123.

Fulton, Samuel, and W. Fla. Rev., v.21, p.708n.; noted, v.22, p.91.

Fulton, William, Protestant minister banished by Butler, v.27, p.501.

Fulton, William T., N. O. minstrel, sketch of, v.30, p.139-140.

Fundamental Orders of Connecticut, noted, v.24, p.701.

"Funeral Ceremony of Napoleon in New Orleans," by A. A. Fossier, v.13, p.246.

Fuqua, James O., proposed substitute for ordinance of secession, v.26, p.1001.

Furniture, purchased by Americans in Europe, v.24, p.945; in early houses, v.32, p.32-34.

Furrate, Gustave, noted, v.24, p.770.

Fur Trade, in St. Louis, v.22, p.88; export, v.22, p.663; disagreement over cargo, v.23, p.392-398.

Fur Traders, Spanish fear of British, v.21, p.54; on Miss. River, 1795, v.21, p.70ff.

Fuselier de St. Clair, Gabriel, v.28, p.818n.

Fusion Board, or Warmoth Board, v.29, p.409.

Fusionist Com. of Citizens, to appeal to Pres. Grant, v.27, p.564, 571.

Fusion Party, headed by McEnery for gov., v.27, p.553-554, 563; meeting of Dec. 10, 1872, v.27, p.564, 567, 568, 569, 571, 572, 573, 574, 579; supports Sheridan, v.27, p.581, 583, 586, 588; dispute over vacancy in U. S. Senate, v.27, p.590.

Futch, William, Confed. soldier, v.26, p.954.

GABICI, LEON, NEW ORLEANS MUSICIAN, v.31, p.132.

"Gaceta de Texas," first Tex. newspaper, v.23, p.1001n.

Gage, Gen., wanted Manchac opened, v.25, p.935.

Gaiennie, General, noted, v.24, p.766.

Gaiety Theatre, noted, v.25, p.375.

Gaillardet, quoted, on Murat, v.25, p.997; gives dinner in Soule's honor, v.25, p.1073.

Gaines, Edmund Pendleton, marriage to Myra Clark, v.20, p.23; est. Fort Jesup, v.20, p.183; and Indians on S. Western frontier, v.20, p.184; ordered army to Sabine, v.20, p.186; and W. Fla., v.21, p.154; and Andrew Jackson, v.21, p.386; and Spanish insurgents in Fla., v.21, p.816-817; noted, v.23, p.477; marriage to Myra Clark, v.27, p.51; death of, v.27, p.52-53; picture of, v.27, p.50, 176, 184, 190; picture, v.27, p.212; Major-General, v.32, p.253.

Gaines, James, noted, v.25, p.295.

Gaines, Myra Clark, heritage and early life, v.20, p.5-14; marriage to W. W. Whitney, v.20, p.19; suits against Relf & Chew, et al., v.20, p.21ff.; marriage to E. P. Gaines, v.20, p.23; litigation in Supreme Court, v.20, p.26ff.; description of, v.20, p.38-39; noted, v.27, p.7, 9; motives of, v.27, p.10; father's will, v.27, p.12-13; issue of legitimacy, v.27, p.13-15; issue of recovery of property, v.27, p.15-16; birth of, v.27, p.25; circumstances concerning birth, v.27, p.41-44; picture of, v.27, p.42; placed in care of and reared by S. B. Davis, v.27, p.43-47; discovers papers relating to birth, v.27, p.47; marriage to W. W. Whitney, v.27, p.47; learns from Bellechasse of last will of father, v.27, p.48; proceedings to probate will, v.27, p.48-51; marriage to E. P. Gaines, v.27, p.51-53, 62; evidence for, v.27, p.62-86; presents marriage certificate of Desgrange as evidence, v.27, p.86-91, 91, 96, 103, 110; negative evidence in case of, v.27, p.115-133; conflicting evidence, v.27, p.133-178; references to in "Court Circles," v.27, p.176-178; list of cases, v.27, p.178-179; petition to probate will of 1813 denied, v.27, p.180; bill of equity filed in Circuit Ct. of U. S. to recover property, v.27, p.180; Ct. grants petition that defendants be supplied copies of bill in Fr., v.27, p.180-181, 185-186; procedure delayed, v.27, p.182; applies in Sup. Ct. for writ of mandamus, v.27, p.182-183; writ denied, v.27, p.183-184, 186; Gaines vs. Relf, opinion, v.27, p.187-189; demurrers filed against bill of, v.27, p.189;

allegations of bill, v.27, p.190; statement of case by Circuit Ct., v.27, p.190-195; questions in re case again certified to Sup. Ct., v.27, p.195; opinions rendered in favor of, v.27, p.196-204; opinion in Patterson Case rules Mrs. Gaines legitimate, v.27, p.205-210, 211; decision reversed in suit vs. Relf, Chew, etc., v.27, p.211-241; dissenting opinion, v.27, p.226-232, 235-241; picture of, v.27, p.242; favorable decision in case of vs. Hennan, v.27, p.243-274; dissenting opinion, v.27, p.274-276; favorable decisions in case of vs. City of N. O., v.27, p.278-293; attempt to revoke Clark's will of 1813, v.27, p.293-304; sales of property by Relf and Chew illegal, v.27, p.304-307; Gaines vs. De La Croix, v.27, p.307-311; Davis vs. Gaines, v.27, p.311-314; other cases to recover rents, profits, and damages, v.27, p.314-322.

"Gaines vs. N. O.," also "The Gaines Case," v.27, p.6-322.

Gain, Hugh, printer, v.22, p.370, 374.

Gaisergues, Francis, deposition of, v.23, p.699-700.

Galapagos Islands, guano on, v.23, p.162-169.

Galbraith, Thomas Brabazon, noted, v.22, p.314.

Galerido, Dr. J., noted, v.26, p.76.

Gallatin, Albert, on sugar, v.23, p.1016; noted, v.24, p.727, 939, 946, 1005, 1015, 1018, 1019, 1022, 1062, 1071, 1075, 1143; in London, v.24, p.1007-1008; and Oneida Indians, v.24, p.1056; Sec. of Treasury, noted, v.31, p.276, 279, 384; instructions to Trist, v.31, p.277; idea of Clark, v.31, p.313; concerning Lyman, v.31, p.317.

Gallatin Street, in N. O., v.29, p.44, 45, 46.

Gallaudet, ———, noted, v.23, p.1237, 1238.

Gally, Louis B., noted, v.23, p.477.

Galveston Bay, named, v.22, p.795; filibuster base, v.22, p.737; located, v.24, p.632.

Galveston Island (Campeache), base for privateers, v.24, p.16, 641.

Galveston, Laffites at, v.21, p.213-219; documents concerning establishment of privateers, 1816-1817, v.21, p.1086-1109; headquarters of filibusters, v.23, p.762ff., 780, 850; storm of 1818, v.23, p.795-796; (Galveztown) noted, v.24, p.638, 641.

Galvez, Bernardo de, "Diary of Operations Against Pensacola," Trans. from the Spanish by Gaspar Cusachs, v.1, sec. 1, p.44; noted, v.23, p.429-439; papers in Bibliotheca Parsoniana, v.24, p.310, 311; Sp. Gov. appoints Bouligny Lt. Gov. of La., v.25, p.939; his conquest of W. Fla., v.26, p.311; siege of Pensacola as revealed in Robt. Farmar's Journal, v.26, p.315-329; Gov. of Sp. La., v.26, p.740; his military campaigns against Manchac, Baton Rouge, Mobile, Pensacola, v.26, p.740-745; receives Sp. declaration of war on Eng., v.26, p.762-763; announces falsely that Sp. has recognized U. S., v.26, p.763-764; writes to Grand Pre of recognition, v.26, p.764-766; learned error, v.26, p.767; Sp. Gov., v.27, p.338; in re trade with Indians, v.27, p.647, 648, 649; agreement with Blommart, v.27, p.649-650; treatment of contraband traders, v.27, p.653-654; aid to Am. in Rev. War, v.27, p.655, 656, 657, 659; led army of Sp. against British, v.27, p.661; siege of Pensacola, v.27, p.663, 664, 665; plans to release Gen'l Campbell, v.27, p.665-666; learns of Campbell's treachery and orders detention of, v.27, p.666-667; promotion of, v.27, p.668; suspends Blommart's sentence, v.27, p.668, 669; release of John Campbell, v.27, p.670; relieved de Villiers of Ark. post, v.27, p.672; conceded equal rights to all traders, v.27, p.692, 702, 854-927 passim.; Sp. Gov. of La., v.28, p.64, 693; and Don Pedro, v.28, p.694ff.; noted, v.28, p.721; and N. O. Charity Hospital, v.31, p.18-20; noted, v.31, p.612.

"Galvez, Dario de," by Gaspar Cusachs, v.1, sec.1, p.9.

Galvez, Don Jose de, urged opening of road and seaport in Tex., v.28, p.1076.

"Galveston, A Spanish Settlement of Colonial Louisiana," by V. A. Scramuzza, v.13, p.553; noted, v.25, p.163, 940; post at, v.26, p.745.

Gambi (Gambio), noted, v.24, p.13, 14.

Gambi, Vincent, privateersman, v.22, p.734, 1035-1038, 1085; privateer, v.23, p.810.

Gambling, in Sp. N. O., v.22, p.691.

Ganienne, Urbin, deposition of, v.23, p.719-720.

Garcia, Felix, and the const. con. of 1844, v.25, p.1077ff.; pres. pro tem. of the senate, 1846, v.25, p.1039; and the senatorial election of 1848, v.25, p.1096-1100; vice-pres. Society of Nat'l Hist. and the Sciences, v.26, p.61.

Garcia y Muniz, Manuel, noted, v.23, p.429, 818, 821, 822; mission to check on Laffites, v.23, p.808; letter to viceroy, v.23, p.811.

Gardema, G., sheriff of St. Martin, appeal to lottery co., for aid in flood, v.27, p.1028.

"Garden of Fray Antonio de Sedella," ed. by Stanley Faye, v.21, p.1069-1074.

Gardette, James, husband of Zulime Carriere, v.27, p.46, 58, 59, 60, 62, 70, 71, 78, 79, 82, 86, 88, 99, 120, 122, 132, 143, 151, 167-168, 170, 172, 175, 191, 193, 194, 216, 281, 285, 288.

Gardette, Jas., Jr., v.27, p.59, 60; testimony of in regard to marriage certificate of Desgrange, v.27, p.86.

Gardner, L. H., named in Kellogg impeachment, v.31, p.713.

Gardoqui, Diego, sketch, v.21, p.21n.; treaty with U. S., v.21, p.42-43; approves Ouachita settlement, v.31, p.613; opinion of situation, v.31, p.623.

Garfield, James A., noted, v.29, p.733, 735; elected Pres. of U. S., v.29, p.744; killed by assassin, v.29, p.745.

Garic, Flojac, noted, v.22, p.808; sketch, v.22, p.812.

Garic, Francois, noted, v.24, p.358-359.

Garic, Juan Bautista, noted, v.22, p.388.

Garland, ———, noted, v.24, p.775.

Garland, Henry Lestrapes, noted, v.23, p.1003.

Garland, Kate, collection in L.S.U. Archives, v.24, p.342.

Garland, Rice, on La. Sup. Ct., v.23, p.1029; scandal involving, v.23, p.1035.

Garland, W. H., noted, v.23, p.204.

Garnier, John, noted, v.22, p.151.

Garreau, Armand, Louisiana novelist, v.31, p.992.

Garrison, William Lloyd, noted, v.24, p.521.

Garrot, V., Laffites agent, v.21, p.213; Col., aide to Lallemand, v.23, p.785, 807.

Garrow, Joseph, noted, v.23, p.357, 368.

Garza, Don Ysidro de la, expedition to clear neutral ground, v.28, p.1068.

"Gas Bank," noted, v.24, p.48.

Gasquet, James A., noted, v.23, p.213.

Gassen, J. B., St. Charles Parish merchant, v.21, p.1114.

Gastinel, Arthur, and Lottery, v.31, p.760-761.

Gates, Ada Favrot, collection in Howard-Tilton Memorial Library, v.24, p.330.

Gates, Judge Fred, v.28, p.1136.

Gates, William, collection in Institute of Middle American Research, v.24, p.332.

"Gatlin Gun" Conv., see Custom House Conv.

Gaudet, Mrs. Frances Joseph, noted, v.25, p.789.

Gaudet Normal and Industrial School, History of, v.25, p.789-790.

Gaudin, Edouard, elected St. Louis Church Warden, v.31, p.986.

Gauld, George, and W. Fla. Assembly, v.23, p.23ff.; noted, v.23, p.357, 368, 377.

Gautier, Captain, noted, v.24, p.660.

"Gavilan," brigantine, v.24, p.676.

Gaw, Alexander, noted, v.22, p.1003.

"Gayarre, A Last Evening with Judge" (with picture), by Frank D. Richardson, v.14, p.81.

"Gayarre, An Evening With," by Rudolph Matas, v.33, p.269-293.

Gayarre, Antonio, noted, v.22, p.815.

Gayarre, Charles, manuscripts in Bibliotheca Parsoniana, v.24, p.311; correspondence in Xavier University Archives, v.24, p.336; collection in L.S.U. Archives, v.24, p.342; noted, v.24, p.316; and nullification, v.25, p.91; noted, v.25, p.681, 1004, 1044, 1075, 1087, 1106, 1107; his "History of La.," v.25, p.1055; supported "tree theory" of origin of name B. R., v.28, p.45; and state banking controversy, v.28, p.979; writes letter to De Bow, v.29, p.360-361; noted, v.29, p.362; work on "Review," v.29, p.371, 372, 376, 383; idea of Bastrop's identity, v.31, p.608; quoted, v.31, p.612; born, v.33, p.159; baptised, v.33, p.160; childhood, v.33, p.161; schooling, v.33, p.168, 169, 170; practice of law in La., v.33, p.170; "Essai Historique sur la Louisiane," v.33, p.171, 172; illness, v.33, p.173; travels in France, v.33, p.173, 174; works on Hist. of La., v.33, p.174; Returns to La., v.33, p.175; publishes history, v.33, p.175; Series of lectures, v.33, p.176; Sec. of State, v.33, p.177, 178; revives La. Hist. Soc., v.33, p.178; Retires from position of Sec. of State, v.33, p.180; Publication of third vol. of Hist., v.33, p.180; writes vol. "Amer. Domination," v.33, p.181-182; during Civil War, v.33, p.183-184; works on last vol. of Hist., v.33, p.184;

returns to N. O., v.33, p.185; appointed Reporter by Sup. Ct., v.33, p.186; his last book, v.33, p.187; List of Hist. articles, v.33, p.187-188; death, v.33, p.188; brief description of characters in his novel "Quevedo," v.33, p.193-204; lectures, v.33, p.257; publishes two novels, v.33, p.258; physical description, v.33, p.272.

"Gayarre, Charles, A Biographical Sketch," by Grace King, v.33, p.159-88.

"Gayarre, Charles, Autobiography of", Introduction by Henry P. Dart, v.12, p.5; "Biographical Sketch," by a Louisianian, v.12, p.9; "Four Letters From Gayarre, 1878-1889," v.12, p.28.

"Gayarre, Charles Etienne, Some Letters of, on Literature and Politics, 1854-1885," v.33, p.223-254.

Gayarre, Charles, "Historical Notes on Commerce and Agriculture of Louisiana, 1720-1766," v.2, p.286.

"Gayarre, Charles, Louisiana's Literary Historian," by Wilford B. Yearns, Jr., v.33, p.255-268.

Gayarre, Charles, "Reports on Louisiana Archives in Spain, 1850," v.4, p.466.

Gayarre, Charles, "Tribunals of Criminal Jurisdiction in Ancient Rome," v.33, p.205-222.

Gayarre, Don Juan Antonio, v.33, p.167.

Gayarre, Ferdinand, and dueling, v.23, p.453-454.

Gayarre, Luis, noted, v.22, p.815.

"Gayarre Manuscripts, Some Unedited," by Edward Alexander Parsons, v.33, p.189-204.

"Gayarre, The Last Days of Charles," by John S. Kendall, v.15, p.359.

Gaylord Box Company, set up in Bogalusa, v.29, p.130; merges with Bogalusa Paper Company, v.29, p.107, 130-131, 183.

Gayoso de Lemos, Manuel, made Gov. of Natchez, 1789; v.21, p.15; trip to states of Franklin and Cumberland, v.21, p.18; letter to Carondelet noted, v.21, p.24n., 33n.; and Treaty of Nogales, v.21, p.28n.; fortifies post of Las Barrancas de Margot, v.21, p.55; noted, v.23, p.429, 432, 695, 702; land grant to, v.23, p.1090; marriage, v.23, p.1090-1091; noted, v.28, p.703, 705; becomes Gov., v.28, p.710; and Favrot, v.28, p.711; death, v.28, p.715; noted, v.28, p.943; treaty with Indians, v.28, p.1013; replaces Carondelet, v.31, p.623; suspends Bastrop contract, v.31, p.624.

Gayoso, Fernando, suit to recover land, v.23, p.1090-1093.

Gazzo, John, noted, v.23, p.553.

Geale, Herbert, case challenging constitutionality of Act No. 9 of 1874, v.27, p.985.

Gebbia, Leonardo, and Mafia, v.22, p.828-831.

Geissler, Ludwig, noted, v.24, p.133.

"General Bank's Red River Campaign," by Richard Hobson Williams, v.32, p.103.

"General Benjamin F. Butler and the Widow Mumford," by Louis Taylor Merrill, v.29, p.341-354.

"General Bolivar," Laffite's ship sold in N. O., to Duncan, v.21, p.205; privateer of the Laffites, v.23, p.751; privateer vessel, v.24, p.367, 368.

"General Edmund P. Gaines and the Protection of the South Western Frontiers," by James W. Silver, v.20, p.183-191.

General Education Board, v.25, p.793-795.

"General Gates," changed to the "Dardo" under British registry, v.24, p.616.

"General Jackson," Laffite's vessel, v.21, p.205.

"General James Wilkinson — The Last Phase," by Thomas R. Hay, v.19, p.407, 435.

"General Morelos," pirate schooner, v.23, p.851.

"General San Martin," brig, v.24, p.647, 651.

"Genesis of Germantown, Louisiana, The: Or the Mysterious Past of Louisiana's Mystic, Count de Leon," by Karl J. R. Arndt, v.24, p.378-433.

"Genessee," federal boat, v.29, p.1108, 1118, 1124.

Genet Affair and Spanish Fla., mentioned, v.21, p.30-31.

Genet, Citizen, effect of in La., v.28, p.704-705.

Genet, Edmond Charles, activities in La., v.22, p.52-56; noted, v.23, p.431.

Genndry, Gustave, noted, v.23, p.566.

Genois, Charles, N.O. recorder, v.25, p.358, 1053, 1075.

Genois, Joseph, noted, v.22, p.1139n., 1154.

Genova, see Matesi, Francisco.

Gens de couleur libres, v.25, p.305, 301.

"Gentlemen of Pointe Coupee, A," by Henry Plauche Dart, v.5, p.462.

Gentlemen's Hebrew Benevolent Association, noted, v.24, p.326.

Geology, of Avoyelles and Rapides Parishes, noted, v.25, p.398; of Caldwell and Winn Parishes, noted, v.25, p.398.

George III, Commission of George Johnstone as gov. of W. Fla., v.21, p.1025-1033.

"George Graham's Mission to Galveston in 1818," ed. by Walter Prichard, v.20, p.619-650.

George, John, noted, v.23, p.419, 420.

"George Washington Cable's Literary Apprenticeship," by Arlin Turner, v.24, p.168-186.

Gerard, Francesca, marriage to Pedro Favrot, v.28, p.699.

Gerault, John, noted, v.22, p.982; v.23, p.29.

German Catholic Churches in New Orleans, noted, v.24, p.136; listed, v.24, p.137.

German Coast, plan for colonization, 1795, v.21, p.61; noted, v.26, p.669.

German Colonists of John Law, in and around New Orleans, v.26, p.367-369; hardships of, v.26, p.663-665; at Ark. post, v.26, p.667-669; departure to lower Miss., v.26, p.671; noted, v.26, p.680.

"German Drama on the N.O. Stage, The," by Arthur Henry Moehlenbrock, v.26, p.361-627.

German instruction in New Orleans, 1866, table, v.24, p.151-152.

"German Liberals in N.O., 1840-1860," by Robert T. Clark, Jr., v.20, p.137-151.

German Protestant Churches in New Orleans, noted, v.24, p.136; listed, v.24, p.137.

German schools in New Orleans, v.24, p.148-149.

German Society of New Orleans, organized 1847, v.26, p.378-379.

Germans, of N.O., v.20, p.137-151, 925ff.; in the Civil War, v.20, p.990-1015; emigrants in La., v.21, p.57; redemption case of Sally Miller, v.22, p.155-165; truck farmer, v.22, p.671; coast, v.22, p.815; in W. Fla., v.23, p.373; trip of immigrant to New Orleans and Nacogdoches, v.23, p.485-500; in New Orleans and Reconstruction, v.23, p.501-524.

German Theatre, in N.O., noted, v.24, p.156; table of performances, v.24, p.159; Magazine St., first in N.O., v.28, p.228; Chapman's Co. at, v.28, p.251; becomes New Am. Theatre, 1840, v.28, p.252.

Germantown, "first La. Share-Our-Wealth community," v.24, p.379, 380, 391, 382, 429, 431, 432, 433.

Germany, James, Indian trader, v.23, p.372.

Gerstacker, Friedrich, noted, v.23, p.485.

Gholson, William Y., counsel Morse vs. O'Reilly, v.31, p.463.

Giacona, ———, and Mafia, v.22, p.833.

Giannini, Vittorio, photostats of music in Xavier University, v.24, p.336.

Gibson, John, editor "True American," letter from, v.26, p.90; noted, v.26, p.91, 92; description of, v.26, p.98; editorials, v.26, p.98-101, 101-102.

Gibson, Randall L., and the founding of Tulane U., v.20, p.1045-1047; Col., v.27, p.784; election of successor to Senate, v.27, p.791, 792; attacked by Anti-Lotteryites, v.27, p.1065; U.S. Senator, 1882, v.28, p.1161; end of term, v.28, p.1164; death, v.28, p.1167; Brig. Gen'l, v.29, p.724, 727, 781; Confederate officer, v.29, p.1056, 1193.

Giffen, Adam, commissioner of lottery drawings, v.27, p.977.

Gifford, George, counsel Morse vs. O'Reilly, v.31, p.471.

Giquel, E., noted, v.23, p.193.

Gilbert Academy and Industrial School, history of, v.25, p.787-788.

Gilbert, and expedition against Laffite, v.24, p.19.

Gilbert, James, Confed. soldier, v.26, p.949.

Gilbert, T. B., favored lottery bill of 1890, v.27, p.1033.

Gili, Fray Sebastian, noted, v.22, p.106; letter from Casa Calvo, v.22, p.132-133; letter to Casa Calvo, v.22, p.138-140.

Gillett, R. H., counsel Morse vs. O'Reilly, v.31, p.471.

Gilliot, Marcellin, noted, v.22, p.1068.

Gilmer, Mrs. E. M., (Dorothy Dix), "Talks on Grace King," v.6, p.359.

Gilmore, James R., sketch of, v.29, p.1251; peace conference with Pres. Davis, v.29, p.1253-1257; results of conference, v.29, p.1257-1258.

Ginn, Mildred Kelly, "A History of Rice Production in La. to 1896," v.23, p.544-588.

Girard, John, noted, v.22, p.982.

Girard, Pierre, noted, v.23, p.851.

Girard, Stephen, and the Spanish Land Grants, v.20, p.440-445.

Giraud, Ernest, N.O. musician, v.31, p.131.

Gird, H. H., president of Centenary College, v.31, p.882.

Girod, Claude, and Batture controversy, v.23, p.695, 699-700, 701.

Girod, Francis, noted, v.23, p.683.

Girod, Nicholas, letter from Andrew Jackson, v.21, p.380-382; letter to Casa Calvo, v.22, p.125-128; letter from Casa Calvo, v.22, p.140-141; buys land of B. Gravier, v.22, p.397, 407, 412; noted, v.22, p.808; sketch, v.22, p.812; documents in Bibliotheca Parsoniana, v.24, p.311; noted, v.24, p.373.

"Gironde," ship bringing settlers to N.O., 1724, v.21, p.981; boat brings Nuns to La., v.29, p.564, 565, 570.

Gladstane, Mary, noted, v.23, p.509.

Gladstone, William E., cited, v.24, p.532.

"Glass, The Trial of Mary," by Henry P. Dart, Translated from the original by Heloise H. Cruzat, Laura L. Porteous and J. Franklin Jameson, v.6, p.589.

Glendora Plantation, site of Indian burial ground, v.25, p.627.

Glen, James, noted, v.23, p.546.

Glenk, Robert, handbook cited, v.24, p.320, 350.

Globe Ball Room, v.33, p.392-393, 405.

Glover, William B., "A History of the Caddo Indians," v.18, p.872-946.

Goan, Thomas, noted, v.23, p.404.

Godchaux, Frank, "rice king," head of La. State Rice Milling Co., v.27, p.1166, 1167.

Godley, William, noted, v.23, p.42, 354ff.

Godoy, Manuel de, El Duque de la Alcudia, Principe de la Paz, and Supreme Council of State, v.21, p.68; sketch, v.21, p.23n.; letter from Carondelet noted, v.21, p.28n.; and treaty of 1795, v.23, p.86.

Gogreve, Henry H., mayor of Carrollton, v.21, p.251; noted, v.22, p.203.

Goldwaite, Alfred, senator, on Lottery Bill, v.27, p.1042; speaker at Prog. League meeting, v.27, p.1063; sen. leader of pro-lottery forces, v.28, p.1145.

Goldwater, Dr. Sigismund S., survey of Charity Hospital, v.31, p.84-85.

Gondre, Pierre, noted, v.24, p.371.

Gonon, French inventor of telegraph, v.31, p.427; estimates cost, v.31, p.428.

Gonsoulin, Francois, sketch, v.28, p.813n.; claims on Belle Isle, v.28, p.915.

Gontgen, Dr., secretary of Count de Leon, v.24, p.384, 420, 423, 428, 430.

Gonzales, Ambrosia J., Lopez's lieut., noted, v.22, p.1122.

Gonzales, John Edmunds, "William Pitt Kellogg, Reconstruction Governor of Louisiana, 1873-1877," v.29, p.394-495.

Gonzales, Mateo, noted, v.22, p.1052.

Good Government League, organized, v.28, p.1223; noted, v.28, p.1228.

Goodrich, Charles, pastor in N.O., v.22, p.462, 463; Protestant minister banished by Butler, v.27, p.501.

Goodwin, Cardinal, "The Louisiana Territory, 1682-1803," v.3, p.5.

Goodyear, A. C., of Great Southern Lumber Co., v.29, p.91, 93, 120, 121, 171.

Goodyear, Charles W., of Great Southern Lumber Co., v.29, p.90, 94n., 121, 122, 181.

Goodyear, Frank H., of Great Southern Lumber Co., v.29, p.90, 91, 93, 94n., 154, 155, 181, 186.

Gordon, Arthur, noted, v.22, p.364, p.451; and W. Fla. Assembly, v.23, p.5ff., 377, 391.

Gordon, William, noted, v.23, p.368.

Gosson, Antoine, noted, v.22, p.629.

Gottschalk, Edward, father of Louis, v.31, p.866.

Gottschalk, Louis Moreau, collection, v.24, p.317; N.O. musician, early life, v.31, p.866; career, v.31, p.867; personal life, v.31, p.867-868; work, v.31, p.869; relics of, v.31, p.869-871.

Gottschalk, Paul, collection cited, v.24, p.330, 350.

Gouberg, M., diploma in wrestling, New Orleans Public Library, v.24, p.325.

Goudeau, J. B., Agreement with LeBreton Employing Goudeau as Overseer, v.9, p.590.

Gounod, autograph of, in Howard-Tilton Memorial Library, v.24, p.330.

Government and individual contacts, Edward Livingston's views upon, v.24, p.723-725.

"Government by Treaty," by William H. Fitzpatrick, v.33, p.299-316.

"Government Employees and Salaries in Spanish La." by A. P. Nasater, v.29, p.885-1040.

"Governor Perier's Expedition Against the Natchez Indians, Dec. 1730, Jan. 1731," by John A. Green, v.19, p.547-577.

"Governor Peter Chester's Observations on the Boundaries of British W. Fla. about 1775," ed. by James A. Padgett, v.26, p.5-11.

Gower, Benjamin, noted, v.23, p.389, 391.

Grace, Hon. Fred J., Reg. of State Land Office, report in 1912 on act 215 of 1908, v.28, p.315; reports quoted, v.28, p.316, 317; Supervisor of Mines and Minerals, v.29, p.67.

Gracien, Geo., v.27, p.989; substantiated charges of Wilde of bribery of Lottery Co., v.27, p.990.

Graham, co-manager Am. Theatre on death of Russell, 1838, v.28, p.228.

Graham, George, mission to Galveston in 1818, v.20, p.169-150; documents of proposals to Jean Laffite, v.21, p.213-219; mission to Galveston, v.23, p.794ff.; sketch, v.28, p.820n.

Graham, George Mason, autobiography of, v.20, p.43-57; noted, v.25, p.699; General, and Louisiana State Seminary, v.31, p.517.

Graham, James, candidate for auditor, v.31, p.535.

Graham, John, Sec. of Territory of Orleans, v.20, p.44; Sec. of Legation to Spain and later minister to Portugal, v.20, p.45; and W. Fla. Rev., v.21, p.79; letter from Skipwith, v.21, p.156-158, 162-171; noted, v.22, p.721n., 763.

Graham, L., and Company acquires property of "De Bow's Review," v.29, p.393.

Graham, Lewis E., Prog. League Com., v.27, p.1062.

Graham, Richard, aide-de-camp to Gen'l Harrison, Indian agent and planter on Ohio R., v.20, p.45.

Grailhe, Alexander, duels of, v.33, p.150-151.

"Grambling," La. Negro Normal, v.25, p.811.

Grand Caillou, fort of, v.26, p.1022; noted, v.28, p.807, 885.

Grandchamps, Francois, one of first registered pharmacists, v.26, p.336, 337.

Grand Cheniere, dam built to prevent salt from killing rice, v.27, p.150-160.

Grand Coteau, Convent, v.25, p.730.

Grand Ecore, noted, v.24, p.78, 88, 92, 93, 94, 99, 429, 431, 432; 1873 sketch of, v.24, p.430; noted, v.25, p.400.

"Grand Era," confederate boat, v.29, p.1100, 1102.

"Grandfather Clause," Negro disfranchised by, v.26, p.1121.

Grand Island, noted, v.24, p.23.

Grand Isle, v.28, p.884, 885.

Grand Lake, noted, v.24, p.73; noted, v.25, p.165, 932; Cathcart's inspection, v.28, p.761, 765, 766ff.

"Grand Masonic Lottery," noted, v.31, p.717.

Grand Opera House, Bernhardt's appearance there, v.26, p.772, 777.

Grand Pre, Carlos, noted, v.22, p.75, 77; tenant, v.22, p.1121n., 1122ff.; at Natchez, v.28, p.703, 704, 705, 708, 715; death, v.28, p.721; sketch, v.28, p.721-722; noted, v.28, p.943.

Grand Pre, Charles de, commandant at Baton Rouge, v.25, p.13, 19, 941.

Grand Pre, Louis de, loses hand, v.21, p.121; death of, v.21, p.188n.; and W. Fla. Rev., v.21, p.720n.; killed in W. Fla. Rev., v.28, p.722, 724.

Grand River, noted, v.25, p.163, 165, 205.

Grand Terre, during Civil War, v.23, p.462-463.

Grand Terre Island, noted, v.24, p.12, 23; base for privateers, v.24, p.14, 15.

Granger, Francis, noted, v.24, p.1153.

Granger, Gordon, noted, v.23, p.1212.

"Gran Sultan," Aury schooner, v.24, p.629, 636, 637.

Grant, Alex. J., Jr., Confed. naval officer, v.27, p.483, 484.

Garnt, Gen. U. S., message to Gen. Banks from, v.32, p.116, 127; noted, v.32, p.130, 138; plan of operations, v.32, p.139.

Grant, J. G., Anti-Lottery League Fin. Com., v.27, p.1056.

"Grant, Major William, 1838-1919," Henry P. Dart, v.7, p.658.

Grant, Michael, noted, v.23, p.357, 368.

Granton, Chambellan, name appears on cornerstone of Convent as architect, v.29, p.577; stepson of governor, v.29, p.578.

Grant Parish, Indians of, v.23, p.1107-1131; populist legislator from, v.26, p.1109.

Grant, Ulysses S., and capture of Vicksburg, v.23, p.1205, 1206, 1208; noted, v.24, p.74, 84, 114, 115, 116, 117; backs Kellogg administration in La., v.29, p.401, 404, 405, 411, 413, 424, 431, 434, 437, 441, 442, 487, 489; restores Kellogg to office in La., v.29, p.723; noted, v.29, p.725, 732, 736, 1241, 1242, 1244, 1246, 1251, 1252.

Grappe, Francis, noted, v.23, p.1115.

Gras, Antonio, identified, v.21, p.727n.

Grassin, Alexis, noted, v.24, p.614.

Gravel Hill, Wells' plantation, v.31, p.999.

Gravier, Bertrand, Jr., noted, v.22, p.407.

Gravier, Bertrand, land grant in wife's will, v.22, p.391; sketch, v.22, p.399; inventory, v.22, p.408; and Batture controversy, v.23, p.683ff.; noted, v.23, p.1064.

Gravier, Father, acc'ts of Houma way of living, v.28, p.51, 52, 54; judgment of Natchez, v.31, p.578; quoted, v.31, p.601.

Gravier, Jean, and Faubourg Ste. Marie, v.22, p.385-427; sketch, v.22, p.401-403; and Batture controversy, v.23, p.682ff.

Gravier, Jean, Jr., noted, v.22, p.390, 397.

Gravier, Jeanne, noted, v.22, p.407.

Gravier, Nicholas, administrator of B. Gravier's estate, v.22, p.397.

Gravier, Pere James, and Fort de la Boulaye, v.19, p.853-857.

"Graviers and the Faubourg Ste. Marie," by F. P. Burns, v.22, p.385-427.

Grayer, J. C., state tax assessor named in Wickliffe impeachement, v.31, p.694.

Gray, James, noted, v.23, p.376.

Gray, John H., and W. Fla. Rev., v. 21, p.109, 112; letter from Skipwith, v.21, p.156-158, 162-171; letter to Kemper, v.21, p.118.

Grayson, Annie Boyd, noted, v.24, p.346.

Grayson, John B., noted, v.22, p.462.

Graz-Lauzin family papers, in L.S.U. Archives, v.24, p.342.

Great Britain, policy of toward former Spanish Colonies, v.24, p.951-952; negotiations against Russian campaign, v.24, p.992, 1141; and Portuguese refugees, v.24, p.1141.

"Great Fire of 1788 in New Orleans," by L. A. de Rojas, v.20, p.578-589.

Great Raft, v.25, p.399-401.

Great Southern Lumber Co., work in Bogalusa, v.29, p.90-96, 101-107, 120-122, 123, 125-126, 169, 177, 182-183.

"Great Storm of 1722 at Fort Louis, Mobile, The," Translated by Heloise H. Cruzat, v.14, p.567.

"Great Stroke of Pierre Laffite," by S. Faye, v.23, p.733-826.

Greece, struggles of for independence, v.24, p.939, 952, 955-956, 966-968, 978-979, 987, 991, 1003, 1009, 1043, 1045, 1049, 1104; question of British aid, v.24, p.957ff., 966-968, 969, 1016; mediation by European powers, v.24, p.1065-1066, 1069-1071, 1074-1075, 1077-1078, 1080, 1081-1082, 1085, 1090, 1092-1093, 1094-1095.

Greeley, Horace, visits to New Orleans, v.24, p.169; noted, v.29, p.1249, 1250, 1252; supported by Hebert, v.31, p.534, 536-537; supported by Fusionists, v.31, p.700.

Greenage, Aaron, noted, v.23, p.421.

Green, Gen. Thomas, noted, v.32, p.111, 113, 118, 119, 123, 125, 126.

Green, H. N., Confed. soldier, v.26, p.972.

Green, John A., "Governor Perier's expedition against the Natchez Indians, Dec., 1730-Jan., 1731," v.19, p.547-577.

Green, John, noted, v.22, p.190; councilman of Crowley, v.27, p.1131.

Green, K. J., school board member of 1st Bogalusa school, v.29, p.100.

Greenville, located, v.22, p.190.

Greenwald, Henry, controlled Dauphine Theatre at which Bernhardt appeared, v.26, p.782.

Greenwald Theatre, Bernhardt at, v.26, p.775.

Greer, James Kimmins, B.A., M.A., "Louisiana Politics, 1845-1861," First installment, v.12, p.381; Second installment, v.12, p.555; Third, Fourth, Fifth and Sixth installments, (Conclusion), v.13, p.67, 257, 444, 617; "A Texas Ranger and Frontiersman, The Last Days of Buck Barry in Texas," (Review), v.15, p.711.

Gregg, Alla, daughter of John Gregg, v.29, p.11.

Gregg, John, joins brother Josiah, v.29, p.8-9; in La., v.29, p.11, 13; death, v.29, p.13n.

Gregg, Josiah, sketch of, v.29, p.5-7; first visit to La., v.29, p.7-11; member of firm of Pickett and Gregg, v.29, p.11; visits brother in La., v.29, p.11-12; in Mexico, v.29, p.12.

Gregory, Francis H., noted, v.22, p.1024.

Gregory, Thomas, noted, v.23, p.384.

Gremillion, Jas. A., bid for erection of Crowley City Hall, v.27, p.1140; Sec. of State, address at Crowley rice festival, v.27, p.1212.

Grenada, noted, v.24, p.648.

Greneaux, Charles E., candidate for state treasurer on Dem. ticket, 1855, v.25, p.680; nominee for state treasurer, v.31, p.501.

"Grenier's Journal of His Voyage to Vera Cruz in 1745," ed. by Charmion Clair Shelby, v.21, p.631-655.

Grice, Warren A., noted, v.23, p.199.

Griffe, defined, v.25, p.301.

Griffin, Max L., "A Bibliography of New Orleans Magazines," v. 18, p.493-556.

Griffin, William F., noted, v.24, p.56; Moore's senatorial colleague, v.26, p.979; pres. pro. tem. of Sen. 1857; v.26, p.981, 982, nominated for Dem. cand., v.26, p.988.

Griffith, Llewellyn Colville, sketch, v.21, p.162n.; and W. Fla. Rev., v.21, p.720n.; Kemper's letter to concerning Beaudin claim, v.25, p.948-949; his answer, v.25, p.949-950; noted, v.29, p.76.

"Gri-Gri Case, The," A Criminal Trial in Louisiana During the Spanish Regime, 1773, by Laura L. Porteous, v.17, p.48.

Grillo, Oscar, noted, v.24, p.134.

Grima, Edgar, "Notarial System of Louisiana," v.10, p.76.

Grima, Felix, noted, v.22, p.424.

Grimble Bell School, v.25, p.361.

Gropp, Arthur E., research bulletin for Middle American Research, v.24, p.331, 333, 350.

Gros, Dr. ———, noted, v.22, p.813.

Gross, Dr. Samuel D., praises Luzenberg, v.26, p.50.

Grosse Tete Railroad, noted, v.21, p.1140.

Grosz, Agnes Smith, "The Political Career of Pinckney Benton Stewart Pinchback," v.27, p.527-612.

Gruis, de, noted, v.22, p.1024.

Grundy, Felix, noted, v.24, p.924, 928.

Grunewald, Benedict M., pres. of N.O. Grand Opera Association, v.29, p.676-677.

Grunewald, L., N.O. publisher, v.31, p.147.

Grunewald Opera House, first public meeting place of Anti-Lottery League, v.27, p.1055; reception honoring Legislators voting against lottery, v.27, p.1056, 1063.

Grunewald's Music Store, Bernhardt makes first N.O. public appearance at, v.26, p.774.

Gruss, Louis, "Judah Philip Benjamin," v.19, p.964-1068; "The 'Mission' to Ecuador of J. P. Benjamin," v.23, p.162-169; ed. and tr., "Jose Julian Marti on J. P. Benjamin," v.23, p.259-264.

Grymes, John Randolph, N.O. lawyer, v.19, p.331; and Firebrand Affair, v.21, p.206, 208, 210; and Spanish filibusters, v.21, p.814; and German redemptioners, v.22, p.158; noted, v.23, p.437n.; and New Orleans Assoc., v.23, p.763; and Jean Laffite, v.24, p.13-14; noted, v.24, p.365, 371, 376; and New Orleans Associates, v.24, p.631; defense in duel trial, v.24, p.758; duel with Alcee LaBranch, 1837, v.24, p.765; and tariff, v.25, p.94; noted, v.25, p.999, 1008, 1044; on the Guerrero pirate case, v.25, p.1078, 1079, 1083; pres. bar association, v.25, p.1086; Jones' council, v.25, p.1102; denounced S. C. Ord. of Nullification, v.28, p.951.

Grymes, Philip, letter to Skipwith, v.21, p.89; noted, v.23, p.437.

Guadeloupe, privateers of, at Barataria, v.23, p.458; base for privateers, v.24, p.10.

Guadiana, Jose Maria, Comdt. Nacogdoches, v.28, p.1051; search for smugglers in neutral ground, v.28, p.1060-1061; opinion of House of Barr and Davenport, v.28, p.1102.

Gual, Dr. Pedro, noetd, v.23, p.755; fled (1812) to the U.S. from Venezuela, v.24, p.613, 615; to Cartagena, v.24, p.616; activities in Philadelphia, v.24, p.628, 634, 639, 646; plans presented to Aury, v.24, p.645; to St. Bart's, v.24, p.647; with Aury in negotiations with Brion, v.24, p.650; visit to Madariaga, v.24, p.656; rising position, v.24, p.667; governor of Santa Marta, v.24, p.690; secretary of the treasury, v.24, p.696.

Guano, on Galapagos Islands, v.23, p.162-169.

Guard of Night Watch, payrolls in Bibliotheca Parsoniana, v.24, p.310.

Guatemala, as dependency of Mexico, v.24, p.655.

Guerard, Capt. R. G., replaced Lamothe, v.26, p.835.

Guerine, Francis, petition of, v.23, p.382.

Guerra y Poseda, Jose, noted, v.24, p.367.

Guerrero, Father Francisco, noted, v.31, p.902, 903.

Guerrero, Francisco Perez, noted, v.21, p.101, 102; letter from Bishop of Havana, v.22, p.114-115.

Guerrero pirates, Soule's first case, v.25, p.1077-1078.

"Guerrero," schooner, v.24, p.653, 684, 687.

Gueydon, ———, noted, v.23, p.569.

Guice, T. J., the cotton bagging question, v.26, p.1065-1066; Farmers' Alliance leader, v.26, p.1070; cand. for Cong., 1890, v.26, p.1077; Third party leader, v.26, p.1084; defeated, v.26, p.1090; address at Anti-Lottery League conv., v.27, p.1057; obtains ruling of Nat'l Farmers' Union in re combine, v.27, p.1087.

Guichard, Maglorio, noted, v.22, p.815.

Guichard, Robert F., opinion of Lottery Bill, 1890, v.27, p.1042.

Guides to manuscript collections, by Work Projects Administration, v.24, p.306, 312, 314, 320, 345, 349, 350, 352.

"Guide to Depositories of Manuscript Collections in Louisiana," by the Historical Records Survey, Work Projects Administration, v.24, p.305-353.

"Guido and Ginevra," excerpt from opera in L.S.U. Music School Library, v.24, p.347.

Guilday, Peter, historian of church, v.31, p.898.

"Guillaume," noted, v.23, p.436.

Guillot, Pierre, educator, v.31, p.852.

Guion, George S., "Gov. Luther E. Hall," v.6, p.51; noted, v.25, p.1008.

Guion, Walter, cand. Atty.-Gen'l, 1900, v.28, p.1191.

Guiraud, Ernest, N.O. composer, v.31, p.873-874.

Guirot, A. J., collector of customs, v.26, p.1003.

Gulf Blockading Squadron, noted, v.24, p.449.

Gulf of Mexico, Spanish Coastguard in, v.23, p.429; Wickliffe advocates U.S. supremacy in, v.25, p.687, 688.

Gulf Refining Company, leased oil land in Caddo field, v.29, p.65, 68, 69n.

Gulotta, John, one of early Bogalusa Italians, v.29, p.93.

Gunby, Judge A., moving spirit behind bagging factory, v.26, p.1065; defeated in Cong. race, 1892, v.26, p.1090; suggested to head fusion ticket, v.26, p.1100; La. rep. to Nat'l Populist Conv., v.26, p.1119.

Gunther, Catharina, account of conversion to Catholicism, v.24, p.408-410; noted, v.24, p.412.

Gurley, Henry H., and 1824 tariff bill, v.25, p.39; and 1826 tariff measure, v.25, p.43; and 1828 tariff, v.25, p.46; and tariff, v.25, p.57, 58.

Gurley, John W., noted, v.22, p.433, 435; noted, v.24, p.731, 732; killed in duel, v.24, p.773-782.

Gurley, Rev. R. R., letter of John McDonogh to, v.25, p.385.

Gurlie and Guillot, architects and contractors, v.29, p.626, 631, 633, 650, 651, 652, 655, 659.

Guth, E., N.O. musician, v.31, p.143.

Gutierrez, Jose Bernardo, de Lara, and revolt in Mexico, v.22, p.719ff.; noted, v.22, p.806; expedition of, v.23, p.758, 773, 853, 1000-1001; noted, v.24, p.635; filibuster expedition into neutral ground, v.28, p.1053, 1054-1055; bandit leader, v.28, p.1069; filibuster in Fla., v.21, p.807.

Gutierrez-Magee expedition, v.25, p.294-297; v.28, p.1103.

Guttheim, Rabbi James Koppel, sketch, v.22, p.166-180.

Guyol, Louise Hubert, "A Southern Author in her New Orleans Home," v.6, p.365.

"G. W. Sentell," Steamer, picture of, v.25, p.456.

HABINE, LOUIS, NOTED, v.22, p.808; sketch, v.22, p.811.

Hachard, Marie Madeline, her acc't of voyage of nuns from France to La., v.29, p.565-566; noted, v.29, p.569; refers to progress of work on convent, v.29, p.573, 574-575.

Haddon, Marie, mother of Fulwar Skipwith, v.31, p.299.

Hadley, J., noted, v.23, p.1185.

Hagan, John, suit over land, v.23, p.1093-1094.

Hagan, William H., noted, v.23, p.1099.

Haggard, J. Villasana (co-author), "Handbook for Translators of Spanish Historical Documents," rev'd, v.25, p.536; "The Neutral Ground Between La. and Tex., 1806-1821," v.28, p.1001-1128.

Hahn, Michael, Gov. of La., v.20, p.995ff; noted, v.23, p.503, 511, 515, 1136, 1221, 1222; noted, v.24, p.506; Gov. of La., 1864, v.25, p.748, 749; elected to Cong. from Second District of La., 1862, v.27, p.254; gov., v.27, p.989; substantiated charges by Wilde of bribery by Lottery Co., v.27, p.990; Republican nominee for Congress, v.29, p.744, 752; turns unionist, v.31, p.1010; candidate for governor, v.31, p.1012, 1015-1016; U. S. Senator, v.31, p.1023; noted, v.31, p.1081, 1100.

Hair, Velma Lea, "The History of Crowley, La.," v.27, p.1119-1225.

Haiti, as port for privateers, v.23, p.443.

Halevy, Jacques Francois, "Guido and Ginerva," in L.S.U. Music School Library, v.24, p.347.

Haley, John J., contractor for Washington and New Orleans telegraph, v.31, p.430.

Haldiman, Brig.-Gen. Frederick, noted, v.23, p.5, 357, 389.

Half Moon Bluff Church on Bogue Chitto before 1812, v.29, p.83.

Hall, A. Oakey, "The Manhattaner in N. O.," about McDonogh, v.26, p.142; on New Orleans, v.31, p.394, 398, 417-418, 419.

Hall, Basil, noted, v.22, p.151; v.23, p.877.

Halleck, Major-Gen. Henry, W., order to Gen. Banks, v.32, p.103; noted, v.32, p.130, 132, 133.

Hallett, Robert W., noted, v.23, p.244.

Hall, G. A., letter from G. S. Denison, v.23, p.1233.

"Hall, Gov. Luther E.," by Walter J. Burke, George Seth Guion and Donelson Caffery, v.6, p.46; cand. for Gov., v.28, p.1222, 1228; noted, v.29, p.108, 109; Gov. of La. visits Bogalusa, v.29, p.110-112; and Charity Hospital, v.31, p.84-86.

Hall, James, noted, v.23, p.180.

"Hall, Judge Dominick Augustine, Andrew Jackson and" (Report of the Committee of Louisiana Senate, 1843), v.5, p.509; and Andrew Jackson, v.21, p.369ff.,

399n.; noted, v.22, p.439, 1049, 1083-1084, 1085; noted, v.23, p.436; noted, v.24, p.731, 732, 740, 776; judge, Orleans District Court, v.31, p.324-325.

"Hallucinations, The Nature of," by F. Legge (The London Academy), v.1, p.292.

Hall, William P., in the Cong. Campaign of 1890, v.26, p.1077.

Halphen, Dr. Michael, noted, v.26, p.62.

Halsey, J. T., early N. O. newspaperman, v.29, p.782.

Halsey, Thomas Lloyd, noted, v.22, p.1092, 1093.

Ham, Capt. Hillory H., confed. sold., v.26, p.957.

Ham, H. H., confed. sold., v.26, p.955, 974.

Hamilton, Alexander, noted, v.23, p.430-431; noted, v.24, p.699, 701, 703.

Hamilton, Martena, wife of Thomas Ellis, v.29, p.683.

Hamilton, Thomas, noted, v.23, p.874.

Hamilton, William S., candidate for Gov. of La., 1830, v.25, p.60-61.

Hammerstein, Rev. Herman, cited, v.24, p.138.

Hammond, Abner, and Genet Affair, v.21, p.30-31.

Hammond, Andres, identified, v.21, p.30.

Hammond, Samuel, and Genet plans, v.21, p.30n., 31.

Hammond, William J., on N. O. "Item," v.31, p.785.

Hampson, John, Mayor of Carrollton, v.21, p.244, 245; and Carrollton, v.22, p.196, 197, 202; noted, v.23, p.204.

Hampton, Chas. P., on Lottery bill, v.27, p.1042.

Hampton Roads, noted, v.24, p.449.

Hampton, Wade, noted, v.22, p.448; noted, v.28, p.843, 844n., 883; Comd. U. S. Troops Orleans Ter., action to clear neutral ground, v.28, p.1065-1066.

Hancock, Winfield Scott, noted, v.24, p.114; Gen'l, nominee for Pres. of U. S., v.29, p.743; loses election for presidency, v.29, p.744.

"Handbook for Translators of Spanish Historical Documents," by Villasana Haggard and Malcolm Douglas McLean, rev'd, v.25, p.536.

Handy, Thomas H., and Reconstruction, v.23, p.466-467.

Hannay, John, noted, v.22, p.313.

Hannay, Samuel, noted, v.22, p.370, 374, 945, 986; noted, v.23, p.12, 73.

Hanson, Octave, Sen. of McEnery faction, v.28, p.1137.

"Hans Sachs," manuscript in L.S.U. Music School Library, v.24, p.348.

Haralson, A. D. M., Wickliffe's law partner, v.25, p.675.

Hardesty, B. F., People's Party elector, v.26, p.1087.

Harding, George, counsel Morse vs. O'Reilly, v.31, p.471.

Hardin, J. Fair, "The First Great River Captain, Henry Miller Shreve," v.10, p.25; "The Early History of the Louisiana State University," v.11, p.5; "Thoughts, Visions and Sketches of North Louisiana," by Luther Logino, M.D. (Review), v.14, p.239; "G. P. Whittington, In Memoriam," v.15, p.655; "Fort Jessup, Fort Selden, Camp Sabine, Camp Salubrity, Four Forgotten Army Posts," I, II, III, IV, v.16, p.5, 279, 441, 670; "The Diary of a Young Lawyer of Natchitoches of 1836, William S. Toumey," I, II, edited by, v.17, p.64, 315; "An Outline of Shreveport and Caddo Parish History," v.18, p.759-871; "Don Juan Filhiol & the Founding of Fort Miro, the Modern Monroe, La.," v.20, p.436-485.

Hardin, M. D., Wickliffe studied law in office of, v.25, p.670.

Hardy, J. H., candidate for secy. of state, v.31, p.1055.

Hardy, Richardson, noted, v.22, p.1122.

Hardy, Thomas, noted, v.23, p.24, 380, 381, 391.

Hardy, Thomas Robert, noted, v.22, p.313, 980.

Hargrave, Major William H., and W. Fla. Rev., v.21, p.85, 118, 119, 799n.

Harlan, Dr., Charter member medical soc., v.26, p.59, 60.

Harmanson, John H., Congressman from La. in support of bill for re-claiming swamp land, v.28, p.279; and sugar tariff, v.25, p.138, 139.

Harman, Thomas L., noted, v.22, p.418.

Harmon, B. H., mayor of Rayne, v.27, p.1120.

Harmonists, noted, v.24, p.422, 423.

Harmony Society, picture of Great House of, v.24, p.423.

Harper, D. Clinton, noted, v.24, p.1161.

Harper, Mrs. Harriet, nurse of Myra Clark, v.27, p.44, 45, 46, 47, 56, 71, 72, 75, 84, 85, 90; testimony of, v.27, p.64-68; evidence against, v.27, p.115, 125, 133, 169;

evidence of, v.27, p.137, 161, 164, 165, 172, 173, 190, 191, 195, 208, 214, 224, 235-236, 262, 271, 280, 285.

Harper, Samuel H., member of St. Helena Police Jury, v.23, p.407ff.

Harper, William, colored leader from Caddo, v.26, p.1082; noted, v.27, p.43, 44, 64, 71.

Harpin, Capt., early slave trader, v.23, p.866.

Harrington, Fred Harvey, author of "Fighting Politician, Major General N. P. Banks," v.31, p.557-563.

Harris, A. B., pres. Senate, 1873, v.27, p.576.

Harris, Dr. E. B., noted, v.26, p.76.

Harris, G. D., of La. Geol. Survey, v.29, p.502-503.

Harris, Isham G., noted, v.24, p.111; Gov. of Tenn., v.29, p.1063.

Harrisonburg, in 1860, v.21, p.1203-1205; noted, v.24, p.80, 102; location of Fort Beauregard, v.26, p.974n.

Harrison, Dr. J., noted, v.26, p.76.

Harrison, Fairfax, "The Virginians on the Ohio and the Mississippi in 1742" (Reprinted from the Virginia Magazine of History), v.5, p.316.

Harrison, George, noted, v.23, p.404; v.24, p.1147.

Harrison, J. Burton, and La. Hist. Soc., v.23, p.1039, 1040, 1044.

Harrison, Joseph, noted, v.23, p.404.

Harrison, J. P., noted, v.23, p.204, 226.

Harrison, Rev. J. H., of Vanderbilt, pres. of S. Univer., 1883, v.25, p.770.

Harrison, William Henry, and international complications of the Mafia incident, v.20, p.1096-1101; and tariff, v.25, p.76; and 1836 campaign, v.25, p.108; La. support in 1840, v.25, p.112-113.

Harris, Prof. C. C., agricultural school at Calhoun recommended by, v.26, p.1065.

Harris, Rufus C., "Address in Memory of Henry Plauche Dart," v.18, p.251-252.

Harris, T. H., cited on Lusher, v.25, p.750; concerning educational system under Conway, v.25, p.755-756, 762, 806.

Harris, William H., noted, v.23, p.514, 559.

Harris, W. L., noted, v.23, p.204.

"Harrod, Benjamin Morgan," W. O. Hart, v.8, p.668; noted, v.23, p.1240.

Harrod, Charles L., and B. F. Butler, v.23, p.1241-1257.

Harrod, Morgan, noted, v.23, p.528.

Hart, Colonel Thomas, noted, v.24, p.923.

Hartford Convention, noted, v.24, p.698.

"Hartford," federal boat, v.29, p.1108, 1109, 1110.

Hartford, Oliver T., Sg't of Troop "E" of La. Inf., v.29, p.82.

Hart, Harriet, last Negro born in slavery in Bogalusa section, v.29, p.87n.

Hart, Henry, noted, v.24, p.1138, 1155.

Hart, Jacob, Jr., and Barataria, v.22, p.803-804, 1024.

Hart, J. M., and W. S. Pike, named by Wickliffe to head penitentiary, 1856, v.25, p.703.

Hart, Joel Tanner, creater of statue of Clay, sketch of, v.27, p.771-775.

Hart, John W., early N. O. police reporter, v.29, p.54-55.

Hart, Mrs., noted, v.24, p.1151, 1152; money from James Brown, v.24, p.1165; death of, v.24, p.1166.

Hart, W. O., "New Orleans," v.1, p.353; "Clark Mills," v.3, p.614; "Constitutions of Louisiana, with Some Observations on the Constitutional Convention of 1912," v.3, p.570; "History of the Louisiana Historical Society," v.3, p.112; "Rights of Women in Louisiana," v.4, p.437; "The Confederate Die for the Coinage of Silver Half Dollars," v.5, p.505; "Mrs. Louise Livingston, Wife of Edward Livingston," v.5, p.352; "The Napoleon Inkstand," v.5, p.501; "Report of Treasurer of Louisiana Historical Society for 1921," v.5, p.238; "J. Sanford Saltus," v.5, p.499; "Frederick D. King," v.6, p.195; "Presentation of Loving Cup to Grace King," v.6, p.363; "Retirement of Chief Justice Monroe, F. A.," v.6, p.107; "Remarks on Retirement of Chief Justice Provosty," v.6, p.216; "Flag Legislation in Louisiana," v.7, p.449; "History of the Events Leading Up to the Battle of the 14th September, 1874," v.7, p.571; "An Interesting Incident in Connection with New Orleans Premium Bonds," v.8, p.248; "Benjamin Morgan Harrod," v.8, p.668; "New Orleans Times and New Orleans Democrat," v.8, p.574; "A Boy's Recollection of the War Between the States," v.11, p.253; "Death of, Treasurer of Louisiana Historical Society," by H. P. Dart (Editor's Chair), v.13, p.117.

Hartzell, Dr. Joseph C., papers in L. S. U. Archives, v.24, p.342; noted, v.25, p.779.

Harvard College, in 1807, v.23, p.1000.

Hasset, Canon Thomas, letter from Bishop of Havana, v.22, p.113-114; noted, v.27, p.93, 95, 96, 97, 98, 152, 153, 154, 156, 157, 159, 160, 217, 220, 258, 264.

Hassett, Father Tomaso, noted, v.31, p.902, 903.

Hassinger, Geo., fusion cand. treasurer, 1900, v.28, p.1192.

Hassinger, Jacob, noted, v.23, p.502, 519.

Hatcher, C. F., slave dealer, v.22, p.152, 153-154.

Hatcher, William B., "Edward Livingston," rev'd. by William O. Lynch, v.24, p.542-543; "Edward Livingston's View of the Nature of the Union," v.24, p.698-728.

Hatch, F. W., on Returning Board, v.27, p.558; appt'd by Warmoth to Returning Board, v.28, p.1134; member of Warmoth Returning Board, v.31, p.700.

Hauck, Minnie, musical career, v.31, p.861, 862-863; early life, v.31, p.862; and Curto, v.31, p.865.

"Haunted House," and Lafitte, v.24, p.15-16.

Havana, Bishop of (Juan Jph.), letter to Casa Calvo, v.22, p.111-113; letter to Hasset, v.22, p.113-114; letter to Guerrero, v.22, p.114-115; letter to Marques de Someruelos, v.22, p.115-116; letter to Solana, v.22, p.116-117.

"Havana, Louisiana Troops at Occupation of," John S. Kendall, v.7, p.40.

Hawes, Edmund, and W. Fla. Rev., v.21, p.131, 688n.

Hawes, J. M., noted, v.24, p.75.

Hawkes, Charles K., noted, v.23, p.1232.

Hawkins, Jacob, on Repub. Returning Board, v.27, p.558; judge of Superior District Ct. renders decision in favor of P. H. Morgan, v.27, p.578; on Lynch Returning Board, v.28, p.1135; member of Lynch Returning Board, v.31, p.700.

Hawkins, Joseph, noted, v.22, p.750.

Hawks, Rev. Francis Lister, pastor in New Orleans, v.22, p.457, 466-467, 468-469.

Hawsey Memorial School, v.27, p.1180.

Hawthorne, Nina Emily, wife of P. B. S. Pinchback, v.27, p.606.

Haydel, Mrs. A. M., noted, v.24, p.764.

Haydn Mass in C, in L. S. U. Music School Library, v.24, p.347.

Hayes Creek Church, organized in Washington Parish in 1813, v.29, p.83.

Hayes, C. W., chief geologist of U. S. G. S. in 1908, v.29, p.63, 64.

Hayes, R. B., recorder, Acadia Parish, v.27, p.1127.

Hayes, Rutherford B., visit to N. O., 1891, v.33, p.334.

Hay, John, sent to Niagara Falls by Lincoln with peace terms, v.29, p.1249.

Hayne, Robert Y., at issue with views of Edward Livingston, v.24, p.700, 703; noted, v.24, p.1135; speech of, v.24, p.1163.

Haynie, Martin L., and W. Fla. Med. Soc., v.21, p.722n.

Hays, Gilbert, noted, v.23, p.391.

Hay, Thomas R., "Gen'l James Wilkinson—The Last Phase," v.19, p.407-435.

Hayton, John, noted, v.23, p.386, 404.

Hayton, Joseph, v.23, p.404.

"Hayward, Attempted Escape of John and Josiah, from the Jail in N. O.," by Henry P. Dart, Translated by Heloise H. Cruzat, v.9, p.361.

Head of the Passes, noted, v.24, p.450.

Heard, Joseph, noted, v.23, p.409.

Heard, S. S., Col. Confed. Army, v.26, p.958, 960.

Heard, Wm. W., anti-lotteryite cand. for auditor, v.26, p.1081; Dem. cand. for auditor, 1896, v.26, p.1101; Dem. gov., 1900, v.26, p.1124; gov. of La., v.27, p.847; nominated cand. for auditor, v.27, p.1090; suggested cand. auditor, v.28, p.1158, 1173; cand. gov., 1900, v.28, p.1190ff.; elected, v.28, p.1194.

Hearn, Lafcadio, noted, v.23, p.146; **v.24,** p.182; early N. O. newspaperman, v.29, p.786-787.

Hearsey, Clem G., "The Vengeance of the Natchez," v.12, p.266.

Hearsey, Major H. J., loses control of "Democrat," v.27, p.1001-1002; editor of N. O. "Democrat," v.31, p.740; resigns, v.31, p.781; "Daily States," v.31, p.786.

Heath, J. L., Confed. soldier, v.26, p.959.

Hebard, George T., noted, v.23, p.1206.

Heberard, John, testifies for Bastrop, v.31, p.617.

Hebert, Paul Octave, and railroads, v.23, p.236; Governor of Louisiana, v.31, p.491-552; antecedents, v.31, p.491-493; education, v.31, p.493-494; marriage, v.31, p.494; state engineer, v.31, p.494-495; aid-de-camp to Isaac Johnson, v.31, p.495; Mexican War, v.31, p.495-496; candidate for state legislature, v.31, p.497; in Europe, v.31, p.497-498; 1852 Constitutional Convention, v.31, p.498-500; elected gov., v.31, p.500-504; platform, v.31, p.501-502; inauguration, v.31, p.505; internal improvements, v.31, p.510-514; railroads, v.31, p.510-512; levee legislation, v.31, p.512-514; educational legislation, v.31, p.514-515; Louisiana State Seminary of Learning, v.31, p.516-517; and library legislation, v.31, p.518; militia reorganized, v.31, p.518-519; sanitary legislation, v.31, p.519-520; Charity Hospital, v.31, p.520; penal institutions, v.31, p.520-522; U. S. Senate candidacy, v.31, p.522-524; attitude toward Civil War, v.31, p.526-528; Confederate commission, v.31, p.627; second marriage, v.31, p.528; commands Trans-Mississippi Department, v.31, p.528-530; commands District of Texas, v.31, p.530; politics under Warmoth, v.31, p.534-538; supports Grant, v.31, p.538-539; Commission of Engineers, v.31, p.542-545; opposes Ead's jetties, v.31, p.543-545; death, v.31, p.546.

Hebert, Penelope Lynch Adams Andrews, child of P. O. Hebert, v.31, p.528.

Hebert, Robert O., son of Paul Octave Hebert, v.31, p.494.

Hebert, Thomas, son of P. O. Hebert, v.31, p.494.

Hecker, John, P., noted, v.22, p.202.

Heelein and Jennings, Commission Merchants, v.21, p.1127.

Heller, Dr. May, In Memoriam, v.12, p.461.

Heller, Rabbi Max, speech against lottery, v.27, p.1061, 1070.

Helphen, Dr., Ger. physician from N. O., v.28, p.1093.

Hemphill, Joseph, noted, v.24, p.1040.

Hempstead, O. H., named in Wickliffe impeachment, v.31, p.692.

Henderson, ————, noted, v.23, p.400.

Henderson, John, and Lopez expedition, v.22, p.1121n., 1122ff., 1132; trial of, v.22, p.1135-1138.

Henderson, Jonas, noted, v.25, p.786.

Henderson Plantation, near N. O., involved in suit of Davis vs. Gaines, v.27, p.311.

Henderson, Raymond A., pastor in New Orleans, v.22, p.455-457, 465, 470.

Henderson's Hill, noted, v.24, p.86.

Henderson, Stephen, noted, v.22, p.472; and manumission, v.25, p.339, 340, 351.

Hendricks, John, People's Party cand. for auditor, 1892, v.26, p.1081.

Hendricks, Thomas A., noted, v.24, p.116.

Hennen, Alfred, noted, v.23, p.204.

Hennen, Duncan, Myra Clark's suit against, v.27, p.176; opinions, v.27, p.241-276.

Hennepin, Father Louis, Early exploration in La., v.19, p.26-28; accompanies La-Salle, v.25, p.922; his misleading book, v.25, p.932-933, 934.

Hennessy, David C., N. O. Supt. of Police killed by Mafia, v.20, p.1067ff.; murdered by Mafia, v.22, p.492ff.; noted, v.24, p.187.

Heno, George, noted, v.22, p.624.

"Henrique," privateer vessel, v.23, p.431-432.

Henry, ————, noted, v.22, p.980.

"Henry Adams Bullard; First Pres. of the La. Hist. Soc.," ed. by Walter Prichard, v.19, p.7-42.

"Henry Clay Visits N. O.," by Francis P. Burns, v.27, p.717-782.

"Henry Clay Warmoth, Reconstruction Governor of Louisiana," by Francis Byers Harris, v.30, p.523-653.

"Henry de Tonty: Fur Trader of the Miss.," by Murphy, rev'd, v.25, p.226-227.

Henry, J. C., Farmers' Alliance leader, v.26, p.1070.

Henry, John, sketch, v.28, p.791n.

Henry, Nicholas, and Superior Council, v.21, p.1000.

Henry, O. (Sidney Porter), noted, "Old Days on the N. O. Picayune," v.33, p.329.

Henry, S. J., Chairman Populist Nom. Conv., v.28, p.1175.

Henry, S. P., Speaker of the House, v.27, p.1056.

Herault, Francis, identified, v.21, p.728n.

Herman, Dr., delivered eulogy at Luzenberg's grave, v.26, p.103.

Hermitage, located, v.21, p.1139; noted, v.28, p.883, 884.

Hernandez, Carlos, noted, v.22, p.1018, 1019.

Herndon, Samuel McC., Sergeant Major, v.26, p.795, 798, 801; promoted, v.26, p.835.

Hero, Andrew, Jr., old-line Repub., v.26, p.1099.

Herrera, Don Simon de, noted, v.24, p.644; assigned by Sp. to La. Frontier, v.28, p.1035; dispute over neutral ground, v.28, p.1036; neutral ground agreement, v.28, p.1039-1041; noted, v.28, p.1080; council to discuss Indian trade, v.28, p.1088.

Herrera, Jose Manuel de, leader of Mexican insurgents, v.21, p.207; activities in N. O., v.21, p.1086-1087; noted, v.22, p.734, 737, 740; noted, v.23, p.754, 834n., 851.

Herries, George, mentioned, v.21, p.78; and W. Fla. Rev., v.21, p.696n.

Herries, Wm., and W. Fla. Rev., v.21, p.696n.

Herrisse, William Herries, noted, v.31, p.303-305, 306.

Herron, A. S., candidate for sec. of state on Dem. ticket, 1855, v.25, p.680; favored by Wickliffe for Congress, 1860, v.25, p.704; Soule's cand. for gov., 1859, v.26, p.985; nominated, v.26, p.988; candidate for sec. of state, v.31, p.501; for atty.-genl., v.31, p.1055.

Herron, F. D., deposed by Warmoth as sec. of state, v.28, p.1135.

Herron, F. J., removed by Warmoth as sec. of state, v.27, p.557; removed by Warmoth, v.31, p.700; forms rival board, v.31, p.700.

Hervey, Saly, noted, v.24, p.941.

Hervier, Sieur, and trade in Gulf of Mexico, v.21, p.1744, 631ff.

Hester, Dr., charter member Med. Soc., v.26, p.59.

Heustis, Jabez, author, v.31, p.394, 407.

Hewitt, E. S., noted, v.23, p.1180.

Hewitt, Ira L., noted, v.23, p.1177, 1195.

Hewlett's Exchange, noted, v.25, p.79.

Heywood Brothers Oil Corp., of Jennings, La., v.29, p.496-497, 498, 499.

Hickey, Edward, noted, v.23, p.554.

Hickey, Philip, and W. Fla. Rev., v.21, p.71ff., 687n.; ancestry of, v.21, p.89n.

Hidalgo, Miguel, and revolt in Mex., v.22, p.719.

Hierliky, Major, ——————, in W. Fla., v.22, p.33.

Highlands, Nicholas, noted, v.23, p.421.

"Highway Progress in Louisiana," by C. M. Kerr, v.2, p.56.

Hill, Bennett Haskin, noted, v.23, p.1711.

Hiller, Ferdinand, German musician, v.31, p.857.

Hill, F. S., Co-manager of Am. Theatre on death of Russell, 1838, v.28, p.228.

Hill, H. R. W., and railroads, v.23, p.200.

Hilliard, Mrs. Isaac H., copy of diary in Shreve Memorial Library, v.24, p.339; copy of diary in L. S. U. Archives, v.24, p.342.

Hill, James Davidson, "Address at the Dedication of the Vicksburg Memorial Monument," v.3, p.503; In Memoriam, v.11, p.116; on Anti-Lottery League Ex. Com., v.27, p.1056; Anti-Lottery delegate to Farmers' Union meeting, v.27, p.1086; Anti-Lottery League Com., v.28, p.1152; pres. La. Sugar Planters Assoc., v.28, p.1225.

Hill, Jim, Conf. soldier, v.26, p.950.

Hillsborough, Earl of, noted, v.23, p.6, 7.

Hillyard, M. B., staff member N. O. "Times-Democrat," v.27, p.1128.

Hine, Daisy, married M. J. Foster, v.28, p.1132.

Hines, Thomas H., confederate secret agent, v.29, p.1246.

"Hinge or duck-foot paddle," patent granted to Richard Claiborne, v.24, p.733.

Hire, William H., treasurer of Charity Hospital, named in Wickliffe impeachment, v.31, p.693.

Hiriart, Emile, duel of, v.23, p.154-155.

Hispano-Orleanians, distinguished, v.18, p.40-55.

"Histoire de la Louisiane Francais, 1673-1939," by Emile Lauvriere, rev'd by Andre Lafargue, v.24, p.207-210.

"Historian, Charles Gayarre, Louisiana's Literary," by Wilford B. Yearns, Jr., v.33, p.255-268.

Historical and World War Museum, L. S. U., v.24, p.346.

Historical Documents, "A Letter from the Battle of New Orleans from John A. Fort," with Introductory Note by E. A. Parsons, v.32, p.225.

Historical Records Survey, in La., v.24, p.307-308; "Guide to Depositories of Manuscript Collections in Louisiana," v.24, p.305-353; guides published by, v.24, p.330, 333, 345, 346, 350, 351.

"Historical Sketch of Art in La.," by Ben Earl Looney, v.18, p.382-396.

Historical Society, The Louisiana, Minutes of, for 1918, v.2, p.217; Report of, for 1918, by Bussiere Rouen, v.2, p.208.

"History of Bogalusa, the 'Magic City' of La.," by Amy Quick, v.29, p.73-201.

"History of Caddo Oil and Gas Fields," by Gerald Forbes, v.29, p.59-72.

"History of Carrollton," by W. H. Williams, v.22, p.181-215.

"History of Concordia Parish, Louisiana," by Robert Dabney Calhoun, I, II, III, IV, v.15, p.44, 214, 428, 618; V, VI, VII, VIII, v.16, p.92, 309, 454, 598; IX (Conclusion), v.17, p.96.

"History of Crowley, La.," by Velma Lea Hair, v.27, p.1119-1225.

"History of Eastern La.," by Frederick W. Williamson, v.25, p.629.

"History of Madison Parish, Louisiana," by W. M. Murphy, v.11, p.39.

"History of Negro Education in La.," by

Betty Porter, v.25, p.728-821.

"History of Rapides Parish, Louisiana," by G. P. Whittington, I, v.15, p.567, II, III, IV, V, v.16, p.27, 235, 427, 628; VI, VII, VIII, IX, v.17, p.112, 327, 537, 737; X (Conclusion), v.18, p.5-39.

"History of Rice Production in La. to 1896," by M. K. Ginn, v.23, p.544-588.

"History of St. Mary Parish, A Social, 1845-1860," by Jewell Lynn de Grummond, v.32, p.16.

"History of the American Party in Louisiana," by W. Darrell Overdyke, I, v.15, p.581; II, III, IV, V, v.16, p.84, 256, 409, 608.

"History of the Caddo Indians," by William B. Glover, v.18, p.872-946.

"History of the City of Lafayette," by Kathryn C. Briede, v.20, p.895-964.

"History of the Eng. Theatre at N. O., 1806-1842," by Nelle Smither, v.28, p.85-276, 361-572.

"History of the La. State Lottery Company," by Berthold C. Alwes, v.27, p.964-1118.

"History of the Washington Artillery of New Orleans," by P. A. Casey, v.23, p.471-484.

"History of Washington Parish, Louisiana, as Compiled from the Records and Traditions, The," by Hon. Prentiss B. Carter, v.14, p.36.

H. M. S. "Northumberland," noted, v.24, p.311.

Hobbes, Thomas, noted, v.24, p.701.

Hockett, Dr. A. J., noted, v.24, p.326.

Hodgdon, Capt. Geo. M., Commander Co. A under Wood, v.26, p.791; noted, v.26, p.793; made major 2nd La. Regt., v.26, p.794.

Hodge, B. L., Confed. soldier, v.26, p.958.

Hodge, David, noted, v.22, p.1009; member of W. Fla. Council, v.23, p.23, 353ff.

Hoeffer, Dr. M., N. O. musician, v.31, p.136-137.

Hoepner, Ernst, newspaper artist, "Old Days on the N. O. Picayune," v.33, p.328, 330.

Hoey, John, noted, v.22, p.188.

Hoffman, Beekman Ver Planck, noted, v.22, p.1086.

Hoffman, Capt. Walter H., resigned, v.26, p.836.

Hoffman, Frederick L., inventory of maps in collection in Middle American Research, v.24, p.332, 333, 350.

Hoffman, M. W., on Charity Hosp. Board, 1836, v.26, p.58.

Hogan, William Ransom, guide to manuscripts in L. S. U. Archives, v.24, p.340, 346, 350.

Hoge, ———, partner of J. Robb, v.23, p.174; has to leave New Orleans, v.23, p.244.

Hogg-Swayne Syndicate, v.29, p.499.

Holbrook, A. M., and "Picayune," v.31, p.740-741.

Holbrook, Franklin F., guide to research activities, v.24, p.317, 320, 330, 333, 346, 351.

Holbrook, Mrs. A. M., takes over "Picayune," v.31, p.741; noted, v.31, p.790.

Holcombe, ———, newspaperman, "Old Days on the N. O. Picayune," v.33, p.337-338.

Holcombe, James P., noted, v.23, p.1176; assistant to Confederate secret agents, v.29, p.1247, 1249, 1250.

Holland, Geo., director of Vauxhall Garden, v.28, p.234-235; noted, v.28, p.240.

Holliday, Dr. Daniel C., Board of Administrators, Charity Hospital, v.31, p.72-75.

Hollingsworth, James M., Confed. Lieut. Col., v.26, p.958.

Hollins, Commodore, noted, v.24, p.446.

Holloway, Robert, noted, v.23, p.420, 421.

Holly, ———, noted, v.23, p.422.

Holmes, Andrew, and expedition against Lafittes, v.24, p.19.

Holmes, David, and W. Fla. Rev., v.21, p.142n., 718; letter to W. Fla. Convention, v.21, p.735.

Holmes, Theophilus H., noted, v.24, p.68.

Holmes, William C., "The Exalted Enterprise (The Miss. Question: The La. Answer)," v.23, p.78-106.

Holt, Dr. F., noted, v.26, p.76.

Holy Alliance, noted, v.24, p.384, 939; and Great Britain, v.24, p.980-981.

"Home Plantation," or Principal Plantation, of Joseph Erwin, v.27, p.354; description, v.27, p.354-355, 361-363, 374, 375, 376, 380, 381, 385, 386, 387, 388, 390, 393, 397, 398; inventory of, v.27, p.415-425; appraisal, v.27, p.429; statement of crops, v.27, p.466.

Homer College, v.25, p.789.

Homer, in 1860, v.21, p.1183.

Homeyer, H. C., chairman of 1st Bogalusa school, v.29, p.100.

Honduras rice, noted, v.23, p.557-558.

Hood, Duncan N., promised command of a

La. Reg't by Gov., v.26, p.792, 794; noted, v.26, p.804.
Hood, John B., noted, v.24, p.104, 106.
Hood, Thomas, noted, v.24, p.180.
Hood, Walter, election of, v.23, p.377.
Hook, Eleanor, marriage contract with Abraham Morhouse, v.20, p.454-456.
Hoos, Johannes, identified, v.24, p.385-386; sermons of, v.24, p.387-400.
Hootsell vs. L. F. Mason, Sup. Ct. decision that neither Legis. nor Sec. of State could go behind election returns, v.26, p.1110.
Hope & Co., noted, v.24, p.512, 514.
Hopewell culture, v.25, p.398.
Hopkins, James, noted, v.22, p.449.
Hoppen, H. E., in charge of sports for Bogalusa inaugural day, v.29, p.110.
Horner, Joseph P., counsel for Lottery Co., 1879, v.27, p.998, 1008.
Horse racing, in Carrollton, v.21, p.232-233; and Richard Taylor, v.24, p.54.
Horton, James, and W. Fla. Rev., v.21, p.84; mentioned, v.21, p.90; noted, v.21, p.106.
Hospitals, in Sp. New Orleans, v.22, p.647; director of, in 1807, v.23, p.695; See, also, Charity Hospital.
Hotel Dieu, New Orleans, brief history of, v.24, p.312.
Hotel St. Louis, noted, v.33, p.147.
Hough, Judge Wade, People's Party cand. for atty.-general, 1892, v.26, p.1081.
Houin, ———, complaint against, v.23, p.393.
Houma Indians, at site of present B. R., v.28, p.5, 6, 15, 33, 34, 35, 40, 45, 66-68; origin of culture, customs and beliefs of, v.28, p.48-57; noted, v.28, p.58, 83; sketch of settlement, v.28, p.757n.
Houma, La., city named after Houma Indians, v.28, p.57.
"Housing in Creole St. Louis, 1764-1821, an Example of Cultural Change," by Marshall Smelser, v.21, p.337-348.
Houston, Felix, noted, v.22, p.1143-1161.
Houston, J. D., sheriff of N. O., v.27, p.984.
Houston, Sam, noted, v.23, p.1172, 1175; documents in Bibliotheca Parsoniana, v.24, p.311.
Houston, W. J., N. O. judge, and the Agusti Case, v.27, p.984-985.
Hovia, Josef de, noted, v.22, p.393.
Howard Association, charitable group, v.31, p.765; noted, v.33, p.388-394, 398, 399, 401.

Howard, Carlos, mentioned, v.21, p.30; noted, v.22, p.85n.; expedition to Ill., v.22, p.93-97.
Howard, Charles T., noted, v.24, p.314, 327; first pres. La. State Lottery Co., v.27, p.971; sketch, v.27, p.972-973, 975; accused of bribery, v.27, p.976; rights of incorporation of Lottery Co. transferred to, v.27, p.976; assurance of fairness, v.27, p.977; law suit against, v.27, p.982-983, 987, 990, 991; effort to secure favorable action on lottery in Washington, v.27, p.992; alleged control of press, v.27, p.993; reported approached by Nicholls for financial aid in overthrowing Packard, v.27, p.997-998; control of "Democrat," v.27, p.1002; newspaper accounts of death of, v.27, p.1013-1014; improvements to court popular favor, v.27, p.1025, 1102; and the La. Levee Co., v.28, p.307-310; of La. Lottery Co., v.29, p.746, 747; lottery agent, v.31, p.718-719; new company, v.31, p.729; officer La. State Lottery Co., v.31, p.730; noted, v.31, p.743, 749, 750.
Howard, C. N., "The Interval of Military Gov't in W. Fla.," v.22, p.18-30.
Howard, Frank T., noted, v.24, p.314; erection of Confed. Memorial Building, v.27, p.1025-1026.
Howard, General O. O., first commissioner of Bureau of Refugees, Freedman and Abandoned Lands, v.25, p.740-741, 745, 746; commander of "Army of Tennessee," v.32, p.152, 153, 154.
Howard, J. B., named in Wickliffe impeachment, v.31, p.692.
Howard Memorial Library, erection and endowment of, v.27, p.1025.
Howard, Miss Annie T., had Howard Memorial Library erected to her father, v.27, p.1025.
Howe, George, and African slave trade, v.23, p.882-884.
Howe Institute, History of, v.25, p.786-787.
Howell, General A. G., v.28, p.957.
Howell, J. D., La. midshipman, v.27, p.483.
Howell, J. T., Dem.-Populist elector, v.26, p.1116.
Howell, Peytona L., noted, v.24, p.314.
Howell, Rufus K., justice of State Sup. Ct., concurring in decision in favor of P. H. Morgan, v.27, p.578; Louisiana Supreme Court Justice, v.31, p.1026; noted, v.31, p.1080.
Howell, Sen. W. E., requested investigation

of election returns, v.28, p.1181, opposition leader in Sen., 1896, v.28, p.1184; opposed election law, v.28, p.1186.

Howe, Peter, noted, v.25, p.786.

Howe, W. W., resignation of Associate Justice of State Sup. Ct., v.27, p.578.

"How the Louisiana Purchase was Financed," by James E. Winston and R. W. Colomb, v.12, p.139.

Hoyt, D. W., sec.-supt. of Acadia Parish school board, v.27, p.1175.

Hozey, Charles F., noted, v.23, p.475.

Hubert-Robert, Regine Marie Ghislaine, "L'Histoire Merveilleuse de la La. Francaise: Chronique des XVIIe et XVIIIe Siecles et de la Cession aux Etats-Unis," rev'd by A. Lafargue, v.28, p.351-354.

Hudspeth, G. W., district judge in St. Landry Parish, v.27, p.1121.

Huerta, Fray Jose Maria, opinion of Barr and Davenport, v.28, p.1102-1103.

Hueston, ———, in duel, v.24, p.764, 766-767.

Hufty, Joseph, Am. party cand. for sheriff in N. O., 1855, v.25, p.690-691.

Huger, Benjamin, and 1816 tariff bill, v.25, p.30, 32.

Hughes, Christopher, noted, v.24, p.946.

Hughes, Thomas, noted, v.24, p.927.

Hughes, W. L., Violette's staff captain, v.26, p.793; made major 2nd La. Reg't, v.26, p.794; noted, v.26, p.806, 835.

Hugot, Sieur, and lease of Pailloux plantation, v.21, p.996-997.

Hull, Rev. James F., Episcopal rector in N. O., v.21, p.825; v.22, p.447-454.

Hulse, B. M., cited, v.24, p.378.

Humbert, Jean-Joseph-Amable, and Mex. expeditions, v.22, p.739, 748, 749, 1038, 1078, 1087, 1088; noted, v.25, p.298, 299, 300; Fr. filibuster in neutral ground, v.28, p.1056; meeting with Onis, v.23, p.733-734; filibuster, v.23, p.741, 758, 773; and Jackson, v.23, p.753; last days of, v.23, p.783-784, 786; military commandant at Galveston, v.23, p.789; captured at New Orleans, v.23, p.794; returns to Galveston, v.23, p.812; offer to return to Spanish allegiance, v.23, p.832; arrest of, v.23, p.824; expedition, v.23, p.850; noted, v.24, p.365, 366, 373.

Humble, Sallie Lacy, "The Ouachita Valley Expedition of DeSoto," v.25, p.611-643.

"Humors of the Duello," by J. S. Kendall, v.23, p.445-470.

Humphreys, J. B., suit against heirs of to secure money due Brown estate, v.27, p.742-745.

Humphreys, John, nephew of James Brown, v.24, p.941, 1039, 1145, 1146, 1147, 1150, 1161, 1163, 1164, 1170, 1171, 1172, 1173, 1174, 1175.

Huner, John, Jr., noted, v.25, p.398.

Hunt, Carleton, noted, v.22, p.218; quoted on Soule, v.25, p.995-996; orator on occasion of relaying of cornerstone of Clay monument, v.27, p.779; noted, v.29, p.715.

Hunt, Dr. Thomas, noted, v.24, p.768; first dean of Medical College of La., v.26, p.57; noted, v.26, p.75, 76; challenged to duel by Luzenberg, v.26, p.79-80; noted, v.26, p.85.

Hunter, George, diary in L. S. U. Archives, v.24, p.342.

Hunter, Henry D., recommended telegraph, v.31, p.p.427.

Hunter, J. W., noted, v.25, p.807.

Hunter, R. A., La. state treasurer, v.25, p.695; Senate com. on public schools, v.25, p.1042-1043; on Wells, v.31, p.1005-1006.

Hunter, Sherod, noted, v.24, p.76.

Hunter, Thos. T., Confed. naval officer, v.27, p.481.

Hunter, William Walker, papers in the La. Hist. Assn. depository, v.24, p.315.

"Hunt Family, The," by James Renshaw, v.5, p.339.

"Hunt, Gaillard," James A. Renshaw, v.8, p.84.

Hunt, Judge T. G., noted, v.24, p.767; v.25, p.996.

Hunton, Logan, noted, v.22, p.1125; v.23, p.1095.

Hunt, Randall, noted, v.23, p.1056, 1061, 1081, 1082; noted, v.25, p.681, 998, 1078; a tribute to Soule, v.25, p.1081, 1082; senatorial election of 1848, v.25, p.1095, 1107; noted, v.29, p.683, 684; chairman of Elliott investigation, v.31, p.684; elected U. S. Senator, v.31, p.1069.

"Huntsmen of Black Ivory, The," by John Smith Kendall, v.24, p.9-34.

Hunt, T. G., noted, v.23, p.180, 1080.

Hunt, Wm. H., principal orator for unveiling of Clay's statue, v.27, p.774-775.

Hurlburt, Gen. ———, and Christ Church, New Orleans, v.23, p.1246ff.

Hurlbut, Gen., Wells inaugural, v.31, p.1023; quoted, v.31, p.1036-1037.

Huskisson, William, noted, v.24, p.1108.

Huso, Charles, noted, v.22, p.191.
Hutchins, Anthony, and Natchez in Am. Rev., v.22, p.45-46.
Hutchins, John, noted, v.23, p.1232.
Hutchinson, Benjamin, member of St. Helena Police Jury, v.23, p.406ff., 420.
Hutchinson, Alexander C., donation to Charity Hospital, v.31, p.80.
Hutton, James, Com. with Cathcart to survey timber in La. and Ala., v.28, p.735-736; salary, v.28, p.737-738; sketch of survey, v.28, p.738ff.; noted, v.28, p752n., 764, 765, 766, 770, 772, 776, 825, 828, 830, 835, 845, 867, 868, 880, 883, 890, 892; correspondence in resurvey, v.28, p.893ff.; letters to from Cathcart, v.28, p.895-896, 902-904; in re-planned survey of Mermentau, v.28, p.899-902.
Hyams, H. M., on Wells, v.31, p.1055.
Hyams, Judge, editor of the "Sugar Planter," v.21, p.1130.
Hyatt, Arthur W., collection in L. S. U. Archives, v.24, p.342.
Hyman, W. B., on Wells, v.31, p.1006; noted, v.31, p.1008, 1026.

IATTS INDIANS, NOTED, v.23, p.1120.
Iberia Parish, La., noted, v.25, p.162.
"Iberville and Bienville, 1699-1712," by Henry Plauche Dart, v.2, p.72.
"Iberville Coast," v.25, p.163.
"Iberville County," v.25, p.163.
Iberville Parish, in 1860, v.21, p.1125-1130; meeting of Dem., v.25, p.113, 121, 150, 164, 165, 172, 174, 181, 182, 201, 202, 207, 214, 215, 216, 320, 321; history of, v.25, p.162-163; fertility of soil, v.25, p.184-185; sugar area, v.25, p.187, 196, 200; hunting in, v.25, p.205-206; Randolph estate in, v.25, p.213.
Iberville, Pierre Le Moyne, v.25, p.162, 924; discovery of mouth of Miss. by sea, v.25, p.933-934; discovered Miss. Mouth, v.26, p.639; founded post of La. at Biloxi Bay, v.26, p.640; led expedition from Biloxi Bay to build Fort Miss., v.26, p.644; persuaded Tonti to join him, v.26, p.644; advised Fr. court against Tonti, v.26, p.645-646; planned to seize region Tonti controlled, v.26, p.646; noted, v.26, p.648, 687; erected Fort Maurepas, v.26, p.725; built Fort at Eng. Turn, v.26, p.726; sent Bienville to Mobile River, v.26, p.726; left colonies for last time, v.26, p.1702; noted, v.26, p.731, 753; explorations of Red Pole Area, v.28, p.31-34, 35, 37, 40, 44, 45, 46, 48, 50, 51, 52, 55, 66; in re change in course of Miss. at False R., v.28, p.69ff.
Iberville River, See Bayou Manchac, v.25, p.933.
Icks, Adolph, stage manager first German theatre group in N. O., v.26, p.372; one of 1st actors, v.26, p.372; noted, v.26, p.375, 401; unimportant German playwright, v.26, p.436-437.
Idell, Anthony, noted, v.23, p.423.
Illinois, appeals from, to Superior Council, v.21, p.1002-1003, 1013-1020.
Illinois Cattle, export of salt meat, v.22, p.668.
Illinois, garrison at, and fever epidemic, 1769, v.23, p.388.
"Illinois Indians' Visit to France in 1725," by William Beer, v.6, p.189.
Illustrations: Bienville's Seal, v.1, sec.3, p.4; The Choctaws, v.1, sec.1, p.13; Joan of Arc, the Maid of Orleans, v.1, p.262; Andres De Almonaster, v.2, p.402; Baron Joseph Xavier De Pontalba, v.2 p.394; Sedella, De, Fray Antonio (Pere Antoine), v.2, p.368; Bienville, Jean Baptist Le Moyne De, v.3, p.178; Gulf of Mexico, 1744, Map of, v.3, p.167; Gulf of Mexico, Sketch of, v.3, p.202; Louisiana in 1722, Map of, v.3, p.165; Map, original card which figured in Name of New Orleans in 1718, v.3, p.183; New Orleans, A Small Island of (after Dumont of Montigny), v.3, p.243;

New Orleans, as seen from Quincampoix, v.3, p.200; New Orleans in 1725, Plan of, v.3, p.245; New Orleans in 1756, Plan of, v.3, p.249; New Orleans in 1718, Sketch of (after Dumont of Montigny), v.3, p.191; New Orleans in 1721, Sketch of (after Dumont of Montigny), v.3, p.221; Shreve, Captain Henry Miller, v.3, p.136; Baron Marc de Villiers Du Terrage, v.5, p.286; John Dymond, late Editor of La. Hist. Quarterly, v.5, p.187; Portrait of Miss Grace King, v.6, p.345; Map of Bienville's Concessions, v.10, p.8; Map of Caddo Indian Cession, v.10, p.39; Louisiana State Seminary of Learning and Military Academy, v.11, p.10; Site of La. State Seminary as it appears today, v.11, p.28; Du Pratz's map of La., v.11, p.446; Population Map of La., v.12, p.386; Chief Agric. Money Products Map of La., v.12, p.398; La. Map of Pres. election, 1848, v.12, p.556; La. map—Vote on the Const., v.12, p.590; La. map—Pres. election, 1856, v.13, p.111; La. Map—Pres. Election, 1860, v.13, p.482; Maps of Galveztown, v.13, p.560, 580; Map of La.—Popular vote on secession, 1861, v.13, p.638; The Last Photograph of Charles Gayarre, v.14, p.80; photostat of "Extrait de la lettre du Roi," printed by Denis Braud, v.14, p.300; Map of the Delta of the Miss. River, v.14, p.304-305; Copy of entry of baptism of La Salle, 1643, v.14, p.318; Picture of Commemorative Plaque at Rouen, v.14, p.319; Map of E. and W. Fla., v.15, p.392; Map of W. Fla., v.15, p.393; Map of portion of La., v.15, p.396; Portrait of George Purnell Whittington, v.15, p.657; Map showing location of Fort Selden, Camp Salubrity, Adias and Fort Jesup, v.16, p.8; Ruins of Fort Jesup, v.16, p.12; Land Office Map showing Fort Jesup, v.16, p.18; Map of Camp Sabine and Gaine's Military Road, v.16, p.278; Land Office Map of Fort Jesup, v.16, p.674; marker at Fort Jesup, v.17, p.160; View of Fort Jesup Hist. Park, v.17, p.155; Map of Fort Jesup, v.17, p.152; Map of Natchitoches in 1850, v.17, p.142; Portrait of General Solomon Weathersbee Downs, v.17, p.7; View of Fort Jesup, v.17, p.164, 167; First French Map of Lower Miss. R., v.17, p.424; Portraits of Henry Plauche Dart, v.18, p.238, 254; Map of site of Caddo Indian Agency, v.18, p.780; Map of Shreveport, v.18, p.864; Map of La. in 1733, Section of "Carte de la Louisiane," v.19, p.570; Map of Route of French Army in La., 1731, v.19, p.569; Map of Sicily Island, La., v.19, p.568; Map of property of John Lovelace, 1813, v.19, p.565; Plan of Natchez Fort, v.19, p.560; Plan of two Natchez Forts, v.19, p.548; Map of lower Ouachita Valley, v.19, p.548; Map of Natchez, Miss., 1729, v.19, p.548; Map of Fort de la Boulaye, v.19, p.833, 835; "The Logs" of Fort de la Boulaye, v.19, p.836; "Cannon Ball," v.19, p.840; Seven maps of region of Fort de la Boulaye, v.19, p.878; Picture of Document by Laussat, establishing 1st fire department in N. O., v.20, p.181; Carondelet's original Passport to Maison Rouge, v.20, p.300; Map of Maison Rouge Grant, v.20, p.306; Carondelet's "Grant" to Maison Rouge, v.20, p.306; handwriting and signature of Marquis de Maison Rouge, v.20, p.332; Trudeau's plan of Bastrop Grant, v.20, p.374; Map showing Maison Rouge and Bastrop Grants, v.20, p.374; two maps of Ouachita River, v.20, p.395; Map of Bastrop Grant, v.20, p.406; signatures of Bastrop, Morhouse and Filhiol, v.20, p.436; Plan of Fort Miro, v.20, p.464; Survey of Filhiol's Lands, v.20, p.466; Plan of Fort Miro, v.20, p.472; Plan of Faubourg Ste. Marie, 1796, v.22, p.394; Plan of the Vieux Carre and Faubourg Ste. Marie, v.22, p.404; Map of Jesuit Plantation, 1763, v.22, p.408; Carrollton Court House, v.22, p.201; Portrait of Albert G. Brice, Mayor of Carrollton, v.22, p.205; First Catholic Church in Carrollton, v.22, p.210; Portrait of William H. Williams, v.22, p.182; Map of portion of Carrollton, v.22, p.184; Carrollton Hotel, v.22, p.192; N. O. and Carrollton R. R. Depot and Shops, v.22, p.194, 195; deserted cabins of the Germantown settlers, v.24, p.379, 380, 381, 382; View of Wurzburg, Germany, v.24, p.401; "The Crown," v.24, p.403; View of Miltenberg am Main, Germany, v.24, p.414; Count Leon's home in Offenbach, v.24, p.419; The Great House of the Harmony Society, v.24, p.423; Count Leon's house in Philippsburg, v.24, p.425; Church at Monica, Pa., v.24, p.427; Cabin at Germantown, La., v.24, p.428; Grand Ecore, La., 1873, v.24, p.430; cemetery of Germantown settlers, v.24, p.433; Steamer Col. A. P. Kouns, v.25, p.432; Steamer Columbia, v.25, p.433; Steamer D. L. Tally, v.25, p.441; Steamer Era No. 2, v.25, p.447; Steamer G. W. Sentell, v.25, p.456; Steamer La Belle, v.25, p.468; Steamer R. T. Bryarly, v.25, p.492; Steamer Valley Queen, v.25, p.504; Portrait of Mrs. Myra Clark Gaines, v.27, p.42; Portrait of Major General Edmund Pendleton Gaines, v.27, p.42; Portrait of Mrs. General Gaines, v.27, p.242; The Cenotaph, designed by Mr. A. Mondelli (honoring Clay, Calhoun and Webster), v.27, p.766; The Funeral Car, designed and executed by Mr. Dubuque, v.27, p.768; Canal Street—West from Chartres St., v.27, p.772; Map of East B. R. Parish area, v.28, p.11; Map of Baton Rouge Reach, v.28, p.36; Map of D'Artaguette Concession, v.28, p.39; Maps concerning early Baton Rouge, v.28, p.41, 43; Map showing Cathcart's Routes in La., v.28, p.748; Map of Neutral Ground, v.28, p.1002; Map showing the First Neutral Ground in Am. Terr., 1739-1763, v.28, p.1007; Early map of N. America, v.28, p.1022; Map of Neutral Ground between Tex. and La., v.28, p.1044; Triumphal Arch, to honor Lafayette, erected in Jackson Sq., v.29, p.302; Plan and elevation of Hospital, v.29, p.561; plan and elevation of Chapel at Balize, v.29, p.567; plan and elevation of corps de Garde at the Balize, v.29, p.579; plan and elevation of building for Ursuline Nuns, v.29, p.581; Section of building for Ursuline Nuns, v.29, p.583; elevation of building for Ursuline Nuns, v.29, p.585; Section of building for Ursuline Nuns, v.29, p.586; plan of building for Ursuline Nuns, v.29, p.587, 588, 589; plan and elevation of Hospital for Ursuline Nuns, v.29, p.598; plan and elevation for wing for Hospital, v.29, p.598; plan of Chapel for Ursuline Nuns, v.29, p.603; elevation of Ursuline Convent, v.29, p.604; plan of Ursuline Convent, v.29, p.605; section of Ursuline Convent, v.29, p.606; plan and elevation for kitchen for Ursuline Nuns, v.29, p.607; elevations, plans, details and section of Ursuline Convent, v.29, p.608; Photograph of Ursuline Convent, v.29, p.611; Map showing location of Old Ursuline Convent property, v.29, p.617; details of roof construction, v.29, p.619; Bird's eye View of the old Ursuline Convent, v.29, p.633; Photographs of portions of the Old Ursuline Convent, v.29, p.634, 635, 636; Plan of Ursuline Convent, v.29, p.646; Plan of Old Ursuline Convent, v.29, p.655; Map of La. coastal marshlands, v.30, p.655; Map of portion of La. showing Delta Farms project, v.30, p.664; Map showing location of La. Marshlands reclamation projects, v.30, p.676; sketch of N. O. Lake Shore Land Co. project, v.30, p.678.

Immigrants, school for, in N. Y., v.24, p.724; to La. in 1840's, v.25, p.129.

"Impregnable," fort, opposite Old Providence, v.24, p.657.

"Imprisonment for Debt in French Louisiana," Henry P. Dart, v.8, p.549.

Incarcaterra, Frank, noted, v.22, p.830.

"Incident of the Joan of Arc Statuette Presentation, A Pleasing," v.1, p.288.

"Independence," corsair of Cartagena, v.24, p.367.

"Independence," old Fort Santa Teresa, v.24, p.657.

"Independencia del Sur," pirate vessel, v.24, p.362.

Index to Records of Superior Council of Louisiana, v.1, sec.1, p.103, v.1, sec.3, p.224; V, VI, VII, VIII, v.2, p.104, 193, 328, 463; IX, X, v.3, p.141, 403; XI, XII, v.4, p.218, 324, 481; XIV, XV, XVI, XVII, v.5, p.76, 329, 377, 571; XVIII, XIX, XX, XXI, v.6, p.114, 283, 482, 657; XXII, XXIII, XXIV, v.7, p.334, 485, 676; XXV, XXVI, XXVII, XXVII, v.8, p.118, 271, 478, 673; XXIX, XXX, XXXI, XXXII, v.9, p.113, 288, 502, 705; XXXIII, XXXIV, XXXV, XXXVI, v.10, p.96, 252, 409, 566; XXXVII, XXXVIII, XXVIX, XL, v.11, p.119, 288, 478, 625; XLI, XLII, XLIII, XLIV, v.12, p.134, 304, 467, 647; XLV, XLVI, XLVII, XLVIII, v.13, p.119, 307, 488, 660; XLIX, L, LI, LII, v.14, p.119, 254, 446, 570; LIII, LIV, LV, v.15, p.120, 507, 653; LVI, LVII, LVIII, v.16, p.135, 330, 504; LIX, LX, LXI, v.17, p.183, 364, 556.

Index to Spanish Judicial Records of Louisiana, I, II, III, IV, v.6, p.145, 311, 513, 683; V, VI, VII, v.7, p.144, 524, 706; VIII, IX, X, XI, v.8, p.149, 308, 508,

704; XII, XIII, XIV, XV, v.9, p.143, 321, 533, 746; XVI, XVII, XVIII, XIX, v.10, p.129, 281, 438, 588; XX, XXI, X, XXII, v.11, p.153, 314, 508, 654; XXIII, XXIV, XXV, XXVI, v.12, p.166, 331, 498, 675; XXVII, XXVIII, XXIX, XXX, v.13, p.161, 333, 519, 683; XXXI, XXXII, XXXIII, XXXIV, v.14, p.155, 271, 461, 606; XXXV, XXXVI, XXXVII, v.15, p.156, 532, 675; XXXVIII, XXXIX, XL, v.16, p.151, 339, 516, XLI, XLIII, v.17, p.203, 385, 572; XLIV, March, 1782, v.18, p.193-233; XLV, April, 1782, v.18, p.456-485; XLVI, May, 1782, v.18, p.727-758; XLVII, June, 1782, v.18, p.1004-1035; XLVIII, July-Aug., 1782, v.19, p.241-272; LXIX, Sept.-Nov., 1782, v.19, p.510-546; LXX, Nov., 1782, v.19, p.778-827; LI, Dec., 1782, v.19, p.1119-1139; LII, Jan., 1783, v.20, p.245-287; LIII, Feb., 1783, v.20, p.518-555; LIV, March, 1783, v.20, p.840-879; LV, April, 1783, v.20, p.1141-1175; LVI, May-June, 1783, v.21, p.319-336; LVII, July, 1783, v.21, p.610-628; LVIII, Aug., 1783, v.21, p.905-957; LIX, Sept., 1783, v.21, p.1253-1283; LX, Oct., 1783, v.22, p.259-309; LXI, Nov., 1783, v.22, p.575-621; LXII, Dec., 1783, v.22, p.903-931; LXIII, Jan.-Feb., 1784, v.22, p.1211-1247; LXIV, March, 1784, v.23, p.295-347; LXV, April, 1784, v.23, p.635-674; LXVI, May, 1784, v.23, p.945-994; LXVII, June, 1784, v.23, p.1299-1331; LXVIII, June, 1784, v.24, p.258-300; LXIX, July, 1784, v.24, p.601-605; LXX, August, 1784, v.24, p.838-915; LXXI, Sept., 1784, v.24, p.1232-1280, cited, v.24, p.320, 321; LXXII, Oct, 1784, v.25, p.260-285; LXXIII, Nov.-Dec., 1784, v.25, p.589-606; LXXIV, Jan., 1785, v.25, p.873-916; LXXV, Jan., 1785, v.25, p.1184-1223; LXXVI, Jan., 1785, v.26, p.257-305; LXXVII, Feb., 1785, v.26, p.842-909; LXXVIII, Feb.-March, 1785, v.26, p.1187-1236; LXXIX, Feb., 1785, v.27, p.854-927; v.28, p.573-673, 1244-1324; v.29, p.208-270, 510-554, 797-880; LXXXV, v.31, p.157-263.

Index to the French and Spanish Archives (Editor's Chair), v.10, p.407.

"Index to the Publications of the La. Hist. Society, 1895-1917," v.5, p.431.

Indian Mounds, in Catahoula Parish, v.21, p.1204; in Ouachita Valley, v.25, p.617-618, 619, 627-628, 631, 632-633, 638; in B. R. area, v.28, p.24-30; theories as to origin of, v.28, p.26-30; on Berwick plantation, description of, v.28, p.793-795.

"Indianola," an ironclad, v.24, p.72; federal gunboat, v.29, p.1097, 1098, 1101; capture by Confederates and destruction of, v.29, p.1102-1107.

"Indian Place Names in Louisiana, More," by Wm. A. Read, v.11, p.445.

Indians, Caddo, history of, v.18, p.872-946; manners and customs, v.18, p.880-885; Caddo country and range, v.18, p.885-888; relations with French and Spanish, v.18, p.888-897; in La., v.18, p.897-910; treaty of 1835 with the U. S., v.18, p.910-923; in Texas, v.18, p.923-940.

Indians, Land Titles of, v.4, p.134; French expedition against the Natchez, v.19, p.547-577; on the Southwestern frontier, v.20, p.183ff.; instruction to Filhiol regarding, v.20, p.296-297, 309-311, 473-474; in Ouachita, v.20, p.334; trade of Creeks and William Panton, v.21, p.13n.; relations with U. S., v.21, p.17; treaty of Nogales mentioned, v.21, p.28n.; treaties with Gov. of W. Fla., v.21, p.1023; treatment of in W. Fla., v.22, p.21, 25, 36, 381-382; slaves, v.22, p.61, 654-656; aid to Spain, v.22, p.817; sale of liquor to, v.22, p.959; sale of rum to in W. Fla., v.23, p.18ff.; fight of Creeks and Choctaws, v.23, p.371-372; complaint of traders, v.23, p.379; gifts to, v.23, p.387; treaty with Creeks, v.23, p.400; policy of U. S. at Natchitoches, v.23, p.843; as slaves, v.23, p.864; houses for agents, v.23, p.1011; noted, v.23, p.1043; classification of, v.23, p.1110; mounds in Grant Parish, v.23, p.1125-1129; bibl. on, v.23, p.1129-1131; folklore of, in La., v.24, p.749-750; tribes, and location of each in Tex.-La. region, v.28, p.1082n.

"Indians of Grant Parish," by A. N. Ethridge, v.23, p.1107-1131.

"Indians, The Taensa," I, II, by R. D. Calhoun, v.17, p.411, 642.

Indian Trade, rivalry between Am. and Sp., v.28, p.1082-1089.

Indigo, growth of encouraged, v.21, p.1063; trade in, v.22, p.663; export of, v.22, p.667; cultivation in La., v.25, p.25, 185; attempted in Natchez district, v.25, p.153; noted, v.32, p.21.

Indirect voyage, question of, v.24, p.1046-1047, 1050-1051.

Individual and government, Edward Livingston's ideas upon, v.24, p.723-725.

"Induction of Laurent MacMahon as Councillor, 1730," by Heloise H. Cruzat, v.10, p.529.

Industry, in Sp. New Orleans, v.22, p.672-673.

"Infatigable," Spanish brig, v.24, p.629.

Influence of German Culture in New Orleans since 1865; introduction, v.24, p.127-128; German immigration to New Orleans, v.24, p.131-136; German churches, v.24, p.136-148; German schools and instruction in German, v.24, p.148-155; German theatre, v.24, p.156-159; German organizations, v.24, p.159-160; conclusion, v.24, p.160-162; appendix, v.24, p.162-164; bibliography, v.24, p.165-167.

Ingersoll, Charles, noted, v.24, p.1163, 1173.

Ingersoll, Mrs., noted, v.24, p.1165.

Ingham, Samuel D., report on La. sugar industry, v.25, p.62, 70, 71, 72.

Ingraham, Joseph Holt, author on Louisiana, v.31, p.398, 408.

In Memoriam: Baron Marc de Villiers du Terrage, by Andre Lafargue, v.19, p.1069-1074.

In Memoriam: Colonel Hugues J. de la Vergne, v.7, p.121; John F. C. Waldo, v.7, p.125.

In Memoriam: Henry E. Chambers (Editor's Chair), v.12, p.300; Dr. Max Heller, v.12, p.461.

In Memoriam: James Davidson Hill, v.11, p.116.

In Memoriam: William Beer (Editor's Chair), v.10, p.249; William R. Irby (Editor's Chair), v.10, p.95.

Innerarity, James, of Forbes & Co., v.21, p.92n.

Innerarity, John, and W. Fla. Rev., v.21, p.114-115.

Innis, Patrick, v.23, p.357, 368, 388.

"Installation of De Kerleric as Governor of Louisiana, of de Membrede as King's Lieutenant and of de Bellisle as Town Major of New Orleans, 1753," Introduction by Henry P .Dart, translated by Heloise H. Cruzat, v.14, p.235.

"Institutions of Louisiana, Legal," by Henry Plauche Dart, v.2, p.72.

Intendancy of La., an institution, v.21, p.19.

Internal improvements, railroad movement, v.23, p.196-243; question of, v.24, p.714-716.

"International Fibre and Juice Extracting Co.," E. John Ellis, pres., v.29, p.748-749.

"Interregnum in Louisiana in 1861, The," I, II, III, by Lane C. Kendall, v.16, p.175, 374, 639; IV, V, VI, v.17, p.124, 339, 524.

"Interval of Military Government in W. Fla.," by C. H. Howard, v.22, p.18-30.

"Intrepide," privateer, v.23, p.436, 441-442, 772.

"Introduction of Jean Francois Pasquier as Councillor-Assessor in the Superior Council of Louisiana," Translated by by Heloise H. Cruzat, with introductory note by Henry P. Dart, v.10, p.68.

"Inventory of de Vaugine's Plantation in the Attakapas on Bayou Teche," Translated by Laura L. Porteous, with introduction by Henry P. Dart, v.9, p.565.

"Inventory of the Estate of Sieur Jean Baptiste Prevost," Translated by Edith Dart Price and Heloise H. Cruzat, with introduction by Henry P. Dart, v.9, p.411.

"Inventory of the Paris Duverney Concession in La., 1726," ed. by Walter Prichard, v.21, p.979-994.

Iowa, La., v.32, p.588.

Irby, William R., In Memoriam (Editor's Chair), v.10, p.95; noted, v.24, p.318.

Ireland, Joseph, biographer of Mrs. Duff, v.28, p.926.

Ireland, Prof. Ed. J., sponsor of Museum of Pharmacy, v.26, p.337.

Iriarte, noted, v.22, p.940.

"Irion Plantation," of Erwin, v.27, p.354, 368-369, 380, 387, 388, 390, 391, 394, 397, 398; inventory of, v.27, p.425-428; appraisal, v.27, p.430, 432, 434, 436; statement of crops, v.27, p.466.

Irish Bend, noted, v.24, p.73.

"Irish Company," v.25, p.212.

Irish, in New Orleans, v.23, p.870; laborers in La., v.25, p.120.

"Irresistible," buccaneer vessel, v.24, p.361.

Irrigation, of rice in Southwest La., v.23, p.567-571.

Irvine, Marie Hunter, noted, v.24, p.307.

Irving, C. F., Challenge to New Orleans "Crescent," v.24, p.770-772.

Irving, William Templar, noted, v.24, p.941.

Irwin, J. A., trustee of Franklin Academy, 1838, v.39, p.84.

Irwin, Jesse R., stated bribes made by How-

ard, v.27, p.974; incorporator of La. Lottery Co., v.27, p.975, 976.
Irwin, John Lawson, marries Martha Mitchell, children of, v.29, p.292; noted, v.29, p.1042.
Irwin, Martha Mitchell (see Mitchell, Martha), daughter of Philomela Smith Mitchell, v.29, p.292.
Irwin, Mary Philomela (see Kendall, Mary P. Irwin), daughter of Martha Mitchell Irwin, v.29, p.292; marries Wm. Gray Kendall, children of, v.29, p.292-293; mother of John Irwin Kendall, v.29, p.1042.
Irwin, Richard Biddle, noted, v.23, p.1200.
"Isabella," schooner, v.24, p.369, 370, 422.
Isabelle, Thomas, on De Freret Returning Board, v.28, p.1135.
Isla de Culebra, noted, v.24, p.638.
Islands of Caillou and Timbalier, Petitions for Concessions of, 1793, v.2, p.303.
Isle Brevelle, settlement of free Negroes, v.25, p.361, 362, 733.
Islenos, origin of settlers, v.24, p.44-45; place of settlement, v.24, p.45; occupation of settlers, v.24, p.45-47; social customs, v.24, p.47-48.
Isle of Orleans, noted, v.26, p.6-11passim.
Israel Academy, v.25, p.789.
"Istrouma," by William A. Read, v.14, p.503.
Istrouma, former Indian name of site of B. R., v.28, p.5, 34, 44, 46, 47, 54; suburb of present B. R., v.28, p.6.
Italian Opera Co., inaugurated by Caldwell, v.28, p.209, 219, 222-223, 267, 268.
Italians, in N. O., v.20, p.1067ff.; Mafia in New Orleans, v.22, p.493ff., 819-856.
Italo-American incident of 1891, press reaction, v.24, p.187ff.
Iturribarria, Luis, noted, v.22, p.1067; at Galveston, v.23, p.768, 771; issues privateer commissions, v.23, p.789; noted, v.24, p.635.
"Ivanhoe Plantation," of Don Caffery, v.27, p.784.
Izabal, prize goods taken from by Aury, v.24, p.664; noted, v.24, p.671, 678.

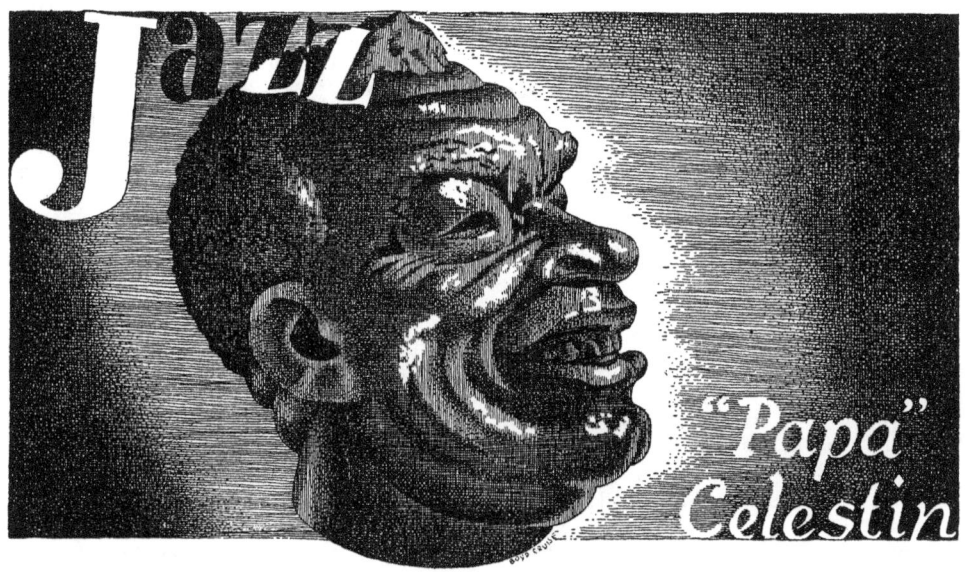

JACK, MADAME, NOTED, v.24, p.612.
"Jackson, Andrew, and Judge D. A. Hall" (Report of the Committee of Louisiana Senate, 1843), v.5, p.509; "Correspondence with James W. Breedlove," by John S. Kendall, v.6, p.179; "Reflections on Campaign, 1814-1815," by Bernard Marigny, v.6, p.61; "And the Louisiana Legislature, 1814-1815," by Henry P. Dart, v.9, p.221; "Report of the Committee of Inquiry of the Military Measures Executed Against the Legislature of Louisiana, December 28, 1814," v.9, p.223; and Firebrand Affair, v.21, p.210-211; difficulties in N. O. and dispute with Fulwar Skipwith, v.21, p.367-417; comments on Reid's biography, v.21, p.411-419; statistics in battles, v.21, p.419; and free Negroes of N. O., v.21, p.1079; and Barataria pirates, v.22, p.1032; letter to Claiborne, Nov. 12, 1806, v.23, p.160; and Humbert, v.23, p.753; takes Amelia Island and Pensacola, v.23, p.794; and Jean Lafitte, v.24, p.14, 21; and Dominique You, v.24, p.26; collection in Bibliotheca Parsoniana, v.24, p.311; noted, v.24, p.373, 700, 1018, 1019, 1065, 1090; and nullification, v.24, p.703, 721; Senatorial criticisms of, v.24, p.711-712; estimate of by James Brown, v.24, p.937-938, 1155; supporters of in Congress, v.24, p.1004; political standing of, v.24, p.1050, 1097, 1137; Beverly letter, v.24, p.1063, 1064; speculation on appointments by, v.24, p.1143, 1148; noted, v.25, p.44, 156, 300, p.1136; Early administration, v.24, 327, 328, 329, 384, 662, 1016, 1083; influence of tariff on campaign, v.25, p.47-48; supporters of in La., v.25, p.59, 60, 77-78, 79, 89-90, 92; and nullification, v.25, p.91; tariff message, 1832, v.25, p.96; and removal of deposits, v.25, p.108; issue of fine, v.25, p.124; noted, v.26, p.727; at the Battle of N. O., v.26, p.960; noted, v.26, p.961, 966, 967, 976; duel with Dickinson, v.27, p.347-348, 397, 489, 495; enemy of Clay, v.27, p.722, 728-729; pres. of U. S., v.27, p.722-723; contest with Calhoun over nullification, v.27, p.728; Clay's attack upon in re Seminole War, v.27, p.733-734, 735, 736, 751; erection of statue in N. O., v.27, p.764; part played by Bogalusians in his success at Battle of N. O., v.29, p.80-81; and Skipwith, v.31, p.307, 309, 315; candidate for Governor of Orleans, v.31, p.347-351; early life, v.31, p.346; noted, v.33, p.228.

Jackson Barracks Library, history of depository, v.24, p.313.

Jackson, Charles B., named in Kellogg impeachment, v.31, p.713.

Jackson, James, petition of, v.23, p.402-403.
Jackson, John, noted, v.24, p.370.
Jackson, La., meeting place of const. con. of 1844, v.25, p.1007ff.; noted, v.32, p.777-779, 781.
Jackson, Moses, Negro Repub. elected Rep. from St. Mary, v.28, p.1140.
Jackson Parish, in 1860, v.21, p.1190-1194; and the bagging factory, v.26, p.1065; noted ,v.26, p.1073, 1104; Populist legislator from, v.26, p.1109.
Jackson railroads, noted, v.24, p.454.
"Jackson Square," by Henry Renshaw, v.2, p.38.
Jackson, S. T., agreed lottery question should be submitted to people, v.27, p.1036-1037.
Jackson, Thomas J. (Stonewall), noted, v.24, p.63.
"Jacobinism in Spanish La., 1792-1797," by E. R. Liljegren, v.22, p.47-97.
Jacobins in La., mentioned, v.21, p.46.
Jacobs, John Hall, noted, v.24, p.324.
Jails, in Pensacola, v.23, p.363, 390-391; at St. Helena, v.23, p.425; in St. Mary Parish, v.32, p.88-89.
Jamaica, noted, v.24, p.9, 654.
"Jamaica Pirates and Louisiana Commerce, The, 1739," by Sallie Dart and Edith Dart Price in Collaboration (documents translated by late Heloise H. Cruzat), v.16, p.209.
James, C. I., vice-pres. of Great Southern Lumber Co., 1905, v.29, p.91.
James, James Alton, "Oliver Pollock," rev'd, v.21, p.561-563.
"James Kirke Paulding's Creole Tale," by Dr. Floyd C. Watkins, v.33, p.364-379.
Jameson, J. Franklin, Translation by "Trial of Mary Glass for Murder," v.6, p.589.
Jameson, Mrs. John Alexander (Eliza Denison), noted, v.23, p.1138n.; letters from G. S. Denison, v.23, p.1142ff.
"James Robb, Banker and Pioneer Railroad Builder," by H. H. Evans, v.23, p.170-258.
Jamey, Father Victor, noted, v.31, p.916, 917, 918, 922, 948.
Jamison, Irwin, Prog. League Com., v.27, p.1062.
Janauchek, Fanny, actress, v.23, p.509; noted, v.24, p.156.
Janin, Albert C., ed. N. O. "Democrat," Lottery Co.'s suit against for libel, v.27, p.987; sued by lottery, v.31, p.746.
Janizaries, noted, v.24, p.999, 1008, 1009, 1111; suppression of, v.24, p.1011-1016.
Jannet, Jean, noted, v.22, p.1067.
Jansenists, controversy with Jesuits, v.24, p.1010.
Janssens, Archbishop Francis, opposed Lottery Co., v.27, p.1070-1071, 1191.
January, D. P., mayor of Crowley, v.27, p.1126, 1171.
Japan rice, description of, v.23, p.571.
Jaquess, James F., sketch, v.29, p.1251-1252; peace conference with Pres. Davis, v.29, p.1253-1257; results of conference, v.29, p.1257-1258.
Jarvis, Nathan, noted, v.23, p.1048.
Jarvis, Russell, attack on John Adams, v.24, p.1106.
Jastremski, Gen'l Leon, headed McEnery Com., v.28, p.1157; McEnery Chairman, v.31, p.837.
Jaurequi, Jacinto de Barrios y, Gov. of Tex., v.28, p.1753; investigated U. S. Tex. border, v.28, p.1021.
Javins, Charles, of Richmond Provost-Guard, v.29,p .1252.
Jayhawkers, in La., v.24, p.83, 95.
Jay, John, noted, v.24, p.699, 700.
Jay's Treaty, noted, v.21, p.52; v.24, p.711.
Jeanerette, La., noted, v.32, p.52, 71.
Jeanes, Miss Anna T., established fund for Negro education, v.25, p.795-99, 810.
Jean-Jacques, Captain, noted, v.23, p.436.
Jeanjean, Father Auguste, refuses bishopric, v.31, p.906.
"Jeanne D'Arc," French Ship, Address to Commander and Officers of, by Andre Lafargue, v.3, p.120.
Jeannin, J. B., Louisiana educator, v.31, p.852.
Jean Vatin's Restaurant, noted, v.26, p.774.
Jeff Davis Cadets, v.29, p.1047-1048, 1052.
"Jefferson and Government by Party, Thomas," by Percy Saint, v.8, p.41.
Jefferson, Charles B., son of Joseph Jefferson, manager of St. Charles Theatre, v.26, p.1155.
Jefferson, City of, collection in Howard-Tilton Memorial Library, v.24, p.330.
Jefferson College, in 1860, v.21, p.1121.
Jefferson Comedy Co., organized theatrical talent, v.26, p.1155.
"Jeffersonian Diplomacy in the purchase of La., 1803," by R. A. McLemore, v.18, p.346-53.
Jeffersonian Republicans, noted, v.24, p.717.
Jefferson, Joseph, his monument in St. Charles Theatre, v.26, p.1150; first visits

to N. O., v.26, p.1150-1151; member stock co., St. Charles, v.26, p.1151; influenced by performance of John E. Owens, v.26, p.1152; visits Australia, v.26, p.1153-1154; performance in N. O., 1870, v.26, p.1154; in N. O., 1893, v.26, p.1155, 1159; Jeff. Comedy Co. organized, 1899, v.26, p.1155; his performance of "The Rivals," v.26, p.1156; his Orange Island estate, v.26, p.1156-1159; as a lecturer, v.26, p.1160; characteristics, v.26, p.1161-1164; at Buzzards Bay, v.26, p.1165; his final appearance in N. O., v.26, p.1165-1166; death, v.26, p.1166.

Jefferson Parish, La., election disturbances in, v.20, p.1108; noted, v.25, p.192.

Jefferson, Thomas, plough used in La., v.21, p.167n.; noted, v.23, p.440, 1049; noted, v.24, p.49, 701, 703, 727, 935; documents in Bibliotheca Parsoniana, v.24, p.311; letter in Ursuline College Museum, v.24, p.335; financial difficulties of, v.24, p.1013; death of, v.24, p.1014; letter of, v.24, p.1140; noted, v.25, p.11, 20, 26, 154, 293, 645; and La. Purchase, v.28, p.1017; cited documents providing that Rio Grande was Western boundary of La., v.28, p.1020, 1021; and Louisiana transfer, v.31, p.270-280; given power to appoint governor, v.31, p.272; attitude toward Sumter, v.31, p.289, 293; and Skipwith, v.31, p.397-398, 301; and Clark, v.31, p.310, 313, 315, 317, 322, 325, 334, 343; and Lyman, v.31, p.317, 319; and Lafayette, v.31, p.327-328, 332-334; and Monroe, v.31, p.335-337, 339-345; and Jackson, v.31, p.347-348; and Claiborne, v.31, p.353-534, 361, 365, 369, 370-380; "Donation by State of Louisiana to the Family of Thomas Jefferson, 1827, v.8, p.52.

Jenkins, B. F., opposed lotteries, v.27, p.1040.

Jenkins, Donelson Caffery, early N. O. newspaperman, v.20, p.777-778.

Jenkins, Dr. William, note book of in Rudolph Matas Medical Library, v.24, p.334.

Jenkins Ferry, noted, v.24, p.100.

Jenkins, John C., and family, collection in L. S. U. Archives, v.24, p.342-343.

Jenkins, P. E., sketch, v.21, p.1127-1128.

"Jennings, First Louisiana Salt Dome Pool," by Gerald Forbes, v.29, p.496-509.

Jennings, Henry, noted, v.24, p.9.

Jennings, La., early history of, v.23, p.559; suit involving oil field handled by Caffery, v.27, p.850, 1161, 1167, 1191, 1218, 1220; Heywood Bros. drill for oil, v.29, p.496; sale of stock to promote oil field, v.29, p.496-497; 4th well is financial success, v.29, p.497; transportation of Jennings oil to market, v.29, p.498; method of drilling, v.29, p.498-499; year of 1902 marks excitement in field, v.29, p.499; production doubles in 1903, v.29, p.500; year of 1904 brings high point of production, v.29, p.500-501; production triples in 1905 but revenue decreases, v.29, p.501-502; year of 1906 brings salt water menace, v.29, p.502; production declines in 1907, v.29, p.502-503; resume of 25 yrs. presented in 1926, v.29, p.503; cumulative resume presented in 1934, v.29, p.503-504; Jennings area reveals great deal of geological information, v.29, p.504-509; noted, v.32, p.591-592.

Jere, C. H., cashier first German theatre group in N. O., v.26, p.372.

Jesuits, and early education, v.19, p.601-607; land grant to, v.22, p.386; sale of plantation, v.23, p.681, 689; in France, v.24, p.978, 1000, 1010, 1011-1012, 1032, 1122, 1136; and sugar cane in La., v.25, p.24.

Jeter, W. L., member of Delta Rifles, v.29, p.105.

Jewell, Edwin L., opponent of Pinchback for Legis., 1868, v.27, p.535; newpaper editor, v.31, p.1041; defeated for state printer, v.31, p.1074; against lottery, v.31, p.723; charges Warmoth, v.31, p.727.

"Jewish Agricultural Colony in La.," by Leo Shpall, v.20, p.821-831.

Jews, in La., v.21, p.518-531; in N. O., v.22, p.166-180; laws concerning, v.24, p.1032.

Jiron, Antonio, noted, v.22, p.1026.

Joachum, Dr. Otto, letter from in Touro Infirmary Library, v.24, p.327.

Joan of Arc, "Celebration held by Louisiana Historical Society, May 1, 1918, Address on," by E. F. Genoyer de Bournety, French Consul, v.1, p.277; "Statuette of Joan of Arc; Its Presentation and Acceptance" (From N. Y. Museum of French Art to Louisiana Historical Society), "Acceptance Address," by Andre Lafargue, v.1, p.279; "Presentation of the Statuette to L. H. S.," v.1, p.285; "Pleasing Incident of the Presentation," v.1, p.288; "Fete of, May 16," v.1, p.295; "Maid of Orleans, The," by Heloise Hulse Cruzat, v.1, p.263.

"Joaquin Miller in New Orleans," by A. Turner, v.22, p.216-225.

Johannes, Father, noted, v.24, p.384; sermons of, v.24, p.385ff.

Johannot, privateer, v.24, p.17.

"Johann von Paris," manuscript in L. S.U. Music School Library, v.24, p.327.

"John Hampden Randolph, A. La. Planter," by Paul Everett Postell, v.25, p.149-223.

"John Howard Payne in New Orleans," by Lewis Leary and Arlin Turner, v.31, p.110-122.

John Law Company, noted, v.25, p.934.

"John McDonogh: Man of Many Facets," by Dr. Arthur G. Nuhrah, v.33, p.5-144.

"John McDonogh and the Miss. River Trade," by Lewis E. Atherton, v.26, p.37-43.

Johnness, privateer, v.24, p.17.

Johnny, Capt., noted, v.22, p.1061-1063.

Johns, John, law partner of E. Johns Ellis, v.29, p.753.

Johnson, Andrew, contemporary opinion of, v.23, p.1225, 1236, 1238; noted, v.24, p.112, 113, 114.

Johnson, Bowling Arthur, feature writer of "American Lumberman," v.29, p.101.

Johnson, Cecil, "The Distribution of Land in British West Florida," v.16, p.539; "A Note on Absenteeism and Pluralism in British W. Fla.," v.19, p.196-198; "British W. Fla., 1763-1783," rev'd, v.26, p.1181-85.

Johnson, Charles, commander of post of Baton Rouge, v.21, p.138.

Johnson, Charles Grandpre, sketch, v.28, p.942n.

Johnson, Dave C., lottery agent, v.31, p.719; suit against, v.31, p.731.

Johnson, Delos R., Representative from Washington Parish, v.29, p.108.

Johnson, Henry, noted, v.23, p.1007; candidate, 1850, v.23, p.1080ff.; and 1819 tariff bill, v.25, p.34; and nullification, v.25, p.92, 114, 115, 1004, 1060, 1061; on the Wilmot Proviso, v.25, p.1070, 1072, 1075; senatorial election of 1848, v.25, p.1093, 1095; Gov., v.29, p.79; La. senator, v.27, p.733; against lotteries, 1826, v.27, p.969; U. S. Sen. supporting bill for reclaiming swamp land, v.28, p.279.

Johnson, Howard Palmer, "New Orleans under General Butler," v.24, p.434-536.

Johnson, Isaac, Jr., and W. Fla. Rev., v.21, p.708n.; uncle of Gov. Isaac Johnson, sketch, v.28, p.942n.

Johnson, Isaac, noted, v.23, p.1049, 1097; noted, v.25, p.128, 129, 130, 136, 139, 140, 142, 673; candidate for Gov., 1846, v.25, p.1037; elected, v.25, p.1038; inaugural message, v.25, p.1040; noted, v.25, p.1053, 1107; on the slavery question, v.25, p.1116; gov. of La., v.27, p.752; meeting in N. O. to aid in Irish potato famine, v.27, p.755; ancestors, v.28, p.941-945; early life, v.28, p.945, 946; becomes lawyer, v.28, p.946-947; marriage to Charlotte McDermott, v.28, p.947; children of, v.28, p.947; member of legal prof. W. Fel., v.28, p.948; mil. career, v.28, p.949; in local politics, v.28, p.949-950; description, v.28, p.950; elected to La. Lower House, v.28, p.950; on Judiciary Com. and special com. to study S. C. ord. of nullification, v.28, p.950-951; seeks to amend charter of W. Fel. R. R., v.28, p.951; second Legis. session, v.28, p.951-952; resumes law practice and local interests, v.28, p.952-953; judge of 3rd district, v.28, p.954-955, 956; app't sec. of state, v.28, p.955-956; resigns, v.28, p.956; appt'd Court of Errors and Appeals in Criminal Cases, v.28, p.956-957; suggested as cand. for gov., v.28, p.957-958; rec'd Dem. nom., v.28, p.958-959; campaign and election of, v.28, p.959-963; inauguration, v.28, p.963-965; oath of office questioned, v.28, p.961; capital moved to B. R., v.28, p.967, 974-975; interest in Mex. War, v.28, p.967-968; appt'd state supt. of ed., v.28, p.969; gen'l assembly, 1847, v.28, p.969-970; State Univ., N. O., v.28, p.970; public school bill, v.28, p.970-971; day of thanksgiving and prayer, v.28, p.972; death of wife, v.25, p.972; message to Legis., 1848, v.28, p.972-973; denounces Wilmot Proviso, v.28, p.973; Board of Health provided for, v.28, p.973; condition of school system, v.28, p.973-974; flood of 1849, v.28, p.974; personal popularity of, v.28, p.975; last message to Legis., v.28, p.975-977; att'y gen'l, v.28, p.977-978; remarriage, v.28, p.978; settlement of McDonogh estate, v.28, p.978; urged to be cand. for Cong., v.28, p.978-979; state banking controversy, v.28, p.979; Orleans Navigation Co. case, v.28, p.979; Const. Conv., 1852, v.28, p.979-980; retirement, v.28, p.980;

cand. for ass't justice of state sup. ed., v.28, p.980; death and burial, v.28, p.980-981; estate of, v.28, p.981; summary, v.28, p.982-983; bibl., v.28, p.984-989.

Johnson, Isaac, grandfather of later gov., settled in Natchez, v.28, p.941-942; family of, v.28, p.942-943; moved to Bayou Sara region, v.28, p.943.

Johnson, J. K., on committee to incorporate Bogalusa, v.29, p.108, 109; designated Comm. of Accounts and Finances in Bogalusa, v.29, p.113; takes charge of Bogalusa cut-over lands, v.29, p.125-126.

Johnson, John Hunter, and W. Fla. Rev., v.21, p. 76, 107n., 687n.; commander at Bayou Sara, v.21, p.93, 94; letters from A. L. Duncan, v.21, p.115-116, 122; sketch, v.21, p.161n.; father of Gov. Isaac Johnson, v.28, p.942; noted, v.28, p.943; family and life, v.28, p.944-945; death and estate of, v.28, p.946-947.

Johnson, John, sketch, v.28, p.832n.

Johnson, Joseph Eugenius, and W. Fla. Rev., v.21, p.707n.; sketch, v.28, p.942n.; and W. Fla. Rev., v.28, p.944; noted, v.28, p.946, 947.

Johnson, Joseph, v.29, p.76.

Johnson, Manie, "The Colfax Riot of April, 1873," v.13, p.391.

Johnson, M. C., attorney in Morse Case, v.31, p.463.

Johnson, Peter, noted, v.23, p.480.

Johnson, Reverdy, noted, v.24, p.514, 515; lawyer in Gaines Case, v.27, p.9; death of, v.27, p.300; Commissioner sent to N. O., v.27, p.511.

Johnson, Richard M., noted, v.24, p.1157, 1161.

Johnson, Robert, privateersman, v.22, p.1083-1084.

Johnson, Sir William, noted, v.22, p.25, 801.

Johnson's Island, Union army military prison, v.29, p.706-707, 1214-1215.

"Johnson's Journal, William" (A Voyage from Pittsburgh to New Orleans and thence to New York in 1801). Reproduced from the New Jersey Historical Society's Quarterly Magazine, v.5, p.34.

Johnson, Wm. H., v.28, p.750n., 751.

Johnson, William T., and family, collection in L.S.U. Archives, v.24, p.343.

Johns, Paul Emile, N. O. musician, and Chopin, v.31, p.857; businesses, v.31, p.858-859; private life, v.31, p.859; composer, v.31, p.859; death, v.31, p.860; memorial, v.31, p.860.

Johnston, Albert Sidney, and New Orleans, v.24, p.445, 448.

Johnston, Chapman, noted, v.24, p.1090.

Johnston, Col. Wm. Preston, presiding over Anti-Lottery meeting, v.27, p.1060.

Johnston, Dave C., tells story of bribery in getting Act 25 of 1868 passed, v.27, p.976; La. Lottery Co's attack on, v.27, p.977.

Johnston, Dave P., La. man conducting lottery in Ohio, v.27, p.1079.

Johnstone, George, Gov. of W. Fla., commission, orders and instructions, v.21, p.1021-1068; and W. Fla. Assembly, v.22, p.34, 311, 312n.; speech to W. Fla. Assembly, v.22, p.314-316, 943; and W. Fla. Assembly, v.23, p.22, 357, 380.

Johnstone, James, noted, v.22, p.316, 317, 322-323.

Johnstone, William, noted, v.22, p.38; v.23, p.404.

Johnston, Gen'l Geo., aided in interesting out-of-state people in Anti-Lottery League, v.27, p.1059.

Johnston, Joseph E., noted, v.24, p.61, 62, 107.

Johnston, Joseph, noted, v.29, p.1242.

Johnston, Josiah Stoddard, noted, v.23, p.874, 1003, 1021, 1108; v.24, p.1060; and tariff, v.25, p.46, 74, 87, 102, 58, 71, 72, 73; Clay's second in duel with Randoplh, v.27, p.727; reelected to U. S. Senate, 1831, v.27, p.735-736; noted, v.28, p.820n.

Johnston, Mrs. William Preston, Tribute by Quarante Club, v.9, p.281; pres. Women's Anti-Lottery League, v.27, p.1061.

"John Warren," transport, v.24, p.96.

Joiner, Sil, Conf. Soldier, v.26, p.756.

Joly, Nicolas Maurice, noted, v.24, p.643, 653; with Venezuelan squadron, v.24, p.662; marriage, v.24, p.666; command of Margaritan fleet, v.24, p.666; admiral, v.24, p.666; supplanted by Brion, v.24, p.667.

Jonas, B. F., Address at Laying of Cornerstone of Monument, September 14, 1874, v.7, p.640; Chairman Com. of Finance, favored bill for lotteries for charity, v.27, p.971; explanation of postponed lottery bill of 1867, v.27, p.971-972, 990; and election of 1872, v.28, p.1134; supported McEnery forces, 1892, v.28, p.1161; opponent of Foster in U. S. Sen. races, v.28, p.1196-1197; noted, v.28, p.1171; candidate for Lt. Gov., v.29, p.399, 400; noted, v.29, p.437, 715,

749, 751; backer of N. O. "Democrat," v.31, p.739; noted, v.31, p.739.

Jonas, George, noted, v.22, p.180.

"Jonchere Concession, The," Translated from the Book of Concessions by Heloise H. Cruzat, Introduction by Henry P. Dart, v.11, p.553.

Jones, Dr. J., noted, v.26, p.76.

Jones, Dr. Thomas Jesse, national survey of schools for Negroes, v.25, p.768, 777, 1101-1104.

Jones, Evan, noted, v.22, p.433, 435, 973; petition of, v.23, p.366.

Jones, Guillermo, father-in-law of Abner Hammond, v.21, p.32.

Jones, James C., noted, v.23, p.200.

Jones, James, member of W. Fla. Council, v.23, p.353ff., 366.

Jones, Joseph, report in Rudolph Matas Library, v.24, p.334.

Jones, Michael, and W. Fla. Rev., v.21, p.82, 739n.

Jones, Philip Livingston, prominent position of, v.24, p.773; duel with Gurley, v.24, p.774-781.

Jones, Philip, noted, v.22, p.433.

Jones, Rev. Benjamin, member Centenary College Board, v.31, p.126-127.

Jones, Robert B., Louisiana Supreme Court Justice, v.31, p.1025.

Jones, Sam H., reform of Charity Hospital, v.31, p.96-97.

Jones, T. Sambola, requests withdrawal of Adams as Gov. Cand., v.28, p.1154-1155.

Jones, William, noted, v.22, p.191.

Jorda, Jayme, deposition of, v.23, p.701-702.

Jordan, Juan, noted, v.22, p.941.

"Jose Alvarez de Toledo's Reconciliation with Spain," Tr. and ed. by H. G. Warren, v.23, p.827-863.

"Jose Julian Marti on J. P. Benjamin," ed. and tr. by L. Gruss, v.23, p.259-264.

"Joseph Jefferson in N. O.," by John Smith Kendall, v.26, p.1150-1167.

Josephson, Manuel, noted, v.23, p.384.

Joubert, Dr., Great Fr. surgeon of N. O., v.28, p.330-331; honored by Fr. gov't for services rendered Fr. sailors, v.28, p.333.

Jourdan, Noel, candidate for St. Louis Church Warden, v.31, p.913.

"Journalism in New Orleans between 1880 and 1900" by John S. Kendall, v.8, p.557.

"Journal of James Leander Cathcart," v.28, p.735-921.

"Journal of the Comm. of the Convention of Fla.," v.21, p.95-97.

"Journal of W. Fla. Convention," v.21, p.686-755.

Juando, Christobal, noted, v.24, p.366.

"Judah Philip Benjamin," by Louis Gruss, v.19, p.964-1068.

"Judah P. Benjamin: Confed. Statesman," by Robert Douthat Meade, rev'd, v.26, p.1170-1171.

"Judicial Auction Sale in Louisiana, 1739," by Henry P. Dart, v.8, p.382.

Judiciary, of Sp. La., v.22, p.698-700; reform in La., and the Const. Con. of 1844, v.25, p.1028-1033; in the legislative session, 1846, v.25, p.1044-1052.

Jumel, Allen, candidate for state treasurer, v.31, p.535.

Jumel, Allen, Jr., physician replacing Chalaron, v.26, p.824, 835.

Junta de Estados, origin of, v.21, p.7.

"Jurisdiction of Settlement of Neustra Senora Del Pilar de Nacagdoches. House Located East side of Sabine River, Year 1805," v.28, p.1105-1109.

"Jurisdiction of the Consuls, Tribunals of Criminal Jurisdiction in Ancient Rome," by Charles Gayarre, v.33, p.209-210.

"Jurisdiction of the Dictator, Tribunals of Criminal Jurisdiction in Ancient Rome," by Charles Gayarre, v.33, p.211.

"Jurisdiction of the Senate, Tribunals of Criminal Jurisdiction in Ancient Rome," by Charles Gayarre, v.33, p.210.

"Jurisdictions, Special, Tribunals of Criminal Jurisdictions in Ancient Rome," by Charles Gayarre, v.33, p.217.

Jurisprudence in La., v.19, p.57-63.

"Jurisprudence of the Supreme Court of Louisiana," Chas. Payne Fenner, v.4, p.71.

Jusan, Gabriel, noted, v.21, p.1008.

KAISER, SARAH MARIA, MARRIES H. A. Bullard, v.23, p.1003.

Kane, Harnett T., "The Bayous of La.," rev'd, v.28, p.349-351; "Deep Delta Country," rev'd, v.28, p.990-92; "Plantation Parade: The Grand Manner in Louisiana," rev'd, v.29, p.203-207.

Kane, T. H., noted, v.25, p.807.

Kanki, Pazos, noted, v.24, p.645.

Karlin, J. Alexander, "New Orleans Lynchings of 1891 and the American Press," v.24, p.187-203.

Karl, Landgrave, of Hessen, v.24, p.418, 419.

Kathman, J. C., named in Wickliffe impeachment, v.31, p.692.

Kautz, Albert, noted, v.24, p.459.

Keachie, noted, v.24, p.87.

Keaton, Ilous, recalls early Bogalusa days, v.29, p.93.

Keaton, Mrs. Dollie, early Bogalusa settler, v.29, p.88n., 92n.

Keaton, Mrs. R. E., early Bogalusa settler, v.29, p.88-89.

Keaton, R. E., trustee of 1st Bogalusa school, v.29, p.100.

Keep's Cavalry Co., noted, v.25, p.212.

Keith contributions, noted, v.25, p.795.

Keller, Fidel, noted, v.24, p.490.

Keller, Mathias, opera collection in L.S.U. Music School Library, v.24, p.348.

Keller, Miss Melba, queen of rice festival, 1940, v.27, p.1212.

Kellogg, William Pitt, noted, v.23, p.1137; collector of customs, v.23, p.1224, 1226; noted, v.24, p.115; papers in L.S.U. Archives, v.24, p.343; nominated by Radical Repub. for gov., 1872, v.27, p.553, 554; gubernatorial race, v.27, p.563; appeal to att'y-gen'l of U. S., v.27, p.565, 572, 575; inauguration of, v.27, p.576; noted, v.27, p.579, 580, 584, 588; faction of, elected Pinchback senator, v.27, p.589; visit to mid-western states, v.27, p.591, 593, 594, 596, 599, 778, 787; failed to sign Acts No. 9 and 10, v.27, p.981; headed lottery Repub., v.27, p.1092; and the La. Levee Co., v.28, p.309; and election of 1872, v.28, p.1134ff.; birth, ancestry, education and early life, v.29, p.394-395; enters politics and becomes Chief Justice of Nebraska Territory, v.29, p.395; appointed Collector of Port at N. O., v.29, p.396; rise to power in La., v.29, p.393-399; nominated custom house Republican candidate for Gov., v.29, p.400-401, 403; many oppose nomination, v.29, p.402, 404-405; Kellogg's supporters uphold him, v.29, p.405-406; campaign tour, v.29, p.406-408; controversy over election returns, v.29, p.409-

412; dual government for La., v.29, p.411, 415; both parties struggle for control, v.29, p.412-413; two governors inaugurated, v.29, p.414-415; rival governments struggle for control, v.29, p.417-418; race riot at Colfax, v.29, p.419-420; attempted assassination of, v.29, p.421-422; Grant publicly recognizes Kellogg regime, v.29, p.424-425; goes to Alabama, v.29, p.426-427; addresses State Colored Men's Convention, v.29, p.427; proposes law dealing with registration and elections, v.29, p.428; deals with Coushatta riot, v.29, p.431; appeals for Federal troops in La., v.29, p.431-432; opposition high against him, v.29, p.432-433; overthrow of Kellogg gov't by arms, v.29, p.433-434; restoration of Kellogg gov't by Federal forces, v.29, p.434-436; prepares for Congressional election, v.29, p.436-439; his account of occupation of State House by U. S. forces, v.29, p.442-444; Congress takes definite action recognizing Kellogg gov't, v.29, p.446; calls extra session of Legislature and presents objects, v.29, p.446-448; visit North to create confidence in La. among Northerners, v.29, p.449-450; impeached, tried and reinstated, v.29, p.452-460; financial history during administration, v.29, p.460-473; efforts to improve N. O., v.29, p.473-477; internal improvement efforts, v.29, p.477-480; work on institutions, v.29, p.480-481; educational problems, v.29, p.481-482; pardoning power, v.29, p.482-483; executive patronage, v.29, p.483; problem of registration and election laws, v.29, p.483; absences from La. during governorship, v.29, p.484; judged by traveler to La., v.29, p.485; delegate to Rep. State Conv., v.29, p.485-486; orders state house occupied by armed police, v.29, p.489; introduces next gov. of La. at inaugural ceremony, v.29, p.490; nominated to U. S. Senate, v.29, p.490; seated in Senate, v.29, p.491; retires from political life, v.29, p.492; death, v.29, p.492; bibl., v.29, p.493-495; noted, v.29, p.715, 723, 727, 729, 755, 756, 757, 760; noted, v.31, p.67, 702, 734; candidate for governor, v.31, p.536, 539, 700; and Clinton impeachment, v.31, p.704-705; governor, v.31, p.705; investigation of, v.31, p.708; impeachment, v.31, p.708; dismissed, v.31, p.710-711; articles of impeachment, v.31, p.712-714.

Kelly, Alexander D., noted, v.23, p.204, 212, 226.

Kelly, E. H., noted, v.28, p.471.

Kemp, David, assessor of St. Helena, v.23, p.409.

Kemp, Dempsey, noted, v.23, p.420.

Kemp, Jonathan, member of St. Helena Police Jury, v.23, p.407ff.

Kemp, Thomas, treas. of St. Helena Police Jury, v.23, p.424.

Kemper, Bishop Jackson, visit to New Orleans, v.22, p.463, 471.

Kemper, Nathan, and W. Fla. Rev., v.21, p.81ff.

Kemper, Reuben, W. Fla. Rev., v.21, p.80ff., 747n., 795-96; letter to Rhea, v.21, p.90-93, 101-107, 113-114, 153, 155-156; letter to Perez, v.21, p.100; letter to J. P. Kennedy, v.21, p.101; letter from Stirling Dupree, v.21, p.109-110, 118; letter to Dupree, v.21, p.110-112, 119; letter to John H. Gray, v.21, p.112, letter to Alex McMullen, v.21, p.116-117; letter from John H. Gray, v.21, p.118; collector of claims in W. Fla., v.25, p.944-970.

Kemper, Samuel, and W. Fla. Rev., v.21, p.81ff.; noted, v.25, p.295, 298.

Kendall, Amos, supports southern telegraph, v.31, p.428-429; forms company, v.31, p.430; noted, v.31, p.435; relation with O'Reilly, v.31, p..455-457; applies for injunction, v.31, p.458.

"Kendall, George Wilkins, and the Founding of the New Orleans Picayune," by John S. Kendall, v.11, p.261; noted, v.23, p.216; v.24, p.35; letter to, v.24, p.37.

Kendall, John Irwin, son of Mary Irwin Kendall, sketch of, v.29, p.293, 1042-1043; joins Jeff Davis Cadets, v.29, p.1047; leaves cadets and joins 4th La. Reg't, v.29, p.1048; assigned as pv't in Delta Rifles of the 4th La. Reg't, v.29, p.1052; life and fighting in the 4th La. Reg't, v.29, p.1052-1088, 1089-1097, 1108, 1109-1124, 1147, 1149-1155, 1160-1176, 1196-1214; made orderly sg't, v.29, p.1074; appointed 2nd Lt., v.29, p.1090; participates in capture of "Indianola," v.29, p.1098-1107; captured and held prisoner in N. O., v.29, p.1132-1133; events in prison and escape, v.29, p.1133-1137; events during return to Confederate lines, v.29, p.1137-1142;

visits father in Ocean Springs, v.29, p.1142-1143; rejoins reg't at Mobile, v.29, p.1147; detached from reg't and placed on Gen'l Cantey's staff, v.29, p.1168; work on Canety's staff, v.29, p.1181-1189; captured, v.29, p.1212-1214; prison life, v.29, p.1214-1224; released and returns to civilian life, v.29, p.1224; short sketch of army data and order of promotion, v.29, p.1224-1225.

Kendall, John Smith, "The Municipal Elections of 1858," v.5, p.357; "Correspondence of Andrew Jackson with James W. Breedlove," v.6, p.179; "Louisiana Troops at Occupation of Havana," v.7, p.40; "Diary of Surgeon J. M. Craig, The, 4th La. Regt., C.S.A., 1864-65," v.8, p.53; "Journalism in New Orleans Between 1880 and 1900," v.8, p.557; "Piracy in the Gulf of Mexico, 1816-1823," v.8, p.341; Review of Prof. Louis Martin Sears' "John Slidell," v.9, p.598; "Early New Orleans Newspapers," v.10, p.383; "George Wilkins Kendall and the Founding of the New Orleans Picayune," v.11, p.261; "The Foreign Language Press of New Orleans," v.22, p.363; "Irwin Russell in New Orleans," v.14, p.321; "The Last Days of Charles Gayarre," v.15, p.359; "Documents Concerning West Florida Revolution, 1810," I, II, III, v.17, p.80, 306, 474; "Old New Orleans Houses," v.17, p.680; "Some Distinguished Hispano-Orleanians," v.18, p.40-55; "A New Orleans Lady of Letters," v.19, p.436-465; "The Pontalba Buildings," v.19, p.119-149; "The Strange Case of Myra Clark Gaines," v.20, p.5-42; "Old N. O. Houses and Some of the People Who Live in Them," v.20, p.794-820; "Paul Tulane," v.20, p.1016-1066; "The World's Delight: The Story of Adah Isaacs Menken," v.21, p.846-868; "Shadow Over the City," v.22, p.142-165; "Who Killa de Chief?", v.22, p.492-530; "Blood on the Banquette," v.22, p.819-856; "According to the Code," v.23, p.141-161; "The Humors of the Duello," v.23, p.445-470; "New Orleans' 'Peculiar Institution,'" v.23, p.864-886; "Christ Church and Gen. Butler," v.23, p.1241-1257; "The Huntsmen of Black Ivory," v.24, p.9-34; "Historical Collections in New Orleans," cited, v.24, p.312, 317, 320, 331, 351; "The Successors of Lafitte," v.24, p.360-77; "Pistols for Two, Coffee for One," v.24, p.756-782; "N. O.'s Miser Philanthropist: John McDonogh," v.26, p.138-161; "World's Delight" quoted on Adah Isaacs Menken's parentage, v.26, p.162; "Sarah Bernhardt in N. O.," v.26, p.770-782; "Joseph Jefferson in N. O.," v.26, p.1150-1167; "The Am. Siddons," v.28, p.922-940; "Old-Time N. O. Police Reporters and Reporting," v.29, p.43-58; "Chronicles of a Southern Family," v.29, p.277-295; "New Orleans Newspapermen of Yesterday," v.29, p.771-790; "Recollections of a Confederate Officer," v.29, p.1041-1228; "New Orleans Musicians of Long Ago," v.31, p.130-149; "The Friend of Chopin and Some Other New Orleans Musical Celebrities," v.31, p.856-876; "Old Days on the New Orleans Picayune," v.33, p.317; "Old Days on the Times-Democrat," v.33, p.406.

Kendall, Lane C., "John McDonogh, Slave Owner," I, v.15, p.645; II, v.16, p.125; "Interregnum in Louisiana in 1861, The," I, II, III, v.16, p.175, 374, 639; IV, V, VI, v.17, p.124, 339, 524.

Kendall, Mary P. Irwin, daughter of Martha Mitchell Irwin, v.29, p.292; marriage to W. G. Kendall, children of, v.29, p.292-293.

Kendall, Miss Julia, noted, v.25, p.784.

Kendall, N. J., noted, v.23, p.1257.

"Kendall of the Picayune: Being His Adventures in N. O. on the Texan Santa Fe Expedition, in the Mexican War, and in the Colonization of the Texas Frontier," by Fayette Copeland, rev'd, v.26, p.1168-70.

Kendall, Wm. Gray, father of John Irwin Kendall, v.29, p.1042, 1043, 1046.

Kendall, Wm. Gray, Jr., noted, v.29, p.1043.

Kennard, J. H., suit of P. H. Morgan against, for office of Associate Justice, v.27, p.577-578.

Kennedy, Dr. Hugh, early N. O. newspaperman, v.29, p.773; sketch, v.29, p.774-775.

Kennedy, Hugh, New Orleans mayor, reform, v.31, p.1028-1035; at odds with Canby, v.31, p.1072; noted, v.31, p.1102.

Kennedy, J. M., against lottery bill, 1890, v.27, p.1034, 1040.

Kennedy, Joseph C. G., and the 7th Census, v.22, p.479ff.

Kennedy, Joseph Pulaski, letter to convention of State of W. Fla., v.21, p.98-99; mentioned, v.21, p.103-104, 122n.; letter to Kemper, v.21, p.117; letter from Robert Caller, Jr., v.21, p.117-118; and Mobile Soc., v.21, p.153n.; and W. Fla. Rev., v.21, p.799n.

Kenner and Henderson, noted, v.22, p.151.

Kenner, Duncan F., noted, v.23, p.1080; v.24, p.98-99; on tariff, v.25, p.136; head of Public Education Committee, v.25, p.675; and the Const. Com. of 1844, v.25, p.1007ff.; noted, v.25, p.1053, 1083; vice-pres. Bar Association, v.25, p.1086; Whig Candidates for Senate, 1848, v.25, p.1095-1104; debate with Soule, v.25, p.1108; Cand. for U. S. Sen., v.26, p.978; La. delegate to Conv. of seceding states, v.26, p.1002; noted, v.31, p.988, 1000; Wells investigation, v.31, p.1107.

Kenner estate, noted, v.24, p.1161.

Kenner, La., brief sketch, v.28, p.756n.

Kenner, Louis M., returning board, v.31, p.1093; indicted, v.31, p.1108.

Kenner, Mrs. Butler, noted, v.24, p.519.

Kenner, William, noted, v.22, p.439, 440, 449; v.24, p.975, 988, 994.

Kent, Chancellor John, noted, v.24, p.699.

Kenton, Simeon, noted, v.24, p.927.

Kentucky and Spain, v.22, p.817.

Kentucky Resolutions, noted, v.24, p.698.

Ker, Dr. David C., noted, v.26, p.51, 95.

Ker, Dr. J. H., noted, v.26, p.76.

Ker, Dr. John J., letter to Bee, v.26, p.69-70.

Ker, Dr. O. C., noted, v.26, p.76.

Ker, Rose Routh, wife of M. J. Foster, v.28, p.1132.

"Kerlerec, Installation of De, as Governor of Louisiana," Introduction by Henry P. Dart, translated by Heloise H. Cruzat, v.14, p.235.

Kerlerec, Louis Billouart, Chevalier de, and Paul Rocheblave, v.18, p.337-343; documents in Bibliotheca Parsoniana, v.24, p.311; Gov. of La., v.26, p.704, 705; dispatch to concerning trade with Sp., v.26, p.705-706; correspondence with Sp. Viceroy, v.26, p.706-707, 712; restored fortifications at Natchez, v.26, p.730; succeeded Vaudreuil, v.26, p.736; became Gov. and writes Minister concerning enlargement of Hospital, v.29, p.612; quarrel with Ordonnateur over building ends in recall, v.29, p.613-614.

Kerner, Justinus, noted, v.24, p.383.

Kernion, George C. H., "Reminiscences of Chevallier Bernard de Verges," v.7, p.56; "Jacques de la Chaise," v.7, p.447; Tr. by, "Documents Concerning the History of the Indians of the Eastern Region of Louisiana" by Baron Marc de Villiers, v.8, p.28; "The Chevalier de Pradel," v.12, p.238.

Kernion, Jean Francois Huchet de, app't to Superior Council of La., 1762, v.21, p.669.

Kernochan, H. P., noted, v.22, p.218; cand. for auditor second Populist ticket, 1896, v.26, p.1102; cand. auditor, 1896, v.28, p.1177.

Kerr, C. M., Highway Progress in La., v.2, p.56.

Kerrish, W. T. J., Confed. naval engineer from La., v.27, p.485.

Kerr, J. W., "Memorial of John Perkins, 1868," ed. by P. L. Rainwater, v.20, p.965-989.

Key, D. N., Postmaster Gen'l, declared Lottery Co. fraudulent, v.27, p.1003; forbade payment of money orders or delivery of registered letters to Dauphin, v.27, p.1007; sued by Dauphin, v.27, p.1007-1008.

Kidd, Captain, noted, v.24, p.9.

Kidd, E. E., chairman of Com. to investigate state debt, v.27, p.786; submits bill calling for const. conv., v.27, p.989; address to Prog. League, v.27, p.1063.

Kierns, C. A., patented process for making paper from rice straw, v.27, p.1168.

Kilbourne, Annie Sanderson, "War Times in and Around Clinton, Louisiana," v.13, p.64.

Kilbourne, Chas., opposed lotteries, v.27, p.1040.

Killion, Joseph, noted, v.23, p.420.

Kimball, Frederick, and W. Fla. Rev., v.21, p.740n.

Kinchen, William, assessor of St. Helena, v.23, p.409, 425.

Kindrick, Charles, newspaperman, "Old Days on the N. O. Picayune," v.33, p.331.

King, Fred, Anti-Lottery League Ex. Com., v.27, p.1056.

King, George R., Justice of La. Supreme Court, v.25, p.1050, 1086; app'td to Ct. of Errors and Appeals, v.28, p.957.

King, Grace, "Notes on the Life and Service of Bienville," v.1, sec.3, p.39; "Abstracts by William Price of State Papers Preserved in the Louisiana Historical Society with Notes," v.1, sec.1, p.10; tr. of "Address of Celebration of the Founding of New Orleans," by Charles Barrett, v.2, p.258; "Creole Families of New Orleans, Notes on Her Book," v.3, p.612; "Selections from Her Scrap Book: Interesting Fossils of Louisiana," v.4, p.130; "Old St. Louis Hotel," v.4, p.128; "Last Captured Slaves," v.4, p.132; "Ye Olden Tyme," v.4, p.125; "Baron Marc de Villiers du Terrage," v.5, p.287; "Commerce of Louisiana During the French Regime, 1699-1763," Critique on, by N. M. Miller Surrey, Ph. D., Columbia University, v.5, p.19; Minutes of Meetings, 1920-1921 (Recording Secretary), v.5, p.208; Beer, William (List of Writings of Grace King), v.6, p.378; Cocks, Reginald S., "The Fiction of Grace King," v.6, p.353; Dart, Henry P., "Miss King's Historical Works," v.6, p.347; "Dorothy Dix Talks on Grace King," v.6, p.359; Guvol, Louise Hubert, "A Southern Author in Her New Orleans Home," v.6, p.365; Hart, W. O., "Presentation of Loving Cup," v.6, p.363; Illustration (Portrait), v.6, p.344; Louisiana Historical Quarterly Tribute to Grace King, v.6, p.345; Pope, Katherine, "The Distinction of Grace King," v.6, p.374; Rowland's "Varina Howell, wife of Jefferson Davis" (Book Review), v.11, p.466; Death of Grace King: Ideals of Grace King, v.15, p.339; Memorial Services of Le Petit Salon, v.15, p.330; Memorial Services Louisiana Historical Society, v.15, p.338; "Memories of a Southern Woman of Letters" (Book Review by Henry P. Dart), v.16, p.164; "A Bio-Bibliography of Grace Elizabeth King," by Bess Vaughan, v.17, p.751; family and early life in N. O., v.19, p.439-446; friendship with Charles D. Warner, v.19, p.450-451; literary work, v.19, p.453-459; work on La. sources cited, v.24, p.317, 320, 351; papers in Howard-Tilton Memorial Library, v.24, p.329; noted, v.24, p.531; "Charles Gayarre, A Biographical Sketch," v.33, p.159-188.

King, John, noted, v.24, p.1097.

King, John Haskell, noted, v.23, p.1171.

"King, Judge Frederick D.," by Henry Renshaw, W. O. Hart, F. A. Monroe, Edw. A. Parsons, E. K. Skinner and John St. Paul, v.6, p.194.

King, Miss Annie R., Translation from the original by, "An Original Autograph of Henry De Tonty," v.6, p.576.

King, Richard, Claimant of Maison Rouge Grant, v.20, p.353ff.

King, Rufus, noted, v.24, p.962, 1005.

King, secret agent of Claiborne in Baton Rouge, v.21, p.163.

King's Hospital, noted, v.31, p.11, 12, 13.

Kingston, Stephen, claim on French government, v.24, p.1017.

Kinkel, Gottfried, visit to N. O., v.20, p.143, 145.

"Kinno," federal boat, v.29, p.1108.

Kinsman, Lieutenant, noted, v.24, p.315.

Kipp & Rausch, rice firm, v.23, p.555.

Kirkland, W. A., Confed. sold., v.26, p.950.

Kirkland, William, and W. Fla. Rev., v.21, p.108, 120n., 721; mentioned, v.21, p.138.

"Kitchen Middens," shell formation giving evidence of prehistoric Indians in B. R. area, v.28, p.25.

Kittredge, Dr., noted, v.26, p.76.

Kitzinger, Fred, N. O. musician, v.31, p.143.

Klaw and Erlanger "syndicate" fight against its dictatorship, v.26, p.781.

Klaw, Mark, in partnership with Erlanger and Charles Jefferson in management of St. Charles Theatre, v.26, p.1155.

Kleinhagen, Rev. Henry, noted, v.24, p.142, 144.

Kleinpeter, John B., candidate for Lt.-gov. second Populist ticket, 1896, v.26, p.1102; auditor, v.28, p.1176; cand. Lt.-gov., v.28, p.1177, 1181.

Kleinpeter, J. P., candidate for auditor 1st Populist ticket, 1896, v.26, p.1101.

Kleinpeter, Josiah, Farmers' Alliance leader, v.26, p.1070.

Klock, Remy, "Regular" cand. for Supt. of Ed., v.26, p.1081.

Kneeland, Ira, and W. Fla. Rev., v.21, p.84; mentioned, v.21, p.106; identified, v.21, p.737.

Kniffen, Dr. Fred B., in re "kitchen middens," v.28, p.25; co-ed; "Southern Ala. in 1818: The Journal of James Leander Cathcart," v.28, p.735-921.

"Knighthood Was in Flower, When," by Heloise Hulse Cruzat, v.1, p.367.

Knight, Mrs. Edward, and N. O. theatre, v.21, p.498.

Knoblock, Clay, chairman McEnery State Nom. Conv., v.28, p.1158.

Know-Nothings, and Judah P. Benjamin, v.19, p.993-996; in San Antonio, 1855, v.23, p.1158; Party noted, v.25, p.679, p.686; the campaign of 1855, v.25, p.680-

682; decline of, v.25, p.682-683.
Knox, Mrs. James, noted, v.29, p.1229.
Koch, Christian D., and family collection in L.S.U. Archives, v.24, p.343.
Kohlman, Samuel J., Dem. Populist elector, v.26, p.1116.
Kohn, Samuel, land titles in Carrollton, v.21, p.228; history of Carrollton, v.22, p.190.
Kolling, Fritz, noted, v.24, p.134.
Konigshofen, noted, v.24, p.415.
Konrad, William Robinson, "The Diminishing Influences of German Culture in New Orleans Life Since 1865," v.24, p.127-167.
Kostheim, noted, v.24, p.381.
Koune, Jean-Pierre, noted, v.22, p.106, 111, 117, 121.
Kramer, Wilbur, supt., v.25, p.805.
Kremer, George, controversy with Clay, v.24, p.1063.
Krouse, F. O., picture of Germantown cabin of, v.24, p.428; noted, v.24, p.432, 433.
Krudener, Count, minister from Russia to the U. S., v.24, p.1034, 1057, 1067, 1072.
Kruttschnitt, E. B., treasurer, Dem. Anti-Lottery St. Ex. Com., v.27, p.1059, 1091, 1093.
Ku Klux Klan, supported by Germans, v.23, p.505.
Kummel, Charles, noted, v.23, p.521.
Kuss, Rev. E. W., cited, v.24, p.145.

LABADIEVILLE, NOTED, v.24, p.71.
Labatut, Dr. I., charter member Med. Soc., v.26, p.59; on Med. board of Censors, v.26, p.76, 82.
Labatut, Isadore, noted, v.23, p.226.
Labatut, Jean-Batiste, letter to Casa Calvo, v.22, p.129.
Labatut, J. B., on Charity Hosp. Board, 1836, v.26, p.58; noted, v.26, p.75.
"LaBelle," steamer, picture of, v.25, p.468.
Labor, artisans as colonists, 1795, v.21, p.62; strike of 1892 in N. O., v.21, p.547-560; apprentice system, v.22, p.685; white, in W. Fla., 1769, v.23, p.383; slave, in rice fields of S. C., v.23, p.546; on Randolph plantation, v.25, p.176-182, 183, 184.
Laborde, J. J., noted, v.22, p.1154.
Laborde, J. M., noted, v.22, p.1108.
Labourette, ———, noted, v.24, p.756, 757.
LaBranche, Alcee, description of, v.24, p.764-765; engagement with John R. Grymes, v.24, p.765; duel with Hueston, v.24, p.764, 766-767; noted, v.25, p.124, 125, 131, 134.
LaBranche, Alexander, noted, v.23, p.721; v.24, p.764.
Labuzan, Chas. A., Grand Marshal of funeral procession in N. O. honoring Clay, Webster and Calhoun, v.27, p.767.
"La Caridad," Spanish merchant vessel, v.24, p.366-367.

Lacaze (alias Bernardo Ferrero), noted, v.24, p.645, 676.
LaCaze, Pierre, vice consul of Fr., 1914, efforts in locating and rebuilding monument to Fr. sailors, v.28, p.336-337, 340ff.
Lacey, James E., lumberman, v.29, p.91.
Lacey, J. D., v.29, p.92.
La Chaise, Auguste, agent of Genet in La., v.28, p.704.
Lachine, monument to LaSalle, v.22, p.5-17.
Lacoste, clerk of the senate, v.25, p.1039.
Lacoste, Mrs. A. S., noted, v.24, p.147.
Lacoste, Pierre, noted, v.22, p.815.
Lacroix, Irenee Amelot de, the revolutionist, v.25, p.657; his arrest, v.25, p.658; Robinson's suspicious of, v.25, p.662.
LaCroix, Jacques, noted, v.24, p.366.
"Ladies', The, Farewell to Brutal Ferocity Butler," quoted, v.24, p.529.
Lafargue, A. D., anti-lotteryite cand. for Supt. of Ed., v.26, p.1081; Anti-lottery cand. for supt. of Ed., v.27, p.1090; nominated Foster as anti-lotteryite cand. for gov., v.27, p.1090; member Farmers' Alliance Com., v.28, p.1152; cand. supt. of ed., v.28, p.1158.
Lafargue, Andre, Acceptance Address, on Presentation and Acceptance of Statuette of Joan of Arc, v.1, p.279; Address in Paris, at Bi-Centennial Celebration

of Founding of New Orleans, v.1, sec.3, p.24; Address at Raising the American Flag in Jackson Square, New Orleans, Jan. 8, 1918, v.1, sec.3, p.212; The New Orleans French Opera House, v.3, p.368; The Foundation of Biloxi, v.3, p.617; Address to Commander and Officers of "Jeanne d'Arc," v.3, p.120; Biloxi Bi-Centennial, v.4, p.459; The New Orleans Bi-Centennial Medallion, v.7, p.87; Bienville, A Genealogical Sketch, v.8, p.252; A Reign of Twenty Days, v.8, p.398; Manuscript of General Richard Taylor's "Destruction and Reconstruction," v.13, p.46; "La Salle Takes Possession of Louisiana," by Baron Marc de Villiers du Terrage, translation by, v.14, p.301; La Salle's House at Lachine, Province of Quebec, v.14, p.315; Address in memory of Henry Plauche Dart, v.18, p.247-249; In Memoriam, Baron Marc de Villiers du Terrage, v.19, p.1069-1074; Pierre Clement de Laussat, Colonial Prefect and High Commissioner of France in La.: His Memoirs, proclamations and orders, v.20, p.159-182; A Man of God and a servant of Humanity: The Rev. Marie Arthur Guillaume le Mercier du Quesnay, v.20, p.680-689; "The Robert Cavelier de la Salle Monument at Lachine, Canada," v.22, p.5-17; "The La. Purchase: The French Viewpoint," v.23, p.107-117; Pierre Clement de Laussat: An Intimate Portrait, v.24, p.5-8; rev's "Historie de la Louisiane Francaise, 1673-1939," by Emile Lauvriere, v.24, p.207-210; Louisiana Linguistic and Folklore Backgrounds, v.24, p.744-755; The Little Obelisk in the Cathedral Sq. in N. O., v.28, p.326-348; rev's Kane's "The Bayous of La.," v.28, p.349-351; rev's Hubert-Robert's, "L'Histoire Merveilleuse de la Louisiane Francais," v.28, p.351-354; rev's Kane's "Deep Delta Country," v.28, p.990-992; rev's Robert's, "Royal Street: A Novel of N. O.," v.28, p.992-995; Opera in New Orleans in Days of Yore, v.29, p.660-678; rev's Bromfield's, "Wild Is the River," v.29, p.791-793; rev's Robert's, "Brave Mardi Gras: A New Orleans Novel of the '60's," v.29, p.793-796.

Lafargue, J. B., noted, v.25, p.807.

Lafayette: "Celebration by the Louisiana Historical Society of the Centennial Anniversary of the Visit of Lafayette," reported by James A. Renshaw, v.9, p.190; "Dedication of Lafayette Public School in New Orleans," address by James J. A. Fortier, v.9, p.204; "His Visit to New Orleans in 1825," compiled by James A. Renshaw, v.9, p.182.

Lafayette, City of, early history and annexation to N. O., v.20, p.895-964; case, concerning land in, v.23, p.1025-1027; levees of, v.23, p.1036.

"Lafayette Combine," agreement between Anti-Lotteryites and Farmers' Union, v.27, p.1086-1087; fusion of Farmers' Alliance and Anti-Lottery League, v.28, p.1152ff.

"Lafayette, General, "Land Ventures of, in the Territory of Orleans and State of Louisiana," by Kathryn T. Abbey, v.16, p.359; grant of land to, v.23, p.1093, 1094; acts of Congress honor him, v.29, p.296, 297; Nolte's account of reasons for Lafayette's visit, v.29, p.297-299; invited to visit New Orleans, v.29, p.299-300; accepts invitation to N. O., v.29, p.300; city hall made into house for him, v.29, p.301; Triumphal Arch honoring him erected, v.29, p.301-303; tours America, v.29, p.303-307, 310-311; N. O. prepares for his visit, v.29, p.311-313; detailed account of six day visit, v.29, p.313-323; Masonic dinner honors him, v.29, p.321-322; leaves N. O., v.29, p.324-325; Nolte's account of his visit, v.29, p.325-328; dispute between militia and La. Legion, v.29, p.329-330; dispute settled by Lafayette, v.29, p.330-332; legislative and judicial history of land grants allotted Lafayette by Congress, v.29, p.332-335; made citizen of U. S., v.29, p.335-336; leaves Am. for last time, v.29, p.337-338; bibl., v.29, p.339-340; land grants on Lake Lafayette, v.21, p.1140; visit to the U. S., v.24, p.964; return from the U. S., v.24, p.968; withdrawal from politics, v.24, p.988-989, 1005, 1027; in French politics, v.24, p.1036, 1045-1046, 1076; marriage of granddaughters, v.24, p.1044, 1046, 1107; conversation with Brown, v.24, p.1065; noted, v.24, p.1106, 1115; early career, v.31, p.325; land bounty, v.31, p.326-327, 328-329; candidate for governor of Orleans, v.31, p.327-328; refuses nomination, v.31, p.330-331; noted, v.32, p.253-254n.

Lafayette, George Washington, suit over land, v.23, p.1093-1094.

Lafayette, La., description of, v.24, p.41;

noted as Vermillionville, v.24, p.83; collection in Howard-Tilton Memorial Library, v.24, p.330; noted, v.27, p.843; State Farmers' Union meeting in, 1891, v.27, p.1086, 1087, 1120; test case of, involving bonds issued against special tax for municipal improvement, v.27, p.1146, 1153, 1183, 1212, 1218, 1220, 1221.

Lafayette Square, history of, v.22, p.415-416; statues of, v.26, p.138-140.

"Lafayette's Visit to Baton Rouge, April, 1825," translated by R. W. Colomb, v.14, p.178.

"Lafayette's Visit to New Orleans, 1825," by Henry Renshaw, v.1, sec.2, p.5.

Lafayette Theatre, noted, v.26, p.375.

"Lafayette, The Lost City of," by James A. Renshaw, v.2, p.47.

"Lafayette Visits New Orleans," by Francis P. Burns, v.29, p.296-340.

Laffite, Antoine, noted, v.24, p.13, 14.

"Lafitte, A Visit to," contributed by Elliot Snow, v.11, p.434.

Laffite, Eugene, noted, v.23, p.745, 748.

Laffite, Jean, establishment at Galveston, v.20, p.627ff.; expedition against, v.21, p.205; documents of proposals of Geo. Graham, v.21, p.213-219; as Spanish agent, v.21, p.1088ff., 1097-1102; diary of voyage to Galveston, v.21, p.1102-1107; plan to capture corsairs, v.21, p.1107-1109; and Long's expedition, v.22, p.745; and Champ D'Asile, v.22, p.747; and Claiborne, v.22, p.756-758; and Bishop of Chiapa, v.22, p.1064-1066; noted, v.22, p.1026ff., 1068, 1070, 1075, 1077, 1079, 1082, 1088; ancestry and early life, v.23, p.739-741; letter to Madison, v.23, p.752; sketch, v.23, p.753; aids Jackson at New Orleans, v.23, p.753; expedition west of Ark. Post, v.23, p.754-755; Spanish agent, v.23, p.754ff.; boss at Galveston, v.23, p.768; letter to Sedella, v.23, p.769; letters from P. Laffite, v.23, p.773-775, 785-787; and French emigres, v.23, p.778ff.; return to Galveston, v.23, p.780; goes to New Orleans, v.23, p.789; letter from Gen. Long, v.23, p.813; letters to Gen. Long, v.23, p.814-815, 816-817; letter to Capt.-Gen., v.23, p.819-820; moved to Yucatan, v.23, p.825; and piracy, v.24, p.9; description of, v.24, p.13-14; operates blacksmith shop, v.24, p.14; becomes privateer, v.24, p.14-15; conflicts with Claiborne, v.24, p.18-19; expeditions against by the U. S., v.24, p.19-20; and War of 1812, v.24, p.20-22; refuses British bribe, v.24, p.20-21; serves under Jackson, v.24, p.21; pardoned by the U. S., v.24, p.21; returns to privateering, v.24, p.21-22; death of, v.24, p.22; at Galveston, v.24, p.22-24; and smuggling of slaves, v.24, p.22-24; documents in Bibliotheca Parsoniana, v.24, p.311; noted, v.24, p.360-361.

Laffite, Louis, noted, v.23, p.745.

Laffite, Lt. Jacques de L., friend of Wood, and member of Nat'l Guard, v.26, p.792; refused as Col., v.26, p.793; as Commissary Officer, v.26, p.808; noted, v.26, p.811.

Laffite, Marc, noted, v.22, p.1026.

Laffite, Pierre, as Spanish agent, v.21, p.213-219, 1088ff.; noted, v.22, p.1026ff., 1080; won as Spanish agent, v.23, p.739-741; ancestry and early life, v.23, p.744-745; as Baratarian smuggler, v.23, p.746-750; jailed, v.23, p.751; and Battle of New Orleans, v.23, p.753; plans to aid royalist, v.23, p.757, 758, 764, 782-783, 788, 789-792, 802-808; letter to Cienfuegos, v.23, p.765; letters to J. Laffite, v.23, p.773-775, 785-787; captured by U. S., v.23, p.794; meeting with Graham, v.23, p.795-797; trip to Baltimore and Washington, v.23, p.799; letter to Capt.-Gen., v.23, p.819-820; last days in New Orleans, v.23, p.826; description of, v.24, p.13; noted, v.24, p.14, 26; indictment against, v.24, p.17, 18, 19; and smuggling of slaves, v.24, p.23-24; documents in Bibliotheca Parsoniana, v.24, p.311; noted, v.25, p.300.

"Lafitte's Biography, The Controversy on," by Gaspar Cusachs, v.3, p.100.

"Lafitte, The Louisiana Pirate and Patriot," by Gaspar Cusachs, v.2, p.418.

"Lafitte the Pirate," by Lyle Saxon, rev'd by J. Fair Hardin, v.14, p.441.

Lafon, Bartholome, engineer at Galveston, v.21, p.1095; civil engineer and smuggler, v.22, p.1017ff., 1066; sketch, v.22, p.1068-1070; architect and pirate, v.23, p.768, 773, 776; noted, v.28, p.760n.

Lafon, Bernard, privateersman, v.22, p.1017ff.

Lafon Map, of La., 1806, v.25, p.628.

Lafon, Thomy, Negro philanthropist, v.21, p.1080; free negro, v.25, p.319, 364, 732.

Lafosse, Santiago, noted, v.24, p.371.

"Lafourche Lottery," river improvement lottery, v.31, p.717.

Lafourche Parish, rice crop of, v.23, p.554; sugar region, v.25, p.54-55; Houma Indians in, v.28, p.57; natural resources, v.28, p.321-322.

La France, Marie, noted, v.24, p.357.

Laftman, R. H., begins papermaking in Bogalusa, v.29, p.128.

Lagautray, ———, noted, v.23, p.379.

La Harpe, Benard de, explorer in La. for gold, v.26, p.655-660; noted, v.26, p.665; at the Ark. Post, v.26, p.668, 669; his journey to make friends with the Indians, v.26, p.689; noted, v.26, p.693; recommended strong reinforcements to Ark. Post, v.26, p.720.

Laimengre, Teresa, noted, v.23, p.767.

Lakanal, Joseph, manuscripts in Howard-Tilton Memorial Library, v.24, p.329; birth, v.31, p.553; education and profession, v.31, p.553; member of French Convention, v.31, p.553; Committee of Public Instruction, v.31, p.554; educational system, v.31, p.554; Council of Five Hundred, v.31, p.554-555; jobs after 1797, v.31, p.555; flight to America, v.31, p.555; accepts presidency of College of Orleans, v.31, p.556; settles in Mobile, v.31, p.556; returns to France, v.31, p.557; death, v.31, p.557; praetor, v.31, p.850; College d'Orleans, v.31, p.853.

"Lakanal the Regicide: A Biographical and Historical Study of the Career of Joseph Lakanal," by Charles Dawson, reviewed by Walter Prichard, v.31, p.553-557.

Lake Bistineau, noted, v.24, p.432; v.25, p.400.

Lake Borgne, v.28, p.825, 846, 883.

Lake Charles, La., noted, v.24, p.423, 432; political riot, v.27, p.842, 843, 1120, 1130, 1145, 1163; rice mill, v.27, p.1167, 1183, 1193; alkali works in, v.27, p.1170, 1175, 1200, 1203, 1218; noted, v.32, p.575-584.

Lake Chetimaches, v.28, p.835ff., 889; See also Grand Lake.

Lake Chico, v.28, p.837ff.

Lake Izabal, noted, v.24, p.664.

Lake Kernan, v.28, p.12, 35, 36, 38, 67; old Indian Village located near, v.28, p.42.

Lake Lafayette, located, v.21, p.1140.

Lake Maurepas, noted, v.26, p.5-11passim, 665; v.28, p.740, 825, 846, 883.

Lake Natchez, noted, v.25, p.205.

"Lake of the Taensa, The," by John C. Parish (Reprinted from "The Palimpsest," March, 1922), v.5, p.201.

Lake Palourde, Cathcart's survey, v.28, p.761, 785ff.

Lake Platt, Cathcart's survey, v.28, p.785ff.

Lake Pontchartrain, noted, v.25, p.14; v.26, p.5, 7, 665, 747; v.28, p.33, 740, 825, 846, 883; letters in re timber on, v.28, p.917-21.

Lake Providence, La., in 1860, v.21, p.1212; noted, v.23, p.1140; v.25, p.184, 924.

Lake Verrett, v.28, p.754, 755, 787, 789, 796.

La Lande, app't to Superior Court of La., 1762, v.21, p.669.

Lallemand, General Charles-Francois-Antoine, leader of French refugee settlement on Trinity River, v.20, p.619ff.; and Laffite, v.21, p.215, 219; and Champ D'Asile, v.22, p.747-749; French emigre, v.23, p.778ff.; leader of French raiders in Texas, v.24, p.649, 656, 674.

Lallemand, Henri, colony in Texas, v.23, p.778ff.

L'Alouette, ———, noted, v.23, p.146; duels of, v.23, p.445-446, 461-462.

La Maison, Capt. Pierre, noted, v.22, p.1037, 1054, 1085-1088; privateer, v.23, p.123, 789, 794, 810, 811.

Lamana, Peter, and Mafia, v.22, p.826ff.

Lamana, Walter, and Mafia, v.22, p.826ff.

Lamar, L. Q. C., Congressman from Miss., v.29, p.733.

Lambert, Dr. P. A., Charter member Med. Soc., v.26, p.59; and leg. acts 1804-1824 regulating doctors, apothecaries, lawyers, v.26, p.917-920; foods, v.26, p.921; gambling, v.26, p.924-925; slaves and Indians, v.26, p.926-927; protection of inventors, v.26, p.935-936.

Lamberton, P. M., promotion of, v.26, p.836.

Lambremont, Paul M., lt.-gov., v.28, p.1222.

Lambre, Remigio, noted, v.22, p.73n., 77n.

"L'Ami des Lois," and Sp. Am. revolts, v.22, p.783.

Lamm, Emile, noted, v.22, p.196.

Lamothe, Capt. Louis, his first company sworn in, v.26, p.803; resigned, v.26, p.835.

Lampton Literary and Industrial College, Negro institution, v.25, p.789.

La Nana, Sp. post, v.28, p.1029, 1030, 1033, 1034, 1051, 1060; land grant of Barr and Davenport, v.28, p.1089, 1090.

Land Claims, in W. Fla., v.21, p.199-200.

Landers, Colonel H. L., "Wet Sand and Cotton—Banks' Red River Campaign," v.19, p.150-195.

Land Grants, v.11, p.87, 209, 463, 553; in Ouachita, v.20, p.289-462; in and around N. O., v.20, p.902-904; speculation in, v.21, p.166-167; in Carrollton, v.21, p.222ff.; in W. Fla., v.22, p.26, 32ff., 380; fraudulent sale of, in W. Fla., v.22, p.1003ff.; policy of W. Fla., 1769, v.23, p.361ff.; for educational uses, v.23, p.1004-1006.

Landreaux, Dr. J. U., Charter member Med. Soc., v.26, p.59; noted, v.26, p.76.

Landreth, John, surveyor of La. and Ala. timber for naval purposes, v.28, p.736; salary, v.28, p.738; sketch of survey, v.28, p.738ff.; Cathcart's letter of instruction to, v.28, p.894-895; correspondence with Cathcart concerning planned survey of Mermentau, v.28, p.899-902; noted, v.28, p.771, 772, 825, 830, 835, 850, 866, 867, 868, 910.

Landrum, William J., noted, v.24, p.89.

Landry, Aristide, nomination of, v.23, p.1080.

Landry, E. A., cand. for Sen., 1879, v.28, p.1139.

Landry, Louis, inspector of Bayou Plaquemine palisade, v.25, p.937-938.

Landry, Severin, and family, collection in L.S.U. Archives, v.24, p.343.

Landry, Thomas R., "The Political Career of Robert Charles Wickliffe, Gov. of La., 1856-1860," v.25, p.670-727.

Landry, Trasimond, cand. for Lt.-Gov., 1846, v.25, p.1037; elected, v.25, p.1038; noted, v.25, p.1075; and the senatorial election of 1848, v.25, p.1095; nom. for Lt.-Gov., v.28, p.959, 960; inauguration, v.28, p.963.

Lane, Joseph, noted, v.24, p.59.

Lane, Ricardo, mentioned, v.21, p.31.

Lanfear, Ambrose, noted, v.23, p..1245.

Lange & Legendre, rice firm, v.23, p.555.

L'Ange, Joseph, noted, v.24, p.672.

Langlois, Francois, noted, v.22, p.89.

Langloisiere, Suzanne Piot de, case against Pasquier, v.21, p.1006, 1013-1020.

Langres, Father Bruno de, first New Orleans Capuchin superior, v.31, p.899, 900.

Lanier, J. S., v.27, p.1050; chairman St. Central Com., v.27, p.1088, 1089, 1090; chairman State Central Com., 1891, v.28, p.1153, 1154; noted, v.28, p.1175.

Lanman, Charles, author on Louisiana, v.31, p.398, 409, 417, 419.

Lansing, John, instructed Edward Livingston in Law, v.24, p.699.

Lanusse, Arnaud, Negro philanthropist, v.25, p.734, 790.

Lanusse, Charles Barthelemy, land titles of, v.21, p.228.

Lanusse, Paul, mentioned, v.21, p.227; letters to Casa Calvo, v.22, p.125, 128, 129, 140-141; letter from Casa Calvo, v.22, p.140-141.

Lanux, G. A., noted, v.23, p.557.

Lapeyre, J. M., noted, v.23, p.204.

Laporte, Antoine, noted, v.22, p.756.

Laporte, J. B., noted, v.23, p.776.

Lapouse, ———, duel with Bermudez, v.23, p.449-451.

Lara, Jose Bernardo Gutierrez de, activities in N. O., v.21, p.206.

Lara, Manuel Diaz de, teacher in Sp. school, v.22, p.683.

Laresche-Bossiere duel, 1859, v.24, p.769.

Larmatier, noted, v.24, p.367, 368.

Larned, Rev., noted, v.33, p.70.

Laroche, ———, noted, v.23, p.719.

La Roche, Mary, noted, v.24, p.1154.

La Ronde, Pierre Denis, deposition of, v.23, p.724-725.

Larrive, ———, noted, v.22, p.387.

Lartiga, Don Pedro, Sp. practitioner, v.28, p.1093.

Larto, Luke, noted, v.23, p.1125.

La Rue, Antonio, settler in neutral ground, v.28, p.1052.

"Larue, Etienne, Trial of before the Superior Council of Louisiana, 1747," translation by Heloise H. Cruzat, v.13, p.377.

Larue, John C., noted, v.22, p.1110, 1133.

Larue, Mrs. Anna, defied Butler, v.27, p.513-514.

Larue, Mrs. John, imprisonment by Federal troops, v.24, p.493-494.

La Salle, Cavelier de, monument at Lachine, v.22, p.5-17; noted, v.22, p.939; explorer, v.25, p.399, 921; authorized to find way to Mexico, v.25, p.922, 923; ignored forks of river, v.25, p.925-926; claimed Miss. Valley for France, v.25, p.926; falsified "Rio Grande," v.25, p.927; return trip, v.25, p.928; leads expedition by sea, v.25, p.928; death of, v.25, p.928; his survivors reached Ark. post, v.26, p.663; noted, v.26, p.636; plan for opening the Miss., v.26, p.640; noted, v.26, p.641, 642, 643, 645, 687; early explorations and forts erected by, v.26, p.722; Fort Niagara, v.26, p.723; Fort Michilimackinac, v.26, p.723-724; his expedition to find Miss. from Gulf, v.26, p.725; noted, v.26, p.731, 736, 753; explorations in lower Miss., v.28, p.31; noted, v.28, p.32, 50, 72, 83; attempt to spread Fr. influence to Tex., v.28, p.1075.

"La Salle du Spectacle" or "Le Spectacle de la Rue St. Pierre," first Fr. Theatre, v.28, p.89.

"La Salle's House at Lachine, Province of Quebec," by Andre Lafargue, v.14, p.315.

"La Salle Takes Possession of Louisiana," by Baron Marc de Villiers du Terrage, translated by Andre Lafargue, v.14, p.301.

Las Casas, letter to from Miro, v.26, p.745; from Carondelet, v.26, p.745; Carondelet's letters to, v.26, p.748, 749.

La Sere, Emile, noted, v.23, p.226; noted, v.25, p.139, 1038, 1074, 1075; disputed election of, v.25, p.1008, 1010; chairman St. Cen. Com., address on Odd Fellows Hall meeting, v.26, p.987-988.

Lasiere, Jean de, noted, v.22, p.815.

"Las Ormigas," Davenport's tract of land, v.28, p.1052, 1089, 1090, 1101.

Lassassier, Timoleon, mayor of Carrollton, v.21, p.244; noted, v.22, p.202.

Lassiter, W. R., Conf. soldier, v.26, p.949.

Lassure, ———— de, noted, v.22, p.812.

Lassus, Carlos de, v.29, p.76.

"Last Ditch" Democrats, election of 1872, v.28, p.1134.

"Last Evening With Judge Gayarre, A" (with picture), by Frank D. Richardson, v.14, p.81.

"Last Island, Disaster of August 10, 1856, personal narrative of his experiences by one of the survivors," intro. by Walter Prichard, v.20, p.690-737; noted, v.24, p.23; resort for wealthy planters, v.25, p.204, 205; disaster of, v.25, p.705.

"La Superbe, Wreck of, 1745," translated by Heloise H. Cruzat, Introduction by Henry P. Dart, v.11, p.179; wreck of 1745, v.21, p.40.

Latham, Captain, noted, v.24, p.40.

Latherthwaits, William, noted, v.22, p.317, 944.

Lathrop, Barnes F., "An Autobiography of Francis T. Nicholls, 1834-1881," v.17, p.246.

Lathrop, Charles C., noted, v.23, p.189.

Latin America, relations with New Orleans, 1810-1824, v.22, p.710-794.

"Latin City, The (New Orleans)," by Edward Alexander Parsons, v.3, p.361.

Latour, Arsene Lacarriere, "Historical Memoir of the War in West Florida and Louisiana, 1814-1815," v.2, p.143; and Laffite, v.21, p.1105; Spanish agent, v.23, p.755, 763, 764-765, 766.

Latour, ————, noted, v.24, p.757.

Latrobe, Benjamin Henry Boneval, noted, v.24, p.742; granted exclusive right to supply water to N. O., v.26, p.928.

Latrobe, H. S. B., survey for erection of lighthouse at mouth of Miss., v.28, p.748n.

Latrobe, William Henry, in New Orleans, v.22, p.142.

Lattimore, Dr. David, noted, v.24, p.731.

Laurence, Wm., and W. Fla. Rev., v.21, p.746n.

Laurent, Lubin F., "History of St. John the Baptist Parish," v.7, p.316.

Laurier, Charles Fremont de, noted, v.22, p.87.

Laussat, Citizen, Fr. Rep. transferring La. to U. S., v.27, p.329.

Laussat, Pierre Clement de, dinner party of, v.22, p.693; coat of arms of, v.24, p.5; portrait of, v.24, p.6; birth of, v.24, p.6; description of, v.24, p.6-7; later career, v.24, p.8; documents in Bibliotheca Parsoniana, v.24, p.311; commission to William Miller, v.24, p.734; his impressions of the balize, v.26, p.752; his reception at San Felipe, v.26, p.752-753; Napoleon's messenger, v.26, p.753, 754.

Lauvriere, Emile, "Histoire de la Louisiane Francois, 1673-1939," rev'd by Andre Lafargue, v.24, p.207-210.

Lavard, ————, noted, v.22, p.1067.

Laveau, Marie, queen of the Voodoos, v.24, p.752.

Lavergne, D. C., heads Agricultural Dep't in Bogalusa High School, v.29, p.143-144.

La Vergne, Pierre de, "Early Econ. Life in La., 1804-1824," (An Historical Dialogue), v.26, p.915-936.

Lavigne, Dame Eugenie, noted, v.24, p.358-359.

Law digest, of Bullard and Curry, v.23, p.1031.

"Lawd Sayin' the Same, The," by Hewitt Leonard Ballowe, rev'd by Yvonne P. Tison, v.31, p.154-156.

Law, John, mentioned, v.21, p.980; and slavery in La., v.23, p.865-867; and the "Miss. Bubble," v.26, p.651-653; concession of, v.26, p.667-670, 680; the site of his Ark. post, v.26, p.681, 682; noted, v.26, p.732, 739.

Lawrason, S. McC., Sen. favoring election law, v.28, p.1186; vice-pres. Const. Conv., v.28, p.1188; noted, v.28, p.1191.

Lawrence, Luther, noted, v.23, p.1000.

Lawrence, William Beach, noted, v.24, p.1101, 1111, 1119, 1128.

Laws, early La., levee and road, v.18, p.126-132.

"Lawsuit in the Court of the Governor at New Orleans Involving Land in Opelousas, 1764, A," translated by Laura L. Porteous, v.12, p.533.

"Lawsuit over the right to sell the Office of Notary in Louisiana During the French Regime, 1769," transcription by the late Heloise H. Cruzat, translation by Sally Dart, v.16, p.587.

Lawton, Peter S., approved Lottery Bill, v.27, p.1036; Rep. from Orleans, his vote on Lottery issue, v.28, p.1144.

Layssard, Etienne Maraffret, militia commander at Rapides, v.27, p.633, 645; at Ark., v.27, p.647.

Layton, Robert, noted, v.22, p.466.

Lazaret, Quarantine Station below N. O., v.28, p.329-330; monument to Fr. sailors, 1857, v.28, p.334, 335, 337.

Lazarist Fathers, noted, v.24, p.139.

Lazarus, Felix, noted, v.24, p.173.

Lea, Charles E., resolution to investigate charges of bribery by Lottery Co., v.27, p.989.

Leach, Margaret T., "The Aftermath of Reconstruction in Louisiana," v.32, p.631.

Leach, William, member of St. Helena Police Jury, v.23, p.406ff.

Leacock, Dr. W. T., noted, v.23, p.1242; Protestant minister banished by Butler, v.27, p.501.

Lead, of upper La., v.22, p.83.

Lea, Fannie Heaslip, noted, v.29, p.782.

League, Edward Livingston's definition of, v.24, p.705.

Lea, James J., early N. O. newspaperman, v.29, p.782-783.

Leake, Dr. William W., dismissed as superintendent of Charity Hospital, v.31, p.88.

Leary, Lewis, "John Howard Payne in New Orleans," v.31, p.110-122.

"Lease of a La. Plantation and Slaves, 1727," ed. by Walter Prichard, v.21, p.995, 997.

Lebeau, Monsieur, in duel, v.24, p.758.

LeBlanc, Dudley, public service commissioner, ordered installation of new telephone system in Crowley, v.27, p.1154.

Le Blanc, Joseph, noted, v.22, p.815.

Le Blanc, Packinham, noted, v.24, p.769.

Le Blanc, Paul, noted, v.22, p.815.

Le Blanc, Paul O., cap't from Washington Parish, v.29, p.82.

LeBreton, Dagmar Renshaw (Illustrated by) "France d'Amerique," Book review by Edith Dart Price, v.16, p.168.

Le Breton, Jean Baptiste Cesaire, land grants of, v.21, p.225; and Superior Council, v.21, p.1000.

Le Breton, Louis Cezard, Agreement to Employ Jean Baptiste Goudeau as Overseer, v.9, p.590.

Le Breton, N. B., noted, v.22, p.424.

LeBretton, Louis Caesar, plantation of, v.22, p.187.

LeCarpenter, noted, v.24, p.367, 368.

Le Changeur, Pierre, sues B. Gravier, v.22, p.399-400.

Leclerc, expedition noted, v.24, p.25.

LeClerc, Jean, noted, v.22, p.802, 813.

Leclerc, E. V., named in Kellogg impeachment, v.31, p.713.

LeConte, ———, noted, v.23, p.374.

Ledet, Wilton P., "History of the City of Carrollton," v.21, p.220-281.

Lee, A. L., noted, v.24, p.90; noted, v.32, p.117, 119, 120, 121, 122, 128, 137.

Lee, E. Jeff., Conf. soldier, military record, v.26, p.937-938; letters from, v.26, p.950-967, 967-971, 973-974; noted, v.26, p.940, 942, 947; letters to from W. C. Lee, v.26, p.943.

Lee, Elizabeth, noted, v.24, p.49.

Lee, George M., Conf. soldier, military career, v.26, p.937, 938; letters from, v.26, p.940-943, 943-949; death of, v.26, p.949n.; noted, v.26, p.943n.

Lee, Henry C., Conf. soldier, father of Mrs. Sallie Lee Boner, v.26, p.937, 938; letters of, v.26, p.967, 971-972; noted, v.26, p.945, 949, 953, 968, 970.

Lee, Jesse, member of St. Helena Police Jury, v.23, p.407ff.

Lee, Robert E., noted, v.24, p.67, 110, 112; noted, v.29, p.1242, 1245, 1246, 1249, 1251, 1252.

Lee, Rufus L., noted, v.26, p.937, 945, 949, 953, 967.

Lee, Starling C., noted, v.26, p.937, 945, 947, 950, 951, 956, 959, 961.

Lee, Wm. C., Confed. soldier, his military career, v.26, p.937, 938; letters from, v.26, p.943; noted, v.26, p.940n., 963, 968.

Lefebvre-Desnouettes, Gen., French emigre, v.23, p.778.

Lefleur, Henry, letter from, v.23, p.386-387.

Leflore, Greenwood, Indian Chieftain, friend of Philomela Smith, v.29, p.291.

Lefort, Luis Francisco, teacher in New Orleans, v.22, p.685.

"Lefort, Petition of Don Luis Francisco, 1800," by Laura L. Porteous, v.11, p.244.

"Legal Institutions of Louisiana," by Henry Plauche Dart, v.2, p.72.

Le Gardeur, J., Jr., reviewed, "A La Poursuite des Aigles," by Simone de la Souchere Delery, v.33, p.151.

Legendre, Ernest, noted, v.24, p.770.

Legendre, Jas., address to Prog. League, v.27, p.1063.

Legge, F., "The Nature of Hallucinations," v.1, p.292.

LeGrand, Miss Julia, quoted, v.24, p.530, 531.

Lehmann, H. E., New Orleans musician, v.31, p.133.

Lehmann, Hugo, noted, v.24, p.133.

Leiris, Rev. ———, pastor in New Orleans, v.22, p.456.

Leitch, William, noted, v.22, p.313.

Leland College, v.25, p.782-783, 792.

Leland, Waldo G., "Guide to Material for American History in the Libraries and Archives of Paris," Book review by Henry P. Dart, v.16, p.168.

"Le Marechal d'Estrees," ship list of passengers bound from France to La., 1719, v.21, p.970-974.

Lemonier, Dr. Rene, on Med. Board of Censors, v.26, p.60.

"Le Moniteur de la Louisiane," established v.22, p.58.

LeMonnier, Dr. Y. R. (and W. O. Hart), "The Confederate Die for the coinage of Silver Half Dollars," v.5, p.505.

Lemos, Domingo de, noted, v.22, p.393.

Lemos, Manuel Gayoso de, and French Rev., v.22, p.57; sketch, v.22, p.79n.

Le Normand, Marin, and Superior Council, v.21, p.1000.

Leonard, Albert, U. S. att'y, v.27, p.1008; Lottery Repub. cand. for Gov. of La., v.27, p.1092; Rep. of McEnery faction, v.28, p.1137; Rep. Lotteryite cand. for Gov., v.28, p.1159.

Leonard, Bethia, wife of Thomas O. Moore, v.26, p.977.

Leonard, Don Gilberto, Spanish treasurer of army, v.31, p.621; countersigns contract, v.31, p.622; abrogates Bastrop contract, v.31, p.626.

Leonard, Gilbert, and W. Fla. Rev., v.21, p.700n.

Leonard, Henry Percy, leads N. O. "Bee's" attack on Payne, v.31, p.115.

Leonard, James, headed Repub. faction, v.26, p.1088; Populist cand. for Cong., 1894, v.26, p.1095.

Leonard, John, petition of, v.23, p.383.

Leonard, John W., auth. of letter on W. Fla. Revolution, v.18, p.359-362; and W. Fla. Rev., v.21, p.131, 688n.

Leonard, Judge Gilbert, in duel with Toca, v.24, p.762-764.

Leonard, Judge John, and Plaquemines Fraud, v.27, p.724.

Leonard, Patrice, named in Wickliffe impeachment, v.31, p.692.

Leon, Count de, plans for ideal life, v.24, p.418-419; home in Offenbach, v.24, p.419; arrival in Economy, Pa., v.24, p.424; house in Phillippsburg, v.24, p.425; library, v.24, p.430; death of, v.24, p.431.

Leon, Nicholas, collection in Institute of Middle American Research, v.24, p.332.

Leon, Prince, noted, v.24, p.423.

Leovy, Mrs. Henry J., vice-pres. Women's Anti-Lottery League, v.27, p.1061.

Le Prevost, Bourgerel, suit of, v.21, p.1012.

"Le Propagateur Catholique," suppressed by Butler, v.27, p.500.

Leprosy, in Sp. New Orleans, v.22, p.679-680.

Lerch, Dr. Otto, birth and early education, v.33, p.243; introduced Wasserman reaction here, v.33, p.345; published "Rational Therapy," v.33, p.346; "Dr. Otto Lerch, 1855-1948," by Dr. A. E. Fossier, v.33, p.343-348.

Les Allemands (Ger. Coast), v.26, p.665.

L'Espinase, Pierre-Francois, noted, v.22, p.106ff.

Lesseps, Alexander, noted, v.23, p.204, 212.

"Les Sirenes," defined, v.25, p.306.

Lestage, Oscar H., "The White League in La. and Its Participation in Reconstruction Riots," v.18, p.617-695.

Lestrapes, Alphonse, noted, v.23, p.1003.

"Les Trois Capalins," dueling at, v.25, p.310.

"Lesueur Collection, The," by Henry P. Dart, v.6, p.585.

"Letter, A, From the Battle of New Orleans from John A. Fort," With Introductory Note, by E. A. Parsons, v.32, p.225.

"Letter in Answer to Dr. Stenberg's Article," by Arthur S. Aiton, v.19, p.1075-1077.

"Letters of a Confederate Soldier," by Mary Elizabeth Sanders, v.29, p.1229-1240.

"Letters of Edward Livingston to Presidents of the U. S.," ed. by James A. Padgett, v.19, p.938-963.

"Letters of James Brown to Henry Clay, 1804-1835," edited by James A. Padgett, v.24, p.921-1177.

"Letters of Judah P. Benjamin to Ambrose Dudley Mann, Minister of the Confederacy to Belgium," ed. by James A. Padgett, v.20, p.738-93.

"Letters of Nathaniel Cox to Gabriel Lewis," v.2, p.179.

"Letters of Pontalba to Miro," Trans. by Heloise H. Cruzat, v.2, p.393.

"Letters, Some, of Charles Etienne Gavarre on Literature and Politics, 1854-1885," v.33, p.223-254.

Letz, Paul, Crowley city engineer, v.27, p.1153.

Levees, contract for, in Carrollton, v.21, p.248-249; in New Orleans, v.22, p.198-199, 643; repair of, v.22, p.669; as promenade, v.22, p.688; at Baton Rouge, v.28, p.14-15; early attempts to build, v.28, p.277-278; opinions in re national aid in building, v.28, p.280-282; the Swamp Land Act, v.28, p.282ff.; state provisions for, v.28, p.286ff.; Board of Public Works, v.28, p.293ff.; other agencies, v.28, p.300ff.; La. Levee Co., v.28, p.307-310; swamp lands donated to levee district, v.28, p.312-323; Miss. R. Com., v.28, p.323-325.

Leveque, Joseph Mark, newspaperman, "Old Days on the Times-Democrat," v.33, p.414, 416.

Leverer, Peter, noted, v.22, p.996.

Levering, Andrew, agent for Randolph, v.25, p.168.

Levert, Augusta, v.27, p.391, 473, 475; opposed lottery, v.27, p.1043; pressure brought to bear on, v.27, p.1047.

Levert, Madam Octave Walter, address in honor of Clay, v.27, p.770.

Levine, Sadie, 1st Jew to be married in Bogalusa, v.29, p.120.

Levy, Alphonse, pres. Southwest La. Land Co., v.27, p.1123, 1171.

Levy, J., noted, v.22, p.180.

Levy, Ulrich Phillips, noted, v.24, p.1126.

Lewis, A. C., and Negro education in La., v.25, p.794, 808.

Lewis, Capt. Meriwether, U. S. agent among Indians, v.28, p.1028-1029.

Lewis, Dr. Ernest S., defies General Butler, v.31, p.61-62; on Board of Administrators of Charity Hospital, v.31, p.75.

Lewis, Dr. H., Charter member Medical Soc., v.26, p.59; noted, v.26, p.55, 62, 63.

"Lewis, Gabriel, Letters of Nathaniel Cox to," v.2, p.179.

Lewis, Guinea, founder of Franklin, La., v.28, p.1130.

Lewis, Jacob, noted, v.24, p.620.

Lewis, J. H., Acadia Parish supt. of schools, v.27, p.1178.

Lewis, Joseph, messenger of early Bap't Church in Wash. Parish, v.29, p.83.

Lewis, Joshua, noted, v.22, p.785.

Lewis, Maximilian Bernhard, noted, v.24, p.381.

Lewis, Micajah, duel with Sperry, v.23, p.156-160.

Lewis, Thomas H., in La. Con. Conv. of 1844, v.25, p.1012, 1016, 1033.

Lewis, William T., noted, v.23, p.478.

Lewis, W. L., documents in Bibliotheca Parsoniana, v.24, p.311.

"L'Histoire Merveilleuse de la Louisiane Francais; Chronique des XVIIe et XVIIIe siecles et de la cession aux Etats-Unis," by Regine Marie G. Hubert-Robert, rev'd by A. Lafargue, v.28, p.351-354.

Liaison, arrangements of quadroons, v.25, p.307, 309, 310-312.

Libano, Lt. A. J., resigned, v.26, p.836.

Liberal Republican Party, Warmoth allied with, v.27, p.551; conv. in Cincinnati, v.27, p.551; Banks' activity in, v.31, p.562.

Liberia, noted, v.25, p.341, 344, 345, 346, 350, 351, 354, 355, 372, 385, 386, 387.

"Liberty Monument," by James A. Renshaw, v.3, p.259.

"Liberty," redoubt behind "Independence" fort, v.24, p.657.

"Libraries, in N. O., 1771-1833," by Roger Philip McCutcheon, v.20, p.152-158; of Ante-Bellum La., v.23, p.131-140; of New Orleans Lyceum, v.23, p.1047; in Calcasieu Parish, v.32, p.616; of Sp. school, v.22, p.683.

Liddell, Moses, noted, v.25, p.159, 165, 183, 190, 192, 195, 203; to Miss., v.25, p.160; in legislature, v.25, p.160; death of, v.25, p.167; settlement of estate, v.25, p.168; collection in L.S.U. Archives, v.24, p.343.

Liddell, St. John Richardson, collection in L.S.U. Archives, v.24, p.343; noted, v.25, p.160, 165, 168, 184, 187, 188, 192, 196, 205, 206, 212.

Lieutaud, Albert, jt. auth., "The Miss. Fort Called Fort de la Boulaye, 1700-1715; The First French Settlement in Present Day La.," v.19, p.829-899.

Lieutenant senior grade (teniente de navio), noted, v.24, p.614.

"Life and Public Service of E. John Ellis, The," by Robert Cinnamond Tucker, v.29, p.679-770.

"Life of Richard Taylor," by Jackson Beauregard Davis, v.24, p.49-126.

Lightner, John, Populist cand. for Cong., 1894, v.26, p.1095.

"Lightning," fort, v.24, p.657.

"Lights and Shadows of a Great Event," James A. Renshaw, v.8, p.657.

Ligneville, Madame la Duchesse de, compositions in Howard-Tilton Memorial Library, v.24, p.330.

Liljegren, Ernest R. (ed.), "Materials Relating to the History of the Miss. Valley from the Minutes of the Spanish Supreme Council of State, 1787-1797," v.21, p.5-75; "Jacobinism in Spanish La., 1792-1797," v.22, p.47-97.

Lilley, Thomas, and W. Fla., v.21, p.77ff., 687n.

Limburg, Nicolas, noted, v.24, p.653, 660, 671.

Lincoln, Abraham, letter to N. P. Banks, v.23, p.1212; noted, v.24, p.59, 435, 505, 517; ideas of reconstruction, v.27, p.494-495; attitude toward slavery, v.27, p.511; Emancipation Proclamation, effect on N. O., v.27, p.514-515, 520; hoped to reinstate La. in U. S., v.27, p.522-523.

Lincoln Parish, La., and the Cong. election of 1894, v.26, p.1097; Populist legislator from, v.26, p.1109.

Lindauer, Chris, newspaperman, "Old Days on the N. O. Picayune," v.33, p.325-326.

Lindoe, Dr. Robt. F., noted, v.26, p.75; challenged Campbell to duel in behalf of Luzenberg, v.26, p.80-81; his letter to the public in his own defense, v.26, p.82-83; testimonial signed by, v.26, p.88-89, 91.

Lindsey, Richard, noted, v.23, p.536.

Lindsley, Percy W., Cap't of troop "E" of La. Inf., v.29, p.82.

Lineberger, Rev. R. F., cited, v.24, p.143.

Lintot, William, noted, v.23, p.1091.

Liotaud, Louis, noted, v.23, p.1093, 1094.

Liquet, Pedro, noted, v.24, p.367.

Lislet, Louis Moreau, noted, v.22, p.399, 418, 749, 808, 813; noted, v.23, p.700, 730; N. O. lawyer, v.19, p.331; noted, v.25, p.979, 980.

"List of Foreigners or Their Children, Who Are Considered Within Jurisdiction of Nacogdoches and Who Are Living in Bayou Pierre," v.28, p.1109-1110.

"List of Ranches and Settlers Pertaining to the jurisdiction of Nacogdoches and Situated East of the Sabine R.," v.28, p.1104.

"List of Ranches Recognized as Lying Within Jurisdiction of Nacogdoches, together with name of Ranch, name of Owner, Distance and Direction from Nacogdoches," v.28, p.1111-1112.

"Literary Travellers in Louisiana Between 1803 and 1860," by Florence Roos Brink, v.31, p.394-422.

"Literature, and Politics, Some Letters of Charles Etienne Gayarre on, 1854-1885," v.33, p.223-254.

Literature, in New Orleans, v.22, p.216-225; ante-bellum library, v.23, p.131-140; German, in New Orleans, v.23, p.510; in St. Mary Parish, v.32, p.94-96.

"Little Obelisk in the Cathedral Sq. in N. O.," by Andre Lafargue, v.28, p.326-348.

Little River, noted, v.24, p.75; noted, v.25, p.215, 361.

Little Rock, noted, v.24, p.84.

Livaudais, Jacques Esnoul de, fils, buys property, v.21, p.674-676.

Livaudais, Jacques, pere, and Jesuit plantation, v.23, p.681; in charge of galley slaves, v.23, p.695; noted, v.23, p.717; deposition of, v.23, p.731-732.

Livaudais, Louis A., resigned, v.26, p.836.

Livestock, in Duverney Concession, v.21, p.987-988; in La., noted, v.32, p.10.

"Livingston, Edward," by Merrill Moores, v.3, p.486; defeated by Shreve in attempt to monopolize river navigation, v.18, p.822-829; arrival in La., v.19, p.330-331; marriage, v.19, p.333-334; N. O. Lawyer, v.19, p.334ff.; and Aaron Burr, v.19, p.336, 337; and Lafittes, v.19, p.337-340; Codifier of La. Laws, v.19, p.342-357; batture controversy, v.19, p.357-374; in La. legislature, v.19, p.374-378; prison reform, v.19, p.354-357, 381; cases before La. Supreme Ct., v.19, p.385-386; bibliography of, v.19, p.388-389; early life, v.19, p.938-939; removal to La., v.19, p.939; letters to Jeff., v.19, p.940ff.; to Madison, v.19, p.943ff.; to Monroe, v.19, p.946ff.; ancestry, v.19, p.900-937; and John Maison Rouge's suit in 1817, v.20, p.338-339; sales of land in Ouachita, v.20, p.407ff.; and Spanish filibusters, v.21, p.814; batture case, v.22, p.411ff.; noted, v.22, p.434ff.; and privateers, v.23, p.437, 761, 763; noted, v.23, p.1006, 1064; documents in Bibliotheca Parsoniana, v.24, p.311; noted, v.24, p.365, 933, 1134, 1135, 1139, 1143, 1150; member of New Orleans Association, v.24, p.631; early life, v.24, p.699; expressions of political philosophy, v.24, p.700-701, 703-707, 709-716, 719-728; and 1824 tariff bill, v.25, p.39, 40, 42, 43; and 1826 tariff bill, v.25, p.43; and 1828 tariff, v.25, p.46, 47, 78; noted, v.28, p.770n.; opposed Claiborne, v.31, p.287, 315, 369, 378, 379.

Livingston, Mrs. Edward, noted, v.24, p.1134.

"Livingston, Mrs. Louise, Wife of Edward Livingston," by W. O. Hart, v.5, p.352.

Livingston, Peter N. B., noted, v.22, p.35.

Livingston, Philip, noted, v.22, p.31, 33.

Livingston, Robert, of Clermont, grandfather of Ed. Livingston, v.19, p.919ff.

Livingston, Robert R. (Judge), father of Ed. Livingston, v.19, p.920-21.

Livingston, Robert R., and the purchase of La., v.18, p.347-353; defeated by Shreve in attempt to monopolize river navigation, v.18, p.822-829; son of Judge Robert R. Livingston, v.19, p.924-925; collection in Bibliotheca Parsoniana, v.24, p.310-311; noted, v.24, p.699, 932; acquired La. from France, v.25, p.939; minister to France, v.31, p.290, 311, 326, 331; candidate for Governor of Orleans, v.31, p.351-352, 384.

Lizano, Nicholas, deposition of, v.23, p.706-708.

Lizars, Henry, and W. Fla. Assembly, v.22, p.317, 946; noted, v.23, p.19, 357, 368, 377.

Llaguno, Eugenio de, y Amirola, identified, v.21, p.22n.

Lloyd, William B., and telegraph, v.31, p.431-432, 459; attacks O'Reilly, v.31, p.460-462.

Llulla, "Pepe" Jose, sketch, v.23, p.460-470.

Lobrano, Jacinto, member of Laffite's crew, v.24, p.28-29; death of, v.24, p.29; and General Butler, v.24, p.29.

Locke, John, noted, v.24, p.701.

Lockett, S. H., sketch of Grand Ecore, 1873, v.24, p.430.

Lockett, Thomas, noted, v.25, p.295.

Lockhart, Henry, noted, v.22, p.458.

Lockyer, Captain, British attempt to bribe Laffite, v.24, p.20-21.

Locofocos, origin of term, v.23, p.1086n.; noted, in La., v.25, p.128, 129, 130, 131, 142, 1035-1036, 1038, 1039, 119.

Locquet, E., duel of, v.23, p.154-155.

Loeb, Harry Brunswick, one time impresario of Fr. Opera House in N. O., v.29, p.663.

Loftus, Major Arthur, expedition up Miss. R., v.22, p.22-27.

Logan, George W., noted, v.24, p.80.

Logan, Thomas M., cited from his "Memoir of Luzenberg" on his appointment as House Surgeon, Charity Hosp., v.26, p.50-51; on his marriage, v.26, p.51; on his visit to Paris, v.26, p.51-52; Franklin Infirmary, v.26, p.55, 56; on the old staff of Franklin Inf., v.26, p.56, cited on Luzenberg's disassociation with the college, v.26, p.58; noted, v.26, p.61; on Luzenberg's surgical achievements, v.26, p.62-63; on his work with yellow fever, v.26, p.64, 65; on his work with small pox, v.26, p.65; his "Memoirs" quoted, v.26, p.105, 106, 107; quoted on La. Pharmacy laws, v.26, p.335-336.

Loggy Bayou, noted, v.25, p.399, 400.

L'Olonnois, pirate, v.24, p.9.

Lombard, Augustin, noted, v.23, p.423.

Lomine, Charles, privateersman, v.22,

p.1038-1041, 1076, 1078; privateer, v.23, p.810; noted, v.24, p.612, 613, 615.

London Associates, noted, v.24, p.647.

Long, Huey P., noted, v.31, p.86; and Charity Hospital Board, v.31, p.87-88; corruption in management, v.31, p.88-90; tiffs with Tulane and Loyola, v.31, p.90; moves female medical building, v.31, p.91; keeps federal funds from Charity, v.31, p.93; assassination noted, v.31, p.93; impeached, v.31, p.682; noted, v.32, p.15.

Long, James, expeditions of, v.22, p.743-746, 1078-1079; expedition to Tex., v.23, p.812ff.; letter to J. Laffite, v.23, p.813; letter from J. Laffite, v.23, p.814-815, 816-817, 822; filibuster into neutral ground, v.28, p.1053, 1057-1059.

Long River, La Salle discovers, v.25, p.927; Sp. interest in, v.25, p.937.

Longino, Luther, M. D., "Thoughts, Visions and Sketches of North Louisiana," reviewed by J. Fair Hardin, v.14, p.239.

"Longstreet's, A. B., Brief Sojourn in Louisiana," by Arthur Marvin Shaw, v.32, p.777.

Longstreet, Augustus B., president of Centenary College, v.31, p.126.

Longstreet, James, in 1873, v.23, p.531; orders of in Jackson Barracks Library, v.24, p.313; on Repub. Returning Board, v.27, p.558; placed by Pinchback in command of Militia, v.27, p.569; on Lynch Returning Board, v.28, p.1135; arrest of members of McEnery Legis., v.28, p.1137; member of Lynch board, v.31, p.700; member of returning board, v.31, p.1093.

Lonsdale, Henry T., noted, v.23, p.240, 244.

Loomis, Capt., ———, noted, v.22, p.1083.

Looney, Ben Earl, "Historical Sketch of Art in La.," v.18, p.382-396.

L'Opera Francais de la Nouvelle Orleans (The French Opera House of N. O.), v.29, p.668-676.

Lopez, Francisco, noted, v.22, p.1018.

Lopez, Juan, noted, v.22, p.934.

Lopez, Juan Elias, noted, v.24, p.659; re-established independent government of New Granada, v.24, p.661; death in attack on Porto Bello, v.24, p.662.

Lopez, Manuel, and W. Fla. Rev., v.21, p.687n.

Lopez, Narciso, expedition to Cuba, v.22, p.1095-1167; sketch, v.22, p.1121-1122; expedition to Cuba, v.23, p.1071-1079.

Loppinot, Carlos Joseph, noted, v.22, p.624, 632.

Loppinot's, Case: "Civil Procedure in Louisiana Under the Spanish Regime as Illustrated in Loppinot Case, 1774," translated by Laura L. Porteous, v.12, p.38.

Loret, Joseph A., opinion on lottery question, v.27, p.1040.

Lorimer, John, and W. Fla. Assembly, v.22, p.317-318, 322, 943; noted, v.23, p.13, 357, 368, 377.

Lorimer, Louis, sketch, v.21, p.36n.; noted, v.22, p.84, 87.

Lorrains, Jacques, suit against, v.21, p.1007-1008.

Lortzing, Gustavo Alberto, manuscripts in L.S.U. Music School Library, v.24, p.347-348.

Los Adaes, Sp. post and the disputed neutral ground, v.28, p.1023, 1024, 1029, 1030, 1033, 1038, 1046, 1050.

"Lost City of Lafayette, The," by James A. Renshaw, v.2, p.47.

Lottery Bill of 1890, provided for submitting question to the people, v.27, p.1033; arguments pro and con, v.27, p.1033-1035, 1036-1041, 1042, 1043; gov.'s veto, v.27, p.1043-1044; attempt to override veto, v.27, p.1044-1045; gov.'s signature declared not necessary, v.27, p.1045; analysis, v.27, p.1045-1046; struggles in Legis., v.27, p.1045-1049; primary demanded, v.27, p.1050; in the courts, v.27, p.1050-1052.

Lottery, for building church, v.22, p.445, 447, 449; attack upon by Cable, v.24, p.170; documents in La. State Museum, v.24, p.319; in Savannah, v.24, p.759; in New Orleans, v.24, p.760; definition of, v.27, p.966; early lotteries and their purposes, v.27, p.966-968; objections to, v.27, p.968; purposes in La., v.27, p.969; opposition to in La., v.27, p.969; legalized in La., v.27, p.969; La. State Lottery Co., chartered, v.27, p.969, 975; history of La. State Lottery Co., v.27, p.969-1103; bill providing for other lotteries in La., v.27, p.971-972; attempt to incorporate lottery Co. in opposition to La. Lottery Co., v.27, p.980; denied use of mails, v.27, p.991-992; attempt to incorporate other lotteries, v.27, p.1004; early fathers favored, v.27, p.1067; foreign lotteries, v.27, p.1067-

1068; swindling schemes, v.27, p.1068; condemned as evil, v.27, p.1070; early laws against, v.27, p.1073; La. Lottery Co., v.32, p.490, 508.

Lott, Hiram R., senator, v.27, p.1058; temporary chairman Anti-Lottery Nominating Conv., v.27, p.1090; Temp. Chairman Anti-Lottery State Nom. Com., v.28, p.1157.

Louaillier, Louis, and Andrew Jackson, v.21, p.369ff, 375.

Loubat, Walter, head of N. O. opera house ass'n, v.29, p.678.

Lougborough, P. S., attorney in Morse case, v.31, p.463.

Louis XIV, decrees in Bibliotheca Parsoniana, v.24, p.310.

Louis XV, decrees in Bibliotheca Parsoniana, v.24, p.310.

Louis XVIII, death of, v.24, p.938.

"Louis DeClouet's Memorial to the Spanish Gov't, Dec. 7, 1814," ed. by S. Faye, v.22, p.795-818.

Louisiana: "Admission into the Union of," by Lillie Richardson, v.1, p.333; "Boundary of Louisiana, Western," by Gaspar Cusachs, v.1, sec.1, p.9; "Boundaries of Texas and Louisiana, Report to Mexican Republic Concerning," by Fray Jose Maria Puelles, 1828, v.1, sec.1, p.21; "Data of, Recently Acquired by the U. S. Congressional Library," by William Beer, v.1, sec.1, p.116; "Early Episodes in History of," by Wm. Kernan Dart, v.1, sec.3, p.190; "Families of, History of Some of the Leading," v.1, sec.1, p.95; Introduction—Resume of Activities of L.H.S., by the Editor, v.1, sec.1, p.5; "Notes on, in 1778," (From Chas. Theo. Middleton's "System of Geography," pub. in London, 1778), v.1, p.375; "Old Portage Between Bayou St. John and the Mississippi River," v.1, p.372; "Some Rare Historic Data of," (Old Book concerning Grant from Louis XIV to Crozat), v.1, sec.1, p.118; "Works Published on Ancient," (See A. L. Boimare), v.1, sec.2, p.9; "Sidelights on Louisiana History," Trans. by Heloise H. Cruzat: Bienville's Land Near New Orleans, 1726, v.1, sec.3, p.123; "Bienville's Land Titles, 1719," v.1, sec.3, p.121; "Bienville Secures German Families for His Lands, 1722," v.1, sec.3, p.122; "Bienville Sells Plantation Adjoining Old New Orleans," v.1, sec.3, p.116; "Bill for Services Rendered Mr. Pailhoux's Negroes," 1726, v.1, sec.3, p.153; "Census of 1721," v.1, sec.3, p.97; "Census of 1726," v.1, sec.3, p.134; "Certificate of Freedom," v.1, sec.3, p.103; "Church and Education in New Orleans," v.1, sec.3, p.87; Consultation and Diagnosis of Physicians Over Swiss Soldiers in 1727, v.1, sec.3, p.105; "Contact with Surgeon in 1724," v.1, sec.3, p.104; "Decree Forbidding Deportation of Vagabonds, Smugglers and Criminals to Louisiana, 1720," v.1, sec.3, p.124; Destruction of Animals, 1724, v.1, sec. 3, p.111; Foundation of Hospital in New Orleans from Memorial by Bienville, 1737, v.1, sec.3, p.96; Friendly Note in 1726, v.1, sec. 3, p.126; "Gentilly, A Summer Suburb of New Orleans, 1726," v.1, sec.3, p.120; Indian Tribes Appearing in Bienville's Colonial Life, v.1, sec.3, p.148; Jean Louis' Will—Bequest which was the Nucleus of present Charity Hospital, 1735, v.1, sec.3, p.94; "Judgement of Superior Council in Suit of Pauger vs. Bienville, 1724," v.1, sec.3, p.140; "Lead Mines in Upper Louisiana, Documents Relative to," v.1, sec.3, p.111; Lead Mines in Illinois in 1719, v.1, sec.3, p.113; Lead Mines of La-Mothe, 14 miles from Kaskaskia, v.1, sec.3, p.113; Memorial of Bienville Asking for his Recall, 1740, v.1, sec.3, p.114; Memorial of Bienville and Salmon to Establish a College in New Orleans, 1742, v.1, sec.3, p.93; Memorial of Mr. Ceard vs. Chauvin Bros., 1724, v.1, sec.3, p.142; Military Companies in New Orleans in 1724, v.1, sec.3, p.133; Murder Sentence, v.1, sec.3, p.111; Address on, by Col. H. J. de la Vergne, v.2, p.174; "Archives of," by Henry Plauche Dart, v.2, p.349; "Bird of, Emblematic," by Stanley Clisby Arthur, v.2, p.248; "Cession of, by France; Treaty Between French Republic and United States, 1803," v.2, p.139; "Concession of Ste. Catherine at the Natchez," Trans. from the French, by Heloise H. Cruzat, v.2, p.164; "Flags of, The," by Milledge L. Bonham, Jr., v.2, p.439; "Fiscal System for, A New," by L. E. Thomas, v.2, p.129; "Highway Progress in," by C. M. Kerr, v.2, p.56; "Historical Notes on Commerce and Agriculture of, 1720-

1766," by Charles Gayarre, v.2, p.286; Historical Society, Minutes of The, for 1918, v.2, p.217; "Historical Society, Report of The, for 1918," by Bussiere Rouen, v.2, p.208; "Legal Institutions of," by Henry Plauche Dart, I—1699-1712, Iberville and Bienville, v.2, p.72; II—1712-1717, Crozat's Charter, v.2, p.74; III—1717-1732, Company of the West, The, v.2, p.85; IV—1731-1762, Crown Colony, v.2, p.98; Origin of the Name of, (from New Orleans Picayune), v.2, p.230; "Ursulines of, The," by Heloise H. Cruzat, v.2, p.5; Address by the House of Representatives of Louisiana to the People of France (1831), v.3, p.399; Books on Louisiana during Colonial Days, Sold at Anderson Galleries, New York, v.3, p.139; "Constitutions of Louisiana, with some Observations on the Constitutional Convention of 1921," by W. O. Hart, v.3, p.570; "History of Louisiana Historical Society," by W. O. Hart, v.3, p.112; "Louisiana Completa, A Centenary Relation of West Florida and the Treaty with Spain, 1819-1821," by Edward Alexander Parsons, v.3, p.455; Louisiana Historical Society, Minutes of, 1919-1920, v.3, p.373; "Louisiana Territory, The, 1682-1803," by Cardinal Goodwin, v.3, p.5; Cabildo Archives, I, II, III, IV, v.3, p.71, 279, 322, 509; 1725 Anti-Liquor Ordinance for Soldiers and Sailors, v.3, p.73; 1726 Petition of Attorney General Regarding Absconding Debtor, v.3, p.74; 1730 Ordinance Concerning Slaves, v.3, p.75; 1730 Petition in Succession of de la Chaise, v.3, p.77; 1730 Petition of Marie Barbe Edelmaire to Annul Exchange of Slave, v.3, p.78; 1731 Report of Attorney General Concerning Management of Jail, v.3, p.80; 1733 Decree Prohibiting Sale of Real Property Without Permission from the Council, v.3, p.83; 1739 Recorded Act of Sale of Negro Slave, v.3, p.84; 1743 Ordinance Regulating Practice of Medicine, Surgery and Obstetrics, v.3, p.86; 1748 Petition of Owner for Permission to sell Real Property, v.3, p.88; **1753 Ordinance Suppressing Cattle** Stealing by Slaves, v.3, p.89; 1753 Petition of Jean Pierre Hingle for Permission to Sell Real Property, v.3, p.91; 1763 Petition for Criminal Prosecution of Dupre Terrebonne, Jr., for Killing a Slave, v.3, p.93; 1763 Summary of Facts in Controversy Over a Cow, v.3, p.95; 1769 Decision of Council Concerning Seizure of Vessel from Manchac, v.3, p.96; Petition and Order for Selection of Tutor and Curator for Minor, v.3, p.98; "Criminal Trials, Louisiana, 1720-1766," by H. P. Dart, v.3, p.279; Case No. 1, Porcher and Bahu, charged with Larceny, 1720, v.3, p.281; Case No. 2, Jean Melum, charged with Stabbing, 1728, v.3, p.284; Case No. 3, Sieur Loquet de la Pommeraye, Charged with Illegal Burying of a N e g r e s s, 1738, v.3, p.291; Case No. 4, Michel Degout, charged with Murder, v.3, p.294; "First Succession Opened in Louisiana, The," by Henry P. Dart, v.3, p.322; 1738, Family Meeting to Select Tutor and Curator, v.3, p.543; Letters of Sieur Terrisse de Terman, v.3, p.509; 1744 Emancipation of Marie Aram, A Slave, v.3, p.551; 1745-1747, Two Nuncupative Wills, v.3, p.564; Family Meeting to Decide on Exchange of Horn Island for a City Lot, v.3, p.547; First Charity Hospital for the Poor of New Orleans, v.3, p.554; Supplement to Emancipation of Marie Aram, v.4, p.366; Cabildo Archives VII—Supplement to First Charity Hospital, v.4, p.361; Cabildo Archives IX—Passport to ship "Apollo," v.4, p.216; "Confederate M i l i t a r y Records," by A. B. Booth, v.4, p.369; "Courts and Law, Colonial," by Henry P. Dart, v.4, p.255; Indian Land Titles, v.4, p.134; Servinien's Case, 1752, v.4, p.290; Dart, Henry P., Editor, See Cabildo Archives, Records of Superior Council; Gayarre Report on La. Archives in Spain, 1850, v.4, p.466; Gov. Unzaga's Fire Ordinance, v.4, p.201; Indian Land Title, v.4, p.134; "Mathews, George, President Louisiana Supreme Court," by Etienne Mazureau, v.4, p.154; "Mazureau's Oration on," by H. P. Dart, v.4, p.149; Watts Discourse on, v.4, p.189; New Orleans Fire Protection, Spanish Period, v.4, p.201; "Servinien's Case, 1752," by Henry P. Dart, v.4, p.290; Spain, Allegiance to, Oath of, v.4, p.205; Supreme Court of La., v.4, p.5; Cabildo Archives: "A Gentleman of Pointe Coupee," by H. P. Dart, v.5, p.462; "Nuncupative Will of Philip Haynaud," Trans. by Heloise H. Cruzat, v.5, p.466; "Politics in Louisiana in 1724," by H. P. Dart, v.5, p.298; "Suit for Damages for Personal Injuries to a Slave, 1724," Trans. by Heloise H. Cruzat and Dr. E. Dupaquier, v.5, p.58; "Ceard's Case, 1724," by H. P. Dart, v.5, p.155; "Commerce of, During the French Regime, 1699-1763," by N. M. Miller Surrey, Ph. D., Columbia University, Critique by Grace King, v.5, p.19; "Webster, Daniel, in Louisiana History," by J. M. Pilcher, v.5, p.478; Colonial Archives (See Editor's Chair), v.6, p.111; "Conventional Mortgages of Spanish Colonial Period," by Henry P. Dart, v.6, p.255; "Early Louisiana Inquest, An" (Translated from the original by Mrs. Heloise H. Cruzat), v.6, p.269; "Episodes of Colonial Life," by Henry P. Dart, v.6, p.35; "Life in Middle of Last Century," (An Old Lady's Gossip) Edited by Cecile Willink, v.6, p.380; Louisiana Historical Society, Minutes of Meeting, 1922, v.6, p.164; "Nicholls Family, The," v.6, p.5; "Superior Council of Louisiana, Session of the, in 1744," by Henry P. Dart, v.6, p.571; "Calendar Of Documents," Mrs. N. M. Surrey, v.7, p.551; "Case in Admiralty, 1741," Henry P. Dart and Heloise H. Cruzat, v.7, p.5; Destrehan's Slave Roll, v.7, p.302; "Documents Relating to O'Reilly," David K. Bjork, v.7, p.20; Editor's Chair, v.7, p.141, 332, 480, 674; "Flag Legislation," W. O. Hart, v.7, p.449; "Jacques de la Chaise," George C. H. Kernion, v.7, p.447; "Louisiana Historical Society Fifty Years Ago," Cecile Willink, v.7, p.667; "Louisiana Troops at Occupation of Havana," John S. Kendall, v.7, p.40; Minutes Louisiana Historical Society, 1923, v.7, p.128; "Mississippi Valley Beginnings," Caroline Richardson, v.7, p.672; "Morse Family," Dr. Edward C. Morse, v.7, p.441; "Municipal Legislation by Superior Council," Heloise H. Cruzat, v.7, p.567; "Pages from Journal of Voyage Down Mississippi to New Orleans," Felix Flugel, v.7, p.414; "Reminiscences of Chevallier Bernard de Verges," George C. H. Kernion, v.7, p.56; Semi-Centennial 14th September, 1874, v.7, p.570; "Slavery on Louisiana Sugar Plantations," V. Alton Moody, v.7, p.191; "Smuggler St. Michel," Henry P. Dart, v.7, p.371; "St. John the Baptist Parish, Its History," Lubin F. Laurent, v.7, p.316; "Tchoupitoulas Plantation," Meloncy C. Soniat, v.7, p.308; "Uncle Tom's Cabin" and "The Spanish Post of the Adaias," Phanor Breazeal, v.7, p.304; "West Feliciana, A Glimpse of Its History," Louise Butler, v.7, p.90; "Documents Concerning the History of the Indians of the Eastern Region of Louisiana," by Baron Marc de Villiers, George C. H. Kernion, v.8, p.28; "Eighteenth Century in Louisiana, The," Henry P. Dart, v.8, p.474; "French Colonial Procedure in Louisiana for the Appointment of Tutors to Minors," Heloise H. Cruzat, v.8, p.218; "Great Louisiana Plantation of the French Colonial Period, A," Henry P. Dart, v.8, p.589; "Imprisonment for Debt in Louisiana," Henry P. Dart, v.8, p.549; "Judicial Auction Sale in Louisiana" 1739, Henry P. Dart, v.8, p.382; "Torture in Spanish Criminal Procedure in Louisiana, 1771," Laura L. Porteous, v.8, p.5; "Wills of the French Colonial Period in Louisiana," Heloise H. Cruzat, v.8, p.411; "Elections in 1860 in Louisiana," by Mary Lilla McLure, v.9, p.601; "'Jackson and the Louisiana Legislature, 1814-1815," by Henry P. Dart, v.9, p.221; "Louisiana Indigo Plantation on Bayou Teche, 1773," v.9, p.565; "Regulations to be Observed by the Syndics and Alcalds of the Jurisdiction of Baton Rouge, 30 October, 1804," by Governor Vincente Folch, v.9, p.405; "Report of the Committee of Inquiry of the Military Measures Executed Against the Legislature of Louisiana, December 28, 1814," v.9, p.223; "Following the Spanish Trail Across Neutral Territory in Louisiana," by Leon Sugar, v.10, p.86; "Induction of Laurent MacMahon as Councillor in the Superior Council of Louisiana, 1730-1731," v.10, p.529; "Introduction of Jean Francois Pasquier, as Councillor-Assessor in the Superior Council of Louisiana, 1737," v.10, p.68; "Louisiana Planter and His Home, The," by Louise Butler, v.10, p.317; "Notarial System of Louisiana, The," by Edgar Grima, v.10, p.76; "A Louisiana Will of the Spanish Era, 1766," by Laura L. Porteous, v.11, p.607; "Distribution of Land in Louisiana by the Company of the Indies," Translated by Heloise H. Cruzat, Introduction by Henry P. Dart, v.11, p.553; "Documents Concerning Bienville's Lands in Louisiana," Translated by Heloise H. Cruzat, Introduction by Henry P. Dart, v.10, p.5, 161, 364, 538; v.11, p.87, 209, 463; "Governor Claiborne and the Public School System of the Territorial Government of Louisiana," by Stewart Grayson Noble, v.11, p.535; "History of Madison Parish, Louisiana," by W. M. Murphy, v.11, p.39; "O'Reilly's Ordinance of 1770," v.11, p.237; "Spanish Land Laws of Louisiana, The," by Francis P. Burns, v.11, p.557; "Governor Ungaza Decides that the Family Meeting Has no Place in Spanish Probate Procedure in Louisiana, 1771," translated by Laura L. Porteous, v.12, p.288; "How the Louisiana Purchase was Financed," by James E. Winston and R. W. Colomb, v.12, p.189; "Louisiana in 1724—Banet's Report, 1774," Translated by Heloise H. Cruzat, v.12, p.121; "Louisiana Politics, 1845-1861," James Kimmins Greer, B.A., M.A., 1st and 2nd Installments, v.12, p.381, 555; "Splendid Work of Rowland and Sanders on the French Archives of Louisiana" (Editor's Chair), v.12, p.464; "System of Redemption in the State of Louisiana," by J. Hanno Deiler, Translated by Rev. Louis Voss, D. D., v.12, p.426; "Criminal Trial before the Superior Council, May, 1747," Introduction by H. P. Dart, Translation by Heloise H. Cruzat, v.13, p.367; "French Literature of Louisiana," Caulfield's, v.13, p.484; "Early Census Tables of Louisiana," Introduction by William Beer, Translation by J. K. Ditchey, v.13, p.205; "Dreamy Bayous," by Evelyn Soule, v.13, p.253; "Politics, 1845-1861," by James Kimmins Greer, 3rd, 4th, 5th and 6th Installments (Conclusion), v.13, p.67, 257, 444, 617; "Moore, Thomas O., Governor of Louisiana, 1860-1864," by G. P. Whittington, v.13, p.7; "Moore, Thomas O., Papers of," Introduction by G. P. Whittington, v.13, p10; "War Times in and Around Clinton, Louisiana," by Annie Sanderson Kilbourne, v.13, p.64; "Concerning the Loyalty of Slaves in North Louisiana in 1862, Letters from John H. Ransdell to Governor Thomas O. Moore," Introduction by G. P. Whittington, v.14, p.487; "First Cargo of African Slaves for Louisiana, 1718," Introduction by Henry P. Dart, Translated by A. G. Sanders, v.14, p.163; "First Law Regulating Land Grants in French Colonial Louisiana," Translated by Henry P. Dart, v.14, p.346; "Installation of de Kerlerec as Governor of Louisiana, 1753," Introduction by Henry P. Dart, Translated by Heloise H. Cruzat, v.14, p.235; "Louisiana in the Disputed Election of 1876," I, II, by Fanny Z. Lovell Bone, v.14, p.408, 549; "Ship Lists of Passengers Leaving France for Louisiana, 1718-1724," I, Translated by Albert Laplace Dart, v.14, p.516; "Spanish Procedure in Louisiana in 1800 for Licensing Doctors and Surgeons," Introduction by Henry P. Dart, Translated by Laura L. Porteous, v.14, p.204; "Documents Concerning the Crozat Regime in Louisiana, 1712-1717," Translated by A. G. Sanders, Introduction by Henry P. Dart, v.15, p.589; "History of American Party in Louisiana," by W. Darrell Overdyke, v.15, p.581; "History of Concordia Parish," I, II, III, IV, by Robert Dabney Calhoun, v.15, p.44, 214, 428, 618; "History of Rapides Parish," I, by G. P. Whittington, v.15, p.567; "Louisiana Purchase and West Florida," by Francis P. Burns, v.15, p.319; "Louisiana in the Disputed Election of 1876," III, IV (Conclusion), by Fanny Z. Lovell Bone, v.15, p.93, 234; "Office of Councillor-Assessor in the Superior Council of Louisiana in the French Regime" (Editor's Chair), v.15, p.117; "Savage Law of the French Regime in Louisiana," Translated by Heloise H. Cruzat, Introduction by Henry P. Dart, v.15, p.482; "Ship Lists of Passengers Leaving France for Louisiana, 1718-1724," II, III, Translated by Albert L. Dart, v.15, p.68, 453; "Spain's Report of the War with the British in Louisiana," by Jac. Nachbin, note by Henry P. Dart, v.15, p.468: "Documents Concerning the Crozat Regime in Louisiana, 1712-1717," Translated by A. G. Sanders, Introduction by Henry P. Dart, v.16, p.293; "Domestic Animals and Plants of French Louisiana as Mentioned in the Literature with Reference to Sources, Varieties and Uses," by Lauren C. Post, v.16, p.554; "Education in Louisiana in the Closing Decades of the Nineteenth Century," by Edwin L. Stephens, v.16, p.38; "Four Forgotten Army

Posts," by J. Fair Hardin, v.16, p.5, 279, 441, 670; "History of the American Party in Louisiana," by W. Darrell Overdyke, v.16, p.84, 256, 409, 608; "History of Concordia Parish," by Robert D. Calhoun, v.16, p.92, 309, 454, 598; "History of Rapides Parish," by G. P. Whittington, v.16, p.27, 235, 427, 628; "Interregnum in Louisiana in 1861," by Lane C. Kendall, v.16, p.175, 374, 639; "Jamaica Pirates and Louisiana Commerce, 1739," by Sally Dart and Edith Dart Price in Collaboration, v.16, p.209; "Land Ventures of General Lafayette in the Territory of Orleans and State of Louisiana," by Kathryn T. Abbey, v.16, p.359; "Lawsuit over the Right to Sell the Office of Notary in Louisiana During the French Regime, 1769," Translated by Sally Dart, v.16, p.587; "Documents Concerning the Crozat Regime in Louisiana, 1712-1717," III, IV, Translated by Albert Godfrey Sanders, v.17, p.268, 452; "Gri-Gri Case, The, A Criminal Trial in Louisiana During Spanish Regime, 1773," by Laura L. Porteous, v.17, p.48; "History of Concordia Parish, Louisiana," VI, VII, VIII, IX, by G. P. Whittington, v.17, p.112, 327, 537, 737; "Interregnum in Louisiana in 1861," IV, V, VI, by Lane C. Kendall, v.17, p.124, 339, 524; "Marriage Contracts of French Colonial Louisiana," by Henry P. Dart, v.17, p.229; "Wilde, Richard Henry, and the Establishment of the University of Louisiana," by Aubrey Starke, v.17, p.605; early History of, v.19, p.23-42; Process of Jurisprudence, v.19, p.35-38; Indians in, v.19, p.38-41; made Captaincy-General, v.21, p.54; description of in 1860, v.21, p.1110-1214; promise of aid for Aury, v.24, p.622; question of property titles, v.24, p.713; State Bank, v.24, p.735; flags, v.24, p.744-745; French culture, v.24, p.745-749; Spanish influence, v.24, p.748; language of original settlers, v.24, p.748-749; Indian folklore, v.24, p.749-750; Negro folklore, v.24, p.750-752; voudouism, v.24, p.751-752; Acadian folklore, v.24, p.752-755; climate, v.24, p.925-926, 928; French sentiment, 1810, v.24, p.931-932; support for John Quincy Adams, v.24, p.1044; 1828 election in, v.24, p.1125; plans of James Brown to visit, v.24, p.1147ff.; succession laws in, v.24, p.1149-1150; land values, v.24, p.1173; admitted to Union, v.25, p.27; 1816 tariff, petition, v.25, p.28-29; memorial to Cong., v.25, p.76; refuge for Santo Domingans, v.25, p.302, 303; attitude toward immigrants, v.25, p.303; laws on free Negroes, v.25, p.317, 331-333, 334, 369-370; laws on manumission, v.25, p.337-338; Bank of, v.25, p.384; Dept. of Conservation, v.25, p.398; and Negro education, v.25, p.728-821; Conditions in under Butler, v.26, p.355; Lincoln's hope to "reconstruct," v.26, p.356-357; the search for treasure in, v.26, p.647-661; divided into 9 districts, 1723, v.26, p.730; leg. solutions to problems of, 1804-1824, v.26, p.915-936passim; economic and social conditions in post-bellum days, v.26, p.1055-1062; her contribution to the Confed., v.26, p.1005-1009, 1111-1112, 1117, 1030; financial conditions of, v.26, p.1009-1010, 1012, 1014-1016, 1038-1041, 1043; early explorations and transfer of to the U. S., v.27, p.329-342; description of agriculture, people, political districts, etc. after its transfer to U. S., v.27, p.349-353; secession from Union, v.27, p.487, 489-490; wealth of, v.27, p.487-489; contribution to Confed., v.27, p.491; conditions in during war, v.27, p.491-493, 493-494; Cong. election of 1862, v.27, p.523-524; Fr. gift to Sp., v.27, p.629; first bishop of, v.27, p.713-714; ceded to Fr. by Sp., v.27, p.715; conveyed to U. S., v.27, p.935; retroceded to Fr., 1800, v.27, p.935; history of the state lottery, v.27, p.964-1117; fed'l aid for levee improvement, v.27, p.1026-1027, 1028; Hy. W. Allen's official report of conduct of Fed'l troops in Western part of, v.27, p.1226-1228.

"Louisiana, A. B. Longstreet's Brief Sojourn in," by Arthur Marvin Shaw, v.32, p.777.

"Louisiana and the Annexation of Texas," by James E. Winston, v.19, p.89-118.

"Louisiana and the Tariff, 1816-1846," by Joseph George Tregle, Jr., v.25, p.24-148.

"Louisiana, Ante Bellum Suffrage and Representation in," v.19, p.390-406

"Louisiana Anticipates Sp's Recognition of the Independence of the U. S.," by J. Horace Nunemaker, v.26, p.755-769.

Louisiana Bank, noted, v.25, p.987.

Louisiana Bureau of Agriculture, organized by State Agr. Society, v.26, p.1063;

noted, v.26, p.1069.

"Louisiana Cession and the Family Compact," by Richard R. Stenberg, v.19, p.204-207.

"Louisiana Completa" (West Florida Centenary), by Edward A. Parsons, v.3, p.455.

"Louisiana Confederate Memorial, Dedication Address at Vicksburg of," by Col. J. D. Hill, v.3, p.503.

"Louisiana Courier," and Sp. Am. revolts, v.22, p.785-786.

Louisiana Democratic Association, v.25, p.123.

"Louisiana, Education in Colonial," by Stuart G. Noble, v.32, p.759.

Louisiana Elections of 1878, Results of, v.32, p.649-667; Elections of 1879, Results of, v.32, p.667-684; Elections of 1880, v.32, p.684-715.

"Louisiana Gazette," and Sp. Am. revolts, v.22, p.780ff.

Louisiana Guard, noted, v.24, p.438.

Louisiana Historical Association, history of depository, v.24, p.314; business papers of, v.24, p.315.

"Louisiana Historical Society, History of," by W. O. Hart, v.3, p.112; "Fifty Years Ago," by Cecile Willink, v.7, p.667; Minutes of Meetings, 1923, v.7, p.128; Minutes of Meetings, 1924, v.8, p.89; Reception by Society to Southern Medical Association, 1924, v.8, p.449; "Celebration by the Louisiana Historical Society of the Centennial Anniversary of the Visit of Lafayette," reported by James A. Renshaw, v.9, p.190; the tenth year of the Quarterly (Editor's Chair), v.10, p.94; "First Meeting of the Sala Capitular at the Cabildo," by H. Gibbs Morgan, v.14, p.60; activities during past year (1934-35), v.18, p.966-971; approaching centennial, v.18, p.972; new editor completes his first volume, v.18, p.973-975; Bullard first president, v.19, p.7-42; centennial celebration, v.19, p.5-6; org. of and address delivered at 1st annual meeting, v.19, p.21-42; formation of, v.23, p.1039-1040, 1046; address to, by Bullard, v.23, p.1040-1044; provisions of Const., v.23, p.1044, 1045-1046; reorganization of, 1846, v.23, p.1045-1046; sketch of, v.24, p.316; publications of, v.24, p.317.

Louisiana History, romance of research in, v.20, p.557-577.

"Louisiana in 1724—Banet's Report," Translated by Heloise H. Cruzat, v.12, p.121.

"Louisiana in the Confederacy," by Jefferson Davis Bragg, rev'd, v.25, p.823-824.

"Louisiana in the Disputed Election of 1876," by Fanny Z. Lovell Bone, I, II, v.14, p.408, 549; III, IV (Conclusion), v.15, p.93, 234.

"Louisiana in the Sp.-Amer. War, 1898-1899, As Recorded by Col. Elmer E. Wood, Commander of the 2nd Reg't of the La. Volunteer Inf.," ed. by Walter Prichard, v.26, p.783-841.

"Louisiana," ironclad vessel, v.24, p.446; U. S. revenue cutter, v.24, p.370.

Louisiana Irrigation & Mill Co., v.27, p.1129.

Louisiana Legion, noted, v.24, p.27.

Louisiana Levee Co., under control of Howard & Morris, v.28, p.307-310.

"Louisiana Linguistic and Folklore Backgrounds," by Andre Lafargue, v.24, p.744-755.

Louisiana Lottery Company and the election of 1892, v.25, p.715; and Farmers' Alliance, v.26, p.1070; anti-lottery campaign, v.26, p.1077-1083; noted, v.28, p.307; the fight against rechartering, v.28, p.1141-1151; an issue in 1892 campaign, v.28, p.1152ff.; discontinued, v.28, p.1163, 1164; noted, v.29, p.746. See La. State Lottery Co.

Louisiana Map of 1732, 1733, v.19, p.571.

Louisiana Medio—Chirurgical Soc., Luzenberg instrumental in organizing, v.26, p.59; noted, v.26, p.64; resolution of on death of Luzenberg, v.26, p.103-104.

Louisiana National Guard, Wood helped organize fourth battalion of, v.26, p.785; 4th battalion of becomes part of regular army, v.26, p.791-794.

"Louisianian," Pinchback's newspaper, v.27, p.539.

"Louisiana Officers of the Confed. Navy," by Geo. T. Ness, Jr., v.27, p.479-486.

"Louisiana People's Party," by Lucia Elizabeth Dainel, v.26, p.1055-1149.

"Louisiana Pioneer in the Regulation of Pharmacy," by David L. Cowen, v.26, p.330-340.

"Louisiana Planter and His Home, The," by Louise Butler, v.10, p.317.

"Louisiana Politics, 1845-1861," by James Kimmins Greer, B.A., M.A., 1st and 2nd Installments, v.12, p.381, 555; 3rd, 4th, 5th, and 6th Installments (Conclusion), v.13, p.67, 257, 444, 617.

"Louisiana Populist," official organ of People's Party, v.26, p.1092, 1118.

"Louisiana Press and the Lottery, The," by Richard H. Wiggins, v.31, p.716-841.

Louisiana Purchase: "How the Louisiana Purchase was Financed," by James E. Winston and R. W. Colomb, v.12, p.189; "And West Florida," by Francis P. Burns, v.15, p.391; "Jeffersonian Diplomacy in," v.18, p.346, 353; motives for sale, v.21, p.354-361; a consequence of, v.21, p.362-366; and Jefferson, v.23, p.78-106; "The French Viewpoint," by A. Lafargue, v.23, p.107-117.

Louisiana, reconstruction in, v.19, p.668-750.

Louisiana Reform Press, comprised Populist newspaper, v.26, p.1118.

"Louisiana's Administration of Swamp Land Funds," by Sam Mims, v.28, p.227-325.

Louisiana Standard Oil and Pipe Line Co., organized, v.29, p.497.

Louisiana State Agricultural Society, organized, v.26, p.1063-1064; meeting and resolutions of 1889, v.26, p.1065.

Louisiana State Bank, Controversy over, v.28, p.979.

Louisiana State Colonization Society, object of, v.23, p.1049-1050.

Louisiana State Lottery Co., campaign against, v.27, p.788-790; introduction, v.27, p.964-965; chartered, v.27, p.969, 975; Act No. 21 of 1866, v.27, p.970; Acts No. 40 and 154, v.27, p.971; bill providing for other lottery drawings in La., 1867, v.27, p.971-972; C. T. Howard, first pres., v.27, p.972; Act No. 25 of 1868, provisions of, v.27, p.974, 975; arguments against, v.27, p.974-975; organization, v.27, p.975-976; open for business, v.27, p.976-977; attack on other lotteries on legal grounds, v.27, p.977; absolved from city license by court decision, v.27, p.978; scheme of early monthly drawings, v.27, p.978-979; Beauregard and Early, commissioners, v.27, p.979; sentiments against, v.27, p.979-980; attempt to incorporate other lottery in opposition to, 1874, v.27, p.980; acts to prevent sale of foreign tickets in N. O., v.27, p.980-981; attempts to repeal lottery acts, v.27, p.981-982, 985; legal cases challenging methods of, v.27, p.982-985; opposition to, v.27, p.985-987; Beauregard and Early in defense of, v.27, p.987; troubles in court, v.27, p.987-988; agitation for Const. Conv., 1878, v.27, p.988-989; bills to repeal fail, v.27, p.989, 991; investigation of charges of bribery, v.27, p.989-991; fed'l interference, v.27, p.991-992; arguments favoring, v.27, p.992; arguments against, v.27, p.993-994; Act No. 44 of 1879; an attempt to abolish Co., v.27, p.994-995, 997; Co. defends itself, v.27, p.995-996; purported financial aid to Nicholls in overthrow of Packard, v.27, p.997-998; Act 44 ruled unconstitutional, v.27, p.998-999; Const. Conv. of 1879, Article 167, v.27, p.999-1001; obtained control of "Democrat," v.27, p.1001-1002; attempts to charter other companies, v.27, p.1004-1005, 1006; attacks against, 1882-1890, v.27, p.1005-1007; victory in courts, v.27, p.1007-1010; suits against McClure, v.27, p.1010-1011; out-of-state attacks on, v.27, p.1012-1013; Forman answers attack, v.27, p.1013; death of Howard, v.27, p.1013-1014; financial returns, v.27, p.1014-1015, 1020-1021; description of drawings, v.27, p.1016-1020; daily drawings, v.27, p.1021-1024; methods of advertising through mails, v.27, p.1024-1025; courted popular favor through donations to charity and public enterprise, v.27, p.1025-1026; gives aid in floods of 1890, v.27, p.1027-1029; other charities, v.27, p.1029; offers of Morris for recharter of, v.27, p.1030, 1032; Nicholls' warning against, v.27, p.1030-1032; Lottery Bill of 1890 to submit question to people, introduced, v.27, p.1033; arguments pro and con, v.27, p.1033-1035, 1036-1041, 1042-1043; gov's veto, v.27, p.1043-1044; attempts to override veto, v.27, p.1044-1045; gov's signature declared unnecessary, v.27, p.1045; analysis of bill, v.27, p.1045-1046; struggle in Legis., v.27, p.1046-1047; court decision forcing promulgation of Lottery Bill, v.27, p.1050-1052; the Anti-Lottery League, v.27, p.1054-1062; Women's Anti-Lottery League, v.27, p.1061-1062; Prog. League, v.27, p.1062-1063; campaign highlights, v.27, p.1063-1066; contributed money to Nicholls' campaign, v.27, p.1065-1066; state finance, strongest motive in favor of, v.27, p.1066-1067; other arguments for, v.27, p.1067-1070; called moral evil, v.27, p.1070; opposed by Churchmen, v.27, p.1070-1071; opposed for too high profits, daily drawings, etc., v.27, p.1071-1072; Cong. Anti-Lottery Postal Bill, 1890, v.27, p.1072-1077; attacks on Co., v.27, p.1076-1077; effects of Postal Bill, v.27, p.1077-1083; conducts business by express, v.27, p.1077, 1080; Sup. Ct. rules postal law constitutional, v.27, p.1081-1082; Co. to abide by law, v.27, p.1083; Cong. law to suppress lottery traffic through interstate commerce, v.27, p.1083; law constitutional, v.27, p.1084; Farmers' Union and Anti-Lottery League combine against, v.27, p.1086-1087; supporters name McEnery for gov., v.27, p.1088; caucus of faction supporting, v.27, p.1089; ticket supporting, v.27, p.1090; McEnery faction campaigns, v.27, p.1091-1092; Morris withdraws offer, v.27, p.1093; efforts to unite party, v.27, p.1093-1094; bill fails to pass electorate, v.27, p.1095; bill to prohibit sale of tickets after Dec. 1893, v.27, p.1096-1097; final drawing, v.27, p.1098; business transferred to Honduras, v.27, p.1098-1099; method of conducting business, v.27, p.1099-1101; officers arrested and tried, v.27, p.1101-1102; bibl., v.27, p.1113-1117; established, v.31, p.718; opening, v.31, p.730; abolished, v.31, p.763; seeks injunction, v.31, p.763; vs. John Fitzpatrick, v.31, p.764; attacks by "Democrat," v.31, p.743-768; defeats "Democrat," v.31, p.774-778; woos public, v.31, p.786-791, 799-812; struggle for Charter, v.31, p.794-797; final defeat, v.31, p.838. See La. Lottery Co.

Louisiana State Museum, holdings, v.24, p.317-320; reports cited, v.24, p.320, 351.

Louisiana State Normal College, noted, v.25, p.730.

"Louisiana State Register," Republican newspaper, v.30, p.230.

Louisiana State Rice Milling Co., consolidation of Mills, v.27, p.1166, 1167.

Louisiana State Seminary of Learning, early history, v.20, p.53ff.; authorized, v.31, p.516; Sherman president, v.31, p.517.

"Louisiana State University, The Early History of The," by J. Fair Hardin, v.11, p.5; noted, v.25, p.204.

Louisiana Sugar Planters Association, collection in L. S. U. Archives, v.24, p.343.

Louisiana Supreme Court, case of Morris vs. Mason, v.27, p.1050-1052; approved bonds on special tax for municipal improvements, v.27, p.1146.

Louisiana Teche Seminary, see Gilbert Academy and Industrial School, v.25, p.787-788.

"Louisiana, The Aftermath of Reconstruction in," by Margaret T. Leach, v.32, p.631.

"Louisiana, The Freedmen's Bureau of," by John Cornelius Englesman, v.32, p.145.

Louisiana Treaty, used in negotiations for claims, v.24, p.946, 977, 984, 1042, 1051, 1086, 1128, 1132.

"Louisiana, Twentieth Century," by Dr. G. W. McGinty, v.32, p.5.

Louisiana Volunteer Reg't, second formation and acceptance, v.26, p.792-796; called into active service, v.26, p.796; at Camp Foster, v.26, p.797-810, 811-815; at Mobile, v.26, p.815-817; at Miami, v.26, p.817-823; near Jacksonville, v.26, p.823-827; in Savannah for embarkation, v.26, p.827; in Cuba, v.26, p.825-834; mustering out of, in Savannah, v.26, p.835; list of promotions, v.26, p.835-837; general behavior of, v.26, p.837-840; mortuary, list of, v.26, p.841.

Louisiana Volunteers Light Artillery, money voted for, v.25, p.1053.

"Louisiana Will of the Spanish Era, 1776," by Laura L. Porteous, v.11, p.607.

Louis, Jean, died leaving wealth to found hospital, v.29, p.597; bequeaths funds to establish first New Orleans Charity Hospital, v.31, p.9-12.

Louisville Medical Club, minutes in Rudolph Matas Medical Library, v.24, p.333-334.

Lourier, Peter, noted, v.22, p.983.

Louvre, exhibits at, v.24, p.1067.

Lovell, James, noted, v.23, p.386, 404.

Lovell, Joseph, noted, v.22, p.455, 461, 466, 468, 469-470, 472.

Lovell, Mansfield, noted, v.24, p.442, 443, 444, 458, 473; defense of New Orleans, v.24, p.445-446, 452, 454; Confed. general of N. O., v.26, p.958; supervisor of defense preparations in N. O., v.26, p.1008; request to Davis for better defense, v.26, p.1019; seige of N. O., v.26, p.1019-1020; Confed. Gen'l at N. O., v.27, p.487.

Love, Sam, Confed. soldier, v.26, p.952; noted, v.26, p.954.

Lowden, Andrew, Confederate soldier captured at Gettysburg, v.29, p.1215; pris-

oner at Johnson's Island, v.29, p.1215-1218.
Lowe, Frank, Confed. soldier, v.26, p.949.
Lowell, C. W., postmaster, led opposition movement to Gov. Warmoth, v.27, p.541; speaker of the Louisiana House, against lottery, v.31, p.725.
Lowndes, William, noted, v.24, p.935.
Lowrey, Walter McGehee, author, "The Political Career of James Madison Wells," v.31, p.995-1123.
Loyal Leagues, Negro organization, v.30, p.178, 194, 558.
Loyola, Joseph de, letters concerning gov't in Sp. La., v.29, p.915-917.
Loyola University, noted, v.24, p.154, 155; historical sketch, v.24, p.321; library, v.24, p.322; bulletin, v.24, p.323, 351.
Lozano, Joaq'n, interpreter, v.23, p.698.
Lozano, Juan Domingo, Captain of the "Indefatigable," v.21, p.1090-1091.
Luciano, Salvatore, and Mafia, v.22, p.820ff.
Luciano, Tony, and Mafia, v.22, p.820ff.
Lucie, Mr. and pirates, v.24, p.32, 33.
Luckett, Philip M., incorporator of La. Lottery Co., v.27, p.975.
"Luck, The, of Roaring Camp," Cable's comment on, v.24, p.173-174.
Ludeling, John T., Chief Justice, 1873, v.27, p.576; judgment in favor of Morgan, v.27, p.578; pres. North La. and Texas Railroad Co., v.30, p.1193-1196, 1204-1209; Chief Justice of Louisiana Sup. Court, presides at Wickliffe impeachment, v.31, p.691; and Kellogg impeachment, v.31, p.709.
Ludlow and Smith, management of St. Charles Theatre, v.26, p.1151, 1152.
Ludlow, Noah M., director of Am. Theatrical Commonwealth Co., v.28, p.96ff.; noted, v.28, p.252, 253; co-manager of Am. Theatre, Poydras St., v.28, p.257; season 1840-1841, v.28, p.257-263; 1841-1842, v.28, p.269-274; dominated theatrical scene, 1843, v.28, p.274; noted, v.28, p.935.
Ludwig I, King of Bavaria, v.24, p.384, 420.
Ludwig II, Grand Duke, v.24, p.421.
Lugano, G., transcription by, "Savage Law of the French Regime in Louisiana, 1765," v.15, p.482; Trans., "Minutes of Superior Council of La., March 5, 1746," v.21, p.1006-1020; "Records of the Superior Council of La.," LXXXII, Jan., 1760-Dec., 1761, v.23, p.265-94; LXXXIII, Jan.-Feb., 1762, v.23, p.589-634; LXXXIV, March-Apr., 1762, v.23, p.889-994; LXXXV, May-June, 1762, v.23, p.1258-1298; LXXXVI, July-Sept., 1762, v.24, p.211-257; LXXXVII, Oct.-Dec., 1762, v.24, p.544-600; LXXXVIII, Jan.-March, 1763, v.24, p.783-837; LXXXIX, April-May, 1763, v.23, p.1178-1231; XC, June, 1763, v.25, p.228-259; XCI, July, 1763, v.25, p.537-588; XCII, Aug., 1763, v.25, p.831-872; XCIII, Sept., 1763, v.25, p.1128-1183; XCIV, Oct., 1763, v.26, p.169-256.
Lumber, export of, v.22, p.663, 668; importation of, v.22, p.971; duty on, v.23, p.13, 58; journal of saw mill, v.23, p.729; Lutcher and Moore Cypress Lumber Co., v.30, p.1013-1014, 1027; Industry in Calcasieu Parish, v.32, p.548-558; in Louisiana, noted, v.32, p.12.
Lumsden, Francis Asbury, noted, v.24, p.35; v.30, p.254, 256; establishes "Picayune," v.31, p.719.
Luna, Tristan de, expedition of, v.22, p.936-938.
Lusher, Robert M., State supt. of ed., 1865-1868, v.25, p.750, 784, 804; educator in charge of Peabody Fund, v.30, p.755; N. O. Boys' Grammar and High School, v.30, p.869-870; noted, v.30, p.845, 867, 873, 971; cand. for supt. of education, v.31, p.535, 1055.
Lutcher, J. H., pioneer cypress lumberman, sketch of, v.30, p.1013-1014.
Lutherans, in Calcasieu Parish, v.32, p.625.
Lutcher and Moore Cypress Lumber Company, v.30, p.1013-1014, 1027.
Luther College, v.25, p.789.
Luxuries, importation of, v.22, p.669, 674.
Luzenberg, Dr. Charles Aloysius, ancestry and early life of, v.26, p.49-50; emigrated to U. S., v.26, p.50; attended Jeff. Med. College and graduated with honors, v.26, p.50; established in N. O., v.26, p.50; made House surgeon Charity Hosp., v.26, p.50-51; married, v.26, p.51; tour of Europe, v.26, p.51-52; return to N. O. and his philanthropy there, v.26, p.52-53; his proposal for and building of new hospital, v.26, p.53-55; physician in U. S. Marine Hosp. Service, 1843, v.26, p.55-56; his friendship with Henry Clay, v.26, p.56; and the typhus epidemic of 1847, v.26, p.56; his work in the establishment of the Medical College of La., v.26, p.57; his resignation, v.26, p.58; appointed administrator of Charity

Hosp., v.26, p.58-59; organized La. Med. Soc. 1843, v.26, p.59-60; on Med. Board of Censors, 1836, v.26, p.60; his activities other than Medical, v.26, p.60-61; his ability as a surgeon, v.26, p.61-63; his work with yellow fever, v.26, p.64-65; smallpox, v.26, p.65-70; case of Seminole Woman and his fight with Physico-Med. Soc., v.26, p.71-102; his death, v.26, p.102-104; characterization of, v.26, p.105-108; appendix, v.26, p.109-136; bibliog., v.26, p.136-137.

Luzenburg, Charles, attorney for lottery company, v.31, p.776.

Lyceum Library, noted, v.24, p.324.

Lyceum, People's, in New Orleans, v.23, p.1047.

Lyell, Charles, noted, v.23, p.869, 873; on Louisiana, v.31, p.400, 409, 412, 415.

Lyman, General Phineas, in W. Fla., v.22, p.33.

Lyman, Thaddeus, noted, v.22, p.45.

Lyman, William, birth and early career, v.31, p.317-318; candidate for governor of Orleans, v.31, p.317-319; consul at London, v.31, p.319.

Lynch, B. L., judge in disputed election of Pinchback to House, v.27, p.587.

Lynch Board, Repub. Returning Board, v.27, p.558; noted, v.29, p.409, 410; Anti-Warmoth returning board, formed, v.31, p.700.

Lynch, Charles, buys Bastrop lands, v.31, p.628.

Lynching, of Italians in New Orleans, v.22, p.492-525; comments upon, v.24, p.188-201.

Lynch, John, and the Returning Board in election of 1872, v.28, p.1134-1135; heads Anti-Warmoth returning board, v.31, p.700; anti-lottery bill, v.31, p.723.

Lynch, Judge, noted, v.24, p.187.

Lynch, William O., rev's "Edward Livingston," by William B. Hatcher, v.24, p.542-543.

Lyon, Dr. William, identified, v.21, p.733n.

Lyon, E. Wilson, "The Man Who Sold La.," rev'd, v.25, p.828-830.

Lyons, D. B., councilman of Crowley, v.27, p.1126.

Lyons, E. W., sheriff of Acadia, v.27, p.1127.

Lyons, J. L., Rep. of St. Landry Parish, introduced bill for creation of new parish, v.27, p.1121.

Lyons, Lucien E., Prog. League com., v.27, p.1062.

Lyons, R. B., assessor, Acadia Parish, v.27, p.1127.

Lyons, Sister Mary, La. educator, at Sacred Heart Convent in Grand Coteau, v.30, p.960, 965.

Lyons, Theodore H., treas. Prog. League, v.27, p.1062.

MACARTHY, VICTOR EUGENE, N. O. MUSICIAN, v.31, p.135.

Macarty, Augustin, noted, v.22, p.418.

Macarty, Barthelemy, land grant to, v.21, p.226.

Macarty, Bartholome, noted, v.22, p.814.

Macarty et al. vs. Mandeville, v.25, p.370-371.

Macarty, Eugene, noted, v.25, p.304, 370, 371.

Macarty, Jean Baptiste, land grant to, v.21, p.226; noted, v.23, p.684, 694; deposition of, v.23, p.730-731.

Macarty, Louis, noted, v.22, p.814.

Macauley, Dr., La. educator, organizes New Orleans Female Collegiate Institute, v.30, p.853-856; noted, v.30, p.967.

MacDonough, Thomas, noted, v.24, p.979.

MacGregor, Gregor, noted, v.24, p.623, 644, 647, 660; expedition against Panama, 1818, v.24, p.649; failure to join Aury, v.24, p.658; at Aux Cayes, v.24, p.659; with Aury, v.24, p.661-665; against Rio Hacha, v.24, p.671.

Machen, M. F., editor and business manager "La. Populist," v.26, p.1093.

Mackay, Charles, author on Louisiana, v.31, p.397, 417.

Mackey, Alexander, noted, v.23, p.877.

Mackey, T. G., noted, v.23, p.1080.

Mackie, Dr. J. M., noted, v.26, p.54, 76, 86, 87; his letter against Luzenberg, v.26, p.92-96; noted, v.26, p.99, 100.

Mackie, Harry A., Wood's adjutant, v.26, p.791; enlisted as private, v.26, p.796; made 2nd Lt., v.26, p.810.

MacLean, Dr. Basil, investigation of Charity Hospital, v.31, p.96.

Maclellan, Alexander, and W. Fla. Assembly, v.22, p.312.

"MacMahon, Laurent, Induction as Councillor, 1730," Text and translation by Heloise H. Cruzat, v.10, p.529.

"MacMahon, Laurent, First Councillor in the Superior Council of Louisiana, Director of the Company of the Indies at New Orleans, 1730-1731," by Henry P. Dart, v.10, p.517.

Macon, Bayou, course of, v.25, p.929, 930, 932.

Macon Bill No. 2, noted, v.24, p.613.

Macon Ridge, v.25, p.929; Tonti reaches, v.25, p.932.

Macri, blockade of, v.24, p.1069.

MacYntosh, Don Juan, mentioned, v.21, p.31.

MacYntosh, ———, Vincennes revolutionist, v.22, p.86.

"Madam Girard," Miss Grace King's, A review by H. P. Dart, v.5, p.51.

Madariaga, Rev. Jose Cortes, in Jamaica, v.24, p.640, 641, 646, 654, 667; "Canon of Chile," v.24, p.655; noted, v.24, p.642, 689; commissions to Aury, v.24, p.656; quoted, v.24, p.657; with Aury at Old Providence, v.24, p.670-671; letter to

Aury, v.24, p.679; death of, v.24, p.696.
Maddox, Joseph, and Well's bribery, v.31, p.1106.
Madison, Charles T., Quartermaster, v.26, p.795; his efforts to obtain supplies, v.26, p.808-809; change in rank, v.26, p.837.
Madison, James, proclamation claiming W. Fla., v.21, p.149n.; letter from Skipwith, v.21, p.141-144, 147-148; noted, v.23, p.440; and smuggling, v.23, p.442-443; letter from J. Laffite, v.23, p.752; noted, v.24, p.26, 49, 703, 709, 727, 935, 1137; documents in Bibliotheca Parsoniana, v.24, p.311; letter in Ursuline College Museum, v.24, p.335; failure to prosecute privateers from Spain, v.24, p.630; ideas of sovereignty, v.24, p.708; and Va. Resolutions, v.24, p.719; administration of, v.25, p.293, 294, 303; letters from Robinson, v.25, p.663; cited, v.25, p.664, 667, 668; declares status of West Florida, v.29, p.77; instructions to Claiborne, v.31, p.275, 277; noted, v.31, p.289, 293, 307, 325, 334, 370; appointed Sumter, v.31, p.294; and Monroe, v.31, p.337, 345; and Claiborne, v.31, p.372, 381; election, v.31, p.343; Livingston candidacy, v.31, p.352.
"Madison Parish, Louisiana, History of," by W. M. Murphy, v.11, p.39.
Maduel, Carlos, N. O. musician, v.31, p.132-133.
Maeder, James G., teaches Cushman, v.31, p.973; Cushman's voice, v.31, p.976.
Maeder, Mrs. James G., noted, v.31, p.975; Cushman's voice, v.31, p.976.
Maenhaut, Father Constantine, noted, v.31, p.913; appointed pastor, v.31, p.914; attacks by papers, v.31, p.916; to Prieur, v.31, p.919; recognized, v.31, p.963.
Mafia, incident in N. O., v.20, p.1067-1110; and murder of David Hennessy, v.22, p.492-530; history of, v.22, p.502-507; in New Orleans, v.22, p.819-856.
Magee, Augustus, noted, v.22, p.725, 726; filibuster, expedition into neutral ground, v.28, p.1053, 1055; bandit leader, v.28, p.1068-1069; Comd. Am. detachment against bandits, v.28, p.1062; comdr. filibustering expedition, v.28, p.1094.
Magee, A. W., noted, v.25, p.294, 295; U. S. leader of insurgents, v.25, p.651, 652.
Magee, Hezekial, trustee of Franklin Academy, 1838, v.29, p.84.

Magee, Rob't M., Lt. of Troop "E" of La. Inf., v.29, p.82.
Magee, T. A., appointed to Bogalusa police force, v.29, p.113; noted, v.29, p.118.
Maginnis, Col. A. A., secured aid in many ways for La. Reg'ts, v.26, p.807.
Maginnis, John, business mgr. "Daily True Delta," v.30, p.304; sketch of, v.30, p.305-306.
Magne, Jules, noted, v.23, p.1046.
"Magnolia" plantation, v.25, p.216.
Magruder, John Bankhead, noted, v.23, p.1202; v.24, p.74, 78, 79, 101.
Magruder, W. H. N., La. educator, organizes Collegiate Institute at Baton Rouge, v.30, p.774-775; at Feliciana High School in Jackson, v.30, p.828; noted, v.30, p.966; Louisiana educator, v.31, p.126.
Maguire, Francis, noted, v.23, p.26.
Mahoney, John, People's Party cand. for Treas., 1892, v.26, p.1081.
Maillard, Jacques, noted, v.22, p.685.
Maillot, Francois, case against, v.21, p.1009-1010.
Mail service, to diplomats, v.24, p.942, 976, 996-997, 999, 1020, 1026, 1042, 1051, 1060, 1069, 1076, 1088, 1092, 1094, 1107, 1110, 1114, 1125, 1140; in N. O. in 1836, v.25, p.108.
Maire, Laurent, and filibusters, v.23, p.742, 757, 766.
Maison de Sante, noted, v.24, p.312.
Maison Rouge land grant, v.20, p.289-462; owned by Skipwith and Daniel Clark, v.21, p.166; noted, v.25, p.631, 632.
Maison Rouge, Margaret, and claim to land in Ouachita, v.20, p.337.
Maison Rouge, Marquis de, plans colony, v.31, p.612.
Maissionabe, Jean Baptiste, La. educator, establishes Jesuit High School, v.30, p.956.
Maistre, Father Claude Pascal, attempt to incite Negroes against whites, v.27, p.502, 512.
Maitland, John, noted, v.23, p.29, 366.
Major, Hoguet A. (tr.), "Inventory of Duvernay Concession in La., 1726," v.21, p.985, 994; (tr.), "Lease of a La. Plantation and Slaves, 1727," v.21, p.995-997.
Major, James P., noted, v.24, p.76.
Malabar Cane, noted, v.25, p.186.
Malaria, and early rice culture, v.23, p.549.
Maligre, Joseph, noted, v.22, p.70.
Mallalieu, Bishop W. F., noted, v.25, p.779.
Malvern Hill, battle of, v.24, p.66-67.

Mamou Oil Field, v.27, p.1169, See also Evangeline.

Manassas Junction, noted, v.24, p.61, 62, 63.

Manchac, District of, established, v.22, p.40; duel of Claiborne and Clark, v.23, p.160-161; in 1769, v.23, p.394, 396; noted, v.26, p.11; Eng. troops at, v.26, p.741; Galvez's attack upon, v.26, p.742; Descoudreaux in command, v.27, p.630; reported captured by Willing, v.27, p.656; recaptured by British, v.27, p.656, 657; John McGillivray in command, v.27, p.658.

Mandeville College, v.30, p.916-917.

Mandeville de Marigny, Col. ———, duel of, v.23, p.150-151.

Mandeville, duel site, v.24, p.759, 762.

Mandeville, Henry D., and family collection in L.S.U. Archives, v.24, p.343.

Mandeville, Madame, noted, v.22, p.661n.

Mangan, Rev. Patrick, noted, v.22, p.99.

"Mangoree," pirate vessel, v.24, p.362.

Mangourit, Michel Ange Bernard de, noted, v.22, p.56.

"Manhattaner in N. O.," A. Oakey Hall, about McDonogh, v.26, p.142.

"Manifest Destiny," by A. Curtis Wilgus, v.15, p.486; and Cuban question, v.22, p.1095-1167; noted, v.25, p.1110.

"Manigault," plantation, description of, v.23, p.547.

Mann, Ambrose Dudley, letters to, from J. P. Benjamin, v.20, p.738-793.

Mannerchor, noted, v.24, p.160.

Manning, M. C., quoted, v.24, p.101.

Manning, Thomas C., report of Committee of Credentials, v.26, p.988; managed Moore's plantation, v.26, p.1045; noted, v.27, p.1227; sketch, v.27, p.1227-1228; Wells default, v.31, p.1002-1003; on Wells, v.31, p.1005; White League, v.31, p.1096; Anderson decision, v.31, p.1112.

"Man of God and a Servant of Humanity: The Rev. Marie Arthur Guillaume Le Mercier du Quesnay," by Andre Lafargue, v.20, p.680-689.

"Manon Lescaut, The Real Versus the Ideal," by Victorin Dejan, Trans. from the French by Heloise H. Cruzat, v.2, p.313.

Manouvrier, G. P., N. O. musician, v.31, p.131-132.

Mansfield Academy, v.30, p.820.

Mansfield Baptist Academy, v.25, p.789.

Mansfield, battle of, v.24, p.88-90, 92; noted, v.24, p.99, 100.

Mansfield, Edward, noted, v.24, p.654.

Mansfield, in 1860, v.21, p.1172.

Mansura, located, v.21, p.1147.

Mansuy, ———, engineer, v.23, p.681.

Mansvelt, noted, v.24, p.10.

Mantegue, ———, noted, v.22, p.815.

Manufacturing, ills of poor in England, v.24, p.998-999; progress in France, v.24, p.1067-1068.

Manumission of slaves, v.25, p.336-356.

"Manuscript of General Richard Taylor's 'Destruction and Reconstruction,'" by Andre Lafargue, v.13, p.46.

Manuscripts, collection in La., v.24, p.305, 353; other collections cited, v.24, p.316, 320, 331, 333, 349-353.

"Manuscripts, Some Inedited Gayarre," by Edward Alexander Parsons, v.33, p.189-204.

"Man Who Sold La.: The Career of Francois Barbe-Marbois," by E. Wilson Lyon, rev'd, v.25, p.828-830.

Maps, collection in Howard-Tilton Memorial Library, v.24, p.329; of La., noted, v.21, p.53, 64; Latourette's of St. Mary Parish, noted, v.32, p.23, 24, 63.

Marabon, defined, v.25, p.301.

Marbois, Vincente de, noted, v.22, p.666.

Marchand, Nicholas, accompanied Cathcart expedition, v.28, p.739, 752, 754, 755, 757, 770, 811.

Marchand, Sidney A., "Story of Ascension Parish," rev'd by Edith Dart Price, v.14, p.569.

Marchese, Paulo, and Mafia, v.22, p.836.

Marciacq, J. L., owner of "Le Vigilant," v.31, p.981-982, 983-986.

Marcos, Capt. ———, noted, v.22, p.1026ff.

Marcy, Lena Gomez, noted, v.24, p.322.

Marcy, William L., noted, v.23, p.162.

Mardi Gras Creek, noted, v.26, p.749.

Mardi Gras, noted, v.24, p.169; in New Orleans, 1862, v.24, p.447; in N. O., v.26, p.404; noted, v.26, p.449.

Mareuil, Baron de, noted, v.24, p.946, 1023, 1053, 1063, 1080.

Margarita Island, noted, v.24, p.651, 665, 669, 688.

Margil, Antonio, noted, v.25, p.362.

"Margry, Pierre," by Bussiere Rouen, v.5, p.192.

Marienat, John, noted, v.22, p.419.

Marigny, Bernard, "Reflections on Jackson's Campaign, 1814-1815," v.6, p.61; land titles of, v.21, p.228; noted, v.22, p.808; sketch, v.22, p.811; collection in

Howard-Tilton Memorial Library, v.24, p.330; noted, v.25, p.984, 1007, 1010, 1022, 1075, 1083; pres. pro. tem. of const. conv. of 1844, v.25, p.1007; on the rights of foreign born citizens, v.25, p.1012, 1014, 1016, 1019-1020; the campaign of 1846, v.25, p.1037; noted, v.30, p.446.

Marimon, Juan, noted, v.24, p.616, 626, 636.

Marin, E., noted, v.24, p.48.

"Marine Survey of Schooner Charlotte, 1777," translation by Laura L. Porteous, v.13, p.230.

Marin, Louis, de la Marque, case against Thibierge, v.21, p.1003, 1013-1020.

Marinos, Pedro, noted, v.22, p.815.

Markey-Pickard Institute, v.30, p.874-875.

Marks, I. N., noted, v.24, p.767.

Marks, Samuel F., auditor on Dem. ticket, 1855, v.25, p.680; teller of the senate, v.25, p.1039; nominated for Dem. Cand. for Gov., v.26, p.988, 989.

Marksville Complex, v.25, p.398.

Marksville Female Academy, sketch of, v.30, p.762-763.

Marksville High School, sketch of, v.30, p.763-764.

Marksville, La., in 1860, v.21, p.1147; noted, v.24, p.95; noted, v.25, p.398.

"Maronne" plantation, location of, v.23, p.439.

Marquez, Frank, opposed lottery, v.27, p.1040, 1056.

"Marquis de Maison Rouge, the Baron de Bastrop and Col. Abraham Morhouse: Three Ouachita Valley Soldiers of Fortune. The Maison Rouge and Bastrop Spanish Land 'Grant'" by Jennie O'Kelly Mitchell and Robert D. Calhoun, v.20, p.289-462.

Marraro, Howard R., "Auguste Davezac's Mission to the Kingdom of the Two Sicilies, 1833-1834," v.32, p.791.

"Marriage Contract between Pierre LeMoine D'Iberville and Marie Therese Pollet de la Combe," Translated by Heloise H. Cruzat, v.17, p.242.

"Marriage Contracts of French Colonial Louisiana," by Henry P. Dart, v.17, p.229.

"Marriage Contracts of the Spanish Period in Louisiana," Translated by Laura L. Porteous, v.9, p.385.

Marr, Rob't H., supports claims of McMillen for Senate, v.27, p.592; judge denouncing Kellogg, v.27, p.778; noted, v.29, p.718; of committee of seventy, v.29, p.721; noted, v.29, p.722.

Marshall, ———, noted, v.23, p.402.

Marshall, Henry, La. delegate to conv. of seceding states, v.26, p.1002.

Marshall, John, in bad health, v.24, p.1160.

Marshall, Mary Louise, study of Thomas Wade, v.24, p.333, 334, 351.

Marshall, Mrs. Eliza, money from James Brown, v.24, p.1145.

Marshall, Thos. A., noted, v.23, p.204.

Marshall, Thos. A., Jr., Sec. Prog. League, v.27, p.1062.

Marshall, William, noted, v.23, p.42, 361, 368, 377, 391.

Marsh Island, v.28, p.800ff.

"Marte," Spanish brig, v.24, p.664, 665.

Martial Law, in New Orleans, 1862, v.24, p.447.

Marti, Jose Julian, tribute to Benjamin, v.23, p.259-264.

Martindale, Daniel, sketch, v.31, p.123; affiliates with Centenary College, v.31, p.124; founds chapter of "Mystic Seven," v.31, p.125; charged with corruption, v.31, p.126-127; board investigation, v.31, p.127-128; continues work, v.31, p.129; sketch, v.31, p.129.

Martineau, Harriet, noted, v.31, p.56; author on Louisiana, v.31, p.397, 406, 407.

Martinez, Francisco, noted, v.22, p.1026ff.

Martinez, Pizarro Francisco, sec. to Morphy, v.23, p.827.

Martin, Father, noted, v.25, p.362.

Martin, Francois Xavier, second pres. of the La. Hist. Soc., v.19, p.42-69; early life in France, v.19, p.46-47; printer and lawyer in N. Car., v.19, p.47-48; wrote history of N. Car., v.19, p.49-50; Judge of Superior Court of the Territory of Orleans, v.19, p.51-55; published digest of decisions of the Supreme Court and History of La., v.19, p.56-57; developed jurisprudence in La., v.19, p.57-63; and Andrew Jackson, v.21, p.369; noted, v.22, p.749; on La. Sup. Ct., v.23, p.1027, 1028, 1029, 1035; as historian, v.23, p.1043, 1045; Bullard's eulogy on, v.23, p.1051-1053; believed Iberville responsible for change in course of Miss. at Pointe Coupee, v.28, p.70; ruled Johnson's oath of office valid, v.28, p.966; noted, v.33, p.171; his History of La., v.33, p.171; noted, v.33, p.256.

Martinique, privateers of, v.23, p.433; base for privateers, v.24, p.10.

Martin, James, noted, v.22, p.434, 435.

Martin, John Allen, and W. Fla. Assembly, v.23, p.23, 357, 358, 368.

Martin, Judge F. X., and nullification, v.25, p.91, 351; noted, v.25, p.979, 980; quoted on slavery agitation, v.25, p.999, 1000-1001.

Martin, R. C., noted, v.23, p.189.

Martin, Rev. A. M., noted, v.25, p.362.

Martin, Rev. F., noted, v.25, p.362.

Marx, Max, "Grand Old Man of Bogalusa," v.29, p.99.

Mary, Aristide, noted, v.25, p.364, 734.

Maryland, free Negroes in, v.25, p.319; emigration of McDonogh, v.25, p.340.

Mary Madeline Sophie, Sister, noted, v.24, p.336.

Mary Redempta, Sister, noted, v.24, p.337.

Mary Reginald, Sister, noted, v.24, p.325.

Mason, A. H., noted, v.24, p.104.

Mason, Benjamin, mayor of Carrollton, v.21, p.252; noted, v.22, p.203.

Mason, George, noted, v.24, p.118.

Masonic Institute of Clinton, v.30, p.829-831.

Mason, John, and W. Fla. Rev., v.21, p.79, 156.

Mason, Leonard F., "Regular" cand. for Sec. of State, v.26, p.1081; refused promulgation of Lottery Bill, v.27, p.1050; sued by Morris, v.27, p.1050-1052; Lotteryite cand. for Sec. of State, v.27, p.1090; refused to promulgate lottery amendment, v.28, p.1149; cand. Sec. of State, v.28, p.1185; Sec. of State, v.31, p.826.

Masons, at Frankfort, v.24, p.418; noted, v.24, p.1153, 1154.

Masons, Grand Lodge of N. O., honors Calhoun, Webster, Clay, v.27, p.765; ceremonies for laying cornerstone of Clay's monument, v.27, p.770; in charge of dedicating and unveiling of Clay's statue, v.27, p.774; La. Grand Lodge, v.27, p.969, 1194, 1195.

Masot, Jose, and Spanish filibusters, v.21, p.809; and Job Northrup, v.22, p.1056-1058.

Maspero, Pierre, first manager of St. Louis Hotel, v.25, p.991.

Massachusetts, Body of liberties of, v.24, p.701.

Massenet, Father, noted, v.22, p.941.

Masse, Opelousas trader attempted to settle in Sp. territory, v.26, p.713.

Massicot, Louis, and Gutierrez-Magee expedition, v.22, p.783-784.

"Master of the Mississippi: Henry Shreve and the Conquest of the Miss.," by Florence L. Dorsey, rev'd, v.25, p.824-827.

Matagorda, noted, v.24, p.637, 641, 642, 643.

Matanzas, Cuba, port, v.24, p.629.

Matas, Rudolph, M. D., "Address at Reception by Louisiana Historical Society to the Southern Medical Association, 1924," v.8, p.449; "Yellow Fever Retrospect and Prospect, A," v.8, p.454; "An Evening With Gayarre," v.33, p.269-293.

"Material for Poems," quoted, v.24, p.183.

Matesi, Francesco, and New Orleans Mafia, v.22, p.819ff.

Mather and Panton, traders, v.21, p.13.

Mather and Strother Co., identified, v.21, p.13n., 27.

Mather, Geo. Jr., and W. Fla. Rev., v.21, p.688, 696n.

Mather, James, mayor of New Orleans, attempts to establish provisional hospital, v.31, p.35-38, 40; buys plantation to house hospital, v.31, p.42-43.

Mather, Joseph, diary in L.S.U. Archives, v.24, p.343.

Mather, Santiago, granted trading privileges, v.21, p.13.

"Mathews, George, Panegyric on," by Etienne Mazureau, v.4, p.154.

Mathews, George, sketch, v.21, p.91n.; noted, v.23, p.1027.

Mathews, Leonard, noted, v.23, p.204.

Mathias, William, noted, v.22, p.364.

Mathieson Alkali Works, in Lake Charles, v.27, p.1170.

Matranga, Charles, and Mafia, v.22, p.510-512.

Matranga, Tony, and Mafia, v.22, p.510-512.

Matthews, Charles, noted, v.24, p.371.

Matthews, O. J., noted, v.23, p.405.

Matthews, R. Bowman, early N. O. newspaperman, v.29, p.781-782.

Maudet, Lt. Fr. naval officer, saved from death in Yellow Fever epidemic in N. O., v.28, p.329-331; gets money to build memorial to lost comrades, v.28, p.332-333.

Maunsell, Edward, noted, v.23, p.527.

Mauns, Rev. N. A., noted, v.24, p.140.

Maurian, Charles, chairman of House Com. on Int. Impvts., v.30, p.29; committees served on, v.30, p.30, 33, 63; noted, v.30, p.28; parish judge, v.31, p.950; decision, v.31, p.953.

Maury, Dabney H., noted, v.24, p.104, 109, 118.

"Mauseturm" legend, quoted, v.24, p.420.
Maverick, Lewis, noted, v.23, p.1161, 1234.
Maverick, Sam, noted, v.23, p.1234.
Maximiliano, Don, noted, v.22, p.1014.
Maxwell, Barry, N. O. minstrel, sketch of, v.30, p.140-141.
May, Albert H., Jr., noted, v.23, p.527.
Mayas, noted, v.24, p.331-332.
Mayfield, J. T., Conf. soldier, v.26, p.955.
Mayfield, Robert, N. O. newspaperman and painter, v.33, p.422.
Mayflower Compact, noted, v.24, p.701.
Mayo, George, noted, v.25, p.1022; on Comm. for support of schools, v.25, p.1042-1043; conference committee, v.25, p.1046, 1051, 1052, 1054.
Mayo, Henry M., newspaperman, noted, v.33, p.423-424.
Mayo, W. T., pioneer N. O. music publisher, v.31, p.132, 147-148; buys Johns' business, v.31, p.859.
May, Thomas P., founder of "N. O. Times," v.30, p.280.
Mazange, Leonardo, noted, v.22, p.631.
"Mazeppa," and Theatre, v.21, p.846ff.
Mazureau, Adolphe, noted, v.22, p.413.
Mazureau, Etienne, "Panegyric on George Mathews," v.4, p.254; N. O. lawyer, v.19, p.332; noted, v.22, p.808, 813; v.24, p.371, 757, 1152; noted, v.25, p.980; antagonist of Soule, v.25, p.999, 1007; Civil Code of, v.25, p.1049; and the Guerrero pirate case, v.25, p.1078, 1081, 1084, 1085; and College of Jefferson, v.31, p.853.
"Mazureau's Oration on Mathews," by Henry P. Dart, v.4, p.149.
McAlpin, Lee, Dem.-Populist elector, v.26, p.1116.
McCain, J. M., opposed lottery question, v.27, p.1040.
McCain, William D., "Papers of the Food Administration for La., 1917-1919, in the Nat'l Archives," v.21, p.869-874.
McCaleb, E. Howard, on com. to supervise primary, v.27, p.1094; v.28, p.1161.
McCaleb, Theodore H., Judge, noted, v.22, p.1133; v.23, p.1056, 1060, 1066, 1067; spoke in memory of Calhoun, v.27, p.769; oration on Clay, v.27, p.770.
McCall, Gen'l G. A., noted, v.29, p.345-346.
McCall, Henry, proposed cand. for Gov., v.28, p.1175.
McCall, Miss Kate, corresponding sec., Women's Anti-Lottery League, v.27, p.1061.
McCalmont, Maggie, La. educator, organ-
izes Millwood Institute, v.30, p.827.
McCargo, Thomas, and "Creole" case, v.23, p.1033.
McCarthy, Harry, musician, writes, "Bonnie Blue Flag," v.31, p.145-146.
McCarthy, Terrence, N. O. newspaperman, v.33, p.332.
McCarty, Jean Baptiste, history of plantation, v.22, p.187-189.
McCaskey, Benjamin P., boatswain in Confed. navy, v.27, p.485.
McCausland, Robert, and W. Fla. Rev., v.21, p.108, 709n.; recommendation of, v.21, p.201-202.
McCerran, Landry and Co., slave dealers, v.22, p.152, 153.
McClelland, George B., nomination of, v.23, p.1215; noted, v.24, p.63, 486.
McClendon, J. L., of Bogalusa, v.29, p.92.
McCloskey, Dean John F., sponsor of Museum of Pharmacy, v.26, p.337.
McCloy, Shelby T., "French Charities to the Acadians, 1755-1799," v.21, p.656-668; "Government Assistance in Eighteenth-Century France," rev'd, v.30, p.350-352.
McClure, Col. A. K., opposed lottery, v.31, p.783; v.27, p.1010-11, 1012.
McClure, J. E., co-founder of "N. O. Crescent," v.30, p.268; noted, v.30, p.296.
McComb, Henry S., pres. N. O., Jackson and Great Northern Railroad, v.30, p.1143-1148.
McConnell, Jas., amended lottery bill to provide revenue for disabled veterans, v.27, p.970; opposed bill authorizing lotteries for charitable institutions, v.27, p.971; McClure's counsel in N. O., v.27, p.1011; attacked monopolistic features of lottery, v.27, p.1055; address to Dem. Anti-Lottery St. Com., v.27, p.1091; anti-lotteryite, v.28, p.1158.
McCormack, Thomas, noted, v.22, p.434.
McCormeck, Simon, v.23, p.404.
McCormick, Dr., noted, v.26, p.56.
McCulloch, Henry E., noted, v.24, p.75.
McCulloch, Hugh, letters from G. S. Denison, v.23, p.1221, 1223, 1229-1231.
McCullar, Ben, Conf. soldier, v.26, p.954.
McCutcheon, Roger Philip, "Libraries in N. O., 1771-1833," v.20, p.152-158; "Books and Booksellers in N. O., 1730-1830," v.20, p.606-618.
McDaniel, Hilda Mulvey, "Francis Tillou Nicholls and the End of Reconstruction," v.32, p.357.
McDermott, Bryan, identified, v.21, p.162;

and W. Fla. Rev., v.21, p.707n.

McDermott, Charlotte, marriage to Isaac Johnson, v.28, p.947; ancestry, v.28, p.947n.

McDermott, John Francis, "Diary of Charles Dehault Delassus from New Orleans to St. Louis, 1836," v.30, p.360-438.

McDonald, Joe, Confed. soldier, v.26, p.954.

"McDonogh, John, Slave Owner," by Lane C. Kendall, I, v.15, p.646; II, v.16, p.125; will broken by Judah P. Benjamin, v.19, p.989-992; agent of W. Fla., v.21, p.151; colonization of Slaves, v.21, p.1082-1083; noted, v.22, p.434, 435, 438, 439; slaves of, v.23, p.872, 882; noted, v.23, p.1035, 1049; documents in Bibliotheca Parsoniana, v.24, p.311; collection in Tilton Memorial Library, v.24, p.329, 330; philanthropist, and manumission, v.25, p.339, 340-346; will of, v.25, p.350-351; sketch of career, v.25, p.384-385; letter to Rev. Gurley, v.25, p.385-388, 790-791; Succession case, v.25, p.1079; and Miss. R. Trade, v.26, p.37-43; statue of, v.26, p.139-140; body removed to Baltimore, v.26, p.140; subsequent history of his grave, v.26, p.140-141; erection of monument in Lafayette Sq., v.26, p.141-142; became a legend, v.26, p.142-143; early life in N. O., v.26, p.143; possible reasons for his becoming a recluse, v.26, p.143-148; his life and habits in McDonoghville, v.26, p.145-150; the manumission of slaves, v.26, p.151; his great wealth, v.26, p.151; N. O. prejudice against, v.26, p.152-153; an interview with the Baroness de Pontalba, v.26, p.153-156; his death and the reading of his will, v.26, p.156-158; description of the McDonogh tomb, v.26, p.158-161; controversy over estate, v.28, p.978; from apprentice to successful trader, v.33, p.16-40; the Land Colossus, v.33, p.40-63; Soldier, Politician and Man of Religion, v.33, p.64-71; Educator and Dabbler in Science and Technology, v.33, p.71-116; Foster Father of Liberian Colonists, v.33, p.117-129; And as it Must to All Men, v.33, p.129-144; sent to N. O., v.33, p.181; opened store, v.33, p.18; associated with John and William Taylor, v.33, p.20-37; land holdings, v.33, p.41-43; land speculation, v.33, p.43-46; Fla. land claims, v.33, p.44-53; sale and purchase of plantations, v.33, p.55-56; City real estate, v.33, p.56-57; trouble with surveying, v.33, p.58; McDonoghville, v.33, p.61; Religious education, v.33, p.64-65; work in religion, v.33, p.66-67; education, v.33, p.72; theories of education, v.33, p.73, 76; relations with his brothers, v.33, p.75-82; education of slaves, v.33, p.86-88; interest in possibilities of steamboats, v.33, p.91; interest in railroad development, v.33, p.92; brickyard, v.33, p.94; place in N. O. society, v.33, p.96-100; moves to McDonoghville, v.33, p.100; reasons for move, v.33, p.101; health, v.33, p.102-103; Almonester Legend, v.33, p.104-106; living quarters, v.33, p.108-109; clothing, v.33, p.110; travels, v.33, p.112; work, v.33, p.113; gardens, v.33, p.114; relation with colonists, v.33, p.117-129; death, v.33, p.129-130; newspaper accounts of death, v.33, p.131-133; funeral, v.33, p.134-136; robbery of house, v.33, p.138-139; monument, v.33, p.140-141; "Man of Many Facets," by Dr. Arthur G. Nuhrah, v.33, p.4-144.

McDonough, John, authorized financial agent for West Fla., v.29, p.77.

McDowell, F. B., "Reminiscenses of Days That are Gone," v.2, p.321 (From an old copy of Charleston Observer, by the courtesy of Miss Grace King).

McDuffie, George, and tariff of 1832, v.23, p.1012; scene in House of Representatives, v.24, p.996-997; and tariff, v.25, p.50, 63, 65, 66, 81, 83, 84, 85, 88-89, 90, 105, 131.

McDuffie, H. E., Confed. naval officer, v.27, p.484.

McElroy, John, only Catholic in Bogalusa until 1906, v.29, p.89.

McEnery, John, noted, v.24, p.115; nominated by "fusion" ticket for gov., v.27, p.553-554; declared elected by DeFeriet Returning Board, v.27, p.558; gubernatorial race, v.27, p.563; pleadings to Grant, v.27, p.568, 569, 572, 574, 575; inauguration of as gov., v.27, p.575-576, 579, 580; Lottery Co. admits interference in election of 1872, v.27, p.996; noted, v.28, p.312; and election of 1872, v.28, p.1134ff.; supported by Warmoth, v.29, p.398; Democratic candidate for Gov., v.29, p.400; N. O. "Republican" comments on him, v.29, p.405-406; claims election, v.29, p.411, 412; noted, v.29, p.413; inaugurated one of dual gov's of La., v.29, p.414; election investigated, v.29, p.416; resists Kellogg gov't, v.29, p.418, 419, 423; noted, v.29, p.427; declared gov. by his party, v.29, p.432; noted, v.29, p.433, 434, 437, 438; publishes protest over election, v.29, p.440; letter concerning taxes, v.29, p.462; noted, v.29, p.488, 715, 717, 722, 723, 727, 728, 729; Demo. cand. for gov. reform ticket, v.30, p.218, 638; election of, v.30, p.220; events following election of, v.30, p.220-223, 645-646; cand. for gov., v.31, p.535, 700, 837; noted, v.31, p.67, 705, 739, 836.

McEnery, Samuel D., headed ticket for lottery Democrats, 1892, v.25, p.716; Wood on staff of, v.26, p.785; called meeting of farmers, v.26, p.1063-1064; "Regular" cand. for gov., 1892, v.26, p.1078, 1080, 1081; speech to Democrats, v.26, p.1106, 1109; named U. S. Senator by Leg., v.26, p.1111; noted, v.27, p.789, 790; senator from La., 1897, v.27, p.818; voted for treaty with Sp., v.27, p.832-833; resolution of regarding Philippines, v.27, p.833; supported Heard for gov. of La., 1900, v.27, p.847; justice concurred in opinion that gov's signature not necessary on bill proposing const. amendment, v.27, p.1052; announced as cand. for gov. by Lottery-ites, v.27, p.1088, 1089, 1090, 1091; campaign, v.27, p.1091-1092; efforts to unite factions, v.27, p.1093-1094; campaign, v.27, p.1094; election disputed, v.27, p.1094-1095; cand. for gov., 1892, v.28, p.1155ff.; noted, v.28, p.1171, 1172; appt'd U. S. sen., v.28, p.1184; efforts to save La. sugar industry, v.28, p.1209-1210; death of, v.28, p.1222; elected Lt. Gov. of La., v.29, p.744, 751.

McFarland, A. D., noted, v.23, p.560, 568.

McFarland, J. W., Farmers' Alliance leader, v.26, p.1070; People's Party elector, v.26, p.1087; cand. for Sec. of State on 1st Populist ticket, 1896, v.26, p.1101; on 2nd Populist ticket, v.26, p.1102; Dem.-Populist elector, v.26, p.1116; temp. chairman Populist nom. Conv., v.28, p.1175; cand. Sec. of State, v.28, p.1176-1177.

McFarland, Leander, Confed. soldier, v.26, p.968.

McGillivray, Alexander, sketch, v.21, p.18n.; and Carondelet, v.21, p.25n.

McGillivray, John, and Am. Rev., v.22, p.43-44; noted, v.22, p.317; noted, v.23, p.361, 368, 379, 401.

McGinn, Wallace, Jr., postmaster of Crowley, v.27, p.1156.

McGinty, G. W., "Changes in La. Agriculture, 1860-1880," v.18, p.407-429; "Twentieth Century Louisiana," v.32, p.5.

McGloin, Frank, introduced ordinance on lotteries and monopolies, 1879, v.27, p.999; speaker at anti-lottery meeting, May, 1890, v.27, p.1055; presiding Anti-Lottery League meeting, v.27, p.1055; Ex. Com. Anti-Lottery League, v.27, p.1056.

McGrath, John, noted, v.29, p.1041, 1042.

McGuire, R. F., copy of diary in Shreve Memorial Library, v.24, p.339.

McHenry, Judge John, noted, v.24, p.758; v.25, p.1051, 1084; Soule sentenced by for contempt of court, v.25, p.1089-1093.

McHenry, Mathew, noted, v.22, p.981; and W. Fla. Assembly, v.23, p.5ff.

McIntosh, Alexander, noted, v.22, p.981; and W. Fla. Assembly, v.23, p.25, 42, 357, 368; election of, v.23, p.377; petition of, v.23, p.403.

McIntosh, John, noted, v.23, p.357, 368.

McIntosh, Mrs. L. J., La. educator, v.30, p.842.

McIntyre, John, noted, v.22, p.191.

McKay, Zuinglius, noted, v.22, p.204.

McKean, Ed., Ass't Paymaster, v.27, p.480.

McKean, Rev. ———, pastor in New Orleans, v.22, p.450.

McKee, John, sketch, v.21, p.102n.

McKinley, Judge, ruled Bain telegraph legal, v.31, p.470.

McKinney, Samuel, La. educator, supervisor Castleton Female Seminary, v.30, p.778-779.

McKnight, D. A., Law partner of E. John Ellis, v.29, p.753.

McKnight, George, poem by, v.29, p.1220-1222.

McLean, Malcolm Douglas (co-author), "Handbook for Translators of Spanish Historical Documents," rev'd, v.25, p.536.

McLean, William J., noted, v.23, p.240.

McLemore, R. A., "Jeffersonian Diplomacy in the Purchase of La., 1803," v.18, p.346-353.

McLoughlin, Mrs. James J., "Zachary Taylor: A Sketch of his Life," v.18, p.377-381.

McLure, Mary Lilla, "The Elections of 1860 in Louisiana," v.9, p.601; "General

Solomon Wethersbee Downs (1801-1854), v.17, p.5.

McManus, Hugh, Anti-Lottery League financial com., v.27, p.1056.

McMillen, James A., noted, v.24, p.320; "A Rare Confed. La. State Document and Its History," v.27, p.1226-1228.

McMillen, Wm. L., Fusionist claimant for Senate, v.27, p.579; elected U. S. senator by McEnery Legis., v.27, p.590; right to seat in Senate referred to com. on Privileges and Elections, v.27, p.592; no decision reached, v.27, p.592; withdraws credentials, v.27, p.600.

McMullen, Alexander, letter from R. Kemper, v.21, p.116-117.

McMurtrie, Douglas C., "The French Press of La.," v.18, p.947-965; work on early printing in New Orleans, v.24, p.312, 351.

McNair, John, state supt. of public ed. in La., 1864-1865, v.25, p.749.

McNeil, Joseph, noted, v.22, p.434, 435, 439, 449; v.23, p.1243.

McNeil, S. D., Sec. Soc. of Nat. History and the Sciences, v.26, p.61.

McPhelin, John, v.29, p.716.

McPherson, Alexander, noted, v.23, p.26, 358, 360, 380.

McPherson, James, noted, v.22, p.37.

McPherson vs. Robinson et al., v.25, p.318.

McQueen, John, introduced ribbon cane, v.25, p.54.

McRea, Major, O'Reilly agent, v.31, p.439.

McShane, ———, and Jones-Gurley duel, v.24, p.778-779.

McStravick, People's Party Cand. Sec. of State, 1892, v.26, p.1081.

McWaters, Benjamin, and W. Fla. Rev., v.21, p.131.

McWhorter, George C., noted, v.25, p.1046, 1051, 1052, 1098; cand. for State Treasurer, v.31, p.501.

McWhortle, Geo., State treasurer and state banking controversy, v.28, p.979.

Meader, Herman, Anti-Lottery League financial com., v.27, p.1056.

Meade, Robert Douthat, "Judah P. Benjamin, Confed. Statesman," rev'd, v.26, p.1170-1171.

Meamelouc, defined, v.25, p.301.

Means, Edward J., letterbook in L.S.U. Archives, v.24, p.343.

Mease, Edward, noted, v.23, p.382.

Mechanics' Institute, meeting in of Repub. Returning officers, v.27, p.560, 564, 566; Legis. assembled at recognition by Fed'l gov't, v.27, p.569, 573, 574, 575, 579; meeting in to devise means of erecting statue honoring Clay, v.27, p.764; riot at, v.29, p.47-48.

Mechanics' Society of N. Y., letter the germ of the Livingston Criminal Code, v.24, p.724.

Mecklin, A. W., N. O. newspaperman, v.33, p.331.

"Medallion, The New Orleans Bi-Centennial," Andre Lafargue, v.7, p.87.

Medical College of Louisiana (now Tulane), establishment and first years of, v.26, p.57-58; uses Charity Hospital facilities, v.31, p.69-70.

Medical Committee in New Orleans, register in Rudolph Matas Medical Library, v.24, p.334.

"Medical Science, Original Contributions of Louisiana to" (A Bibliographic Study), by Edmond Souchon, M. D., v.1, sec.1, p.85.

Medical Society of W. Fla., v.21, p.710-711.

Medicine, doctor of Colonial La., v.22, p.402, 425; in Sp. New Orleans, v.22, p.677ff.; tropical, in N. O., v.23, p.735; history of in N. O., 1830-1848, v.26, p.49-137.

Medlenka, J. G., sponsored developments of shipping facilities in Crowley, v.27, p.1175.

Meegel, Edward, noted, v.22, p.203.

Meeker, S. F., thought lotteries morally evil, v.27, p.1039.

Meeks, Theodore, noted, v.22, p.201, 204.

Meigs, Quartermaster-General, noted, v.24, p.535.

Mejan, Count, Fr. Consul in N. O., 1857, v.28, p.330, 335.

"Membrede, Installation of De, as King's Lieutenant," Introduction by Henry P. Dart, Translated by Heloise H. Cruzat, v.14, p.235.

Membre, Father Zenobe, his account of LaSalle's voyage down the Miss., v.26, p.723.

"Memoir of the War in West Florida and Louisiana, 1814-1815, Historical," by Major A. Lacarriere Latour, v.2, p.143.

"Memorialists to Congress, 1804, Orleans Territory," by Everett S. Brown, v.1, sec.1, p.99.

"Memorial of John Perkins," ed. by P. L. Rainwater, v.20, p.965-989.

Menard, J. W., named in Wickliffe impeachment, v.31, p.693.

Menchaca, Jose, and revolt in Mexico, v.22, p.719n., 721.

Mendez, Lopez, noted, v.24, p.649, 650.

Menendez de Aviles y Marquez, Pedro, noted, v.22, p.938.

Menillon, Louis Augustin, deposition of, v.23, p.721-722.

Menken, Adah Isaacs, actress in N. O., v.21, p.846-868; identity of her father questioned, v.26, p.162; letter from concerning her faith, v.26, p.163; education, v.26, p.163; her marriage to Alexander Isaac Menken, v.26, p.164; her poetic and other contributions to her faith, v.26, p.164-165; her theatrical career, v.26, p.166-167; her illness and death, v.26, p.168.

Menou, Count de, and claims, v.24, p.1022-1024, 1034, 1063.

Mentz, E. B., Assistant Sec. of State, v.27, p.582.

Mentzinger, Henry, deposition of, v.23, p.694-696.

Mercer, Dr. W. H., noted, v.24, p.489; helped pay mortgage on Clay's home, v.27, p.721; Clay's reception at home of, v.27, p.739, 749

Merchants Bank of N. O., v.25, p.989.

Merchants Exchange of N. O., noted, v.24, p.761; v.25, p.174.

Merchant, W. B., N. O. postmaster, suit against, v.27, p.1008-1009.

Mercier, Alfred, quoted on Soule, v.25, p.974, 975, 976, 991, 993; on American "intrusion" in Fr. affairs, v.25, p.982; on the burning of the St. Louis Hotel, v.25, p.991-992; on Soule's interest in education, v.25, p.1040; on his maiden senatorial address, v.25, p.1065, 1067-1068; quoted on Guerrero pirates trial, v.25, p.1077-1078; noted, v.25, p.1079; describes Soule's oratorical method, v.25, p.1080-1081, 1082.

Mercier, Amatine, Soule's bride, v.25, p.980.

Mercier and Company, book dealers, v.22, p.686.

Mercier, Dr. Armand, and case of Sally Miller, v.22, p.162; Charter member of Med. Soc., v.26, p.59; noted, v.26, p.103; noted, v.33, p.281.

Mercier, Jean Baptiste, deposition of, v.23, p.705.

Mercier, Jean, pere, noted, v.23, p.696.

Merida, Rafael Diego, noted, v.24, p.622.

Merle, John A., noted, v.22, p.458.

Mermentau, v.28, p.739, 765, 811, 817, 826, 829, 830, 845, 886, 1023, 1024, 1027, 1046.

Merrill, Louis Taylor, "General Benjamin F. Butler and the Widow Mumford," v.29, p.341-354.

Merry, J. F., noted, v.23, p.559.

Metairie Association, noted, v.24, p.117.

"Metairie," plantation, sold, v.21, p.1070.

Methodists, in N. O., v.21, p.826-828; Church in Carrollton, v.22, p.209; in Calcaiseu Parish, v.32, p.620; in St. Mary Parish, v.32, p.75; Episcopal (North) in Calcasieu Parish, v.32, p.625.

Metif, defined, v.25, p.301.

Metivier, John, noted, v.22, p.982.

Metoyer, Augustin, noted, v.25, p.347, 362.

Metoyer, family name of free negroes, v.25 ,p.321.

Metoyer, Jean Baptiste Augustin, v.25, p.319, 371, 383.

Metropolitan Police, and the White League, v.23, p.530ff.; v.29, p.47, 48, 418, 420, 421, 435, 452, 474, 475, 476; created by Warmoth, v.31, p.698; used against Wickliffe, v.31, p.688-689.

Metternich, diplomatic actions of, v.24, p.940; in Paris, v.24, p.943.

Metz, Dr. Abraham L., Chemist of board of health, v.26, p.819.

Metzinger, Juan Baptiste Antoniette, and W. Fla. Rev., v.21, p.720n.

Meullion, Dr. Ennemond, noted, v.24, p.733.

Meullion family, papers in L.S.U. Archives, v.24, p.343.

Meunier, ————, noted, v.22, p.624.

Mexican Association of N. O., v.25, p.9, 18, 20.

Mexican Gulf Railroad Company, history of, v.30, p.1130.

"Mexican or Petit Gulf Cotton," v.25, p.175.

Mexican Revolution, Firebrand affair, v.21, p.203-212.

Mexican War, noted, v.25, p.317; La's attitude toward, v.25, p.1052-1055; U. S. Senate debates peace negotiations, v.25, p.1060-1072; Trist draws Treaty, v.25, p.1072; Soule's views on, v.25, p.1073-1074, 1107; peace offers refused, v.25, p.1110; return to N. O. of sick and wounded soldiers of, v.26, p.56; its lack of influence on the N. O. stage, v.26, p.1153.

"Mexican War, General Beauregard and General Blanchard in," Address by Milo B. Williams, v.1, p.299.

Mexico, trade with La., v.21, p.362-366; filibuster expeditions, v.21, p.1086ff.; commercial land route from N. O. to Mex. City, v.22, p.777; measures to save for Spain, v.23, p.844, 848-853; documents in Institute of Middle American Research, v.24, p.332; republican patriots in, v.24, p.621; threats of French conquest, v.24, p.1101; and Burr conspiracy, v.25, p.8; plots against, v.25, p.16, 291, 296, 298, 399.

Meyer, Adolph, Dem. cand. for Cong., 1894, v.26, p.1095; Dem. congressman, v.26, p.1116; Dem. congressman, 1898, v.26, p.1123.

Meyer, F., noted, v.24, p.141.

Meyer, Robert, N. O., musician, v.31, p.133.

Mezieres, Athanase de, noted, v.22, p.69; comd. at Natchitoches, v.27, p.1769; instruction from O'Reilly, v.27, p.633, 636; Osage raid on district of, v.27, p.647, 657; Capt. at Natchitoches, v.28, p.1083.

Mezieres, Josef de, noted, v.22, p.73n., 77n.

Mezieres, Santiago de, noted, v.22, p.73n., 77n.

M'Gary, Mary, noted, v.23, p.1036.

Michaux, Andre, noted, v.22, p.85.

Michel, arrived in La., as Intendant, v.29, p.609; noted, v.29, p.612.

Michel, Francis Louis, pastor in New Orleans, v.22, p.460.

Michel, Francois Moreau, sketch, v.23, p.431.

Michel, Honore, ordonnateur, v.26, p.698-699.

Michel, John T., Dem. cand. for Sec. of State, 1896, v.26, p.1101; v.28, p.1172-1173, 1191, 1222, 1228, 1229.

Micheli, Vicente, trader, v.28, p.1098.

Michell, James, noted, v.22, p.985.

Middens, noted, v.23, p.1127.

Middle American languages, documents in Institute of Middle American Research, v.24, p.332.

Middle American Research Institute, Tulane University, v.24, p.327, 331-333.

Middleton, Henry, noted, v.24, p.949, 1031, 1092, 1094, 1114.

"Mid-June," by Cable, v.24, p.178.

Mier, Servando Teresa de, noted, v.24, p.635.

Mignonette, pen-name of Cable, v.24, p.171.

Milam, Benjamin R., and Long's expedition, v.22, p.745.

Miles, Benjamin, impressed by pirates, v.22, p.1021-1023.

Miles, Gen'l W. K., sent from Port Hudson to relieve Col. Powers, v.29, p.1111-1112; noted, v.29, p.1122, 1129.

Miles, J. J., Populist cand. for Lt.-Gov., v.28, p.1160.

Miles Planting and Mfg. Co., of La., suit against gov't for bounty due, v.27, p.817.

Milfort, Gen'l Louis, description of Mobile, 1783, v.28, p.699; opinion of relative efficiency of Fr. and Sp. rule, v.28, p.701.

Milfort, Le Clerc, Indian agent, v.22, p.91.

Milfort, sketch, v.21, p.46n.

Milhet, Jean, noted, v.23, p.110.

Military history, the Washington Artillery of New Orleans, v.23, p.471-484.

Militia, at St. Louis, v.22, p.88-89.

Millaudon, Laurent, land titles of, v.21, p.228n; and beginnings of Carrollton, v.22, p.190-196.

Mille, Miss S., noted, v.24, p.322.

Miller, ———, and W. Fla., v.22, p.46.

Miller, Bonnamy and Co., noted, v.21, p.22n.

Miller, Henry C., attack on Lottery Co., v.27, p.1055; address to Women's Anti-Lottery League, v.27, p.1061.

Miller, Joaquin, in New Orleans, v.22, p.216-225.

Miller, John D., address in memory of Henry Plauche Dart, v.18, p.244-245; on La. Bar Assoc. committee which prepared memorial of Henry Plauche Dart, v.18, p.255-266.

Miller, John F., and case of Sally Miller, v.22, p.158ff.

Miller, John, petition of, v.23, p.383-384.

Miller, M. N., school board member of 1st Bogalusa school, v.29, p.100.

Miller, Sally, case of German redemptioner, v.22, p.155-165; noted, v.25, p.303.

Miller, William, noted, v.23, p.404; identified, v.24, p.733-735.

Milliken, D. A., donates memorial building to Charity Hospital, v.31, p.77.

Milliken's Bend, noted, v.24, p.75, 82.

"Mills, Clark," by W. O. Hart, v.3, p.614.

Mills, I. J., La. rep. to Cincinnati conv., v.26, p.1077-1078; People's Party cand. for Lt.-gov., v.26, p.1080.

Mills, J. C., appointment as commissioner urged, v.29, p.109; designated Comm. of Public Health, Bogalusa, v.29, p.113.

Mills, John, and W. Fla. Rev., v.21, p.76, 94n., 13n., 687n.; letter to Skipwith, v.21, p.139-141.

Mills, John, Beaudin claim, v.25, p.949-950.

Mills, John H., founder Bayou Sara, v.28, p.942, 943.

Mills, regulations of in St. Helena, v.23, p.412.

Mills, Thos. B., skipper from La. on "Sampson," v.27, p.483.

Millwood Institute, v.30, p.827-828.

Milne, Alexander, Jr., noted, v.22, p.434, 435.

Milneburg, noted, v.22, p.435.

Miltenberg am Main, picture of, v.24, p.414; noted, v.24, p.415.

Miltenberger, Corinne L., donation to Charity Hospital, v.31, p.80.

Milton, John, noted, v.24, p.701.

Mims, J. H., chosen ass't City Clerk of Bogalusa, v.29, p.114.

Mims, Sam, "La.'s Admin. of Swamp Land Funds," v.28, p.277-325.

Mina, Francisco Xavier, filibuster in New Spain, v.21, p.808ff.; in N. O. 1817, v.21, p.1087; and revolt in Latin Am., v.22, p.735, 736-739, 1063, 1090; filibusterer, v.23, p.759, 764, 861; execution of, v.23, p.777; Toledo's plan to betray, v.23, p.829; denounced by Toledo, v.23, p.830; expedition to Mex., v.23, p.1071, 1072n.; noted, v.24, p.635, 644; contacts with Aury, v.24, p.639-642; death by assassination, v.24, p.662.

Minden Academy, v.30, p.929.

Minden Female College, sketch of, v.30, p.930-933.

Minden Female Seminary, v.30, p.930.

Minden, La., in 1860, v.21, p.1184.

Minden Male Academy, v.30, p.933-934.

Minerals, in Ouachita according to Filhiol, v.20, p.481.

Minister of the Hanse Towns, noted, v.24, p.1047; see also Rumpff.

Ministry of Marine, correspondence in La. State Museum depository, v.24, p.317.

Minor, Stephen, suit of heirs of, v.23, p.1091-1093.

Minor, William J., and family collection in L.S.U. Archives, v.24, p.343.

"Minutes of the Assembly of W. Fla., 1767-1768," ed. by J. A. Padgett, v.22, p.943-1011.

"Minutes of the Council of West Florida, April 3-July 22, 1769," ed. by J. A. Padgett, v.23, p.353-404.

"Minutes of the First Session of the Assembly of W. Fla.," ed. by J. A. Padgett, v.22, p.311-384.

Minutes of the Louisiana Historical Society, for 1918, v.2, p.217; for 1920-21, v.5, p.208; for 1922, v.6, p.164; v.7, p.128.

"Minutes of the Police Jury of St. Helena Parish, August 16-19, 1812," ed. by W. Prichard, v.23, p.405-427.

"Minutes of the West Florida Assembly, 1768, 1769," ed. by J. A. Padgett, v.23, p.5-77.

Miranda, Francisco Antonio Gabriel, expedition of, v.22, p.715; noted, v.23, p.430; offer to Haitian patriots, v.24, p.620-621.

"Miro, Estevan, Letter from Pontalba to," Trans. by Heloise H. Cruzat, v.2, p.393; and Ouachita land grants, v.20, p.295ff.; letter to from de Maison Rouge, v.20, p.313; established Fort Miro, v.20, p.464; instruction to Filhiol, v.20, p.473-475; sketch, v.21, p.18n.; and Catholic Church, v.21, p.1071; noted, v.22, p.398; v.23, p.429; documents in Bibliotheca Parsoniana, v.24, p.311; Sp. Gov. of La., v.25, p.183, 307, 938; at Sp. Council of War, v.26, p.741; succeeded Galvez as Gov. of La., v.26, p.745; awarded promotion, v.27, p.663; acting gov. of La., trial of rebels from Ark., v.27, p.671; report of to Galvez concerning Ark. and de Villiers, v.27, p.672, 673; orders Madame de Villiers released, v.27, p.674; efforts to Clear Miss. R. for Sp. trade, v.27, p.677; deals with Chickasaw for peace, v.27, p.678-679, 679-680, 681; reinforcements to Ark., v.27, p.682, 683; became gov., v.27, p.686, 687, 689; regarding sale of rum to Indians, v.27, p.692, 693; issued order prohibiting, v.27, p.694; Lopez's story to in re Indian brawl resulting from sale of rum, v.27, p.696, 697; land grant policy, v.27, p.698, 699; in re the repair of Ark. post, v.27, p.699, 700, 701, 702, 703, 704; Cruzat's warning of Am. expedition, v.27, p.705; invited immigration of Am., v.27, p.706; sends squadron to Natchez, v.27, p.706-707; orders Ark. lookout post abandoned, v.27, p.708; end of rule in La., 1791, v.27, p.708, 709, 712, 854-927passim.; and N. O. Charity Hospital, v.31, p.19-22, 28.

Miro Fort, est. 1790 by Filhiol, v.20,

p.464ff.; renamed Fort Monroe, v.20, p.472.

Misotiere, Pierre, deposition of, v.23, p.728-729; noted, v.23, p.730.

"'Mission' to Ecuador of Judah P. Benjamin," by L. Gruss, v.23, p.162-69.

"Mississippi and Pacific Railroad, Louisiana Central Stem of, History of," v.30, p.1217-1225.

Mississippi, and tariff question, v.25, p.76-77; admitted to Union, v.25, p.156; and cotton production, v.25, p.175; gulf coast of, v.25, p.204.

Mississippi Balize, noted, v.24, p.629.

Mississippi Bubble, John Law and, v.26, p.651-663.

Mississippi City, resort of wealthy planters, v.25, p.205.

"Mississippi," federal boat, v.29, p.1108, 1109.

"Misssissippi Fort called Fort de la Boulaye (1700-1715): The First French Settlement in Present Day La." by Maurice Reis, v.19, p.829-99.

"Mississippi in the Transfer of the Louisiana Purchase," by Dunbar Rowland, L.L.D., v.13, p.235.

"Mississippi," ironclad vessel, v.24, p.446, 457.

"Mississippi Provincial Archives, 1729-1740, French Dominion," by Dunbar Rowland and A. G. Sanders (Reviewed by Henry P. Dart), v.11, p.111.

Mississippi question, v.23, p.79.

Mississippi River Commission, and cut offs of Miss., v.28, p.77, 79, 81; Cong. provided for, v.28, p.323-324.

Mississippi River, navigation of, v.21, p.14, 65, 42-45, 53; levees at Red River landing, v.21, p.1143-1144; crevasse of, v.22, p.189; Delta survey of, v.22, p.208-209; noted, v.25, p.162, 163, 164, 170, 172, 173, 184, 185, 189, 202, 207, 292, 385, 398; and its forks, v.25, p.921-942; noted, v.26, p.5-8passim; the right to navigate, v.26, p.12-36; McDonogh and trade on, v.26, p.37-43; still generally in Southern hands, 1861-1862, v.26, p.341; noted, v.26, p.344, 633-671 passim; N. O. located on, v.26, p.364; trade and traffic on, v.26, p.365-366; noted, v.26, p.641-642; course of, v.26, p.642-643; noted, v.26, p.722; LaSalle trip to find mouth of, Iberville ascends, v.26, p.725; Fort Boulaye, 1st settlement on lower part of, v.26, p.726; noted, v.26, p.728, 729, 730, 823, 952; the "Manassas" on, v.26, p.952n.; noted, v.26, p.974, 977; ordinance in La. granting free navigation to friendly states and foreign powers, v.26, p.1002; Federal fleet seizes forts on, v.26, p.1019; noted, v.26, p.1023, 1024; controlled by Federals, v.26, p.1032; noted, v.26, 1151; noted, v.27, p.330, 331; discovery, v.27, p.332, 333, 334, 336, 337, 338; free navigation of, v.27, p.339, 340, 341, 348, 350, 351, 353, 355, 361, 363, 364, 374, 375, 377, 397, 428, 429, 481, 486, 487, 488, 489, 494, 522, 540, 629, 630, 631, 639, 640, 641, 642, 643, 644, 646, 647, 648; in control of Am., v.27, p.661; floods of, v.27, p.661-662; left bank claimed for Sp., v.27, p.622, 665, 676; Sp. meet no hostility, v.27, p.677, 679, 683; Ga. claims land to, v.27, p.699; Am. given right to navigate, v.27, p.700, 712, 701; floods of, v.27, p.702, 709, 706, 707, 710, 711, 715, 717, 724; Am. right to navigate, v.27, p.734, 742; Eads' improvement of jetties, v.27, p.841, 842; dredging of Southwest Pass, v.27, p.842; bill for improving South Pass, v.27, p.843; investigation of comparative merits of South Pass and Southwest Pass, v.27, p.843-844; development of transportation on, v.27, p.939-941; competition with railroads, v.27, p.957; floods of 1890, v.27, p.1026, 1034, 1039; flood control, v.27, p.1056, 1164, 1174; noted, v.28, p.5, 9-10; straight course of at B. R., v.28, p.10, 12; noted, v.28, p.13, 14, 31, 33, 34, 35, 40, 42, 49, 50, 51, 59, 61, 62, 65, 66; changes in course of, v.28, p.38; causes of changes, v.28, p.69-75; possible data of change at False R., v.28, p.75-77; other cut offs, v.28, p.77-78; human interference not necessary, v.28, p.77-81; time required for cut off, v.28, p.81-84; U. S. purchased La. to secure control of, v.28, p.277; early efforts to prevent overthrow, v.28, p.277-278; U. S. gov't accepts no responsibility in control of, v.28, p.278; early fed'l attempts to control, v.28, p.279-282; provision by La. for levees, v.28, p.287-289; noted, v.28, p.297; La. Levee Co., v.28, p.307-310; nat'l aid unavailable, v.28, p.310-312; flood of 1927, v.28, p.322-323; Miss. R. Com., v.28, p.323-324; Flood Control Act, v.28, p.324-325; Cathcart's impressions of and surrounding territory, v.28, p.748-750; alluvial valley of, location of, v.30, p.656-657; extent of, v.30, p.656-659; characteristics of soil of, v.30, p.659-665; history of reclamation of, v.30, p.665-709.

"Mississippi River Ice at N. O.," by John C. L. Andreassen, v.21, p.349-53.

Mississippi River Packet Co., Pinchback secured passage of act establishing, v.27, p.540; v.30, p.1093.

"Mississippi Valley Beginnings," Review by Caroline Richardson, v.7, p.672.

"Mississippi Valley, Calendar of Documents," Mrs. N. M. Miller Surrey, v.7, p.674.

Mississippi Valley Hist., Minutes of Spanish Supreme Councils of State, 1787-1797, v.21, p.5-75.

Mississippi Valley, Sp. activities in, v.22, p.933-942.

"Mississippi Valley, 1763-1803, Contest for Ecclesiastical Supremacy," by Clarence Wyatt Bispham, v.1, sec.3, p.154.

Missolonghi, noted, v.24, p.966, 999, 1000.

Missouri, housing in 1764-1821, v.21, p.337-348.

Missoury, Francoise, Case involving, v.21, p.1003, 1013, 1020.

Mitchell, Ben, Dem. Populist elector, v.26, p.1116.

Mitchell, Captain, noted, v.24, p.662.

Mitchell, D. L., Assistant Sec., Anti-Lottery Legaue of La., v.27, p.1054-1055.

Mitchell, Harry A., "The Development of N. O. as a Wholesale Trading Center," v.27, p.933-963.

Mitchell, James, noted, v.23, p.26, 45, 391.

Mitchell, Jennie O'Kelly (co-author), "The Marquis de Maison Rouge, the Baron de Bastrop and Col. Abraham Morhouse: Three Ouachita Valley Soldiers of Fortune, The Maison Rouge and Bastrop Spanish Land 'Grants,'" v.20, p.289-462.

Mitchell, John, noted, v.23, p.391.

Mitchell, Martha, marries John L. Irwin, children of, v.29, p.292.

Mitchell, M., revolutionary agitator, v.22, p.82n.

Mitchell, Philomela Smith (see Smith, Philomela), daughter of Rev. Jedediah Smith, v.29, p.291-292.

Mitchell, Thomas (or Medad) and Clark's expedition, v.21, p.34.

Mitchell, William, trial of, v.22, p.766; privateersman, v.2, p.759, 760, 762, 1051-1056, 1087; noted, v.23, p.391.

Mithoff, Henry, mayor of Carrollton, v.21, p.244-245; noted, v.22, p.202.

"'Mobile Landing,' The Old, Head of the Basin in New Orleans," by Charles Patton Dimitry, v.3, p.131.

Mobile River, land grants on, v.23, p.404.

Mobile, Society in 1810, W. Fla. Rev., v.21, p.99n., 100-101n., 122n., 153n., and W. Fla. Rev., v.21, p.84-88, 90-91, 98-99, 136; conditions of Fort, 1810, v.21, p.103; expeditions against Fort by W. Fla., v.21, p.752, 753, 761; District in W. Fla. Assembly, v.22, p.41, 312; made county, v.22, p.335; improvements in, v.22, p.340; election of vestry, v.23, p.16; in 1863, v.23, p.1207; Farragut's attack on, v.23, p.1212, 1213; noted, v.24, p.85, 103, 106, 107, 108, 109; described by Cathcart, v.28, p.852; Cathcart's survey of surrounding region, v.28, p.853ff., 871ff.

Mobley, James William, "The Academy Movement in Louisiana," v.30, p.738-978; sketch of, v.30, p.738n.

Mob Spirit, in New Orleans, 1862, v.24, p.456, 460.

"Modern Quasimodo, A" (from old issue of Times-Democrat), v.2, p.318.

Moehlenbrock, Arthur Henry, "The German Drama on the N. O. Stage," v.26, p.361-627.

Moise, E. W., noted, v.23, p.226; candidate for attorney general on Dem. ticket, 1855, v.25, p.680, 996, 1058.

Moise, J. C., Anti-Lottery delegate to Farmers' Union meeting, v.27, p.1086; on com. to supervise primary, v.27, p.1094; Anti-Lottery League com., v.28, p.1152; member com. to supervise election, v.28, p.1161; appt'd judge Crim. Dist. Ct. of N. O., v.28, p.1162.

Molina, Antonio, noted, v.22, p.1015, 1016.

"Molinary, Andres," Flo Field, v.7, p.455.

"Molinary, The Grave of" (Poem), Lilita Lever Younge, v.7, p.465.

Monaca, Pa., noted, v.24, p.426; pictures of church and house of Leon, v.24, p.427.

Monaghan, John J., helps with plans of Great Southern Lumber Co., v.29, p.105.

Mona Passage, noted, v.24, p.646, 653, 676.

Moncla, La., v.25, p.397.

Moncure, J. C., Speaker of House of McEnery factions, v.28, p.1137.

Mondelli, A., designed St. Charles Theatre, v.28, p.205.

Monett's Ferry, noted, v.24, p.94.

Money, value of paper reduced, v.21, p.1008; problem of Carondelet, v.22, p.62; paper in W. Fla., v.22, p.376; specie from Mex., v.22, p.777-778; scarce in N. O., v.22, p.1012-1013; specie from New Spain, v.22, p.1013-1016; rice bills in N. C., v.23, p.546; in N. O., 1864, v.23, p.1212.

Mongino, Louis, revolutionary agitator, v.22, p.66, 76.

Monier, Jean, noted, v.22, p.1050, 1051.

Moni, Father Louis Leopold, appointed pastor, v.31, p.906; death, v.31, p.907; funeral, v.31, p.908.

"Moniteur de la Louisiane," and Sp. Am. revolts, v.22, p.781.

"Monongahela," federal boat, v.29, p.1108.

Monroe, Ben, attorney in Morse case, v.31, p.463.

Monroe Doctrine, contemporary reactions to in Europe, v.24, p.952ff., 1002-1003.

Monroe, F. A.; "King, Frederick D.," v.6, p.199; Retirement of Chief Justice, v.6, p.107; N. O. Sup. Ct. justice, v.27, p.984; aid in organizing league in N. O., v.27, p.1056, 1091; presentation of floral offering to Nicholls from Women's Anti-Lottery League, v.27, p.1096.

Monroe, James, policy toward Fla. and Tex., v.23, p.780-782, 827; noted, v.24, p.934, 1137; noted, v.25, p.36, 296, 297, 298; and Robinson, v.25, p.650ff.; appointed Kemper collector of claims, v.25, p.944; letter to Kemper, v.25, p.946; Jefferson's choice for governor of Orleans, v.31, p.286; friendship with Sumter, v.31, p.292-293, 294; correspondence with Madison, v.31, p.293; contact with Skipwith, v.31, p.297, 299, 302, 305, 308; noted, v.31, p.301, 320, 323, 326; and Dawson, v.31, p.328; candidate for governor of Orleans, v.31, p.335-346, 358; to Jefferson, v.31, p.338, 341; reappointed Minister to Spain, v.31, p.340; elected president, v.31, p.346.

Monroe, John T., noted, v.23, p.151; Mayor of New Orleans, v.23, p.1236; noted, v.24, p.457, 532; quoted, v.24, p.458, 459, 461; protest against Butler's Order No. 28, v.24, p.496-497; Mayor of N. O. during Civil War, v.27, p.492; refused to surrender, v.27, p.493; attitude toward Butler, v.27, p.497-498, 499; appeal to food stores to open, v.27, p.505; gov't of called "thug rule," v.27, p.508; denounces "woman order," v.27, p.512; taken into military custody by Butler, v.27, p.512; candidate for mayor of N. O., v.31, p.1075, removed, v.31, p.1089.

Monroe, La., early history of, v.20, p.463-485; diary of schoolteacher, 1835-1837, v.20, p.651-679; in 1860, v.21, p.1195-1196; noted, v.26, p.916, 938, 939, 967, 968; army training camp there, v.26, p.1022; and bagging factory, v.26, p.1065; Farmers' Alliance meeting in 1892, v.26, p.1084-1085; noted, v.26, p.1104.

Monroe, Thomas Bell, noted, v.23, p.1058, 1061; Judge, heard Morse vs. O'Reilly, v.31, p.462-463.

Montanary, Elena, Marriage contract with Juan Benoit, v.9, p.385.

Montberault, ———, noted, v.23, p.56.

Montegut, Gabriel, "Regular" cand. for State Treasurer, v.26, p.1081; Lotteryite cand. for Treas., v.27, p.1090; cand. Treas., v.28, p.1158.

Montejo, Jesse A., daughter of P. O. Hebert, v.31, p.494.

Montemart, Duke de, noted, v.24, p.1144.

Montero, Don Bernardino, Sp. Comdt. at Nacogdoches, v.28, p.1067; noted, v.28, p.1093.

Montez, Lola, German liberal in N. O., v.20, p.146-147.

Montezuma, Count of, v.18, p.47-49.

Montgomery, Emmett L., promoted, v.26, p.837.

Montgomery Free Institute, v.30, p.831-832.

Montgomery, Geo. W., on Lottery Bill, v.27, p.1042; pressure on to vote for lottery, v.27, p.1047; compromise plan for voting on lottery bill, v.27, p.1050.

Montgomery, R. W., noted, v.23, p.204, 212.

Monthiarch, ———, noted, v.23, p.148.

Montiasse, ———, noted, v.23, p.146.

Montilla, Mariano, and insurgents, v.21, p.1094-1095; noted, v.22, p.1066; noted, v.24, p.618, 622, 628, 639, 640, 641, 642, 643, 679, 688; commission to act with Brion, v.24, p.667-668.

Montmorenci, Count de, noted, v.24, p.1144.

Montmorency, Duke de, noted, v.24, p.961.

Montpelier Academy, papers in L.S.U. Archives, v.24, p.344; noted, v.30, p.903-905.

Montville Bridge Act, authorizes Montville inhabitants to construct bridge on Bayou Carron, v.30, p.66-67.

"Monument, Liberty," by James A. Renshaw, v.3, p.259.

Moody, V. Alton, "Slavery on La. Sugar Plant.," v.7, p.191.

Mooney, Frank, and Mafia in New Orleans, v.22, p.827.

Moore, Alexander, and W. Fla. Assembly, v.22, p.317, 943; noted, v.23, p.23, 77, 353ff.

Moore, Arthur K., "Specimens of the Folktales from Some Antebellum Newspapers of La.," v.32, p.723.

Moore, Clarence B., "Antiquities of the Ouachita Valley," v.25, p.627, 632.

Moore, J. J., cand. for Rep. from St. Mary, v.28, p.1136.

Moore, John, noted, v.23, p.26; v.25, p.112, 115, 116, 117, 124, 140; v.28, p.767n., 818n.

Moore, Joseph H., candidate for Mayor of New Orleans, v.31, p.1075.

"Mooreland," Thomas O. Moore's plantation, v.26, p.977; wrecked by war, v.26, p.1043-1044, 1045; his return to, v.26, p.1047-1049.

Moore, Lawrence H., member of St. Helena Police Jury, v.23, p.407ff.

Moore, R. Woods, author, "The Role of the Baron de Bastrop in the Anglo-American Settlement of the Southwest," v.31, p.606-681.

Moores, Merrill, "Edward Livingston," v.3, p.486.

"Moore, Thomas O., Papers of," Introduction by G. P. Whittington, v.13, p.10; "Governor of Louisiana, 1860-1864," by G. P. Whittington, v.13, p.7; "Letters from John H. Ransdell, 1863," Introduction by G. P. Whittington, v.14, p.487; noted, v.23, p.1176n.; noted, v.24, p.59, 68, 114, 441, 442, 446; letter from Judge Barthes Egan, v.24, p.100-101; papers in L.S.U. Archives, v.24, p.344; appeal for aid against Federal invasion, v.24, p.452; quoted, v.24, p.453; address to "Loyal People and True," v.24, p.474-475; Wickliffe's successor, v.25, p.705; birth, early life, v.26, p.975-977; state rep., v.26, p.978-979; state senator, v.26, p.979-983; interest in public ed., v.26, p.979, 980, 981-982; nominated for gov., v.26, p.989; inauguration, v.26, p.991-993; first months of governorship, v.26, p.993-994; and La. secession, v.26, p.994-1004; seizure of U. S. property, v.26, p.1005; preparation for war, v.26, p.1005-1009; message to Legis., Nov., 1861, v.26, p.1009-1010; veto of Cotton Bill, v.26, p.1015-1017; efforts for Welfare of La. troops and for adequate defense, v.26, p.1017-1019; moved capital to Opelousas, v.26, p.1020; ordered supplies burned, v.26, p.1021; requested General in La., v.26, p.1021-1024; organized "Partisan Rangers," v.26, p.1022; complaint of at seizure of supplies, v.26, p.1023; meeting of gov's of Tex. and Ark., v.26, p.1023-1024; cooperated with Taylor, v.26, p.1025-1026; called special Legis. sess., v.26, p.1026, 1028; his address to regular sess., May, 1863, v.26, p.1029-1030, 1039-1041; his recommendations acted upon, v.26, p.1030-1032, 1041, and the fall of Vicksburg, v.26, p.1032; conv. of gov's for defense of Confed. west of Miss., v.26, p.1032; farewell address to Legislature, 1864, v.26, p.1033, 1043-1044; and civil and economic conditions, v.26, p.1034-1042; returned to his plantation, v.26, p.1043-1044; migrated to Texas, Sept. 1864, v.26, p.1044, 1045; fled to Mexico and Cuba, v.26, p.1045-1046; parole and pardon granted, v.26, p.1046-1047; return to La., v.26, p.1047-1049; death of, v.26, p.1049; bibliography, v.26, p.1050-1053; gov. of La. in re secession, v.27, p.489; preparation for war, v.27, p.490-491; proclamation of suspending payment of metallic currency, v.27, p.492; forbade interchange of goods with Union controlled N. O., v.27, p.506-507, 521, 508; suspended metallic money, v.27, p.509; directed the fight of La. against the Federals, v.27, p.520, 774, 1227.

Mora, Jacinto, land grant to, v.28, p.1052; trader, v.28, p.1090, 1099.

Morales, Antonio, letter to King of Spain, 1803, v.21, p.1069-1074.

Morales, Juan Ventura, raids gambling house, v.22, p.691, 692n.; noted, v.22, p.811; closes port of New Orleans, v.23, p.79, 80; closed Am. right of deposit at N. O., v.28, p.1017; acting Int. Gen'l, v.28, p.1244-1324passim.; Spanish Intendant, letter from Carondelet, v.31, p.620; raises money, v.31, p.621; objection to Bastrop grant, v.31, p.622-623; succeeded, v.31, p.626.

Moran, Blas, noted, v.23, p.771n.

Moran, D., noted, v.22, p.1075.

Morea, French attacks upon, v.24, p.1121.

Morehouse, Abram, Bastrop's proposed

partner, v.31, p.625; receives Bastrop lands, v.31, p.628.

Morehouse Parish, in 1860, v.21, p.1197-1200; bagging factory, v.26, p.1065; noted, v.26, p.1087.

"More Indian Place Names," by William A. Read, v.11, p.445.

Morellos, ———, noted, v.23, p.852.

Morel, P. L., and Andrew Jackson, v.21, p.369.

Moreno, Francisco Ildefonso, See Sedella, Antonio.

Moreno, Manuel, and the Laffites, v.23, p.807.

"Morganalia," by Milledge L. Bonham, Jr., v.17, p.706.

Morgan, Benjamin, and W. Fla. Rev., v.21, p.113; noted, v.22, p.432, 435, 439, 722, 724; member of New Orleans Association, v.24, p.631; N. O. merchant, opinion of Daniel Clark, v.31, p.312-313.

Morgan, Charles, railroad magnate, buys Pontchartrain Railroad, v.30, p.1120-1122; purchases New Orleans, Opelousas and Great Western Railroad, v.30, p.1172-1179; sells stock in Pontchartrain Railroad, v.30, p.1312-1313; complaint against N. O., Mobile and Texas Railroad, v.30, p.1315-1316; noted, v.30, p.1155, 1257.

Morgan City, La., name changed from Brashear City, v.30, p.1068n.

Morgan Collection, in La. State Museum, v.24, p.319.

Morgan, George W., noted, v.22, p.434.

Morgan Head, on Catalina, v.24, p.657, 622.

Morgan, Henry, noted, v.24, p.9, 654, 655, 657, 659, 664.

Morgan, H. Gibbs, "Dual Between Diplomats, A," v.14, p.385; "First Meeting of the Louisiana Historical Society in the Sala Capitular at the Cabildo," v.14, p.60.

Morgan, J. M., La. midshipman, v.27, p.483.

Morgan, John, and W. Fla. Rev., v.21, p.94n., 688n.

Morgan, John H., noted, v.29, p.1246.

Morgan, Morris, correspondence in Xavier University Archives, v.24, p.336.

Morgan, O. Bery, noted, v.25, p.765.

Morgan, Pat, petition of, v.23, p.384.

Morgan, Philip Hickey, noted, v.24, p.769; suit against J. H. Kennard for office of Assoc. Justice, v.27, p.577.

Morgan, S. C., in shooting affray with Pinchback, v.27, p.536-537.

"Morgan's, Gen. David B., Defense of the Conduct of the Louisiana Militia in the Battle of New Orleans on the Left Side of the River," v.9, p.16.

Morgan, Sir Henry, noted, v.23, p.428.

Morgan's Louisiana and Texas Railroads, v.30, p.1172.

Morgan-Sparks duel, noted, v.24, p.769.

Morgan, Thomas Gibbs, noted, v.24, p.769.

Morgan, Thomas N., noted, v.22, p.462.

Morganza, in 1860, v.21, p.1142; noted, v.24, p.78, 80.

Morhouse, Col. Abraham, heritage and early life, v.20, p.387; land grants in Ouachita, v.20, p.388ff.; death, family and estate, v.20, p.424-428; land sales in Bastrop grant, v.20, p.449-453; marriage with Eleanor Hook, v.20, p.454-456.

Morillo, at Cartagena, v.24, p.617-620, 669; noted, v.24, p.621.

Moro, Manuel Gonzales, noted, v.22, p.799, 815, 818.

Morphy, Alonzo, noted, v.23, p.1029.

Morphy, Diego, Sp. vice-consul at N. O., v.21, p.679ff.; noted, v.22, p.726, 742, 788; noted, v.23, p.827; Sp. consul at N. O., v.28, p.1063.

Morrill Act, S. Univ., land-grant College under terms of, v.25, p.771.

Morris, Charles, noted, v.24, p.978, 988, 994.

Morrises, of New York, v.24, p.700.

Morrissey, John, lottery agent, v.31, p.719; files suit, v.31, p.728.

Morris, John A., lottery official, 1892, v.25, p.716; lottery privilege withdrawn, v.26, p.1079; pres. Lottery Co., Caffery's attack against, v.27, p.788, 789; corporation rights of Lottery Co. transferred to, v.27, p.976; suit against, v.27, p.982-983; charges of bribery against, v.27, p.909, 991, 997; offered increased license fee to secure recharter of Lottery Co., v.27, p.1030; additional offer, v.27, p.1032, 1034; letter to Legis. offering levee aid, v.27, p.1036, 1040, 1041, 1042, 1045, 1046; favored over Newgass, v.27, p.1049; suit against Sec. State Mason to force promulgation of Lottery Bill, v.27, p.1050-1052, 1054, 1055; aid to Nicholls' campaign, v.27, p.1066, 1068, 1088; revoked offer, v.27, p.1093, 1094; transfer of Co. to Honduras, v.27, p.1079, 1102; letter of, withdrawing offer, v.27, p.1110-1113;

and the La. Levee Co., v.28, p.1142ff., 1160; and lottery co., v. 31, p.729, 832; noted, v.31, p.742, 790, 825.

Morrison, James, noted, v.24, p.925.

Morse, Dr. Edward C., "The Morse Family in Louisiana," v.7, p.441.

"Morse Family in Louisiana," by Dr. Edward C. Morse, v.7, p.441.

Morse, Isaac E., noted, v.25, p.139, 140, 141; Johnson's successor as atty. gen'l, v.28, p.982; candidate for atty. gen'l., v.31, p.501.

Morse, M. D., Edw. Clarke, "Captain Ogden's Troop of Horse in the Battle of New Orleans," v.10, p.381.

Morse, Samuel F. B., inventor of telegraph, v.31, p.425.

Morse vs. O'Reilly, case between O'Reilly and Kendall, v.31, p.458; trial, v.31, p.463; decision, v.31, p.463-464; appeal, v.31, p.469; Supreme Court hearing, v.31, p.470-473.

Morton, Oliver P., noted, v.24, p.115; Ind. senator, investigation of La. politics, 1873, v.27, p.580; champions admission of Pinchback to U. S. Senate, v.27, p. 592, 593-594; asks for recommitment, v.27, p.594-595, 596; again defends Pinchback, v.27, p.598-599.

Mortuary list, members 2nd La. Vol. Inf., May 2, 1898, to Ap. 18, 1899, v.26, p.841.

Morvant, Francois, trader of Natchitoches, v.27, p.634, 652.

Moscoso, Luis de, noted, v.22, p.936; noted, v.25, p.399, 630, 639-641.

Mosquito Coast, of Nicaragua, v.24, p.654.

"Mosquito," noted, v.23, p.436.

Mossu, Joseph, suit of, v.21, p.1007.

Mother De Ricci Memorial Fund, noted, v.24, p.326.

Moton, Robert, Negro educational leader, v.25, p.801-802.

Mount Carmel Convent, Lafayette, La., v.30, p.946.

Mount Carmel Convent, N. O., La., v.30, p.951-952.

Mount Carmel Convent, Thibodaux, La., v.30, p.947.

Mount Carmel School, v.30, p.956-957.

Mount Lebanon, in 1860, v.21, p.1191.

"Moustique," privateer, v.23, p.436.

Mouton, Alexander, and New Orleans railroad convention, v.23, p.221; noted, v.23, p.1020, 1021; noted, v.24, p.41, 59-60; to U. S. senate, v.25, p.108, 115, 142; gov. of La., v.25, p.121, 989; on Texan annexation, v.25, p.1003-1004; presiding officer of secession conv., v.26, p.998, 1000; declared La. seceded, v.26, p.1001; praises Moore for veto of Cotton Bill, v.26, p.1016-1017; appt'd Johnson sec. of state, v.28, p.955; appt'd Johnson to Ct. of Errors and Appeals, v.28, p.956; noted, v.28, p.965.

Mouton, Alfred, operations under Richard Taylor, v.24, p.71, 73, 76; noted, v.24, p.89, 90.

Mouton, Charles H., noted, v.24, p.56; Dem. candidate for Lt. Gov., 1855, v.25, p.680; Lt. Gov. resigned, v.26, p.982; noted, v.26, p.987.

Mowry, John, noted, v.22, p.801.

Mueller, Dr., resident physician of Franklin Infirmary, 1847, v.26, p.56; eulogy at Luzenberg's grave, v.26, p.103.

Mugeres Island, and the Laffites, v.23, p.801, 824.

Muhlenberg, Rev., ———, pastor in New Orleans, v.22, p.450.

"Muir, John, British Consul at New Orleans, 1860, Report to Lord John Russell on Financial and Economic Disturbance in New Orleans on the Eve of Secession," contributed by Milledge L. Bonham, v.13, p.32.

Mulatto, defined, v.25, p.301.

Mullen, Father Jas. Ignatius, defied Butler, v.27, p.501.

Muller, Adam, noted, v.24, p.381.

Muller, Bernhard (Count de Leon), noted, v.24, p.381, 383, 384, 385, 418; difficulties with organized church, v.24, p.397-402, 406-409, 415-416; see also Count de Leon.

Muller, George, noted, v.24, p.133.

Muller, Irvan, manuscript in L.S.U. Music School Library, v.24, p.347.

Muller, Salome, see Miller, Sally.

Mullings, C. K., trustee of 1st Bogalusa school, v.29, p.100.

Mullins, Thomas, General Court Martial for Trial of Brevet Lieutenant-Colonel, v.9, p.33.

Mumford, Mrs. Wm. B., pleas clemency for doomed husband, v.29, p.343; Gen. Butler pledges aid to her, v.29, p.343-344; forgives Butler, v.29, p.344; secures Butler's aid through the years, v.29, p.347-351; son plots revenge against Butler, v.29, p.352-353; death noted, v.29, p.353.

Mumford, W. B., Jr., v.29, p.352.

Mumford, William B., punishment for flag

offense, v.24, p.488-490; Butler refused to commute sentence, v.27, p.505; hanging of, v.27, p.518; sentenced to be hanged for treason, v.29, p.342, 343; accounts of the execution, v.29, p.344-345.

Mumfre, "Doc," and Mafia, v.22, p.839-843.

Munday, Gen., S. W., temp. chairman of state Dem. Conv., 1859, v.26, p.987.

Munday, Mrs. S. E., La. educator, v.30, p.823, 970.

"Municipal Elections of 1858, The," by John S. Kendall, v.5, p.357.

"Municipal Legislation by Superior Council of Louisiana," Heloise H. Cruzat, v.7, p.567.

Munson, Thenia, mother of Gov. Isaac Johnson, v.28, p.942, 944.

"Murder Case Tried in New Orleans in 1773," ed. by H. P. Dart, v.22, p.623-641.

Murdock, James, noted, v.31, p.977; opinion of Cushman, v.31, p.979.

Murphy, Edward, noted, v.22, p.70; organized trading firm, v.28, p.1089, 1096; sketch, v.28, p.1090; death, v.28, p.1103; secures possession of land, v.28, p.1051-1052.

Murphy, Edward R., "Henry de Tonty," rev'd, v.25, p.226-227.

Murphy, Helen Spann, "The Souls of Old Houses," v.13, p.59.

Murphy, John B., sheriff of St. Mary Parish, marriage of daughter to Caffery, v.27, p.784; noted, v.28, p.1130.

Murphy, Martha, wife of Thomas J. Foster, v.28, p.1130-1131.

Murphy, Mrs. W. M., "The Old Pecan Tree on Eureka Plantation, East Carroll Parish, Louisiana," v.17, p.625.

Murphy, Smith, Barr, and Davenport, Commercial partnership, v.28, p.1052.

Murphy, W. M., "History of Madison Parish, Louisiana," v.11, p.39.

Murray, A. M., author on Louisiana, v.31, p.397, 400-402, 412-413.

Murray, Amelia, noted, v.23, p.873.

Murray, Charles, author on Louisiana, v.31, p.397.

Murray, Charles H., incorporator of La. Lottery Co., v.27, p.975; corporation rights transferred to, v.27, p.976; suit against, v.27, p.982-983; lottery agent, v.31, p.729; officer of lottery, v.31, p.730.

Murray, Marguerite, crowned Silver Jubilee Queen of Bogalusa, v.29, p.116.

Murray, William, noted, v.23, p.1003, 1007.

Murrell, Cornelia Randolph, noted, v.25, p.150, 157, 216.

Murry, John, petition of, v.23, p.365.

Museo, Guatemalteco, noted, v.24, p.331.

Music, German, in New Orleans, v.23, p.510.

Music School Library, L.S.U., v.24, p.347.

Muskhogean Indians, in Grant Parish, v.23, p.1109.

Musquito Isles, Cathcart's survey, v.28, p.785ff.

"Muster Rolls of the Fourth Louisiana Regiment of Volunteers, Confederate States Army," by John Smith Kendall, v.30, p.481-522.

Muston, Mathew, noted, v.22, p.982; v.23, p.29.

Muter, George, noted, v.24, p.929.

Muxo, Leandro, and Mexican Association, v.25, p.18.

Myer, H. C., judge, Pinchback witness, v.27, p.587.

Myers, John F., member of St. Helena Police Jury, v.23, p.406ff.

Myles, Isaac A., Whig representative, v.25, p.1095, 1096, 1098; accused of fraud, v.25, p.1101-1104.

Myrtle Bayou, v.28, p.780, 781, 783.

Myrtle Isle, v.28, p.775, 779, 780.

"Mystic Seven," college fraternity, v.31, p.125.

NACHBIN, JAC, "SPAIN'S REPORT OF the War with the British in Louisiana," v.15, p.468.
Nachon, Father, noted, v.24, p.463.
Nacogdoches, and revolutionary agitators, v.22, p.73, 725, 727; travel account of J. Eder, 1854, v.23, p.496-500; and Long expedition, v.23, p.812, 817; and the disputed neutral ground, v.28, p.1029-1112passim.
Nadaud, D. O., candidate for St. Louis Church Warden, v.31, p.913.
"Names 'False River' and 'Pointe Coupee,' The: An Inquiry in Historical Geography," by Hilgard O'Reilly Sternberg, v.31, p.598-605.
Nancarrow, John, noted, v.25, p.299; files claim for Bastrop, v.31, p.617, 628-29.
Nantachie, Indians, in Grant Parish, v.23, p.1109.
Napoleon, noted, v.24, p.6; attempts at rescue, v.24, p.27, 373-76; secret report in Bibliotheca Parsoniana, v.24, p.310; noted, v.33, p.146-150; funeral of, v.33, p.147; proposed funeral service in New Orleans, v.33, p.148.
Napoleonic Fever, noted, v.33, p.145.
"Napoleon Inkstand, The," by W. O. Hart, v.5, p.501.
"Napoleon's Cession of La.: A Suggestion," by R. R. Stenberg, v.21, p.354-61.
"Napoleon, The Funeral of, in New Orleans," by A. E. Fossier, v.13, p.246.

Narvaez, Panfilode, expedition of, v.22, p.933-34.
Nasater, Abraham P., "Gov't Employees and Salaries in Sp. La.," v.29, p.885-1040; (ed.) "Materials Relating to the History of the Miss. Valley from the Minutes of the Spanish Supreme Councils of State, 1787, 1797," v.21, p.5-75; acknowledgement to, v.22, p.49.
Nashville, Tenn., railroad mission of Robb to, v.23, p.217.
Nassau Hall, Princeton University, v.24, p.699.
Natchez (Fort Rosalie) map of, v.19, p.548, 560, 569; life in early, v.20, p.972-75; Gayoso de Lemos made gov., v.21, p.15; religious toleration, v.21, p.58; district established, v.22, p.40; and Am. Rev., v.22, p.45; and French Rev., v.22, p.79-83; pro-Spanish feeling, v.22, p.814; meeting of Indians at, v.23, p.386-87; noted, v.24, p.80; health conditions, v.24, p.928; district history of, v.25, p.152-54; fertility of, v.25, p.152-53; plantation center, v.25, p.175; noted, v.25, p.54, 152, 153, 154, 160, 294, 295, 297, 299, 661, 667, 668; trading post established by Fr., v.28, p.58-59; noted, v.28, p.61, 64, 65; Favrot in comd., v.28, p.702ff.; on telegraph, v.31, p.449-50.
Natchez Indians, Perier's expedition against, v.19, p.547-77; in Grant Parish, v.23, p.1109; description of, v.23, p.1117-

1119; ethical precepts of, v.31, p.569-97; French judgments of, v.31, p.576-85; human sacrifice, v.31, p.583, 584; native testimonials, v.31, p.585-94.

"Natchez Massacre and Governor Perier, The," by Rev. John Delanglez, S. J., v.17, p.631.

"Natchez Rebellion of 1781 and its Aftermath, The," by John Caughey, v.16, p.57.

"Natchez, The Vengeance of the," by Clem G. Hearsay, v.12, p.266.

"Natchez Trace, The," by R. S. Cottrell, v.6, p.259.

Natchitoches, and French Rev., v.22, p.65-79; plots against Mex., v.22, p.717ff.; Argote's expedition to, v.22, p.796-97; noted, v.22, p.805, 806, 816; noted, v.24, p.74, 88, 94, 100; cotton area of La., v.25, p.27, 294, 295, 296, 297, 298, 299, 320, 324, 361, 397, 399, 400, 649, 651; noted, v.26, p.661, 688, 689, 694, 698, 702; post established, v.26, p.728; erection and description of fort, v.26, p.731; noted, v.26, p.736; noted, v.26, p.753, 1094; proposed Cane River docks, v.26, p.1119; dispute over transfer of post, v.28, p.1021-23; and the disputed neutral ground, v.28, p.1024-1103passim; noted, v.23, p.429; Indian agents at, v.23, p.843; headquarters for filibusters, v.23, p.1001, 1002; noted, v.27, p.336, 541; Mezieres in command, v.27, p.630, 633; produce of, v.27, p.635, 636, 637, 639, 644, 645; raided by Osage, v.27, p.647, 650, 651, 652, 657; problem of preventing sale of rum to Indians, v.27, p.691, 708; N. O. trade with, v.27, p.953.

Natchitoches Academy, sketch of, v.30, p.844-845.

"Natchitoches, History of," by Milton Dunn, v.3, p.26.

Natchitoches Indians, in Grant Parish, v.23, p.1109; culture of, v.23, p.1114-1116; noted, v.25, p.398, 399; noted, v.26, p.687.

Natchitoches Parish, overthrow of radicals during reconstruction, v.18, p.649-57; in 1860, v.21, p.1165-70; Grant Parish a part of, v.23, p.1108; noted, v.25, p.319, 320, 322, 323, 325, 335, 337, 347, 348, 361, 362, 371; and the Cong. election of 1894, v.26, p.1097; Populist legislator from, v.26, p.1109; noted, v.26, p.1073, 1077.

"National Advocate," v.30, p.280.

National Bank and 1837 panic, v.25, p.112.

National Democratic Convention, partial proceedings, v.24, p.58-59.

National Democratic Party, Caffery's part in the organization of, v.27, p.803; refused to nominate ticket, 1900, v.27, p.805.

National Guards, of La., and their part in the Civil War, v.29, p.1050-1051, 1074, 1195, 1201.

National Republicans, v.25, p.48, 51, 53, 60, 77; in La., v.25, p.74, 78, 79, 89.

Native Americanism, v.25, p.129; in La., v.25, p.130.

Native Guards, noted, v.24, p.523.

Natta, Captain, noted, v.24, p.676, 677.

"Nature of Hallucinations, The," by F. Legge (London Academy), v.1, p.293.

Navarino, engagements at, v.24, p.373, 978, 1069, 1070, 1074-75.

Navigation of Red River, History of, v.25, p.398-406.

Navy Commissioners Islands, v.28, p.783ff.; good live oaks, v.28, p.888; noted, v.28, p.889.

Neander, Professor, noted, v.24, p.421.

Neckere, Leo de, Bishop of New Orleans, v.31, p.906.

Negro education, in La., v.25, p.728-821; under the slave regime, v.25, p.728-37; the Catholic church in relation to, v.25, p.729-31; vocational training, v.25, p.736-37; under the Freedman's Bureau, v.25, p.737-47; Banks General Order #38, v.25, p.738; organization of schools, 1864, v.25, p.738-39; teachers salaries, v.25, p.739; educational policy of Bureau, v.25, p.742; attendance, v.25, p.742; support of, v.25, p.742-43; made permanent, 1866, v.25, p.744; under Pres. and Cong. plans of Reconst., v.25, p.748-767; first const. provision for, 1864, v.25, p.748; provisions for by local authorities, v.25, p.750-52; in const. of 1868, v.25, p.753; under Supt. Conway, v.25, p.754-62; dishonesty and illiteracy of early officials, v.25, p.756-60; the problem of mixed schools, v.25, p.760-64; accomplishments, v.25, p.764-67; institutions of higher learnings, v.25, p.768-90; philanthropy in, v.25, p.790-802; recent develop., v.25, p.802-815; training of teachers, v.25, p.806-12; vocational and industrial training, v.25, p.812-14; bibl., v.25, p.815-21.

Negroes, commerce in, 1787, v.21, p.14; public education in N. O., v.21, p.264-65;

free, in N. O., 1803-1860, v.21, p.1075-85; free, settlement of in Rapides Parish, 1860, v.21, p.1160; free, as witnesses, v.22, p.64; legislation against, v.22, p.147; in Sp. New Orleans, v.22, p.656-62; in Territory of Orleans, v.22, p.721; expedition against Bowles, v.22, p.795; in Natchez, v.22, p.814; as soldiers, v.22, p.1068; fear emancipation of, v.22, p.58; in New Orleans, v.2, p.142-65; and Sp. judicial system, v.22, p.623-41; duty on import in W. Fla., 1769, v.23, p.61; free, as skilled swordsmen, v.23, p.146; as servants in W. Fla., 1769, v.23, p.365ff.; taxes on, 1812, v.23, p.412; free, of Haiti, rejected by New Orleans, v.23, p.444; free, troops in New Orleans, 1873, v.23, p.531; in Union Army at New Orleans, v.23, p.1192, 1194, 1196, 1197, 1207; free, in New Orleans, 1807, v.23, p.707, 708-709; slavery in New Orleans, v.23, p.865; effort to Colonize, v.23, p.1048-1050; contraband trade in, v.24, p.12; attitude of Richard Taylor toward, v.24, p.55; laws regarding, v.25, p.303, 304; introduced into Illinois, v.26, p.736; sharecroppers, v.26, p.1056; and cotton culture, v.26, p.1058; suffrage of, v.26, p.1059, 1060; in the Black Belt, v.26, p.1061; their vote in 1894 Cong. election, v.26, p.1097; Gov's election 1896 and question of suffrage, v.26, p.1103-1107; disorder in St. Landry Parish, v.26, p.1107-1108; and election reform, v.26, p.1111; suffrage amendment, v.26, p.1117-1118; grandfathers clause, v.26, p.1121; in the St. Legis., 1867, v.27, p.533; Civil Rights Article giving equal rights on public conveyance, etc., v.27, p.534; see also Slaves.

Negro folklore, in La., v.24, p.750-52.

Negro problem, in New Orleans, v.24, p.517-24.

Negro Rural School Fund, established by Anna T. Jeanes, v.25, p.795-99.

Negro soldiers, mentioned, v.24, p.82-83, 108.

Negro theatre, attempt to establish, 1838, v.28, p.229.

Neil, Arthur, and W. Fla. Assembly, v.22, p.956, 981; noted, v.23, p.42, 76; member of Council of W. Fla., 1769, v.23, p.353ff.

Neilson, James, and W. Fla. Rev., v.21, p.96, 97, 131, 720n., 750.

Nelson, A. T., cand. for treasurer, first Populist ticket, 1896, v.26, p.1101; reasons for opposing lottery question, 1890, v.27, p.1040.

Nelson, H. E., cand. treasurer, v.28, p.1176.

Nelson, Hugh, noted, v.24, p.946.

Nelson, James, v.29, p.76.

Nelson, John D., death of, v.26, p.820, 835.

Nelson, Miss Kate Page, v.30, p.970.

Nelson's Bridge, noted, v.24, p.79.

Nelson, William Stuart, president of Dillard, 1936, v.25, p.781.

Neps, Capt. ———, noted, v.22, p.1045.

Neri, Felipe Enrique, see Baron de Bastrop.

Ness, Geo. T., Jr., "La. Officers of the Confed. Navy," v.27, p.479-86.

Nettelrode, Lake Charles business man, v.24, p.423, 432.

Nettles, Mrs., noted, v.23, p.421.

Neutral Ground Agreement of 1806, v.25, p.292, 294.

"Neutral Ground Between La. and Tex., 1806-1821," by J. Villasana Haggard, v.28, p.1001-1128.

Neutral Ground Between La. and Tex., noted, v.22, p.719n., 721; background, v.28, p.1002-18; map of, v.28, p.1003, 1022, 1044; first neutral ground in Am., v.28, p.1004-1009, map of 1st neutral ground, v.28, p.1007; boundary conflict, v.28, p.1009-10; Indian barrier, v.28, p.1010-14; Treaty of San Lorenzo, v.28, p.1014-15; La. purchase and its aid in creation of, v.28, p.1016-18; disputed Western Boundary of La. purchase, v.28, p.1018-28, neutral ground proposals, v.28, p.1024-28; attempts to enforce opposing claims, v.28, p.1028-34; agreement, v.28, p.1034-43; boundaries of, v.28, p.1043-47; physical aspects, v.28, p.1047-49; factors working against, v.28, p.1049-50; settlers, v.28, p.1050-53; filibusters, v.28, p.1053-59; bandits in, v.28, p.1059-60; fugitive slaves in, v.28, p.1069-73; Sp. restrictions on Tex.-La. trade, v.28, p.1074-82; Indian trade, v.28, p.1082-89; House of Barr & Davenport, v.28, p.1089-1103, list of ranches, settlers and families, v.28, p.1104-12.

Neutrality acts, of 1797 and 1817, v.24, p.630.

"Neutral Territory in Louisiana, Following the Spanish Trail Across the," by Leon Sugar, v.10, p.86.

Neuville, Hyde de, noted, v.24, p.991; correspondence with Adams, v.24, p.1086.

Neuville, Labourdonaye de, noted, v.24, p.993, 996.

Neuville, Madame de, injured from a fall, v.24, p.1089.

Neville, Julian, slave dealer, v.22, p.152, 153.

New American Theatre, built, 1835, v.26, p.371; noted, v.26, p.375; 1824, Camp St., v.28, p.116-121; description, v.28, p.121-22; became Am. Theatre, v.28, p.121.

New Bern, N. C., noted, v.24, p.621.

Newcomb College, noted, v.24, p.153, 155.

"New Delta," Anti-Lottery League newspaper, v.27, p.788, 1058, 1059, 1077; established, v.31, p.790; quoted, v.31, p.798, 801, 802, 805, 813, 814, 818, 823, 825, 828, 829, 834; noted, v.33, p.406.

New England, and tariff on sugar, v.25, p.141.

New England Society of N. O., purpose of, v.23, p.1047-1048; organization and activities, v.27, p.739; Clay guest of honor of, v.27, p.740; annual banquet, 1843, v.27, p.747; fifth conv. and banquet, Clay guest of honor, 1846, v.27, p.751-54; 765.

"New Enterprise," privateer of Laffites, v.23, p.782, 812.

"New Fiscal System for Louisiana, A," by L. E. Thomas, v.2, p.129.

Newgass, Benjamin, lottery offer, v.27, p.1035-36, 1049; offer of Mex. Lottery Co., v.28, p.1143, 1144.

New Granada, federation of, v.24, p.614-15.

New Harmony, Ind., noted, v.24, p.429.

New Iberia, founding of, v.22, p.795; noted, v.24, p.69, 70, 73, 79, 83; noted, v.25, p.140; military camp there, v.26, p.1025; noted, v.26, p.1156; noted, v.28, p.810, 821ff., 834, 835.

Newlin, A. W., newspaperman, "Old Days on the N. O. Picayune," v.33, p.334-35.

"New Liners," Soule faction, v.26, p.987.

New Madrid Fort, mentioned, v.21, p.33, 35-36; fortified by Carondelet, v.22, p.84.

Newman, Francis, trial of, v.22, p.716-17.

Newman, Mary, noted, v.24, p.454.

Newman, S. B., Jr., noted, v.23, p.528.

Newmark, Bishop George Augustus, noted, v.24, p.323; correspondence in Newmark Library, v.24, p.324.

Newmark, Dr. Gertrude W., noted, v.24, p.323.

New Orleans and Carrollton Railroad, History of, v.30, p.1125-1127.

New Orleans and Nashville Railroad, sketch of, v.30, p.1128-1130.

New Orleans and Ohio Line, route, v.31, p.437; consolidated, v.31, p.453-54.

New Orleans and Ohio Telegraph Lessees, lease Morse-O'Reilly consolidation, v.31, p.473.

New Orleans and Opelousas Railroad Convention, 1852, v.23, p.220-21.

New Orleans and Texas Railroad and Steamship Line, v.30, p.1078.

"New Orleans and the Cuban Question during the Lopez Expeditions, 1849-1851," by C. S. Urban, v.22, p.1095-1167.

"New Orleans and the Texas Revolution," by James E. Winston, v.10, p.317.

"New Orleans and the War of 1812," by R. McC. B. Adams, I, II, III, v.16, p.221, 479, 681; IV, V, VI, v.17, p.169, 349, 502.

New Orleans Associates, relations with Aury, v.24, p.627; membership, v.24, p.631; relations with Gual, v.24, p.634; noted, v.24, p.641; rejection of Mina plan, v.24, p.642.

New Orleans Association, and Spanish filibusters, v.23, p.737, 740, 750; expedition to Pensacola, v.23, p.763.

New Orleans Banking and Improvement Co., v.25, p.987-988, 989, 990; financing of St. Louis Hotel, v.25, p.991.

New Orleans, Baton Rouge and Vicksburg Railroad, history of, v.30, p.1225-1242; noted, v.30, p.1216.

New Orleans "Bee," v.29, p.50.

"New Orleans Bulletin," established, v.30, p.293; is sold to Vinton, v.30, p.294; staff of, v.30, p.295.

New Orleans Canal & Banking Co., land titles in Carrollton, v.21, p.228.

New Orleans Charity Hospital, First in 1736, v.4, p.359.

New Orleans "Chronicle," v.29, p.50.

New Orleans Citizens League, reform organization in N. O., v.26, p.1107; carried city election, 1896, v.26, p.1109; noted, v.26, p.1110.

New Orleans College of Pharmacy of Loyola U., v.26, p.337.

"New Orleans Commercial Bulletin," founding of, v.30, p.288; policy of under Seymour, v.30, p.289; suspension of by Butler, v.30, p.289; re-established, v.30, p.290; policy under Jewell, v.30, p.291; and Bartlett, v.30, p.292-293.

"New Orleans Crescent," v.30, p.267; early partners in, v.30, p.268-269; political affiliations of, v.30, p.270, 271, 272;

under Nixon, v.30, p.270-273; confiscation of, v.30, p.273; purchase of by Barker, v.30, p.273; revival of, v.30, p.274; staff of, v.30, p.274-275; policy after war, v.30, p.275-278; closes down, v.28, p.278-279; bought by "Times," v.30, p.285.

"New Orleans Daily Crescent," suppressed by Butler, v.27, p.500.

New Orleans "Daily Delta," established, v.20, p.296; policies of, v.30, p.296-297; connection with Walker, v.30, p.298-299; confiscation by Butler, v.30, p.301; reopening of, v.30, p.301; becomes "Era," v.30, p.302; plant reopened, v.30, p.303.

New Orleans "Daily Southern Star," v.30, p.255, 290-291.

New Orleans "Daily True Delta," v.30, p.303; becomes Demo. organ, v.30, p.304; confiscated by Butler, v.30, p.304; resumes pub., v.30, p.305; purchased by Hahn, v.30, p.306; becomes organ of state, v.30, p.306; closing of, v.30, p.307n.

New Orleans "Delta," noted, v.32, p.727.

"New Orleans Democrat," launched by Dem. leaders, v.30, p.311; policies of, v.30, p.311-314; suspension of, v.30, p.312; reestablishment of, v.30, p.313-314; editorial from, v.30, p.333-334.

New Orleans Drainage Co., Luzenberg director of, 1841, v.26, p.61.

New Orleans "Era," v.30, p.302-303.

New Orleans Female Academy, v.30, p.865.

New Orleans Gas Light and Banking Co., hist. of, v.23, p.173-74.

"New Orleans German Colony in the Civil War," by Robert T. Clark, Jr., v.20, p.990-1005.

New Orleans "German Gazette," v.29, p.50.

New Orleans Great Northern Railroad, v.29, p.94, 170, 171.

New Orleans "Herald," v.29, p.50; v.30, p.264.

"New Orleans in the Spanish Period, Life in," by M. Wood, v.22, p.642-709.

New Orleans "Item," v.29, p.50, 53, 54.

New Orleans, Jackson and Great Northern Railroad, noted, v.23, p.179; building of, v.23, p.215; noted, v.25, p.696, 697; history of, v.30, p.1133-1148.

"New Orleans Lady of Letters, A," by John S. Kendall, v.19, p.436-65.

New Orleans Lake Shore Land Co., drainage project, v.30, p.688-689.

New Orleans Lottery Co., attempt to create, v.27, p.980, 1004.

"New Orleans Lynchings of 1891 and the American Press," by Alexander J. Karlin, v.24, p.187-204.

"New Orleans Mafia Incident," by John E. Coxe, v.20, p.1067-1110.

New Orleans Magazines, bibliography of, v.18, p.493-548; chronological check list, v.18, p.549-52; index of editors and principal contributors, v.18, p.552-55; addenda, v.18, p.555-56.

"New Orleans Medical and Surgical Journal," comments on Medical Society, v.26, p.59; voiced need for reform in pharmacy laws, v.26, p.335, 336, 339.

"New Orleans' Miser Philanthropist: John McDonogh," by John S. Kendall, v.26, p.138-61.

New Orleans, Mobile and Chattanooga Railroad Company, history of, v.30, p.1242ff.; name and destination changed, v.30, p.1257; and state bonds, v.30, p.1262-1273.

New Orleans, Mobile and Texas Railroad, history of, v.30, p.1242-1325; division from N. O. to Mobile, v.30, p.1242; guarantee of bonds by state, v.30, p.1262; and subsidy by state, v.30, p.1273; and stock subscription, v.30, p.1282; road from N. O. to Houston, v.30, p.1298; from N. O. West, v.30, p.1306; from Brashear to Texas, v.30, p.1312; and new contract, v.30, p.1318; and N. O. subscription, v.30, p.1320.

"New Orleans Musicians of Long Ago," by John Smith Kendall, v.31, p.130-49.

New Orleans National Bank, cases against Merchant, v.27, p.1008-1009, 1074.

"New Orleans' Negro Minstrels," by John Smith Kendall, v.30, p.128-148.

New Orleans Netherlands Company, reclamation project, v.30, p.676, fig.3, 701.

New Orleans "News," v.29, p.50.

"New Orleans Newspapermen of Yesterday," by John Smith Kendall, v.29, p.771-790.

New Orleans, Opelousas and Great Western Railroad, v.25, p.697; incorporated, v.30, p.1068; during Civil War, v.30, p.1069-1070; historical sketch, v.30, p.1071-1078; sold at sheriff's sale, v.30, p.1078; history of, v.30, p.1148-1172; construction corporation formed, v.31, p.511.

New Orleans Opera, beginning of in N. O., v.29, p.662-663.

New Orleans Orphan Asylum, aid for, v.25, p.1052.

New Orleans Pacific Railroad, v.30, p.1092;

legislation to aid, v.30, p.1100-1105.

"New Orleans' 'Peculiar Institution,' " by J. S. Kendall, v.23, p.864-86.

New Orleans "Picayune," v.29, p.50, 51, 54, 55; noted, v.30, p.225; political associations of, v.30, p.256-257; purchase of, v.30, p.258; direction of by Jenkins, Rhett, v.30, p.258-260; staff of, v.30, p.261-263; purchase of by "Herald," v.30, p.264-265; under Holbrook, v.30, p.265-267; excerpt from, v.30, p.331-332; noted, v.30, p.135, 144, 146.

"New Orleans Picayune, George Wilkins Kendall and the Founding of the," by John S. Kendall, v.11, p.261.

"New Orleans Press and Reconstruction," by Fayette Copeland, v.30, p.149-339.

"New Orleans Price-Current," v.30, p.149, 160, 164.

New Orleans Public Service Company, v.23, p.174.

New Orleans, Red River and Texas Telegraph Company, noted, v.31, p.450; plans, v.31, p.451.

New Orleans "Republican," v.29, p.50, 51; leading radical journal of South, v.30, p.307; established, v.31, p.720; quoted, v.31, p.731.

"New Orleans Sanitary Conditions Under Spanish Regime, 1799-1800," translated by Laura L. Porteous, introduction by Henry P. Dart, v.15, p.610.

New Orleans "States," v.29, p.50.

New Orleans "Sunday Delta," v.30, p.310.

New Orleans Theatre, St. Philip St., v.28, p.113.

"New Orleans Times," v.29, p.50, 53, 54; founding of, v.30, p.280; policies of, v.30, p.280-283; purchases "Crescent," v.30, p.285-287; purchase of by Mrs. King, v.30, p.287; under Stoutemeyer, v.30, p.288; noted, v.30, p.310; established, v.31, p.719; quoted, v.31, p.721, 724, 725, 726, 728, 729, 730-31, 762, 772; purchased by Clinton, v.31, p.775; merged with "Democrat," v.31, p.785.

New Orleans "Times-Democrat," v.29, p.50, 56, 57, 58.

New Orleans "Truth," v.29, p.50.

"New Orleans Under General Butler," by Howard Palmer Johnson, v.24, p.434-536.

New Orleans Union Association, noted, v.24, p.506.

New Orleans University, v.25, p.778-80, 792.

New Orleans vs. Houston, withdrew granting of lottery charters from police power of state, v.27, p.1010, 1030.

"New Orleans Yellow Fever Epidemic of 1853, The," by Donald E. Everett, v.33, p.380-405.

New Orleans, "Bi-Centennial of New Orleans," Meeting of Louisiana Historical Society, Oct. 24, 1917, Address on, by T. P. Thompson, v.1, sec.3, p.13; Address on, by E. F. Genoyer de Bournety, Consul-General of France, v.1, sec.3, p.9; Celebration of, in Paris, of the Founding of New Orleans, v.1, sec.3, p.18; "Life and Services of Bienville, Notes on," by Grace King, v.1, sec.3, p.39; "Bienville, New Orleans Under," by Heloise Hulse Cruzat, v.1, sec.3, p.54; "Flag, First Official, of," Address by W. J. Waguespack, v.1, sec.3, p.210; "Flag, Raising of American, in Jackson Square," Address by Andre Lafargue, v.1, sec.3, p.212; "La Spectacle de la Rue St. Pierre," by Nellie W. Price, v.1, sec. 3, p.215; "Life in New Orleans An Indian Treaty," by William Kernan Dart, v.1, sec.3, p.193; "New Orleans," by W. O. Hart, v.1, p.353; "Old Orleans Greets," July 4, 1918, v.1, p. 298; Old Portage Between Bayou St. John and Mississippi River, v.1, p.372; "Jackson Square," by Henry Renshaw, v.2, p.38; "Treasure House for Historians, A," by Clarence Wyatt Bispham, v.2, p.237; "Celebration of the Founding of," Address by Charles Barrett, Trans. from French by Miss Grace King, v.2, p.258; Battle of Sept. 14, 1874; Recollections by Col. F. L. Richardson, v.3, p.498; "Bonded Debt of, 1822-1920, Inclusive," by H. P. Phillips, v.3, p.596; "Charity Hospital, First, for the Poor of," by H. P. Dart, v.3, p.554; "Creole Families of," Notes on Miss Grace King's Book, v.3, p.612; "Custom-House, Historical Sketch on Construction of," by Charles A. Favrot, v.3, p.467; "French Opera House, The," by Andre Lafargue, v.3, p.368; "Founding of, The," by Delaville H. Theard, v.3, p.68; "History of the Foundation of," by Baron Marc de Villiers, Translated from the French by Warrington Dawson, v.3, p.157; Contents: Forward, v.3, p.157; Mississippi Portage, The, v.3, p.161; Naming and the Foundation of New Orleans, v.3, p.173; Mississippi Flood in 1719. Consequences of the Capture of Pensacola, The Year 1720, v.3, p.189; New Orleans Bluff — The Real Manon — "Princess Charlotte" — Mademoiselle Baron, v.3, p.197; Adrien de Pauger Traces the Plan of New Orleans, v.3, p.218; New Orleans, the Capital of Louisiana—the Cyclone of 1722—D'Artaguette's Chronicle, v.3, p.230; Vieux Carre and the First Engineers of New Orleans, v.3, p.241; Briefly Statistical, v.3, p.248; For Illustrations contained in Baron Villier's Book, see Illustrations; "Latin City, The," by Edward Alexander Parsons, v.3, p.361; "Liberty Monument," by James A. Renshaw, v.3, p.259; "The Old 'Mobile Landing,' Head of the Basin in," by Charles Patton Dimitry, v.3, p.131; "New York Yankee in New Orleans, Sept. 14, 1874," by John J. Colvin, Jr., v.3, p.502; Charity Hospital, First in, 1736, v.4, p.359; Fire Protection in Spanish Period, v.4, p.201; Cabildo of, The, v.5, p.279; Experiences of William Perry in 1758 in, v.5, p.53; "Early Commercial Prestige of," by Henry E. Chambers, v.5, p.451; "New Orleans and Bayou St. John in 1766," by William Beer, v.6, p.19; "New Orleans in 1867," by Guilio Adamoli, v.6, p.271; "Reflections on Jackson's Campaign, 1814-1815," by Bernard Marigny, v.6, p.61; "Bi-Centennial Medallion," Andre Lafargue, v.7, p.87; "Charles S. Waterman, Mayor of New Orleans," Francis P. Burns, v.7, p.466; Semi-Centennial, 14th September, 1874, v.7, p.570; "Interesting Incident in Connection with New Orleans Premium Bonds, An," W. O. Hart, v.8, p.248; "New Orleans Bee," Buissiere Rouen, v.8, p.585; "New Orleans Times and New Orleans Democrat," W. O. Hart, v.8, p.574; "Suit for Debt in the Governor's Court, New Orleans, A, 1770," Laura L. Porteous, v.8, p.240; Battle of New Orleans, v.9, p.5-112; "Contract to Build a Ship in New Orleans, 1769," translated by Laura L. Porteous, v.9, p.593; Slave Depot of the Company of the Indies at N. O. (Editor's Chair), v.9, p.286; "Early New Orleans Newspapers," by John S. Kendall, v.10, p.383; "New Orleans and the Texas Revolution," James E. Winston, v.10, p.317; "Ogden's Troop of Horse in the Battle of New Orleans, Capt.," by Edw. Clarke Morse, M.D., v.10, p.381; "Procedure for Sale of an American Vessel in New Orleans, 1803," by Laura L. Porteous, v.10, p.185; "Faithful Picture of the Political Situation in New Orleans at the Close of the Last and Beginning of the Present Year, 1807," by James E. Winston, v.11, p.359; "Kendall and the Founding of the New Orleans Picayune," by John S. Kendall, v.11, p.261; "Public Education in New Orleans in 1800," by Henry P. Dart, v.11, p.241; "Petition of Don Luis Francisco Lefort to Open a House of Education in New Orleans," by Laura L. Porteous, v.11, p.244; "Foreign Language Press of New Orleans, The," by John S. Kendall, v.12, p.363; "Lawsuit in the Court of the Governor at New Orleans Involving Land in Opelousas, 1764, A," translated by Laura L. Porteous, v.12, p.533; "Financial and Economic Disturbance on the Eve of Secession," by John Muir, contributed by Milledge L. Bonham, v.13, p.32; "Duel in the Dark in New Orleans, 1747," by H. P. Dart, v.13, p.199; "Criminal Trial of Etienne La Rue, May, 1747," translated by Heloise H. Cruzat, v.13, p.377; "Funeral Ceremony of Napoleon in New Orleans," by A. E. Fossier, v.13, p.246; "Early Census Tables of Louisiana," introduction by William Beer, translated by J. K. Ditchey, v.13, p.205; N. O. Cabarets, v.19, p.578-83; financial statement for 1789, v.19, p.584-94; the Pontalba Buildings, v.19, p.119-49; German liberals in 1840-1860, v.20, p.137-51; libraries in 1771-1833, v.20, p.152-158; arrival of de Laussat, v.20, p.168; first mayor and council, v.20, p.168-72; archives of, v.20, p.171-72; militia in 1803, v.20, p.173-76; Charity Hosp., v.20, p.177; fire dept., v.20, p.179-80; faubourgs forming upper section of, v.20, p.192-211, fire of 1788, v.20, p.578-89; books and booksellers, 1730-1830, v.20, p.606-18; early houses, v.20, p.794-820; hist. of the City of Lafayette, v.20, p.895-964; Germans in, v.20, p.925ff.; education in, v.20, p.935-43, 1016-66; transportation in, v.20, p.943-945; religion in, v.20, p.945-47; fires and floods in, v.20, p.950-51; crime in, v.20, p.952-953; trade in early, v.20, p.1025ff.; Mafia in, v.20, p.1067-1110; fire of 1783, v.21, p.13; fire of

Dec. 8, 1794, v.21, p.53; history of City of Carrollton, v.21, p.220-81; ice in Miss. River, in 1783, v.21, p.349-53; Andrew Jackson in, v.21, p.367ff.; strike of 1892, v.21, p.547-60; Spanish consuls in 1804-1821, v.21, p.677-84; filibustering expedition to Pensacola, v.21, p.807ff.; Protestants in, v.21, p.823-45; theatre, v.21, p.846ff.; meeting of Southern Hist'l Ass'n, v.21, p.959; free negro in, 1803-1860, v.21, p.1075-1085; schism of 1805, v.22, p.98-141; slaves in, v.22, p.142-65; history of Carrollton, v.22, p.181-215; history of Faubourg Ste. Marie, v.22, p.385-427; history of Episcopal Church, v.22, p.428-78; Mafia affair, v.22, p.492-530, 819-56; trial of slave for murder, v.22, p.623-41; life in Sp. period, v.22, p.642-709; fires of 1788, 1794, v.22, p.666; health and sanitation in Sp. period, v.22, p.676-82; education, v.22, p.682-87; amusements, v.22, p.687-94; crime, v.22, p.694-700; relations with Latin Am., 1810-1824, v.22, p.710-94; newspapers, v.22, p.685; economic conditions, 1800, v.22, p.1012-13; first city directory, v.22, p.1068; riots of 1851, v.22, p.1149-59; municipal gov't of, v.23, p.177; charter of 1852, v.23, p.190; settlers from in W. Fla., v.23, p.375, 379; French vice-admiralty prize court established, 1799, v.23, p.431; privateers in, v.23, p.435, 437; hist. of Washington Artillery, v.23, p.471-84; travel account of German immigrant, 1853, v.23, p.492-95; German colony and Reconstruction, v.23, p.501-24; White League in, v.23, p.525-43; rice mills in, v.23, p.556; no longer La. rice market, v.23, p.574; Batture controversy, v.23, p.679-732; three municipalities of, v.23, p.1064n.; in 1854, v.23, p.1146; G. S. Denison as Special Agent of Treas. Dept. and Acting Collector of Customs, v.23, p.1178ff.; customhouse in 1862, v.23, p.1182ff.; removal of mayor, 1865, v.23, p.1222; B. Butler and Christ Church, v.23, p.1241-1257; description of c. 1812, v.24, p.27; noted, v.24, p.76; German population in, v.24, p.130; German newspapers in, v.24, p.131-36; German schools in, v.24, p.148-49, 151-52; German theatre in, v.24, p.159; table of newspaper reactions to lynchings in, v.24, p.202-04; guide, v.24, p.312, 314, 320, 349; Public Library, v.24, p.324, 325, 352; life in the early Confederacy, v.24, p.438-40; press comments on Federal invasion, v.24, p. 452-56, 460, 462, 464; 1862 capture described, v.24, p.457; clean-up by Butler, v.24, p.477-78; and privateers, v.24, p.638; yellow fever in, v.24, p.739; healthfulness, v.24, p.928; Sp. officials in, v.25, p.6; and revolutionary activities, v.25, p.9-11; noted, v.25, p.50, 62, 123, 126, 127, 191, 204, 207, 208, 213, 214, 215, 239, 242, 293, 294, 297, 298, 300, 305, 308, 315, 317, 321, 323, 329, 333, 338, 339, 340, 344, 345, 350, 355, 359, 361, 364, 365, 366, 371, 372, 373, 384, 385; memorial to Congress, v.25, p.73; visited by Clay, v.25, p.74; and tariff, v.25, p.79, 90, 135-36; and nullification, v.25, p.91; cotton center, v.25, p.175; free colored population, v.25, p.302, 310, 319-20, 327, 349; immigrants from Santo Domingo, v.25, p.306; archdiocese of, v.25, p.362; description of, v.25, p.980-83; the anglo creole struggle in, v.25, p.981-86; the financial history of, v.25, p.986-94; representation in Leg., v.25, p.1022-27; removal of state capital from, v.25, p.1044; judiciary reform of, v.25, p.1045, 1048, 1049; her part in the Mexican War, v.25, p.1053-54; noted, v.26, p.7, 8; history of medicine in, v.26, p.49-137; and Miss. R. trade, v.26, p.37ff.; the German drama in, v.26, p.361-627; noted, v.26, p.635, 665-721 passim, p.722, 732, 736, 737; capital moved to, v.26, p.730; given to Sp., 1762, v.26, p.739; forts of, v.26, p.737, 740, 745-47; noted, v.26, p.748; the Wood family in, v.26, p.784-85; noted, v.26, p.786; filibustering center against Cuba, v.26, p.788n.; Legis. solution to problems of 1804-1824, v.26, p.915-36; noted, v.26, p.937, 947; expected attack on, v.26, p.951, 953, 957, 959; noted, v.26, p.985, 986, 988, 991; question of moving capital, v.26, p.993; noted, v.26, p.994, 996, 997; secession conv. reassembles in, v.26, p.1002-1004; noted, v.26, p.1005, 1007, 1008; defense preparations in, v.26, p.1008; federal threat of attack, v.26, p.1018; siege and capture of by Federals, v.26, p.1019-1020; noted, v.26, p.1032; illegal trade in with federal soldiers, v.26, p.1034-37; noted, v.26, p.1041; riot in, v.26, p.1059; two governors, v.26, p.1059-60; agr. exp. station, v.26, p.1064, Joseph Jefferson in, v.26, p.1150-67; Myra Clark Gaines' suit against, v.27, p.176, 276-93; Gaines vs., suit decided in favor of Mrs. Gaines, v.27, p.315-17, 319-20, 321, 330, 331, 336, 337, 338, 340, 341, 342, 348, 350, 351, 361, 365, 366, 367, 371, 372, 374, 375, 378, 379, 380, 382, 386, 389, 390, 393, 395; surrender of, 1862, v.27, p.487; population and wealth of, v.27, p.488; went secessionist, v.27, p.490; conditions before surrender, v.27, p.492-93; fall of, v.27, p.494, 495; Butler's reception in, v.27, p.496, 497, 498, 499; economic conditions improved by Butler, v.27, p.505-10; Butler's attitude toward slaves, v.27, p.511-12; Monroe taken into custody and military gov't established in, v.27, p.512-13; Butler "cracks down," v.27, p.514-18; celebration of July 4, 1862, v.27, p.519; conscription in, v.27, p.519-20, 527; Pinchback's arrival in, v.27, p.529; recruiting of men in, v.27, p.529-30, 630, 635, 636, 638, 640, 642, 643, 644, 646, 647, 648, 649, 650, 651, 652, 655, 656, 657; shipments of goods from, v.27, p.659, 665, 671, 672, 676, 677, 678, 682, 689, 690, 691, 693, 695, 697, 700, 701, 706, 711; statue of Clay, v.27, p.717, 718, 721, 723, 724, 725; Clay's interests in, v.27, p.732-33; his first visit, v.27, p.734-35; second visit, v.27, p.735-36; visit in 1842, v.27, p.736-47; Clay appears before Sup. Ct., v.27, p742-45; Clay Ball, v.27, p.745-47; fourth visit, v.27, p.747-50; final visit, v.27, p.756, 757; ball in honor of Taylor, v.27, p.758-59; social activities of 1849, v.27, p.759-60; laying of cornerstone of Custom House, v.27, p.760; reception of Polk, v.27, p.761; mourns death of Clay, v.27, p.762; mourns death of Webster, v.27, p.763; formation of Clay Monument Assoc., v.27, p.764-65; funeral procession in honor of Clay, Calhoun, Webster, v.27, p.765-69; erection of statue to Clay, v.27, p.769-75, 776; Butler's regime in, v.27, p.777; Cotton Centennial Exposition, 1884, v.27, p.777, 778; cornerstone of Clay Monument relaid in Lafayette Sq., v.27, p.779; Univ. of La. in, v.27, p.784, 843; development as a wholesale trading center, origin of, v.27, p.933; trade monopolized by Western Co., v.27, p.934; leading trade center of Miss. Valley, v.27, p.935; Sp. restrictive policy in re trade in, v.27, p.935, 936-37; lack of initiative in, v.27, p.935; limited wholesale trade in before 1812, v.27, p.936-37; development of Miss. Valley affects trade in, v.27, p.937-39; U. S. receives right of deposit in, v.27, p.938; trade of affected by development of river transportation, v.27, p.939-41; table showing value of down river shipments to, v.27, p.939; Jefferson's prophecy for, v.27, p.940; triangular trade, v.27, p.941-44; two-way trade with Pittsburgh, v.27, p.942-43; first city directory, 1822, v.27, p.943, 952; wholesale house in N. O., 1822, v.27, p.943; value of produce received, 1830, 1860, v.27, p.944; a world port, v.27, p.944; results of failure to recognize importance of railroads, v.27, p.944-46; wholesale merchants in, prior to Civil War, v.27, p.947-951; laws regulating auction sale, v.27, p.948-49; comparison with N. Y., v.27, p.949; specialties of Commission Merchants, v.27, p.949-50; table showing kinds of businesses in, 1844, v.27, p.950; factorage system, v.27, p.951; wholesale trading area of, v.27, p.951-53; table showing, v.27, p.952-53; competition with other trade centers, v.27, p.954-57; table showing investment of in materials for trade territory of, v.27, p.956; effect of Civil War on trade in, v.27, p.957; effect of railroad development, v.27, p.957-58; yellow fever adverse factor in trade of, v.27, p.958; changes in after Civil War, v.27, p.958-60; table showing trading areas and kinds of business, 1904, v.27, p.960-61; decline of wholesaler, v.27, p.961-63; churches of, benefited by lotteries, v.27, p.969; lottery to reduce evils in, v.27, p.970, 972, 973; demand for city license from Lottery Co., rejected, v.27, p.978; sentiments against Lottery Co., v.27, p.979, 980; attempt to establish lottery co. of, v.27, p.980; acts to prevent sale of foreign lottery tickets in, v.27, p.980-81; courts of, busy handling cases of violation of lottery act, v.27, p.984; Citizens petition Washington for enforcement of law denying lottery use of mails, v.27, p.992; assessors of, denied right to levy assessment against Lottery Co., v.27, p.1009; McClure visits, v.27, p.1011; Crevasses near, v.27, p.1026; Lottery Co. donates money to fight floods, v.27, p.1027, 1050, 1056; headquarters Dem. Anti-

Lottery St. Ex. Com., v.27, p.1059, 1065; foreign lottery operating in, v.27, p.1068, 1077, 1079, 1080; Dem. St. Central Com. meets in, v.27, p.1088, 1089, 1091; meeting of rival Dem. Central Com. in, v.27, p.1093; efforts to eradicate lotteries, v.27, p.1103; yellow fever epidemic, 1905, v.27, p.1135, 1136, 1145, 1163; held rice trust, v.27, p.1164, 1165, 1199; noted, v.28, p.59, 57, 61, 65; a hist. of the Eng. theatre in 1806-1842, v.28, p.85-276, 361-572; Pedro Favrot's plan for defense of, v.28, p.694-95; Cathcart's impression of v.28, p.749; capital removed, "Country vs. City" affair, v.28, p.967; clearing house for troops of Mex. War, v.28, p.967; crime in N. O., 1865-1898, v.29, p.43-49; beginning of police reporting, v.29, p.48; list of police reporters in N. O. between 1870-1895, v.29, p.50; Lafayette's visit to, v.29, p.306-307, 308-309, 310-325, 326-328; telegraph reaches, v.31, p.444, 447.

New Philadelphia Congregation, laws of, v.24, p.426.

"New Providence," Netherlander schooner, v.24, p.629.

New Roads, La., v.25, p.211.

New Santander, province of, v.24, p.642.

Newsom, H. C., v.27, p.1036; opposed lottery question, v.27, p.1039.

Newspaper Row, noted, v.33, p.407.

Newspapers, "Old Days on the New Orleans Picayune," by John Smith Kendall, v.33, p.317-34; "Old Days on the Times-Democrat," by John Smith Kendall, v.33, p.406-429.

"Newspapers, Specimens of the Folktales from Some Ante Bellum, of La.," by Arthur K. Moore, v.32, p.723.

Newspapers, French, in La., bibliography of, v.18, p.947-65; German in La., v.20, p.139-41; in N. O., v.20, p.947; in Carrollton, v.21, p.267-69; in St. John the Baptist Parish, v.21, p.1117; in St. James Parish, v.21, p.1121; at Marksville, 1860, v.21, p.1147, 1149; of Ascension Parish, v.21, p.1124; in Iberville Parish, v.21, p.1127; in W. Baton Rouge Parish, v.21, p.1132; in W. Feliciana, v.21, p.1136; in Pointe Coupee, v.21, p.1139; in Alexandria, v.21, p.1156; in Natchitoches, v.21, p.1169; in Mansfield, v.21, p.1173; in Shreveport, v.21, p.1177; in Bossier, v.21, p.1179-80; in Minden, v.21, p.1184; in Bienville, v.21, p.1187; in Jackson Parish, v.21, p.1191; in Bastrop, v.21, p.1198; in Catahoula, v.21, p.1207; in Concordia, v.21, p.1209; in Carrol, v.21, p.1212-13; first in New Orleans, v.22, p.58; in Carrollton, v.22, p.211; in Sp. N. O., v.22, p.685-86; source of revolts in New Spain, v.22, p.780-86; Spanish, v.22, p.802; German, in N. O. during Reconstruction, v.23, p.501ff.; first in Tex., v.23, p.1001; and publications in New Orleans, 1866-1877, list of, v.30, p.314-331; in Calcasieu Parish, v.32, p.717-20; in St. Mary Parish, v.32, p.89-94.

New Town (Nova Iberia), description, v.24, p.41.

"New York Yankee in New Orleans, Sept. 14, 1874," by John J. Colvin, Jr., v.3, p.502.

"Neyrada," Spanish brig, v.24, p.361.

Niblett's Bluff, noted, v.24, p.74, 77, 78; v.32, p.593.

Nicaragua, Mosquito Coast of, v.24, p.654; engagements off the coast, v.24, p.660.

Nicholas I, noted, v.24, p.983; difficulties in Russia, v.24, p.986-87, 989; war against Turkey, v.24, p.991-92.

Nicholas, R. C., noted, v.25, p.123, 1039, 1044, 1095.

"Nicholls, An Autobiography of Francis T., 1834-1881," by Barnes F. Lathrop, v.17, p.246.

"Nicholls Family in La., The," v.6, p.5.

Nicholls, Francis T., and Mafia incident, v.22, p.527; gov. of La., v.25, p.710, 767; v.26, p.1060; became gov. of La., 1877, v.27, p.605, 787, 985, 996; delay in signing Act No. 44, v.27, p.997; accused of "bad faith" by Lottery Co. because of purported aid to by Co., v.27, p.997-98, 1011; levee improvements, v.27, p.1026; rejects lottery co. offer to aid in flood control, v.27, p.1027; message of May 12, 1890, to Legis. warning against recharter of lottery co., v.27, p.1030-32; vetos Lottery Bill, 1890, v.27, p.1043-44; power of veto of bill passed by Const. majority challenged, v.27, p.1044, 1045; Legis. attack on, v.27, p.1046-47; charge members of Legis. with bribery, v.27, p.1047, 1050, 1056; Anti-Lottery League's resolution of confidence in, v.27, p.1058, 1061, 1064, 1065; accused of accepting campaign money from Lottery Co., v.27, p.1065-66; overtures to State Farmers' Union, v.27, p.1086, 1092, 1094; final message to Legis., v.27, p.1095-96; original name suggested for Acadia Parish, v.27, p.1121; end of the La. Levee Co., v.28; p.309-10; Dem. Cand. Gov., v.28, p.1138; called Const. Conv., v.28, p.1139; opposition to rechartering lottery co., v.28, p.1142, accused of receiving money from lottery co., v.28, p.1144-45; vetoed lottery bill, v.28, p.1147-48; noted, v.28, p.1151, 1157, 1159; named Chief Justice of La. Sup. Ct., v.28, p.1166-67; noted, v.28, p.1185; nominated for gov. of La., v.29, p.485; inaugurated, v.29, p.490; noted, v.29, p.730, 732, 733, 737, 751, 754; and Charity Hospital, v.31, p.68; Governor of La., v.31, p.778, 794; vetoes lottery recharter, v.31, p.796; and Wells indictment, v.31, p.1109.

"Nicholls, Francis Tillou, and the End of Reconstruction," by Hilda Mulvey McDaniel, v.32, p.357.

Nicholls, Richard, petition of, v.23, p.403.

Nicholls, Thomas C., and nullification, v.25, p.93, 95; report on S. C. Ord. of Nullification, v.28, p.950; apt'd to Ct. of Errors and Appeals, v.28, p.957.

Nichols, Edward, letter in Bibliotheca Parsoniana, v.24, p.311.

Nicholson, George, manager of N. O. "Democrat," v.31, p.741; state printer, v.31, p.778; noted, v.31, p.786.

Nicholson, John, and W. Fla. Rev., v.21, p.116, 153n.; letters to Rhea, v.21, p.154-55; identified, v.21, p.798.

Nicholson, J. W., La. educator, organizes Arizona Academy, v.30, p.817, 818; noted, v.30, p.970.

Nicholson, Mrs. E. J. (Pearl Rivers), by Jas W. Renshaw, v.6, p.580.

Nicolle, ———, noted, v.22, p.1018.

Niggerville, name for Washington, La., v.25, p.360.

Nilco, now Jonesville, La., v.25, p.626; see also Anilco, v.25, p.629-30.

Niles, Hezekiah and tariff, v.25, p.57, 60; editor of "Niles Register" and publication of Robinson's Map, v.25, p.667-68.

"Niles' Register," and Sp. Am. revolts, v.22, p.782; publication of Robinson's Map, v.25, p.667-68.

Nim, Ormand F., noted, v.24, p.89.

Nitalbany (River), noted, v.23, p.410.

Nixon, J. O., owner of "N. O. Daily Crescent," v.27, p.500; first assis. Grand Marshall of parade for unveiling of Clay Statue, v.27, p.774; early N. O. newspaperman, v.29, p.773; proprietor of "Crescent," sketch of, v.30, p.270-271; fights duel, v.30, p.271; military service of, v.30, p.272; revives "Crescent," v.30, p.274-275; sues state, v.30, p.278; loses "Crescent," v.30, p.279; death, v.30, p.279; noted, v.30, p.181, 254, 273, 284.

Noble, James, noted, v.23, p.1177.

Noble, Jane, noted, v.23, p.1145.

Noble, Stuart Grayson, "Governor Claiborne and the Public School System of the Territorial Government of Louisiana," v.11, p.535; "Schools of New Orleans During the First Quarter of the Nineteenth Century," v.14, p.65; co-author, "Education in Colonial Louisiana," v.32, p.759.

Noeli, Luis, Spanish agent, v.23, p.789; letter to Cienfuegos, v.23, p.789-92.

Nogales, Creeks cede to Spanish, v.21, p.24n.; Treaty of, v.21, p.28n.

Nolan, Philip, noted, v.22, p.730; v.25, p.292.

Nolan, Thomas J., newspaperman, "Old Days on the N. O. Picayune," v.33, p.335.

Nolte, Vincent, duel of, v.23, p.446-47; N. O. Merchant, v.24, p.16, 18; banker, importer, v.27, p.941-42; Eng. dry goods a specialty, v.27, p.950; friend of Lafayette, v.29, p.297; his accounts of Lafayette, v.29, p.297-299, 325-328; noted, v.33, p.54.

Nootka Sound Affair, noted, v.21, p.15ff.

Norden, W. Van, Pres. La. Saving Bank, v.27, p.547.

Nordhoff, Charles, noted, v.23, p.523-24.

Norgress, Joseph, pioneer in cypress lumber industry, sketch of, v.30, p.1012-1013; officer Red Cypress Lumber Company, v.30, p.1017-1018; noted, v.30, p.1025.

Norgress-Menefee Cypress Company, v.30, p.1013.

Norgress, Rachel Edna, "The History of the Cypress Lumber Company in Louisiana," v.30, p.976-1059.

Norman, N. Philip "Red River of the South," v.25, p.397-535.

Norsworthy, W. F., Chairman Farmers' Alliance, v.28, p.1152.

North Louisiana Agr. Society organized at Calhoun, v.26, p.1064; meeting, v.26, p.1066.

North Louisiana and Texas Railroad Company, v.30, p.1197-1209.

"North Pole," noted, v.24, p.650.

Northrup, Captain, noted, v.24, p.662.

Northrup, Job, privateer, v.21, p.809; threatens Pensacola, v.22, p.1057-61, 1087.

"Northumberland," British ship, v.24, p.311.

Norton, E. E., La. Repub. divulged secrets of election of Pinchback to U. S. Senate, v.27, p.595.

Norton, James, noted, v.23, p.409.

Norton, "Wash," N. O. minstrel, sketch of, v.30, p.133-135.

Norvilla Collegiate Institute, v.30, p.907-908.

Norwood, S. S., La. educator, founder Norvilla Collegiate Institute, v.30, p.907-908.

Norwood, Charles, noted, v.22, p.434, 439.

"Notarial System of Louisiana, The," by Edgar Grima, v.10, p.76.

"Notaries in Louisiana during the French Colonial Period, Ordinance of 1717 Governing," translated by the late William K. Dart, v.10, p.82.

"Note on Absenteeism & Pluralism in British West Fla," by Cecil Johnson, v.19, p.196-98.

"Notes on Legislation and Litigation affecting the Title of St. Louis Cathedral," by Francis P. Burns, v.18, p.363-76.

"Notes on the Life and Services of Bienville," by Grace King, v.1, sec.3, p.39.

Notre Dame, Sisters of, v.24, p.149, 154.

"Nottaway," Randolph plantation, v.25, p.150, 167, 174, 196, 197, 200, 201, 210, 211, 213, 215, 216, 217.

Nott, G. Wm. "Adrien Rouquette: Poet and Mystic," v.6, p.388.

Nouveau, ———, noted, v.23, p.394.

Nova Iberia (New Town), description of, v.24, p.41.

"Noveau Nain Jaune," Soule's French paper, v.25, p.975.

Nugent, Gordon Richard, noted, v.23, p.361, 368; letter from, v.23, p.388; petition of, v.23, p.404.

Nuhrah, Arthur G., co-author, "Education in Colonial La.," v.32, p.759-76; "John McDonogh: Man of Many Facets," v.33, p.5-144.

Nullification, answer to Ordinance framed by Livingston, v.24, p.721; and Calhoun, v.24, p.1159; in S. C., v.24, p.1168; reaction to in La., v.25, p.91-96.

Nunemaker, J. Horace, "La. Anticipates Spanish Recognition," v.26, p.755-69.

Nunez, Adrien, Cand. for Sen., v.28, p.1139; elected, v.28, p.1140.

Nunez, Vincente Jose, and fire of 1788, v.22, p.666.

Nunez, Vincent, noted, v.24, p.356.

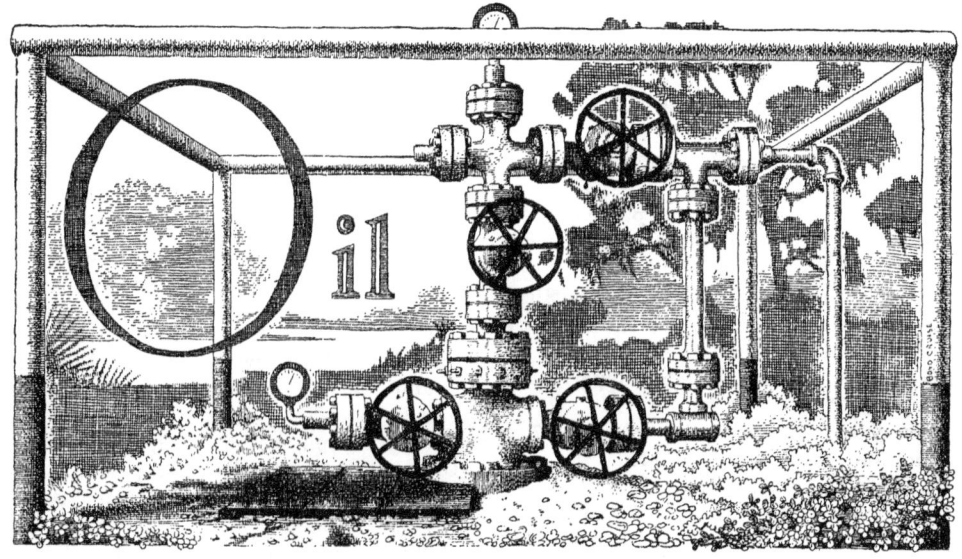

OAKEY, ———, IN DUEL WITH Wright, v.24, p.759-62.
Oak Grove Academy, v.30, p.807.
"Oakland" Plantation, production of rice on, v.23, p.554.
"Oak Lawn," description of, v.24, p.41; v.32, p.30.
Oaks, The, dueling at, v.25, p.310.
Obelisk, in Cathedral Sq., in N. O., story of, v.28, p.326-48; names of Fr. Sailors inscribed on, v.28, p.325; description of, v.28, p.334; removed to N. O., v.28, p.338ff.
O'Brian, Christopher, sketch, v.28, p.791n.
O'Brien, Matthew, Confed. naval engineer from La., v.27, p.484-85.
O'Brien, Wm. V., Catholic priest, certificate of marriage of Desgrange and Barbara Orci, v.27, p.61, 87, 90, 98, 143, 215, 224.
Occupations of free colored in N. O., 1854, chart, v.25, p.390-392.
O'Conner, Stella, "The Charity Hospital at New Orleans: An Administrative and Financial History, 1736-1941," v.31, p.1-109.
O'Conner, William, and Mafia, v.22, p.512.
O'Connor, Thos., favored lottery bill of 1890, v.27, p.1033; approved submission of lottery question to people, v.27, p.1037.
Odd Fellows Hall, meeting of Soule Faction, v.26, p.985-86; delegates not admitted to State Dem. Conv., v.26, p.988; meeting repudiated, v.26, p.988-89; conv. at, v.26, p.989; Fusionist assembly in, v.27, p.574, 769, 997.
Odoardo, Cecilio, and murder case of slave, v.22, p.626.
Odom, John, noted, v.26, p.953, 965, 968.
Odom, Van D., "The Political Career of Thomas Overton Moore, Secession Gov. of La.," v.26, p.975-1054.
O'Donnell, Mary Agnes, first Director of Nurses, New Orleans Charity Hospital, v.31, p.75.
O'Donnell, Will I., approved submission of lottery question to people, v.27, p.1037.
O'Fallon, Dr. James, noted, v.21, p.25n., 34.
"Official Expression of Manifest Destiny Sentiment Concerning Hispanic America, 1848-1871," by A. Curtis Wilgus, v.15, p.486.
Ogden, Abner N., noted, v.25, p.1075, 1083, 1086, 1087; Judge, marries into Smith family, v.29, p.290.
Ogden, F. N., and White League, v.23, p.528ff.; supported claims of McMillen for Senate, v.27, p.592; heads opposition to Kellogg in N. O., v.29, p.432, 433; noted, v.29, p.722.
Ogden, H. N., att'y gen'l recognized by Fusionists, v.27, p.567; in re enforcement of Act No. 44, v.27, p.998; cand.

for att'y-Gen'l, v.31, p.535; noted, v.31, p.764.

Ogden, H. W., Dem. cand. for reelection to Cong., 1894, v.26, p.1093, 1095, 1097; Dem. Congressman, v.26, p.1116.

Ogden, Isaac, noted, v.22, p.466.

Ogden, Peter V., and Andrew Jackson, v.21, p.383.

Ogden, R. H., noted, v.23, p.1095.

Ogden, R. N., candidate for att'y-gen'l., v.31, p.501.

"Ogden's Troop of Horse in the Battle of New Orleans, Capt.," by Edw. Clarke Morse, M. D., v.10, p.381.

"O. Henry," William Sidney Porter, noted, v.33, p.329.

O'Higgins, Bernardo, noted, v.24, p.657.

Ohio, and Spain, v.22, p.817.

Oil City, La., v.29, p.62, 67.

Oil, discovery in Acadia, v.27, p.1134; development of in Acadia, v.27, p.1169-70; fields in Calcasieu parish, v.32, p.561-567.

Okracoke Inlet, noted, v.24, p.614.

"Old Bill Taylor," Confed. soldier, v.26, p.950.

Old Catholic Churches in America, statistics on, v.24, p.324, 353; papers on movement in Newmark Library, v.24, p.323-24.

"Old Days on the New Orleans Picayune," by John Smith Kendall, v.33, p.317-342.

"Old Days on the Times-Democrat," by John Smith Kendall, v.33, p.406-429.

Old Documents: From the Collection of Gaspar Cusachs, v.2, p.447; Letter from Gen. Robert E. Lee to Gen. G. T. Beauregard, v.2, p.450; Letter from David B. Morgan to Andrew Jackson, 1815, v.2, p.449; Letter from John Miller to William Panton, 1800, v.2, p.453; Letter from Timothy Pickering, 1813, v.2, p.447; Note from General G. T. Beauregard, 1861, v.2, p.451; Ordinance of Unzaga, 1770, v.2, p.448.

"Old Lady's Gossip, An," Edited by Cecile Willink, v.6, p.380.

"Old Liner," follower of Slidell, v.26, p.986.

"Old New Orleans Houses," by John S. Kendall, v.17, p.680.

"Old New Orleans Houses & Some of the People Who Lived in Them," by John S. Kendall, v.20, p.794-820.

Old New Orleans, manuscripts in Howard-Tildon Memorial Library, v.24, p.329-30; work by Arthur on, v.24, p.320, 349.

"Old Orleans Greets New Orleans, July 4, 1918," v.1, p.289.

"Old Pecan Tree on Eureka Plantation, East Carroll Parish, Louisiana, The," by Mrs. W. M. Murphy, v.17, p.625.

"Old Portage Between Bayou St. John and Mississippi River," v.1, p.372.

Old Providence, island off New Granada, v.24, p.622; described, v.24, p.654-55; action noted, v.24, p.656-65, 670, 671, 674, 675, 677-79, 681-87, 693-95; reports of 1819 personnel, v.24, p.672; return of Aury to, v.24, p.696-97.

"Old-Time New Orleans Police Reporters and Reporting," by John S. Kendall, v.29, p.43-58.

Oliver, Joseph, noted, v.22, p.1026.

Oliver, Mary, noted, v.23, p.404.

"Oliver Pollock," by James Alton James, rev'd, v.21, p.561-63.

Olivier, George M., noted, v.24, p.355.

Olivier, Nicholas Godefroy, noted, v.24, p.355.

Olivier, Pedro, sketch, v.21, p.25n.

Olmos, Father, noted, v.22, p.936.

Olmsted, Frederick, noted, v.23, p.869; author on Louisiana, v.31, p.398, 412, 417.

Olympic Circus, N. O. theatre, v.28, p.94, 95.

O'Malley, Dominick C., and the Mafia, v.22, p.518.

Omoa, fortified town, v.24, p.663, 675, 682-83.

Onate, Don Juan de, noted, v.22, p.938.

"One Hundred Great Years: The Story of the Times Picayune from its Founding to 1940," by Thos. E. Dabney, rev'd, v.27, p.1229-31.

O'Neil, James, Tax assessor named in Wickliffe impeachment, v.31, p.693.

O'Neill, Arturo, sketch, v.21, p.25n.

O'Neill, W. A., Repub. leader in the House, v.28, p.1183; noted, v.28, p.1186.

O'Niell, Charles A., address in memory of Henry Plauche Dart, v.18, p.242-44; v.28, p.1129, 1130.

Onis, Gonzales Lopez y Vara, Don Luis de, and Laffite, v.21, p.213-19; noted, v.22, p.806; and privateering, v.23, p.442; and P. Laffite, v.23, p.733ff.; letter from Picornell, v.23, p.741; sketch, v.23, p.759, 802-803; and Napoleonic emigres, v.23, p.778-79; sends agent to check on Fatio, v.23, p.789; letter from Fatio, v.23, p.793-794; letters to Ramirez, v.23, p.803-804; 807-808; promoted to European post, v.23, p.815; meets Toledo, v.23, p.828-29; tries to circulate proclamation, v.23, p.830; noted, v.25, p.293, 658, 659; cited on Robinson, v.25, p.669.

Opdenweyer, John W., pioneer cypress lumberman, v.30, p.1014.

"Opelousas, A Lawsuit in the Court of the Governor at New Orleans Involving Land in, 1764," translated by Laura L. Porteous, v.12, p.533.

Opelousas Female College, v.30, p.909.

Opelousas Female Institute, v.30, p.910.

Opelousas, La., plan for colonization of, v.21, p.61; noted, v.22, p.816; v.23, p.558; description of country c. 1838, v.24, p.39-42; noted, v.24, p.67, 68, 73, 74, 84; cotton area of La., v.25, p.27; and nullification, v.25, p.92, 121, 360, 361; noted, v.25, p.937, 938; capital moved to, v.26, p.1020; special Legis. sess. at, v.26, p.1026, 1037, 1040; army training camp, v.26, p.1022; endangered and capital removed from, v.26, p.1028; noted, v.26, p.1108; riots in 1896, v.28, p.1179.

Opelousas Railroad, noted, v.24, p.473.

"Opera, and Duels in New Orleans," v.23, p.151-55.

Opera, collection by Mathias Keller in L.S.U. Music School Library, v.24, p.348.

"Opera in New Orleans in Days of Yore," by Andre Lafargue, v.29, p.660-678.

Opportunism, in "allegiance" under Butler in New Orleans, v.24, p.506.

Orange County Court House, noted, v.24, p.63.

Orange Island (later Jefferson Island) Joseph Jefferson's estate, v.26, p.1156-58; found to be "salt dome," v.26, p.1158-59; noted, v.26, p.1164, 1165.

Orci, Barbara m, first wife of Desgrange, v.27, p.61, 86-91, 92, 94, 97, 106, 153, 215, 220, 238, 257.

Order No. 28, quoted, v.24, p.494; discussed, v.24, p.494-98.

Order of the Sacred Heart, Sisters of, established schools in La., 1821, v.25, p.730.

Order of Ursuline Nuns, account of voyage to La., v.29, p.565-566; journey to N. O. by pirogue, v.29, p.568-69; history of work in N. O., v.29, p.569-574, 590-595, 597, 602, 611-612, 616-617, 620, 622-624, 626-628, 627, 631.

Ordinance of Free Commerce Sp. Comm. policy, 1778, v.28, p.1074.

Ordinance of Secession, proposed, v.26, p.1000; adopted, v.26, p.1001.

"Ordinance of 1717 Governing Notaries in Louisiana During French Colonial Period," Translated by the late William Dart, v.10, p.82.

Ordinance of 1787 made part of organic law of Orleans Territory, v.18, p.71.

Ordozgoity, Vincente, sketch, v.22, p.1025.

O'Reilly, Alexander, in La., v.19, p.32-36; Sp. gov. of La. first legal recognition of pharmacy as a separate branch of the medical arts, v.26, p.330-31; on poisons, v.26, p.331; Ulloa's successor, v.26, p.739-40; second Sp. Gov. of La., v.27, p.632; instructions concerning commerce, v.27, p.633-34, 638, 645; placed tax on distilled liquors, v.27, p.691; issued trading licenses in N. O., v.27, p.691, 936; grants of land in present Acadia, v.27, p.1119; and N. O. Charity Hospital, v.31, p.17, 18; documents in Bibliotheca Parsoniana, v.24, p.311.

O'Reilly, Black Code of, in Bibliotheca Parsoniana, v.24, p.311.

"O'Reilly, Documents Relating to Alexandro," David K. Bjork, v.7, p.20.

"O'Reilly's Ordinance of 1770 Concerning Grants of Land in Louisiana to New Settlers, Fencing of Same, etc." Reprinted from Translation by Gustavus Schmidt in Louisiana Law Journal I, Part 2, Page 61, August, 1841, v.11, p.237.

O'Reilly, Henry, promoter of the People's Line, propaganda campaign, v.31, p.438-39, 441; contractor for Kendall, v.31, p.455-56; break with Kendall, v.31, p.457; in defense of enterprise, v.31, p.459-60; appeals case, v.31, p.465; noted, v.31, p.476.

O'Reilly, John, noted, v.22, p.70; Capt., builder of O'Reilly line, v.31, p.441.

Oriental Republic (Uruguay), flag of, v.24, p.669.

"Original Contributions of Louisiana to Medical Science," by Edmond Souchon, M.D. (A Bibliographic Study), v.1, sec.1, p.85.

Original settlers of La., language of, v.24, p.748-49.

"Origin and Early Development of County-Parish Government in Louisiana, 1805-45," by Robert D. Calhoun, v.18, p.56-160.

"Origin and Early Settlement of B. R.,

La.," by Andrew C. Albrecht, v.28, p.5-68.

"Origin of Class Struggle in Louisiana," by R. W. Shugg, rev'd by E. A. Davis, v.23, p.887-88.

"Origin of the Name of Louisiana" (From New Orleans Picayune), v.2, p.230.

Orleans Artillery, noted, v.24, p.28.

Orleans Board of School Directors, v.25, p.751.

Orleans Guard, and Cathedral question, v.31, p.931, 935-36.

Orleans, Isle of, health conditions, v.24, p.926.

Orleans Navigation Co., case of, v.28, p.979.

Orleans Parish, La., and Granger movement, v.26, p.1063; noted, v.26, p.1081, 1087; martial law under Butler, v.27, p.499, 522, 561; new court in, established by Pinchback, 1872, v.27, p.567-68, 724, 999, 1036, 1037, 1040, 1047, 1057, 1086.

Orleans Parish Med. Soc., v.26, p.70.

"Orleans Territory Memorialists to Congress 1804," by Everett S. Brown, v.1, sec.1, p.99.

Orleans, Territory of, created, v.18, p.65; divided into counties and parishes, v.18, p.57; pen sketch of, v.18, p.61-65; divided into parishes, 1807, v.24, p.729; importance to the U. S., 1800, v.24, p.930-34.

Orleans Theatre, v.28, p.103, 104, 107ff., 110-13, 114-20.

Orpheum Theatre, Bernhardt's final appearance here, v.26, p.776.

Orso, Zenon, and Mobile Society, v.21, p.153n.

Ortega, Juan Gualberto de, Spanish vice-consul to St. Louis, v.21, p.684.

Ortiz de Alaya, Tadeo, Mexican agent, v.22, p.740-41.

Ortiz, Juan, interpreter for DeSoto, v.25, p.624; death of, v.25, p.626.

Osage Indians, shown in Europe, v.24, p.1056-57; diplomatic difficulties concerning, v.24, p.1076-77, 1107.

Osborne, Audley L., Agent of Claiborne, v.21, p.163.

Osborne, Dr. J. J., Charter member Med. Soc., v.26, p.59; noted, v.26, p.75, 76.

Osborne, J. N., named in Wickliffe impeachment, v.31, p.693.

Osborne, Samuel, noted, v.23, p.404.

Oswald, Miss Julia, cited, v.24, p.150.

Otaheite cane, noted, v.25, p.186.

Ott, C. Ellis, on committee to incorporate Bogalusa, v.29, p.108, 109.

Ott, Edward Stanley, Bogalusa's 1st general, v.29, p.83.

Ott, Eleanore, writes pageant for Bogalusa Silver Jubilee, v.29, p.116.

Ott, Jacob, v.29, p.83.

Ottis, James, noted, v.24, p.701.

Otto, Rev. Martin, noted, v.24, p.140.

Ouachita Female Academy, v.30, p.887-888.

Ouachita Indians, in Grant Parish, v.23, p.1109; description of, v.23, p.1125.

Ouachita Lake, canal from Miss. R., v.23, p.438.

Ouachita Parish Academy, v.30, p.887.

Ouachita Parish, in 1860, v.21, p.1194-97; and the bagging factory, v.26, p.1065; and the Cong. election of 1894, v.26, p.1097.

Ouachita, post established by Filhiol, v.20, p.464; description of, v.20, p.476-85; colony of, v.21, p.59; settlement planned, v.31, p.612-13; settlement, v.31, p.616; mill built, v.31, p.617; controversy over, v.31, p.621-23; contract suspended, v.31, p.724; rights sold, v.31, p.628; significance, v.31, p.628-29.

Ouachita River, course of, v.25, p.625, 929, 930, 931.

Ouachita Valley, early history of, v.20, p.289-462; DeSoto's expedition in, v.25, p.611-41; bibl., v.25, p.642-43.

Ouachita Valley Historical Society of Monroe, La., v.25, p.611.

"Ouida," plantation, v.28, p.1132.

Ould, Robert, agent of exchange for Confederate gov't, v.29, p.1249, 1251, 1252.

Outlaw, Edward W., noted, v.24, p.490.

"Outline of Shreveport and Caddo Parish History," by J. Fair Hardin, v.18, p.759-871.

Overall, John W., early N. O. newspaperman, v.29, p.778-779.

Overdyke, W. Darrell, "History of the American Party in Louisiana," I, v.15, p.581; II, III, IV, V, v.16, p.84, 256, 409, 608; noted, v.24, p.338.

Overseer, problems concerning, v.25, p.183-84.

Overton, Gen. Walter H., aide to Gen. Jackson at Battle of N. O., v.26, p.976; settled in Rapides Parish, v.26, p.976; Capt., comd. garrison at Natchitoches, v.28, p.1067.

Owen, Allison, noted, v.24, p.315.

Owen, Christiana (see Smith, Christiana

Owen), wife of Ebenezer Smith II, v.29, p.282.
Owen, Dr. Whyte G., noted, v.25, p.150, 209, 217.
Owen, Robert, noted, v.24, p.429.
Owen, William Miller, compiler of work on La. Hist. Assn., v.24, p.316, 352.
Ozanne, Rev. Wm., noted, v.26, p.103.
Ozanne, Thomas D., pastor in New Orleans, v.22, p.458.
"Ozone Special," old Bogalusa train, v.29, p.94.

PACHA, IBRAHAM, NOTED, v.24, p.967, 968, 995, 1070.

Packard Government, v.32, p.407, 409.

Packard, S. B., leader of Custom House Party, v.27, p.552; directs seizure of State House, v.27, p.560, 561; adherents demanded that Pinchback relinquish claims to Senate, 1874, v.27, p.597; opposed by Pinchback, v.27, p.604; Lottery Co's part in overthrow of, v.27, p.996, 997-98; Rep. cand. for gov., 1876, v.28, p.1138; Kellogg supporter, Republican leader, v.29, p.398, 399, 400, 428, 433, 434, 437, 449, 485, 486, 489; noted, v.29, p.715, 722, 731; at Repub. convention, v.30, p.616-617; takes possession of State House, v.30, p.644; noted, v.30, p.604, 615, 648; takes possession of Mechanics Institute, v.31, p.701; took oath of office, v.32, p.399-400; noted, v.32, p.405, 410, 411, 434, 436, 636.

Packenham, Gen. Sir Ed. and Battle of N. O., v.26, p.960.

Paddon, John, opinion of Charlotte Cushman, v.31, p.974.

Padgett, James A., "Letters of Edward Livingston to Presidents of the U. S." (ed.), v.19, p.938-63; "Ancestry of Edward Livingston of La.; The Livingston Family," v.19, p.900-37; (ed.) "Some Letters of James Brown of La. to Presidents of the U. S.," v.20, p.58-163; A Decree for La. issued by the Baron Carondelet, June 1, 1795, v.20, p.590-605; "A Yankee School Teacher in La., 1835-1837; The Diary of Caroline B. Poole," v.20, p.651-79; "The letters of Judah P. Benjamin to Ambrose Dudley Mann...," v.20, p.738-93; "The Constitution of the W. Florida Republic," v.20, p.881-94; (ed), "The W. Fla. Rev. of 1810, as Told in the Letters of John Rhea, Fulwar Skipwith, Ruben Kemper and Others," v.21, p.76-202; (ed) "Difficulties of Andrew Jackson in N. O. Including His Later Dispute with Fulwar Skipwith, as Shown by the Documents," v.21, p.367-419; (ed) "Official Records of the W. Fla. Rev. and Rep.," v.21, p.685-805; (ed) "Commission, Orders and Instructions Issued to George Johnstone, British Gov. of W. Fla., 1763-1767," v.21, p.1021-68; (ed), "Minutes of the First Session of the Assembly of W. Fla.," v.22, p.311-84; "Minutes of the Assembly of W. Fla., 1767-1768," v.22, p.943-1011; "The Reply of Peter Chester, Gov. of W. Fla. to Complaints Made Against His Administration," v.22, p.31-46; (ed), "Minutes of the W. Fla. Assembly, 1768, 1769," v.23, p.5-77; "Minutes of the Council of W. Fla., April 3-July 22, 1769," v.23, p.353-404; "Some Documents Relating to the Batture Controversy in New Orleans," v.23, p.679-732;

"Letters of G. S. Denison, 1854-1866," v.23, p.1132-1240; (ed), "Letters of James Brown to Henry Clay, 1804-1835," v.24, p.921-1177; (ed), "The Documents Showing That the U. S. Ultimately Financed the W. Fla. Revol. of 1810," v.25, p.942-70; (ed), "Gov. Peter Chester's Observations on the Boundaries of British W. Fla.," v.26, p.5-11; "Discussion in the Continental Congress Relative to Surrendering the Right to Navigate the Miss. R.," v.26, p.12-36; "Repairing the La. Gov't Buildings in 1811," v.26, p.44-48; "Bernard de Galvez's Siege of Pensacola in 1781 (As Related in Robert Farmar's Journal)," v.26, p.311-29.

Padilla, Antonio, noted, v.31, p.673; Bastrop executor, v.31, p.676.

Pailloux, Paul, mentioned, v.21, p.995-97.

Paine, Thomas, noted, v.24, p.701.

Palfrey, John, sketch, v.28, p.828n.

Palmer, Confed. fleet surgeon, v.27, p.482.

Palmer, Rev. B. M., noted, v.22, p.415; noted, v.24, p.435; sermon quoted, v.24, p.436; Methodist minister, sermon in defense of slavery, v.27, p.511; speaker at Anti-Lottery meeting, v.27, p.1060-61, 1070; address to Women's League, v.27, p.1061-62; address to Dem. Anti-Lottery St. Com., v.27, p.1091; anti-lotteryite, v.28, p.1158.

Palmerston, Lord, noted, v.24, p.1108.

Pamlico Sound, noted, v.24, p.614.

Pampero, noted, v.22, p.1146-48.

Panama Congress, noted, v.24, p.714.

Panama Mission, interest in Europe, v.24, p.992-93, 998; discussed by Brown, v.24, p.1002-03; and Henry Clay, v.24, p.1004; noted, v.24, p.711, 1018, 1091.

"Panchita," prize schooner, v.23, p.789, 810, 811.

Paniagua, Flavio Antonio, Collection in Institute of Middle American Research, v.24, p.332.

Panics, slave, fear of New Orleans, v.22, p.142-65.

Panis, Jacinto, noted, v.22, p.625.

Panni, F., unpublished music of in L.S.U. Music School Library, v.24, p.347.

Panton, Forbes & Co., trading firm in E. Fla., v.21, p.13n.

Panton, Leslie and Co., trading firm in W. Fla., v.21, p.13n.; noted, v.21, p.22n., 25n.; British firm Having Sp. Indian Trade Monopoly, v.28, p.1012, 1014.

Panton, Wm., commercial activities in W. Fla., v.21, p.13n.; trade with Indians, v.21, p.71.

Paola, San Francisco di, engravings by in Howard-Tilton Memorial Library, v.24, p.330.

Paomene, Ana Basbaze, noted, v.22, p.391.

Papin, Jean Marie, noted, v.22, p.89; sketch, v.22, p.94.

Pardee, Don A., judge Fed'l Circuit Court, decision in case of Merchant vs. N. O. Nat'l Bank, v.27, p.1009.

Pardo, Ambroise, New Orleans merchant, v.22, p.687n.

Parham, Wm. S., noted, v.25, p.1039; committee on support of schools, v.25, p.1042-43; suggested legislation on Mex. War, v.25, p.1054; and the election of U. S. Senator, 1848, v.25, p.1096, 1098-99, 1100.

Parish History, "History of Madison Parish, La.," by W. M. Murphy, v.11, p.39; "History of Washington Parish, La., as Compiled from the Records and Traditions," by Hon. Prentiss B. Carter, v.14, p.36; "Story of Ascension Parish," by Sidney A. Marchand, Book Review by Edith Dart Price, v.14, p.569; "History of Concordia Parish, La.," by Robert Dabney Calhoun, I, II, III, IV, v.15, p.44, 214, 428, 618; V, VI, VII, VIII, v.16, p.92, 309, 454, 598; IX (Conclusion), v.17, p.96; "History of Rapides Parish, La.," by G. P. Whittington, I, v.15, p.567; II, III, IV, V, v.16, p.27, 235, 427, 628; VI, VII, VIII, IX, v.17, p.112, 327, 537, 737; X (Conclusion), v.18, p.5; "History of Caddo Parish, La.," v.18, p.759-871; "A Social History of St. Mary Parish, 1845-1860," by Jewell Lynn de Grummond, v.32, p.16; "Economic and Social Development of Calcasieu Parish," by Grace Ulmer, v.32, p.519.

Parish, John C., "The Lake of the Taensa," v.5, p.201.

Parish jury in E. Baton Rouge Parish, v.21, p.200-201.

Parish, Origin and early development of county-parish government, v.18, p.56-160.

Parisi, Capt. ————, noted, v.22, p.1067.

Paris Island, v.28, p.829, 833, 887, 891.

Paris, Joseph, sketch, v.21, p.979ff.

Paris, social life in, v.24, p.963, 1034; Bi-Centennial Celebration in, of Founding of New Orleans, v.1, sec.3, p.18.

Parker, C. Harrison, attack on Lottery Co., v.27, p.1055; Executive Com. Anti-

Lottery League, v.27, p.1056, 1091; established "New Delta," v.31, p.790.

Parker, John M., La. Fed'l Food Administrator, 1917, v.21, p.869-74; Gov. of La., noted, v.25, p.772.

Parker, Joshua, petition of, v.23, p.365.

Parkerson, John R., v.28, p.1129, 1130.

Parkerson, W. S., leader of citizens in N. O. Mafia incident, v.20, p.1086ff.; and the Mafia, v.22, p.518; address to Dem. Anti-Lottery St. Com., v.27, p.1091; noted, v.27, p.778; Anti-Lotteryite, v.28, p.1158.

Parker, Walter, address in memory of Henry Plauche Dart, v.18, p.249-50; noted, v.33, p.410, 412, 421.

Parkhurst, Helen, "Don Pedro Favrot, a Creole Pepys," v.28, p.679-734.

"Parkman, The Centenary of Francis," by Henry P. Dart, v.6, p.655.

Parlange, Charles, anti-lottery cand. for lt.-gov., v.26, p.1081; noted, v.27, p.789, 1056; first Anti-Lottery meeting held in office of, v.27, p.1054; on League Ex. Com., v.27, p.1056; chairman, Dem. Anti-Lottery St. Ex. Com., v.27, p.1059; chief author Anti-Lottery Postal Bill, v.27, p.1075; nominated cand. for lt.-gov., v.27, p.1090; address to Dem. Anti-Lottery St. Com., v.27, p.1091, 1093; formation of Anti-Lottery League, v.28, p.1150; suggested cand. for lt.-gov., v.28, p.1158.

Parry, William, noted, v.23, p.41.

Parsons, Edward Alexander, "Louisiana Completa, A Centenary Relation of West Florida and the Treaty with Spain, 1819-1821," v.3, p.455; "The Latin City (New Orleans)," v.3, p.361; "Stones of Reims," v.4, p.425; "Henry Vignaud: A Personal Sketch," v.5, p.63; "J. Sanford Saltus: A Remembrance," v.5, p.493; "Frederick D. King," v.6, p.206; Address in memory of Henry Plauche Dart, v.18, p.240-41; noted, v.24, p.310, 316; Introductory Note to "A Letter from the Battle of New Orleans from John A. Fort," v.32, p.225; "Some Inedited Gayarre Manuscripts," v.33, p.189-204.

Parsons, Mosby M., noted, v.24, p.88, 90, 91, 93, 96.

"Partisan Rangers," organized in La. for home defense, v.26, p.1022; noted, v.26, p.1025.

Parton, James, quoted, v.24, p.466, 486, 532-35; noted, v.33, p.223, 251.

Pasa Caballos, noted, v.24, p.617, 643, 689.

Pascagoula Indians, in Grant Parish, v.23, p.1109; description of, v.23, p.1123.

"Pascagoula, The Mysterious Music of," v.32, p.727-29.

Pasquier, Francoise Antoine, case against, v.21, p.1006-1007.

"Pasquier, Jean Francoise, Introduction of, as Councillor-Assessor in the Superior Council of Louisiana, 1737," text and translation by Heloise H. Cruzat, introduction by Henry P. Dart, v.10, p.68.

Pass Caballos, noted, v.24, p.648.

Pasta, Madame, aided by James Brown, v.24, p.987, 1017.

Pastor, Billy, sketch of, v.30, p.147.

Patorno, Philip, noted, v.22, p.828.

Patout, Isadore, sketch, v.28, p.767n.

Patrick, Walton R., "A Circulating Library of Ante-Bellum La.," v.23, p.131-40.

"Patriota," brig, v.24, p.643, 651.

Patriot, case of, v.22, p.1083-84.

Patterson, and Ross expedition against Pirates, v.24, p.13, 18, 19-20, 24.

Patterson, Chas., suit against Myra G. Gaines decided against, v.27, p.205-10, 211.

Patterson, Commodore, ———, takes Barataria, v.22, p.1036.

Patterson, Daniel T., and Fire Brand Affair, v.21, p.205, 206; naval officer in comd. at N. O., v.28, p.738-39; survey for erection of lighthouse at mouth of Miss., v.28, p.748n.; noted, v.28, p.751n., 752, 754, 760, 844ff., 883; letters of, v.28, p.908-909, 910, 914-15, 920-21.

Pattersonville, La., description of, v.24, p.40; noted, v.32, p.22, 51, 71, 76, 83.

Patti, Adelina, appeared on stage of Fr. Opera House, v.29, p.674; singer, v.31, p.134.

Patti, Carlos, N. O. musician, v.31, p.134-35.

Patton, Charles, noted, v.22, p.434; declines a duel, v.23, p.453.

Patton, J. D., Peoples Party cand. for Supt. of Ed., 1892, v.26, p.1081.

Pauger, Adrien de, engineer arrives in N. O. to lay out plans of city, v.29, p.559; notes taken as engineer concerning conditions in N. O., v.29, p.560, 562; succeeded as engineer-in-chief by Deverges, v.29, p.566.

"Paulding's, James Kirke, Creole Tale," by Dr. Floyd C. Watkins, v.33, p.364-79.

Paullin, Charles O., The Father of Admiral Farragut, v.13, p.37.

"Paul Tulane," by John Smith Kendall, v.20, p.1016-66.

Pavie, Pierre, noted, v.22, p.71.

Paw Paw Bend, old Mississippi River channel, v.31, p.600.

Paxton, W. E., La. educator, head of Shreveport University, v.30, p.797.

Payne, Billy, N. O. musician, sketch of, v.30, p.141.

Payne, Dan M., confed. sold., v.26, p.960.

Payne, John Howard, noted, v.31, p.110; solicitor, v.31, p.111; reception in New Orleans, v.31, p.112-13; attacked by "Bee," v.31, p.113ff.; defended by "Advertiser," v.31, p.115ff.; given benefit, v.31, p.118-21; leaves New Orleans, v.31, p.122.

Payne, John N., noted, v.23, p.528.

Payne, Richard, noted, v.23, p.77.

Pazos, Vicente, noted, v.24, p.646.

Peabody, George, noted, v.24, p.171; instituted Peabody Fund, v.25, p.791, 795.

Peabody High School for Girls, v.30, p.873-874.

Peabody Normal School, v.25, p.784, 791.

"Peace Overtures of July, 1864," by Howard T. Dimick, v.29, p.1241-1258.

Peak, D. L., confed. soldier, v.26, p.964.

Pearce, Wm., conf. soldier, v.26, p.954.

Pearl River, noted, v.25, p.936; v.29, p.73, 77, 78, 79, 80, 87, 88, 94, 103, 114, 122; navigation project of, v.29, p.172-174, 184.

Pearsall, N. G., general mgr. of N. O. Great Northern Railroad, v.29, p.91.

Pearson, Jesse, confed. soldier, v.26, p.964, 969.

Peck, Col. F. L., lumberman and Pres. of Miss. Central Railroad, v.29, p.90-91.

Pedesclaux, Pedro, noted, v.22, p.391, 395, 813.

Pedesclaux, Peter, duels of, v.23, p.149; noted, v.23, p.695; deposition of, v.23, p.718.

Pedro, Constitution for Portugal, v.24, p.1008; See Portugal.

Peire, Henry D., and Spanish filibusters, v.21, p.814, 1092; and filibusters, v.23, p.761; member of New Orleans Assn., v.24, p.631, 632, 636, 637.

Pelican flag of La., v.26, p.997.

Pelletier, Citizen, noted, v.22, p.56.

Pelot, Samuel, noted, v.22, p.1061.

Pemberton, William, petition of, v.23, p.404.

Penal Codes, by Edward Livingston, v.24, p.725.

Penal legislation, v.25, p.1046-47.

Penalosa Briceno y Berdugo, Don Diego Dionisio de, noted, v.22, p.938.

Penalver y Cardenas, Luis de, and Catholics in N. O., v.21, p.1071-72; noted, v.22, p.100, 684; noted, v.31, p.20; first Bishop of La., v.31, p.902.

Penicaut, M. Jean, acc't of Iberville exploration, v.28, p.32; early mention of Red Pole site, v.28, p.34, 37; acc't of origin of name of B. R., v.28, p.44-45, 46, 47; in re Pointe Coupee Cut-off, v.28, p.73, 74, 75; noted, v.28, p.52, 56.

Penn, Alfred, noted, v.23, p.240.

Penn, D. B., and election of 1872, v.28, p.1134; cand. for La. Lieut. Gov., v.29, p.400; noted, v.29, p.423; declared Lt. Gov. by McEnery forces, v.29, p.432; declares himself Lt. Gov. when McEnery forces drive Kellogg from power, v.29, p.433; surrenders office to Kellogg, v.29, p.434; noted, v.29, p.437; acts in absence of Gov., v.29, p.721, 722; cand. for Lt. Gov., v.31, p.535.

"Pensacola and the Filibusters, 1816-1817," by Harris Gaylord Warren, v.21, p.806-22.

"Pensacola, Diary of Bernardo de Galvez of Operation Against," trans. by Gaspar Cusachs, from the Spanish, v.1, sec.1, p.44.

Pensacola, in 1810, v.21, p.91; W. Fla. Conventions expedition against, v.21, p.752-53, 762; District of, and W. Fla. Assembly, v.22, p.311ff.; trade of, v.22, p.672; plan to attack, v.22, p.733; Colonization of, v.22, p.941; internal improvements, v.22, p.968, 970; prison, v.22, p.978; fire prevention in, v.23, p.13, 50; vestry elected, v.23, p.16; bill concerning parish vestries, v.23, p.50; jails in, v.23, p.51; failure of plot to attack by New Orleans Assoc., v.23, p.764; Latour's plan to settle near, v.23, p.766; in 1860, v.23, p.1167; in 1863, v.23, p.1198; noted, v.25, p.19, 20, 21; proposed attack on, v.25, p.664; noted, v.25, p.935.

"Pensacola," Union war vessel, v.29, p.341.

Pentagon Barracks of B. R., v.28, p.8, 68.

People's Lyceum, purpose of, v.23, p.1047.

"People's News," Bogalusa's youngest newspaper, v.29, p.168, 169.

People's Party, noted, v.26, p.1061, 1062; organizations and conditions leading to, v.26, p.1062-74; the Omaha platform, v.26, p.1074-76; cong. campaign of

1890, v.26, p.1077; aims of, v.26, p.1077-78; anti-lottery campaign, v.26, p.1077-83; pres. campaign of 1892, v.26, p.1083-91; depression of 1893, v.26, p.1092; "La Populist," official newspaper, v.26, p.1092; cong. election of 1899 and free coinage of silver, v.26, p.1092-98; gov's election, 1896, v.26, p.1099-1111; Legis. sess., 1896, v.26, p.1111-12; Dem.-Populist fusion in cong. and pres. election, 1896, v.26, p.1113-17; La. Reform Press, v.26, p.1118-19; local reforms, v.26, p.1119-20; Const. Conv. of 1898 and work of, v.26, p.1120-22; decline of, v.26, p.1122-24; appendix, v.26, p.1124-44; bibliography, v.26, p.1144-49; named Tannehill cand. for gov. in La., 1892, v.27, p.1092; election of 1892, v.28, p.1160, 1162-63.

People's Telegraph Company, route, v.31, p.437; success in gaining support, v.31, p.438-41; halted by Kendall injunction, v.31, p.444; begins operations, v.31, p.447-48; in Mississippi, v.31, p.449; financial reserves, v.31, p.452; leased by Reid, v.31, p.452-53; consolidated, v.31, p.453-54; employees arrested, v.31, p.468; noted, v.31, p.476; prices, v.31, p.477.

Pepitone, Mike, and Mafia, v.22, p.837-39.

Pepitone, Pietro, and Mafia, v.22, p.835.

Pepper, George H., collection in Institute of Middle American Research, v.24, p.332.

Peralta, Juan, deposition of, v.23, p.696-97.

"Percenod," Spanish vessel, v.24, p.368.

Perche, Father Napoleon Joseph, noted, v.31, p.898, 923; quoted, v.31, p.911, 923; edits Catholic paper, v.31, p.923; imprisoned by Butler, v.27, p.500.

Perchet, Don Juan Marie, of Fort Nogales chosen to prepare defense plans for Baton Rouge, Natchez, Galveztown, v.26, p.745.

Percival, Dr. J., N. O. musician, v.31, p.132.

Percy, Ferdinand, noted, v.22, p.405, 419.

Percy, Miss, wife of Peter Randolph, v.25, p.156.

Percy, Pierre, noted, v.22, p.406.

Percy, Robert, and W. Fla. Rev., v.21, p.707n.

Perera, Manuel, noted, v.22, p.1018.

Perez, Cayetano, letter from R. Kemper, v.21, p.100.

Perez, Luis, noted, v.22, p.934.

Perier, Boucher de la, Gov. of La., expedition against the Natchez, 1730-1731, v.19, p.547-77; noted, v.26, p.670, 672-74, 732, 733.

Perier, M. de, succeeds Bienville as Gov. of La. Colony, v.29, p.563; noted, v.29, p.564, 569; announces arrival of nuns from Fr., v.29, p.570; writes on problem of wayward girls, v.29, p.573; letters on progress of construction work on convent, v.29, p.575; noted, v.29, p.577, 578, 579, 580.

"Perier, The Natchez Massacre and Governor," by Rev. John Delanglez, S. J., v.17, p.631.

Perilhe, M., course in medicine in Rudolph Matas Medical Library, v.24, p.334.

Periodicals, bibliography of New Orleans magazines, v.18, p.493, 556; (French) of La., bibliography of, v.18, p.947-65.

Perique tobacco, culture of in La., v.20, p.565.

Perkins, A. J., cand. for Sen., 1879, v.28, p.1139.

Perkins, George, noted, v.24, p.457, 458, 459.

Perkins, Jacob, developments in steam engine, v.24, p.1058-59.

Perkins, John, Jr., N. O. lawyer, v.19, p.82; Sec. of the La. Hist. Soc., v.19, p.82; delegated by Hist. Soc. to do research in France, v.19, p.82; district judge, v.19, p.83; delegate to La. Secession Convention, v.19, p.84; member of Confederate Congress, v.19, p.85; emigre to Mexico, v.19, p.85-87; proposed Ordinance of Secession, v.26, p.1000; proposed sending 6 delegates to Confed. Conv., v.26, p.1002; and La. Hist. Soc., v.23, p.1046.

Perkins, John, Sr., moved to Natchez, v.19, p.71; parish judge, v.19, p.71; plantation estates in Concordia parish, v.19, p.72-73; will, v.19, p.75-79; est. professorship in Columbia Theological Seminary, S. Car., v.19, p.80-81.

Perkins, John, and De Bow, v.22, p.483.

Perkins, John, memorial of by J. W. Kerr, v.20, p.965-89.

"Perla Oriental," noted, v.24, p.676.

"Permanent Tribunals, or Quaestiones Perpetuae, Tribunals of Criminal Jurisdiction in Ancient Rome," by Charles Gayarre, v.33, p.217-222.

Permoli, Father Bernard, noted, v.31, p.917; arrested, v.31, p.923, 927, 937.

Perpeet, Hermann, noted, v.24, p.140.

Perriliat, Francois, noted, v.24, p.421.

Perrin, Henri W., of Confed. navy, prisoner, v.27, p.482.

Perry, Gerard, mentioned, v.21, p.1011.

Perry, Henry, mentioned, v.21, p.1092, 1094; argument with Aury and Mina, v.21, p.1098, 1099n.; noted, v.23, p.850; member of New Orleans Assn., v.24, p.631, 634, 638, 641, 642, 644; noted, v.25, p.295, 296.

Perry, Judge R. S., on Anti-Lottery League Com., v.28, p.1152.

Perry, ———, expedition of, v.22, p.735-36.

Peru, importance of trade, v.24, p.655.

Pery, Judge R. S., of Iberia, Anti-Lottery delegate to Farmers' Union, meet., v.27, p.1086.

Peso de Borgo, Josef, privateer, v.23, p.435n.

Peters, Benjamin Franklin, son of Samuel Jarvis, v.30, p.445-473.

Peters, Hugh, sketch of, v.30, p.439-441.

Peters, J. F., helps on inaugural day in Bogalusa, v.29, p.110.

Peters, Mrs., on Gottschalk, v.31, p.866-67, 870.

Peters, Samuel, grandfather of Samuel Jarvis, sketch of, v.30, p.441-42.

Peters, Samuel Jarvis, noted, v.23, p.178, 180, 1049; and railroads, v.23, p.200; Am. leader in Anglo-Creole Controversy, v.25, p.983, 1053; ancestry and early life, v.30, p.439-444; travels to N. O., v.30, p.444; marriage and children of, v.30, p.445; assists in purchase of Faubourg Marigny, v.30, p.446-447; elected to N. O. City Council, v.30, p.447-449; endorses improvements, v.30, p.405; director of Pontchartrain Rwy. Co., v.30, p.451-452; pres. City Bank of N. O., v.30, p.452; improvements of water supply, v.30, p.453; chairman, Chamber of Commerce, v.30, p.453; leader in construction of St. Charles Hotel, v.30, p.454-455; creation of First Municipality, v.30, p.456; improvements of Second Municipality, v.30, p.457-462; activities in education, v.30, p.462-464; erection of Municipal Hall, v.30, p.465; activities during war with Mexico, v.30, p.465-466; activities in nomination of Zachary Taylor, v.30, p.466; appointed collector of customs, v.30, p.467; fight against city consolidation, v.30, p.467-469; career as aldermen, v.30, p.468-470; is honored by leading citizens of N. O. at dinner, v.30, p.470; election to presidency Louisiana State Bank, v.30, p.471; political affiliations, v.30, p.472; later life, death, v.30, p.473-475; description of, v.30, p.474; bibl., v.30, p.476-480.

Peters, William Birdseye, father of Samuel Jarvis, v.30, p.442.

Petion, Alexandre, noted, v.24, p.620, 621, 622, 627.

Petit Caillou, v.28, p.765, 806, 885.

"Petite-Chance," noted, v.23, 436.

"Petition for Concession of Islands of Caillou and Timbalier, and Order of Survey, 1793," v.2, p.303.

"Petition of Don Luis Francisco Lefort to open a house of Education in New Orleans," by Laura L. Porteous, v.11, p.244.

"Petition of Widow Donna Anna Judith Chenal, to Prevent the Inhabitants of Opelousas from Killing the Straying Cattle Belonging to her at her Dairy Farm, 1773," by Laura L. Porteous, v.11, p.233.

Petrie, George, noted, v.23, p.404.

Peychardiere, Father de la, and Jefferson College, v.31, p.854.

Peyroux, Henri, de la Coudreniere, sketch, v.22, p.85n.

Pez, Andres de, noted, v.22, p.940, 941.

Pfaff, Caroline S., "Henry Miller Shreve, A Biography," v.10, p.192.

Pfeiffer & Hassinger, publishers, v.23, p.502.

Pfeiffer, Peter, noted, v.24, p.131.

Pharmacy, regulation of in La., v.26, p.330-340; O'Reilly's edict concerning, 1770, v.26, p.330-31; 1808 Act, Sec. 1, required licenses for pharmacists, v.26, p.331-32; Sec. 2, concerned deteriorated drugs, v.26, p.332; Sec. 3, selling of poisons, v.26, p.332-33; revision of 1808 Act, v.26, p.333-35; Logan quoted on, v.26, p.335; list of licensed apothecaries, v.26, p.336; motivation forces for early legis., v.26, p.337-39; reasons for repeals of legis., 1852, v.26, p.339-40.

Pharr and Williams' Saw Mill, v.30, p.1009.

Pharr, John N., collection in L.S.U. Archives, v.24, p.344; cand. for gov. second Populist ticket, v.26, p.1102-04, 1108, 1109-11; cand. gov. 1896, v.28, p.1177ff.; cypress lumberman, organizes Pharr and Williams' sawmill, sketch of, v.30, p.1009-1010.

Pharr, John, and Eugene, reclamation project at Avoca Island, v.30, p.1055-1056.

Phelps, Ashton, v.33, p.420.
Phelps, Gen., at Carrollton, v.23, p.1195.
Phelps, John, noted, v.26, p.972.
Phelps, John W., in charge of camp for Negroes, v.24, p.519; controversy with Butler, v.24, p.520-23; noted, v.24, p.524.
Phelps, Peleg B., columnist, "N. O. Times," v.30, p.285.
Phelps-Stokes Fund, v.25, p.795.
Philadelphia, Cholera in, v.24, p.1168; as refuge for Venezuelan revolutionists, v.25, p.7; medical study in, v.25, p.203, 298; the meeting of the Revolutionary junta in, v.25, p.657.
"Philanthrope," privateer of Laffites, v.23, p.747.
Philanthropy in Negro education, v.25, p.790-802.
Philharmonic Soc., Luzenberg pres. of, v.26, p.61; noted, v.26, p.103.
Philibot, Charles, noted, v.22, p.624.
Philipe, Father, administrator of first N. O. Charity Hospital, v.31, p.10-13.
Philippsburg, noted, v.24, p.426, 428, 429.
Philipps, Capt. William, letter from, v.23, p.385.
Phillips, Aaron J., owner theatrical co., v.28, p.103ff.
Phillips, Eugene, La. midshipman, v.27, p.483.
Phillips, Henry, nominated for Dem. cand., v.26, p.988, 989.
Phillips, Horace P., "Bonded Debt of New Orleans, 1822-1920, Inclusive," v.3, p.596.
Phillips, Mrs. Philip, imprisonment on Ship Island, v.24, p.493.
Phillips, Ulrich B., noted, v.25, p.149, 1113; cited on education of slaves, v.25, p.728.
Phillisee, Jacob, noted, v.23, p.404.
"Phosphorescent Sea, A," quoted, v.24, p.182-83.
Physico-Medical Society of N. O., cited on Luzenberg's disassociation with the Medical College, v.26, p.58; in reaction to the case of Mary the Seminole, v.26, p.73-75; Luzenberg's letter to, v.26, p.75; Luzenberg expelled from, v.26, p.76-77; noted, v.26, p.79-100passim; disbanded, v.26, p.101; noted, v.26, p.102, 105; report of the proceedings in relation to trial and expulsion of Luzenberg, v.26, p.109-36.
"Picayune," sketch of, v.24, p.35; quoted on discussions, v.25, p.1005; on Const. Con. of 1844, v.25, p.1023; in praise of Soule as Senator, v.25, p.1060; noted, v.32, p.724, 727; noted, v.33, p.407; rivalry with Times Democrat, v.33, p.427; "Old Days on the New Orleans Picayune," by John Smith Kendall, v.33, p.317-342. See N. O. Picayune.
Pickens, Wyatt, A. (tr.), "Inventory of Duvernay Concession in La., 1726," v.21, p.985-94; (tr.) "Lease of La. Plantation and Slaves, 1727," v.21, p.995-97.
Picket, John, Conf. soldier, v.26, p.952, 954.
Pickett, A. B., installed first telephone in Crowley, v.27, p.1153.
Pickett and Gregg, noted, v.29, p.7, 9, 10, 11.
Pickett, John, anti-lotteryite cand. for Treasurer, v.26, p.1081; cand. for Treasurer, second Populist ticket, 1896, v.26, p.1102; Anti-Lottery cand. for Treas., v.27, p.1090; v.28, p.1158, 1177.
Picornell, Juan Bautista, refugee from Caracas, v.25, p.5, 6, 7; to West Indies, v.25, p.8; unclaimed letter to, v.25, p.9; in N. O., v.25, p.9ff.; noted, v.25, p.296, 299, 300.
Picornell, Juan Mariano, insurgent, v.21, p.683, 1087, 1088; and Toledo's expedition, v.22, p.730; v.23, p.734ff.; sketch, v.23, p.735; applies for royal amnesty, v.23, p.736; Spanish agent in N. O., v.23, p.736; enlists P. Laffite as Spanish agent, v.23, p.739ff.; letter to Onis, v.23, p.741-42; and Aury's expedition, v.23, p.761-62; goes to Tampico, v.23, p.777; estimate of by Laffite, v.23, p.806, 811; pres. Mex. Rev. govt. in exile, v.28, p.1056; see Juan Bautista Picornell.
Picton, Dr. J. M. W., quoted on Luzenberg's theory about small pox, v.26, p.66-67, 68, 69; signed Luzenberg's expulsion from Medical Society, v.26, p.76.
Pierce, ———, noted, v.23, p.1066.
Pierce and Payne's College, v.30, p.1066.
Pierce, B. W., of Bienville Parish, v.26, p.987.
Pierce, LeRoy, of Bogalusa, v.29, p.88, 91.
Piernas, Luis, and Spanish filibusters, v.21, p.815-16.
"Pierre Clement de Laussat, Colonial Prefect and High Commissioner of France in La.: His Memoirs, proclamations and orders," by Andre Lafargue, v.20, p.159-82; "Pierre Clement de Laussat: An

Intimate Portrait," by Andre Lafargue, v.24, p.5-8.
Piesantino, Jean-Joseph (Pepe), noted, v.22, p.1025ff.
Piggott, Tom, parish surveyor of Bogalusa, v.29, p.92.
Pikens, Israel, letters to and from Cathcart, v.28, p.912-14.
Pike, William S., and J. M. Hart named by Wickliffe to head penitentiary, 1856, v.25, p.703; noted, v.30, p.1216-1217.
Pike, Zebulon Montgomery, and the "Neutral Ground," v.22, p.721; noted, v.22, p.729; v.25, p.297; expedition of 1806, v.25, p.645-49; intercession for Robinson, v.25, p.650; cited on Robinson, v.25, p.668-69; cleared out neutral ground of bandits, v.28, p.1066-68.
Pilcher, Dr. William, N. O. musician, v.31, p.141.
Pilcher, Joseph Mitchell, "Judah Philip Benjamin or Jewish Prophecy Fulfilled," v.3, p.478; "Daniel Webster in Louisiana History," v.5, p.478.
Pinac Institute, v.30, p.866-867.
Pinchback, P. B. S., noted, v.25, p.762; instrumental in establishing S. Univer., v.25, p.769; graduate of Straight College, v.25, p.776; birth and parentage, v.27, p.527-28; ed. and early life, v.27, p.528; arrival in N. O., v.27, p.529; in the Union Army, v.27, p.529-30; applies for commission and is denied, v.27, p.530-31; goes to Washington, v.27, p.531; returns to La., v.27, p.531; organized Fourth Ward Repub. Club. in N. O., v.27, p.532; a delegate to Repub. St. Conv., v.27, p.532; member Central Ex. Com., v.27, p.532; declines position of Insp. of Customs, v.27, p.532; delegate to Const. Conv., 1867-1868, v.27, p.532-35; author of Civil Rights Article of Const., v.27, p.534; becomes senator in contested election, v.27, p.535-36; delegate to Nat'l Repub. Conv., v.27, p.537-38; civil rights legis., v.27, p.538; declined offer of position of Register of Land Office in N. O., v.27, p.538; forms factorage concern, v.27, p.538-39; responsible for passage of election law of 1870, v.27, p.539-40; other work in the Senate, 1871, v.27, p.540-41; cand. for U. S. Senate, 1871, v.27, p.542; shared in Legis. plundering, 1871, v.27, p.543-44; joins Warmoth faction, v.27, p.544-45; named lt.-gov., v.27, p.546-48; election confirmed, v.27, p.550; fed'l investigation of, v.27, p.550-51; unites with Customhouse Party, v.27, p.551-53; cand. for Cong., v.27, p.554; railroad race with Warmoth, v.27, p.554-57; election of Nov. 1872, v.27, p.557-59; declined organization of Legis., 1872, v.27, p.560; made acting gov. pending trial of Warmoth, v.27, p.561; authority questioned, v.27, p.561-63; attempt to get fed'l support, v.27, p.563; struggle with Warmoth for authority, v.27, p.563; message to gen'l assembly, Dec. 10, 1872, v.27, p.563-64; appeal to Grant, v.27, p.564-66; legis. of, v.27, p.566-68; given fed'l recognition, v.27, p.568-69; conflict of Militia and city police, v.27, p.569-70; legis. of, v.27, p.570-71; appointments of, v.27, p.571; threat against Fusion Legis., v.27, p.572-74; dissension in Repub. ranks, v.27, p.574-75; farewell address, v.27, p.576-77; St. Sup. Ct. decision on legality of gov't of, v.27, p.577-78; investigation of La. affairs by U. S. Senate, v.27, p.579-80; Repub. Congressman-at-large, 1872, v.27, p.581-28; debate in House as to right to seat in, v.27, p.582-83; referred to Com. of Elections, v.27, p.583-85; speech to House of Rep., v.27, p.585-86; majority report of Com. of elections adopted, excluding Pinchback from House, v.27, p.586; gives testimony, v.27, p.587-88; disputed election against referred to Com., v.27, p.588-89; defeated, v.27, p.589; concurrent contest for recog. by Senate, v.27, p.589; elected U. S. Senate by Kellogg faction, v.27, p.589; credentials presented to Senate, v.27, p.589-90; La. commissioner to Vienna Exposition, 1873, v.27, p.590; trip to mid-west, v.27, p.591; right to seat in Senate referred to Com. on Privileges and Elections, v.27, p.592; Morton champions admission of, v.27, p.592; debates in re, v.27, p.593; case postponed, v.27, p.594; election reaffirmed by Kellogg Legis., v.27, p.594; consideration of case resumed, v.27, p.594; motion for recommitment, v.27, p.594-96; case tabled, v.27, p.597; attempt to bolster prestige in La., v.27, p.597; reelected U. S. Senator, 1875, v.27, p.597; case referred to com., v.27, p.598; majority report in favor of, v.27, p.598; senatorial debate, v.27, p.598-99; case tabled, v.27, p.599; further debate, v.27, p.599; case against postponed, v.27, p.600; consideration

resumed, v.27, p.601; claim rejected, v.27, p.602; given monetary compensation, v.27, p.602-603; delegate to Repub. Nat'l Conv., 1876, v.27, p.604; chairman St. Ex. Com., v.27, p.604; opposes Packard, v.27, p.604; recognizes Nicholls gov't, v.27, p.605; holds Fed'l offices, v.27, p.605; delegate to Repub. Nat'l Conv., v.27, p.605; supports measure for colored university, v.27, p.606; member Board of Trustees of Southern U., v.27, p.606; passed bar exam., v.27, p.606; private life, v.27, p.606; leaves La., v.27, p.606-607; death and burial in N. O., v.27, p.607; estimate, v.27, p.607; bibl., v.27, p.607-612; lt-gov, v.28, p.1132; and election of 1872, v.28, p.1134; noted, v.29, p.393; Negro leader allied with Warmoth, leaves him, v.29, p.400; merges with Kellogg followers, v.29, p.403; supports Kellogg among Negroes, v.29, p.408; noted, v.29, p.409; elevated to gov. when Warmoth is impeached, v.29, p.410; Pres. Grant recognizes Pinchback gov't, v.29, p.411; struggles for control of gov't, v.29, p.412, 413; noted, v.29, p.414, 427, 458, 485; elected permanent pres. of Rep. State Conv., v.29, p.486; noted, v.29, p.715; elected lt-gov., v.30, p.626; Pinchback convention, v.30, p.637-639; tricked by Warmoth, v.30, p.640; recognized by Grant as gov., v.30, p.646; noted, v.30, p.213, 245, 253, 547, 605, 620, 634; cand. for Congress, v.31, p.536; disqualified for Returning Board, v.31, p.700; acting governor, v.31, p.701; mentioned in Warmoth impeachment articles, v.31, p.702.

Pinckney, Charles, views similar to Edward Livingston, v.24, p.703.

Pineda, Alonzo de, noted, v.22, p.933.

Pine Grove Academy, sketch of, v.30, p.804-807.

Pinatdo, Vincent Sebastian, succession of, v.25, p.388-389.

Pintado, Vizente, and W. Fla. Rev., v.21, p.120.

Pintard, John, report to Gallatin on Louisiana government, v.31, p.279.

Pipes, D. W., introduced bill regarding Newgass Lottery offer, v.27, p.1036; and the lottery question, v.28, p.1143.

Piquet, John, noted, v.22, p.982.

"Piracy, in the Gulf of Mexico," John S. Kendall, v.8, p.341; in Gulf of Mexico, v.22, p.751ff.; accounts of, v.24, p.9-34, 360-77; scare in 1842, v.24, p.30-34; extent in La., 1814, v.24, p.360-69.

Pirates, Laffites plan to capture, v.21, p.215-17.

Pirogue, derivation of, v.23, p.123.

Pironneau, A., Jr., noted, v.22, p.1066.

Pirtle, Henry, attorney in Morse case, v.31, p.463.

Pisgignoux, Jean Pierre, arrest of, v.22, p.81-82, 82n.; mentioned, v.21, p.37n., 46.

"Pistols for Two, Coffee for One," by John Smith Kendall, v.24, p.756-82.

Pitot, James, mayor of New Orleans, v.31, p.31-32.

Pitot, Judge Hilant, and Gravier suits, v.22, p.413, 425.

Pitou (Pitot), James, judge of Ct. of Probates, N. O., v.27, p.23, 48, 66, 67, 69, 70, 72, 73, 75, 76, 119, 173.

Pittman, M., and W. Fla., v.22, p.28.

Pius VII, letter of in Ursuline College Museum, v.24, p.335.

Pizarro, Jose Garcia de Leon y, and Toledo, v.23, p.831.

Place, ———, noted, v.22, p.1067.

"Placee," definition of, v.25, p.311.

Place, F. L., La. midshipman, v.27, p.483.

Place, James, Manager Am. Theatre, v.26, p.1153.

Place, Josephine Clifton, sketch, v.30, p.130-131.

Placide, Jane, and N. O. theatre, v.21, p.498.

Plague in Eastern Europe, 1828, v.24, p.1120.

Plandem Guillermo, mentioned, v.21, p.32.

"Plantation, Dr. James G. Carson's Canebrake: A View of an Ante-Bellum Louisiana," by Dr. Robert C. Reinders, v.33, p.353-363.

"Plantation Experience of Joseph and Lavinia Erwin, 1807-1836," by Alice Pemble White, v.27, p.343-78.

"Plantation Life in the Fla. Parishes of La., 1836-1846, as Reflected in the Diary of Bennet H. Barrow," by Edwin A. Davis, rev'd, v.26, p.1173-79.

"Plantation Parade: The Grand Manner in Louisiana," by Harnett T. Kane, rev'd by Walter Prichard, v.29, p.203-207.

Plantations, inventory of Duvernay Concession, v.21, p.985-94; lease of 1727, in Pailloux succession on, v.21, p.995-97; of St. James Parish, v.21, p.1119; of Concordia, v.21, p.1207; descriptions, v.32, p.29-34.

Planters Bank of Woodville, Miss., noted, v.25, p.159.

"Planters' Banner," 1836--1872, Franklin newspaper, v.32, p.89-94.

Planters notes, investment of James Brown in, v.24, p.1146.

Planters' Telegraph Company, noted, v.31, p.451.

Plaquemine Academy, v.30, p.833.

Plaquemine, La., in 1860, v.21, p.1126-27; noted, v.24, p.80, 85; v.25, p.163, 204, 207, v.28, p.755, 757, 758.

Plaquemine Seminary, v.25, p.207; v.30, p.834-835.

"Plaquemines Frauds," noted, v.24, p.763; v.25, p.1005, 1013; lost Clay the electoral vote of La., 1844, v.27, p.723.

Plaquemines Jefferson Draining District, v.30, p.688-689.

Plaquemine "Southern Sentinel," noted, v.25, p.206.

"Plaquemines Parish, La., Election Frauds in, 1844" ("The Nation"), N. Y., 1879, v.10, p.402; production of rice in, v.23, p.554; meeting of planters, v.25, p.73; charges of fraud in, v.25, p.126-27; noted, v.25, p.371; noted, v.26, p.1102; election disturbances in, v.26, p.1108.

Plaquemines post, noted, v.26, p.745; Favrot in comdt., v.28, p.708ff.; transferred to Fr., v.28, p.719-20.

Plauche, John B., disputed election of, v.25, p.1008, 1010; the Dem. campaign. of 1846, v.25, p.1037; defeated for nomination as lt.-gov., v.28, p.959.

Player List of the Eng. theatre at N. O., 1806-1842, v.28, p.542-63.

Play List of the Eng. Theatre at N. O., 1806-1842, v.28, p.490-541.

Playwright List of the Eng. Theatre at N. O., 1806-1842, v.28, p.563-72.

Pleasant Hill Academy, v.30, p.819.

Pleasant Hill, noted, v.24, p.84, 88, 91, 92, 94, 95, 99, 100.

Pleasant Hill, Battle of, v.32, p.119-125.

Pleasanton, Stephen, noted, v.24, p.994, 1034, 1037, 1041, 1057, 1091, 1102, 1107, 1125, 1130, 1138-39.

Pleasants, R. B., and White League, v.23, p.528, 533.

Pleyle Company, music publishers, v.31, p.857, 859, 860.

Plotton, L. F., Donaldsonville artist, v.31, p.990.

Plumb Island, v.28, p.765, 798ff., 808, 809, 886.

Plumer, Mr. and Mrs. Cramer and N. O. Theatre, v.21, p.502.

Plumley, B. Rush, chairman of Board of Education, 1864, v.25, p.739.

Pluralism in Br. West Fla., v.19, p.196-198.

Poe, Edgar Allan, comment upon by Cable, v.24, p.174, 175.

Poeyfarre, Juan Bautista, noted, v.22, p.393.

Poinsett, Joel Roberts, noted, v.24, p.1072, 1076, 1135.

Poinsett, Joe R., noted, v.23, p.1046n.

Point au Fer, v.28, p.765, 810, 829, 886ff.

Point Chevreuil, v.28, p.810, 829, 830.

"Pointe Coupee Cut Off in Hist'l Writings," by Hilgard O'Reilly Sternberg, v.28, p.69-84.

Pointe Coupee Cut Off Cause, v.28, p.69-75; date, v.28, p.75-77; human interference unnecessary and ineffective for, v.28, p.77-81; length of time for change, v.28, p.81-84.

Pointe Coupee, conspiracy of negroes, 1795, v.21, p.54; de Chaufret as Commandant, v.21, p.984; Parish in 1860, v.21, p.1137-44; slave insurrection planned, v.22, p.63; cotton area of La., v.25, p.27, 121, 162, 361; fortifications of, v.26, p.740, 745; origin of name, v.31, p.600.

Point Pleasant, La., v.25, p.163.

Poisseau, Athanase, noted, v.22, p.73n., 77n.

Polhamus, J. Nelson, newspaperman, "Old Days on the N. O. Picayune," v.33, p.331.

Police Jury, genesis of, v.18, p.93-94; powers, v.18, p.120.

Police, Reporting, in N. O., 1865-1898, v.29, p.43-58; in Carrollton, v.21, p.255; system in Sp. New Orleans, v.22, p.697-98.

Polignac, Charles, noted, v.24, p.80, 83, 85, 90, 91.

Polignac, Prince de, noted, v.24, p.1128, 1150.

"Political Career of James Madison Wells, The," by Walter McGehee Lowrey, v.31, p.995-1113.

"Political Career of Murphy James Foster, Gov. of La., 1892-1900," by S. J. Romero, Jr., v.28, p.1129-1243.

"Political Career of Pinckney Benton Stewart Pinchback," by Agnes Smith Grosz, v.27, p.527-612.

"Political Career of Robert Charles Wickliffe, Gov. of La., 1856-60," by Thomas R. Landry, v.25, p.670-727.

"Political Career of Senator Donelson Caffery," by Lucile Roy Caffery, v.27, p.783-853.

"Political Career of Thomas Overton Moore, Secession Gov. of La.," by Van D. Odom, v.26, p.975-1154.

"Politics in Louisiana in 1724," by Henry Plauche Dart, v.5, p.298.

"Politics in Louisiana, 1845-1861," by James K. Greer, I, II, v.12, p.381, 555; III, IV, V, VI (Conclusion), v.13, p.67, 257, 444, 617.

"Politics, Some Letters of Charles Etienne Gayarre on Literature and, 1854-1885," v.33, p.223-54.

Polk, James K., and tariff issue, v.25, p.125, 126, 127, 134, 140; noted, v.25, p.1004, 1066, 1070, 1110; selects Trist Commissioner to Mex., v.25, p.1072; annual message, 1847, v.25, p.113.

"Polk, Leonidas, The Ante-Bellum Career of," by Vera Lea Dugas, v.32, p.245.

Polk, Leonidas, pioneer Bishop of Shreveport, v.18, p.832-33; noted, v.22, p.470; v.23, p.1049; v.24, p.101; letter to his father, 1828, v.32, p.245-47; early education, v.32, p.249; at West Point, v.32, p.250-265; early ministry, v.32, p.265-287; travels, v.32, p.268; preached first sermon, v.32, p.275; European travel, v.32, p.277-282; life of farmer, v.32, p.282; illness, v.32, p.284; consecrated Bishop, v.32, p.286; Missionary Bishop, v.32, p.287-310; arrives in Shreveport, v.32, p.293; arrives in N. O., The Bishop Planter of La., v.32, p.310-325; a Bishop of the South, v.32, p.325-345; at Christ Church, v.32, p.326; at Trinity Church, v.32, p.325-26, 339; Polk family genealogy, v.32, p.345-349; noted, v.33, p.396.

Polk, William Mecklenburg, noted, v.23, p.1230.

Pollock, Hugh, noted, v.22, p.434.

Pollock Institute, v.30, p.832.

Pollock, Oliver, in W. Fla., v.22, p.38; documents in Bibliotheca Parsoniana, v.24, p.311; Am. agent, v.26, p.740; spread false news of Sp. recognition of U. S., v.26, p.764; commercial agent in N. O., v.27, p.643, 650, 651, 652, 656; supplies for Willing, v.27, p.657, 659; letter to Patrick Henry, v.27, p.660; led army of Sp. subjects against British, v.27, p.661, 667, 668, 938.

"Polyanthus," theatrical "scandal sheet," v.30, p.129-131.

Pompieres, Labbay, noted, v.24, p.1112.

Poncet, Lt. John E., resigned, v.26, p.836.

Pond, Adam, noted, v.22, p.1089-91, 1093.

Pond, Col. Preston, noted, v.26, p.953.

Pontalba, Baron Joseph Xavier de, noted, v.23, p.113.

"Pontalba Buildings," by John S. Kendall, v.19, p.119-49.

Pontalba, Madame de, v.19, p.127-49.

"Pontalba to Miro, Letters of, 1792," Trans. by Heloise H. Cruzat, v.2, p.393.

Pontchartrain Railroad, history of, v.30, p.1117-1122.

Pont, Don Nicholas, trader sent to Indians, v.28, p.1099.

Pool, Carleton, newspaperman, "Old Days on the Times-Democrat," v.33, p.419.

Poole, Caroline B., diary of, 1835-37, v.20, p.651-79.

Poole, G. F., mortuary in Boglusa, v.29, p.99.

"Popa," a privateer, v.24, p.619, 621.

Popa Hill, near Cartagena, v.24, p.618.

Pope, Col. H. H., negro Sheriff of St. Mary, v.28, p.1134.

Pope, John, noted, v.24, p.736.

Pope, Katherine, "The Distinction of Grace King," v.6, p.374.

Popular government, Edward Livingston's theories of, v.24, p.704.

Populists and election of 1896, v.28, p.1171, 1174ff.

Poree, Charles, letter to Casa Calvo, v.22, p.125-28, 129.

Porro y Peinado, Fray Francisco, noted, v.22, p.102.

Portage, the Old, Between Bayou St. John and the Mississippi River, v.1, p.372.

Portalis, Count, noted, v.24, p.1036, 1144.

Port-au-Prince, noted, v.24, p.620.

Portell, Thomas, sketch, v.21, p.37n.; and revolutionary agitators, v.22, p.85.

Porteous, Laura L., Tr. by "Trial of Mary Glass," v.6, p.589; "A Suit for Debt in the Governor's Court, N. O., 1770," v.8, p.240; "Torture in Spanish Criminal Procedure in Louisiana, 1771," v.8, p.5; "Trial of Pablo Rocheblave before Governor Unzaga, 1771," v.8, p.372; Tr. by, "Contract to Build a Ship in N. O., 1769," v.9, p.593; "Inventory of De Vaugine's Plantation in the Attakapas on Bayou Teche, 1773," v.9, p.565; "Marriage Contracts of the Spanish Period in Louisiana," v.9, p.385; Tr. by,

"Governor Carondelet's Levee Ordinance, 1792," v.10, p.518; "Procedure for Sale of an American Vessel in New Orleans, 1803," v.10, p.185; Tr. by, "A Louisiana Will of the Spanish Era, 1776," v.11, p.607; "Petition of Don Luis Francisco Lefort to Open a House of Education in New Orleans," v.11, p.244; "Petition of Widow Donna Anna Judith Chenal to prevent Inhabitants of Opelousas from Killing the Straying Cattle Belonging to Her at Her Dairy Farms, 1773," v.11, p.233; Tr. by, "Documents in Loppinot's Case," 1774, v.12, p.38; "Governor Unzaga Decides that the Family Meeting Has no Place in Spanish Probate Procedure in Louisiana, 1771," v.12, p.288; "Lawsuit in the Court of the Governor at New Orleans Involving Land in Opelousas, 1764," v.12, p.533; Tr. by, "Marine Survey of Schooner Charlotte, 1777," v.13, p.230; Tr. by, "Spanish Procedure in Louisiana in 1800 for Licensing Doctors and Surgeons," Introduction by Henry P. Dart, v.14, p.204; Tr. by, "Sanitary Conditions in New Orleans Under the Spanish Regime, 1799-1800," v.15, p.610; Tr. by, "The Gri-Gri Case, A Criminal Trial in Louisiana During the Spanish Regime, 1773," v.17, p.48; tr. by, "Account of the Credit and Debit of the Funds of the City of N. O. for the Year 1789," v.19, p.584-94; Tr. by, "Murder Case Tried in New Orleans, 1773," v.22, p.624-41; Tr. by, Index to the Spanish Judicial Records of Louisiana, v.8, p.149, 309, 508, 704; XII, XIII, XIV, XV, v.9, p.143, 321, 533, 746; v.10, p.129, 281, 438, 588; v.11, p.153, 314, 503, 654; v.12, p.166, 331, 398, 675, v.13, p.161, 333, 519, 683; XXXV, XXXVI, XXXVII, v.15, p.156, 532, 675; XXXVIII, XXXIX, XL, v.16, p.151, 339, 516; XLI, XLII, XLIII, v.17, p.203, 385, 572; XLIV, March, 1782, v.18, p.193-233; XLV, April, 1782, v.18, p.456-85; XLVI, May, 1782, v.18, p.727-58; XLVII, June, 1782, v.18, p.1004-35; XLVIII, July-Aug., 1782, v.19, p.241-72; LXIX, Sept.-Nov. 1782, v.19, p.510-46; LXX, Nov. 1782, v.19, p.778-827; LI, Dec. 1782, v.19, p.1119-39; LII, Jan., 1783, v.20, p.245-87; LIII, Feb., 1783, v.20, p.518-55; LIV, March, 1783, v.20, p.840-79; LV, April, 1783, v.20, p.1141-75; LVI, May-June, 1783, v.21, p.319-36; LVII, July, 1783, v.21, p.610-28; LVIII, Aug., 1783, v.21, p.905-57; LIX, Sept., 1783, v.21, p.1253-83; LX, Oct., 1783, v.22, p.259-309; LXI, Nov., 1783, v.22, p.575-621; LXII, Dec., 1783, v.22, p.903-31; LXIII, Jan.-Feb., 1784, v.22, p.1211-47; LXIV, March, 1784, v.23, p.295-347; LXV, April, 1784, v.23, p.635-74; LXVI, May, 1784, v.23, p.945-94; LXVII, June, 1784, v.23, p.1299-1331; LXVIII, June, 1784, v.24, p.258-300; LXIX, July, 1784, v.24, p.601-05; LXX, Aug., 1784, v.24, p.838-915; LXXI, Sept., 1784, v.24, p.1232-80; LXXII, Oct., 1784, v.25, p.260-85; LXXIII, Nov.-Dec., 1784, v.25, p.589-606; LXXIV, Jan., 1785, v.25, p.873-916; LXXV, Jan., 1785, v.25, p.1184-1223; LXXVI, Jan., 1785, v.26, p.257-305; LXXVII, Feb., 1785, v.26, p.842-909; LXXVIII, Feb.-March, 1785, v.26, p.1187-1236; LXXIX, Feb., 1785, v.27, p.854-927; v.28, p.573-673, 1244-1324; v.29, p.208-270, 510-554, 797-880; LXXXV, v.31, p.157-263.

Porter, Admiral, ———, list of fleet under his command, v.32, p.108; report to Sec. of Navy, v.32, p.112; message to Gen. Sherman, v.32, p.127; noted, v.32, p.111, 130, 134, 136, 137.

Porter, Alexander, noted, v.23, p.1021, 1023, 1082n.; and the La. Hist. Soc., v.23, p.1040; eulogy on by H. A. Bullard, v.23, p.1050-1051; description of home, v.24, p.41; noted, v.24, p.1170; and nullification, v.25, p.91; noted, v.25, p.108; letter of, v.25, p.119; judge, host of Clay, v.27, p.737; named to U. S. Senate, v.27, p.741; death of, 1844, v.27, p.748; sketch, v.28, p.817n.

Porter, Betty, "History of Negro Education in La.," v.25, p.728-821.

Porter, Chauncey, noted, v.22, p.197.

Porter, David, Commodore, noted, v.23, p.436.

Porter, David D., and the Red River Campaign, v.18, p.6ff., 855-58; noted, v.24, p.84, 86; attack upon New Orleans, v.24, p.448-51.

Porter, James, noted, v.25, p.76; and nullification, v.25, p.93, 95; minority report on S. C. Ord. of Nullification, v.28, p.950.

Porter, Moses, Mil. Comd't at Natchitoches efforts to enforce U. S. Claims, v.28, p.1031, 1036.

Porter, Sidney, "O. Henry," noted, v.33, p.329.

Porter, Stone & Co., case concerning U. S. mail, v.23, p.1024-1025.

Port Hazard, noted, v.24, p.37.

Port Hudson, noted, v.24, p.68, 69, 72, 74, 82; military operations by Richard Taylor, v.24, p.76-77; in 1862 and 1863, v.23, p.1196, 1202; assault on, v.23, p.1203-1204.

Portneuf, Louis Robineau de, suit of, v.21, p.1008, 1009.

Porto Bello, noted, v.24, p.650, 657, 659, 670.

Portoin, Mathew, noted, v.22, p.982.

Port Republic, military operations, v.24, p.65.

Port Royal, noted, v.24, p.448.

Portsmouth Agreement, noted, v.24, p.701.

Portugal, representative government in, v.24, p.1009, 1011, 1012, 1071; influence of constitution on Europe, v.24, p.1015-16; influences of disturbances on Europe, v.24, p.1025-33, 1035-36, 1049-50, 1055-56, 1066-67, 1141-42; policy of Don Miguel, v.24, p.1105, 1114, 1115, 1121.

Posadas, Father, noted, v.22, p.939.

"Poschelianer," noted, v.24, p.394, 395, 402.

Posey, Lloyd, approved Lottery Bill, v.27, p.1043; proposed voting in hotel to secure vote of sick senator, v.27, p.1044-45; Orleans Parish Sen., v.28, p.1148.

Postal System, U. S., case concerning, v.23, p.1024-1025.

Post-Civil War, documents in La. Hist. Assn. depository, v.24, p.315.

Postell, Paul Everett, "John Hampden Randolph, A La. Planter," v.25, p.149-223.

Postell, William Dostie, study of school of medicine, v.24, p.320, 321, 352.

Postion's Settlement, Cathcart's survey, v.28, p.781-82, 783.

Post, Lauren C., "Domestic Animals and Plants of French Louisiana as Mentioned in the Literature with Reference to Sources, Varieties and Uses," v.16, p.554.

Poston, John, conf. soldier, v.26, p.952, 954.

Post Rapide, noted, v.25, p.399.

Potthof, Charles, noted, v.23, p.518.

Poulaga, ———, noted, v.23, p.148.

Poultney, John, noted, v.22, p.434, 435; v.23, p.1025.

Pounds, Inez, teacher in 1st Bogalusa school, v.29, p.100.

Poussett, Francis, and W. Fla. Assembly, v.22, p.312, 317, 949ff.; and W. Fla. Assembly, v.23, p.5ff.; Clerk of Council of W. Fla. and Rep. Provincial Sec., 1769, v.23, p.353ff.; petition of, v.23, p.366; land granted, v.23, p.383.

Powell, Alexander, letter to Lindoe, v.26, p.83.

Poydras Academy, v.30, p.889-891.

Poydras College, mentioned, v.21, p.1139.

Poydras, Julien, mentioned, v.21, p.1139; buys land from B. Gravier, v.22, p.407; and manumission, v.25, p.339, 340; presented petition to House of Rep. asking for admission of Ter. of Orleans, as State, v.27, p.726.

Pradel, Charles (fils), identified, v.22, p.390.

"Pradel, The Chevalier de," by George C. H. Kernion, v.12, p.238; Book Review by Edith Dart Price, v.12, p.134.

Pradel, Jean Charles de, noted, v.22, p.387, 388, 389-90.

Pradel, Jean Charles de (fils), buys part of Jesuit plantation, v.23, p.68.

"Prados, Major John B., A Confederate Soldier," by James A. Renshaw, v.10, p.241.

Prairie Hayes, La., bid for county seat of Acadia, v.27, p.1122, 1125.

"Prairie Place," rented to Randolph and Hudson, v.25, p.198.

Prat, and Superior Council, v.21, p.1000.

Prats, Emile, noted, v.23, p.163.

Pratt, Julius A., Confed. naval officer, v.27, p.484, 1192.

Pratte, Bernardo, noted, v.22, p.88, 95.

Preaux, Robert, noted, v.22, p.1108.

"Precieuse Ridicule," coasting schooner, v.25, p.940.

Prentice, G. D., incorporator of O'Reilly line, v.31, p.467.

Prentiss, S. S., noted, v.22, p.1133; v.25, p.979, 999, 1079, 1087; counsel of Myles, v.25, p.1102.

Prentiss, Sergeant S., eulogy on, by H. A. Bullard, v.23, p.1054-1055.

Prentiss, Sergeant S., address to Whig Conv. in N. O., 1844, v.27, p.749, 750, 755.

Presbyterian Church, in New Orleans, v.22, p.432, 450-51.

"Presbyterian Lottery," noted, v.31, p.717.

Presbyterians, in N. O., v.21, p.825, 826; in San Antonio, v.23, p.1153; in Calcasieu Parish, v.32, p.623.

Presentation of the Statuette of Joan of Arc to the Louisiana Historical Society, May 1, 1918, v.1, p.285.

Press, French control of, v.24, p.1032, 1043, 1105, 1113.

Press, the New Orleans, during Reconstruction, v.30, p.114-339; bibl., v.30, p.334-339.

Preston, C. C., organizer of Bellevue Academy, v.30, p.900-901; noted, v.30, p.968.

Preston, Isaac T., noted, v.22, p.209; v.23, p.204, 212; v.24, p.1152; v.25, p.1008ff., 1027, 1075, 1083; v.27, p.740; executor of Brown estate, v.27, p.742.

Preston, Rev., noted, v.26, p.103.

Preval, Gallien, N. O. justice of the peace, certificate of death of Clark, v.27, p.118-19; noted, v.22, p.420.

Prevost, Barton, noted, v.24, p.777.

Prevost, Eugene, N. O. musician, v.31, p.131.

"Prevost, Jean Baptiste, Inventory of Estate of," Translated by Edith Dart Price and Heloise H. Cruzat, with introduction by Henry P. Dart, v.9, p.411.

Prevost, Jean Baptiste, attorney, v.21, p.1007; noted, v.22, p.434, 439; inventory of, v.22, p.674; library of, v.22, p.686n.

Prevost, John Bartow, criticism of Claiborne, v.31, p.369.

Prewet, J. B., noted, v.23, p.1243.

Price, Andrew, Dem. Can. for Cong., 1894, v.26, p.1095; defended morality of Louisiana, v.27, p.1076; Cand. U. S. Sen., v.28, p.1184.

Price, Edith Dart, "Inventory of Sieur Jean Baptiste Prevost," v.9, p.411; "Famous Event in the French Colonial History of Louisiana," v.15, p.376; "France d'Amerique," by Simone de la S. Delery and Gladys Anne Renshaw (Book Review), v.16, p.168; "Jamaica Pirates and Louisiana Commerce, 1737," v.16, p.209; Tr. "The Expense Account of a Grande Dame of French Colonial La.," v.21, p.629-30; (co-author), "La Dame de Ste. Hermine," v.21, p.671-73.

Price, Mrs., money from James Brown, v.24, p.928, 941, 1039, 1145, 1165, 1173; noted, v.24, p.1153.

"Price, William, Abstracts of, From State Papers," by Grace King, v.1, sec.1, p.10.

Prichard, Walter, ed., "An Original Letter on the West Florida Revolution of 1810," v.18, p.354-62; The New Editor completes his first volume, v.18, p.973-75; ed. "Henry Adams Bullard; First Pres. of the La. Hist. Soc.," v.19, p.7-42; ed. "Francois Xavier Martin; Second Pres. of the La. Hist. Soc.," v.19, p.43-69; ed. "The Experiences of a Federal Soldier in La. in 1863," v.19, p.635-67; "The Romance of Research in La. History," v.20, p.557-77; ed. "Notes on the Great Fire of 1788 in N. O.," v.20, p.584-89; ed. "George Graham's Mission to Galveston in 1818," v.20, p.619-50; ed. "The Last Island Disaster of Aug. 10, 1856; Personal Narrative of his Experience by One of the Survivors," v.20, p.690-737; ed. "Inventory of the Paris Duvernay Concession in La., 1726," v.21, p.979-94; ed. "Lease of a La. Plantation and Slaves, 1727," v.21, p.995-97; ed. "A Tourist's Description of La. in 1860," v.21, p.1110-1214; "Minutes of the Police Jury of St. Helena Parish, August 16-19, 1813," v.23, p.405-27; "The Origin and Activities of the 'White League' in New Orleans," v.23, p.525-43; ed. "Some Interesting Glimpses of Louisiana a Century Ago," v.24, p.35-48; ed. "Three Letters of Richard Claiborne to William Miller, 1816-1818," v.24, p.729-43; revs. "The Stewardship of Don Esteban Miro, 1782-1792," by Caroline Maude Burson, v.24, p.537-41; revs. Bragg, Jefferson D., "La. in the Confederacy," v.25, p.823-34; revs. Caldwell, Norman W., "The French in the Miss. Valley, 1740-1750," v.25, p.827-28; revs. Carter's "Territory of Orleans," v.25, p.224-26; revs. Dorsy, Florence L., "Master of the Miss.," v.25, p.824-27; revs. Lyon, E. Wilson, "The Man Who Sold La.," v.25, p.828-30; revs. Murphy's "Henry de Tonty," v.25, p.226-27; revs. Williamson, Frederick W., "Yesterday and Today in La. Agriculture," v.25, p.822-23; ed. "La. in the Sp. Am. War," v.26, p.783-841; revs. Davis, Edwin A., "Plantation Life in the Fla. Parishes of La., 1836-1848, as Reflected in the Diary of Bennett H. Barrow," v.26, p.1173-79; revs. Warren, Harris G., "The Sword Was Their Passport," v.26, p.1179-81; revs. Johnson, Cecil, "British W. Fla., 1763-1783," v.26, p.1181-85; revs. Forbes, Gerald, "Flush Production," v.26, p.1185-86; Introduction to "Gaines

Case," v.27, p.5-8; revs. Dabney, Thos. E., "One Hundred Great Years: The Story of the Times Picayune from its Founding to 1940," v.27, p.1229-31; co-ed "Southern La. and Southern Ala. in 1819: The Journal of James Leander Cathcart," v.28, p.735-921; revs. Kane's "Plantation Parade: The Grand Manner in La.," v.29, p.203-207; ed. "A Forgotten Louisiana Engineer: G. W. R. Bayley and his 'History of the Railroads of Louisiana,'" v.30, p.1065-1325; revs. "The Famous Case of Myra Clark Gaines," v.30, p.338-342; revs. "History of Avoyelles Parish, Louisiana," v.30, p.342-346; revs. "The Heart of the Sugar Bowl: The Story of Iberville," v.30, p.346-349; revs. "Zachary Taylor," v.30, p.349-350; revs. "Government Assistance in Eighteenth-Century France," v.30, p.350-352; revs. "The Beleaguered City: Richmond" (1861-1865), v.30, p.352-353; revs. "The South During Reconstruction," v.31, p.150-54; author, "Selecting a Governor for the Territory of Orleans," v.31, p.269-393; revs. "Lakanal the Regicide," v.31, p.553-57; revs. "Fighting Politician: Major General N. P. Banks," v.31, p.557-59; ed. "Records of the Superior Council of La.," v.21, p.282-318, 564-609, 875-908; LXXXII, Jan., 1760-Dec., 1761, v.23, p.265-94; LXXXIII, Jan.-Feb., 1762, v.23, p.589-634; LXXXIV, March-April, 1762, v.23, p.889-944; LXXXV, May-June, 1762, v.23, p.1258-1298; v.24, p.211-57, 544-600, 783-837, 1178-1231; v.25, p.228-59, 537-88, 831-72, 1128-83; v.26, p.169-256; ed. "Index to the Spanish Judicial Records of La.," v.21, p.610-628, 909-59, 1253-83; LXIV, March, 1784, v.23, p.295-347; LXV, April, 1784, v.23, p.635-74; LXVI, May, 1784, v.23, p.945-94; LXVII, June, 1784, v.23, p.1299-1331; v.24, p.258-300, 601-05, 838-915, 1232-80; v.25, p.260-85, 589-606, 873-916, 1184-1223; v.26, p.257-305, 842-909, 1187-1236; v.27, p.854-927; v.28, p.573-673, 1244-1324; v.29, p.208-270, 510-554, 797-880; LXXXV, v.31, p.157-263.

Pride, Charles, noted, v.23, p.226.

"Pride," ship of Laffite, v.24, p.21, 22.

Prien, v.32, p.593.

Priestley, Herbert Ingram, Ph. D., "Spanish Colonial Municipalities," v.5, p.125.

Priestly, Orville E., ed. "Signal," v.27, p.1188.

Priests, in Philadelphia, v.24, p.1139-40.

Prieto, Casimiro, noted, v.23, p.430.

Prieur, Denis, noted, v.24, p.769; and nullification, v.25, p.91; noted, v.25, p.1086; mayor of New Orleans during Cathedral Controversy, v.31, p.919.

Prim, Father Francis, noted, v.24, p.138.

Primo, Bishop Feliciano Marin, noted, v.22, p.102.

Primogeniture, question of in France, v.24, p.991.

"Prince Eugen," manuscript in L.S.U. Music School Library, v.24, p.348.

Prince, Louis, noted, v.23, p.441.

"Princess," steamer, v.25, p.191, 331, 705.

Printing, in W. Fla., v.22, p.326, 374.

Prison reform in La., Livingston and, v.19, p.354-57, 381; in Sp. N. O., v.22, p.699.

Privateering, in Gulf of Mex., v.22, p.751ff.; accounts of, v.24, p.9-34; schooner to New Orleans, 1810, v.24, p.611; effect of War of 1812 upon, v.24, p.614; in New Orleans, v.24, p.638, 737-38.

Privateers, in W. Fla. Rev., v.21, p.146-47; documents in re-establishment at Galveston, v.21, p.1086-1109; origin of and laws concerning, v.23, p.428; in Barataria, v.23, p.428-44; prosecution of cases in New Orleans, v.23, p.437.

"Privateersmen of the Gulf and Their Prizes," by S. Faye, v.22, p.1012-94.

"Privateers of Guadeloupe and their Establishment in Barataria," by S. Faye, v.23, p.428-44.

Privateer vessels, in Gulf of Mex., v.23, p.118-30.

Privy Council, of Council of State in Paris, a Court of Review, v.21, p.1000.

"Procedure for Sale of an American Vessel in New Orleans, 1803," Text and translation by Laura L. Porteous, v.10, p.185.

"Proceedings of the Physico-Med. Soc. of N. O. in Relation to the Trial and Expulsion of Charles Luzenberg (with Comments on the Same), Published by Order of the Society: N. O., 1839," noted, v.26, p.97-98; reprinted, v.26, p.109-36.

Proclamation, British, of 1763, Creating West Florida, v.13, p.610.

Profiteers, in the Civil War, v.24, p.472.

Progressive League, pro-lottery party, organization, v.27, p.1062; first meeting, v.27, p.1062-63; later meeting, v.27, p.1063; campaign highlights, v.27, p.1063-65, 1086; pro-lottery organization, v.28, p.1151.

"Propagateur Catholique, Le.," established, v.31, p.923; Cathedral Controversy, v.31, p.923-31, 932-36, 938, 939-40.

Property, in France, 1827, v.24, p.1071; in 1828, v.24, p.1113.

Property titles, in La., v.24, p.713, 933.

"Proserpina," Spanish schooner, v.23, p.430.

Protectionism, issue in La., 1842, v.25, p.122ff.

"Protestant Beginnings in N. O.," by John K. Bettersworth, v.21, p.823-45.

Protestants, French Church in New Orleans, v.22, p.455; in N. O., noted, v.24, p.136-37.

Provenzanos, and the Mafia, v.22, p.510ff.

Providence Academy, v.30, p.808.

Providence Agreement, noted, v.24, p.701.

Providencia, noted, v.24, p.654.

Province of La., relation to State of La., v.24, p.745.

Provosty, Oliver O., pressure on to vote for lottery, v.27, p.1047; Ceremonial in Supreme Court on his retirement, v.6, p.209; Remarks on his retirement as Chief Justice of Louisiana, v.6, p.210.

Prudhomme, Antoine, noted, v.22, p.77n.

Prudhomme, Denis, noted, v.22, p.77n.

Prudhomme, Dominico, noted, v.22, p.73n.

Prudhomme, Manuel, noted, v.22, p.73n., 77n.

Pruett, Paulin, duel with Trouett, v.24, p.756-58.

Pruit, Uriah, noted, v.23, p.420.

Pruyn, R. L., brief sketch of life in Confederate army, v.29, p.1050-1051; noted, v.29, p.1059; at battle of Shiloh, v.29, p.1065; finds fife and plays "Dixie" to inspire men at Shiloh, v.29, p.1068; promoted to Cap't, v.29, p.1074; releases men from guardhouse who had refused to answer roll call, v.29, p.1075; assigned to gun at Fort Hill, v.29, p.1076; commands expedition taking barges to Vicksburg, v.29, p.1079; noted, v.29, p.1089, 1095; on detached duty at Port Hudson, v.29, p.1108; scheme to blow up enemy vessel with torpedo, v.29, p.1110; daring trip through enemy lines, v.29, p.1124-1126; noted, v.29, p.1128; escapes being taken prisoner by swimming Miss., v.29, p.1132; noted, v.29, p.1147; promoted to major, v.29, p.1195.

"Public Education in New Orleans in 1800," by Henry P. Dart, v.11, p.241.

Public lands, and Clay, v.24, p.1166.

"Public School System of the Territorial Government of Louisiana, Governor Claiborne and The," by Stewart Grayson Noble, v.11, p.535.

Public Service, James Brown's views of, v.24, p.1007-08.

Puckett, Dr. C. McD., sugar planter rep., v.26, p.1099.

Puelles, Fray Jose Maria, "Report to President of Mexican Republic, Concerning Boundaries of Texas and Louisiana, 1828," v.1, sec.1, p.21.

Pufendorf, Samuel von, noted, v.24, p.701.

Pugh, E. N., sugar—Dem. nominee for gov., v.26, p.1100; Repub. cand. for gov., v.28, p.1175.

Pugh, L. H., severed Dem. connections, v.26, p.1094.

Pugh, W. W., Temporary Chairman State Dem. Conv., 1859, v.26, p.987; permanent chairman, v.26, p.988; Dem. cand., v.26, p.988.

Puglia, James Philip, noted, v.22, p.60.

Puissan, Dr., Charter member Med. Soc., v.26, p.59.

Pujo, Arsene P., opposed Sanders as Sen., v.28, p.1223.

Pullen, E. J., Capt. Co. K, 4th La. Reg't muster roll given, v.30, p.515-518.

Pursell, Samuel, noted, v.22, p.203, 204.

Purvis, Jack, Jr., winner in baby contest in Bogalusa, v.29, p.112.

QUADROONS IN LA., v.25, p.305-312; balls, v.25, p.308, 309.

"Quadrupeds of North American," by Audubon, noted, v.25, p.206.

Quarante Club, Tribute to Mrs. William Preston Johnston, v.9, p.281.

Quarles, Maj. Gen'l, confederate officer, v.29, p.1108, 1152, 1168, 1181, 1189-1191, 1206.

Quarterly (January, 1923, issue), Editor's Chair, v.16, p.112; The Tenth Year of the, (Editor's Chair), v.10, p.94.

Quateron, defined, v.25, p.301.

Queen, John, last of N. O. minstrels, sketch, v.30, p.144-146.

"Queen of the West," federal gunboat, v.24, p.72; v.29, p.1097, 1100; captured by confederates, v.29, p.1100-1101; used in capture of "Indianola," v.29, p.1102-1107.

Querre, Juan, noted, v.22, p.1067.

Quesada, Juan Nepomuceno de, Gov. of E. Fla., v.21, p.29n., 30.

Questi, Giovano, sketch, v.28, p.758n.

Quevedo, Francisco Gomez de, y Villegas, born, v.33, p.189; education, v.33, p.190; holds diplomatic offices, v.33, p.191; satirist, v.33, p.192.

"Quevedo," novel by Charles Gayarre, brief description of main characters, v.33, p.193-204.

Quick, Amy, "The History of Bogalusa, the 'Magic City' of La.," v.29, p.73-201.

Quillan, John, noted, v.23, p.409.

Quilling, ———, noted, v.23, p.419.

Quinn, Dr. James P., letter to Thompson, v.26, p.81-82.

Quintanilla, Vincente, noted, v.22, p.1035.

Quintero, Jose, and dueling code, v.23, p.453-60; early N. O. newspaperman, v.29, p.779-780.

Quintero, Joseph A., v.30, p.262.

Quintero, Lamar, N. O. newspaperman, "Old Days on the N. O. Picayune," v.33, p.321.

Quitman, John A., and Lopez expeditions, v.22, p.1122; noted, v.22, p.1132, 1137-39.

Rosedown

RABUN, CHARLEY, CONF. SOLDIER, v.26, p.952, 954, 969.

Raby, Keder, noted, v.23, p.420.

Race Riots, in La. during reconstruction, v.18, p.619ff.

Rader, Perry Scott, "The Romance of Am. Courts, Gaines vs. N. O.," v.27, p.5-322; sketch of, v.27, p.6-7.

Radical Republicans, Custom House group, v.27, p.552; nominated Kellogg, v.27, p.553; united with Regulars, v.27, p.553.

Radziwill, Prince, influences Chopin, v.31, p.856.

Raguet, Abbe, director of company for religious matters, v.29, p.570-571; director first N. O. Charity Hospital, v.31, p.10-13.

Raguet, Jean Baptiste, and Superior Council, v.21, p.1000.

Railey, Col. Chas. R., quarrel with Kellogg, v.29, p.421, 422; tried on charges of conspiracy to assassinate Kellogg, v.29, p.422; noted, v.29, p.422n.

Railroads, early, in La., v.18, p.854-55; interest in 1850's in New Orleans, v.23, p.179; movement in La., 1829-1851, v.23, p.196-243; in New Orleans, 1865, v.23, p.1219; expansion of in La., v.25, p.696-98; in Calcasieu Parish, v.32, p.543-44; New Orleans and Carrollton R. R. Co., v.21, p.230, 234-44; in W. Feliciana, 1860, v.21, p.1135; in Pointe Coupee, v.21, p.1140; planned in Ascension Parish, v.21, p.1125; in Alexandria, 1860, v.21, p.1157; in La., 1860, v.21, p.1194; noted, v.22, p.195-96.

Rainer, Daniel, noted, v.23, p.419.

Rainold, Dr. Mozart W., assistant surgeon, v.26, p.795.

Rainwater, P. L., ed. "The Memorial of John Perkins," v.20, p.965-89.

"Rainy Days," essay by Cable, v.24, p.170.

"Raising American Flag at Jackson Square, New Orleans, Jan. 8, 1918," Address by Andre Lafargue, v.1, sec.3, p.212.

Ramage, James, noted, v.24, p.1138.

Ramirez, Alexandro, noted, v.23, p.766; letters from Onis, v.23, p.803-804, 807-808.

Ramiz, Pedro, noted, v.22, p.73.

Ramke, Diedrich, "Edward Douglas White, Sr., Gov. of La., 1835-1839," v.19, p.273-327.

Ramos, Antonio, noted, v.22, p.1026ff.

Ramos, ———, director of hospital, v.23, p.695.

"Rampant Individualism in an Ante-Bellum Southern College," by Arthur Marvin Shaw, Jr., v.31, p.877-96.

Ramsford, Andrew, noted, v.22, p.39.

Randall, David A., candidate for gov. of La., 1830, v.25, p.60; sketch, v.28, p.754n.

Randall, Horace, noted, v.24, p.75, 80, 92.

Randall, James Ryder, in La., v.21, p.532-46.

Randazzo, see Esposito, Guiseppe.

Randolph, Algernon Sidney, noted, v.25, p.156, 158, 202, 203-204, 211.

Randolph, Dr. Peter, noted, v.25, p.156, 157.

Randolph, Edward, and W. Fla. Rev., v.21, p.82, 104, 107n.

Randolph, Elizabeth, widow of Judge Peter Randolph, v.25, p.158.

Randolph, Emily Jane Liddell, noted, v.25, p.157, 162, 198, 202, 203, 205; suit for property, v.25, p.200-201; administration of estate, v.25, p.215-217.

Randolph, Frank, ed. "Daily Signal," v.27, p.1187.

Randolph, John, in duel, v.24, p.997; trouble with Clay, v.24, p.999, 1001, 1002; noted, v.24, p.1018, 1019; and 1816 tariff, v.25, p.33; and 1824 tariff, v.25, p.40; and 1828 tariff, v.25, p.43, 154; attack on Claiborne, v.31, p.340, 377.

Randolph, John Hampden, Jr., v.25, p.202, 204, 211, 213, 216.

Randolph, John Hampden, collection in L.S.U. Archives, v.24, p.344; sources for study, v.25, p.150-51; ancestry of, v.25, p.155-56; early life, v.25, p.156-58; an executor of his father's will, v.25, p.158; administrator of brother's estate, v.25, p.158-59; married Emily Jane Liddell, v.25, p.159; plantation ventures, v.25, p.160-62, 164, 165-67, 170-71, 172-73, 174-75, 196, 201-202, 213-215; financial status, v.25, p.164-65, 168, 172, 173, 174, 188, 194-97, 199-201, 213, 215; trip to Baltimore, v.25, p.167; land in North, v.25, p.168-70; executor of Liddell estate, v.25, p.168; slaves of, v.25, p.173, 176ff., 183, 192-93, 197, 211; plantation ideas, v.25, p.177, 178, 179, 181-82, 184, 188-189, 190-92; partnership with Thornton, v.25, p.189-90, 192; Texas during Civil War, v.25, p.197ff., 211-12; contracts with free negroes, v.25, p.199; family life, v.25, p.202ff.; pleasure of, v.25, p.204-206; church connections, v.25, p.206-207; building of mansion, v.25, p.207-11; confederate sympathies, v.25, p.211-12; oath of allegiance, v.25, p.212-213; death of and settlement of estate, v.25, p.215-217; bibl., v.25, p.218-23.

Randolph, Judge Peter, to Miss., v.25, p.154, 155, 156; appointment from Jackson, v.25, p.156, 157, 158, 210.

Randolph, Moses Lidell, noted, v.25, p.201, 204, 211, 212, 213, 216, 217.

Randolph, Mrs. Peter, v.28, p.756n.

Randolph, Virginia, noted, v.24, p.782.

Randolph, V. M., noted, v.22, p.1116.

Randolph, W. M., noted, v.23, p.517.

Ranney, H. L., noted, v.23, p.180, 204.

Ranney, R. H., La. educator, pres. Baton Rouge College, v.30, p.771-772.

"Ransdell, John H., Letters from, to Governor Thomas O. Moore, 1863," Introduction by G. P. Whittington, v.14, p.487.

Ransdell, Jos. E., secured relief for flood sufferers, v.28, p.1219; cand. U. S. sen., v.28, p.1223ff.; noted, v.28, p.1229.

Ransom, Gen. ———, noted, v.32, p.109, 115, 120.

Ranson, Thomas E. G., noted, v.24, p.89.

Raphael, Father, v.29, p.570, 571, 572.

Rapho, Capt. Louis, famous N. O. huntsman, v.26, p.777-78.

Rapides Academy for Girls, v.30, p.898.

Rapides, College of, v.24, p.735; sketch of, v.30, p.891-893.

Rapides Female Seminary, v.30, p.896-897.

Rapides Parish, in 1860, v.21, p.1153-61; noted, v.22, p.816; Grant Parish formed from, v.23, p.1107; cotton center of La., v.25, p.27; noted, v.25, p.120, 337; Moore family in, v.26, p.976-77; Moore representative from, v.26, p.978-79; State Seminary of Learning in, v.26, p.980; Senator from, v.26, p.981; noted, v.26, p.983, 988, 991, 1003, 1029; Moore leaves, v.26, p.1044, 1045; Moore's return to, v.26, p.1046; Moore delegate to Dem. Conv., 1874, v.26, p.1049; and the cong. elect. of 1894, v.26, p.1097.

"Rapides Parish, Louisiana, History of," by G. P. Whittington, I, v.15, p.567; II, III, IV, V, v.16, p.27, 235, 427, 628; VI, VII, VIII, IX, v.17, p.112, 327, 537, 737; X (Conclusion), v.18, p.5.

Rapier, John L., officer of Confed. Marine Corps from La., v.27, p.485-86; case involving violations of Anti-Lottery Postal Law, v.27, p.1082.

Rapier, Thomas G., newspaperman, "Old Days on the N. O. Picayune," v.33, p.318-19.

Rapp, Frederick, noted, v.24, p.424, 428.

Rapp, George, noted, v.24, p.422, 423, 424, 425, 426, 428, 429.

Rapp, Henry B., privateersman, v.22, p.1071-72.

Ratcliff, Cyrus, in const. con. of 1844 in La., v.25, p.1005ff.

Rathborne, Joseph, founder La. Cypress

Lumber Co., v.30, p.1002; sketch of, v.30, p.1007-1008; noted, v.30, p.1004, 1020.

Rathbun, George, and sugar tariff, v.25, p.137.

Rauhman, Henry C., Capt. Co. A, 4th La. Reg't, muster roll given, v.30, p.485-487.

Raulan, Joseph, noted, v.22, p.983.

Rausom, Thomas Edward Greenfield, noted, v.23, p.1206.

Ray, Henry W., Confed. naval officer, v.27, p.484.

Ray, John, candidate for lt.-gov., v.31, p.501.

Ray, R. R., introduced bill to repeal lottery acts, v.27, p.982.

Raymond, Father Gilbert, noted, v.31, p.952.

Rayne Board of Health, fight against yellow fever, v.27, p.1136.

Rayne, Louisiana, construction of rice mill at, v.23, p.562; noted, v.27, p.1119, 1120, 1121, 1122; bid for parish seat of Acadia, v.27, p.1122, 1125, 1134, 1155, 1162, 1164, 1167; bank of, merged with that of Crowley, v.27, p.1171, 1191, 1194, 1199, 1205, 1211, 1218, 1220, 1221.

Rayner, James A., pres. N. O., Mobile and Chattanooga Railroad, v.30, p.1242-1245; noted, v.30, p.1247, 1259.

"Rayne Sentinel," feud with "Signal," v.27, p.1185-86.

"Rayne Signal," founded, v.27, p.1184; sold to Duson, v.27, p.1184; favored division of St. Landry and Rayne as county seat of new parish, v.27, p.1120, 1185; moved to Crowley, v.27, p.1123, 1185.

Rayneval, Count de, noted, v.24, p.1128; and claims question, v.24, p.1132, 1135.

Raynor, Daniel, and W. Fla. Rev., v.21, p.707n.

R. D. Wilson's School, sketch of, v.30, p.782-783.

Read, John H., noted, v.24, p.459.

Read, Mrs. Mary W., La. educator, pres. Readvilla Academy, v.30, p.772-774; noted, v.30, p.966.

Readvilla Academy, sketch of, v.30, p.772-774.

Read, William A., "Louisiana Place Names of Indian Origin," revd. by Henry P. Dart, v.11, p.286; "More Indian Place Names," v.11, p.445; "Istrouma," v.14, p.503; "Louisiana—French" (review),
v.15, p.710; Address in Memory of Henry Plauche Dart, v.18, p.250-51; student of La. Indians, v.24, p.749.

Read, William, lawyer, v.31, p.941; to Blanc, v.31, p.950-51.

Real estate, of Sp. New Orleans, v.22, p.672.

Real Estate Owners' and Taxpayers' Union of N. O., advocated const. conv., 1878, v.27, p.988.

Re-apportionment Act of 1842, v.25, p.121.

"Rebecca," slaver, illegal, v.23, p.881-84.

"Rebeccah," slave ship, v.24, p.362.

"Rebel Reefer Furls His Last Sail, The," by Milledge L. Bonham, Jr., v.11, p.582.

Reception by La. Hist. Soc. to Sou. Medical Assn., v.8, p.449.

"Recollections of a Confederate Officer," by John Smith Kendall, v.29, p.1041-1228.

"Recollections of the Battle of the 14th of September, 1874, in New Orleans," by Col. Frank L. Richardson, v.3, p..498.

"Reconstruction and the New Orleans German Colony," by R. T. Clark, Jr., v.23, p.501-24.

"Reconstruction, Francis Tillou Nicholls and the End of," by Hilda Mulvey McDaniel, v.32, p.357.

"Reconstruction, The Aftermath of, in Louisiana," by Margaret T. Leach, v.32, p.631.

Reconstruction era in La., disfranchisement in, v.18, p.557-80; white supremacy in the South, the battle for constitutional government in New Orleans, July 30, 1866, v.18, p.581-616; the White League in La., v.18, p.617-695; women in public affairs in La., v.19, p.668-750; end of in La., v.23, p.466-67; White League in New Orleans, v.23, p.525-43; Lincoln's plan, v.23, p.1135-1136; in La., 1864, v.23, p.1210; in La., v.24, p.114-15; in La., v.25, p.709-14; Negro education during, v.25, p.748-67; in La. and the South, v.26, p.1055-62; in La. under Warmoth, v.28, p.1132-34; election of 1872, v.28, p.1134ff.; New entry Red River, v.28, p.31, 49, 52, 71, 297, 845; red cedar on, v.28, p.890-892; noted, v.32, p.145.

Records of the Superior Council of Louisiana, see Superior Council, Records of.

Red Chute, noted, v.25, p.400.

Redden, William, noted, v.23, p.420.

"Redemption System in the State of Louisiana, The," by J. Hanno Deiler, translated by Rev. Louis Voss, D.D., v.12, p.426.

Redemptorist Fathers, noted, v.24, p.138, 154.

Red Land Seminary, v.30, p.793.

Red Pole, Iberville's exploration of site of, v.28, p.32-34, 50; location of site, v.28, p.35-44; origin of name, v.28, p.44-47; Indian origin and settlement, v.28, p.48-57, 66-68.

Red River Bay, noted, v.25, p.398.

"Red River Campaign, General Bank's," by Richard Hobson Williams, v.32, p.103.

Red River Campaign, raids of Banks, v.18, p.5-15, 855-58; of Banks, v.19, p.150-95; noted, v.24, p.84-101.

"Red River of the South," by N. Philip Norman, v.25, p.397-535.

Red River Parish, White League in, v.18, p.657-70; and the Cong. election of 1894, v.26, p.1097.

Red River, plantation area, v.25, p.186; description of, v.25, p.397-98; noted, v.25, p.361, 930, 931, 932, 937; appropriation to clear obstruction, v.23, p.1011; first American expedition up, v.18, p.765-69; the great raft removed, v.18, p.769-75; century of steamboating on, v.18, p.845-63; noted, v.32, p.103, 144, v.21, p.1151, 1154, 1161ff.; noted, v.26, p.633; mine hunting on, v.26, p.650; noted, v.26, p.655, 687, 688, 694, 707, 714; Fort St. Jean Baptiste on, v.26, p.731; campaign of Gen. Banks, v.26, p.974n.; effort to get guns for defense of, v.26, p.1025; bill passed for defense of, v.26, p.1026-27; campaign of 1863, v.26, p.1028, 1039, 1041, 1043, 1044, 1048.

Red River raft, noted, v.24, p.37, 38.

Red River Valley, historical sketch of, v.25, p.398-406.

"Red Stick," meaning of name B. R., v.28, p.5, 6; conjectures as to origin of name, v.28, p.7-8.

Reeder, Captain George Washington, and expedition against pirates, v.24, p.32-34.

Reed, Isaac, sketch of, v.28, p.763n.

Reeds Island, Cathcart's survey, v.28, p.782, 783, 793.

Reese, D. M., La. educator, pres. Acadia College, v.30, p.757.

Rees, James, dramatist, v.31, p.980.

Reeves, L. V., nominated Dem. cand. for gov., v.26, p.988.

Refugio, noted, v.24, p.641.

Regan, W. D., Confed. soldier, v.26, p.973.

Reggio, Judith Helene Anastasie de, noted, v.24, p.354, 355.

Register of State Land Office, v.28, p.300; creation and duties of, v.28, p.301-302; noted, v.28, p.314; reports of, v.28, p.314, 315, 316-19.

Register, R. C., commissioned judge by Kellogg, v.29, p.419.

Regottez, Sieur Louis, diploma in Wrestling in New Orleans Public Library, v.24, p.325.

"Regulations to be observed by the Syndics and Alcalds of the Jurisdiction of Baton Rouge, October 30, 1804," by Governor Vincente Folch, v.9, p.405.

"Regulators," v.25, p.709.

Reichard, August, Brig. Gen'l of Civil War, v.20, p.1001; noted, v.23, p.503.

Reid, James K., lessor of O'Reilly route, v.31, p.452-3, 473.

Reid, Samuel Chester, noted, v.24, p.979.

"Reign of Twenty Days, A," by Andre Lafargue, v.8, p.398.

"Reims, Stones of," by Edward A. Parsons, v.4, p.425.

Reinders, Dr. Robert, "Dr. James G. Carson's Canebrake; A View of an Ante-Bellum Louisiana Plantation," v.33, p.353-63.

Reinecke, J. A., Jr., "Diplomatic Career of Pierre Soule," v.15, p.283.

"Relations between New Orleans and Latin America, 1810-1824," by A. T. Wellborn, v.22, p.710-94.

Relf, Richard, noted, v.22, p.434, 435, 439, 453, 461, 466, 470, 471-72; on Charity Hosp. Board, 1836, v.26, p.58; noted, v.27, p.7; partner of Clark, v.27, p.19; finds and probates will of Clark, v.27, p.20, 21, 22, 23; produces letter of Desgrange to Clark, v.27, p.26, 30, 31, 32, 33, 45; opposed probate of will, v.27, p.49-50, 56, 64, 65; charge against, v.27, p.63, 69-70, 73, 75-76; testimony concerning, v.27, p.81, 117, 118-20; petition against, v.27, p.126, 127, 128, 131, 134, 141, 173; defendant in Myra's bill in equity in Circuit Ct. of U. S., v.27, p.180-83; charges against, v.27, p.184-85; filed demurrer, v.27, p.189, 206, 209; opinion in favor of, v.27, p.211-41, 246, 247, 249, 250, 251, 277, 278, 289, 290, 291; illegal sales of Clark estate, v.27, p. 304-307, 308, 309, 310, 211, 312, 315; noted, v.23, p.771n.

Relf & Chew, N. O. Agents for Daniel Clark, v.20, p.7, executors for Clark, v.20, p.16ff.; sued by Myra Clark, v.20, p.22ff.; noted, v.22, p.151.

Religion, in N. O., v.20, p.945-47; toleration in Spanish La., v.21, p.58, 62; in early N. O., v.21, p.823-45; "The Early History of the Episcopal Church in New Orleans," v.22, p.428-78; in Texas, 1854, v.23, p.1150; in Calcasieu Parish, v.32, p.620-27.

"Reminiscences of Days that are Gone" (From old copy of Charleston Observer, by courtesy of Miss Grace King), v.2, p.321.

Remy, Henry, noted, v.25, p.996-97, 1051.

"Remy's Lost History of Louisiana," by Henry P. Dart, v.5, p.5.

Renaud, ———, noted, v.22, p.1067.

Renaud, Pierre, deposition of, v.23, p.710-11.

Rendon, Don Francis, and Spanish land grants, v.20, p.303.

Rendon, Francisco, intendant of La., v.21, p.19n.

Renoudet's School, v.30, p.912-913.

Renovales, Mariano de, noted, v.24, p.647; expedition against Mexico, v.24, p.649.

Renshaw, Gladys Anne, "France d'Amerique" (Book Review by Edith Dart Price), v.16, p.168.

Renshaw, Henry, "Lafayette's Visit to New Orleans, 1825," v.1, sec.2, p.5; "Jackson Square," v.2, p.38; "Judge Frederick D. King, v.6, p.195.

Renshaw, James A., "The Lost City of Lafayette," v.2, p.47; "Liberty Monument," v.3, p.259; "The Hunt Family," v.5, p.339; "The 14th September, 1874, as Viewed by the Supreme Court of Louisiana," v.7, p.618; "Hunt, Gaillard," v.8, p.84; "Lights and Shadows," v.8, p.657; "Recollections of Yesterday," v.8, p.428; Celebration by the Louisiana Historical Society of the Centennial Anniversary of the Visit of Lafayette, reported by James A. Renshaw, v.9, p.190; "Lafayette, his Visit to New Orleans in 1825," compiled by James A. Renshaw, v.9, p.181; "Major John B. Prados, A Confederate Soldier," v.10, p.241; "Judah Touro and His Will," v.11, p.67.

Renshaw, Jas W. (Mrs. E. J. Nicholson), v.6, p.580.

Renthrope, Peter Hy., sketch, v.28, p.781n.

Renthrops Ferry, v.28, p.781n., 793, 795, 812, 814.

"Repairing the La. Gov't Bldgs. in 1811," ed. by James A. Padgett, v.26, p.44-48.

"Reply of Peter Chester, Gov. of W. Fla., to Complaints Made Against His Administration," ed. by J. A. Padgett, v.22, p.31-46.

"Report of Louisiana Historical Society for 1918," by Bussiere Rouen, v.2, p.208.

Report of the Committee of Inquiry of the Military Measures Executed Against the Legislature of Louisiana, December 28, 1814, v.9, p.223.

Report of the Proceedings of the Louisiana Historical Society, 1919-1920, v.3, p.373.

Report of Treasurer (W. O. Hart), Louisiana Historical Society, v.5, p.238.

Report to Congress, January, 1824, From State Papers, v.2, p.119.

"Report to Mexican Republic Concerning Boundaries of Texas and Louisiana," by Rev. Fray Jose Maria Puelles, 1828, v.1, sec.1, p.21.

Representation, in Ante-Bellum La., v.19, p.390-406; apportionment in Fla. parishes, v.21, p.191-92.

"Republicano," Cartagenan schooner, v.24, p.625, 626.

Republican Party, Liberal German element in, v.23, p.517ff.; noted, v.25, p.711, 712, 714, 716, 718; gubernatorial campaign in La., 1872, v.27, p.554, 556, 558; votes to impeach Warmoth, and Pinchback becomes gov., v.27, p.560-61, 562, 563, 565, 566, 568; achieved Fed'l recognition in La., v.27, p.568-69, 571; dissension in, v.27, p.574-75; inauguration of Kellogg, v.27, p.576, 577, 578; Pinchback cand. for U. S. Cong., v.27, p.581, 582, 587; contest to seat Pinchback, v.27, p.590, 593, 595, 597, 601, 602, 604, 605; Pinchback delegate to St. conv., 1867, v.27, p.732; election for state senate, 1868, v.27, p.535; Pinchbacks delegate to Nat'l, v.27, p.537-38; split in ranks of, v.27, p.538, 540, 541, 542, 545; conv., 1872, v.27, p.551, 552; endorsed Pinchback, v.27, p.552-53, 785, 797, 804; in re tariff, v.27, p.806-21 passim; blamed for La. Lottery Co., v.27, p.1013; and the La. Gubernatorial election of 1892, v.27, p.1081, 1092; split over lottery question, v.27, p.1092, 1121.

Republic of Columbia, established by Bolivar, v.24, p.667.

Residual sovereignty, Edward Livingston's ideas of, v.24, p.719.

Resolution Endorsing Bill for Erection of Monument to Louisiana Soldiers who

Served in Vicksburg Campaign, v.1, p.347.

"Retirement" Plantation, v.29, p.295.

Returning Board, and the election of 1876, v.25, p.711-13; in election of 1872, v.27, p.557-59; v.28, p.1134-35.

"Revenants," revolutionary society, v.22, p.69ff.

Revolution of 1876 in Louisiana, The, Editor's Chair by Henry P. Dart, v.14, p.242.

Revolution, tendencies toward, in Europe, v.24, p.940, 1095.

Rewards of Public Service, A Digression on the, (Editor's Chair), v.6, p.281.

Reybaud, Thomas, noted, v.24, p.27, 368, 372.

Rey, Juan Garcia, abduction of, v.22, p.1107.

Reynard, Juan Andres, buys part of Jesuit plantation, v.23, p.681; and Jesuit land grant, v.22, p.388-92, 395, 396, 399.

Reynolds, M. M., noted, v.22, p.1108, 1160.

Rhea, Capt., noted, v.23, p.386.

Rhea, John, and W. Fla. Rev., v.21, p.76ff., 687n.; letter from Kemper, v.21, p.90-93, 101-107, 113-14, 119-21, 153, 155-56; letter from Nicholson, v.21, p.154-55.

Rhett, Col. R. B., ed. Charleston "Mercury," v.30, p.259-260.

Rhett, Col. R. B., Jr., ed. N. O. "Picayune," v.30, p.259-260.

Rhodes, Dr. John, noted, v.26, p.56; Charter member Med. Soc., v.26, p.59.

Rhodes, Myrtle, winner in Bogalusa baby contest, v.29, p.112.

Riano, Francis de, deposition of, v.23, p.716-18.

Ribbon cane, noted, v.25, p.54, 186.

Ricard, Cyprian, noted, v.25, p.320, 732.

Rice, export of, v.22, p.668; noted, v.23, p.514; introduction to U. S., v.23, p.544-45; production in La. to 1896, v.23, p.544-88; bounty on, v.23, p.546; as medium of exchange, v.23, p.546, 548-49; returns on crop, v.23, p.547; states producing, 1839, v.23, p.547-48; introduction into La., v.23, p.548; effect of Civil War on production, v.23, p.548; method of cultivation in S. C., v.23, p.549; description of farm in La., v.23, p.550; method of cultivation in La., v.23, p.550-51; method of harvesting and threshing, v.23, p.551, 552; classification of, v.23, p.552; crop of 1877-1878, v.23, p.556; varieties of, v.23, p.557, 564; combined with sugar planting, v.23, p.557; culture in Southwest La., v.23, p.558-75; early methods of milling, v.23, p.562-63; cost of production, v.23, p.565; soil best fitted for, v.23, p.565; early efforts at irrigation, v.23, p.567-68; use of by-products, v.23, p.571; introduction of Japanese variety, v.23, p.571; marketing of, v.23, p.573; statistics on, v.23, p.577-85; an early export of N. O., v.27, p.938, 1119; importance of in growth of Crowley, v.27, p.1134; Crowley the "rice City of Am.," v.27, p.1157; am't produced in Acadia, v.27, p.1157; history of Acadia, v.27, p.1157; system of irrigation, v.27, p.1157-60; other improvements, v.27, p.1160; new varieties, v.27, p.1161-62; work of Crowley Rice Experimental Station, v.27, p.1161, 1162; Rice Assoc. of Am. organized in Crowley, v.27, p.1162; Nat'l Rice Festival, v.27, p.1162; Fed'l State Grading Office, v.27, p.1162; growth of rice mills in southwest La., v.27, p.1164, 67; trade names of, v.27, p.1167; mills in Crowley, v.27, p.1167; festival, v.27, p.1208-14; in La., noted, v.32, p.9; in Calcasieu Parish, v.32, p.503-38.

"Rice City of Am.," see Crowley.

Rice, "Daddy," early N. O. minstrel, v.30, p.131; noted, v.30, p.134, 138, 140.

Rice, Dr. J., noted, v.26, p.76; on Med. Board of Censors, v.26, p.60.

Rice Irrigation & Improvement Assoc., v.27, p.1159.

Rice mills, establishment of, v.23, p.552; at Rayne, v.23, p.562; rebellion of planters against trust of millers, v.23, p.563; trust of millers, v.23, p.573.

Rice, Samuel Russel, sketch of, v.28, p.792n.

Richardson, Caroline, "Mississippi Valley Beginnings," v.7, p.672.

Richardson, Col. Francis D., Sketch of (New Orleans Picayune, 1896), v.3, p.624; sketch of, v.28, p.817n.

Richardson, Col. Frank L., "My Recollections of the Battle of the 14th of September, 1874, in New Orleans," v.3, p.498.

Richardson, Col. Robert, noted, v.26, p.967, 968.

Richardson, D. C., brief sketch, v.29, p.60n.

Richardson, Frank D., "A Last Evening with Judge Gayarre" (with picture), v.14, p.81.

Richardson, Frank L., "The War as I saw It," introduction by Cecile Wilink, I, II, v.6, p.89, 223.

Richardson, James, orders of, in Jackson Barracks Library, v.24, p.313.
Richardson, Jas. S., vice-pres. Prog. League, v.27, p.1062.
Richardson, J. B., named in Wickliffe impeachment, v.31, p.692.
Richardson, Jim Warren, v.29, p.83, 88.
Richardson, John G., sketch of, v.28, p.817n.
Richardson, Lillie, "The Admission of Louisiana into the Union," v.1, p.333.
Richardson, Mrs. T. L., vice-pres. Women's Anti-Lottery League, v.27, p.1061.
Richardson, R. W., appt'd to rep. La. at Memphis R.R. conv., v.28, p.974.
Richardson, Samuel, noted, v.23, p.422.
Richardson, T. R., noted, v.26, p.955n.
Richardson, Wm., sketch of, v.28, p.817n.
Richard, Warren, N. O. minstrel, v.30, p.146.
Richard, William C., poet, v.31, p.485.
Richarville, Druet de, suit against sucession, v.21, p.1010.
Richelieu, Duke de, noted, v.24, p.961, 1022.
Richen, Rev. L., noted, v.24, p.139.
"Richmond," federal boat, v.29, p.1108.
Richmond, headquarters for Richard Taylor, v.24, p.75.
Richoux, A, et als., sale of Havana lottery tickets prohibited, v.27, p.927; sued by lottery company, v.31, p.731.
Ridgely, Dr., Charter member Medical Soc., v.26, p.59.
Riedy, Pastor Owen, noted, v.24, p.146.
Ries, Maurice, "The Miss. Fort Called Fort de la Boulaye (1700-1715); the First Fr. Settlement in Present Day La.", v.19, p.829-99.
Rieux, Louis Francois de, sketch of, v.22, p.1066.
Rife, George E., noted, v.23, p.480.
Rigau, Gascon Antoine, noted, v.23, p.443n; French emigre, v.23, p.778.
Rigaud, Andre, sketch, v.23, p.443n.
Rigaud, Benoit-Joseph, noted, v.23, p.443n.
Rigaud, General ———, and Champ Asile, v.22, p.748.
Rightor, Henry, work in New Orleans history cited, v.24, p.327, 335, 352; newspaperman, "Old Days on the Times-Democrat," v.33, p.408, 409.
Rightor, Nicholas H., N. O. Sup. Ct. Justice, v.27, p.984.
Rigny, Admiral de, at Scio, v.24, p.108.
Rigolet du Bon Dieu, located, v.23, p.1107; v.25, p.397.

Riley, Martin L., "The Development of Ed. in La. prior to Statehood," v.19, p.595-634.
Ringgold Male and Female Academy, v.30, p.792.
Rio Dulce, described, v.24, p.663.
Rio Hacha, noted, v.24, p.688.
Riordan, B. R., on staff of "Daily Delta," v.30, p.290-300.
Rios, Manuel de los, noted, v.22, p.1040.
Riots, New Orleans, 1851, v.22, p.1149-59.
Ripley, Eliza, quoted on Soule, v.25, p.995.
Ritter, Rev. H. S., cited, v.24, p.142.
Rivas, ———, noted, v.22, p.940.
Rivers, R. H., president Centenary College, v.31, p.126.
River Teche, description of, v.24, p.41-42.
Rivore, Emile, duel with Andre Roman, v.24, p.772-73.
Roachborough, C. A., colored delegate to People's Party Conv., 1892, v.26, p.1080.
Roads, and U. S. politics, v.24, p.1008-09.
Roads, plank, in Carrollton, v.21, p.246-47; shell, v.21, p.252; in La., 1860, v.21, p.1110ff.; in Carrollton, v.22, p.201; in New Orleans, v.22, p.645-46; in W. Fla., v.22, p.957; in St. Helena, 1813, v.23, p.410, 418-24; public, in New Orleans, v.23, p.697.
Robbins Case, noted, v.24, p.711.
Robb, James Hampden, sketch, v.23, p.255.
Robb, James, parentage and early life, v.23, p.170-71; banker in Va., v.23, p.171-72; banker in New Orleans, v.23, p.173-74; business interests in Cuba, v.23, p.175; New Orleans alderman, v.23, p.176, 193-196; elected state senator, v.23, p.180-87; and consolidation of New Orleans, v.23, p.188-89; and Comp. of 1850, v.23, p.189-90; refused U. S. senatorship, v.23, p.192; and railroad movement in La., v.23, p.196-243; private banking of, v.23, p.243-45; art patron, v.23, p.246; loses fortune, 1857; v.23, p.248-49; moves to Chicago, v.23, p.249; railroad official in N. Y., v.23, p.250; as a unionist, v.23, p.250-51; during Civil War, v.23, p.253; returns to New Orleans, 1865, v.23, p.254; refuses cabinet officer, v.23, p.254; death, v.23, p.256.
"Robert Cavelier de la Salle Monument at Lachine Canada," by A. Lafargue, v.22, p.5-17.
Robert, Jean, and Barataria, v.22, p.803-804, 1024; noted, v.23, p.441.

Roberts, Percy, noted, v.29, p.360; De Bow's "European Correspondent," v.29, p.373.

Roberts, Percy S., speaker at Prog. League meeting, v.27, p.1063.

Roberts, Peter, sketch, v.28, p.831n.

Roberts, W. Adolphe, "Royal Street: A Novel of Old N. O.," rev'd, v.28, p.992-95; "Brave Mardi Gras: A New Orleans Novel of the 60's" rev'd, v.29, p.793-796.

Robertson, Colonel, ———, and W. Fla., v.22, p.20, 21.

Robertson, E. W., state auditor, v.25, p.695.

Robertson, S. M., Dem. Cand. for Cong., 1894, v.26, p.1095; congressman, v.26, p.1116, 1898, 1123.

Robertson, Thomas Bolling, marries Lelia Skipworth, v.21, p.78; and W. Fla. Rev., v.21, p.156n; noted, v.22, p.762; and Sp. Am. insurrections, v.22, p.788-90; and 1816 tariff bill, v.25, p.30-34; noted, v.25, p.36, 57, 60, 133; and protection, v.25, p.41; secretary of Territory of Orleans, v.31, p.309, 383, 836.

Robichaux, J. P., collection in L.S.U. Music School Library, v.24, p.348.

Robinson, David, v.29, p.79.

Robinson, Henry W., "The Republican Party after the Battle of Sept. 14, 1874," v.7, p.604; on La. Bar Assoc. which prepared memorial of Henry Plauche Dart, v.18, p.255-66.

Robinson, John B., noted, v.26, p.971.

Robinson, John Hamilton, and Toledo's expedition, v.22, p.729; noted, v.22, p.731, 734, 739, 806; noted, v.25, p.297, 298, 299; life of, v.25, p.644-69; and the Pike expedition, v.25, p.645-49; his military career, v.25, p.649-50, 662-63; as Monroe's agent to Salcedo, v.25, p.650-56; cited on Pan Americanism, v.25, p.567; cited on Mexican independence, v.25, p.658; and his efforts for Mexican independence, v.25, p.159-62, 663-66; as agent to Mexican Congress, v.25, p.663-66; commissioned general in Patriot army, v.25, p.666; publication of maps, v.25, p.667-68; his death, 1819, v.25, p.668-69; becomes interested in filibustering, v.28, p.1054, 1056-57.

Robinson, Major W. M., early N. O. newspaperman, v.29, p.773.

Robinson, S. W., confed. soldier, v.26, p.971n.

Robinson, Tully, noted, v.23, p.437.

Robinson, William Davis, sketch, v.22, p.731-32; his attempt to supply arms to Teran, v.25, p.665; mistaken for John H. Robinson and arrested, v.25, p.666.

Robinson, Wm., Carpenter in Confed. Navy, v.27, p.485.

Rocheblave, Paul de Rastel de, v.18, p.336-43.

Rocheblave, Philippe Francois de Rastel de, v.18, p.334-36.

Rocheblave, Pierre Louis de, v.18, p.334.

"Rocheblaves in Colonial Louisiana," by E. Fabre Surveyor, v.18, p.332-45.

Rochemore, becomes Ordonnateur, quarrels with Gov., v.29, p.613-614.

Rocquiny, Jacques de, author, v.31, p.992.

Rodgers, John, noted, v.24, p.970, 978, 979.

Rodney, Caesar A., noted, v.22, p.763.

Rodon, Juan Francisco, Spanish consular agent, v.21, p.683, 684, 1099.

Rodon, Pablo, Spanish consular agent, v.21, p.684.

Rodriguez, Juan, noted, v.22, p.934.

Rodriguez, Mariano, sent to trade with Indians, v.28, p.1086.

Rodriguez, Sebastian, Sp. comdt. of frontier, v.28, p.1030ff.; Ct.-martialed, v.28, p.1034.

Roger, Ayme, French consul at New Orleans, v.31, p.993.

Roger, Pierre, justice of peace, v.23, p.696ff., 705.

Rogers, Capt. Madison, confed. soldier, v.26, p.955, promoted, v.26, p.967.

"Rogers Compositions," noted, v.25, p.366.

Rogers, Jane Grey, "An Interesting Medico-Historical Exhibit," v.6, p.588.

Rogers, Rev. Walter, noted, v.25, p.365.

Rogers, Walter H., N. O. Sup. Ct. Justice, v.27, p.984; att'y gen'l, counsel for Mason, v.27, p.1051.

Rogers, W. O., La. educator, pres. Sylvester Larned Institute, v.30, p.871.

Roig, Salvator, noted, v.22, p.1023.

"Role, The, of the Baron de Bastrop in the Anglo-American Settlement of the Southwest," by R. Woods Moore, v.31, p.606-81.

Rolland, Jean Baptiste, noted, v.23, p.695; deposition of, v.23, p.714-716.

Rollinger, Augustin, identified, v.24, p.386-87.

Rolling, Hubert, N. O. musician, v.31, p.133-34.

Roman, Andre Bienvenue, noted, v.23, p.1028; duel with Emile Rivore, v.24, p.772-73; noted, v.25, p.60, 112; and tariff, v.25, p.76, 111; and nullification, v.25, p.91, 92, 93; inaugural address, v.25, p.1000; and the Const. Con. of 1844, v.25, p.1006ff; noted, v.28, p.295, 950; and La. internal improvements, v.30, p.41-48; noted, v.30, p.20, 51, 473, 747, 903; gov. of La., v.31, p.937, 1001.

Roman, Henry J., noted, v.21, p.1120.

Roman law, influence upon Edward Livingston, v.24, p.701.

"Romance of Am. Courts, Gaines vs. N. O.," by Perry Scott Rader, v.27, p.5-322.

"Romance of Research in La. History," by Walter Prichard, v.20, p.557-77.

"Romano," schooner, v.24, p.653.

Romero, ———, noted, v.22, p.939.

Romero, Sidney James, Jr., "The Political Career of M. J. Foster, Gov. of La. 1892-1900," v.28, p.1129-1243.

"Rome, Tribunals of Criminal Jurisdiction in Ancient," by Charles Gayarre, v.33, p.205-222.

Ronaldson, Joseph A., La. educator, v.30, p.822; noted, v.30, p.965.

Ronaldson's School, v.30, p.822.

Ronquillo, Juan, Chief pilot at Balize, v.28, p.708, 709.

Root, Wm. H., Civil War Diary of, v.19, p.635-67.

Roques, Charles, noted, v.25, p.320, 371.

"Rouquette, Adrien, Poet and Mystic," by G. Wm. Nott, v.6, p.388.

Roquiere, Francois, noted, v.22, p.77n.

Rory, Jean Louis, noted, v.24, p.366.

Rosati, Father Joseph, New Orleans diocese, v.31, p.905, 906.

Roscio, Juan German, noted, v.24, p.640, 641, 643, 667, 696.

Rose Bluff, v.32, p.593.

Rosecrans, Wm. S., noted, v.29, p.252.

Rose, George, noted, v.23, p.35.

Roselius, Christian, German liberal in N. O., v.20, p.144; and case of Sally Miller, v.22, p.162ff.; noted, v.23, p.183, 516, 1049, 1061, 1095; prof. in Univ. of La. Law School, v.23, p.1063; and Batture controversy, v.23, p.1065, 1067; noted, v.25, p.980, 1079, 1083, 1086; and the Const. Con. of 1844, v.25, p.1007ff.; noted, v.27, p.740; oration on Webster, v.27, p.769; N. O. unionist, v.31, p.1015; Wells nomination, v.31, p.1026.

Rosenberg, Adolf, history of costume in Shreve Memorial Library, v.24, p.339.

Rosenwald Fund, noted, v.25, p.773, 781, 794, 795; organization and plan of, v.25, p.799-902.

Rosiere, Gilbert, noted, v.23, p.146, 147.

Ross, David, noted, v.23, p.26, 45; election of, v.23, p.377.

Ross, Mrs. Eliza, money from James Brown, v.24, p.1145.

Ross, expedition against pirates, v.24, p.13, 18, 24.

Ross, George T., noted, v.22, p.434, 435, 439.

Ross, James, and W. Fla. Assembly, v.22, p.317, 943; v.23, p.5ff.; election of, v.23, p.377.

Ross, Reuben, noted, v.25, p.295.

Ross, Robert, noted, v.22, p.980.

Rosseau, Judge, noted, v.24, p.48.

Rosseau, Pierre, deposition of, v.23, p.698.

Rossman, Walter, noted, v.25, p.681.

Rost, Pierre A., noted, v.23, p.1008; judge of La. Sup. Ct., v.23, p.1028, 1029; noted, v.25, p.980; Justice of La. Supreme Court, v.25, p.1050.

Rouen, Bussiere, Report of Louisiana Historical Society for 1918, v.2, p.208; "Pierre Margry," v.5, p.192; "New Orleans Bee," v.8, p.585.

Rouen, S., La. educator, v.30, p.880; noted, v.30, p.968.

Rouncevall, Robert, noted, v.23, p.419.

Round Island expedition to Cuba, v.22, p.1115-20.

Rouquette, Abbe, missionary to Indians, v.24, p.750.

Rouquette, Francois Dominique, noted, v.33, p.224; manuscripts in Howard-Tilton Memorial Library, v.24, p.329.

Rousseau, Lawrence, officer of the Confed. Navy, v.27, p.479-80, 708, 710, 711.

Rousseau, Lovell H., v.30, p.565-569.

Rousseau, Pedro, sketch, v.21, p.49; fortifies Las Barrancas de Margot, v.21, p.55.

Rousseau, Pierre, noted, v.22, p.50; sketch, v.22, p.82n.; v.23, p.429.

Rousselin, Jean-Pierre, noted, v.22, p.1066.

Rousselon, Father Etienne, noted, v.25, p.363; appointed cure, v.31, p.909; noted, v.31, p.911.

Roussere, Jean Baptiste, deposition of, v.23, p.720-721.

Routh, Mary, Grandmother of Gov. Isaac Johnson, v.28, p.942.

Rowdy Bend, Old Mississippi channel, v.31, p.600.

Rowe, James S., co-manager Am. Theatre,

v.28, p.186; seasons 1833-1835, v.28, p.186-99; death, v.28, p.199.

Rowland, Dunbar, and A. G. Sanders "Mississippi Provincial Archives, 1729-1740, French Dominion" (review by Henry P. Dart), v.11, p.111; Splendid Work on French Archives of Louisiana (Editor's Chair), v.12, p.464; "Mississippi in the Transfer of the Louisiana Purchase," v.13, p.235; "Mississippi Provincial Archives, 1704-1743, French Dominion," Vol. III (review), v.15, p.707.

Rowland, Eron, "Varina Howell, Wife of Jefferson Davis" (review by Grace King), v.11, p.466; (review), v.15, p.350.

Royal Hospital of New Orleans, history of, v.29, p.559-562, 594-595, 597-602, 611-615, 624, 625.

"Royal Street: A Novel of Old N. O.," by W. Adolph Roberts, rev'd, v.28, p.992-95.

Royalton, William, noted, v.23, p.1141.

Rozier, J. Ad., Louisiana party chairman, v.31, p.1053; noted, v.24, p.506; proposed substitute for ordinance of Secession, v.26, p.1000-1001, 1002.

"R. T. Bryarly," steamer, picture of, v.25, p.492.

Rua, Jose de la, noted, v.22, p.1019.

Ruddock, C. H., cypress lumberman, v.30, p.1015-1016.

Ruddock Cypress Co., v.30, p.1002, 1015-1016.

Rudolph Matas Medical Library, Tulane University, v.24, p.327, 333.

Rudrow, E. V., councilman of Crowley, v.27, p.1131.

Ruff, Dr. S. W., noted, v.26, p.76.

Ruffin, Mrs. Minnie Markette, "General Solomon Wethersbee Downs, 1801-1854," v.17, p.5.

Rufignac, Joseph, noted, v.22, p.803, 815.

Rugby School, v.30, p.879.

Rumpff, Mrs., daughter of John Jacob Astor, v.24, p.1042, 1047.

Rumpff, Mr., noted, v.24, p.1042, 1047, 1057, 1076; and commercial treaty for Hanseatic Towns, v.24, p.1048-49.

Rush, Richard, noted, v.24, p.1127, 1150; and Antimasons, v.24, p.1159; remarks on liquidation of W. Fla. claims, v.25, p.946-48.

Rush, Mrs. Richard, noted, v.24, p.1117, 1125, 1127.

Rushton, Dr. W., noted, v.26, p.76.

Russ, William A., Jr., "Disfranchisement in Louisiana, 1862-70," v.18, p.557-80.

"Russell in New Orleans, Irwin," by John S. Kendall, v.14, p.321.

Russell, Jonathan, noted, v.24, p.1040.

Russell, Richard, Co-manager of Am. Theatre, v.28, p.186; seasons 1833-36, v.28, p.186-204; noted, v.28, p.211; season 1836-37, v.28, p.212-18; 1837-38 his last season, v.28, p.224-29.

Russia, war with Turkey, v.24, p.999ff., 1103-04, 1111, 1115, 1135-36; reaction of other powers to war, v.24, p.1104, 1109, 1118, 1121, 1132-33, 1141, 1143.

Ruston College, sketch of, v.30, p.840-841.

Rutherford, C. M., slave dealer, v.22, p.152.

Ryan, Representative, introduced bill locating State Seminary of Learning in Rapides, v.26, p.980.

Ryan, V. A., named in Kellogg impeachment, v.31, p.713.

SABA, NOTED, v.24, p.652.
Sabine Crossroads, or Battle of Mansfield, v.24, p.92; v.32, p.119-125.
Sabine, description of country, v.24, p.35-37.
Sabine Normal and Industrial Institute, v.25, p.788-808.
Sabine Parish, in La., Populist legis. from, v.26, p.1109.
Sabine River, noted, v.25, p.292, 294, 295, 299, 624, 661, 662; v.28, p.826, 886, 890; disputed boundary of neutral ground, v.28, p.1024, 1028ff.
Sacatra, defined, v.25, p.301.
Sackel, Paul, N. O. pianist, v.31, p.867.
Sacred Heart Academy of Natchitoches, v.30, p.948.
Sacred Heart Convent, Grand Coteau, v.30, p.960-962.
St. Aloysius Academy, v.30, p.954.
St. Alphonsus' School, v.30, p.955.
St. Amant, A. Joseph, rep. arrested for bribery, v.27, p.1047-48.
St. Amant, Antoine, noted, v.22, p.815.
St. Amant, Madame, noted, v.22, p.661n.
St. Amant, Pierre, noted, v.22, p.815; v.23, p.441.
St. Ange, Post of, v.23, p.393.
St. Augustine, Mother Marie Tranchepain de, superior of Ursuline Nuns, 1727, v.25, p.729.
St. Bart's, noted, v.24, p.647, 648, 652, 653, 669.

St. Basil's Convent, v.30, p.945.
St. Bernard, settlement at, v.23, p.724.
Saint-Caste, Capt., noted, v.23, p.436.
St. Charles Academy, v.30, p.957.
St. Charles Hotel, headquarters for Butler, v.24, p.465, 466; Butler forces way into, v.27, p.497, 513, 737, 747, 748; New Eng. Soc. of N. O. has banquet in, v.27, p.751-54; meeting of Dem. St. Central Com., v.27, p.1091.
St. Charles Institute, v.30, p.860-862.
"St. Charles Lyceum Lottery," noted, v.31, p.717.
St. Charles Municipal Drainage Dist., v.30, p.690.
St. Charles Parish, in 1860, v.21, p.1113-15; rice crop of, 1874-1875, v.23, p.554.
St. Charles Theatre, meeting at, v.24, p.506; built, 1835, v.26, p.370-71; noted, v.26, p.375, 382, 384, 387, 388; Joseph Jefferson medallion in, v.26, p.1150; Jefferson's appearance in, v.26, p.1151-67 passim.; opened 1835 by Caldwell, v.28, p.204; description, v.28, p.205; season 1835-36, v.28, p.204-12; 1836-37, v.28, p.218-24; 1837-38, v.28, p.229-34; becomes Vauxhall Garden for summer season 1838, v.28, p.234-35; seasons 1838-39, v.28, p.240-45; 1839-40, v.28, p.247-50; 1840-41, v.28, p.253-57; 1841-42, v.28, p.264-68; destroyed by fire 1842, v.28, p.268, 274.
St. Clair, Benoit de, sketch, v.28, p.813n.;

claims on Belle Isle, v.28, p.915.
St. Cosme, Father, French missionary to Natchez Indians, v.31, p.578.
St. Denis, Charles Juchereau de, brother-in-law of LaForest to whom Tonti-LaForest-Accaux partnership was in debt, v.26, p.639; given charge of Ohio, v.26, p.646; mine hunting on Red R., v.26, p.650; his journey up Red R. noted, v.26, p.687, 688; established post at Natchitoches, 1714, v.26, p.731; attacked Natchez Indians, v.26, p.733; established post on Ohio R., v.26, p.737, noted, v.26, p.753.
St. Denis, noted, v.25, p.399, 983.
St. Domingo, recognition by France, v.24, p.947-48, 851, 955, 972; debt of, v.24, p.1006-07.
St. Francis Academy, v.30, p.963.
St. Francis of Sales, Academy of, v.30, p.957.
St. Francisville, and W. Fla. Rev., v.21, p.76ff.; in 1860, v.21, p.1134-35; noted, v.25, p.50, 157; home of R. C. Wickliffe, v.25, p.674, 675, 707; noted, v.28, p.944, 945; anti abolition meeting, v.28, p.952; Dem. barbecue for selecting cand. for Gov., v.28, p.957, 958; noted, v.28, p.972; Johnson's burial place, v.28, p.981.
St. Francis Xavier School, v.30, p.958.
Ste. Genevieve, and French Rev., v.22, p.85.
St. Helena Parish, minutes of Police Jury of, 1813, v.23, p.405-27; rules and regulations governing police jury of, 1813, v.23, p.407-08; taxes for revenue, v.23, p.411-13; laws concerning cattle, v.23, p.414-17; laws regulating fences, v.23, p.417; laws concerning roads and bridges, v.23, p.418-24; payment of members of police jury of, v.23, p.426.
Ste. Hermine, La Dame de, will of, v.21, p.671-73.
St. James Grammer School, v.30, p.897.
St. James Parish, in 1860, v.21, p.1118-22; meeting of planters, v.25, p.114; sugar area, v.25, p.187; and the granger movement, v.26, p.1063; crevasse in, v.26, p.1072.
St. John Bayou, noted, v.25, p.940.
St. John's High School, v.30, p.788.
St. John's Hospital, original N. O. Charity Hospital, v.31, p.9, 13.
St. John's Plains and W. Fla. Rev., v.21, p.77, 685.
"St. John the Baptist Parish, Its History,"
Lubin F. Laurent, v.7, p.316; in 1860, v.21, p.1115-18; slave revolt in, v.22, p.144-46; crevasse in, v.26, p.1072.
St. Joseph, La., noted, v.24, p.81.
St. Joseph's Academy, v.30, p.941.
St. Joseph's College for Boys, v.30, p.948.
St. Joseph's School, v.30, p.962.
St. Katherine's Hall, v.30, p.877.
"St. Landry, Mother of Parishes," Gilbert L. Dupre, v.8, p.420; German colony in, v.23, p.513-14; settlement of, v.23, p.558; noted, v.25, p.121, 162, 319, 321, 371; noted, v.26, p.980, 985; and the Cong. election of 1894, v.26, p.1098; noted, v.26, p.1101, 1102; disorder in 1896, v.26, p.1107; Populist legis. from, v.26, p.1109; riots in 1896, v.28, p.1179.
St. Laurent, Madame de, La. educator, proprietress select school, St. Martinsville, v.30, p.911-912; noted, v.30, p.969.
St. Louis Cathedral, legislation and litigation affecting the titles, v.18, p.363-76; noted, v.25, p.365; trustee problem, v.31, p.897-971; under French, v.31, p.899-900; under Spanish, v.31, p.900-03; under Americans, v.31, p.903-07.
"St. Louis," early slaver, v.23, p.866.
St. Louis Hotel, construction and financing of, v.25, p.990-91; burning and reconstruction of, v.25, p.991-92; description of, v.25, p.992-94; sale of, v.25, p.1056; noted, v.27, p.740; Clay Ball at, v.27, p.745-47; Clay's reception, v.27, p.749-50, 771, 997.
St. Louis, housing of, 1764-1821, v.21, p.337-48; and revolutionary agitators, v.22, p.88, 92; trade with Spanish internal provinces, v.23, p.843; fortification maintained by O'Reilly, v.26, p.740.
St. Louis Institute, v.30, p.858-60.
Ste. Marie, Faubourg, history of, v.22, p.385-427.
St. Martin Parish, meeting of planters, v.25, p.73, 162; formation of, v.28, p.1129; outstanding men of, v.28, p.1129, noted, v.28, p.1131.
Saint Martin, Pierre Bauchet, deposition of, v.23, p.725.
St. Martin's captured by British, v.23, p.434.
St. Martinville, noted, v.22, p.795; description of, v.24, p.41; noted, v.25, p.937; noted, v.28, p.759, 763, 811, 817, 822ff., 835ff., 883.
St. Mary Parish, and nullification, v.25, p.92; sugar area, v.25, p.140, 141, 160, 187; noted, v.27, p.365, 522; Donelson

Caffery a sugar planter in, v.27, p.783; Caffery a parish judge of, v.27, p.783; Murphy, sheriff, v.27, p.784; Sypher, state senator from, v.27, p.785, 790, 821, 843, 980, 1040, 1041; formation of, v.28, p.1129; noted, v.28, p.1130, 1131; reconstruction in, v.28, p.1133-34; 1st post war election in, v.28, p.1134; election of 1872, v.28, p.1136; election of 1876, v.28, p.1138; support of Foster, v.28, p.1140; and 1892 election, v.28, p.1156; geography, v.32, p.17-19; origin of the people, v.32, p.19-20; earlier history, v.32, p.23-23; land holdings, v.32, p.23-26; slaveholdings: Whites: Free Colored, v.32, p.26-28; plantation premises, v.32, p.28-34; plantation discipline, v.32, p.34-38; slave life, v.32, p.38-42; crops, v.32, p.43-44; marketing, v.32, p.44-49; livestock, v.32, p.49-50; location of towns, v.32, p.50-52; Franklin, v.32, p.52-55; civic services, v.32, p.55-59; commercial and social centers, v.32, p.59-62; organizations, v.32, p.62-65; amusements, v.32, p.65-73; religion and education, v.32, p.73-81; health, v.32, p.81-84; crime, v.32, p.84-89; newspapers, v.32, p.89-94; literature, v.32, p.94-96; bibl., v.32, p.96-102; population in 1850, v.32, p.19.

"St. Mary Parish, A Social History of, 1845-1860," by Jewell Lynn de Grummond, v.32, p.16.

St. Mary's Academy of Natchitoches, v.30, p.949.

St. Mary's Academy of New Orleans, v.30, p.952.

St. Mary's Academy, v.30, p.824-25.

St. Mary's Church, Bayou Goula, v.25, p.206, 207.

St. Mary's Dominican Academy, v.30, p.953.

St. Mary's Dominican College, records of, v.24, p.326, 352.

St. Mary's School of Baton Rouge, sketch of, v.30, p.780-82.

St. Maxent, Maximilliano de, and W. Fla. Rev., v.21, p.100n.; commander at Plaquemines post, v.26, p.748.

St. Michael's Convent in St. James, v.25, p.730.

St. Michael's of the Sacred Heart, v.30, p.958-960.

St. Patrick's Hall, Nicholls and Wiltz inaugurated, v.32, p.399.

St. Paul, Henry, and Batture controversy, v.23, p.1064-1067.

St. Paul, John, Remarks on Frederick D. King, v.6, p.203.

Saint, Percy, "Thomas Jefferson and Government by Party," v.8, p.41.

St. Peter and Paul's College, v.30, p.940.

St. Peter's Academy, v.30, p.832-833.

St. Peter Street Theatre in N. O., v.26, p.369.

St. Philip Street Theatre, established 1808, v.26, p.369; Ludlow rented, v.26, p.370; noted, v.28, p.91ff., 102ff.; Allen's Co. at, v.28, p.113-14.

St. Romes, J. C. de, noted, v.25, p.62, 77, 91.

Saint-Saens, autograph of, in Howard-Tilton Memorial Library, v.24, p.330.

St. Simeon's Select School, v.30, p.954-55.

"St. Tammany Parish, The Choctaw of," by David I. Bushnell, Jr., v.1, sec.1, p.11.

St. Tammany Parish, v.29, p.73n., 75, 78, 79, 80, 102, 121.

St. Victoria plantation, v.25, p.216.

St. Vincent's Academy (Ascension Parish), v.30, p.937.

St. Vincent's Academy (Rapides Parish), v.30, p.958.

St. Vincent's Academy (Shreveport), v.30, p.942-43.

St. Vincent's School of New Orleans, v.30, p.953-54.

St. Xavier, Sister de, appointed for officer of Hospitaliere, v.29, p.594-95.

Salcedo, Manuel de, and La. Purchase, v.23, p.80; noted, v.23, p.714; noted, v.24, p.7, 8; transfer of La. to U. S., v.28, p.1018; aid in returning fugitive slaves, v.28, p.1072, 1073; letter to Indians, v.28, p.1086; council on Indian trade, v.28, p.1088; noted, v.28, p.1093; Spanish Gov. of La., v.31, p.632.

Salcedo, Nemesio, comd't-gen'l and the neutral ground, v.28, p.1023, 1024, 1028, 1031, 1033, 1035, 1036, 1038, 1045, 1073.

Salcedo, Nirnecio de, noted, v.22, p.728, 776-777.

"Sale of Real Property in La. in 1769," ed. by Henry P. Dart, v.21, p.674-76.

Sales, Louis de, noted, v.22, p.815, 818.

"Sally," privateer, v.23, p.441.

Salmen, Ella Rose, 2nd wife of Wm. Henry Sullivan, v.29, p.186.

Salmon, Edme Gatien, ordonnation in N.O., v.26, p.693, 694, 710.

Salmon, Sieur, works at Balise in absence of Deverges, v.29, p.579; describes hospital in letter, v.29, p.580; sends plans of progress of work and letter of needs to King, v.29, p.580-583; explains delay of building, v.29, p.584; expresses satisfaction of official chaplain, v.29, p.596-597; expresses gratitude to King in letter, v.29, p.599.

Salt, in La., v.24, p.70; v.32, p.12.

Saltonstall, Leverett, and 1842 tariff, v.25, p.116, 117.

"Saltus, J. Sanford," by W. O. Hart, v.5, p.499; "A Remembrance," by Edward Alexander Parsons, v.5, p.493.

Sambola, Antoine, amendment to lottery bill, v.31, p.719; attacks Campbell, v.31, p.721; noted, v.31, p.747, 793; ousted as senator, v.27, p.536; amendment to bill providing for other lotteries in La. providing license is paid and bond given, v.27, p.971; Agusti counsel, v.27, p.984.

"Samuel Jarvis Peters," by Rita Katherine Carey, v.30, p.439-480.

San Andres, noted, v.24, p.654, 655, 659, 679.

San Antonio, in 1854, v.23, p.1146, 1147; noted, v.24, p.641.

San Blas Indians, noted, v.24, p.678.

Sanders, Albert Godfrey, Splendid Work on French Archives of Louisiana (Editor's Chair), v.12, p.464; Translations by: "Documents Covering the Impeachment of Bienville," Introduction by Henry P. Dart, v.14, p.5; "Documents Covering First Cargo of African Slaves for Louisiana," Introduction by Henry P. Dart, v.14, p.163; "Documents Concerning the Crozat Regime in Louisiana, 1712-1717," Introduction by Henry P. Dart, I, v.15, p.589; II, v.16, p.293; III, IV, v.17, p.268, 452; "Mississippi Provincial Archives, 1704-1743, French Dominion," Vol. III (Review), v.15, p.707.

Sanders, Geo. N., Confederate secret agent, v.29, p.1247, 1249, 1250.

Sanders, J. Y., v.28, p.1129, 1130, 1188; favored primary system, v.28, p.1196; declined to be U. S. senator, v.28, p.1222; noted, v.30, p.1050.

Sanders, Mary Elizabeth, "Letters of a Confederate Soldier," v.29, p.1229-1240.

Sandoval, Manuel, Gov. of Tex., v.28, p.1021.

Sandoz, William J., "A Brief History of St. Landry Parish," v.8, p.221.

Sandridge, John M., returning board, v.31, p.1094.

San Felipe, fort on Lake Izabal, v.24, p.664.

San Fernando Fort, established, v.21, p.55.

"San Fernando," ketch, v.24, p.629, 633, 634, 637.

San Gabriel de Manchac, Sp. fort, v.25, p.936; deserted and reestablished, v.25, p.936-37; goes out of existence, v.25, p.939; built by Sp., v.27, p.630, 631; regarrisoned, 1775, v.27, p.644, 661.

Sang-mele, defined, v.25, p.301.

"Sanitary Conditions in New Orleans Under the Spanish Regime, 1799-1800" (Letter to the Cabildo from El Sindico Procurado General del Publico, dated January 24, 1800), translated by Laura L. Porteous, introduction by Henry P. Dart, v.15, p.610.

Sanitation, in Sp. New Orleans, v.22, p.676-77.

San Luis Potosi, and Spanish insurgents, v.23, p.737.

San Martin y Cuebas, Salvador de, robbed by Laffite, v.22, p.1064-65.

San Maxent, Celestino, expedition of, v.22, p.1014-15.

San Michel, located, v.21, p.1130.

Sansum, O. B., address to Prog. League, v.27, p.1063.

Santa Catalina, described, v.24, p.654; noted, v.24, p.656, 657.

Santa Fe de Bogota, viceroyalty of, v.24, p.655; liberation by Bolivar, v.24, p.666.

Santa Marta, noted, v.24, p.690.

Santander, Francisco de Paula, noted, v.24, p.667, 690; charged with increasing Granadine army, v.22, p.673; reply to petition by Aury, v.24, p.686-87.

Santa Teresa, Spanish fort, v.24, p.654.

Santo Domingo, slave revolt, v.21, p.26, 39-40, 88n.; trade with, v.22, p.779; noted, v.25, p.318, 327, 353, 373, 975; refugees to La., v.25, p.302, 304; mixed races in, v.25, p.306.

San Tomas de Angostura, noted, v.24, p.666.

"Sarah Bernhardt in N. O.," by John Smith Kendall, v.26, p.770-82.

Sargent, Dr. Percy, son-in-law of Gov. Isaac Johnson, v.28, p.947, 981.

Sargent, E. L., noted, v.23, p.1256.

"Sarpis," privateer of Laffites, v.23, p.747.

Sarpy, Bernardo, noted, v.22, p.95.

Sarpy Crevasse, v.26, p.1072.

Sarpy, Juan Bautista, buys land of B. Gravier, v.22, p.397, 406, 407; sues J. Gravier, v.22, p.416.

Sarpy, Mrs. George, noted, v.24, p.764.

Sarrazin, Jean, noted, v.23, p.774.

Satte, ———, noted, v.22, p.1024.

Saucedo, Antoine, Texas political chief, v.31, p.648, 650, 659; charged, v.31, p.658; Bastrop's executor, v.31, p.676.

Saucier, Corinne L., "History of Avoyelles Parish, Louisiana," revd.; v.30, p.342-346.

Saul, Joseph, noted, v.22, p.434, 435, 439; duel with Nolte, v.23, p. 446-47.

Saunders, Judge Lafayette, presiding at const. con., v.25, p.1007.

Saunderson, John P., noted, v.22, p.434, 439.

Sauve, Pierre, presented memorial to congress, v.31, p.366, 367; noted, v.31, p.287.

Sauvinet, Joseph, member of New Orleans Assn., v.24, p.627, 656, 672; mentioned, v.21, p.1092; noted, v.22, p.1034, 1041; noted, v.23, p.436; wrecking of privateer, v.23, p.441-42; and privateers, v.23, p.747, 764, 851.

Sauvole, Gov., left in charge of colony by Iberville, death of, v.26, p.726.

"Savage Law of the French Regime in Louisiana" (Judicial Condemnation of the Body of a Suicide in 1765), translation by Heloise H. Cruzat, introduction by Henry P. Dart, v.15, p.482.

Savannah, brawl in 1810, v.24, p.613.

Savary, Joseph, noted, v.22, p.1068; and filibusters, v.23, p.851; noted, v.24, p.627, 628, 629, 634, 638, 642, 643; noted, v.25, p.327, 328, 329.

Savinilla, noted, v.24, p.686, 688, 690, 695.

"Savior of his Country," title of Brion, v.24, p.652.

Sawyer, Samuel, Conf. soldier, v.26, p.965.

Saxe-Weimer, Duke of, noted, v.23, p.873.

Saxon, Lyle, noted, v.24, p.308; quoted, v.25, p.307, 308; noted, v.25, p.312, 367, 368; "Lafitte the Pirate," reviewed by J. Fair Hardin, v.14, p.441.

Scarborough, Lucy Paxton, "So It Was When Life Began," v.13, p.428.

"Scene of the LeBreton Murder," Frank H. Waddill, v.8, p.266.

Schaffner, T. P., telegraph contractor, v.31, p.437; attorney for Morse, v.31, p.463; describes trial, v.31, p.464-65.

Schaible, Carl, N. O. musician, v.31, p.143.

Schenck, Chas. H., on lottery bill, v.27, p.1042.

Schiller Centenary Festival, noted, v.26, p.380.

Schilling, Rev. Oscar J., cited, v.24, p.144.

"Schism of 1805 in New Orleans," ed. by S. Faye, v.22, p.98-141.

Schlatre, Michael, Genealogy of family, v.20, p.727-37.

Schlenker, Jacob, confed. soldier, v.26, p.969.

Schlicher, R. E., pres. of Rice Festival, v.27, p.1209.

Schlinder, Charles, cited, v.24, p.160.

Schmidt, Gustavus, "O'Reilly's Ordinance of 1770" (Reprinted from Translation in Louisiana Law Journal I, Part 2, Page 61, August, 1841), v.11, p.237.

Schmidt, Gustav, manuscript of "Prince Eugen," in L.S.U. Music School Library, v.24, p.348.

Schmidt, W. B., noted, v.23, p.517.

Schneider, Leonard, proposed N. O. Lottery Co. of State of La., v.27, p.1004.

Schneider, Louis, noted, v.23, p.517, 520.

Schomberg, ———, duel of, v.23, p.447-48.

Schoolcraft, Luke, N. O. minstrel, sketch of, v.30, p.135-138.

School of Citizenship, in N. Y., v.24, p.724.

"Schools of New Orleans During the First Quarter of the Nineteenth Century," by Stuart Grayson Noble, Ph.D., v.14, p.65.

Schreiber, Adolph, noted, v.23, p.517.

Schroeder, Frederick, noted, v.22, p.192.

Schuler, Francis, noted, v.22, p.194.

Schuler, Kathryn R., "Women in Public Affairs in La. During Reconstruction," v.19, p.668-750.

Schuller, Rudolph, collection in Institute of Middle American Research, v.24, p.332.

Schultz, Christian, author on Louisiana, v.31, p.396, 403, 410.

Schuylers, of N. Y., v.24, p.700.

Schwager, Peter, noted, v.23, p.521.

Schwarz, Louis, noted, v.23, p.518.

Schweggman, C. A., noted, v.24, p.150.

Schweickhardt, Rev. Louis, cited, v.24, p.141.

Schwing Lumber and Shingle Company, v.30, p.1039.

Scio, noted, v.24, p.1081.

Scott, Ann Smith (see Smith, Ann), married John Scott, children of, v.29, p.290.

Scott Bluffs, v.28, p.14, 35, 36; Red Pole site believed to be near, v.28, p.38, 40, 42; noted, v.28, p.67. v.21, p.501.

Scott, J. M., and New Orleans theatre,

Scott, John, noted, v.21, p.131n.; identified, v.21, p.766n.

Scott, Luther C., publisher of "Signal," v.27, p.1186; buys "Signal," v.27, p.1186-87; sells "Signal," v.27, p.1187.

Scott, Mary Ann, wife of J. M. Wells, v.31, p.999.

Scott, Mrs. Emily T., collection in L.S.U. Archives, v.24, p.344.

Scott, Sir Walter, popularity in N. O., v.21, p.420-517.

Scott, Susannah, 2nd wife of Philander Smith, v.29, p.285.

Scott, Thos. W., pres. dem. Conv., B. R., v.28, p.958.

Scott, W. E., Councilman of Crowley, v.27, p.1147.

Scott, Winfield, noted, v.24, p.1159.

Scramuzza, V. M., "Galveztown, A Spanish Settlement of Colonial La.," v.13, p.553.

Scroggs, W. O., study of La. archives, v.24, p.317, 320, 352.

Scully, Frederick, and marshland reclamation, v.30, p.685, 697.

Seaman, Mrs. J. E., La. educator, organizer Southern Academic Institute, New Orleans, v.30, p.875.

"Seargent S. Prentiss, Whig Orator of the Old South," by Dallas C. Dickey, rev'd by T. Harry Williams, v.29, p.202-203.

Sebastian, Benjamin, sketch, v.21, p.44n.; arrival in N. O., 1795, v.21, p.66.

Secession, protest against in La. Convention, v.19, p.199-203; sentiment in Tex., v.23, p.1161; in Tex., 1860, v.23, p.1168; in the South, v.23, p.1170-1171; gradually accepted in New Orleans, v.24, p.434-39; Edward Livingston's arguments against, v.24, p.722; Sec. issue and 1833 tariff, v.25, p.97, 99, 104; reaction to in La., v.26, p.994-98; the secession Conv. of 1861, v.26, p.998-1004.

"Secession, Financial and Economic Disturbances in New Orleans on the Eve of," by John Muir, contributed by Milledge L. Bonham, v.13, p.32.

Sedella, Fray Antonio de, Spanish secret agent in N. O., v.21, p.677-78; and filibusters, v.21, p.813; garden of, v.21, p.1069-74; and Laffites, v.21, p.1088, 1097; and Schism of 1805, N. O., v.22, p.98-141; letters to Casa Calvo, v.22, p.117, 124-25, 130-31; letter from Walsh, v.22, p.118-20; letters to Walsh, v.22, p.118, 120-21; letter from Casa Calvo, v.22, p.125; noted, v.22, p.814; and Picornell, v.23, p.736ff.; letter from J. Laffite, v.23, p.769; Spanish agent meets Toledo, v.23, p.827; noted, v.23, p.844; letters in Bibliotheca Parsoniana, v.24, p.311; noted, v.31, p.901, 902.

"Sedella, Fray Antoine de, An Appreciation of," by Clarence Wyatt Bispham, v.2, p.24.

Sedition Law of 1798, noted, v.24, p.711.

Seger, A. B., vice pres. N. O. Opelousas and Great Western Railroad, v.30, p.1074-1075, 1153; pres., v.30, p.1162; noted, v.30, p.1165, 1169.

"Seherin von Prevorst," by Kerner, v.24, p.384.

Seiferth, Hermann J., newspaperman, "Old Days on the N. O. Picayune," v.33, p.338-41.

Seip, Frederick, opposed lottery bill, v.27, p.1043; La. Sen., v.28, p.1145.

Sejour, Victor, noted, v.25, p.359-60.

Selby, minority report on Elliott case, v.31, p.684.

Seldner, Ed. W., designated city clerk of Bogalusa, v.29, p.113.

"Selecting a Governor for the Territory of Orleans," by Walter Prichard, v.31, p.269-393.

Sellers, Ben, brief sketch, v.29, p.120n.

Semet, Antoine, noted, v.22, p.1034.

Semi-Centennial 14th September, 1874, W. O. Hart, J. A. Renshaw, H. W. Robinson, B. F. Jonas, v.7, p.570; Editorial Introduction, Henry P. Dart, v.7, p.570; History of Events Leading up to the Battle, W. O. Hart, v.7, p.571; The Call to Arms, v.7, p.596; General Odgen's Official Report, v.7, p.597; Metropolitan Police Story of the Battle, v.7, p.602; Republican Party After the Battle, Henry W. Robinson, v.7, p.604; The 14th of September, 1874, as viewed by the Supreme Court of Louisiana, James A. Renshaw, v.7, p.618; Roster of Citizen Soldiery, v.7, p.621; Ceremonies Attending Laying of Cornerstone of Monument at Head of Canal Street, September 14, 1891, v.7, p.633.

Semmes, Thomas J., noted, v.22, p.169; counsel for Lottery Co., 1879, v.27, p.998, 1008; Counsel for Morris, v.27, p.1051, 1082; speaker, v.31, p.538; noted, v.31, p.764; defends Wickliffe, v.31, p.696.

Semple, Henry Churchill, study of Ursulines, v.24, p.335.

Semple, W. M., staff of "Crescent," v.30, p.274.

"Senate, Jurisdiction of the, Tribunals of Criminal Jurisdiction in Ancient Rome," by Charles Gayarre, v.33, p.210.

Senet, Joseph, sketch, v.28, p.772n.

Sennegy, Rene de (Father de la Peychardiere), Jefferson College, v.31, p.854.

Sentemanat, Angele de Marigny de, married Neville Soule, v.25, p.980.

Separation of powers, theory of, v.24, p.711.

"Seraphine," and attempt to rescue Napoleon, v.24, p.27; noted, v.24, p.374.

Sergeant, John, noted, v.24, p.1078.

Seringue, Mikel, master carpenter, contractor for building of Convent, v.29, p.575-76.

Serpas, Joseph, Jr., noted, v.24, p.357.

Serpas, Joseph, Sr., noted, v.24, p.357.

Servell, French inventor of telegraph estimates cost, v.31, p.428.

"Servinien's Case, 1752," by Henry P. Dart, v.4, p.290.

Sessums, Davis, Episcopal bishop of La., vice-pres. Anti-Lottery meeting, v.27, p.1060, 1070.

Seton, Elizabeth Ann Bailey, establishes Sisters of Charity, v.31, p.53.

Settoon, D. F., named in Kellogg impeachment, v.31, p.712.

Severn, Robert, noted, v.23, p.146.

Sevet, Sieur, suit against, v.21, p.1012.

Sevier (Seaver, Xavier), husband of Mary Ann Duff, lawyer of N. O., v.28, p.933ff.

Sevin, Felix, noted, v.23, p.556.

Sewall, Cora C., daughter of Paul Octave Hebert, v.31, p.494.

Seward & Thompson, rice firm, v.23, p.555.

Seward, William Henry, noted, v.23, p.1181; v.24, p.114, 511, 515, 516.

Seymour collection, in La. State Museum, v.24, p.319.

Seymour, Horatio, Democratic nominee, v.30, p.569.

Seymour, I. G., ed. "Commercial Bulletin," sketch, v.30, p.289; noted, v.24, p.66.

Seymour, Truman, noted, v.29, p.1241.

Seymour, Wm. J., early N. O. newspaperman, v.29, p.773, 775-76; v.30, p.289, 290.

"Shadow Over the City," by J. S. Kendall, v.22, p.142-65.

"Shady Retreat," Foster plantation, v.28, p.1130.

Shakespeare, Joseph A., and the Mafia, v.22, p.509, 513; mayor of N. O. accepts Lottery Co.'s offer of aid, v.27, p.1027-28.

Shakespeare, Wm., his plays on the N. O. German stage, v.26, p.399-400; noted, v.26, p.427.

Shaler, William, and Mexican Revolution, v.22, p.722n.; and Toledo, v.23, p.827, 855n.; special agent of the U. S., v.23, p.1001; noted, v.25, p.294, 295, 296, 297, 298; special gov't agent, v.25, p.656; his warning to Toledo, v.25, p.662; U. S. agent in Natchitoches, v.28, p.1054, 1055, 1094.

Shannon, Rev. James, pres. Centenary College, v.31, p.884.

"Share system," or "cropping system" and the post bellum negro, v.26, p.1056.

Sharkey, W. L., noted, v.23, p.204.

Sharp, John C., appt'd to rep. La. at Memphis R. R. Conv., v.28, p.974.

Sharpe, Peter, and 1824 tariff bill, v.25, p.39.

Shattuck's Bill, also Lottery Bill or House Bill No. 214, v.27, p.1045, 1050, 1057.

Shattuck, S. O., introduced bill to let people decide on Lottery Question, v.27, p.1033, 1046; v.28, p.1143.

Shaw, Arthur Marvin, Jr., "Wm. Preston Johnston: A Transitional Figure of the Confed.," rev'd, v.26, p.1171-72; "Study of Centenary College," v.24, p.339, 352; "A Threatened Witch Hunt in an Ante-Bellum Louisiana College," v.31, p.123-29; "Rampant Individualism in an Ante-Bellum Southern College," v.31, p.877; "A. B. Longstreet's Brief Sojourn in Louisiana," v.32, p.777.

Shaw, C. L., noted, v.23, p.568.

Shaw, Daniel, commissioned sheriff by Kellogg, v.29, p.419.

Shaw, Kate, N. O. educator, v.30, p.873-74.

Shaw, Matthew, confederate soldier taken prisoner, v.29, p.1215.

"She Adder," letter from, v.24, p.528.

Shea, F. J., contractor, v.29, p.96.

Sheafe, Charles F., Baton Rouge telegraph representative, v.31, p.448.

Shelby, Charmion Clair, ed., "Grenier's Journal of His Voyage to Vera Cruz, 1745," v.21, p.631-55.

Sheldon, Mr., secretary at French legation, v.24, p.948, 952, 956, 962, 975, 979, 993, 997, 998, 1003, 1006, 1014, 1019, 1085-86, 1091, 1094, 1096, 1097, 1098, 1101, 1105, 1108, 1115.

Shell Petroleum Co., v.29, p.504, 507, 508.

Shepherd Brown & Co., conducted trade with interior, v.26, p.37, 38, 40, 41.

Shepherd, Rezon D., noted, v.22, p.439, 449.

Shepley, Geo. F., military comdt. in N. O., v.27, p.506, 508; became acting mayor of N. O., v.27, p.512-13, 523; noted, v.23, p.1135; v.24, p.499.

Sherborne, H. N., district att'y, counsel for Mason, v.27, p.1051.

Sheridan, Geo. A., Fusionist claimant to Cong., 1872, v.27, p.581-82; debate in Cong. regarding claim to seat, v.27, p.583-89, 595.

Sheridan, Phil, noted, v.23, p.1224, 1238.

Sheridan, Philip H., noted, v.24, p.114; commander of La. Mil. Dist. under Reconstruction Acts, v.30, p.546; noted, v.30, p.549; and riot, v.31, p.1083-84; interferes, v.31, p.1088-90; on Wells, v.31, p.1090; dismisses Wells, v.31, p.1091; Wells' statement, v.31, p.1115.

Sherman, Gen. W. T., letter to Gen. Banks, v.32, p.107; noted, v.32, p.105, 107, 108, 109, 111, 113; message to Gen. Banks, v.32, p.116; noted, v.32, p.124, 130, 146; message from Gen. Banks, v.32, p.126; message from Admiral Porter, v.32, p.127.

Sherman, William T., first supt. of La. State Seminary of Learning, v.20, p.55; noted, v.23, p.1213; in Ga., v.23, p.1217; noted, v.24, p.61, 84, 105, 107; first supt. of La. State Seminary, v.25, p.699; appeals for aid for negro, 1861, v.25, p.737-38; noted, v.29, p.1241, 1242, 1244, 1245; first supt. of Louisiana Seminary, v.31, p.517.

Sherwood, William, work on "De Bow's Review," v.29, p.373.

Shields, Bernard C., v.27, p.779; favored bill of 1890, v.27, p.1033; motion in House that Lottery Bill be sent to Sec. of State Mason for promulgation without gov's signature, v.27, p.1045; address to Prog. League, v.27, p.1063; sen. from Orleans, v.28, p.1149.

Shields, Joseph D., collection in L.S.U. Archives, v.24, p.344.

Shields, Thos., purser of the Navy stationed at N. O., v.28, p.871, 872.

Shiloh, effect of battle in New Orleans, v.24, p.448.

Ship Island, noted, v.24, p.440, 450, 531, 533.

Shipley, Captain, noted, v.24, p.512.

"Ship Lists of Passengers Leaving France for Louisiana," translated by Albert Laplace Dart, 1718-1724, I, v.14, p.516; II, III, v.15, p.68, 453; IV, v.21, p.965-78.

Ships, privateer vessels, v.23, p.118-30.

Sholars, D. M., v.28, p.1172; fusion cand., lt.-gov., v.28, p.1900, 1192.

Short, Samuel, noted, v.22, p.191.

Shpall, Leo, "A Jewish Agricultural Colony in La.," v.20, p.821-31; "The First Synagogue in La.," v.21, p.518-31; "Rabbi James Koppel Guttheim," v.22, p.166-80; "Adah Isaacs Menken," v.26, p.162-68; "Louis Moreau Gottschalk," v.30, p.120-127.

Shreve, Henry Miller; "The First Great River Captain," by J. Fair Hardin, v.10, p.25; "A Biography," by Caroline S. Pfaff, v.10, p.192; "Forgotten Service," v.3, p.137; founder of Shreveport, v.18, p.785-91; removed raft from Red River, v.18, p.769-75; champion of free river navigation, v.18, p.822-29; noted, v.23, p.1011; v.25, p.400, 401.

Shreve Memorial Library, Shreveport, v.24, p.339.

Shreveport Female High School, v.30, p.796.

Shreveport Female Institute, v.30, p.798.

"Shreveport Group," noted, v.25, p.212.

Shreveport, La., centennial celebration, v.18, p.759; founding, v.18, p.785-91; founders, v.18, p.811-19; the Confederate capital of La., v.18, p.863-71; in 1860, v.21, p.1175-78; description of, c. 1838, v.24, p.37-39; noted, v.24, p.84, 87, 93, 100; noted, v.25, p.397, 398, 400, 401; noted, v.26, p.973; made capital of La., v.26, p.1028, 1029, 1039; population, 1860, v.27, p.488; Capital of La., v.27, p.520, 541; relief from Lottery Co. in Red R. flood, v.27, p.1028, 1061; Capital of La., v.27, p.1226; Hy. W. Allen's official report of fed'l troops in Western La., v.27, p.1226-28.

Shreveport Seminary, sketch of, v.30, p.801-802.

Shreveport University, v.30, p.796-797.

Shugg, Roger W., "A Suppressed Co-operationist Protest Against Secession," v.19, p.199-203; "Suffrage and Representation in Ante-Bellum La.," v.19, p.390-406; "The New Orleans General Strike of 1892," v.21, p.547-60; "Origin of Class Struggle in Louisiana," rev'd by E. A. Davis, v.23, p.827-88.

Sibley, Cyrus, and W. Fla. Rev., v.21, p.85; noted, v.22, p.788.

Sibley, H. H., noted, v.24, p.69.

"Sibley, Dr. John, of Natchitoches, 1757-1837," by G. P. Whittington, v.10, p.467; "Journal of Dr. John Sibley, July-October, 1802," v.10, p.474; "Letters of Dr. Sibley to his Son, Samuel Hopkins Sibley, 1803-1821," v.10, p.498; "Letters of Dr. Sibley to Christopher C. Baldwin of Worcester, Mass., 1832-1835," v.10, p.508; and Long's expedition, v.22, p.744; noted, v.23, p.1115; explorer of Red River, noted, v.25, p.294, 297, 667n.; quoted, v.25, p.640; sketch, v.28, p.845n.; noted, v.28, p.886; report of, v.28, p.890, 892; Indian agent at Natchitoches, v.28, p.1031, 1082n.; activities among Indians, v.28, p.1086-87; noted, v.28, p.1095.

Sibley, Mary Wells, sister of J. M. Wells, v.31, p.1000.

Sibley, Robert F., trustee of Franklin Academy, 1838, v.29, p.84.

"Sicilies, Auguste Davezac's Mission to the Kingdom of the Two, 1833-1834," by Howard R. Marraro, v.32, p.791.

Sicily Island, in 1860, v.21, p.1204-1205; noted, v.25, p.929, 930; noted, v.26, p.655; Perier's victory, v.26, p.672.

Sickles, Jackson E., levee board member, v.31, p.542.

Sidney, Algernon, noted, v.24, p.701.

"Sieur George," by Cable, v.24, p.168.

"Signal," campaign for electric and water works for Crowley, v.27, p.1145-46; advocate of improved fire dept., v.27, p.1149; urged farmers to support local milling co., v.27, p.1164-65; moved from Rayne to Crowley, 1886, v.27, p.1185; Burkdoll, editor, v.27, p.1185-86; advertising important function, v.27, p.1186; becomes daily, v.27, p.1186-87.

"Signal No. 8," gunboat, v.24, p.96.

Siguenza y Gongora, Carlos de, noted, v.22, p.941.

Sigur, L. J., noted, v.22, p.1134, 1142, 1145, 1146; and Lopez expeditions, v.22, p.1097n., 1121n., 1122, 1123; v.24, p.758; v.30, p.297-298, 303.

Silk, failure of cultivation, v.22, p.996; cultivation of, v.23, p.1043; U. S. study in France, v.24, p.1060, 1068.

Silva, Vicente Pazos, noted, v.24, p.645.

Silver, James W., "Gen. Edmund P. Gaines and the Protection of the S. Western Frontiers," v.20, p.183-91.

Silver question, in La. in 1896, v.28, p.1170-71, 1173-74.

Silver, smuggled out of New Orleans, v.22, p.62n.

Simmons, T. E., Corporation rights of Lottery Co. transferred to, v.27, p.976; suit against, v.27, p.982-83.

Simmons, Wm., trustee of Franklin Academy, 1838, v.29, p.84.

Simmons, Z. E., noted, v.31, p.728, 730; member lottery co., v.31, p.729.

Simms, Richard, on the lottery question, v.27, p.1042.

Simms, Wm. Gilmore, v.29, p.373, 378, 391.

Simon, Edward, judge of La. Sup. Court, v.23, p.1029.

Simons, Dr. James, noted, v.26, p.75, 82; letter to Luzenberg on the success of operation on Seminole, Mary, v.26, p.89; noted, v.26, p.91.

Simpson, George A., "Early History of the Flag of the U. S.," v.28, p.258.

Simpson, John, noted, v.23, p.45, 387; petition of, v.23, p.376, 380.

Sims, Frank, N. O. musician, v.31, p.144.

Simsport, noted, v.24, p.85, 95.

Sisters of Charity, established, v.31, p.52-3; regard for, v.31, p.62-3; assume payment of hospital's debts, v.31, p.67; controversy over establishment of nursing school, v.31, p.70-6; noted, v.31, p.80; relieved of managerial duties, v.31, p.85; investigation of Charity Hospital, v.31, p.96.

Sisters of Divine Providence, noted, v.25, p.362.

Sisters of the Holy Family, Congregation of Negro religious order, v.25, p.363, 364, 731.

Skinner, E. K., remarks on Frederick D. King, v.6, p.207.

Skipper, Ottis Clark, "J. D. B. De Bow and the Seventh Census," v.22, p.479-91; "De Bow's Review after the Civil War," v.29, p.355-393.

Skipwith, Fulwar, and W. Fla. Rev., v.21, p.77ff., 707n., 714; letter from Audibert, v.21, p.87, 145-147, 150-152; letter from Grymes, v.21, p.89; letter from Steele, v.21, p.123; complaint against Dupree, Armstrong and Watter, v.21, p.123-24; inaugural address to Assembly of W. Fla., v.21, p.124-28; letter from Talleyrand, v.21, p.128; reply to inaugural address, v.21, p.129-31; orders to Collins, Baldwin and Johnson, v.21, p.136-38; letter from Audibert and Mills, v.21, p.139-41; letter to Madison, v.21, p.141-44, 147-148; to Ballinger, v.21, p.145; to Claiborne, v.21, p.149-50, 201-202; from Mills and Audibert, v.21, p.150-52; to Graham, v.21, p.156-158, 162-71; address to people of W. Fla., v.21, p.158-

61; letter to his constituents, v.21, p.171-79; owns one-fourth of Maison Rouge Grant, v.21, p.166; compromise with De Lassus, v.21, p.170; address to constituents, v.21, p.190-91; election address, Aug., 1812, v.21, p.193-98; receiver of land office, v.21, p.199n., dispute with Andrew Jackson, v.21, p.401-19; sketch, v.21, p.401n.; letter to Wm. Lewis, v.21, p.402-404; letter to Richmond Enquirer, v.21, p.404-405; letter to Jackson, v.21, p.405-11; noted, v.29, p.75n., 77; early life, v.31, p.298-99; appointed consul at Martinique, v.31, p.299; secretary to Monroe, v.31, p.299; consul general, v.31, p.300; commercial agent, v.31, p.301; secret mission, v.31, p.302-03; settlement in West Florida, v.31, p.303; financial difficulties, v.31, p.304-05; president West Florida Republic, v.31, p.306; enmity with Jackson, v.31, p.307; voyage to France, v.31, p.308; death, v.31, p.309; children, v.31, p.309.

Skipwith, George G., only son of Fulwar Skipwith, v.31, p.309.

Skipwith, Lelia, marries Thomas Bolling Robertson, v.21, p.78; elder daughter of Fulwar Skipwith, v.31, p.309.

Skipwith, P. H., noted, v.23, p.1236n.

Slack, J. L., La. educator, principal Minden Female Sem., v.30, p.930; estab. Minden Female College, v.30, p.931-33; noted, v.30, p.969.

Slade, Dr., Charter member Med. Soc., v.26, p.59, 60.

Slaten Fund, noted, v.25, p.776, 788, 789, 792-93, 795, 796, 808.

Slaughter, Dr. J. H., of Bogalusa Health Unit, v.29, p.86.

Slauson, Daniel D., collection in L.S.U. Archives, v.24, p.344.

"Slave Depot of the Company of the Indies at New Orleans" (Editor's Chair), v.9, p.286.

"Slaver, Last Captured, The," Miss King's Scrap Book, v.4, p.132.

"Slavery, on Louisiana Sugar Plantations," V. Alton Moody, v.7, p.191; Judah P. Benjamin and, v.19, p.986ff.; issue in politics, v.24, p.936; and 1836 election, v.25, p.108; agitation in La., v.25, p.999-1001; and the annexation of Texas, v.25, p.1002-05; in U. S. Senate, v.25, p.1061; Calhoun quoted on, v.25, p.1064; in Cong. sessions, 1847-49, v.25, p.1110.

Slaves, regulations of, by Carondelet's decree of 1795, v.20, p.600-05; Carondelet fears revolt, v.21, p.26n., 39-40; conspiracy at Pointe Coupee, 1795, v.21, p.54; importation to La., v.21, p.62; revolt in Santo Domingo, v.21, p.88n.; on Duverney Concession, v.21, p.987; lease of, in Pailloux succession, v.21, p.995-97; increase in value, 1746, v.21, p.1008; granted freedom, v.21, p.1076; treatment of, v.21, p.1189; fear of insurrection of, v.22, p.58, 61; Indian, v.22, p.61; Carondelet's rules concerning, v.22, p.61; insurrection at Pointe Coupee, v.22, p.63; in New Orleans, v.22, p.142-65; revolt in St. John the Baptist Parish, v.22, p.144-46; slave auctions, v.22, p.147-51; regulation of in W. Fla., v.22, p.358; freedom granted to, v.22, p.392; murder trial in Sp. La., v.22, p.623-41; Indians, in New Orleans, v.22, p.654-56; smuggling of, v.22, p.764-65; Rules of W. Fla. Assembly, v.22, p.958; diseases of, v.22, p.973; Compensation for execution of, v.22, p.966, 995; and Cuban question, v.22, p.1102-1103; compulsory work on roads, v.23, p.421, 423; labor in rice fields of S. C., v.23, p.546; Indian, inefficiency of, v.23, p.549; in New Orleans, v.23, p.864-86; duties of, v.23, p.870, 871; hire of by the day, v.23, p.872; La. State Colonization Soc., v.23, p.1048-1050; smuggling of, v.24, p.22-24; noted, v.32, p.26-28; discipline of, v.32, p.34-38; life of, v.32, p.38-42; value of, at Canebrake, v.33, p.357; dress of, v.33, p.359; medical treatment of, v.33, p.359; Religious services for, v.33, p.359.

Slave trade, in La., early, v.18, p.272-73; in New Orleans, v.22, p.151-54; in Sp. New Orleans, v.22, p.664, 665; and Barataria, v.22, p.809; duty on, v.22, p.967; of privateers, v.22, p.1075; African, in 1810, v.23, p.437, 440; smuggling of Negroes into La., v.23, p.441; domestic, v.23, p.876-78; illicit, with Cuba, v.23, p.879-81; meeting on "Creole," v.23, p.1033-1034; and privateering, v.24, p.11-12; description of, v.24, p.25.

Slidell, John, (Appendix D) in "Elections of Louisiana in 1860"; v.9, p.677; land in Carrollton, v.21, p.228; and beginnings of Carrollton, v.22, p.190; and Charter for New Orleans, v.23, p.187; noted, v.23, p.226, 1187; noted, v.24, p.58, 500; and tariff issue, v.25, p.51, 62, 109, 131, 132-33, 134; memorial to Congress, v.25, p.73; noted, v.25, p.77, 123, 124,

131, 138, 143, 998, 1004-1005, 1044, 1069; and nullification, v.25, p.91; and Plaquemines Fraud, v.25, p.127; leader of Dem. party, 1860, v.25, p.704; pro-administration leader, v.25, p.706; rejected by Mex. Gov't, v.25, p.1053; Dem. nominee for U. S. Senate, v.25, p.1093; as Soule's rival, v.25, p.1104-1105; cand. for U. S. Senate, v.26, p.978; rivalry with Soule, v.26, p.984; Dem. party split, v.26, p.986-87; and the campaign of 1859, v.26, p.990; home of seized by Butler, v.27, p.515; leader of Democrats responsible for "Plaquemines Fraud," v.27, p.723; noted, v.33, p.228.

Slocum, Thomas, noted, v.25, p.295.

"Slow Man, The," by Cable, v.24, p.170.

Smallpox, in Sp. New Orleans, v.22, p.678.

Smelser, Marshall, "Housing in Creole St. Louis, 1764-1821; An Example of Cultural Change," v.21, p.337-48.

Smelser, William B., noted, v.23, p.472.

Smith, ———, and W. Fla. Assembly, v.23, p.5ff.

Smith, A. J., noted, v.24, p.84, 85, 86, 88, 89; v.32, p.113, 115, 116, 123, 124, 126, 130, 131, 132.

Smith, Ann, daughter of Israel Smith, marriage and children of, v.29, p.290.

Smith, Bill, identifies John I. Kendall, v.29, p.1141-1142.

Smith, Calvin, son of Rev. Jedediah Smith, sketch of, v.29, p.293-294; children of, v.29, p.294.

Smith, Catherine, early life, v.31, p.872; career, v.31, p.872.

Smith, Christiana Owen, wife of Ebenezer Smith II, v.29, p.282.

Smith, Ebenezer, son of Samuel Smith, brief sketch, v.29, p.282.

Smith, Ebenezer, II, son of Ebenezer Smith, sketch of, v.29, p.282-283; children of, v.29, p.286.

Smith, Edith, eldest daughter of Elnathan Smith, sketch of, v.29, p.287-288; children by first marriage, v.29, p.288; second marriage and children of, v.29, p.289.

Smith, E. F., resigned, v.26, p.835.

Smith, E. Kirby, v.24, p.62, 63, 73, 76, 84, 90, 102, 104, 111; in Red River Campaign, v.24, p.86-87; relations with Richard Taylor, v.24, p.93, 97-101; noted, v.29, p.1245; letter from General Taylor, v.32, p.110; noted, v.32, p.109, 111, 112, 118; message to Gen. Taylor, v.32, p.119; noted, v.32, p.126, 129, 133, 135, 140, 141.

Smith, Elenathan, son of Ebenezer Smith II, sketch of, v.29, p.287; children of, v.29, p.287.

Smither, Nellie, "A Hist. of the Eng. Theatre at N. O., 1806-1842," v.28, p.85-276, 361-572; "Charlotte Cushman's Apprenticeship in New Orleans," v.31, p.973-80.

Smith family, early La. settlers, v.29, p.277; origin of family, v.29, p.277-279.

Smith, F. O. J., Morse contractor, v.31, p.437, 459.

Smith, Geo. Winston, "The Banks' Expedition of 1862," v.26, p.341-60.

Smith, Hannah Bates, wife of Elnathan Smith, v.29, p.287; children of, v.29, p.287.

Smith, Henry, ancestry, birth, ed. and priesthood, v.29, p.279-280; severs church connections and sails to Am., v.29, p.280; life in Wethersfield, Conn., as "settled" pastor, v.29, p.281; death, v.29, p.281-282; sketch of, v.29, p.282.

Smith, Herman S., gunner on the "Tennessee," v.27, p.482.

Smith-Hughes Act, 1917, and vocational training, v.25, p.813.

Smith, Isaac Wightman, noted, v.24, p.370.

Smith, Israel, son of Jedediah Smith, descendants of, v.29, p.280-290.

Smith, James S., and W. Fla. Rev., v.21, p.132-34.

Smith, Jedediah, birth, ed., and life as church pastorate in Granville, Mass., v.29, p.283; makes boat trip to Natchez, Miss., v.29, p.283-284; death of, v.29, p.284; children of, v.29, p.285-286.

Smith, J. Fisher, pro-lottery Sen. from Sabine, v.28, p.1147, 1148; senator, illness of prevents majority to override veto in Senate, v.27, p.1044; charged with being bribed, v.27, p.1047.

Smith, John, and W. Fla. Rev., v.21, p.81; noted, v.23, p.404; collection of in La. State Museum, v.24, p.319; Toledo's agent, v.28, p.1056-57.

Smith, John K., noted, v.23, p.1035; navy agent in N. O., v.28, p.753n.

Smith, Joseph, noted, v.22, p.991.

Smith, J. Pinckney, Capt., warrant against for violating postal law, v.27, p.1079.

Smith, Kirby, noted, v.23, p.1224, 1230.

Smith, Landgrave Thomas, introduces rice to S. C., 1693, v.23, p.545.

Smith, Ledoux E., cand. treasurer, 1890, v.28, p.1191.

Smith-Lever Agricultural Extension Act, 1913, v.25, p.812.

Smith, Luther, organized trading firm, v.28, p.1089, 1096; sketch, v.28, p.1090.

Smith, Margaret Mackall, noted, v.24, p.49.

Smith, Mary Isabella, 3rd daughter of Israel Smith, married Judge A. N. Ogden, v.29, p.290.

Smith, Nansiette, money from James Brown, v.24, p.1145.

Smith, Persifor F., sketch, v.23, p.472-73; and expedition against pirates, 1842, v.24, p.31-34.

Smith, Philander, son of Jedediah Smith, brief sketch, v.29, p.285.

Smith, Philomela, 9th child of Rev. Jedediah Smith, sketch of, v.29, p.291-292; children of, v.29, p.292.

Smithport Plantation, drainage reclamation project, v.30, p.676, fig. 3, p.695.

Smith, R. A., La. educator, organizes E. A. Seminary, v.30, p.790; leader Homer College, v.30, p.814-815; principal Trenton Institute, v.30, p.888-889; noted, v.30, p.969.

Smith, R. O., noted, v.23, p.481.

Smith, Robert, letter in New Orleans Public Library, v.24, p.325.

Smith, Samuel, noted, v.24, p.1001, 1124; and colonial question, v.24, p.1109; son of Rev. Henry Smith, brief sketch, v.29, p.282.

Smith, Sara Cook, wife of Jedediah Smith, v.29, p.285.

Smith, Sol., noted, v.28, p.252, 253; co-manager of Am. Theatre, Poydras St., v.28, p.257; seasons 1840-41, v.28, p.257-63; 1841-42, v.28, p.269-74; dominated theatrical scene, 1843, v.28, p.274.

Smith, T. C. H., Morse agent, v.31, p.449, 450, 451.

Smith, T. Kilby, Gen., noted, v.32, p.116; steamers in fleet of, v.32, p.117; noted, v.32, p.118, 124, 125, 126.

Smith, Wm. B., ass't paymaster in Confed. navy, v.27, p.485.

Smith, William W., noted, v.22, p.434.

Smugglers, in La., v.28, p.826-27.

"Smuggler St. Michel, The," Henry P. Dart, v.7, p.371.

Smuggling, English, in Spanish Ill., v.21, p.67; privateers at Galveston, 1816-1817, v.21, p.1086-1109; noted, v.22, p.695; in Gulf of Mex., v.22, p.751; at Barataria, v.22, p.1069; loss of profit after cession of La., v.23, p.439, 440; by way of W. Fla., v.23, p.404; across neutral ground, v.28, p.1079, 1080, 1081-82. See also Privateers.

Snake Island (Campeche), noted, v.24, p.21; See Galveston.

Sneed, Bertie (Gordon L.), 2nd Lt. 1st La. Inf., death of, v.26, p.821; newspaperman, "Old Days on the Times-Democrat," v.33, p.426.

Snowden, Dr. C. F., on committee to investigate case of Seminole Mary, v.26, p.73-75; signed Luzenberg's expulsion from Medical Society, v.26, p.76.

Snow, Elliot, "A Visit to Lafitte" (Reprinted from the Knickerbocker Magazine, March, 1847), v.11, p.434.

Snyder, Robert H., Dem. cand. Lt.-gov., 1896, v.26, p.1101; v.28, p.1172, 1173; elected, v.28, p.1181; noted, v.28, p.1191.

"Social, Economic and, Development of, Calcasieu Parish, Louisiana," by Grace Ulmer, v.32, p.519.

"Social History of St. Mary Parish, A, 1845-1860," by Jewell Lynn de Grummond, v.32, p.16.

Social life, New Orleans in Sp. period, v.22, p.642-709; balls in Sp. New Orleans, v.22, p.688-91; decline in New Orleans under Federal Occupation, v.24, p.484-85.

"Societe Medicale," noted, v.26, p.73.

Society for Relief of Destitute Orphan Boys, benefited by McDonogh's legacy, v.26, p.158.

Society of Natural History and the Sciences, organized by Luzenberg, v.26, p.60-61.

Socola, A., noted, v.23, p.555, 557.

Soemeson, Pierre, noted, v.22, p.734.

"So It Was When Life Began," by Lucy Paxton Scarborough, v.13, p.428.

Solana, Domingo Joaquin, letter from Bishop of Havana, v.22, p.116-17.

Solis, Jacob da Silva, and Jews in New Orleans, v.21, p.520-31.

Solis, Joseph, and plot against Mex., v.22, p.717.

Solis, Pedro de, noted, v.22, p.934.

Solomon, Clara E., diary in L.S.U. Archives, v.24, p.344.

Somdal, Dewey A., "A Century of Steamboating on Red River to Shreveport and the Coming of the Railroads," v.18, p.845-63.

"Some Activities of United States Citizens in the South American Wars of Independence, 1808-1824," by Curtis Wilgus, v.14, p.182.

"Some Distinguished Hispano-Orleanians," by John Smith Kendall, v.18, p.40-55.

"Some French Soldiers Who Became Louisiana Educators," by Simone de la Souchere Delery, v.31, p.849-55.

"Some Inedited Gayarre Manuscripts," by Edward Alexander Parsons, v.33, p.189-204.

"Some Interesting Glimpses of Louisiana a Century Ago," edited by Walter Prichard, v.24, p.35-48.

"Some Letters of Charles Etienne Gayarre on Literature and Politics, 1854-1885," v.33, p.223-54.

"Some Letters of George Stanton Denison, 1854-1866: Observations of a Yankee on Conditions in La. and Tex.," ed. by J. A. Padgett, v.23, p.1132-1240.

"Some Letters of James Brown of La. to Presidents of the U. S.," ed. by James A. Padgett, v.20, p.58-136.

Someruelos, Marques de, letter from Bishop of Havana, v.22, p.115-16.

Somerville, William Clarke, noted, v.24, p.969, 975, 978, 979, 981, 985, 987.

Sompayrac, Paul "Gov. Newton C. Blanchard," v.6, p.56.

Soniat, Chas. T., on lottery bill, v.27, p.1042.

Soniat, Meloncy C., "Tchoupitoulas Plantation," v.7, p.308; "The Faubourgs Forming the Upper Section of the City of New Orleans," v.20, p.192-211.

Soniat, Pierre, noted, v.22, p.192.

Sorel, Joseph, noted, v.22, p.813.

Sorrel, Joseph, v.28, p.819n.

Sorrell, Mrs. M. E., Jeanes teacher, v.25, p.797.

Sosa, Fray Mariano, opinion of Barr & Davenport, v.28, p.1102.

Soto, Don Marcelo, established post at Bayou Pierre, v.28, p.1089; noted, v.28, p.1101.

Souchon, Edmond, M.D., "Original Contributions of Louisiana to Medical Science," v.1, sec.1, p.81; quoted on rivalry between Luzenberg and Stone, v.26, p.58.

Soule, Evelyn, "Louisiana's Dreamy Bayous," v.13, p.205.

Soule, Leon, quoted on Pierre Soule, v.25, p.974, 975-76, 980, 985-86, 991; on Pierre Soule's maiden senatorial address, v.25, p.1065, 1068; on Guerrero Case, v.25, p.1078.

Soule, Neville, only child of Pierre, v.25, p.980.

Soule, Pierre, and De Bow, v.22, p.483; noted, v.23, p.1187; letters in Bibliotheca Parsoniana, v.24, p.311; noted, v.24, p.370, 372, 457, 458, 466, 757; report of conversation with Butler, v.24, p.469; noted, v.25, p.142; pro Douglas Dem leader, v.25, p.706; his ancestry, v.25, p.971-73; his birth and early life in France, v.25, p.973-77; leaves France, v.25, p.976-77; arrives in N. O., v.25, p.978; his early struggle in La., v.25, p.978-80; as a member of the City Council, v.25, p.980; and the Anglo-Creole struggle, v.25, p.985-86; the panic of 1837, v.25, p.986-90; and the St. Louis Hotel, v.25, p.990-94; visits France, v.25, p.994; social activities of in N. O., v.25, p.994-97; embarkation into politics, v.25, p.998-99; slavery agitation and Texas annexation, v.25, p.999-1005; in the Const. Con. of 1844 in La., v.25, p.1005-36; on the rights of foreign born citizens, v.25, p.1011-12; on apportionment of representation, v.25, p.1021-27; the problem of judiciary reform, v.25, p.1028-33, 1044-52; his interest in ed., v.25, p.1033-34, 1040-43; elected state Senator, 1846, v.25, p.1036-38; convening of legislature, v.25, p.1038-39; other legislature interests, v.25, p.1052-53, 1055-57; and the Mexican War, v.25, p.1053-55, 1060-63; named U. S. senator, v.25, p.1058-59; his maiden speech, v.25, p.1065-69; and the Wilmot Proviso, v.25, p.1070-71; suggested peace com. to Mexico, v.25, p.1070; minor legislation, v.25, p.1072-73; visits N. Y., v.25, p.1073-75; returns to N. O., v.25, p.1077-93; Cong. Session, 1847 to 1849, v.25, p.1110-15, 1117; his visit to Fr. and Spain, v.25, p.1117-1118; bibl., v.25, p.1120-27; elected U. S. Senator from La., v.26, p.978; rivalry with Slidell, v.26, p.984; the Odd Fellows Hall Meeting, v.26, p.985-87; threatens Butler, v.27, p.498, 740; chosen for Mission to Spain, v.33, p.180.

Soule's College, v.30, p.868-869.

"Souls of Old Houses," by Helen Spann Murphy, v.13, p.59.

Sour Lake, oil field, v.27, p.1169.

Sour, L. J., disputed election, v.27, p.988, 989.

Soutalet, Jean Batiste, noted, v.24, p.671, 676.

Southal, William, noted, v.23, p.391.

South American republican agents, U. S. attitude toward, v.24, p.613.

South American republics, U. S. recognition of, v.24, p.939; question of recognition, v.24, p.947ff., 964, 970-71, 984, 1006; European reactions to, v.24, p.1027; foreign agents in, v.24, p.1076.

"South as a Conscious Minority, The," by Dr. Jesse T. Carpenter, reviewed by Henry P. Dart, v.14, p.637.

South Carolina, ordinance of nullification, v.24, p.721; reply to, in 1832 by Edward Livingston, v.24, p.727.

"South During Reconstruction, The," by E. Merton Coulter, reviewed by Walter Prichard, v.31, p.150-54.

Southern Academic Institute, v.30, p.875.

Southern Cypress Lumber Selling Company, org., v.30, p.1029; manufacturers assoc. with, v.30, p.1029-30; discontinues bus., v.30, p.1036.

Southern Cypress Manufacturers' Association, meetings of, v.30, p.1041-1042; noted, v.30, p.1048.

"Southern Filibusters in the War of 1812," by Harris G. Warren, v.25, p.291-300.

Southern Hist'l Ass'n, meeting in N. O., v.21, p.959-64.

"Southern La. and Southern Ala. in 1819, Journal of Leander Cathcart," ed. by Prichard, Kniffen and Brown, v.28, p.735-921.

Southern Military Institute, v.30, p.831.

Southern Oil Co., v.29, p.499.

Southern Rights Association, noted, v.24, p.437.

Southern Rights mass meeting, 1860, v.24, p.59.

Southern University, established with support of Pinchback, v.27, p.606.

Southwestern La., disorders in, v.25, p.703-704.

Southwest La. Land Co., laid out Crowley, v.27, p.1123, 1125, 1126; donation for school, v.27, p.1176, 1185.

Southwest La. Trades School, v.27, p.1183-84.

Southwood, Marion, noted, v.24, p.478.

Sovereignty, Edward Livingston's ideas about, v.24, p.709.

Spain, consuls of, in New Orleans, 1804-1821, v.21, p.677-841; filibusters in Pensacola, 1816-1817, v.21, p.806-22; Colonial La., Jacobinism in, v.22, p.47-97; life in Colonial New Orleans, v.22, p.642-709; Latin Am. and New Orleans, v.22, p.710-94; plan to regain La., v.22, p.805-818; coastguard squadrons of the Gulf, v.23, p.429; complaint against privateers, v.23, p.442; Toledo's reconciliation with, v.23, p.827-63; position with respect to England and the U. S., v.23, p.839-44; unsatisfactory internal conditions of, v.24, p.940, 950-51, 952-55, 958, 973, 1055-56, 1071, 1080; relations with France, v.24, p.953-54, 959; and Portuguese rebellion, v.24, p.1035-36; interest in keeping Puerto Rico and Balearic Isles, v.24, p.1113.

Spain, New, Trade with, v.21, p.362-66.

"Spain, The Oath of Allegiance to," by People of Illinois and Louisiana, v.4, p.205.

"Spain's Report of the War With the British in Louisiana," by Jac Nachbin (note by Henry P. Dart), v.15, p.468.

Spaniards, in Red River region, v.25, p.399.

"Spanish Activities in the Lower Miss. Valley, 1513-1698," by A. B. Thomas, v.22, p.933-42.

"Spanish American Patriot Activity Along the Gulf Coast of the United States, 1811-1822," A. Curtis Wilgus, v.8, p.193.

Spanish-American War, 1898-1899, La. in, as recorded by Col. Elmer E. Wood, v.26, p.783-841.

Spanish and French Documents Concerning Early History of Louisiana, v.1, sec.1, p.103; v.1, sec.3, p.224.

"Spanish Civil Procedure in Louisiana, 1774" (Loppinot Case), by Henry P. Dart, translated by Laura L. Porteous, v.12, p.33.

"Spanish Colonial Municipalities," by Herbert Ingram Priestly, v.5, p.125.

Spanish Colonial Officials and Filibustering, v.25, p.292-93; Colonial laws, v.25, p.302.

"Spanish Fort, Historical Data of," by Joseph H. De Grange, v.2, p.268; noted, v.26, p.742.

Spanish Indian policy, toward the Caddoes, v.18, p.891-97.

Spanish influences, in La., v.24, p.748.

Spanish Judicial Records of Louisiana, Index to, tr. by Laura L. Porteous, I, II, III, IV, v.6, p.145, 311, 513, 683; V, VI, VII, v.7, p.144, 524, 706; VIII, IX, X, XI, v.8, p.149, 309, 508, 704; XII, XIII, XIV, XV, v.9, p.143, 321, 533, 746; XVI, XVII, XVIII, XIX, v.10, p.129, 281,

438, 588; XX, XXI, XXII, v.11, p.153, 314, 508, 654; XXIII, XXIV, XXV, XXVI, v.12, p.166, 331, 498, 675; XXVII, XXVIII, XXIX, XXX, v.13, 161, 333, 519, 683; XXXI, XXXII, XXXIII, XXXIV, v.14, p.155, 271, 461, 606; XXXV, XXXVI, XXXVII, v.15, p.156, 532, 675; XXXVIII, XXXIX, XL, v.16, p.151, 339, 516; XLI, XLII, XLIII, v.17, p.203, 385, 572; XLIV, March, 1782, v.18, p.193-233; XLV, April, 1782, v.18, p.456-85; XLVI, May, 1782, v.18, p.727-58; XLVII, June, 1782, v.18, p.1004-35; XLVIII, July-Aug., 1782, v.19, p.241-72; LXIX, Sept.-Nov., 1782, v.19, p.510-46; LXX, Nov., 1782, v.19, p.778-87; LI, Dec., 1782, v.19, p.1119-39; LII, Jan., 1783, v.20, p.245-87; LIII, Feb., 1783, v.20, p.518-55; LIV, March, 1783, v.20, p.840-79; LV, April, 1783, v.20, p.1141-75; LVI, May-June, 1783, v.21, p.319-36; LVII, July, 1783, v.21, p.610-28; LVIII, Aug., 1783, v.21, p.909-57; LIX, Sept., 1783, v.21, p.1252-83; LX, Oct., 1783, v.22, p.259-309; LXI, Nov., 1783, v.22, p.575-621; LXII, Dec., 1783, v.22, p.903-31; LXIII, Jan.-Feb., 1784, v.22, p.1211-47; in La. State Museum, v.24, p.319.

Spanish La., list of Gov't employees and salaries of, v.29, p.890-891, 895-914, 917-918, 920-962, 964-1041.

Spanish land grants in Ouachita, v.20, p.289-462.

"Spanish Land Laws of Louisiana," by Francis P. Burns, v.11, p.557.

Spanish Main, noted, v.24, p.614.

"Spanish Procedure in Louisiana in 1800 for Licensing Doctors and Surgeons," Introduction by Henry P. Dart, translated by Laura L. Porteous, v.14, p.204.

Spanish settlement, in St. Helena, v.23, p.419.

Spanish Supreme Councils of State, Minutes of, 1787-1797, v.2, p.5-75.

Sparks, G. W., La. midshipman, v.27, p.483.

Sparks, Jared, letter in New Orleans Public Library, v.24, p.325.

Sparks-Morgan duel, noted, v.24, p.769.

Sparks, Richard, Col., identified, v.21, p.90n.; and W. Fla. Rev., v.21, p.113, 114, 154; Kemper's letter to, v.25, p.945.

Sparrow, Edward, Whig Candidate for Gov., 1846, v.25, p.1038; noted, v.25, p.1044; delegate to conv. of seceding states, v.26, p.1002; Whig Cand. for lt.-gov., v.28, p.959.

Spearing, Frances E., noted, v.23, p.476.

Spearing, Mary, noted, v.23, p.476.

Spears, Abraham, and W. Fla. Rev., v.21, p.708n.; noted, v.23, p.420.

"Specimens of the Folktales from Some Antebellum Newspapers of La.," by Arthur K. Moore, v.32, p.723.

"Spectacle de la Rue St. Pierre," by Nellie Warner Price, v.1, sec. 3, p.215; first N. O. opera venture, v.29, p.662-663.

Spedding, Lieutenant, noted, v.24, p.368.

Speir, A. B., Conf. soldier, v.26, p.954.

Spencer, John T., La. educator, supervisor, Floridian Academy, v.30, p.906; noted, v.30, p.969.

Sperry, Robert, duel with M. Lewis, v.23, p.156-60.

Spiller, William, and W. Fla. Rev., v.21, p.688n.

Spofford, Judge H. H., attacks constitution of 1864, v.31, p.1060.

Spraggins, Samuel M., v.27, p.370, 376, 384; executor of Erwin's will, v.27, p.399, 400.

Spring Creek Academy, v.30, p.894-895.

Springfield Academy, v.30, p.898-899.

Springfield Institute, v.30, p.841.

Springfield Landing, noted, v.24, p.88, 93.

Spyker, Leonidas P., collection in L.S.U. Archives, v.24, p.344.

Stafford, Dr. George M., ed., "The Autobiography of George Mason Graham," v.20, p.43-57.

Stafford, Joseph, noted, v.24, p.643, 651, 652.

Stafford, L. S., noted, v.24, p.66.

Stafford, S. H., in charge of recruiting under Butler, v.27, p.529.

Stahl, Annie Lee West, "Free Negro in Ante-Bellum La.," v.25, p.301-96.

Stallings, J. M., voted to let people decide lottery question, v.27, p.1037; pres. State Farmers' Union, v.26, p.1066; opposed lottery, favored leaving decision to people, v.28, p.1144.

Standard Land Company, Ltd., of Franklinton, v.29, p.93.

Stanislaus, Sister, "New Orleans Most Beloved Woman," v.31, p.97-8.

Stanley, Henry M., life in N. O., v.20, p.815-20.

Stanley, Marcus Cicero, head of C. H. Murray Company, v.31, p.730.

Stanolind Oil Co., owns territory at Jennings, La., v.29, p.507.

Stansbury, William, early N. O. police reporter, sketch of, v.29, p.56-58.

Stanton, Edwin M., Secretary of War, v.24, p.113, 114, 510, 511, 514, 518, 521, 536.

Staples, O. B., fusion cand. supt. of ed., 1900, v.28, p.1192.

Starke, Aubrey, "Richard Henry Wilde in New Orleans and the Establishment of the University of Louisiana," v.17, p.605.

Starns, William, noted, v.23, p.418.

"Star of the West," incident, v.20, p.999.

State Board of Education, creation and composition of, v.25, p.755.

State Board of Engineers, handling of swamp land, v.28, p.299, 300, 305-307.

State Central Committee, 1859 and Odd Fellows Hall meeting, v.26, p.987-88.

"State ex. rel. Morris vs Mason," v.27, p.1050-52.

State Farmers' Union, in conv. at Baton Rouge, 1890, v.27, p.1057, 1058, 1086; alliance wtih Anti-Lottery League, v.27, p.1058; annual meeting in Lafayette, 1891, v.27, p.1086; combine with Anti-Lotteryites, v.27, p.1086-87; discord in, v.27, p.1087; combine denounced by, v.27, p.1087.

State House, N. O., v.32, p.400, 403, 404, 418.

State Lottery Company, revenues go to Charity Hospital, v.31, p.66, 68.

Statement of Ownership of Quarterly, as Required by U. S. Post Office, v.5, p.282.

State Odd Fellows Orphans Home, v.27, p.1196.

State Papers, vol. 4, page 51, No. 113, Report to Congress, Jan. 1824, v.2, p.119.

State Returning Board, noted, v.26, p.1059.

State rights, idea of, v.24, p.716; noted, v.25, p.113; Wickliffe's stand on, v.25, p.685-90.

State Seminary of Learning, Ryan introduced bill to locate in Rapides, v.26, p.980; Moore's plan of gov't of, v.26, p.981-82; becomes State Seminary of Learning and Military Academy, v.26, p.993; to be used as arsenal, v.26, p.996; noted, v.25, p.677; construction and organization of, v.25, p.698-700.

States, N. O. newspaper, noted, v.33, p.407.

Statuette of Joan of Arc, Presentation of, to Louisiana Historical Society, May 1, 1918, v.1, p.285.

Stauffer, Cyrus W., register of voters, v.31, p.1034.

Stauffer, I. H., Jr., treas. Anti-Lottery League of La., v.27, p.1054.

"Steamboats, on Red River, History of," v.25, p.401-409; sources for information, v.25, p.409-13; list of, v.25, p.413-512; list of steamers with Porter in 1864, v.25, p.513; list of gov't snagboats, v.25, p.514; list of steamboat masters, v.25, p.515-26; list of way landings, v.25, p.527-35.

Steam navigation, essay on by Richard Claiborne, v.24, p.738.

Steele, Dr. Andrew, sec'y of Convention, W. Fla. Rev., v.21, p.77; letter to Skipwith, v.21, p.123; and W. Fla. Rev., v.21, p.688n.

Steele, Frank, noted, v.24, p.84, 87, 93, 99.

Steele, General Frederick, noted, v.32, p.105, 109, 113, 116, 126, 129, 141.

Steele, H. R., named in Kellogg impeachment, v.31, p.713, 714.

Steele, Judge Andrew, noted, v.22, p.725.

Steele, O. B., "Regular" cand. for state auditor, v.26, p.1081; Lotteryite cand. for auditor, v.27, p.1090; cand. auditor, v.28, p.1158.

Steele, R. M., Dem. Populist elector, v.26, p.1116.

Stein, Albert, noted, v.29, p.372; work on "De Bow's Review," v.29, p.376.

Steinriede, Joseph, Confed. naval surgeon, v.27, p.486.

Steir, Emile, early N. O. newspaperman, v.29, p.788.

Stenberg, Richard R., "The La. Cession and the Family Compact," v.19, p.204-209; letter in answer to article by, v.19, p.1075-77; "Napoleon's Cession of La.: A Suggestion," v.21, p.354-61.

Stephens, Alexander H., noted, v.24, p.118.

Stephens, Edwin L., "Education in Louisiana in the Closing Decades of the Nineteenth Century," v.16, p.38; "The Story of Acadian Education in Louisiana," v.18, p.397-406; papers of in L.S.U. Archives, v.24, p.344.

Stephenson, John, petition of, v.23, p.367.

Stephenson, Wendell Holmes, "The Civil War Diary of Willie Micajah Barrow, I, II," (Edited by), v.17, p.436, 712.

Sterling, Alexander, and W. Fla. Rev., v.21, 81, 82; sketch, v.21, p.162n.; noted, v.28, p.763n., 818n.

Sterling, Henry, v.28, p.763n.

Sterling, Judge, noted, v.23, p.57.

Sterling, Lewis, v.28, p.763n.

Sternberg, Hilgard O'Reilly, "The Pointe Coupee Cut-Off in Hist'l Writings," v.28, p.69-84; "The Names, 'False River' and 'Pointe Coupee': An Inquiry in Historical Geography," v.31, p.598-605.

Stetson, F. L., lottery lawyer, v.31, p.825.

Stevens, Col. W. L., gives command 1st La. Reg't, v.26, p.793; at Camp Foster, v.26, p.797-99, 801, 809.

Stevens, Thaddeus, noted, v.24, p.113.

Stevenson, Andrew, noted, v.23, p.1022.

Stevenson, William, Chairman of Democratic Parish Committee in N. O., v.29, p.716.

"Stewardship, The, of Don Esteban Miro, 1782-1792, A Study of Louisiana Based Largely on the Documents in New Orleans," by Caroline Maude Burson, revd. by Walter Prichard, v.24, p.537-41.

Steward, J. T., councilman of Crowley, v.27, p.1126.

Stewart, Col. R. A., prominent La. Know Nothing, v.25, p.686.

Stewart, David B., identified, v.21, p.769n.

Stewart, J. J., People's Party elector, v.26, p.1087.

Stewart, Matthew, noted, v.23, p.420.

Sticky, Daniel, noted, v.23, p.371.

Stiel, William, in W. Fla., v.22, p.38.

Stilling, Jung, noted, v.24, p.383.

Stillman, O. D., noted, v.25, p.681.

Stith, Gerard D., Am. party leader in N. O., 1858, v.25, p.692-93; mayor of N. O., v.27, p.774.

Stockman, Geo. W., promoted, v.26, p.836.

Stockton, Isaac F., noted, v.23, p.477.

Stoddard, Amos, on La., 1812, v.25, p.26; describes Ursuline Convent in book, v.29, p.623; surveyor and author, v.31, p.394, 395, 411.

Stone, Dr. Warren, and case of Sally Miller, v.22, p.162; succeeded Luzenberg as prof. of surgery, v.26, p.57; introduced letheon in N. O., 1847, v.26, p.61; noted, v.26, p.76; Gibson's attack on, v.26, p.102.

Stone, Henry, Confed. naval surgeon, v.27, p.486.

Stone, I. C., noted, v.23, p.1251.

Stone, Mrs. Valina G., noted, v.25, p.776.

Stone vs. Mississippi, v.27, p.1030.

Stone, William A., noted, v.23, p.199.

Stopher, Henry W., noted, v.24, p.347.

Story, Joseph, ideas of sovereignty, v.24, p.709-10.

"Story of Acadian Education in Louisiana," by Edwin L. Stephens, v.18, p.397-406.

"Story of the Ancient Cabildo, The," by Charles Patton Dimitry, v.3, p.57.

Stout, and expedition against Laffite, v.24, p.19.

Straight College, v.25, p.775-78, 792.

Straight, Seymour, v.25, p.775, 776.

Straight University, Pinchback studies law in, v.27, p.606.

Strakosch, Maurice, N. O. musician, v.31, p.134.

"Strange Case of Myra Clark Gaines," by John S. Kendall, v.20, p.5-42.

Strattman, O. C., appointed to Bogalusa police force, v.29, p.113.

Stratton, Joseph B., collection in L.S.U. Archives, v.24, p.344.

Strawbridge, George, judge of La. Sup. Ct., v.23, p.1029.

Strelezski, Anton, N. O. musician, v.31, p.133.

Strickland, Milton A., Circuit Judge, House resolution to investigate arrest of St. Amant, v.27, p.1048.

Strike of 1892, in N. O., v.21, p.547-60.

Stromeyer, George, noted, v.23, p.519.

Strong, George C., noted, v.23, p.1206, 1242; v.24, p.502.

Strother, see Mather and Strother Co.

Strother, Sarah Dabney, v.24, p.49.

Strothers, Arthur, noted, v.23, p.357, 368.

Strothers, Thomas, noted, v.23, p.21.

Stuart, Charles, noted, v.23, p.308, 398, 401; letters from, v.23, p.399.

Stuart, Henry, British Indian Agent, v.25, p.937.

Stuart, James, noted, v.23, p.873; author on La., v.31, p.394, 397, 406, 412.

Stuart, John, and W. Fla., v.22, p.25; letter from, v.23, p.399-401.

Stubbs, Frank M., cap't of 1st Reg't of La. Inf., v.29, p.82.

"Study, A, of the Trustee Problem in the St. Louis Cathedral Church in New Orleans, Louisiana, 1842-1844," by Brother Alfonso Comeau, C.S.C., v.31, p.897-971.

Sturcken, H. F., noted, v.23, p.520.

Suarez, Juan, noted, v.22, p.934.

Subsistence Committee Collection, in Howard-Tilton Memorial Library, v.24, p.934.

Succession sale, of estate of Joseph Dubreuil, v.18, p.291-331.

"Successors of Laffite, The," by John Smith Kendall, v.24, p.360-77.

"Sufferage and representation in Antebellum La.," by Roger W. Shugg, v.19, p.390-406.

Sugar cane, in Pointe Coupee in 1860, v.21, p.1141; in Ascension in 1860, v.21, p.1124; early history in La., v.25, p.24-27; expansion in 1820's, v.25, p.54, 55-56; conflict with cotton in La., v.25, p.83-85, 122ff., 127-28; and 1833 tariff, v.25, p.98-99, 100, 101, 103-108, 108-14; and 1836 campaign, v.25, p.109; convention of planters at Donaldsonville, 1842, v.25, p.111-12; and 1842 tariff, v.25, p.117ff.; varieties of, v.25, p.186; in La., noted, v.32, p.9.

Sugar, culture in La., early, v.18, p.276-79; export of, v.22, p.663, 668; competition with Cuba, v.22, p.1101-1102; in 1854, v.23, p.553; combined with rice planting, v.23, p.557; production and importance of, 1832, v.23, p.1015-1016; introduction of ribbon cane, v.23, p.1016n.; planting of, 1865, v.23, p.1224, 1226; crop of 1866, v.23, p.1237, 1238.

Sugar House Chute, noted, v.25, p.398.

Sugarhouse, importance of, v.25, p.187-88.

Sugar industry, in La., v.24, p.1089, 1099, 1157-58, 1163; need for slaves, v.27, p.377-78, 391, 392; in 1860, v.27, p.488; after Civil War, v.27, p.784-85; and tariff, v.27, p.805-21; early export of N. O., v.27, p.938, 949; "factors" in N. O., v.27, p.951, 351-352; production of, v.27, p.363; on Erwin estate, v.27, p.389, 390.

Sugar, Leon, "Following the Spanish Trail Across Neutral Territory in Louisiana," v.10, p.86.

Sugar Planters Assoc., meeting in N. O., 1894, v.27, p.809; faction of Dem. Party, v.28, p.1169-70; election of 1896, v.28, p.1171, 1174ff.

Sugartown Academy, v.30, p.802-803.

Sugartown, La., v.32, p.584-85.

"Suit for Damages for Personal Injuries to a Slave, 1764," Trans. by Heloise H. Cruzat, v.5, p.58.

Sullivan, Ella Rose Salmen, daughter of Wm. Henry Sullivan, v.29, p.186; noted, v.29, p.189.

Sullivan, Frank T., son of founder of Bogalusa, v.29, p.82.

Sullivan, J. J., People's Party elector, v.26, p.1087.

Sullivan, Will H., son of Wm. Henry Sullivan, v.29, p.186; noted, v.29, p.189.

Sullivan, Wm. Henry, "father of Bogalusa," v.29, p.96; general sup't of Great Southern Lumber Co., v.29, p.96, 103; chose name of Bogalusa, v.29, p.107; begins reforestation of, v.29, p.124-126; mayor of Bogalusa, v.29, p.109, 111; plants tung trees in Bogalusa, v.29, p.123; work in Bogalusa, v.29, p.181-182; sketch of, v.29, p.185-190; noted, v.29, p.96, 97, 116, 120, 151.

Sulphur, in Calcasieu Parish, v.32, p.558-61.

Sulphur, La., v.32, p.590.

Summers, H. M., noted, v.23, p.472.

Sumner, Charles, noted, v.24, p.113.

Sumter, Mary, death of, v.24, p.1117-18.

Sumter, Thomas, Jr., early life, v.31, p.289-90; appointed secretary to Paris legation, v.31, p.291; marriage, v.31, p.292; Monroe's secretary, v.31, p.293; return to U. S., v.31, p.294; Minister to Brazil, v.31, p.294.

Sunny Hill Academy, established, 1887, v.29, p.85.

"Sun People," ruling class of Natchez Indians, v.31, p.586.

Sunset Drainage District, v.30, p.690.

"Superieur," noted, v.23, p.436.

Superior Council of La., appt. of members, 1762, v.21, p.669-70; establishment of, v.21, p.998; Decision Day, Mar. 5, 1746, v.21, p.998-1020; minutes of Mar. 5, 1746, v.21, p.1006-20.

Superior Council of Louisiana, Records of, tr. by Heloise H. Cruzat, introduction by Grace King, v.1, sec.1, p.10; I, v.1, sec.1, p.103; II, v.1, sec.3, p.224; III, VII, VIII, v.2, p.104, 193, 328, 463; IX, X, v.3, p.141, 403; XI, XII, v.4, p.218, 324, 481; XIV, XV, XVI, XVII, v.5, p.76, 239, 377, 571; XVIII, XIX, XX, XXI, v.6, p.114, 283, 482, 657; XXII, XXIII, XXIV, v.7, p.334, 485, 676; XXV, XXVI, XXVII, XXVIII, v.8, p.118, 271, 478, 673; XXIX, XXX, XXXI, XXXII, v.9, p.113, 288, 502, 705; XXXIII, XXXIV, XXXV, XXXVI, v.10, p.96, 252, 409, 568; XXXVII, XXXVIII, XXXIX, XL, v.11, p.119, 288, 470, 624; XLI, XLII, XLIII, XLIV, v.12, p.138, 304, 467, 647; XLV, XLVI, XLVII, XLVIII, v.13, p.119, 307, 488, 660; XLIX, L, LI, LII, v.14, p.119, 245, 446, 570; LIII, LIV, LV, v.15, p.120, 507, 659; LVI, LVII, LVIII, v.16, p.135, 330, 504; LIX, LX, LXI, v.17, p.183, 364, 556; LXII, April, 1747, v.18, p.161-92; LXIII, May, 1747, v.18, p.430-55; LXIV, June-Sept., 1747, v.18, p.696-726; LXV, Oct.-Dec., 1747, v.18, p.976-1003; LXVI, Jan., 1748, v.19, p.210-240; **LXVII, Feb.-Mar., 1748, v.19, p.466-509;** LXVIII, April-May, 1748, v.19, p.751-77; LXIX, June-July, 1748; v.19, p.1078-1118; LXX, Aug.-Dec., 1748, v.20, p.212-44; LXXI, Jan.-Dec., 1749, v.20, p.486-517; LXXII, Jan.-Dec., 1750, v.20, p.832-39;

LXXIII, Jan.-June, 1751, v.20, p.1111-40; LXXIV, Jan.-May, 1752, v.21, p.282-318; LXXV, June-July, 1752, v.21, p.564-609; LXXVI, Aug.-Sept., 1752, v.21, p.875-908; LXXVII, Oct.-Dec., 1752, v.21, p.1215-52; LXXVIII, Jan.-March, 1753, v.22, p.226-258; LXXIX, Apr.-July, 1753, v.22, p.531-74; LXXX, Aug.-Sept., 1753, v.22, p.857-902; LXXXI, Oct.-Dec., 1753, v.22, p.1168-1210; LXXXII, Jan., 1760-Dec., 1761, v.23, p.265-94; LXXXIII, Jan.-Feb., 1762, v.23, p.589-634; LXXXIV, March-April, 1762, v.23, p.889-944; LXXXV, May-June, 1762, v.23, p.1258-1298; LXXXVI, July-Sept., 1762, v.24, p.211-57; LXXXVII, Oct.-Dec., 1762, v.24, p.544-600; LXXXVIII, Jan.-March, 1763, v.24, p.783-837; LXXXIX, April-May, 1763, v.24, p.1178-1231; Records cited, v.24, p.320, 352; XC, June, 1763, v.25, p.228-59; XCI, July, 1763, v.25, p.537-88; XCII, Aug., 1763, v.25, p.831-72; XCIII, Sept., 1763, v.25, p.1128-83; XCIV, Oct., 1763, v.26, p.169-256.

Superior Council Records of Louisiana, 1717-69, in La. State Museum, v.24, p.319.

Superior Court, Edward Livingston's ideas of, v.24, p.712-13.

"Superior Diploma of Parisian Wrestling and Fencing," in New Orleans Public Library, v.24, p.325.

"Superior" (late "Flying Fish"), v.24, p.643.

Superior Oil Co., owns territory at Jennings, La., v.29, p.507.

Supervielle, E., duel of, v.23, p.452.

"Suppressed co-operationist Protest against Secession," by Roger W. Shugg, v.19, p.199-203.

Supreme Council of State, Minutes of Spanish, 1787-1797, v.21, p.5-75.

"Supreme Court of Louisiana, The Celebration of the Centenary of," 1913, v.4, p.5.

Supreme Court of Louisiana, hist. of, v.23, p.1022-1023, 1027-1029, 1035-1037; noted, v.25, p.315, 316, 317; noted, v.27, p.18; orders Clark's will of 1813 probated, v.27, p.243, 244, 245, 277, 294-95; suit in to revoke will, v.27, p.297-99; memorial exercises for Clay, v.27, p.762.

Surrey, Mrs. N. M. Miller, "History of Calendar of Documents," v.7, p.551.

Surrey's "Calendar of Manuscripts in Paris Relating to the History of the Mississippi Valley under the French Domination" (Editor's Chair), v.10, p.564.

Surveyor, E. Fabre, "The Rocheblaves in Colonial Louisiana," v.18, p.332-45.

Surveyor, in New Orleans, v.22, p.1069.

Sutherland, E. W., cand. att'y gen'l, v.28, p.1158.

Sutherland, Joel B., noted, v.24, p.1172.

Sutherlin, E. W., "Regular" cand. for att'y-gen., v.26, p.1081; Lotteryite cand. for att'y-gen'l, v.27, p.1090.

Suthon, L. F., cand. for att'y-gen'l second Populist ticket, 1896, v.26, p.1102; Rep. cand. for gov., v.28, p.1175; cand. att'y-gen'l, v.28, p.1177.

Sutton, Isaac, Negro senator defeated Caffery, v.27, p.785; Rep. cand. for Sen. from St. Mary, 1876, v.28, p.1138; Negro Rep. from St. Mary, v.28, p.1136.

Swain, E. A., La. midshipman, v.27, p.483.

"Swamp Land Act," Wickliffe's interest in, v.25, p.678-79; 1850 provision of, v.28, p.279-80; conflicts in the operation of, v.28, p.282, purpose of, v.28, p.282-83; fraud and speculation in application of, v.28, p.282-84.

Swamp Land Funds, handling of in La., v.28, p.285-93; first use of for levee building, v.28, p.287, creation of Swamp Land Commissioners, v.28, p.287-90; Board of Public Works, v.28, p.293-99; other agencies, v.28, p.300-307.

Swamp Land, U. S. aid in reclamation of, v.28, p.278-82; conflicts in application of Swamp Land Act, v.28, p.282-84; how La. handled funds for, v.28, p.285-93; methods of designating, v.28, p.291; Board of Public Works, v.28, p.293-99; other agencies having control over, v.28, p.300-307; donated to levee districts, v.28, p.312-20; transfer to Tensas Basin Levee Board, v.28, p.320-21.

Swanson, Peter, petition of, v.23, p.383-84.

Swanton, Dr. John R., noted, v.25, p.611, 612, 620, 622, 623; quoted on De Soto's possible trail, v.25, p.629-30; author of "Indian Tribes of the Lower Miss. Valley," v.25, p.638-39, 641.

Sweet Springs, health resort, v.24, p.1166.

Swinburne, Algernon Charles, comment upon by Cable, v.24, p.174.

Swords, M. L., charged with allowing irregular registration in St. Landry, v.26, p.1107.

"Sword, The, was Their Passport, A History of American Filibustering in the Mex. Revol.," by Harris G. Warren, rev'd, v.26, p.1179-81.

Sylvester Larned Institute, v.30, p.871-872.

Sylvester, Murphy J., organized Troop "F" at Franklinton, v.29, p.82.

Synagogue, first in La., v.21, p.518-31.

Sypher, J. H., rep. from 1st district of La., v.27, p.582, 583; delivers harangue to Cong. on political situation in La., v.27, p.585; senator from St. Mary, sued Caffery, v.27, p.785.

"System of Redemption in the State of Louisiana, The," by J. Hanno Deiler, translated by Rev. Louis Voss, D.D., v.12, p.426.

TABARY, LOUIS BLAISE, v.29, p.662.
Taber, Fred R., papers in L.S.U. Archives, v.24, p.344.
"Taensa Indians, The," 1, 11, by R. D. Calhoun, v.17, p.411, 642; in Grant Parish, v.23, p.1109; description of, v.23, p.1117-1119.
Taitt, David, petition of, v.23, p.382.
"Tale, James Kirke Paulding's Creole," by Dr. Floyd C. Watkins, v.33, p.364-79.
Taliaferro, James G., protest against secession, v.19, p.199-203; candidate for gov., v.23, p.504; speech against secession, v.26, p.1000; defeated by Warmoth for gov., 1868, v.27, p.535; Assoc. Justice administers oath of office to acting Gov. Pinchback, v.27, p.561; concurs in decision in favor of P. H. Morgan, v.27, p.578; cand. for gov., v.30, p.548; defeated, v.30, p.549; noted, v.30, p.184, 189.
Talley, B. D., on committee to incorporate Bogalusa, v.29, p.108, 109; chosen city attorney of Bogalusa, v.29, p.113.
Talleyrand, Charles Maurice de Perigord, and La. Purchase, v.23, p.86ff.; letter to Skipwith, v.21, p.128.
Talmage, David, noted, v.23, p.557.
Tampa, pen-name of Cable, v.24, p.171.
Tampico, noted, v.24, p.641.
Taney, Roger B., telegraph decision, v.31, p.472; noted, v.31, p.913, 915.
Tangipahoa Parish, and W. Fla. Rev., v.21, p.187n.; noted, v.29, p.73, 79, 81, 102.
Tangipahoa River, ford on, v.23, p.421.
Tannehill, R. H., noted, v.26, p.1124.
Tannehill, R. L., People's Party cand. for gov., 1892, v.26, p.1080, 1082; Third Party leader, v.26, p.1084; People's Party cand. for gov., 1892, v.27, p.1092; Populist cand. for gov., v.28, p.1160.
Tanner, William, telegraph contractor, v.31, p.437; consolidated pres., v.31, p.453.
Tardiveau, Bartholome, and revolutionary agitators, v.22, p.87.
Tardiveau, P., and revolutionary agitators, v.22, p.87.
Tariff, Spanish, on American goods, v.21, p.22-23; on rice, v.23, p.574; of 1832, v.23, p.1012, 1018; of 1833, v.23, p.1021; and Virginia, v.24, p.1124, 1159; and Clay, v.24, p.1166; and nullification, v.24, p.1168; in force, 1812, v.25, p.27-28; raised in War of 1812, v.25, p.28; of 1816, v.25, p.28-33; discussions, v.25, p.33-41; of 1824, v.25, p.41-42; of 1828, v.25, p.43ff.; status in 1830, v.25, p.68; comparison of 1828 and 1832 proposals, v.25, p.82; of 1832, v.25, p.80ff.; of 1833, v.25, p.96ff.; and 1837 panic, v.25, p.112; in 1841-42 campaign, v.25, p.113-14; of 1841, v.25, p.115; 1842, v.25, p.115-120; political issue, v.25, p.119-37; bill of 1844, v.25, p.131-32; bill of 1846, v.25, p.134-42; reactions to 1846

tariff in La., v.25, p.140-42; bibl., v.25, p.144-48.

Tarpley, C. S., noted, v.23, p.204, 221.

Tate, David, noted, v.23, p.26.

"Tatooed-Serpent," leading Natchez war chief, v.31, p.583, 584; address of wife quoted, v.31, p.590-91; judgment of French, v.31, p.592.

Tattnall, Commodore of Confed. navy, v.27, p.483.

Tauche, ———, complaint against, v.23, p.393.

Taverns, regulations of W. Fla., v.22, p.337, 339; In Sp. New Orleans, v.22, p.671; regulated in W. Fla., v.23, p.14; license and rates of, v.23, p.411-12.

Taxation and Negro education, v.25, p.738, 743, 748.

Taxes, parish, in St. Helena, 1813, v.23, p.812-13.

Taylor, Calvin, and family collection in L.S.U. Archives, v.24, p.344.

Taylor, Elizabeth, noted, v.24, p.49.

Taylor, Georgia Fairbanks, "The Early History of the Episcopal Church in New Orleans, 1805-1840," v.22, p.428-78.

Taylor, Hancock, noted, v.24, p.49.

Taylor, J. A., on de Feriet Returning Board, v.28, p.1135.

Taylor, J. B., Capt. Co. F, 4th La. Reg't muster roll given, v.30, p.501-503.

Taylor, James, noted, v.24, p.49; La. representative, v.26, p.961.

Taylor, Jordan Gray, Capt., conf. sold., v.26, p.939, 951, 955, 957, 961, 963, 966.

Taylor, Jordan G., Jr., brother-in-law of Lee brothers, v.26, p.937, 938-39; Confed. letters to, v.26, p.940-43, 948-53, 956-63, 966-68, 970-71.

Taylor, Miles, and election of 1851, v.23, p.182; noted, v.25, p.1011, 1044.

Taylor, Richard, General, The Manuscript of "Destruction and Reconstruction," by Andre Lafargue, v.13, p.46; in Red River campaign, v.18, p.5ff.; ancestry and early life, v.24, p.49; education, v.24, p.50-51; experience as a sugar planter, v.24, p.52-54; marriage, v.24, p.54; political career, v.24, p.54-61; military service for the Confederacy, v.24, p.61-112; life after the war, v.24, p.112-19; bibliography, v.24, p.120-26; noted, v.25, p.707; La. gen. of the Confed., v.26, p.974; Commanding Officer of Dept. of W. La., v.26, p.1024-25; sought pardon for Moore, v.26, p.1046; reported Confed. authority had ceased in La., 1862, v.27, p.520; letter to Gen. Smith, v.32, p.110; noted, v.32, p.113, 118, 119; message from Gen. E. K. Smith, v.32, p.119; noted, v.32, p.120, 121, 122, 123, 124, 125, 126, 128, 131, 132, 140, 142.

Taylor, Sallie C., Mrs., Sister of Lee brothers in the Confed. Army, v.26, p.937; letters to, v.26, p.943-48, 953-56, 963-65, 969-70, 971, 974.

Taylor, Thomas, noted, v.22, p.1073, 1074, 1092.

Taylor, Zachary, sketch of his life, v.18, p.376-81; and Lopez expedition, v.22, p.1115ff.; letter to Adj.-Gen., 1845, v.23, p.478; ancestry of, v.24, p.49; military career of, v.24, p.50; noted, v.25, p.387, 1053, 1055, 1060, 1066, 1109; pres. election, 1848, v.25, p.1110; noted, v.27, p.521; Whig pres. of U. S., v.27, p.725, 755; nominated for pres., v.27, p.757; ball in honor of, v.27, p.758-59; noted, v.30, p.466-467.

"Tchoupitoulas Plantation," Meloncy C. Soniat, v.7, p.308.

Teachers Institute, and Cable, v.24, p.169.

Tebault, Dr. C. H., pres. Real Estate Owners' and Taxpayers' Union of N. O., v.27, p.988.

Tebbe, Henry, noted, v.22, p.202.

Teche Cypress Association, organization of cypress lumbermen, v.30, p.1025, 1028.

Teche, noted, v.25, p.934.

Tehuantepec Railroad, noted, v.23, p.197.

"Telegraphe," Copy of, Newspaper Published in New Orleans in 1804, v.2, p.292.

Tench, Fisher, noted, v.22, p.985.

teniente de navio (lieutenant senior grade), noted, v.24, p.614.

Tensas Parish, La., noted, v.25, p.355; v.26, p.988; and the Cong. election of 1894, v.26, p.1097.

Tepetate Field, oil field, v.27, p.1170.

Teran, ———, noted, v.22, p.941.

Teran, Manuel Mier y, noted, v.23, p.849.

"Ternan, Terrisse de, Letters" (French Period), Edited by H. P. Dart, v.3, p.509.

"Terrage, Baron Marc de Villiers du," by Grace King, v.5, p.287.

Terre au Boeuf, origin of name, v.24, p.46.

Terrebonne Parish, Houma Indians in, v.28, p.57; noted, v.28, p.315.

Territorial Legislature of La., v.25, p.316, 334.

"Territorial Papers of the U. S.," ed. by Carter, Vol. IX, "Territory of Orleans,"

rev'd, v.25, p.224-26.
"Territory Memorialists to Congress, The New Orleans, 1804," by E. S. Brown, v.1, sec.1, p.99.
Terry, Champness and W. Fla. Rev., v.21, p.131, 746n.
Terry, Jeremiah, noted, v.22, p.973; v.23, p.12, 56, 392, 404; petition of, v.23, p.361-62, 372, 373.
Terry, J. Randall, register of voters, report, v.31, p.1023; refuses to resign, v.31, p.1028, 1030, 1033.
Tessier, Charles, noted, v.25, p.337, 389.
Tetts, J. A., Farmers' Alliance leader, v.26, p.1070; advocated educational qualification for voting, v.26, p.1118.
Texada, Louis, candidate for lt.-gov., 1855, v.25, p.681.
Texas and Red River Telegraph Company, noted, v.31, p.451.
Texas Pacific Railroad, v.30, p.1230-1231.
"Texas Revolution, New Orleans and the," by James E. Winston, v.10, p.317.
Texas, relation with Caddo parish, v.18, p.819-821; Caddo-Texas treaty, v.18, p.821; Texas revolution and Shreveport, v.18, p.829-31; international boundary of Caddo parish and Texas surveyed, v.18, p.833-37; Caddoes in, v.18, p.923-40; annexation of and La., v.19, p.89-118; and war for independence, v.20, p.185-91; de Bastrop's trip to, v.20, p.402-05, 416-24; Reuben Kemper and revolt, v.21, p.83; Laffite's plan to capture coast, v.21, p.213-219; road through La. to, v.21, p.1160; colonization of, v.22, p.741, 746-51, 799; filibustering expedition to, 1813, v.23, p.1000-1002; first newspaper, v.23, p.1001; attack on in 1863, v.23, p.1207, 1208; Civil War in, v.23, p.1216; G. S. Denison made special agent for Treas. Dept., 1865, v.23, p.1227; conditions in after Civil War, v.23, p.1227-1231, 1233-1234; French raiders in, v.24, p.649; marine action, 1805, v.25, p.7; issue of annexation, v.25, p.125, 127, 1002-1005, 1006; frontier dangers to, v.25, p.292, 293, 295, 298, 299, 300, 297, 399.
"Texas, Stephen F. Austin, Founder of," by James E. Winston, v.9, p.398.
Thatcher, George C., La. educator, director of Thatcher Institute, v.30, p.798-800; in Shreveport Seminary, v.30, p.801; principal Minden Male Academy, v.30, p.933; noted, v.30, p.970, 971.

Thatcher Institute, sketch of, v.30, p.798-801.
Theard, Delaville H., "The Founding of New Orleans," v.3, p.68.
"Theard, George H.," by Henry P. Dart, v.5, p.333.
Theard, Paul E., major, commander state militia, v.26, p.997.
Theatre, German, in New Orleans, v.23, p.509; v.20, p.147-50, 991, 1006, 1113-14.
Theatre, in N. O., 1818-1832, v.21, p.420-517, 846ff.; v.22, p.692.
"Theatre of St. Peter's Street," by Nellie Warner Price, v.1, sec.3, p.215.
Theatre, Orleans, most famous Fr. theatre, v.26, p.369; noted, v.26, p.375; sketch of, v.28, p.90; noted, v.29, p.665-668.
Theatre, St. Phillipe, v.25, p.309; Fr. theatre erected in 1808, v.28, p.89-90; noted, v.29, p.663-665.
Theatre St. Pierre, v.29, p.663, 664.
Therese, Mother, of St. Xavier Farjon, superioress of monastery at St. Ursula of N. O., v.29, p.620.
Thespian Benevolent Society of N. O., created interest in Eng. drama, v.28, p.92, 93.
Thibaut, Leonce, hospital steward, v.26, p.796.
Thibierge, Louis, petition to Superior Council of La., v.21, p.1005, 1013-1020.
Thibodaux College, v.30, p.946-947.
Thibodaux, Bannon G., noted, v.25, p.125, 139.
Thimecourt, ———, swordsman, v.23, p.148.
Thomas, Alfred B., "Forgotten Frontiers," rev., v.15, p.712; "Spanish Activities in the Lower Miss. Valley, 1513-1698," v.22, p.933-42.
Thomas, Denis, noted, v.22, p.1067; v.24, p.648, 671.
Thomas, Dr., noted, v.24, p.758; charter member medical society, v.26, p.59.
Thomas, Harvey, Confed. soldier, v.26, p.973.
Thomas, Henry Goddard, noted, v.23, p.1211.
Thomas, Joseph, and W. Fla., Rev., v.21, p.108, 131, 688n.; member of Police Jury of St. Helena, v.23, p.407ff.
Thomas, Leonard, noted, v.23, p.502.
Thomas, L. E., "A New Fiscal System for Louisiana," v.2, p.129.
Thomas, Philemon, and W. Fla. Rev., v.21, p.89ff., 131, 708n.; orders from Con-

vention of State of Fla., v.21, p.107-109; noted, v.23, p.1018; and sugar tariff, v.25, p.86, 87, 101, 103.

Thomas, Theodore, in New Orleans, v.23, p.510.

Thomassin, Antonio, trial of slave for murder, v.22, p.624-41.

Thompson, Captain, noted, v.24, p.375, 376.

Thompson, D. W., v.29, p.687.

Thompson, Jacob, confederate secret agent, v.29, p.1247-1248.

Thompson, James, noted, v.22, p.313.

Thompson, Martha, noted, v.24, p.49.

Thompson, Matt, N. O. minstrel, v.30, p.147.

Thompson, Nathaniel, noted, v.22, p.950; v.23, p.74, 391.

Thompson, Peter, noted, v.22, p.962.

Thompson, T. P., "Address on Bi-Centennial of New Orleans," v.1, sec.3, p.13; collection noted, v.24, p.317, 319.

Thornton, John R., U. S. Sen., v.28, p.1222.

Thornton, Nic., Confed. sold., v.26, p.954.

Thorpe, Thomas B., candidate for supt. of public education, v.31, p.501.

Thorps, Dr., v.28, p.330; honored by Fr. gov't for services rendered Fr. sailors, v.28, p.333.

"Thoughts, Visions and Sketches of North Louisiana," by Luther Longino, M. D., reviewed by J. Fair Hardin, v.14, p.239.

"Threatened Witch Hunt, A, in an Ante-Bellum Louisiana College," by Arthur Marvin Shaw, Jr., v.31, p.123-9.

"Three Letters of Richard Claiborne to William Miller, 1816-1818," edited by Walter Prichard, v.24, p.729-43.

Thruston, Buckner, sketch, v.28, p.820.

Thruston, Dr. Alfred, sketch, v.28, p.820n.

"Thunder," Fr. naval vessel during yellow fever epidemic of 1857, v.28, p.329-34.

"Thunder," redoubt of "Lightning" fort, v.24, p.657.

Thurman, Allen G., noted, v.24, p.116.

Thurston, Frances, v.28, p.821n.

Tickfaw River, noted, v.23, p.410.

Tierra Bomba, noted, v.24, p.617, 619.

Tiger Island, v.28, p.789, 791, 792, 829, 833; Cathcart found good live oak on, v.28, p.887, 891.

"Tigers," noted, v.24, p.62.

Tilden, Samuel J., noted, v.24, p.115, 119.

Tilton Memorial Library, Tulane University, noted, v.24, p.327.

Timballier Bay, v.28, p.754, 765, 804, 885.

"Times-Democrat," established, v.31, p.785; quoted, v.31, p.796, 800, 803, 804, 808, 811, 816, 817, 819, 820, 823, 828.

"Times-Democrat, Old Days on the," by John Smith Kendall, v.33, p.406-429; rivalry with Picayune, v.33, p.427.

"Times-Picayune," book by Dabney on, rev'd, v.27, p.1229-31.

Timson, Rev. J., noted, v.25, p.362.

Tindol, Mrs. J. F., noted, v.24, p.337.

Tinker, Edward Laroque, "William Beer, 1849-1927," v.11, p.59.

Tissot, A. L., N. O. Sup. Ct. Justice, v.27, p.984.

Tivoli Garden, small N. O. theatre, v.28, p.274.

Tobacco, bought by gov't, 1790, v.21, p.19; trade in, v.22, p.49; purchased by Spain, v.22, p.66; export of, v.22, p.663-664; cultivation in La., v.25, p.25.

Toby, Samuel, noted, v.22, p.458.

Toby, Thomas, noted, v.22, p.458.

Toca, noted, v.24, p.354.

Toca, Philip, in duel with Judge Leonard, v.24, p.763-64.

Tod, John, and 1824 tariff bill, v.25, p.39-40.

Todd, Andrew, and trade in Miss. Valley, v.21, p.67ff.; petition for reduced duties, v.21, p.70; noted, v.22, p.95.

Todd, Thomas, noted, v.24, p.929.

Toledano, Jules, noted, v.23, p.180.

Toledo, Jose Alverez de, activities in N. O., v.21, p.206; expedition to Boguilla de Piedras, v.21, p.207; plans for expedition, v.21, p.1086-87; expedition of, v.22, p.727-31, 734-35, 739; noted, v.22, p.1065, 1070; expedition to Tex., v.23, p.734, 741, 754, 756, 758, 1000-1002, 1084; meeting with Sedella, v.23, p.827; conference with Onis, v.23, p.828; returns to Spain, v.23, p.831-32; petition for pardon, v.23, p.833-36; advice to King on affairs relating to America, v.23, p.836-48; plan for suppressing rev. in Mex., v.23, p.848-53; justification, v.23, p.853-63; and filibustering in neutral ground, v.28, p.1054, 1055-57.

Toler, J. B., lumberman and councilman of Crowley, v.27, p.1171.

Tomassi, Chevalier, noted, v.23, p.448.

"Tombs of Historical Interest in the Saint Bernard Cemetery," by Calvin A. Claudel, v.24, p.354-59.

Tompkins, Florence Cooney, "Women of the Sixties," v.2, p.282.

Tonti, Henry de, noted, v.25, p.399; accompanies LaSalle, v.25, p.922, 923, 927;

finds bayous short cut, v.25, p.928; his trip down Miss. to meet LaSalle, v.25, p.928; his 3rd voyage, v.25, p.928; and Ark. post, v.26, p.633, 634, 635; LaSalle granted him Ark. R. as seigniory, v.26, p.636; and fur trade, v.26, p.636-39; returns to Ark., v.26, p.639-40; his trip down the Miss., v.26, p.641-44; meets Iberville, v.26, p.644; his petition to Fr. for recognition, v.26, p.645; petition denied because of Iberville's influence, v.26, p.645-46; death of, v.26, p.646; his interest in treasure, v.26, p.647, 648; noted, v.26, p.649, 659, 663, 668, 672, 680, 718, 753; accompanied LaSalle, 1678, v.26, p.772; last commander of Fort St. Louis, v.26, p.722; his acc't of LaSalle's Voyage down the Miss., v.26, p.723; began Ark. post, v.26, p.731-32.

Tooker, Samuel, noted, v.22, p.1088-89.

Tooraen, Charles E., Capt. Co. E, 4th La. Reg't muster rolls given, v.30, p.497-500.

Torices, Rodriguez, noted, v.24, p.367.

Torras, Joseph, noted, v.21, p.1144.

Torrens, Gabriel, at Galveston, v.22, p.1065.

Torrens, Jose, at Galveston, v.22, p.1065, 1066.

Torre, Pierre, merchant owning territory where Fr. sailors were buried, v.28, p.338-39.

"Torture in Spanish Criminal Procedure in Louisiana, 1771," Laura L. Porteous, v.8, p.5.

Totin, Francisco, trader sent to Indians, v.28, p.1099.

Toulmin, Harry, and W. Fla. Rev., v.21, p.107, 113; and Mobile Soc., v.21, p.153, 154.

Toumey, Williams, "The Diary of a Young Lawyer of Natchitoches of 1836," I, II, edited by J. Fair Hardin and Phanor Breazeale, v.17, p.64, 315.

Tour, Le Blond de la, prepares plans of city of N. O. as engineer-in-chief, v.29, p.559; notes taken while engineer concerning unhealthy conditions in N. O., v.29, p.560; death noted, v.29, p.566.

Touro Infirmary Society, noted, v.24, p.326.

"Touro, Judah, and his Will," by James A. Renshaw, v.11, p.67; established Touro Free Library in N. O., v.20, p.157-158; noted, v.22, p.166, 449; v.24, p.326.

Tourscher, Francis E., church historian, v.31, p.898.

Tousard, Louis, noted, v.22, p.807n., 808, 810.

Toussaint, Francois Dominique (L'Ouverture), noted, v.22, p.813.

Toussard, and Battle of N. O., v.21, p.369.

Toutant, Alfred P., noted, v.24, p.355.

Toutant, Jacques, noted, v.24, p.355.

Towles, Dr. Thomas, and W. Fla. Rev., v.21, p.83.

Towles, John, sketch, v.28, p.762n., 821n.

Towne, E. B., Commissioner of Fourth Swamp Land District, v.25, p.695.

Townshend, E. C., telegraph contractor, v.31, p.437.

Tracey, ass't to Grand Marshall in procession in N. O. honoring Clay, Webster and Calhoun, v.27, p.767.

Tracey, Capt., N. O. confed. soldier, v.26, p.956.

Tracy, E. L., noted, v.23, p.472.

Trade, on Red River, v.18, p.845-54; in Sp. N. O., v.22, p.47-48, 662ff.; free trade, 1793, v.22, p.52; upper La., v.22, p.83; N. O. and Latin Am., v.22, p.770-80; in W. Fla., 1768, v.23, p.9; difficulties in, reported by Brown, v.24, p.1012-13; N. O., a center of, v.27, p.933-34; monopolized by Western Co., v.27, p.934; N. O. center of Miss. Valley, v.27, p.934-35; Sp. control restricts, in N. O., v.27, p.935, 936-37; contraband trade, v.27, p.936; limited wholesaling before 1812 in N. O., v.27, p.936-37; development of in Miss. Valley, v.27, p.937-39; effect in N. O. of development of river transportation, v.27, p.939-41; triangular trade, v.27, p.941-44; effect of railroads on N. O. trade, v.27, p.944-46; wholesale traders in, v.27, p.947-48; auction sales, v.27, p.948-49; N. O. commission merchants specialties, v.27, p.949-50; kinds of business in N. O., 1844, v.27, p.950; part of "factor," v.27, p.951; wholesale trading of N. O., v.27, p.951-53; N. O. in competition with other centers of, v.27, p.954-57; in N. O. after Civil War, v.27, p.957-60; by 1900, v.27, p.960-61; decline of wholesaler, v.27, p.961-63; restrictions between La. and Tex., v.28, p.1074-82; Indian trade, v.28, p.1082-89.

"Trailways to the Momentous Transfer," by Isaac Joslin Cox, v.27, p.329-42.

Tranchipain, Mother Augustine, superior of nuns, dies, v.29, p.590.

Trans-Mississippi Department, noted, v.24, p.68.

Transportation in N. O., v.20, p.943-45.

Travel, in the Caddo region, v.18, p.837-45; on Red River, v.18, p.845-54; and description in La. in 1860, v.21, p.1110-1214; German immigrants journey to New Orleans and Nacogdoches, 1853-1854, v.23, p.485-500; observations on slaves and slave trade, v.23, p.869ff.; trip of G. S. Denison from Royalton, Vt., to San Antonio, Tex., v.23, p.1132ff.

Treaty Between French Republic and the U. S., April 30, 1803, concerning Cession of Louisiana, v.2, p.139.

Treaty Between U. S. and Spain, Ceding East and West Florida to U. S., 1821, v.2, p.154.

"Treaty, Government by," by William H. Fitzpatrick, v.33, p.299-316.

Treaty of Paris, 1763, v.22, p.377-78.

Treaty of San Lorenzo, noted, v.21, p.56.

Treaty of 1795 and international boundary, v.25, p.6.

Tregle, Joseph George, Jr., "La and the Tariff, 1816-1846," v.25, p.24-148.

Trellue, N. B., pioneer cypress lumberman, v.30, p.1016.

Tremoulet, Madame, treatment of slaves, v.22, p.142-43.

Trenton Institute, v.30, p.888-889.

Trepagnier, ———, and slave revolt, v.22, p.145.

Trespalacious, ———, Mexican patriot, v.22, p.745.

Trezevant, P. J., v.28, p.1181, 1186; Dem. leader in House, v.28, p.1183.

"Trial and Sentence of Biron, Runaway Negro Slave, 1728," Heloise H. Cruzat, v.8, p.23.

"Trial of Pablo Rocheblave Before Governor Ungaza, 1771," Laura L. Porteous, v.8, p.372.

"Tribunals of Criminal Jurisdiction in Ancient Rome," by Charles Gayarre, v.33, p.205-222.

"Tribunals, Permanent, or Quaestiones Perpetuae, Tribunals of Criminal Jurisdiction in Ancient Rome," by Charles Gayarre, v.33, p.217-222.

"Tribunals, Special and Temporary, as distinguished from those called Permanent Tribunals of Criminal Jurisdiction in Ancient Rome," by Charles Gayarre, v.33, p.213-17.

"Tribuno," Spanish brig, v.24, p.665, 672.

"Tricking the Ear," by Cable, v.24, p.174.

Tricou, Dr., noted, v.24, p.758; charter member med. soc., v.26, p.59.

Trimble, David, noted, v.24, p.996.

Trimble, Isaac R., noted, v.24, p.65.

Trimble, Robert, noted, v.24, p.929.

Trinity, noted, v.24, p.80, 85; v.25, p.215.

Trinity School of New Orleans, v.30, p.870-871.

Trinity School, v.30, p.811.

Trist, Hore Browse, noted, v.24, p.774, 781, 782; collector of Customs, N. O., v.31, p.276, 302, 356, 360.

Trist, Mary Louise Brown, noted, v.24, p.774.

Trist, Nicholas Phillips, noted, v.24, p.782; appointed commissioner to Mex., v.25, p.1072; negotiates treaty, v.25, p.1072.

Triumphal Arch, honoring Lafayette, v.29, p.301; described, v.29, p.301, 303; picture of, v.29, p.302.

Trouett, ———, duel with Pruett, v.24, p.756-58.

"Troy," plantation of Isaac Johnson, v.25, p.215; v.28, p.943, 944.

Trudeau, Carlos, surveyor general of La., v.20, p.305; surveyor of Faubourg Ste. Marie, v.22, p.395-96; certification of Bastrop land, v.31, p.615.

Trudeau, Felix, Spanish vice-consul to Natchitoches, v.21, p.684; commandant at Natchitoches, v.22, p.77; noted, v.22, p.815; Spanish vice-consul, 1812, v.25, p.651.

Trudeau, Francoise, deposition of, v.23, p.704-705.

Trudeau, Jean, suit against, v.21, p.1008-1009.

Trudeau, Therese, mentioned, v.21, p.1008-1009.

Trudeau, Widow, ———, noted, v.23, p.695.

Trudeau, Zenon, letter to Thomas Portell, 1794, v.21, p.36n.; sketch, v.21, p.67; confiscates property of Andrew Todd, v.21, p.71; removes Peyroux, v.22, p.86; and revolutionary agitators, v.22, p.88-89.

Trujillo, noted, v.24, p.663, 675; attack upon by Aury, v.24, p.680-84.

Trumbull, Lyman, noted, v.29, p.396, 397, 416.

Truxton, Thomas, noted, v.24, p.992.

Tubb, Eli, conf. sold., v.26, p.954.

Tucker, A. L., nominated Moore for gov., v.26, p.988; noted, v.28, p.1136.

Tucker, John, sketch of, v.29, p.10n.

Tucker, Robert Cinnamond, "The Life and Public Service of E. John Ellis," v.29, p.679-770.

Tulane, Paul, founder of Tulane University, v.20, p.1016-66; letters in Howard-Tilton Memorial Library, v.24, p.330.

Tulane Theatre, Bernhardt at, v.26, p.775, 778; under Klaw & Erlanger management, 1899, v.26, p.1155, 1904, 1165; noted, v.26, p.1166.

Tulane University, noted, v.23, p.1056n.; v.24, p.151, 153, 155, 327.

Tunica Indians, invasion of at Red Pole site, v.28, p.52, 57; noted, v.28, p.684.

Tureaud family, collection in L.S.U. Archives, v.24, p.345.

Turkey, war with Russia, v.24, p.999ff., 1016, 1103-04.

Turla, Leopoldo, Cuban poet and patriot, v.18, p.50-51; fled to New Orleans, v.18, p.52; death, v.18, p.53.

Turner, Arlin, "Joaquin Miller in New Orleans," v.22, p.216-25; "George Washington Cable's Literary Apprenticeship," v.24, p.168-86; "John Howard Payne in New Orleans," v.31, p.110-22.

Turner, Edward, identified, v.21, p.402n.; Am. soldier at Natchitoches, v.28, p.1030-31, 1032, 1033; mil. comdr. Natchitoches, appeal to for protection of slaves, v.28, p.1069-70.

Turner, Fielding, identified, v.21, p.402n.

Turner Hall Conv., Pinchback pres. of, v.27, p.545, 551.

Turner Hall Republicans, v.27, p.545, 551.

Turner, Henry, claimant to Maison Rouge grant, v.20, p.344, 366-68.

Turner, Hon. F. L., noted, v.26, p.76.

Turner, James, oration delivered at St. Francisville, v.21, p.179-89; identified, v.21, p.402n., 766n.; noted, v.22, p.470.

Turner, William A., director Eng. theatrical Co., v.28, p.102-103.

Turnhalle, noted, v.26, p.374, 375, 386, 387, 391.

Turnverein, in New Orleans, v.24, p.160.

Turpin, Madame, noted, v.22, p.142.

Twain, Mark, comment upon by Cable, v.24, p.172-73.

"Twentieth Century Louisiana," by Dr. G. W. McGinty, v.32, p.5.

Twentieth Regiment La. Militia, Robinson commissioned surgeon in, v.25, p.663.

Twiggs, Gen'l D. E., noted, v.23, p.1170; v.24, p.439, 440, 441, 442, 500; home of seized by Butler, v.27, p.515.

Twitchell, M. H., leader of Radicals in Red River Parish, v.29, p.430-431.

"Two Brothers," schooner of Laffites, v.23, p.756.

"Two Brothers, The," ship bringing passengers to La., 1719, v.21, p.965-70.

"Two Friends," schooner, v.23, p.435n.; privateer, v.23, p.811.

Tyler, John, and the annexation of Texas, v.19, p.90ff.; and tariff, v.25, p.87, 113, 115, 116; noted, v.25, p.673, 1002-1003, 1099.

Tyler, Robert, ed. "N. O. Democrat," sketch of, v.30, p.311; letter of, v.30, p.332-333; edits "N. O. Democrat," v.31, p.739.

"Types of Privateer Vessels, Their Armament and Flags, in the Gulf of Mexico," by S. Faye, v.23, p.118-30.

URSULINES

UCROS, VINCENTE, noted, v.22, p.1068.
Ueber, Jakob, noted, v.24, p.154.
Ueber, John, noted, v.24, p.154.
Uhler, John Earle, "James Ryder Randall in La.," v.21, p.532-46.
Ulloa, Don Antonio de, noted, v.26, p.9; 1st Sp. gov. of La., 1766, v.26, p.739; Sp. gov., 1766, v.27, p.632; interest in Ark. Post, v.27, p.637; attempt to supply religious guidance for La., v.27, p.638; issued trading licenses in N. O., v.27, p.691; system of land grants under, v.27, p.698; salaries of churchmen, v.27, p.714; trade restrictions, v.27, p.935; sent to take possession of Sp. La., v.29, p.887; has difficulty enlisting Fr. soldiers there, v.29, p.887-889; gov. and cap't-gen'l of province of Sp. La., v.29, p.894, 895; noted, v.29, p.916.
Ulloa, Don Pedro Varela y, noted, v.31, p.621; opinion of Bastrop venture, v.31, p.623.
Ulmer, Grace, "Economic and Social Development of Calcasieu Parish, La.," v.32, p.519.
Umminger, Philipp, noted, v.24, p.384; manuscript of, v.24, p.385-417.
"Uncle Tom's Cabin," Phanor Breazeale, v.7, p.304.
Underwood, Thomas, noted, v.23, p.26.
Union Assoc. of N. O., citizen's organization in conquered N. O., v.27, p.518, 519, 522.
Union Bank of Plaquemine, v.25, p.195.
Union Male and Female Academy, v.30, p.921-22.
Union Parish, of La., noted, v.26, p.937, 957; bagging factory, v.26, p.1065; Populist legis. from, v.26, p.1109.
Unitarian Church, and John Quincy Adams, v.24, p.1165.
"United Colonies of America," definition of, v.24, p.705.
United States Bank, noted, v.24, p.924, 1166.
U. S. Circuit Court, and Gaines Cases, v.27, p.9-320 passim; Eastern La. District cases involving use of mail by Lottery Co., v.27, p.1008-1009.
United States Dept. of Agriculture, bulletins of, v.30, p.682-708.
United States, expedition against Barataria, v.24, p.19-20; prosperity in 1825, v.24, p.957.
U. S. Geological Survey, work in Caddo oil and gas fields, v.29, p.59, 61, 63, 64, 66.
U. S. Supreme Court, and Gaines Cases, v.27, p.8-320 passim; suit of Dauphin vs. Key, v.27, p.1007-1008; upheld La. Sup. Ct. in declaring N. O. assessors could not levy taxes on Lottery Co., v.27, p.1009; Dauphin vs. McClure, for libel,

v.27, p.1010-11; ruled Cong. could not designate what may be carried in mails, v.27, p.1081-82; ruled Cong. could regulate Interstate Commerce, v.27, p.1084.

U. S. vs. Richard King and Daniel W. Coxe, v.20, p.353-63.

"University of Louisiana, Richard Henry Wilde in New Orleans and the Establishment of the," by Aubrey Starke, v.17, p.605.

University of Louisiana, establishment of, v.23, p.1056; Law School, early history of, v.23, p.1056-1063; advertisement of, v.23, p.1060-1061.

University School, v.30, p.826.

"Unzaga, Governor, Decides the Family Meeting has no place in Spanish Probate Procedure in Louisiana, 1774," translated by Laura L. Porteous, v.12, p.288.

Unzaga y Amezaga, Luis de, Governor of La., Fire Ordinance for New Orleans, v.4, p.201; Gov. of La., v.27, p.637, 640-41, 643; has San Gabriel de Manchac regarrisoned, v.27, p.644, 645, 648, 669; issue of trading licenses in N. O., v.27, p.691; noted, v.22, p.640; noted, v.26, p.10; in charge of Sp. La., v.26, p.740.

Upper Old River, noted, v.25, p.398.

Upper Terrebonne Drainage District, v.30, p.676, fig.3, 700.

Urban, Chester Stanley, "New Orleans and the Cuban Question during the Lopez Expedition, 1849-1851," v.22, p.1095-1167.

Urguhart, George, noted, v.22, p.981; and W. Fla. Assembly, v.23, p.5ff.; noted, v.23, p.357, 358, 368, 391; election of, v.23, p.377; noted, v.22, p.981.

Urquhart, Thomas, noted, v.22, p.449, 450.

Ursuline College, New Orleans, sketch of, v.24, p.334-35; museum records, v.24, p.334-35; history of, cited, v.24, p.335, 349.

Ursuline Convent of New Orleans, noted, v.22, p.99, 110, 428, 647; first home of Ursulines, v.29, p.569; work on permanent convent, v.29, p.572-573, 574-580, 584-590; described by nun on moving in, v.29, p.590-595; 1st convent deteriorated rapidly, v.29, p.602; work begun on 2nd convent, v.29, p.602-611; 2nd convent completed, v.29, p.611; changes and enlargements, v.29, p.618-621; description of chapel given by writers, v.29, p.622, 623-624; convent property sold when city streets cut through it, v.29, p.626-63; work on new convent begun, v.29, p.631-637; old convent given to Bishop of New Orleans for use, v.29, p.637-643; explanation of plan of convent with picture, v.29, p.647-648; contract and specifications for convent, v.29, p.651-659.

Ursulines, the, in Louisiana, interest in early education, v.19, p.601-607; and land grants in N. O., v.20, p.904-08; noted, v.25, p.363; early Negro education, v.25, p.729, 733; in La. education, v.30, p.936-937; and Ursuline Convent, v.30, p.949-951; and Royal Hospital, v.31, p.8; noted, v.31, p.14. See order of Ursuline nuns.

"Ursulines of Louisiana, The," by Heloise Hulse Cruzat, v.2, p.5.

Uruguay, revolutionary flag of, v.24, p.662.

Usher, Robert J., Rev's James' "Oliver Pollock," v.21, p.561-63; noted, v.24, p.327.

VACA, CABEZA DE, noted, v.22, p.934, 938.
Vahamonde, Joseph Vasquez, noted, v.22, p.72, 75.
Valdes, Antonio, sketch, v.21, p.21n.
Valence Institute, v.30, p.867.
Valenzuela, located, v.22, p.814.
Vales (drafts), in Galveston, v.24, p.639.
Valle, Francois, made commandant at Ste. Genevieve, v.22, p.85n., 86.
Valley Campaign, traced, v.24, p.63-66.
"Valley Queen," steamer, picture of, v.25, p.504.
Van Buren, John, v.23, p.1197.
Van Buren, Martin, noted, v.24, p.703, 1042, 1137, 1164; coalition with Clinton, v.24, p.1050; and 1836 campaign in La., v.25, p.109; noted, v.25, p.1002, 1003, 1063; candidate for pres., 1848, v.25, p.1110.
Vance, John C., Anti-Lottery delegate to Farmers' Union Meeting, v.27, p.1086; anti-lottery league, v.28, p.1152.
Vance, Joseph, noted, v.24, p.996.
Vance, W. W., suggested amendments to lottery bill of 1890, v.27, p.1042; and lottery question, v.28, p.1146.
Vandenbenden, Louis, and revolutionary agitators, v.22, p.87.
Vandenclooster, Louise Barbe, married Fulwar Skipwith, v.31, p.304.
Vandenclooster, Theresa Josephine, married Wm. Herries Herriesse, v.31, p.304.

Vanderhorst, Ellis, petition of, v.23, p.389.
Vandervoort, George W., early N. O. police reporter, v.29, p.55; secretary to chief of police, N. O., v.29, p.55-56.
van de Wall, William, noted, v.24, p.347.
Vandiver, Frank E., ed., "A Collection of La. Confed. Letters," v.26, p.937-74.
Van Dorn, Major-General Earl, noted, v.24, p.63.
Van Hufflen, H., N. O. musician, v.31, p.143-4.
van Limburg, Dutch minister, v.24, p.514.
Van Os, Fides, singer, v.31, p.871.
Van Vleck, Henry, Chief Engr. N. O., Mobile and Chattanooga Railroad, v.30, p.1246-1269.
Van Wooten, Mrs., La. educator, v.30, p.834.
Varela, Don Mariano, sec. council on Indian trade, v.28, p.1088.
Varieties Theatre, Jefferson at, 1870, v.26, p.1154.
Varnado, M. L., purchased Spence and King bus lines, v.29, p.172.
Varna, fortress of, v.24, p.1121; surrender of, v.24, p.1129.
Vatimesnil, Mr., minister of France, v.24, p.1113.
Vaudreuil, Marquis de, and Superior Council, v.21, p.999; succeeded Bienville as Gov. of La., v.26, p.769, 680, 736; ordered rebuilding of Ark. post, v.26, p.686-687; letter to concerning Fabry,

v.26, p.694; and Sp. trade, v.26, p.699, 700; noted, v.26, p.705; gave Ark. post to command of de la Houssaye, v.26, p.708-709; promised reinforcements, v.26, p.701-11; gave trade monopoly to de la Houssaye, v.26, p.711; succeeded by Kerlerec, v.26, p.712; became gov. of La. Colony, v.29, p.602; sends plan for rebuilding of convent to King, v.29, p.602; noted, v.29, p.612.

Vaudry, W. T., and White League, v.23, p.528.

Vaughan, Bess, "A Bio-Bibliography of Grace Elizabeth King," v.17, p.751; noted, v.24, p.339.

Vaughan, H. L., La. midshipman, of Confed., v.27, p.481, 483.

Vaughn, Cora Wills, wife of P. O. Hebert, v.31, p.494.

Vaught, Darrah Albert Shelby, letter to J. R. Ficklen, v.23, p.525-43; sketch, v.23, p.527.

Vaux, Descommes, noted, v.24, p.763.

Vauxhall garden, St. Charles Theatre converted into, v.28, p.234-35.

Veach, A. C., of U. S. Geological Survey, v.29, p.59.

Veeder, Charles H., La. educator, established Minden Academy, v.30, p.929; noted, v.30, p.930.

Velasco, Viceroy, noted, v.22, p.936.

"Velocipede," noted, v.24, p.37.

Venezuela, revolutionary movement in, 1797, v.23, p.430.

"Vengeance," a privateer, v.24, p.612, 629.

"Vengeance of the Natchez, The," by Clem G. Hearsey, v.21, p.266.

Vente, de la, French missionary to Natchez Indians, quoted, v.31, p.478-9.

Vera Cruz, trade with, v.22, p.778.

Verande, Louis, manager of Fr. opera house at time of fire, v.29, p.676.

Verdun, J. B., Jr., negro clerk of ct. in St. Mary, v.28, p.1139.

Verges, Bernard de, inventory of, v.22, p.674.

Vergne, Col. H. J. de la, Address, "General Beauregard Before the Civil War," v.1, p.297; "Louisiana," v.2, p.174.

Vergnolle, J. M., headed com. for reconstruction of memorial to Fr. sailors, v.28, p.339; New entry Vermillion River, v.28, p.739, 817, 822, 826, 833.

Vermilionville Academy, v.30, p.837.

Vermillion Bay, v.28, p.765, 826.

Vermillion Bayou, noted, v.24, p.73.

Vermillionville (Lafayette), noted, v.24, p.83.

Verner, John, identified, v.21, p.767.

Vernon Academy, v.30, p.835-36.

Vernon, John, and W. Fla. Rev., v.21, p.131.

Vernon Parish, of La., in 1860, v.21, p.1191; Populist legislator from, v.26, p.1109.

Verplanck, Julian, and 1833 Tariff, v.25, p.97, 99, 103, 104.

Verret, Bob, leader of Houma Indians, v.28, p.57.

Verret, Philip, v.28, p.834n.

Vertner, Aaron, death noted, v.29, p.1061-62.

Very, Romain, noted, v.22, p.734.

"Veterans Versus Churchwardens," by Simone de la Souchere Delery, v.33, p.145-50.

Vial, Pedro, noted, v.21, p.38.

Viana, Francisco, neutral ground agreement, v.28, p.1039.

Vicksburg Memorial Monument, Address at Dedication of, by Col. J. D. Hill, v.3, p.503.

Vicksburg, Miss., surrender of, v.23, p.1204, 1205; noted, v.24, p.69, 72, 74, 77, 82, 84, 109; noted, v.25, p.152, 211; plantation center, v.25, p.175.

Vicksburg, Shreveport & Texas Railroad, v.25, p.697; history of, v.30, p.1179-1209; name changed, v.30, p.1197; created, v.31, p.512.

Vick, Thomas E., Capt. Co. H, 4th La. Reg't, muster rolls of, v.30, p.508-511.

Victoria, Guadalupe, rebel leader of Vera Cruz, v.23, p.848-49.

"Victoria," schooner of Lafittes, v.23, p.758; v.24, p.648, 684.

Vidalia, La., in 1860, v.21, p.1209; noted, v.25, p.19.

Vidal, Don Jose, Spanish Consul in N. O., v.21, p.679; sketch, v.22, p.800-801, 803; in Natchez, v.25, p.6-7; children to Pa., v.25, p.7; to Texas, v.25, p.7, 13; and Casa Irujo, v.25, p.8, 10; with Burr Boats, v.25, p.11-12; in Natchez, v.25, p.12-13; pursuit of Altamira, v.25, p.13-18; financial difficulties, v.25, p.18-19; death, v.25, p.19-21.

Vidal, Joseph, collection in L.S.U. Archives, v.24, p.345.

Vidal, Nicolas Maria, noted, v.22, p.52n., 126; letters to Casa Calvo, v.22, p.130, 134-38; letter from Casa Calvo, v.22, p.131-32; and Batture controversy, v.23, p.683.

Vidal y Alarcon, Manuel, noted, v.22, p.800.

Vidrine, Dr. Arthur, superintendent Charity Hospital, v.31, p.88.

Viellier, Charles de, noted, v.22, p.815.

Viel, Rev. Alexandre, noted, v.22, p.98.

Vienna Male and Female Academy, v.30, p.839.

Vieux Carre, noted, v.24, p.183; register of chimneys in, in Bibliotheca Parsoniana, v.24, p.310; noted, v.25, p.373; description of, v.28, p.326-28.

Vigilante tradition, noted, v.24, p.201.

"Vigilant, Le," Donaldsonville paper, v.31, p.981-84.

"Vignaud, Henry: A Personal Sketch," by Edward Alexander Parsons, v.5, p.63.

Vigo, Francesco, early life, v.18, p.41-42; aids Clark in capture of Vincennes, v.18, p.43.

Vilemont, Luis de, Colonization of America, v.21, p.57-63.

Villafane, noted, v.22, p.937.

Villalobos, Antonio Argota, Spanish vice-consul at N. O., v.21, p.684.

Villamil, Andrew, deposition of, v.23, p.713-14.

Villamil, Jose Maria, baptismal record, v.18, p.44; leaves New Orleans for Europe, v.18, p.45; joins revolutionaries in Venezuela and Ecuador, v.18, p.45-46; Ecuadorean minister plenipotentiary to Washington, v.18, p.46; noted, v.23, p.162.

Villapinto, Jose Maria, noted, v.23, p.849.

Villavaso, Nicolas Jose de, Spanish Consular sec'y in New Orleans, v.21, p.684.

Villebeuvre, Lt. Juan de la noted, v.25, p.937.

Villele, de, ministry discussed by James Brown, v.24, p.942-43, 947, 961-62, 971-72, 976, 981-82, 984, 1000, 1006, 1020, 1052, 1067, 1077, 1078, 1079-80, 1088-89, 1090, 1109, 1116, 1124.

Villemont, Chevalier de, list of settlers for Concession, v.21, p.966.

Villere, Col., C. J., commissioner of Honduras Lottery Co., v.27, p.1099.

Villere, James, noted, v.22, p.749, 808; sketch, v.22, p.810.

Villere, Joseph, noted, v.23, p.110.

Villere, M. A. Laure, noted, v.24, p.356.

Villere, Omer, noted, v.24, p.146.

Villiers, de, Baron Marc, "A History of the Foundation of New Orleans," v.3, p.157.

Villiers, Jean, Sp. purchasing agent and Philippe Ferret, test Embargo, v.25, p.941.

Vinache, Joseph, engineer, his memoir on fortification of N. O., v.26, p.747; Battalion Chief of Engineers for France, makes inventory, v.29, p.621-22.

Vincennes, Post of, and fur trade, v.23, p.393.

Vincent, G. W., donation to Charity Hospital, v.31, p.80.

Vincent, William G., noted, v.24, p.73, 85, 86, 90, 96; pres. Anti-Lottery League of La., v.27, p.1054, 1055, 1057, 1091; v.28, p.1158.

Vineyards, failure of cultivation, v.22, p.996.

Vinton, La., v.32, p.585-88.

Violette, E. M., "Donelson Caffery, A Louisiana Democrat Out of Line," v.14, p.521.

Violett, Major Ned, of 3rd Batn. of Nat'l Guards, v.26, p.792.

"Virginians on the Ohio and the Mississippi in 1742," by Fairfax Harrison (Reprinted from the Virginia Magazine of History), v.5, p.316.

Virginia Resolutions, noted, v.24, p.698, 719, 1168.

Virginia Springs, resort, v.24, p.1079, 1115; resort of wealthy planters, v.25, p.205.

"Visits of Josiah Gregg to Louisiana, 1841-1847," by Howard T. Dimick, v.29, p.5-13.

"Visit to Lafitte, A," Contributed by Elliot Snow, v.11, p.434.

Viterbo Brothers, noted, v.23, p.568.

Viviat, ―――――, complaint against, v.23, p.393; noted, v.23, p.395; letter from, v.23, p.397-98.

"Vixen," naval brig, v.23, p.442.

Vizcaya, Alva y, noted, v.23, p.821.

Vocational education, beginnings among Negroes, v.25, p.736-37.

Vogel, Rev. Claude L., O. M., Cap. Ph. D., "The Capuchins in French Louisiana, 1722, 1766" (Review by Henry P. Dart), v.11, p.620.

Voisin, Pierre, deposition of, v.23, p.702-03.

Vokes, Campbell, noted, v.23, p.377, 384.

von Dalberg, Karl Theodor, noted, v.24, p.381.

von Gross, Freiherr, noted, v.24, p.405.

von Pufendorf, Samuel, "De Jure Naturae et Gentium," noted, v.24, p.701.

von Reizenstein, Ludwig, German liberal in N. O., v.20, p.145-47, 1014.

von Zincken, Leon, colonel in Civil War, v.20, p.1002; noted, v.23, p.503.

Voodoo, in La., v.24, p.751-52; noted, v.25, p.366-68.

Voodoo Virgin, noted, v.25, p.367.

Voohries, A. P., candidate for lt.-gov., v.31, p.1055; noted, v.31, p.1082.

Voorhies, Albert, Dem.-Populist elector, v.26, p.1116.

Voorhies, Alfred, Sen. of McEnery faction, v.28, p.1137.

Voorhies, Cornelius, and the Const. Con. of 1844 in La., v.25, p.1010ff.

Voss, Rev. Louis, D. D., trans. by, "The System of Redemption in the State of Louisiana," by J. Hanno Deiler, v.12, p.426; quoted, v.24, p.148.

Voudou, see Voodoo.

Vuillet, New Orleans musician, v.31, p.139.

WADDILL, FRANK H., "SCENE OF the LeBreton Murder," v.8, p.266.
Wade, C. J., in charge of sports for Bogalusa inaugural day, v.29, p.110; also general reception, v.29, p.111.
Wade, Thomas H., journal in Rudolph Matas Medical Library, v.24, p.334.
Wade, Thomas M., supported lottery bill, v.27, p.1037.
Wadley, W. M., pres. Vicksburg, Shreveport and Texas Railroad, v.30, p.1183, 1196.
Wagaman, Thos, v.28, p.767n.
Waggaman, Col. Eugene, noted, v.29, p.724, 727.
Waggaman, George A., noted, v.25, p.78, 79, 87, 102; v.28, p.767n.
Wagner, Irene C., study of La. folklore, v.24, p.755.
Wagner, Peter K., noted, v.22, p.785; elected state printer, v.26, p.978.
Wagnon, Thomas P., noted, v.24, p.924.
Waugespack, W. J., Address, "First Official Flag of the City of New Orleans," v.1, sec.3, p.210.
Wailes, Levin, papers in L.S.U. Archives, v.24, p.344; Reg. of Land Office, Ter. of Orleans, v.28, p.845n.; noted, v.28, p.863; letter to from Cathcart & Hutton, v.28, p.904-05, 906-07, 909.
Walcott, Reuben, noted, v.23, p.479.
Waldron, George B., noted, v.23, p.1232.
Waldron, ———, noted, v.23, p.400.
Walker, Alexander, noted, v.22, p.1139n., 1160; v.23, p.200; ed. N. O. "Herald," v.30, p.264; ed. "N. O. Picayune," v.30, p.265; on staff of "N. O. Times," v.30, p.283; sketch of, v.30, p.283-84; and "Daily Delta," v.30, p.298-99; noted, v.30, p.290, 211.
Walker, Brigadier-General H. T., noted, v.24, p.62.
Walker, Charles, petition of, v.23, p.403.
Walker, Clem L., confederate soldier, v.29, p.1114-15.
Walker, Dr. Winslow, "The Troyville Mounds," quoted from, v.25, p.633, 635, 638.
Walker, John, noted, v.23, p.367.
Walker, Joseph M., pres. Const. Con. of 1844, v.25, p.1008; his questionable election as state treasurer, v.25, p.1047; noted, v.25, p.1075; named state treasurer, v.26, p.978; suggested Dem. Cand. for gov., v.28, p.958-59, noted, v.28, p.961, succeeded Johnson as gov., v.28, p.977; Louisiana governor, v.31, p.497; on internal improvements, v.31, p.513; noted, v.31, p.988.
Walker, Judge Alexander, early N. O. newspaperman, v.29, p.776; noted, v.29, p.783.
Walker, L. P., Secretary of War, v.24, p.439, 440.
Walker, Major-General James G., noted, v.24, p.74, 75, 77, 78, 80, 85, 89, 90, 91, 93, 101.

Walker, Mrs. R. F., noted, v.29, p.1229.

Walker, Norman, early N. O. newspaperman, v.29, p.783-85; son of Alexander, reporter "N .O. Picayune," v.30, p.264, 265.

Walker, Robt. J., and 1846 tariff revision, v.25, p.134-35, 137, 139, 140.

Walker Tariff, noted, v.25, p.141, 142, 144.

Walker, William, editor of "Crescent," v.22, p.1110; papers in Institute of Middle American Research, v.24, p.332, 333; early N. O. newspaperman, v.29, p.786.

Wallace, Caleb, noted, v.24, p.929.

Wallace, W. W., N. O. musician, v.31, p.132.

Waller, Edward, noted, v.24, p.68.

Waller, Stephen, noted, v.23, p.420.

Wall, John, noted, v.23, p.204.

Walmsley, T. Semmes, address in memory of Henry Plauche Dart, v.18, p.242.

Walridge, Ernest, N. O. newspaperman, "Old Days on the N. O. Picayune," v.33, p.336.

Walsh, J. M., noted, v.23, p.556.

Walsh, Rev. Patrick, and Schism of 1805 in New Orleans, v.22, p.98-141; vice-vicar-general, v.22, p.102; letter to Sedella, v.22, p.118-20; letters from Sedella, v.22, p.118, 120, 121; letters from Casa Calvo, v.22, p.121, 123-24, 128, 141; letters to Casa Calvo, v.22, p.121-123, 133; noted, v.31, p.903; schism with Antoine, v.31, p.904.

Walteker, John, petition of, v.23, p.366.

Walters, Ethel, teacher in 1st Bogalusa school, v.29, p.100.

Walters, W. W., noted, v.23, p.204, 207.

Walton, Col., noted, v.23, p.1080.

Walton, Joseph B., led parade for unveiling of statute of Clay, v.27, p.774.

Warden, Mr., former consul in Paris, v.24, p.1059.

Ward, Benjamin, noted, v.22, p.317; and W. Fla. Assembly, v.22, p.943; noted, v.23, p.45, 357, 368; election of, v.23, p.377; petition of, v.23, p.382.

Ward, Daniel, noted, v.22, p.317, 981; and W. Fla. Assembly, v.23, p.19ff.; noted, v.23, p.357, 368; election of, v.23, p.377; petition of, v.23, p.403.

Ward, E. B., receives N. O., Mobile and Texas Railroad, v.30, p.1295-96.

Ward, R. H., People's party elector, v.26, p.1087.

Ward, Walter, Farmers' Alliance Com., v.28, p.1152.

Ware, James A., proposed const. conv., v.26, p.1111-12, proposed ballot reform, v.26, p.1112; bill to suppress lotteries. 1894, v.27, p.1097.

Warfield, Perry, noted, v.22, p.1109.

Warfield, Tim, N. O. minstrel, sketch of, v.30, p.146.

"War in West Florida and Louisiana, 1814-15, Historical Memoir of the," by Major A. Lacarriere Latour, v.2, p.143.

"War of 1812, The, Some Florida Episodes," v.1, p.330; services of Jean Laffite, v.24, p.20-22; documents in La. State Museum, v.24, p.319; and sympathy for French privateersmen, v.24, p.614; effects on La., v.25, p.24; noted, v.25, p.327; "New Orleans and the War of 1812," by R. McC. B. Adams, I, II, III, v.16, p.221, 479, 681; IV, V, VI, v.17, p.169, 349, 502.

"War Times in and Around Clinton, Louisiana," by Annie Sanderson Kilbourne, v.13, p.64.

War to the Death in 1816, noted, v.24, p.655.

Warmoth Board, Governor Warmoth's returning board, v.31, p.700; restrained, v.31, p.700.

Warmoth, Henry Clay, elected gov. of La., v.26, p.1059; headed repub. faction, v.26, p.1088; became gov. of La., 1868, v.27, p.535; friend of Pinchback, v.27, p.537; favored election bill of 1870, v.27, p.539-40; opposition to, v.27, p.541-42; opposed Pinchback as U. S. Senator, 1871, v.27, p.542; calls conv. at Turner Hall, v.27, p.544-45; impeachment advocated, v.27, p.546; calls special session of Senate to select lt.-gov., v.27, p.546-48; organization of Legis., 1872, v.27, p.548-50; split with Pinchback, v.27, p.551-54; railroad race with Pinchback, v.27, p.554-57; election of 1872, v.27, p.557-59; call for extra session of Legis., 1872, v.27, p.559; vote to impeach, v.27, p.560; denounced Pinchback's right to governorship, v.27, p.561-62; struggle for authority, v.27, p.563; appeal to Grant, v.27, p.564-66; plan to reconvene Fusionist Legis., v.27, p.572; supports Sheridan for Cong., v.27, p.582, 583, 588, 595; supported by Pinchback for gov., v.27, p.604; denounced Caffery, v.27, p.809, 811, 816; allowed Lottery Co. Bill to become law without his signature, v.27, p.974, 995; headed Anti-Lottery Republicans, v.27, p.1092; contract with La. Levee Co., v.28, p.309; gov't of, v.28, p.1132-33; appt's to Returning Board, 1872, v.28, p.1134-35; opposes Kellogg, v.29, p.398, 400; noted, v.29, p.339, 402, 409; impeached, v.29, p.410; noted, v.29, p.412, 715; and the New Orleans press, v.30, p.200-217; ancestry, v.30, p.530; early life and ed., v.30, p.530-531; military career, v.30, p.531; receives dishonorable discharge but restored to service, v.30, p.532-533; transferred to N. O., v.30, p.533; appointed judge, v.30, p.534; practices law in N. O., v.30, p.535; indicted for embezzlement, v.30, p.536; returns to N. O., v.30, p.537; activities backing Andrew Johnson, v.30, p.537-539; campaign to secure Negro vote, v.30, p.538-541; elected delegate to Cong., v.30, p.541-545; nominated for gov., v.30, p.547-548; campaign and election, v.30, p.548-549; appointed military gov., later civil gov., v.30, p.550; calls Legislature to convene, v.30, p.551; in legislature, v.30, p.552-559, 563-565, 571-598; attempts to organize state militia, v.30, p.559-563; attempts at internal improvements, v.30, p.574-575; Ship Island controversy, v.30, p.576-579; Railroad controversy, v.30, p.581-584; protest against bribery in leg., v.30, p.584-585; efforts for reform, v.30, p.586-598; agitation concerning Nicholson bill, v.30, p.590-591; charges against of corruption, v.30, p.592-594; attack against Wickliffe, v.30, p.594-596; measures giving autocratic power, v.30, p.599-603; and Republican state convention, v.30, p.604-606, 616-620; campaign of 1870, v.30, p.606-607; bargains with Democrats to defeat Dunn, v.30, p.609-611; factions split, v.30, p.612-632; wounded, v.30, p.12; incident with Dunn, v.30, p.614-615; efforts to elect Lt. Gov., v.30, p.624-626; attempt to keep Carter faction out of Leg., v.30, p.626-632; identifies with "reform" party, v.30, p.633; later career, v.30, p.648; death, v.30, p.649; noted, v.30, p.232, 294, 309; bibl., v.30, p.650-653; governor, v.31, p.687; and Wickliffe, v.31, p.688, 689; early career, v.31, p.698; evaluation, v.31, p.699; impeached, v.31, p.701-03; articles of impeachment, v.31, p.702; congressional report of, v.31, p.733; and lottery, v.31, p.752; noted, v.31, p.64, 1042, 1063.

Warmoth, Isaac Sanders, father of Henry Clay Warmoth, sketch of, v.30, p.530.

Warner, Tabitha Emily, wife of Ezekiel Parke Ellis, v.29, p.679.

Warner, Thomas C., first Parish Judge of Washington Parish, v.29, p.79; trustee of Franklin Academy, 1838, v.29, p.84.

Warnick, Charlie, 1st Jew to be married in Bogalusa, v.29, p.120.

Warren, Dr. James, noted, v.26, p.76.

Warren, Harris G., revs. "Diplomacy of the Borderlands," by Philip Coolidge Brooks, v.24, p.205-06.

Warren, Harris Gaylord, "The Firebrand Affair; A Forgotten Incident of the Mexican Rev.," v.21, p.203-12; tr. and ed., "Documents Relating to George Graham's Proposals to Jean Laffite for the Occupation of the Texas Coast," v.21, p.213-19; "Pensacola and the Filibusters, 1816-1817," v.21, p.806-22; "Documents Relating to the Establishment of Privateers at Galveston, 1816-1817," v.21, p.1081-1109; tr. and ed., "Jose Alvarez de Toledo's Reconciliation with Spain and Projects for Suppressing Rebellion in the Spanish Colonies," v.23, p.827-63; "The Sword was Their Passport," rev'd, v.26, p.1179-81; "Southern Filibusters in the War of 1812," v.25, p.291-300; rev's Haggard and McLean's "Handbook for Translators of Spanish Historical Documents," v.25, p.536.

Warren, Major G. K., levee board member, v.31, p.542.

Warren, T. R., work on "De Bow's Review," v.29, p.376.

Warren, William, diary in Bibliotheca Parsoniana, v.24, p.311.

Wartegg, Baron Ernest Von Hesse, married Minnie Hauck, v.31, p.863.

Warwick, Lord, noted, v.24, p.654.

Washington and New Orleans Company, Morse telegraph line, incorporated, v.31, p.430; route proposed, v.31, p.430; reception of agents, v.31, p.431-2; completion, v.31, p.444; abuses monopoly, v.31, p.445, 474; reform, v.31, p.447, 475.

"Washington Artillery, Early History of the, of New Orleans," by Powell A. Casey, v.23, p.471-84; records in La. Hist. Assn. depository, v.24, p.315; noted, v.24, p.438.

Washington, Booker T., noted, v.25, p.795, 812.

Washington, George, letter in Howard-Tilton Memorial Library, v.24, p.330; noted, v.24, p.700, 711; Statue of, by Hiram Powers, made for Louisiana, letter concerning, v.2, p.272.

Washington, La., noted, v.24, p.79; v.25, p.360.

Washington, Mr., noted, v.24, p.967, 968.

Washington Parish Health Unit, organized, v.29, p.86.

"Washington Parish, The History of," by

Hon. Prentiss B. Carter, v.14, p.36.

Washington Parish, Germans in, v.23, p.514; physiographic characteristics of, v.29, p.73; population of from 1810-1940, v.29, p.73-74; one of the "Florida Parishes," v.29, p.74-75; early settlers of, v.29, p.75; government of from 1810-1819, v.29, p.75-78; created from St. Tammany Parish, v.29, p.79; early family names, v.29, p.80; war record from Battle of N. O. to World War II, v.29, p.80-83; religious views of, v.29, p.83-84; school system of, v.29, p.84-86; health program, v.29, p.86.

Washita, see Ouachita.

Water, Charles de, noted, v.22, p.1044.

Waterloo, located, v.21, p.1139.

Waterman, Abbott, newspaperman, "Old Days on the N. O. Picayune," v.33, p.333-34.

Waterman, Capt. M. S., Commander Co. B under Wood, v.26, p.791.

Waterman, Capt. Jno. B., Commander Co. C under Wood, v.26, p.791.

"Waterman, Charles M., Mayor of New Orleans," Francis P. Burns, v.7, p.466; noted, v.25, p.692.

Watkins, Dr. Floyd C., "James Kirke Paulding's Creole Tale," v.33, p.364-79.

Watkins, James, noted, v.23, p.404.

Watkins, J. B., noted, v.23, p.570.

Watkins, John, noted, v.23, p.26; Whig "traitor" defends vote, v.25, p.1100; and S. C. ord. of Nullification, v.28, p.951.

Watkins, Lynn B., judge, opinion in case of Morris vs. Mason, v.27, p.1051-52.

Watkins, Ogden's opponent for Dem. nominee for Cong., 1894, v.26, p.1095.

Watmough, John G. and 1833 tariff, v.25, p.100.

Watson, Dudley, newspaperman, "Old Days on the Times-Democrat," v.33, p.425.

Watson, John F., and Episcopal Church, v.22, p.431, 432, 434, 435.

Watson, William, member of Police Jury of St. Helena, v.23, p.407ff.

Watter, Henry, complaint against, v.21, p.123-24.

Watts, Charles, "Discourse on George Mathews," v.4, p.189.

Watts, Margaret, marriage to Gayoso de Lemos, v.23, p.1090-1091.

Watts, T. H., noted, v.24, p.113.

Waugh, David, noted, v.22, p.980; and W. Fla. Assembly, v.23, p.23ff.; noted, v.23, p.357, 368; election of, v.23, p.377; petition of, v.23, p.383.

Wax, Myrtle, export of, v.22, p.668.

Wayne, Anthony, mentioned, v.21, p.47.

Wayne, Justice James Moore, opinion in case regarding suit for divorce or annulment of marriage of Z. Carriere and Desgrange, v.27, p.110-14; opinion in Patterson Case, v.27, p.208-10; dissenting opinion in case of Gaines vs. Relf, Chew, and others, v.27, p.213, 226-32, 233, 235-41; writes majority opinion in case of Gaines vs. Hennen, v.27, p.243-74, 276.

Webb, Amos, and W. Fla. Rev., v.21, p.751.

"Webb," federal gunboat, v.29, p.1098; manned by confederates, v.29, p.1100; used in capture of "Indianola," v.29, p.1102-1107.

Webb, H. C., physician, councilman of Crowley, v.27, p.1131.

Weber, D. A., Republican supervisor of elections, 1876, v.25, p.711-12.

Weber, Otto, N. O. musician, v.31, p.144-5.

Webster, Daniel, at issue with Edward Livingston, v.24, p.700, 703, 707, 719; ideas on the Union, v.24, p.707-08; theories on the nature of the state, v.24, p.717-18; noted, v.24, p.937, 1155, 1163; and Gaines Case, v.27, p.9-10, 718; death of, v.27, p.763; N. O. honors jointly with Clay and Calhoun, v.27, p.763-64, 765-69; and 1828 tariff, v.25, p.46; quoted on slavery, v.25, p.1002; noted, v.25, p.1060, 1086, 1111; on Three Million Bill, v.25, p.1062; on U. S. acquiring possessions, v.25, p.1071.

"Webster in Louisiana History, Daniel," by Joseph Mitchell Pilcher, v.5, p.478.

Weed, C. A., publisher of "N. O. Times," v.30, p.286-287.

"Weekly Picayune," noted, v.24, p.35.

Weeks, David, and family collection in L.S.U. Archives, v.24, p.345; noted, v.28, p.821; v.32, p.25n., 94.

Weeks, James C., Repub. anti-lotteryite Cand. for lt.-gov., v.28, p.1160.

Weeks, John, v.28, p.821n.

Weeks plantation, noted, v.32, p.38, 48.

Weeks, Wm., v.28, p.821.

Wegener, Rev. G. J., noted, v.24, p.142.

Wegg, Benjamin Rush, noted, v.23, p.25.

Wegg, Edmund Rush, noted, v.23, p.23, 26; Attorney-General of West Fla., 1769, v.23, p.355ff.; election of, v.23, p.377.

Wehrmann, Henri, noted, v.33, p.409.

Wehrmann, Mrs. Henri, N. O. engraver of Music, v.31, p.147-9.

Weir, C. C., Rev., La. educator, principal Evergreen Home Institute, v.30, p.766.

Weir, John, noted, v.22, p.317; and W. Fla. Assembly, v.22, p.943.

Weiss, Carl Theodor, leaves native Munich to become organist and teacher of music in N. O., v.29, p.14-15; experiences on boat trip from Munich to N. O., v.29, p.15-32; life in N. O., v.29, p.32-42.

Weitzel, Alfred, noted, v.24, p.71, 72, 73, 77.

Weitzel, Godfrey, noted, v.22, p.507; U. S. Gen'l captured sugar region of La., v.27, p.522.

Wellborn, Alfred Toledano, "Relations Between New Orleans and Latin Am., 1810-1824," v.22, p.710-94.

Welles, Gideon, Sec. of Navy, noted, v.24, p.449; v.32, p.412.

"Wellington, Letter of the Duke of, on the Battle of New Orleans," v.9, p.5.

Wells, H. F., speaker at Anti-Lottery meeting, v.27, p.1055.

Wells, H. P., against lottery bill of 1890, v.27, p.1034; opposed rechartering of Lottery Co., v.27, p.1047; temporary chairman McEnery State Nom. Com., v.28, p.1158.

Wells, James Madison, as gov., v.23, p.1221-1222, 1230; noted, v.24, p.114; headed state ticket in La. after Civil War, v.25, p.708; as gov., v.25, p.750; active in securing Moore's pardon, v.26, p.1047; Lt. gov. under Hahn, v.30, p.525; becomes gov., v.30, p.528-529; removed from office, v.30, p.546; noted, v.30, p.539, 540; ancestry, v.31, p.995-6; education, v.31 p.997-8; marriage, v.31, p.999; property, v.31, p.999, 1000-01; pre-war politics, v.31, p.1001-04; default, v.31, p.1001-03; reputation, v.31, p.1005-06, 1083-84; during war, v.31, p.1006-09; rise to power, v.31, p.1009-16; lt. governor, v.31, p.1016, 1019-23; governor, v.31, p.1023; conciliation, v.31, p.1024-37; Confederate period, v.31, p.1037-47; family fight, v.31, p.1048-51; campaign of 1865, v.31, p.1051-64; to legislature, v.31, p.1066-68; opposed, v.31, p.1069-78; collapse, v.31, p.1078-92; fight with Sheridan, v.31, p. 1089-92; returning board, v.31, p.1092-98, 1101-04; investigation, v.31, p.1104-08; indicted, v.31, p.1108-12; last years, v.31, p.1114-15; summary of achievement, v.31, p.1116-17.

Wells, Levi, son of J. M. Wells, v.31, p.1091.

Wells, Montfort, brother of J. M. Wells, v.31, p.996, 1000, 1001; family fight, v.31, p.1047-51.

Wells, Thomas Jefferson, brother of J. M. Wells, nominee for gov., 1859, v.26, p.989; campaign and election of 1859, v.26, p.990-91; noted, v.31, p.996, 1000, 1001; elected, v.31, p.1003; scandal, v.31, p.1047-48.

Wells, Thomas M., son of J. M. Wells, v.31, p.1013; member constitutional convention of 1864, v.31, p.1018-19.

Welman, R. M., noted, v.22, p.449, 453, 461, 466, 472.

Welsh, La., v.32, p.589-90.

Werlein, Philip, noted, v.22, p.424; music store, v.31, p.859.

Werner, Rev. Julius, noted, v.24, p.144.

West Baton Rouge Academy, v.30, p.788.

West Baton Rouge Parish, in 1860, v.21, p.1130-33; meeting of planters, v.25, p.121, 126, 162; election disturbances in, v.26, p.1108.

Westbrook, Uriah, conf. soldier, v.26, p.963.

"Western Boundary of Louisiana," by Gaspar Cusachs, v.1, sec.1, p.9.

"West Feliciana, A Glimpse of Its History," Louise Butler, v.7, p.90.

West Feliciana Parish, in 1860, v.21, p.1134-37; noted, v.25, p.137, 206, 388, 676, 683, 710, 711, 717; formation, v.28, p.946; becomes rich, v.28, p.946; the Johnsons in, v.28, p.946; noted, v.28, p.952ff., 961, 970, 1132, noted, v.30, p.54; road districts of, v.30, p.54; Journal of Police Jury of, v.30, p.103-111.

"West Feliciana Railroad Case," v.28, p.955.

West Feliciana Railroad, historical sketch of, v.30, p.1122-1123.

"West Florida and the Louisiana Purchase," by Francis P. Burns, v.15, p.391.

"West Fla. Rev. of 1810, as Told in the Letters of John Rhea, Fulwar Skipwith, Reuben Kemper and Others," ed. by James A. Padgett, v.21, p.76-202.

"West Florida Revolution of 1810, an original letter on," ed. by Walter Prichard, v.18, p.354-62.

"West Florida: The Capture of Baton Rouge by Galvez, September 21, 1779, From Reports of the English Officers," v.12, p.255; "Documents Covering a Royal Land Grant on the Mississippi and Amite Rivers," transcribed from originals in the Cabildo, v.12, p.630.

"West Florida, The Distribution of Land in British," by Cecil Johnson, v.16, p.539.

West Florida, v.2, p.74, 75-78; "British Proclamation of 1763, Creating the Government of," v.13, p.610; "Revolution, 1810, Documents concerning," I, II, III, by John S. Kendall, v.17, p.80, 306, 474; absenteeism and pluralism in British, v.19, p.196-98; Republic, constitution of, v.20, p.881-94; Rev. and Rep. Official records of, v.21, p.685-805; French designs on, v.21, p.30ff.; Journal of Senate and House, v.21, p.755-83; Commission, Orders and Instructions to George Johnstone, Gov., v.21, p.1021-68; mentioned, v.21, p.1098; interval of military gov't, v.22, p.18-30; reply of Gov. Chester to complaints, v.22, p.31-46; House of Assembly, v.22, p.39; minutes of the first Assembly, 1766-67, v.22, p.311-84; fate of Hargrave and Sibley, v.22, p.788; Vidal as Sp. agent in, v.22, p.801, 802; minutes of Assembly, 1767-68, v.22, p.943-1011; minutes of Assembly of, 1768, 1769, v.23, p.5-77; minutes of Council of, April-July, 1769, v.23, p.353-404; noted, v.23, p.405; seizure from Spain, v.23, p.442-43; Jackson's seizure of Spanish territory, v.23, p.798; and Burr conspiracy, v.25, p.8; 1808 incident, v.25, p.13-14; resolution of, v.25, p.293; noted, v.25, p.384; U. S. interest in, v.25, p.939; refused right of importation from La., v.25, p.940-41; claimed for U. S., v.25, p.942; lists of claims, v.25, p.950-70; becomes Sp. possession, v.27, p.338; plans of Galvez to capture, v.27, p.663; surrender of, v.27, p.666, 670; Rebellion of, v.28, p.944, 947.

West, John K., Herrera's expedition, v.21, p.207; noted, v.21, p.1086; noted, v.22, p.1036; and Spanish insurgents, v.23, p.737; member of New Orleans Association, v.24, p.631; noted, v.25, p.300.

West, John, noted, v.23, p.421.

West, Joseph R., Warmoth's cand. for U. S. Senate against Pinchback, v.27, p.542; presents certificate of Pinchback to Senate, v.27, p.589, 594; called for postponement of vote in Pinchback case, v.27, p.599; presents petition of McMillen for withdrawal of credentials, v.27, p.600, 601.

West Lake, La., v.32, p.592.

West, Mr., and debt problems, v.24, p.993-94.

Westrop, Lionel Beecher, noted, v.23, p.368, 398, 400, 402.

Wetherill, Julia K., noted, v.33, p. 421-22.

"Wet Sand and Cotton—Banks' Red River Campaign," by Colonel H. L. Landers, v.19, p.150-95.

"Weyanoke," Percy plantation, v.25, p.157.

Wharton, Edward C., noted, v.29, p.309; account of "Lafayette in N. O.," v.29, p.310-325.

Wharton, Jack, com. as sec. of state in order to serve on Returning Board, v.27, p.557.

Wharton, John, named by Warmoth as sec. of state, 1872, v.28, p.1134.

Wharton, John A., noted, v.24, p.94, 97.

Wharton, J., member Warmoth returning board, v.31, p.700.

Wharton, Judge T. W., noted, v.23, p.180.

Wharton, Theodore, early N. O. newspaperman, v.29, p.788.

Wheat, Chatham R., and Lopez expedition, v.22, p.1121n., 1124; noted, v.22, p.1160, 1161.

Wheat, Rev. J. T., pastor in New Orleans, v.22, p.461, 468.

Wheat, Robert, noted, v.24, p.51, 65.

Wheaton, Dr., noted, v.26, p.76.

Wheaton, Rev. Nathaniel S., pastor in New Orleans, v.22, p.468, 469, 470.

"Wheeler agreement," arbitration of contested legislative seats, v.31, p.706-08.

Wheeler, Joseph, noted, v.24, p.103.

Wheeler, Rev. ———, pastor in New Orleans, v.22, p.453.

Whelan, Edward, of Bogalusa, v.29, p.92.

Whelan, Jimmy, scout for Great Southern Lumber Co., v.29, p.91-92.

"When Knighthood was in Flower," by Heloise Hulse Cruzat, v.1, p.367.

Whicher, Franc, Capt. Co. B, 4th Louisiana Regiment, muster rolls, v.30, p. 488-490.

"Which Way History?", by Henry P. Dart, v.11, p.468.

Whigs, in La., and annexation of Texas, v.19, p.103-107; and suffrage reform, v.19, p.392-406; in 1851, v.23, p.180ff.; Donaldsonville convention of, 1850, v.23, p.1080-1081; in La., v.25, p.41, 79-80, 121, 122, 123, 124, 125, 126, 128, 129, 130, 131, 133, 140, 141, 142, 143; and tariff, v.25, p.119, 121, 675, 680, 998, 1002, 1005, 1006, 1007, 1008, 1013-14, 1015, 1036; the election of 1846, v.25, p.1036-38, 1053; election of senator, v.25, p.1058; support Wilmot Proviso, v.25, p.1070, 1071; on the Three Million Bill, v.25, p.1072; U. S. senatorial election, 1848, v.25, p.1093-1104; pres. campaign, 1848, v.25, p.1105-1110; Clay a leader of, v.27, p.723; and the Plaquemines Fraud in La., v.27, p.724; Z. Taylor nominated by, v.27, p.725, 741, 745, 748; conv., 1844, v.27, p.749, 750.

Whitaker, A. P. "Commercial Policy of

Spain in Florida and Louisiana, 1778-1803" (Review), v.15, p.345.

Whitaker, Judge W. R., noted, v.31, p.1109, 1110.

White, Alice Pemble, "The Plantation Experiences of Joseph and Lavinia Erwin, 1807-1836," v.27, p.343-78.

White, B. F., Rev., La. educator, v.30, p.909.

White Camelia, v.28, p.1130; organized, v.28, p.1133-34.

White, Campbell, and sugar tariff, v.25, p.87, 100-101.

"White Castle of La., The," noted, v.25, p.150.

White Castle, La., noted, v.25, p.150, 207.

"White, Edward Douglas," by Henry Plauche Dart, v.5, p.145; "Installation of Chief Justice White" (From New York Evening Post, Dec. 19, 1910), v.5, p.152.

White, Edward Douglas, Sr., parentage, v.19, p.273-81; lawyer at Donaldsonville, v.19, p.282; city judge in N. O., v.19, p.283; member of Congress, v.19, p.283-89; Governor of La., v.19, p.290ff.; public land policy, v.19, p.307-308; and Texas revolution, v.19, p.309-10; and Panic of 1873, v.19, p.313-14; the bank question, v.19, p.318-22; member of Congress, v.19, p.323-26; noted, v.23, p.1018, 1019, 1082n.; and tariff, v.25, p.70-71, 87, 98-99, 103, 104, 105, 108, 112, 115, 116, 117, 118, 124; campaign against Dawson, v.25, p.104-107; La. Gov., v.25, p.989, 1053; firm champion of sugar planters and tariff, v.27, p.806; elevated to Sup. Ct., v.27, p.806; speech at Anti-Lottery meeting, 1890, v.27, p.1055-56; address at reception for Anti-Lottery legislators, v.27, p.1056; address at Anti-Lottery Conv., v.27, p.1057; League's resolution of confidence in, v.27, p.1058; charges against, v.27, p.1065; accused of taking money from lottery Co., v.28, p.1144-45; had Lottery Co. prohibited use of mails, v.28, p.1150; noted, v.28, p.1151; and the lottery issue, v.28, p.1161; named U. S. Supreme Court Justice, v.28, p.1167; noted, v.28, p.1169; chief justice, v.28, p.1221; proposes internal improvement legislation, v.30, p.49, 52; and lottery battle, v.31, p.835.

White, George W., and Round Island expedition, v.22, p.1115n., 1121n.; noted, v.24, p.769.

Whitehead, S., cand. lt.-gov., v.28, p.1176.

White, H. H., "The Recollections of a Little Rebel," v.17, p.732.

White, James, early life in Penn., v.19, p.273; member of legislature in N. Car., v.19, p.273; member of Congress, v.19, p.274; Supt. of Indian Affairs, v.19, p.275-81; moved to La., v.19, p.281.

White, Joseph, and W. Fla. Rev., v.21, p.84, 90n., 747n.

White, L., Populist cand. for Lt.-Gov. on 1st ticket, 1896, v.26, p.1101.

"White League in Louisiana and its Participation in Reconstruction Riots," by Oscar H. Lestage, Jr., v.18, p.617-95.

"White League in New Orleans (Reminiscences of a Participant in the Movement)," ed. by W. Prichard, v.23, p.525-43.

White League, v.28, p.1130; Foster's work with, v.28, p.1137-38; organized, v.29, p.444; in N. O., v.29, p.717, 718; organized and supported by press, v.30, p.232; denied as existing, v.30, p.232; disclaims blame in Kellogg protest, v.30, p.235.

White, Maunsel, noted, v.22, p.449; noted, v.23, p.145, 1049; and railroads, v.23, p.200, 214; and railroad convention, 1852, v.23, p.220; Dem. from Plaquemines and the election for senator, 1848, v.25, p.1095-98.

White Sulphur Springs, resort, v.24, p.1018; noted, v.25, p.119.

"White Supremacy in the South; The Battle for Constitutional Government in New Orleans, July 30, 1866," by Francis P. Burns, v.18, p.581-616.

Whitfield, Irene Therese, collector of French folk songs, v.24, p.755.

"Whiting," British dispatch boat, v.24, p.614.

Whitin, Wm. C., noted, v.25, p.776.

Whitman, Andrew, noted, v.23, p.749.

Whitman, Walt, comment on by Cable, v.24, p.174.

Whitney, Wm. W., marriage to Myra Clark, v.27, p.47; proceedings to probate will of Clark, v.27, p.48-51; death of, v.27, p.51, 72, 74, 75, 78, 81, 84; appeal to have Clark's will of 1813 probated, v.27, p.180; death of, v.27, p.182.

Whittaker, Aquila, and W. Fla. Rev., v.21, p.709n.

Whittington, G. P., "Dr. John Sibley of Natchitoches, 1757-1837," v.10, p.467; "Thomas O. Moore, Governor of Louisiana, 1860-1864," v.13, p.7; "Thomas O. Moore, Papers of," v.13, p.10; Introduction, "Concerning the Loyalty of Slaves in North Louisiana in 1863, letters from John H. Ransdell to Governor Thomas O. Moore, dated 1863," v.14, p.487; In Memoriam, J. Fair Hardin, Henry P. Dart, v.15, p.655; "A History of Rapides Parish, Louisiana," I, v.15, p.567; II, III, IV, V, v.16, p.27, 235, 427, 628; VI, VII, VIII, IX, v.17, p.112, 327, 537, 737; X (Concluded), v.18, p.5-39.

"Who Killa de Chief?", by J. S. Kendall, v.22, p.492-530.

Wickliffe, George M., loses nomination for Gov., v.30, p.548; charged by Warmoth with corruption, v.30, p.578; discharged, v.30, p.594-596, 206-207; exacts bribe for payment of hospital appropriation, v.31, p.64-5; noted, v.31, p.704; cause for impeachment, v.31, p.687-8; New Orleans trial, v.31, p.689; impeachment articles, v.31, p.692-4; committee investigation, v.31, p.690; suspension, v.31, p.691; trial, v.31, p.695-8; Pinchback's clash with, v.27, p.533.

Wickliffe, John C., noted, v.22, p.519; v.27, p.778; address at reception honoring Anti-Lottery legislators, v.27, p.1056; addressed Anti-Lottery League Conv., v.27, p.1057; resolution of confidence in Nicholls & White, v.27, p.1058; sec. Dem. Anti-Lottery St. Ex. Com., v.27, p.1059; address to Dem. Anti-Lottery St. Com., v.27, p.1091; Anti-Lotteryite, v.28, p.1158; establishes "New Delta," v.31, p.790.

Wickliffe, Robert C., and railroads, v.23, p.238; noted, v.25, p.670-727; his ancestry and early years, v.25, p.670-741; as state senator, 1852-55, v.25, p.674-83; as gov., 1856-60, v.25, p.683-705; his stand on slavery and state rights, 1856, v.25, p.685-90; and the riotous elections in N. O., v.25, p.690-93; and internal improvements, v.25, p.693-98; and public education, v.25, p.677, 698-701; his efforts for sound banks and currency, v.25, p.768, 701-702; minor problems, v.25, p.702-705; a minority party leader, v.25, p.705-714; national election of 1860, v.25, p.705-707; during Civil War, v.25, p.707; reconst., v.25, p.714-20; bibl., v.25, p.720-27; administered oath to Moore, v.26, p.991; "Regular" cand. for Lt.-Gov., v.26, p.1081; Lotteryite cand. for Lt.-Gov., v.27, p.1090; noted, v.28, p.948; suggested for com. to supervise lottery poll, v.28, p.1154; chairman McEnery State Central Com., v.28, p.1158; nom. Lt.-Gov., v.28, p.1158; noted, v.28, p.1161; had B. R. made sub-port of N. O., v.28, p.1222; candidate for Lt.-Gov., v.31, p.837; Democratic convention, v.31, p.1055; governor, v.31, p.517, 525.

Widiger, Rev. Arthur E., cited, v.24, p.144.

Wiedemann, Dr. Edmund, noted, v.26, p.75; testimonial signed by, v.26, p.88-89.

Wiggins, Richard H., author, "The Louisiana Press and the Lottery," v.31, p.716-884.

Wilbert, A., pioneer in cypress shingle manufacturing, v.30, p.1019.

Wilcox, Dr. W., noted, v.26, p.76.

Wilcox, H. H., chairman of committee to incorporate Bogalusa, v.29, p.108, 109, 110; designated Comm. of Education in Bogalusa, v.29, p.113.

Wilcox, Thomas, noted, v.23, p.1176n.

Wilcoxon, Lloyd, v.28, p.767n.

Wilde, Pickersgill & Co., noted, v.24, p.759.

"Wilde, Richard Henry, in New Orleans and the Establishment of the University of Louisiana," by Aubrey Starke, v.17, p.605.

Wilde, Richard Henry, prof. in Univ. of La., v.23, p.1056; noted, v.23, p.1058; early N. O. police reporter, v.29, p.51.

Wilder, F. F., made affidavit of bribery by Howard, v.27, p.974; incorporator La. Lottery, v.27, p.975; commissioner of Drawing, v.27, p.977.

"Wild Is the River," by Louis Bromfield, rev'd by Andre Lafargue, v.29, p.791-93.

Wilgus, A. Curtis, "Spanish American Patriot Activity Along the Gulf Coast of the United States, 1811-1822," v.8, p.193; "Some Activities of United States Citizens in the South American Wars of Independence, 1808-1824," v.14, p.182; "Official Expression of Manifest Destiny Sentiment Concerning Hispanic America, 1848-1871," v.15, p.486.

Wilkerson, Marcus M., study of Thomas Duckett Boyd, v.24, p.321, 348, 353; rev's Fayette Copeland's, "Kendall of the Picayune," v.26, p.1168-70.

Wilkinson County, Miss., noted, v.25, p. 150, 156, 157, 158, 161, 162, 176, 189, 202; from Natchez district, v.25, p.153-54; Probate Court of, v.25, p.159.

"Wilkinson, General James," by his great-grandson, James Wilkinson, v.1, sec.2, p.79. (Refuting the charge that Wilkinson, while Brigadier General of the U. S.

Army sought to betray his country by procuring the secession of Kentucky and effecting an alliance between that territory and Spain); discharged from army, v.19, p.407; applied for pension in Md., v.19, p.411; moved to Louisiana plantation, v.19, p.416-22; removal to Mexico City and aide to Iturbide, v.19, p.422-34; Spanish agent in Ky., v.21, p.14, 65; and W. Fla. Rev., v.21, p.101n.; letter to Carondelet noted, v.21, p.44n.; intimacy with, v.21, p.45, 47; noted, v.22, p.223n., 398; noted, v.24, p.6, 734, 738, 739, 931; documents in Bibliotheca Parsoniana, v.24, p.311; letters in La. State Museum, v.24, p.319; exposed Burr's plot, v.25, p.11; and Burr plot, v.25, p.13, 645; noted, v.25, p.15, 297; and the Pike expedition, v.25, p.644; Comdr. U. S. Army in West, v.28, p.108; brings neutral ground dispute to agreement, v.28, p. 1037-43; Carondelet tries to use, v.31, p.611; military commissioner for transfer of La., v.31, p.275-7; noted, v.31, p.365, 610.

Wilkinson, James, "General James Wilkinson," v.1, sec.2, p.19; tribute to Henry P. Dart, v.18, p.241-42.

Wilkinson, Joseph B., noted, v.25, p.296.

Wilkinson, Theo. S., v.27, p.1062; defended Louisianians, v.27, p.1076-77; pres. Dem. Anti-Lottery St. Conv., v.27, p.1090; address to Dem. Anti-Lottery St. Com., v.27, p.1091; Foster's letter to, v.27, p.1093, 1096; v.28, p.1165; chairman Anti-Lottery State Nom. Conv., v.28, p.1157; noted, v.28, p.1158.

Wilkins, Col. ————, noted, v.23, p.397.

Wilkins, Dr. C. D., and Charity Hospital, v.31, p.85.

Wilkins, William, noted, v.24, p.1164; and sugar tariff, v.25, p.88.

Willard, Emma, noted, v.23, p.1235.

Willemer, friend of Goethe, v.24, p.420.

"William Pitt Kellogg, Reconstruction Governor of La., 1873-1877," by John Edmunds Gonzales, v.29, p.394-495.

"William Preston Johnston; A Transitional Figure of the Confederacy," by Arthur Marvin Shaw, rev'd, v.26, p.1171-72.

Williams, Alpheus S., noted, v.29, p.742; memorial address by E. John Ellis on life and character of, v.29, p.761-767.

Williams, Benjamin O., and W. Fla. Rev., v.21, p.131, 132n., 688n.; noted, v.23, p.421.

Williams, "Captain" W. H., v.33, p.424.

Williams, David, noted, v.22, p.317, 322; v.23, p.391.

Williams, Dr. John C., identified, v.21, p.733n.

Williams, F. A., Capt. Co. D, 4th La. Reg., muster rolls given, v.30, p.494-496.

Williams, Francis Bennett, pioneer in Cypress lumber industry, sketch of, v.30, p.1010-1012; noted, v.30, p.1025, 1039.

Williams, Howell L., noted, v.24, p.761.

Williams, Hugh, noted, v.26, p.797.

Williams, John, alias of Arsene Latour, v.30, p.715, 735; (see Latour, Arsene Lacarriere).

Williams, J. A., first full-time postmaster of Crowley, v.27, p.1155.

Williams, J., duel with Burch, v.24, p.770.

Williams, Kindred, noted, v.23, p.422.

Williams, L. E., Pres. of local Federation of Labor, v.29, p.134.

Williams, Martin C., brief sketch, v.29, p.81-82.

Williams, Milo B., Address, "General Beauregard and General Blanchard in the Mexican War," v.1, p.299.

Williams, Norman, noted, v.23, p.1177.

Williamson, Frederick W., "History of Eastern La.," quoted, v.25, p.629; "Yesterday and Today in La. Agriculture," rev'd, v.25, p.822-23.

Williamson, George, collection noted, v.24, p.317.

Williamson, James C., noted, v.22, p.434, 436; pastor in New Orleans, v.22, p.459.

Williamsport in 1860, v.21, p.1142-43.

Williams, Richard Hobson, "General Banks' Red River Campaign," v.32, p.103.

Williams, Richard, noted, v.23, p.361.

Williams, Roger, noted, v.24, p.701.

Williams, Stephen, noted, v.23, p.409.

Williams, Sylvania, noted, v.25, p.737, 784, 805.

Williams, T. Harry, rev's Robt. D. Meade's, "Judah P. Benjamin: Confed. Statesman," v.26, p.1170-71; rev's Arthur Marvin Shaw's, "Wm. Preston Johnston: A Transitional Figure of the Confederacy," v.26, p.1171-72; rev's Dickey's, "Seargent S. Prentiss, Whig Orator of the Old South," v.29, p.202-203.

Williams, William H., "The History of Carrollton," v.22, p.181-215.

Willing, James, in W. Fla., v.22, p.38.

"Willing's Expedition Down the Mississippi, 1778," by John Caughey, v.15, p.5.

Willink, Cecile: "An Old Lady's Gossip," v.6, p.380; introduction to "War As I

Saw It" by Frank L. Richardson, v.6, p.86; "Louisiana Historical Society Fifty Years Ago," v.7, p.667.

Willow Chute, noted, v.25, p.400.

"Will of the Spanish Era, A Louisiana, 1766," by Laura L. Porteous, v.11, p.607.

Wills, of Sp. colonial La., v.22, p.394-95.

"Wills of the French Colonial Period in Louisiana," Heloise H. Cruzat, v.8, p.411.

"Wills, Two Nuncupative, French Period, 1745-47," edited by H. P. Dart, v.3, p.564.

Wilson, Charles Grant, correspondence of in Xavier University Archives, v.24, p.336.

Wilson, Harry D., Commissioner of Agriculture, v.30, p.681.

Wilson, Henry, collection in L.S.U. Archives, v.24, p.345.

Wilson, James, noted, v.24, p.701, 703, 708, 709, 716.

Wilson, James H., noted, v.24, p.109, 110.

Wilson, Joseph L., paymaster clerk, v.27, p.482.

Wilson, Maj. M. R., Populist cand. for Cong., 1894, v.26, p.1095.

Wilson, Peter, Hospital Steward, v.26, p.795-96.

Wilson, R. D., La. educator, v.30, p.966.

Wilson, Robert, and circulating library, v.23, p.131-40.

Wilson, Samuel F., editorial staff of "Picayune," sketch of, v.30, p.261; noted, v.30, p.268, 268n., 284.

Wilson, Samuel, Jr., "An Architectural History of the Royal Hospital and the Ursuline Convent of New Orleans," v.29, p.559-659.

Wilson's Farm, engagement noted, v.24, p.88.

Wilson's Landing, noted, v.24, p.95.

Wilson's School, R. D., sketch of, v.30, p.782-783.

Wilson Tariff Bill, effect of, v.28, p.1169, 1170.

Wilson, William, and W. Fla. Rev., v.21, p.83.

Wiltz, Louis A., candidate for mayor of New Orleans, 1872, v.23, p.520; noted, v.28, p.312; Dem. Cand. for Lt.-Gov., 1876, v.28, p.1138; election for gov., 1879, v.28, p.1139-40; death in office, v.28, p.1155; elected gov. of La., v.29, p.744; manager of Kellogg impeachment, v.31, p.714; mayor of New Orleans, v.31, p.543; inaugurated lieut.-gov., v.32, p.399-401; noted, v.32, p.636.

Wiltz, P. S., on De Feriet Returning Board, v.28, p.1135.

Wilz, Marguerita, original owner of land becoming Lafayette Faubourg, v.20, p.908ff.

Winans, Rev. William, Methodist preacher in N. O., v.21, p.826-27; ministry in New Orleans, v.22, p.447, 450.

Winchester, Benjamin, noted, v.23, p.1083.

Winchester, millitary operations noted, v.24, p.64.

Winder, Charles, noted, v.24, p.65.

Winder, John H., appointed manager of Confederate Prison at Andersonville, v.29, p.1248, 1249.

Wine industry, U. S. study in France, v.24, p.1068.

Wingfield, Jas. H., Captain Co. C, 4th La. Reg't. muster rolls of, v.30, p.504-507.

Winn, John W., & Co., Printers of Natchez, v.21, p.127.

Winn Parish of La., first step in formation of La. People's Party, v.26, p.1077; Populist legis. from, v.26, p.1109.

Winnsboro, La., land office discontinued, 1861, v.28, p.300.

Winston, James E., "Stephen F. Austin, Founder of Texas," v.9, p.398; Review of Fleming's "The Freedmen's Saving Bank," v.10, p.562; "New Orleans and the Texas Revolution," v.10, p.317; "Faithful Picture of the Political Situation in New Orleans at the Close of the Last and Beginning of the Present Year," v.11, p.359; "How the Louisiana Purchase Was Financed," v.12, p.189; "The Cause and Results of the Revolution of 1768 in Louisiana," v.15, p.181; address in memory of Henry Plauche Dart, v.18, p.246-47; "La. and the Annexation of Texas," v.19, p.89-118; "The Free Negro in N. O., 1803-1860," v.21, p.1075-85.

Winston, William O., and Andrew Jackson, v.21, p.383.

Winterhalder, Louis, newspaper artist, "Old Days on the N. O. Picayune," v.33, p.328.

Winthrop, Robert C., and sugar tariff, v.25, p.139.

Wirt, Mrs. William, noted, v.24, p.1117, 1125.

Wirt, William, nomination of, v.25, p.1158; noted, v.25, p.1159, 1164.

Wise, John, noted, v.24, p.701.

Wisner, Edward, and Reclamation Proects, v.30, p.675, 677, 682.

Witbeck, Capt. A. T., "The Great Raft in the Red River and Its Removal," v.18, p.769-75.

Wolfe King, letter from, v.23, p.375-76.

Womack, Abner, member of Police Jury of St. Helena, v.23, p.407ff.

Womack, William, noted, v.23, p.422.

Womack, W. R., Farmers' Alliance Com., v.28, p.1152.

"Women in Public Affairs in La. During Reconstruction," by Kathryn R. Schuler, v.19, p.668, 750.

Women, of New Orleans, hatred of Yankees, v.24, p.461-62, 492-96.

"Women of the Sixties," by Florence Cooney Tompkins, v.2, p.282.

Women's Anti-Lottery League, formation of and officers, v.27, p.1061; public meeting, v.27, p.1061-62; functions performed by, v.27, p.1062; floral offering to Foster, v.27, p.1096; resolutions to Foster, v.27, p.1113.

Wood, Ann Mackall Taylor, noted, v.24, p.50.

Wood, Benjamin, suit against Howard, v.27, p.982-83.

Wood, Ben, noted, v.23, p.1197.

Woodbury, Levi P., recommends telegraph, v.31, p.427.

Wood, Col. Elmer Ellsworth, introduction to his records, v.26, p.783-84; ancestry, life and characteristics of, v.26, p.784-86; "La. Prepares for War with Spain in 1898," v.26, p.787-810; in La. Nat'l Guard, v.26, p.791; preparation and commission of 2nd La. Vol. Inf., v.26, p.792-96; made colonel, v.26, p.793; at Camp Foster, v.26, p.796-810, 811-15; "Report to Gov. Foster," v.26, p.810-41; in Mobile, v.26, p.815-17; in Miami, v.26, p.811-23; at Jacksonville, v.26, p.823-27; to Savannah for embarkation, v.26, p.827; in Cuba, v.26, p.827-34; acting brigade commander, v.26, p.831; entrance into Havana, v.26, p.832-34; sailed for Savannah, v.26, p.834; his account of his men, v.26, p.835-41.

Wood, Dr. Robert C., noted, v.24, p.50.

Wood, John R., Sr., donated land for Methodist Church, v.29, p.84.

Wood, Joseph, English singer, v.31, p.973.

Wood, Minter, "Life in New Orleans in the Sp. Period," v.22, p.642-709.

Wood, P. N., noted, v.23, p.204, 244.

Wood, Walter, noted, v.23, p.42.

Wood, W. W. W., and election of 1851, v.23, p.186.

Wood, Trist, publisher of Philip Livingston's account of duel, v.24, p.774-75, 781-82.

Woodrow, James Perkins, Professor in Presbyterian Seminary at Columbia, S. Carolina, v.20, p.965.

Woodruff, Chas. E., Chief med. examiner, v.26, p.802; noted, v.26, p.1805.

Woodruff, Clara, noted, v.23, p.202.

Woodruff, Clark, establishes academy near St. Francisville, v.28, p.945.

Woodson, Carter, noted, v.25, p.316, 372.

Woodville, Miss., noted, v.25, p.154, 156, 157, 160, 162; Planters Bank of, v.25, p.159.

Wooley, A. K., attorney in Morse case, v.31, p.463.

Workman, James, leader in library development in N. O., v.20, p.153, 157; and nullification, v.25, p.91.

"Work of the Quarterly in 1930," by Henry P. Dart, v.14, p.86.

Work Projects Administration, Historical Records Survey, "Guide to Depositories of Manuscript Collections in Louisiana," v.24, p.305-53.

World War, Food Adminis. in La., v.21, p.869-74.

"Wreck of La Superbe in Gulf of Mexico, 1745," Introduction by Henry P. Dart, Translated by Heloise H. Cruzat, v.11, p.179.

Wren, B. C., introduced bill which provided for revenue by lottery, v.27, p.974.

Wren, G. L. P., opposed lottery question, v.27, p.1039.

Wright, David, Clerk of Police Jury of St. Helena, v.23, p.408.

Wright, Dr. Roy, director of Charity Hospital, v.31, p.95-6.

Wright, Edith, first rice queen, v.27, p.1223.

Wright, Fannie, author, v.31, p.397.

Wright, Frances, friend of General Lafayette, v.29, p.328.

Wright, Irvin B., noted, v.23, p.1232.

Wright, Judge B. D., noted, v.23, p.1198.

Wright, Miss Sophie B., N. O. educator, v.30, p.877-878.

Wright, Samuel, duel with Oakey, v.24, p.759-62.

Wright, Sol., king of rice, 1927, v.27, p.1223; "Burbank of the Rice Industry," v.27, p.1161.

Wright, William P., noted, v.23, p.1243.

Wrotnowski, Stanislaus, refuses to issue commissions, v.31, p.1029-30.
Wurzburg, view of, v.24, p.401.
Wyatt, G. M., People's Party advocate, v.26, p.1094.
Wykoff, William, Jr., friend of Claiborne, v.21, p.165n.; and W. Fla. Rev., v.21, p.177.
Wyly, W. G., fusion cand. att'y gen'l, 1900, v.28, p.1192; justice, gave opinion against P. H. Morgan, v.27, p.578.
"Wyoming," plantation, v.25, p.674.

XAVIER UNIVERSITY, HISTORICAL sketch of, v.24, p.335-36; archives, v.24, p.336; library, v.24, p.337; bulletin, v.24, p.353, noted, v.25, p.784-86, 792, 811, 814.

X.Y.Z. Pamphlets on commercial treaty, v.24, p.1162.

YAMOKA, PEN-NAME OF CABLE, v.24, p.171.
Yancey, C. D., noted, v.23, p.204.
Yancey, William L., noted, v.24, p.58.
"Yankee School Teacher in La. 1835-1837: the diary of Caroline B. Poole," ed. by James A. Padgett, v.20, p.651-79.
Yankees, in La. and Tex., 1854-1865, v.23, p.1132-1240.
Yatasi (Yatassee) Indians, in Grant Parish, v.23, p.1109; noted, v.23, p.1116.
Yates, Richard, noted, v.29, p.396.
"Yazoo," a steamer, v.24, p.40.
Yearns, Wilford B., Jr., "Charles Gayarre, Louisiana's Literary Historian," v.33, p.255-68.
Yellow Bayou, noted, v.24, p.97.
Yellow Fever, in Sp. New Orleans, v.22, p.679; prevalence of, v.22, p.817; in New Orleans, 1853, v.23, p.499; fear of by Federal troops in New Orleans, v.24, p.478-79; in New Orleans, v.24, p.739; treatment of, v.26, p.373; epidemic, v.25, p.705; epidemic in N. O. and fight against in Crowley, v.27, p.1135-37; in St. Mary Parish, v.32, p.82; description of N. O. during, v.33, p.381-82; treatment of, v.33, p.385-87; funerals, v.33, p.395-96; noted, v.33, p.145, 280.
"Yellow Fever Retrospect and Prospect, A," Rudolph Matas, M.D., v.8, p.454.
"Yellow Fever, The New Orleans, Epidemic of 1853," by Donald E. Everett, v.33, p.380-405.
"Yesterday and Today in La. Agriculture," by Frederick W. Williamson, rev'd, v.25, p.822-23.
Yllar, Maria, testimony of in Desgrange trial, v.27, p.94-95, 220.
York, Zebulon, nominated Moore for Gov., v.26, p.988.
You, Dominique, noted, v.22, p.1027ff., 1088; and Spanish insurgents, v.23, p.737, 750; at Galveston, v.23, p.811-12; subordinate of Jean Laffite, v.24, p.24-28; early life, v.24, p.25; and defense of New Orleans, v.24, p.26; pardon of by the U. S., v.24, p.26; attempt to rescue Napoleon, v.24, p.27; death of, v.24, p.27; burial place, v.24, p.28; noted, v.24, p.672, 684; v.25, p.300.
Younge, Robert, and W. Fla. Rev., v.21, p.709.
Younge, Lilita Lever, "The Grave of Molinary," v.7, p.465.
Young, George W., sec. Anti-Lottery League of La., v.27, p.1054; work in organizing League, v.27, p.1056.
Young, Guilford Dudley, and Spanish insurgents, v.21, p.818.
Young, John S., com. to supervise primary, v.27, p.1094; and election of 1872, v.28, p.1134; member com. to supervise election, v.28, p.1161; appt'd. sheriff of Caddo Parish, v.28, p.1162.

Young Ladies Institute, v.30, p.862-63.
Young's Point, noted, v.24, p.75.
Young, Ventress, gen'l mgr. of Gaylord Corp., v.29, p.86.
Young, William, noted, v.22, p.190.
Yount-Lee Oil Co., complete deepest well in La.-Tex. Gulf Coast area, v.29, p.503; leases on Jennings dome, v.29, p.506-07.
Yucatan, trade with, v.22, p.778; Laffites at, v.23, p.801; J. Laffite repairs to, v.23, p.824.
Yucatecan Letters, in Institute of Middle American Research, v.24, p.333, 350.

"ZABET PHILOSOPHE," noted, v.25, p.373-74.

Zacatecas State Lottery Company, Mexican firm, competition to La. Co., v.28, p.1142, 1143; noted, v.31, p.794.

Zacharie, F. C., v.27, p.1091; on com. to supervise primary, v.27, p.1094; member com. to supervise election, v.28, p.1161; appt'd register of voters of Orleans, v.28, p.1162; noted, v.31, p.760, 1094; against lottery, v.31, p.761.

"Zachary Taylor, A Sketch of His Life," by Mrs. James J. McLoughlin, v.18, p.377-81.

"Zachary Taylor," by Brainerd Dyer, rev'd by Walter Prichard, v.30, p.349-350.

Zea, Bermudez, noted, v.24, p.960, 970, 973, 975.

Zea, Francisco Antonio, noted, v.24, p.622, 626, 666, 667; aid to enemies of Bolivar, v.24, p.683-85.

Zeller, Francis Charles, mayor of Carrollton, v.21, p.252-53; noted, v.22, p.204.

Zepeda, Jose, robbery of, in neutral ground, v.28, p.1063-64.

Zeringue, Maria Barba, Marriage Contract with Francisco Daspit, v.9, p.394.

Zickwolf, rival of Willemer, v.24, p.420, 432.

Zimpel, Charles F., surveyor of Carrollton, v.21, p.228; and beginning of Carrollton, v.22, p.191.

Zirkel, bishop, v.24, p.402.

Zook, Samuel K., inventor of telegraph, v.31, p.437; arrested, v.31, p.468.

"Zum Treuen Schafer," manuscript in L.S.U. Music School Library, v.24, p.348.

Zuniga, Gov., noted, v.22, p.1019.

Acc't	Account	Dec	December
Acc'ts	Accounts	Dept	Department
Adj	Adjutant	Dist	District
Agr	Agriculture	Docu	Documents
Agri	Agriculture	Docs	Documents
Ala	Alabama	Dr	Doctor
Am	America(n)	E	East
Am't	Amount	Ec	Economic
Appt'd	Appoint(ed)	Ed	Editor
Apr	April		Edited
Ark	Arkansas		Education
Assn	Association	Educ	Education
Assoc	Association	Eng	England
Ass	Associate		English
Ass't	Assistant	Engr	Engineer
As't	Assistant	Est	Established
Atty	Attorney	Estab	Established
Aug	August	Ex	Executive
Auth	Author	Exam	Examination
Bap't	Baptist	Exp	Experiment
Bat	Battalion	Feb	February
Bibl	Bibliography	Fed'l	Federal
B. R.	Baton Rouge	Fel	Feliciana
Br	British	ff	Following
Brig	Brigadier	Fig	Figure
Bros	Brothers	Fin	Finance
Bus	Business	Fla	Florida
c	Circa	Fr	France
Cand	Candidate		French
Capt	Captain	Ga	Georgia
Chapt.(s)	Chapter(s)	Geol	Geological
Co-auth	Co-author	Ger	German
C. O.	Commanding officer	Gen	General
Co	Company	Gen'l	General
Co-ed	Co-edited	Gov	Governor
Col	Colonel	Gov't	Government
Com	Committee	Hist	History
Com	Commercial	Hist'l	Historical
Comd	Command	Ill	Illinois
Comdt	Commandant	Impvts	Improvements
Comm	Commission(er)	Ind	Indiana
Comp	Compromise	Ind	Independent
Con	Convention	Inf	Infantry
Conv	Convention	Insp	Inspector
Confed	Confederate	Int	Intendant
Cong	Congress(ional)	Int	Internal
Conn	Connecticut	Intro	Introduction
Const	Constitution(al)	Jan	January
Cont	Continued	Jt	Joint
Conv	Convention	Ky	Kentucky
Corp	Corporation	L	Lake
Crim	Criminal	La	Louisiana
Ct	Court	Leg	Legislature
Dem	Democrat	Legis	Legislative
Demo	Democrat	Lieut	Lieutenant
Dep	Deputy	Lt	Lieutenant
		Lit	Literary

L.H.S.	Louisiana Historical Society	Rep.	Republic
L.S.U.	Louisiana State University	Rep.	Represent(ed)(ative) Republic
Maj.	Major	R. R.	
Mch.	March	Rev.	Reverend
		Rev.	Revolution
Mass.	Massachusetts	Rev.	Revenue
Mch.	March	Rev'd	Review(ed)(s)
Mem.	Memorial	Rwy.	Railway
Mex.	Mexico Mexican	S.	South
		S. C.	South Carolina
Mfg.	Manufacturing	Sec.	Secretary
Mgr.	Manager	Sec'y	Secretary
Mil.	Military	Sec.	Section
Miss.	Mississippi	Sen.	Senate Senator
Mo.	Missouri		
Ms.	Manuscript	Sept.	September
Mt.	Mountain	Sess.	Session
n	Note Footnote	Sg't	Sergeant
		Soc.	Society
N.	North	Sp.	Spain
n.	New	Span.	Spanish
Nat'l	National Natural	Sq.	Square
		St.	Street
N. C.	North Carolina	St.	State
N. O.	New Orleans	St.	Saint
Nom.	Nominated	Ste.	Saint
Nov.	November	Sup.	Superior—Supreme
N. Y.	New York	Supt.	Superintendent
Oct.	October	Temp.	Temporary
Ord.	Ordinance	Tenn.	Tennessee
Org.	Organized	Ter.	Territory
Orig.	Original	Tex.	Texas
p.	page	Tr.	Translated
Pa.	Pennsylvania	Tran.	Translated
passim	The idea—but not quoted word for word	Treas.	Treasury Treasurer
Plant.	Plantation	U.	University
Pres.	President(ial)	Univ.	University
Prof.	Professor	U. S.	United States
Prof.	Profession	v.	Volume
Prog.	Progressive	Va.	Virginia
Pub.	Published Public	Vol.	Volunteer
		vs.	Versus
Pv't	Private	Vt.	Vermont
R.	River Reconstruction	W.	West
		Wash.	Washington
Recog.	Recognition	Y.	Year
Reg.	Register	Yr.	Years
Reg't	Regiment	Yrs.	Years

www.ingramcontent.com/pod-product-compliance
Lightning Source LLC
Chambersburg PA
CBHW080545230426
43663CB00015B/2719